An Introduction to
German Pietism

YOUNG CENTER BOOKS IN ANABAPTIST & PIETIST STUDIES

Donald B. Kraybill, *Series Editor*

An Introduction to German Pietism

Protestant Renewal at the Dawn of Modern Europe

DOUGLAS H. SHANTZ

Foreword by

PETER C. ERB

The Johns Hopkins University Press
Baltimore

Printed in the United States of America on acid-free paper
2 4 6 8 9 7 5 3 1

The Johns Hopkins University Press
2715 North Charles Street
Baltimore, Maryland 21218-4363
www.press.jhu.edu

Library of Congress Cataloging-in-Publication Data

Shantz, Douglas H.
An introduction to German Pietism : Protestant renewal at the dawn of modern Europe / Douglas H. Shantz ; foreword by Peter C. Erb.
p. cm. — (Young Center books in Anabaptist and Pietist studies)
Includes bibliographical references and index.
ISBN 978-1-4214-0830-9 (hdbk. : alk. paper) — ISBN 978-1-4214-0831-6 (pbk. : alk. paper) — ISBN 978-1-4214-0880-4 (electronic) — ISBN 1-4214-0830-9 (hdbk. : alk. paper) — ISBN 1-4214-0831-7 (pbk. : alk. paper) — ISBN 1-4214-0880-5 (electronic)
1. Pietism—Germany. I. Title.
BR1652.G3S53 2013
273'.7—dc23 2012025312

A catalog record for this book is available from the British Library.

The Johns Hopkins University Press uses environmentally friendly book materials, including recycled text paper that is composed of at least 30 percent post-consumer waste, whenever possible.

To my students
past, present, future

Pietismus und Kirchenmusik sind als die beiden letzten großen Schöpfungen des deutschen Protestantismus bezeichnet worden.

Pietism and church music have been characterized as ultimately the two great creations of German Protestantism.

—Carl Hinrichs, *Preußentum und Pietismus* (1971), p. 17

Contents

Part III. *The Social and Cultural Worlds of German Pietism*

Part IV. *Pietism and Modernity*

Figures, Maps, and Tables

FIGURES

MAPS

TABLES

Foreword

It has been almost fifty years since F. Ernest Stoeffler published the first volume of his history of Pietism.[1] During this time, much has occurred to shift views of the movement. Christianity has developed new foci, in both its scholarly and its popular aspects—foci that have shifted the perspective from which the Pietist movement is considered. Pietism was initiated within German Protestantism in the late seventeenth century and remains with us today in the myriad of Protestant movements that began in and were shaped by the Pietist movement. Particularly in North America, Evangelical Protestantism, one of the major inheritors of the Pietist tradition, has determined much of the new outlook that is shaping the recent study of Pietism.

Over recent years, the scope of studies of the Pietist movement has increased, especially in Germany; one may note the publication of the *Geschichte des Pietismus* as just one indication of the work being done.[2] This growth has fostered a broad framework for study of the movement, both in Germany and in the world beyond.[3] The scholarly impact of these studies on the English-speaking world has been somewhat limited, but here, as well, their effects have been increasing—and nowhere is that impact clearer than in this work by Douglas Shantz.[4]

In Shantz's book there is a fine balance between the "old" and the "new" approaches to the movement, keeping what is of proven importance and adding to this the "new" that has opened Pietism to the modern world in the past three decades. As he puts it, "The genius of Pietism lay in the adjectives it employed: *true* Christianity; *heartfelt* . . . faith; a *living* knowledge of God; . . . the *inner* Word . . . the *new* man," and it is to such adjectives, among others, that the inheritors of the tradition responded. This is the framework in which Shantz shapes his study and, in part, reiterates the old. But this pattern is also shaped by the new, with a focus on features of the Pietist movement in the central cities of Germany and on the social and cultural aspects of Pietist reform, including Radical Pietism, Pietism and gender, the new attention to the Bible, and the missionary aspect that reflected a renewed Protestant interest in world Christianity.

Pietism played a significant role in the development of the modern world at large, especially shaping the culture of the West—something we fail to consider carefully to our peril. It is the source and nature of this influence that is this book's principal contribution and most elucidating aspect. The earliest chapters consider the expanse of thought already inherent in the Protestant Reformation, beginning with a detailed historical and critical analysis of the role of Anabaptists, Spiritualists, and alchemists, as well as Lutheran Orthodoxy (all of which, particularly the latter, have been much neglected in the earlier histories of Pietism), and moving on to its Calvinist forms, following the Thirty Years War, in English Puritanism, Jean de Labadie, and the "Second Dutch Reformation."

"Old" and "new" is a difficult balance to frame in a book written a half-century after Stoeffler's initial piece, and it is particularly difficult to manage for an author with the array of information represented in the four volumes of the *Geschichte des Pietismus* and the numerous studies of the past thirty-five years. There is a plethora of approaches to the Pietist era that need to be carefully considered before one can go on to elucidate the scene of Pietism as a whole, and this Shantz does.

Close attention must be directed to those who shaped Pietism within its Protestant framework at the beginning (with Schütz, Spener, and Francke), to how it developed, and, most recently, to the new forms of Christianity that have arisen under the shaping influence of Pietism. All these aspects this book takes seriously, placing the Pietist revival in a much larger framework than ever before, pointing to its role as an early stage in the rise of modern religion and culture in the West. This book goes a long way toward providing a better understanding of "the West"—both what it has to offer and what it must relinquish in its "tendencies to hero worship and anti-intellectualism" and its legacy of divisiveness and misguided prophecy. But Shantz's study does not close with such negative comment; rather, it offers in its conclusion and in its argument a whole strategy for assessing what is of continuing value in the cultural and religious legacy of German Pietism.

Peter C. Erb

Acknowledgments

I thank the University of Calgary Faculty of Arts for granting me a research sabbatical for the academic year 2009–2010. The year of sustained research and writing made this book possible. I am also grateful for the support of the Religious Studies Department Chair, Virginia Tumasz, who makes working at U of C such a great experience. Thanks go to the Faculty of Protestant Theology at Philipps University in Marburg, Germany, for providing a collegial atmosphere and a wonderful library in which to work.

I offer sincere thanks to those who read parts of this book at various stages, especially Jonathan Strom of Emory University, Peter Erb of Wilfrid Laurier University, Mary-Ann Shantz Lingwood of Grant MacEwan University, and my wife, Heather Shantz. Thanks, too, to the anonymous outside reader for his or her suggestions for improvement. I am delighted that Peter Erb kindly agreed to write the foreword. Back in the early 1980s, when I was a graduate student in Waterloo, Peter gave me a copy of his translation of Johann Arndt's *True Christianity*, helping to spark my interest in German Pietism. I want to thank Donald Kraybill and Jeff Bach of Elisabethtown College and Greg Nicholl at the Johns Hopkins University Press for their enthusiasm, patience, and unflagging support for this book. Karola Radler prepared the index, for which I am most grateful. Thanks also go to Robin Poitras, cartographer at the University of Calgary, who created the map of villages and cities where Pietists resided and one of Moravian mission centers in Labrador.

Finally, I thank the students in my graduate course on German Pietism and Enlightenment Thought in Winter 2011 at the University of Calgary.

An early draft of this book was required reading for the course. Their engagement with the material and insightful comments were a great help in the work of revision. The book is dedicated to them, as well as to all the other students over the past twenty years who have studied the Pietists with me and to those, *deo volente*, who will do so in future.

Part of chapter 4 appeared in an earlier version as "Homeless Minds: The Migration of Radical Pietists, Their Writings and Ideas in Early Modern Europe," in Jonathan Strom, ed., *Pietism in Germany and North America, 1680–1820* (Farnham, UK: Ashgate, 2009), 85–99.

Part of chapter 6 appeared in an earlier version as "Radical Pietist Migrations and Dealings with the Ruling Authorities as Seen in the Autobiographies of J. W. Petersen and J. F. Rock," in Wolfgang Breul, ed., *Der radikale Pietismus: Perspektiven der Forschung* (Göttingen: Vandenhoeck & Ruprecht, 2010), 211–227.

In Appendix A, Sources in Translation: Chapter 6 includes Peter Erb, ed., *Pietists: Selected Writings* (New York: Paulist Press, 1983), 220, 226; W. Kelsey, "Letter of Christopher Sower, Written in 1724, Describing Conditions in Philadelphia and Vicinity, and the Sea Voyage from Europe," *Pennsylvania Magazine of History and Biography* 45, no. 3 (July 1921), 243–254; and *The Complete Writings of Alexander Mack*, ed. William R. Eberly (Winona Lake, IN: BMH Books, 1991), 9–12. Chapter 7 includes Anna Maria van Schurman, *Whether a Christian Woman Should Be Educated and Other Writings from Her Intellectual Circle*, trans. Joyce L. Irwin (Chicago: University of Chicago Press, 1999), 76, 79ff., 85, 92. Chapter 8 includes J. A. Bengel, "The Author's Preface," in *Gnomon of the New Testament*, vol. 1, trans. Charlton T. Lewis and Marvin R. Vincent (Philadelphia: Perkinpine & Higgins, 1862), xvi–xix. Chapter 9 includes Marianne P. Stopp, "Eighteenth Century Labrador Inuit in England," *Arctic* 62, no. 1 (Mar. 2009), 54.

Centers of Pietism, 1670–1727.

An Introduction to
German Pietism

INTRODUCTION

Issues in Defining and Describing the Pietist Movement

In the 1670s, a new movement, later known as Pietism, began introducing some dramatic changes to traditional German Protestantism. Figures such as Theodor Undereyck, Gerhard Tersteegen, Johann Jakob Schütz, Philipp Jakob Spener, Maria Juliana Baur von Eyseneck, Johanna Eleonora Petersen, and August Hermann Francke promoted a practical Christianity marked by personal transformation, programs for social betterment, hopes for Christ's kingdom on earth, and calls for an end to denominational strife. Born-again laypeople, most of them women, became agents of their own spirituality, meeting in non-church settings to pray, read and discuss the Bible, and to encourage one another in their faith. In short, Pietism sought to bring reformation to the Reformation. German Pietism arguably represents the most significant Protestant renewal movement since the sixteenth century.

But why a book on Pietism? The case needs to be made, especially for a North American audience. Here it is: German Pietism represents a key, but forgotten, strand of the religious DNA of North American Christianity. Early European settlement on this continent is not just the story of Puritans and immigration from England. Probably the largest group of European immigrants to America in the eighteenth century was German. About one hundred thousand German-speaking migrants arrived in

North America during that century, and their number included the Pietists, especially Radical Pietist dissenting groups. Although comprising less than 10 percent of German immigrants, the Pietists' influence greatly exceeded their numbers, and they often succeeded in proselytizing other German settlers. By 1776, they made up more than a quarter of all German congregations in the New World.[1] These Pietist Christians brought an ethos of hard work and a born-again faith rooted in a well-read, well-marked Bible and a hymnody of Christian experience.

The influence of Pietist religion is evident among the born-again Evangelicals who dominate the continent today. Yet, apart from groups such as the Moravians, Church of the Brethren, and German and Swedish Baptists, North American Protestants suffer from a serious case of amnesia, as the German Pietist heritage continues to be largely forgotten. This is reflected in the relative lack of books in English on German Pietism, compared with the abundant literature on other early modern Christian movements such as the German and English Reformations, the Mennonites, the early Baptists, and English and American Puritanism and Methodism. The present book seeks to address this lack and to provide an up-to-date introduction to German Pietism in the English language that is suitable for college, university, and seminary students and others interested in learning about a defining moment in the Christian story.

For those seeking a general introduction to German Pietism, the resources in English are few. The main options are Ernest Stoeffler's *The Rise of Evangelical Pietism* (1965, 1971) and *German Pietism during the Eighteenth Century* (1973), Dale Brown's *Understanding Pietism* (1978, 1996), Peter Erb's source selections in *Pietism: Selected Writings* (1982, 2006), and Carter Lindberg's edited volume *The Pietist Theologians* (2005).[2] Stoeffler's studies have commanded the field in terms of introducing Pietism to an English-speaking audience, providing an excellent survey that, in the early 1970s, reflected the latest research and close acquaintance with primary sources.[3] Stoeffler's goal was to make Pietism respectable for a North American audience that tended to view it in a negative light. His first volume discusses English Puritan devotional writers and "Reformed Pietism" in the Netherlands and concludes with Johann Arndt and Philipp Jakob Spener. Given his desire to establish Pietism's respectable pedigree, it is not surprising that Stoeffler minimized the importance of mystical Spiritualists such as Caspar Schwenckfeld and Christian Hoburg to the Pietist story, and that he presented Pietism as a vibrant alternative to a cold and lifeless Lutheran Orthodoxy.[4] The second volume covers the spread of German Pietism in the eighteenth century from Halle to Württemberg, Herrnhut, and the New World. One reviewer credited Stoeffler with exceptional insight into the nuances of thought of key figures such as A. H. Francke and F. C. Oetinger.[5]

The past thirty-five years have witnessed impressive vitality and discovery in the Pietism field, so that Stoeffler's works are now less than satisfactory as an introduction to Pietism.[6] International Pietism Congresses were held in Halle, Germany, in 2001, 2005, and 2009, and the new four-volume *History of Pietism* (*Geschichte des Pietismus*) is now complete.[7] In the vibrant subfield of "Radical Pietism," several dissertations have appeared under the direction of Marburg church historian Hans Schneider. The North American Pietism Studies Research Group has been active for more than twelve years, holding sessions at the January meeting of the American Society of Church History. And social historical studies have begun to address issues of gender, social networks, and politics within the Pietist movement. One gender historian sees "light on the horizon for those who have an interest in new perspectives, questions, and methods in Pietism research."[8]

Not surprisingly, this research has yielded a portrait of German Pietism and its impact that stands in marked contrast to the one offered more than a generation ago. There is a new understanding of Pietism's beginnings, worldview, and cultural significance. Recent research shows that the founder of Pietism was neither Spener nor Arndt but a young lawyer in Spener's parish, Johann Jakob Schütz, whose dramatic conversion led to the first Lutheran Pietist conventicle in Frankfurt in August 1670.[9] Pietism is no longer viewed as a consistently Lutheran effort to simply take the Reformation a step further by adding reformation of *life* to Luther's reformation of *doctrine*. Spener's demand that Christians read the Bible for themselves stands in sharp contrast to Luther's notion of the catechism as the layperson's Bible.[10] The movement took on a variety of expressions as its supporters drew in eclectic fashion on theological notions they found in Caspar Schwenckfeld, Paracelsus, Jakob Böhme, Jean de Labadie, and the English Philadelphians. The Pietists joined early Enlightenment thinkers in helping to undermine traditional social and theological norms and to fashion a European culture marked by individualism, new social networks, and new literary media and genres such as journals, newspapers, and memoirs.[11]

So what is Pietism? Does it refer to a religious *type* or to a religious *epoch*? Was it a European-wide tendency in response to seventeenth-century cultural and religious crisis or a distinctly German movement, albeit in close connection with other European religious piety movements?[12] Did Pietism begin with Arndt and flow into the nineteenth century, as Stoeffler and the new *History of Pietism* suggest? Or was it a movement of the late seventeenth and eighteenth centuries, beginning with Schütz and Spener and thriving under the impact of Zinzendorf and Oetinger? Was Pietism an exclusively Lutheran phenomenon or did it include Reformed Christians (Calvinists) as well? Historians still wrestle with issues of definition and scope as they seek to capture the phenomenon of Pietism.[13] Four attempts at defining Pietism deserve consideration here—those by Johannes Wallmann, Hartmut Lehmann, Fred van Lieburg, and Martin Gierl.

Wallmann distinguishes Pietism "in the wider sense" as a concern for piety that goes back to Johann Arndt, and Pietism "in the narrower sense" as a movement within German Protestantism that dates from the founding of the *collegium pietatis* in Frankfurt in 1670. Wallmann is most concerned with Pietism in the narrower sense.[14] He notes three features of the Pietist movement that set it apart from Lutheran Orthodoxy and earlier promoters of piety such as Johann Arndt: conventicle gatherings of the reborn outside regular church services; an eschatology that looked for the imminent arrival of Christ's millennial kingdom on earth; and the central place of Bible reading in association with the practice of the universal priesthood of believers.[15] Wallmann offers a nuanced understanding of Pietism and its unique place in the panorama of German church history.

Wallmann shows that the Pietist movement had its own linguistic setting, historical identity, and trajectory within early modern Germany.[16] *Pietist* was initially a term of disdain—as with so many designations in Christian history, such as Lutheran, Calvinist, Anabaptist, Puritan, Baptist, and Methodist. It was first used in 1674 by critics of Spener's home gathering (*collegium pietatis*) in Frankfurt. Spener's *Pia Desideria* of 1675 was soon recognized as a programmatic statement of Pietist distinctives, offering a sixfold remedy for widespread spiritual decline based on lay Bible reading, meetings in homes for mutual encouragement, and the practice of Christian love and unity. The term *Pietists* came into common parlance in Leipzig in 1689 in the context of a student society devoted to practical Bible study led by August Hermann Francke. The gatherings became controversial when students began leading studies in homes throughout the city. Innumerable pamphlets, books, and government edicts were published in German lands in the 1690s in response to issues relating to the new movement of people called Pietists.[17]

Hartmut Lehmann promotes a definition of Pietism that is "broad and flexible so that Pietism research can unfold as freely and creatively as possible." Lehmann's concern is to encourage international exchange among researchers of religion in early modern Europe by recognizing the international context of Pietism and the interconnectedness of early modern piety movements. Pietists shared with English and American Evangelicals a similar worldview that included a sense of God's coming judgment on the world, fellowship with born-again believers in other denominations and nations, and the demand for repentance and a holy life. There is a need to move beyond Wallmann's distinction of wide and narrow Pietisms and to compare the religious understandings and sociocultural settings of the Pietists with those of English and American Evangelicals. For all of these groups, the notion of new birth played a central role. While Wallmann sees Pietism lasting only into the late eighteenth century, Lehmann sees an essential continuity between the "older Pietism" of Spener and Francke and the "New Pietism" of the nineteenth and twentieth centuries. The Moravians and the Basel Christian Society are key links between early and later Pietism. For Lehmann, "the discussion concerning the definition of Pietism is not over; it has really only begun."[18]

Key features of Pietism, according to Lehmann, include gatherings of born-again believers for mutual fellowship and encouragement; a tradition of biblical interpretation and belief passed down by Spener, Francke, and other "Pietist patriarchs"; and a sense of identity within a wide network of brothers and sisters in the faith, along with a corresponding sense of separation from the world. Pietism had varying regional expressions that reflected local conditions and traditions. Pietists differed on the importance of a conversion experience and on the specific norms for living a disciplined life, separate from the world.[19] There was no single Pietist systematic theology; some held more closely to traditional Lutheran or Calvinist beliefs than others.

Amsterdam church historian Fred van Lieburg picks up where Lehmann leaves off. He supports Lehmann's effort to open up "a transatlantic perspective" for Pietism research. The focus should be on the "social and cultural strategies" of religious groups rather than their origins and national identities. The definition of Pietism should not be limited to churches, confessions, territories, or even continents; a definition that sees Pietism as German and Lutheran stands in the way of seeing similar tendencies in different countries and churches. Van Lieburg wants a flexible definition that allows one to see Dutch Calvinist as well as German Lutheran variants of Pietism. Finally, van Lieburg warns against taking terms such as *Pietism* too seriously: "It is important to realize that all these concepts are abstractions that have little foundation in the social and cultural dimension of the historical reality they pretend to describe."[20] He calls on researchers to refrain from essentializing Pietism as an epoch *or* type. Rather, they should understand it functionally, as a general pattern or model (*Schablone*). Such an approach is less likely to stand in the way of the new cultural research into religious renewal in early modern Europe.[21]

In contrast to van Lieburg, Martin Gierl offers a definition of Pietism that ties it to theological controversy with Orthodox Lutheranism, first in Leipzig in the late 1680s and then in centers throughout the northern German empire. While Wallmann and Lehmann date Pietism's beginnings with Spener and Schütz in Frankfurt in 1670, Gierl offers a "late view of Pietism," dating it from the point at which Orthodox and Pietist parties and debates came into being.[22] "From the perspective of communications history," Gierl writes, "Pietism is . . . a designation for a controversy that began in Leipzig in 1689 and took place in public according to historically defined rules. Lutheran churchly Pietism was the theological construct that stood at the end point of the argument between Orthodox and Pietist-minded theologians."[23] Spener's Pietism was a program to reform theological controversy in which concern for the Christian brother was foremost.[24] Rather than define Pietism in terms of leading theologians, texts, and theology, Gierl defines it in terms of human action and interaction—how Pietists reacted through conflicts, disputations, correspondence, and discourse. Pietism was a new way of engaging for truth in practical social settings. Gierl considers two great controversies to be crucial in the rise of Pietism: controversies in the early 1690s over conventicles and in 1691, in Hamburg, over chiliasm and the writings of Johann Wilhelm Petersen.[25]

The working definition of Pietism in this book is the following:

> *Pietism arose in the late seventeenth-century German empire among empowered laity and clergy in the prosperous urban settings of Frankfurt and Leipzig. The Pietism movement introduced a new paradigm to traditional German Protestantism, one that encouraged personal renewal and new birth, conventicle gatherings for Bible study and mutual encouragement, social activism and postmillennialism, and ecumenical cooperation—in contrast to the polemical Protestantism that gave rise to the Thirty Years War. Pietism included an eclectic mix of esoteric spirituality, radical Reformation traditions, and biblical devotion, with no clear line separating church Pietists, such as Spener, from the Radicals. The cultural legacy of Pietism includes reforms in caring for the poor and the orphan, new Bible translations, new social networks, experiential literature such as the autobiography and memoir, and worldwide mission. Pietism thrived in German lands in the late seventeenth and eighteenth centuries among all social classes within both Lutheran and Reformed Protestantism. It also thrived in Switzerland, Scandinavia, and the Baltic. Early Pietist missionary efforts in South India and Labrador were cooperative German-Danish enterprises. Pietism came to North America as thousands of disillusioned Germans migrated to the New World.*

This definition reflects the insights of recent scholarship as well as the theological nuance achieved by Wallmann. It sees Pietism as a German movement shaped by social and cultural circumstances unique to German lands, but in close relation to renewal movements in England and the Netherlands and to earlier figures such as Johann Arndt and Jakob Böhme.[26] Early Leipzig Pietism was dominated by stude nts, women, and tradesmen; missing were the upper social classes. But eventually the movement reached all social classes—princely courts, universities, theologians, the middle class, the servant class, and those on the land. This definition includes Count Zinzendorf and the Moravians but sees the German awakenings of the nineteenth and twentieth centuries as distinct, despite continuities.[27] Pietism reflects the culture of the early modern period, whereas later German awakenings and missions reflect the modern age of liberalism, nationalism, colonialism, and the two world wars.

The question of the best method of approach in describing the Pietist movement is also contentious. Pietism research is still dominated by German Lutheran church historians for whom Pietism is the story of male leaders and theologians. The methods of social and cultural history have had comparatively little impact on their portrayals of the world of Pietism. The interpretive frameworks of confessionalization, secularization, and gender have only recently begun to shape the research agendas of Pietism scholars.[28]

The traditional approach is illustrated by Johannes Wallmann's conviction that "the history of Pietism is essentially the history of individual leaders and tradition-building figures."[29] This approach structures the Pietist story around three generations of Pietist Patriarchs, including Philipp Jakob Spener (1635–1705) in the first generation; August Hermann Francke (1663–1727) and early Halle Pietism in the second; and Count Nikolaus Ludwig von Zinzendorf (1700–1760) and the Moravians, Johann Albrecht Bengel (1687–1752), Friedrich Christoph Oetinger (1702–1782), and Württemberg Pietism in the third. Wallmann also includes Pietist Radicals and separatists such as Johann Jakob Schütz, Gottfried Arnold, Johann Wilhelm and Johanna Eleonora Petersen, Johann Konrad Dippel, and Heinrich Horch. The advantage of the biographical approach is its focus on the theological beliefs and innovations of Pietist leaders. The disadvantage is that it overlooks the lived experience of ordinary laypeople, especially women. Today, many scholars see this approach as too patriarchal and dismissive of the insights of cultural and social history.[30]

A second approach uses methods predominant in the historical profession today, examining Pietism as a social and cultural world rather than an otherworldly theology and piety. It presents Pietism as a movement that affected, and was affected by, politics, social behaviors, and culture. Examples of this approach are recent studies by Benjamin Marschke on Pietist chaplains in the Prussian army, by Tanya Kevorkian on Pietism in Leipzig in the age of J. S. Bach, and by Ulrike Gleixner on issues of gender and middle-class culture in German Pietism.[31] A criticism of this approach is that it tends to ignore theological issues, a serious matter when investigating a movement such as Pietism.

The approach in this book is to steer a middle course, valuing the theological, devotional, and social dimensions of Pietism. First, it presents Pietism as a full-orbed social reality that affected the way ordinary Christian people experienced their faith and their world. The Pietist story includes leaders and commoners, thought and experience, religious faith and social expression. Under the impact of Pietist reforms, children were educated differently, sermons were preached differently, hymns were sung differently, and community was structured differently. Second, the book's chapters focus on features of Pietism that made it religiously and culturally significant; the concern is not to provide an encyclopedic biography of every notable figure related to the movement. Third, this history draws on the rich variety of disciplines that have made Pietism their focus: church history, political history, sociology, musicology, literary history, and gender history, to name a few. It reflects the questions and insights of recent research, much of it from the perspective of social and cultural history within the past ten years. Finally, this text describes not only the godly intentions but also the failings of the Pietists, noting the real world consequences of their beliefs, ideas, experiences, and actions.[32]

A final consideration is the formidable challenge facing anyone who would write an introduction to German Pietism. One can only echo Martin Brecht's observation.

> Anyone who works closely with the history of Pietism quickly becomes aware of how fragmentary our knowledge of it is. No one can survey the whole field . . . Even the contribution of great Pietist figures has only been researched in part. Our knowledge of its wider connections is likewise full of gaps. This is true for the roots and beginnings of Pietism as well as for its progress through history.[33]

No one can possibly read all the relevant source material or do justice to the complexity of the movement.[34] Three key figures, Spener, Francke, and Zinzendorf, were prolific authors. Spener's productivity outstripped even Luther's, leading one researcher to state flatly, "There is no complete edition of Spener's works and there will never be one."[35] However, a complete edition of Spener's letters is planned and well under way.[36] Francke was almost equally productive: the archive of the Francke Foundations in Halle houses some twenty-five thousand of Francke's letters. The bibliography of his published writings lists 849 titles.[37] Zinzendorf estimated that he had preached some three thousand messages, most of which were transcribed but remain unpublished. The reprint edition of Zinzendorf's works by Beyreuther and Meyer aimed at publishing sixty volumes.[38] A leading Radical Pietist, Johann Wilhelm Petersen, authored more than 160 works.[39] Also demanding attention are the correspondence, biographies, and autobiographies of Pietist figures that can be found in archives in Herrnhut and Halle and in public and private archives in other communities.

Another challenge is finding the best entryway to Pietism: is it by way of leaders and thinkers, such as Spener, Arnold, Francke, Zinzendorf, and Oetinger, or through sources that give us access to popular piety and to women writers within the movement? Any account of Pietism will be selective; choices must be made in terms of the source material and the subject matter it includes.

Here are my choices. Chapters 1 and 2 discuss the social, political, and religious contexts of Pietism, highlighting the creative and eclectic sixteenth- and seventeenth-century background of Pietist spirituality. Chapters 3 to 5 consider early Pietism in three urban settings: Frankfurt, Leipzig, and Halle. The next four chapters are thematic, examining the social and cultural worlds of the Pietists: the migratory individualism of the Radicals (chapter 6), Pietism and gender (chapter 7), Pietists as readers and translators of the Bible (chapter 8), and Pietists as missionaries to the far reaches of the world (chapter 9). The last chapter considers Pietism's impact in shaping the individualism of modern Western religion and culture. Pietism introduced a new paradigm to Protestant Christianity, one that still exercises a strong appeal among North American Christians. The book concludes by reflecting on the cultural and religious legacy of German Pietism.

This book offers a new generation of students and professors a state-of-the-art portrait of German Pietism, relying on the latest research in German and English. It will have achieved its purpose if it provides some idea of the conflicts and debates, hopes and fears, of the Pietists as they lived, worked, prayed, and suffered together in the fellowship of the reborn and in the hope of worldly vindication.

Finally, a brief comment about terminology may be helpful to some readers. It is common in Pietist sources to come across references to *chiliasm* and *chiliasts* and to find Pietist theology described as *chiliastic*. These are roughly equivalent to *millennialism* and *millennialists* and *millenarian*—

terms more commonly used in English. However, eighteenth-century Pietist chiliasts made no distinction in terms of premillennialism, amillennialism, or postmillennialism. In most cases, Pietists held to a postmillennial theology; they believed that better times were ahead for the church and understood this as the coming millennial age represented by the Church of Philadelphia in Revelation 3:7. Many believed that Christ would not appear visibly to assume his millennial kingdom but would exercise rule in a hidden, spiritual manner, through his saints on earth. The Pietists saw signs that the coming restoration of the true church was imminent: Christians had begun gathering together in peace and harmony, the Gospel was being proclaimed, and the heathen and Jews everywhere had begun converting to Christ.

Part I

The Setting and Inspiration for German Pietism

CHAPTER 1

German Radicalism and Orthodox Lutheran Reform

Any discussion of the context of German Pietism must include the currents of radical reform that persisted underground in German lands from the sixteenth into the eighteenth century. This was the age not only of the bright light of reason and rationalism but also of the subtle light of mysticism and sectarian reform.[1] The lives, writings, and ideals of German Mystics, Anabaptists, Schwenkfelders, Spiritualists, Paracelsists, and alchemists in the sixteenth and seventeenth centuries continued to have an impact a century later through small circles of devotees and protest literature. A tradition of radical religious discourse linked Pietists such as Gottfried Arnold and Friedrich Christoph Oetinger with sixteenth-century radicals.[2] Besides examining various forms of sixteenth- and seventeenth-century German radicalism, this chapter also considers Orthodox Lutheran reform as a factor in the rise of German Pietism.

Anabaptists and Spiritualists

By the mid 1520s, some early supporters of Martin Luther were becoming disillusioned with the progress of Evangelical reform. They criticized Luther for his focus on the "outer word" of scripture and preaching and his neglect of the "inner Word" of Christ in the hearts of believers. They called for a more Christian way of life than was evident in the Evangelical churches. These critics included figures such as Andreas Karlstadt, Thomas Müntzer, Sebastian Franck, Caspar Schwenckfeld, David Joris, and the Anabaptists. When later Pietists looked for inspiration in their own quest for renewal, the sixteenth-century radicals served as important models. Gottfried Arnold, Johann Wilhelm Petersen, Johann Konrad Dippel, and many others expressed high regard for the example and writings of German Anabaptists and Spiritualists.

CASPAR SCHWENCKFELD VON OSSIG (1489–1561)

In the Reformation of the sixteenth century, the figure who pointed most clearly in the direction of Pietism was the Silesian nobleman Caspar Schwenckfeld von Ossig.[3] He studied at several European universities and served for a time as an influential adviser to his Silesian prince, Friedrich II of Liegnitz. Schwenckfeld experienced a conversion in 1519 after reading works by Johannes Tauler, Thomas à Kempis, and especially Martin Luther. Like Thomas à Kempis, Schwenckfeld rejected academic learning in favor of ethical living, self-examination, meditation, union with Christ, and imitation of Christ's life.[4] Assisted by his humanist colleague, the Liegnitz Canon Valentin Crautwald (ca. 1465–1545),[5] Schwenckfeld developed a unique piety focused on the "new man" and the Christian's real partaking, by faith, of the body and blood of the risen Christ. The Silesians criticized the lack of ethical improvement among Lutheran Christians, something they attributed to Luther's persistence in tying spiritual renewal to outward material signs and sacraments. Following the Spiritualist principle of Erasmus, Karlstadt, and Zwingli, Schwenckfeld taught that spiritual grace could be received only by spiritual means. Christ's body and blood, *not* the sacramental bread and wine, were the only source of grace and spiritual nourishment. Crautwald interpreted Christ's words at the Last Supper in a way that echoed John 6:55: "My body which is broken for you is [like] this, namely bread." The new man is born when, by faith, the believer receives the actual substance of Christ's heavenly body, which works inward renewal and transformation. "[He is] obedient to God's Word and guided, formed, and walking by the Spirit. He is vivified in his spirit, puts on new life, lives as a New Man in Christ, and each day, looking to Christ the author of life, is formed according to

His image from glory into glory."[6] In a circular letter in April 1526, Crautwald and Schwenckfeld called for *Stillstand*, a temporary suspension of sacramental practice, and a program of catechetical instruction. The sacraments would be reinstituted only when a church of renewed believers and renewed clergy had come into being.[7]

Under Crautwald's influence, the Schwenkfelders followed Joachim of Fiore in looking for the coming age of the Spirit and a properly constituted Philadelphian church marked by Christian love and peace.[8] Some identified the two witnesses of Revelation 11:3, who would gather the restored church of New Men, with Schwenckfeld and Crautwald.[9] Meanwhile, the Schwenkfelders met in conventicles in homes with like-minded believers. Letters became the means of sharing experiences in the school of Christ and of knitting members together in a common identity.[10] The lack of theological system, the stress on the inward partaking of Christ, and the practice of the priesthood of all believers, with women exercising leadership alongside men, made Schwenkfelder circles attractive to a wide variety of social groups in central and southern Germany, especially women. In the seventeenth and eighteenth centuries, members of Schwenkfelder conventicles built ties with Philipp Jakob Spener, Gottfried Arnold, Count Nikolaus Ludwig von Zinzendorf, and various Pietist pastors.[11]

Schwenckfeld's writings were widely read in the seventeenth century by mystical Spiritualists and first-generation Pietists.[12] The Spiritualist ideal of the coming restoration of the true church as the goal of history lived on in Jakob Böhme, the English Philadelphians, and the Radical Pietists.[13] Schwenckfeld's influence was mediated to Pietism by Jakob Böhme, Christian Hoburg, and Friedrich Breckling.[14] As a young man, Hoburg (1607–1675) was converted to a Spiritualist piety, a "living Christianity of the heart," after reading Schwenckfeld's *Heavenly Medicine*. He soon became a vigorous critic of the Lutheran *Amtskirche*, or state churches. He favored Schwenckfeld's emphases on new birth and lay Christianity over the Lutherans' justification teaching and clergy-dominated churches. Hoburg's disciple Breckling effectively transmitted this piety to a host of Pietist figures through his extensive correspondence.[15] It was probably Hoburg or Breckling who first drew the attention of Gottfried Arnold to the writings of Schwenckfeld and David Joris.[16]

THE INFLUENCE OF CASPAR SCHWENCKFELD AND DAVID JORIS ON GOTTFRIED ARNOLD

Gottfried Arnold's *Impartial History of Churches and Heretics* (1699/1700) is a tribute to Spiritualist believers throughout history and their emphasis on inner, heartfelt faith. For Arnold, the true history of Christianity was to be found in the "radical underground," the marginalized and persecuted, including Anabaptists, Spiritualists, Quakers, Behmenists, Quietists, Paracelsist physicians, and women visionaries. Luther, by comparison, gets "relatively short shrift."[17] The leading figures in Arnold's *Impartial History*, judging by the space he devoted to them, are two sixteenth-century Reformation radicals: the Silesian Spiritualist Caspar Schwenckfeld (82 pages) and the Dutch Anabaptist and alchemist David Joris (238 pages).[18] At a time when Europe was exhausted by the Thirty Years War and religious conflict, Arnold found in the writings of Schwenckfeld and Joris an inward Christianity of the heart that minimized differences of sacrament and confession.[19] Their works served as historical witnesses and benchmarks for the Pietist effort to reorient Christianity toward inward experience and a church taught directly by God's Spirit.

CONNECTIONS BETWEEN ANABAPTISM AND PIETISM

Researchers continue to discover connections between the Pietists and various Anabaptists, Hutterites, and Mennonites. Astrid von Schlachta has demonstrated frequent contacts between eighteenth-century Dutch Mennonites and neighboring Herrnhut preachers. Eighteenth-century Hutterites also had close ties with Pietist groups, especially the Herrnhuters. Von Schlachta finds that the Pietists influenced their Hutterite neighbors towards a greater degree of tolerance, openness, and appreciation for the teachings they held in common. Marcus Meier traces connections between Radical Pietists in Schwarzenau (the New Baptists under Alexander Mack) and the Mennonites. He describes the New Baptists as a radical Pietist group that, at decisive points, was affected by contacts with Mennonites and the Amish.[20]

German Alchemists, Spiritual Alchemy, and New Birth

Also influential among the Pietists was the spiritual alchemy of Paracelsus, Johann Arndt, Jakob Böhme, Jane Leade, and their disciples. These figures expressed a yearning for inner, spiritual transformation and the New Man that struck a chord with the Pietists.

> On the material level the alchemists' purpose in the laboratory was the production of gold, the most perfect of all metals, by actualizing all the qualities of gold which were thought to be potentially present in lesser metals. On the spiritual level [their purpose] was to develop the true Self, to "lead out the gold within," as they said, by actualizing the qualities potentially present in the human being.[21]

A connection between alchemy, Rosicrucianism, and German Pietism is not surprising. In German lands in the late seventeenth and early eighteenth centuries, there were strong currents of the alchemical-kabbalistic-hermetic outlook.[22] Yet there has been a reluctance to consider alchemists and Rosicrucians as a significant factor within Pietism. Peter Erb, for example, rejected alchemy as a key influence on either Johann Arndt or Gottfried Arnold. Erb "de-radicalizes Arnold's intellectual life," insisting on Arnold's undying loyalty to Luther and denying any significant dependence of Arnold on Jakob Böhme or radical Spiritualism.[23] Erich Beyreuther likewise warned against granting Böhme too great an influence on Arnold, arguing that Böhme "remained fundamentally foreign" to Arnold's thinking.[24]

The last few years have seen a new openness to finding significant alchemical involvement among the Pietists. W. R. Ward argued that Pietists in Frankfurt, Württemberg, and Wittgenstein were shaped by the "spiritual vitality [of] the radical underworld" represented in Jakob Böhme and assorted mystics, Paracelsists, alchemists, and Jewish Kabbalists.[25] Christa Habrich has shown that "natural magic and alchemy were viewed positively by radical and churchly Pietism alike."[26] A research group in Halle, led by Monika Neugebauer-Wölk and Markus Meumann, is examining relations among esoteric alchemical traditions, Pietism, and the early Enlightenment in the period around 1700.[27] Halle was not only a university town and center of Pietism but also a place of refuge for heterodox thinkers, including alchemists. Gottfried Arnold and Friedrich Christoph Oetinger are notable examples of the connection between alchemy and Pietism. Arnold's *Impartial History* devoted many more pages to Paracelsus, Jakob Böhme, and the Rosicrucians than to Luther and Melanchthon.[28] In Oetinger, "all the traditions of alchemy and theosophy come together."[29] He saw the work of the alchemist as a pious duty and an aid to theological understanding.

The esoteric worldview of the alchemists had at least six elements. First, alchemical practitioners investigated the Book of Nature, alongside the Bible, as a source of higher wisdom, enlightenment, and deeper Christian understanding. The second element is the doctrine of correspondences—the idea that everything in the universe is related to everything else. There is a correspondence between the microcosm of humanity on earth and the macrocosm of the heavens. "Man is a small replica of the entire universe, and all of his parts correspond to features of the world as a whole."[30] Third is the idea of Nature as a living thing—vitalism: Nature is dynamic and points to higher spiritual realities. Fourth is the idea of transmutation, by which beings are raised from potentiality to actuality and fulfillment. This is true in the vegetative, mineral, animal, and human realms. Fifth is the postmillennial conviction that salvation is something to be realized within this world. Christ represents a principle of cosmic redemption and completion. Finally, Christian alchemists understood true Christianity as consisting not of outward rituals but of the invisible society of the reborn.[31]

PARACELSUS (1493–1541)

The spiritual alchemy of Johann Arndt and Jakob Böhme was inspired by the writings and influence of a man who called himself Paracelsus. Christened Philipp Theophrastus, he was born in 1493 in Einsiedeln, Switzerland, the only child of Wilhelm von Hohenheim (1457–1534), a Swabian nobleman and physician, and a peasant mother who died when Philipp was nine years old.[32] His father taught him a love of nature and learning and some rudiments of medicine. Paracelsus claimed that he studied science and medicine "for many years at universities in Germany, Italy, and France." He swore an oath in Basel in May 1527 that he had obtained his doctor's degree from Ferrara, Italy, probably in 1515. In 1529 he began going by the name Paracelsus, the classical approximation of Hohenheim.[33]

Paracelsus spent much of his life as a restless wanderer and itinerant physician. In addition to Italy, France, south Germany, Austria, and Switzerland, his travels took him through Portugal, Spain, England, the Netherlands, Denmark, Sweden, Prussia, Russia, Lithuania, Poland, Hungary, Romania, Ukraine, Slovenia, Croatia, Greece, and Turkey.[34] His search for medical wisdom even took him to Asia Minor, Ethiopia, and Egypt, where he received instruction in ancient remedies and magical arts. His early travels took him directly into war zones, including the Venetian War (1516–1517), the Dutch War (1519), and the Danish War (1520). He went where he could be of greatest help to suffering humanity, gaining valuable experience as an army surgeon.[35] Today's equivalent would be service with the Red Cross or Doctors without Borders.

Paracelsus's curiosity and devotion to medical knowledge knew no bounds.

> Wherever I went I diligently investigated and sought after the tested and reliable arts of medicine. I went not only to the doctors, but also to barbers, bathkeepers, learned physicians, women, and magicians who pursue the art of healing. I went to alchemists, to monasteries, to nobles and common folk, to the experts and the simple . . . This is my vow: to perfect my medical art and never to swerve from it so long as God grants me my office, and to oppose all false medicine and teachings. Then, to love the sick, each and all of them, more than if my own body were at stake . . . I will let Luther defend his cause, and I will defend my cause, and I will defeat those of my colleagues who turn against me.[36]

He insisted that "the supreme reason for medicine is love," grounded in the virtue of the physician.[37] Paracelsus discovered many things about the natural world and used this knowledge to cure a variety of illnesses, including the plague, gout, epilepsy, and bodily wounds. He offered a classification of miners' diseases based on his experience in the mines of Tyrol. Two of his earliest publications, in 1529 and 1530, were pamphlets on the treatment of syphilis, for which he suggested mercury as the best cure.[38] While Hippocrates and Galen attributed disease to an imbalance of the four humors, Paracelsus taught that diseases are caused by a source outside the body that affects specific organs. He was among the first to promote the use of chemicals in curing disease.[39]

Paracelsus's many books, dictated rapidly to his students, include 53 medical treatises and 235 philosophical and theological works, which were translated into most European languages. The modern edition of his writings, a work in progress, will comprise more than sixteen thousand pages in twenty-eight volumes. Only Luther was more prolific among sixteenth-century German authors. But due to the obscurity of Paracelsus's writing style and the lack of published editions in his lifetime, he was "more honored and ridiculed than read."[40]

For Paracelsus, the source of all knowledge lies in God and his creation rather than in Aristotle or the universities. "I have been chosen by God to extinguish and blot out . . . the words of Aristotle, Galen, Avicenna, and the dogmas of their followers." Paracelsus believed that knowledge of the secrets of Nature, once known to the Persians, Egyptians, and Hebrews, had been lost to the Greeks and later Europeans.[41] While scholars based their arts on their own opinions, Paracelsus's book of alchemy was founded "not upon human authorities but upon Nature itself."[42] True science must imitate God's own creative work. In his "Alchemical Catechism," Paracelsus elaborated on this point: the wise philosopher should follow the path of the Architect of the universe, be "a faithful copyist of the Creator," and imitate Nature point by point in every detail. The alchemist must work with Nature's three basic principles: mercury, sulfur, and salt.[43] He must build a furnace for the fire so that he can build a new world: "for after the same manner as God created the Heaven and Earth, the Furnace with the Fire is to be built and governed . . . according to the exigency of Nature, neither too excessive nor too small, but most fit and apt for the motion of the Matter." The goal of the alchemist is to complete Nature's own work, to perfect what God has left imperfect in the created world, and to attain by refining fire the pure gold hidden in base metals. Humans were placed in the world to bring Nature to perfection, and this includes perfecting themselves. This process of fulfillment is best symbolized in alchemy.[44]

Paracelsus challenged the medical orthodoxy of the time just as Luther challenged theological orthodoxy, earning him the title *Lutherus medicorum,* the Luther of the physicians. Both men opposed Aristotle and traditional academic knowledge in the universities. Paracelsus's university lectures in Basel in 1527 were the first medical lectures offered in German rather than Latin.[45] Like Luther, Paracelsus wrote in a context of crisis and debate.[46] His writings are marked by their iconoclasm, biting satire, and challenges to the authoritative knowledge of the day. Both Luther and Paracelsus suffered libel and slander against their character; both were accused of being addicted to drink. Both men had a sense of living at the end of time, with disaster and the last judgment likely to arrive within their own lifetime. Paracelsus, however, looked for a golden age to follow, when the saints would be rewarded for enduring poverty and oppression, an age that reformers such as himself were helping to inaugurate.[47]

Since the 1990s there has been a new wave of Paracelsus research that takes seriously the religious dimension of his work and recognizes that Paracelsus was as much a social and religious controversialist as he was a medical controversialist.[48] The gradual publication of critical editions of his religious writing over the past fifty years is transforming Paracelsus scholarship.[49] Still unpublished are his commentaries on the New Testament, his writings on the Lord's Supper, and his sermons and writings on the Virgin Mary. In 2008, Urs Leo Gantenbein published the first volume of a planned eight-volume edition of Paracelsus's theological works that will bring the corpus to completion.[50]

In a 1525 tract entitled "Concerning Seven Points of Christian Idolatry," Paracelsus sharply attacked the corruption of clergy and church abuses such as indulgences and other money-making practices. He criticized a purely outward piety of churchgoing, fasting, almsgiving, and pilgrimages. In this criticism he joined reformers such as Erasmus, Luther, Zwingli, and Karlstadt, advocating "an individual and spiritual understanding of Christian faith."[51] Paracelsus was driven by a deep religious commitment grounded in his reading of the Christian Bible. "From Holy Scripture," he wrote, "comes the beginning and guide of all philosophy and natural science." "It is Christ from whom everything must be drawn." In his works in the 1530s, Paracelsus leveled his critical gaze at Catholics and Reformers alike; his anticlericalism lumped together the Catholic, Lutheran, and Zwinglian priesthoods as equally corrupt. "Any clerical order was likely to be arrogant, lazy and debauched."[52] He considered the Anabaptists to be misguided zealots. Paracelsus refused to identify with any of the religious parties of his day; he never left the Roman Catholic Church.

There has been no systematic effort to explore links between Paracelsus and the Anabaptists. Charles Webster finds "striking similarities" between notions in the writings of Paracelsus and Anabaptist beliefs. "He regarded baptism as a matter of choice, suitable only for mature persons and for believers."[53] Paracelsus had particular affinities with Anabaptists who had apocalyptic and Spiritualist tendencies, such as Hans Hut, Hans Denck, Jakob Kautz, and the Strasbourg radical Clement Ziegler. Following Caspar Schwenckfeld, Paracelsus waited for God to reinstitute a new church order.[54]

Gantenbein notes that in the early 1520s, Paracelsus adopted ideas of the early Luther, such as the priesthood of all believers and the role of the laity as leaders of reform. Paracelsus's thought was marked, from early on, by anticlericalism, a focus on Christ, and preoccupation with scriptural commentary. His thinking bore distinctly "Spiritualist tendencies," emphasizing individualism, Christ's inner presence, and imitation of Christ's way of life. Paracelsus was not a true Spiritualist, however, for he taught that believers receive the real presence of Christ in the Lord's Supper. Gantenbein dates Paracelsus's break with Luther to 1525 and the Revolution of the Common Man. Paracelsus was in Salzburg when the miners revolted against the mine owners. Thereafter he took the side of the poor and the commoners, among whom he believed a true Christian life and future Christian renewal were most likely to be found. After 1531 he also distanced himself from the Anabaptists. Gantenbein concludes that the most central notion of all in Paracelsus's theology and writing was love of God and neighbor.[55]

Valentin Weigel (1533–1588) helped to transmit Paracelsus's views and writings to seventeenth-century readers.[56] Another key figure in transmitting Paracelsus's writings was Karl Widemann (d. 1638), a Schwenkfelder physician in Augsburg who devoted thirty years to collecting and copying the works of Paracelsus. Thanks to him, many of Paracelsus's unprinted writings were preserved. Paracelsus's medical and philosophical ideas and criticisms of the churches were kept alive within small but influential circles into the seventeenth and eighteenth centuries.[57] His writings and ideas were also promoted by German and French Calvinists, sometimes accompanied by an apocalyptic and millenarian outlook. Thus, "Religious and medical heresy went together."[58] The Calvinist Landgrave Maurice of Hesse served as patron to the Marburg Circle of alchemists that included Johann Heinrich Alsted of Herborn (1588–1638) and Michael Maier (1569–1622), court physician to the landgrave. King Henry

IV of France had Paracelsian doctors, as did the Elector Palatine Frederick V. Paracelsian medicine and chemistry were widely accepted among Puritans in England and America. In his *Anatomy of Melancholy* (1621), the Anglican clergyman Robert Burton indicates that he was steeped in the literature of Paracelsianism and was a believer in chemical treatments.

JOHANN ARNDT (1555–1621)

Johann Arndt is the most significant figure in post-Reformation spiritual renewal and "the most influential Lutheran since the Reformation."[59] His successful devotional writings have made him the most important figure in the history of modern Protestantism, even surpassing Luther. His writings on behalf of true Christianity and a living faith represent a new epoch in the Lutheran church and a new era in the western Christian world. But interpreters of Arndt's legacy remain divided: for some, he brought Luther to completion; for others, he introduced mystical, Spiritualist, and alchemical ideas that stand in clear opposition to Luther. In the past ten years, thanks to the discovery of letters to and from Arndt, a more detailed portrait of his early life and thought is finally possible.

Arndt was born on December 27, 1555, in Ballenstedt, Anhalt, the son of Jakob Arndt, a Lutheran pastor. His father had been ordained to the ministry two years earlier by Johannes Bugenhagen, a friend of Luther. Johann Arndt attended schools in Aschersleben, Halberstadt, and Magdeburg. Arndt's letters clarify some important details of his student life. He studied arts in Helmstedt from April 1575 to February 1577 and in Strasbourg from 1577 to January 1579. From January to September 1579, he studied Paracelsian medicine and traditional Galenic medicine at the University of Basel. There he was especially influenced by Professor Theodor Zwinger, who introduced him to the thought and writings of Paracelsus. Arndt retained an interest in alchemy for the rest of his life; in later years he had a small laboratory beside his study.[60] Among his friends, Arndt counted the Paracelsist physician Heinrich Khunrath.

It is noteworthy that Arndt does not mention theology as a subject of study. His friend Johann Gerhard confirmed that Arndt never completed a program of theological study, although he may have attended lectures in theology, and his book purchases reveal his wide reading in the field. This yields an astounding conclusion: "The most influential figure in Lutheran

Christianity after the Reformation never completed a course of study in theology."[61] This is not entirely surprising, for it was not yet the norm for Protestant pastors to have completed theological studies. It was not unusual, for example, for schoolteachers without theological training to enter clerical ministry and serve in churches. Arndt's father was a schoolteacher before he became a pastor. Accusations that Arndt had no theological training are now, thanks to recently discovered letters, more credible.

From 1581 to 1583, Johann Arndt served as a schoolteacher in Ballenstedt.[62] On October 30, 1583, he was ordained to the Lutheran ministry, and on October 27, 1584, began pastoral ministry in his home province, in the St. Vitus Church in Badeborn. When the Calvinist prince of Anhalt, Johann Georg, prohibited his clergy from practicing the ritual of exorcism, Arndt refused to comply. In September 1590 he was dismissed from his position. That same year he was called to St. Nicholas Church in Quedlinburg, where he remained for nine years. In addition to his pastoral duties, he carried on a medical practice that taxed him to the limit during the plague epidemics in Quedlinburg in 1598, and later in Eisleben in 1610. The Quedlinburg ministerium commended him for his work: "Last year when the plague raged and he had even lost some of his ministerial colleagues, Arndt endured alone the work [among the sick] and the difficulties, endangering his own life on a daily basis, supported and sustained by the great and almighty God."[63]

While in Quedlinburg, Arndt devoted himself to reading the German mystics and the writings of sixteenth-century Spiritualists, including Caspar Schwenckfeld, Paracelsus, and Valentin Weigel. In Arndt's sermons in 1595 and 1596 on the ten plagues of Egypt, there are echoes of Paracelsus: "Humankind is the most ingenious of God's creative work, a microcosm and small world patterned after the greater world . . . The true physician knows that man is a microcosm, the small world, and that everything that is found in nature in the greater world can also be found in man, in the small world."[64] In 1597 Arndt published an edition of *The German Theology*. In the introduction he called for "real penitence and a Christian life in which true Christianity consist."[65] The end of all theology, he wrote, is union with God. The year 1597 marks a significant turning point in Arndt's life, thought, and writing.[66]

In 1599 Arndt moved to Braunschweig to serve in the church of St. Martin. In 1605, Book I of Arndt's most famous work, *Of True Christian-*

ity, appeared at the Easter book fair in Frankfurt.[67] The tone of the work is evident in passages such as the following:

> It is not knowledge that makes the Christian but the love of Christ . . . We must be born again by the Word of God and become new creatures. If this new birth has not happened in us, then we do not have real faith . . . The scholarly study of the Scriptures without love and a holy Christian life is simply worthless.[68]

In early 1606, Arndt published a revised edition that addressed attacks coming from the Braunschweig clergy. His younger colleague at St. Martin's, Martin Denecke, was at the forefront of the attack. In November 1608, Arndt finally left Braunschweig for Eisleben. He lamented, "I would never have thought that there were such evil, poisonous people among the theologians." "Consider what it is like to be publicly slandered before all the churches as a crude, uneducated ass who has never studied theology."[69]

After Arndt had spent two and a half years at St. Andrew's Church in Eisleben, Duke Ernst of Braunschweig-Lüneburg, in July 1611, appointed him general superintendent in Celle. Arndt served in this role until his death on May 11, 1621. He was prolific in his last ten years, publishing the *Garden of Paradise* in 1612, a book of prayer and devotion. In 1616 and 1617, books of his sermons appeared in print: *Gospel Sermons, Catechetical Sermons*, and *An Exposition of the Psalms of David*. In 1620, with his Lutheran orthodoxy under attack, Arndt wrote four tracts defending his belief in the Trinity and rejecting accusations of perfectionism.[70] In 1621 he published an edition of writings by the medieval mystic Johannes Tauler.

In early 1610 Arndt published *The Four Books of True Christianity*, an expanded version of his 1605 book, *Of True Christianity*. It now consisted of the Book of Scripture, Christ the Book of Life, the Book of Conscience, and the Book of Nature.[71] Arndt wrote "not for the heathen and unbelievers but for Christians who did not live as Christians." He sought his readership among educated laity and especially pastors and theology students, hoping to reorient their thinking from doctrine to life.[72] Arndt addressed the lack of true Gospel preaching and the unrepentant and hypocritical behavior of many Christian people. He blamed the theologians, reminding them that theology is concerned not merely with academic study of the scriptures but with practice and the application of God's word to life and experience. The true Christian follows Christ in life.[73]

Unlike Philipp Jakob Spener, Arndt rarely appealed to Luther; there are just a few scattered references to Luther's *Freedom of a Christian Man* and the *Small Catechism*. The traditional Lutheran emphasis on word and sacrament is nowhere to be found.[74] More typical are Arndt's references to notions found in *The German Theology*, *The Imitation of Christ*, Johannes Tauler, the Franciscan mystic Angela da Foligno, Bernard of Clairvaux, and Johann von Staupitz. Indeed, much of *True Christianity* consists of Arndt's compilation of writings by these authors that emphasize living a holy life marked by humility, self-denial, and imitation of Christ through the power of the Holy Spirit. Arndt's critics discovered passages that he had borrowed from Schwenckfeld, Paracelsus, and Weigel.[75] The genre of *Four Books of True Christianity* reflects the "Spiritualist-hermeticist book metaphoric": the Book of Scripture, the Book of Life, the Book of Conscience, and the Book of Nature.[76]

Arndt researchers continue to debate whether his theology should be seen as complementary to Lutheranism or as a radical alternative to the reigning Lutheran Orthodoxy.[77] Hans Schneider and Hermann Geyer argue that *True Christianity* is best understood as teaching a Spiritualist-hermetic theology that is a radical departure from Luther and Lutheranism. Schneider speaks of the "foreign world of thought" that lay hidden behind the traditional portrait of Arndt. "In *The Four Books of True Christianity*," Schneider writes, "there are not only extensive excerpts from Paracelsus, but ideas from Paracelsus play an important role in the whole conception of the work."[78] This influence is evident not only in Book IV but also in Books I and II. Arndt's references to the light of God active in man echo the Paracelsian anthropology. Arndt's earliest and most enthusiastic readers were Paracelsists. Geyer argues that Arndt's *True Christianity* promotes a "clear theological program, an alternative, hidden way to God."[79] Arndt was not merely sympathetic to hermetic ideas; he was, in fact, a full-fledged Paracelsist and hermeticist.[80] Like Paracelsus, Arndt made it his goal to incorporate hermetic teachings within Lutheranism and to expose Lutheran readers to an alternative, hermeticist form of Christian belief.[81]

Arndt's preaching and writing on behalf of Christian renewal were also marked by a consistent Spiritualism; true Christianity was a matter of the heart, the inner man: "For it is *within* [that we find] the kingdom of God with all its benefits; within we find the temple of God; within is all true worship; within is the true house of prayer in spirit and in truth; within is the school of the Holy Spirit, the workplace of the holy Trinity."[82] Although a Lutheran pastor, Arndt demonstrated a remarkable disregard for the outward church and its institutional life.[83] In an effort to keep him within the Evangelical fold, his Lutheran supporters, such as his friend Johann Gerhard, found themselves forced to moderate and domesticate Arndt's writings.[84] They emphasized that Arndt's contribution was to ethics and Christian living, not dogmatic theology.

Arndt's *Four Books of True Christianity* represented a new genre of writing and a new kind of Protestant piety that met with amazing success. It became the most widely read book in German Protestant history. Arndt used biblical stories and images from nature and addressed the Christian reader and his or her everyday experience, making the book well-suited to laypeople and their devotional reading. The impact of *True Christianity* was astounding. The first English edition of the work appeared in 1646. In 1653 Strasbourg professor Johann Conrad Dannhauer felt constrained to admonish Christians not to read Arndt's book to the neglect of the Bible.[85] By the time Spener arrived in Frankfurt in 1666, Arndt's book had gone through sixty-four editions.[86] A Giessen professor wrote in 1715 that the book could be found in every home. It was reported in Württemberg in 1735 that there were "more Arndts than Bibles."[87] By 1740, Arndt's *True Christianity* had reached ninety-five German editions and had been translated into at least twenty-eight more.[88] By 1800, more than 240 editions of the work had appeared in print, more than one per year since it was first published. The book's impact extended across the Atlantic Ocean. John Wesley, in Savannah, Georgia, recorded in his diary on March 24, 1736, that he had begun to read Arndt's book. In reading Arndt he determined that he was not a true Christian but needed a second birth by the Spirit of God.[89] The first German immigrants to the New World took the book with them. Benjamin Franklin published Arndt's work in Philadelphia in 1751.

Readers of Arndt's book covered a wide spectrum, from Orthodox Lutherans to radical separatists. The first category included people such as Johann Gerhard, Heinrich Varenius, Johann Valentin Andreae, and Paul Egard, all of whom came out in support of Arndt. Without Gerhard, *The*

Four Books of True Christianity might never have seen the light of day; it was he who found a publisher for the book and did the final editing.[90] Andreae expressed thanks to Arndt for calling the church to a true and active Christianity; in 1615 Andreae published a fifty-page Latin summary of *True Christianity,* which he called *The Golden Book.*[91] The most detailed and exhaustive defense of Arndt ever produced was by the court preacher Heinrich Varenius in 1624. Varenius sought to distance Arndt from the thought of Schwenckfeld and Weigel. Spener valued Varenius's defense highly.[92] Egard, known as "the Johann Arndt of the Northern Mark," said *True Christianity* was popular among all social classes and edified all who read it.[93]

Radical disciples of Johann Arndt included his executor, the physician Melchior Breler (1589–1627), whom Arndt loved as a son. In 1625 Breler produced a Latin translation of *True Christianity* and added more cross-references to the works of Paracelsus.[94] Christian Hoburg wrote two works promoting Arndt's piety for a new generation of readers. In Hoburg, the piety and criticism inspired by Arndt "found its sharpest expression."[95] Another proponent of Arndt's writings was Friedrich Breckling (1629–1711). Breckling's father and grandfather before him had read and promoted Arndt's work. During a study visit to Hamburg in 1654, Breckling discovered the writings of Johannes Tauler and Christian Hoburg and converted to a form of mystical Spiritualism.[96] In Zwolle and Amsterdam, Breckling's home was a meeting place for various Spiritualists, with Johann Georg Gichtel serving as his assistant for a time.[97] Breckling corresponded with Spener and Francke and a host of other Pietists. He passed on to Gottfried Arnold his outline of a new church history that would recount the stories of persecuted heretics, including a twenty-two-page list of "some other witnesses to the truth."[98]

Although Arndt was a trailblazer for Pietism, he was no Pietist. Key features typical of later Pietism were foreign to him. In Arndt there is no emphasis on gatherings of the godly in conventicles nor the idea of a priesthood of all believers. The importance of personal Bible study is nowhere to be found in *True Christianity.* The promise of better times and conversion of the Jews were also foreign to Arndt: he shared the Orthodox Lutheran belief in the imminent end of the world and the Last Judgment.[99]

JAKOB BÖHME (1575–1624)

The influence of Jakob Böhme was almost universal among the Pietists. August Hermann Francke and Count von Zinzendorf were acquainted with his works and challenged by his reforming ecumenical impulse. Despite his rejection of separatism, Böhme is considered the father of Radical Pietism and the quest for a church of the reborn. His influence in encouraging Pietist engagement with alchemical thought "can scarcely be overestimated."[100]

Jakob Böhme was born in 1575 to peasant parents in Alt-Seidenberg, south of Görlitz, in the region of Upper Lusatia in Silesia. When not tending cattle, he attended a local school where he learned to read and write. He later picked up some Latin. By 1599 Böhme had become a master shoemaker and had started up a shoe business in Görlitz. That same year he married Katharina, daughter of a prosperous Görlitz butcher. Together they raised four sons. Böhme's seventeenth-century biographer described his appearance thus:

> His outward bodily image was sickly, plain in appearance, small in stature, narrow forehead, high temples, a bent nose, gray almost sky-blue shining eyes, a short thin beard, a soft voice but lovely to listen to, modest in bearing, direct with his words, humble in his behavior, patient in suffering, and gentle of heart.[101]

As a young man, Böhme twice experienced a gracious illumination from God. On both occasions, he was surrounded and overcome by divine light. The first instance, in 1595, lasted seven days. He was granted a higher knowledge and perception of the world, as if a veil were removed and he could see into the very secrets of nature. The second time, in 1600, he was examining a pewter vessel and overcome by a gleam of light. Crossing the bridge near his home in Görlitz, he found his way into a nearby field, where the light allowed him to see into the heart of creation, into its essence and power.[102] "In this divine light my spirit came to recognize God in everything and in all creatures, even plants and grass—who he is and how he is and what his will is. In this light I grew in my ability to describe the being of God."[103]

Böhme gained his knowledge of God from the book of nature, whose

Jakob Böhme. Portrait by Gottlob Glymann, dated between 1712 and 1720.

language he read by the divine light. By the knowledge he gained from the book of nature, he was able to supersede the books of the learned and their debates about the Bible. Böhme likewise learned to read the book of conscience—God himself, who resides within: "My knowledge does not derive just from letters found in a multitude of books; rather I have the letters within me, for God himself is within. Should I not be permitted to read the book that is himself?"[104] Those content with academic knowledge never learn to read from this book. Böhme was a critic of all who relied on reason in their pursuit of truth. Reason can touch only the outer physical world; the spiritual realm is hidden from it. It is the light of God in the soul that is the source of all knowledge. This is "the true theosophical Pentecostal school where the soul is taught by God."[105] The Breslau physician

Johannes Scheffler (*Angelus Silesius*) famously described Böhme as a man who lived in the presence of God.

> In the water lives the fish, the plant in the ground,
> The bird in the air, the sun in the sky,
> The salamander must be preserved by fire;
> And Jakob Böhme's element is the heart of God.[106]

The young Böhme was exposed to several currents of radical reform. There were still some followers of Caspar Schwenckfeld in Silesia, especially among the nobility. The Görlitz region was also a center of Paracelsian activity. The town's medical doctors followed Paracelsian medicine, and the mayor was well-versed in Paracelsian thought and allowed the editing and publishing of an edition of Paracelsus's writings in Görlitz. In 1612 Böhme made the acquaintance of Balthasar Walter, a Paracelsist physician and chemist married to a Görlitz woman. Like Paracelsus, Walter had visited Arabia, Syria, and Egypt in search of the wisdom of Kabbalah, magic, and alchemy. Böhme learned much from Walter; Walter, in turn, considered Böhme a true prophet of God.[107]

Böhme finally gained the courage to describe the insights he had gained from his experience of the light of God. Between January and May of 1612, he produced the manuscript of his first book, *Aurora: The Root or Mother of Philosophy, Astrology, and Theology from the True Foundation.* He added *Aurora* (Dawn rising) to the title at Walter's suggestion.[108] Böhme wrote as a simple man to whom had been revealed, within his spirit, the works and creation of God. He offered readers a true philosophy, describing the origin of all things in God; a true astrology, explaining the struggle of good and evil in all things; and a true theology, discussing the kingdom of Christ and how, by faith, humanity can triumph over evil and gain eternal salvation. Gerhard Wehr observed, "Few works in European intellectual history have exercised as profound and enduring an impact as Böhme's *Aurora.*"[109]

Karl Ender von Sercha, a Schwenkfelder nobleman, borrowed the manuscript of *Aurora* and had it copied. The work was soon being read eagerly by any and all in Görlitz who could obtain it. When a copy came into the hands of the town's leading Lutheran minister, Gregor Richter, he immediately accused Böhme of being a false prophet and turned the writing over to the city magistrate. Böhme was questioned about his beliefs and put in the stocks. His house was searched, the book removed, and Böhme released, on condition that he desist from spreading his beliefs. On July 28, 1613, Pastor Richter denounced Böhme from the pulpit and ordered him to appear on the following Tuesday before the Görlitz clergy. He was again questioned and forbidden to do any more writing.[110] These proceedings remained fresh in Böhme's mind as he reflected on them eleven years later, shortly before his death.

> The pastor cried out against me before the whole church, saying that I disrespected the church and holy sacraments. He repeatedly scolded me for being a heretic, *Schwärmer* and rascal . . . and besmirched my good name, and accused me of things that are simply not true. He said that I am always drunk as a pig on brandy and other wines and beers. In fact I do not despise the church but go regularly; nor do I despise the holy sacraments but partake of them. I have written about the sacraments more clearly than I have ever heard from him in the pulpit. I simply confess that we should heed Christ as he teaches in our hearts. I am no despiser of church and sacraments, much less a drunk, but live my life soberly in prayer and meditation, as I call on the whole city to testify.[111]

Richter haunted Böhme for the rest of his life, relentlessly attacking him and his ideas from the pulpit. He viciously denounced a later book by Böhme, *The Way to Christ*: "There are as many blasphemies in this shoemaker's book as there are lines; it smells of shoemaker's pitch and filthy blacking. May this insufferable stench stay far from us."[112]

Böhme, however, had a growing circle of supporters and admirers throughout Silesia. In March 1613, he sold his shoe business and became a yarn dealer, gaining a newfound freedom to travel and to meet for discussions with like-minded friends.[113] He incorporated these discussions into his writings. His associates, in turn, undertook to copy and circulate Böhme's works. The members of these Böhme circles came from the noble and well-educated classes and included several physicians.[114] Some seventy-eight of Böhme's letters to his friends have been preserved.

In 1618 Böhme began his most productive literary period. His best-known work was *The Way to Christ* (1624), the only book published in his lifetime. There he explained the way to true repentance, self-knowledge, and union with the heavenly Sophia. He discussed how to find *Gelas-*

senheit, or inward calm, forsaking all reliance on reason and simply waiting upon God. He included some prayers to aid readers in finding their way. In another tract, *Concerning the New Birth*, Böhme explained how, in Christ, the believer is restored to the image of God and delivered from the effects of Adam's fall into sin.[115] As with Arndt, Böhme's main concern was for new birth and inward transformation through Christ. All of his letters include the heading, "Our salvation in life is Jesus Christ in us."[116] In his later work, *A Compendium of Repentance*, Böhme described the union of the soul with Christ as "espousal with Virgin Sophia." "The marriage of the Lamb is solemnized where Virgin Sophia, the precious Humanity of Christ, is vitally united to the Soul."[117] In this experience, the soul and Christ embrace one another with joy and experience the love of God. The language of union with the Virgin Sophia was taken up by various radical Pietists such as Heinrich Horch, Gottfried Arnold, and Eva von Buttlar.

Böhme's 1620 work *On the Incarnation of Christ* includes a ten-point confession for the reborn. Articles one and six read as follows:

> We confess that the new reborn man, who is hidden in the old one like gold in stone, has a divine tincture and has divine flesh and blood in him. We say that in all men there is the possibility of new birth, otherwise God would be divided up and not the same in one place as in another. Man is drawn by fire and light: where he turns with the scales, there he falls.[118]

The alchemical language in these articles and the imagery of new birth stand in marked contrast to the language of justification in Luther and Orthodox Lutheranism. Böhme taught a Christianity of the transformed life, not Luther's Christianity of forgiveness through the imputed righteousness of Christ. The German Pietists followed Böhme, not Luther, at this point. Like Paracelsus, but unlike Schwenckfeld, Weigel, and Arndt, Böhme retained an important place for Christian community and the sacraments: at the Lord's Supper, reborn believers are united with one another and with Christ.[119]

In *Aurora* one finds Böhme's hope of a new Reformation: "I live in the hope of the day of perfection, which is now close at hand."[120] In his 1622 commentary on Genesis, *Mysterium Magnum*, Böhme speaks of the coming age of the Spirit, when all things will be restored to their eternal essence and paradise will turn green once more. He looked for a new day for the church when reborn believers would come together from all the different confessions: the renewed spiritual church will consist of members in whom Christ dwells, a notion that echoes Schwenckfeld and the Spiritualists.[121] Böhme divided world history into a sevenfold scheme—from Adam in the garden of perfection, to disintegration, toward reintegration and the end of history.[122]

Jakob Böhme's writings and views cannot easily be identified with any one tradition of thought. He was deeply immersed in Luther's translation of the German Bible; his writings are full of biblical citations and scriptural allusions. He read some of Luther's writings and hymns, adapting them to his own thinking. Böhme's eclecticism is evident in his engagement with German mysticism and alchemy. He was especially attracted to the alchemical notions of Paracelsus, believing that the truths of nature discovered by Paracelsus corresponded to the spiritual truths of the invisible world. Although he was not interested in Paracelsian medicine and chemistry per se and never worked in a laboratory, Böhme found the themes and symbolism attractive and incorporated them into a "mystical alchemy" of spiritual transformation. Self-transformation through new birth was the goal of Böhme's inward alchemy.[123]

Between 1644 and 1662, Böhme's works were translated into English by John Sparrow and John Elliston. The writings quickly found new life in England among Jakob Böhme study circles led by John Pordage and later among the Philadelphians under the prophet Jane Leade (1624–1704).[124] In 1694 Leade founded the London Philadelphian Society as a gathering place for the children of God who had forsaken the "Babel" of the various denominational churches. Inspired by Böhme, they looked for God to establish, at the end of time, an interconfessional community marked by the experience of the inward Christ and Christian love.[125] The writings of English Philadelphians such as Leade, Thomas Bromley, John Pordage, and Thomas Beverley were translated into German in the 1690s and eagerly read by German Pietists, especially in the small counties of Wittgenstein, Ysenburg-Offenbach, Solms-Laubach, and Solms-Braunfels.[126]

In 1676 Johann Jakob Schütz worked with a Jakob Böhme circle in Nuremberg to bring Böhme's writings from Holland through Frankfurt into Germany and Austria. Schütz also worked closely with the Amsterdam publisher Heinrich Betke, the most important publisher of Böhme's writings before Gichtel.[127] Schütz acted as Betke's agent in transporting books from Amsterdam to Frankfurt, many of them by Böhme and Hoburg. Books by these authors were available and being read in such numbers that, in February 1678, the Frankfurt clergy lodged complaints.

In 1682 Johann Georg Gichtel (1638–1710) produced the first complete German edition of Böhme's works in fifteen small volumes, totaling more than four thousand pages.[128] Thanks to Gichtel's edition, countless Pietists, "either openly or secretly," were influenced by Böhme's thinking. F. C. Oetinger was affected by his reading of Böhme and by the idea of God as a creative life force at work in the world. As Böhme's works became more readily available, Orthodox denunciations of Böhme became more vehement. During interrogations by Orthodox Lutheran officials, Pietists were routinely asked whether they owned or had read any books by Jakob Böhme.[129]

Orthodox Lutheran Reform

The setting and inspiration for German Pietism also include a contemporary movement that is often portrayed as the archenemy and polar opposite of Pietism—namely, Protestant Orthodoxy. In the century and a half after Luther, Lutheran and Reformed Protestantism developed distinctive features that crystallized in the Lutheran and Reformed confessional traditions.[130] After the Thirty Years War, a group of Orthodox Lutheran preachers, including Heinrich Müller, Theophil Großgebauer, and Christian Scriver, were remarkable for their reforming energy and ideals. Johann Arndt's *True Christianity* struck a chord with these reform-minded Orthodox Lutherans. And they were not alone. Many of the reforms initiated by the Orthodox turn up in Pietism, leading some to argue for Lutheran Orthodoxy as the primary inspiration for Pietism.[131] In the early days of the Frankfurt collegium, Spener used books of devotion authored by two Orthodox Lutheran pastors: Joachim Lütkemann's *Foretaste of God's Goodness* (1653) and Nikolaus Hunnius's *Epitome of Things to Be Believed* (1625), an outline of Orthodox Lutheran dogmatics.[132] In the "Lübeck Project" of 1640, Hunnius preached a series of sermons in which he denounced the low level of morality within the city.[133] Lutheran Orthodox reform must be taken seriously as a context for Pietist reform ideals.

Protestant Orthodoxy has suffered from both neglect and persistent caricature, as church histories continue to portray it as intellectually rigid and spiritually dead.

> The old Protestant Orthodoxy has been seriously neglected in scholarly research right up to the present day, so that between the investigation of the Reformation period and of Pietism there yawns a huge gulf. One still frequently hears the sparrows singing from the rooftops the old scholarly caricatures: Protestant Orthodoxy was stubbornly dogmatic and dead and placed little value on piety and the ministry.[134]

Research into Orthodox Lutherans has been outstripped by far by research into early modern radicals, including mystical Spiritualists such as Christian Hoburg, Valentin Weigel, and Jakob Böhme. There is a need to do a better job of setting the radicals in the context of the Orthodoxy from which they deviated. Johann Anselm Steiger has published new interpretations of leading Orthodox figures and modern editions of their writings, hoping to encourage a more accurate understanding of Orthodoxy.[135] A more nuanced picture of Orthodoxy is gradually emerging that highlights currents of Orthodox reform before the age of Spener and Pietism.[136]

JOHANN GERHARD (1582–1637)

The reform-minded spirit of Lutheran Orthodoxy is well-represented by the Jena theology professor Johann Gerhard. Gerhard's writings on behalf of the *Formula of Concord* and his nine-volume systematic theology, *Theological Commonplaces,* made him the leading spokesman for early seventeenth-century Orthodox Lutheranism.[137] Recently described as "a Church Father of Lutheran Orthodoxy," Gerhard is often ranked after Martin Luther and Martin Chemnitz as "the third great man of the Reformation."[138] As a young man in Quedlinburg, Gerhard's pastor was Johann Arndt. In 1597 Arndt provided medical care to the young Johann when he was seriously ill and, a year later, comforted him when his father died.[139] For the rest of Arndt's life, he took a fatherly interest in Gerhard. In the introduction to an edition of Arndt's sermons, Gerhard expressed his appreciation: "For more than sixteen years I have esteemed Arndt as my spiritual father."[140]

Although not sharing Arndt's esteem for Paracelsus, Gerhard did share

Arndt's aim of bringing renewal of theology, piety, and Christian life to the German church. For Gerhard, "Theology is not a purely speculative science but a practical one because it deals with the question of how mankind can be healed from the sickness of sin."[141] In *Sacred Meditations* (1606), Gerhard emphasized that Orthodox Lutheran theology, medieval mysticism, and the new piety were complementary and an indivisible unity. Theological reflection should carry through to practical piety. Just as medical science aims at improving bodily health, theological doctrine should aim to benefit the everyday life of Christian people.[142] *Sacred Meditations*, published when Gerhard was only twenty-three years old, met with amazing success in Germany and beyond, going through 115 editions in twelve languages by 1700.[143]

In 1615 Duke Johann Casimir von Heldburg appointed Gerhard general superintendent in Coburg. Like Arndt, Gerhard provided medical advice and medicines to his parishioners. During church visitations he became disturbed by what he saw: poorly educated pastors, a confused mess of worship liturgies, superstitions, drunkenness, and sexual immorality among the people. He addressed these issues in the new *Church Order* of 1615. The spirit of the *Order* is expressed in his admonition: "To confess sins and be reconciled to God and the Church are the greatest privilege a person can experience."[144]

VALENTIN ERNST LÖSCHER (1673–1749)

Valentin Ernst Löscher was the son of Kaspar Löscher, professor of theology and general superintendent of the churches in Wittenberg. Like his father, Valentin Ernst combined both academic positions and pastoral ministry in the church. He became superintendent in Jüterbog in 1698, theology professor in Wittenberg in 1707, and superintendent in Dresden and councilor to August the Strong in 1709. In 1725 he became theology professor at the University in Kiel.[145] Löscher wrote books defending the Lutheran faith against both Roman Catholic and Calvinist opponents. He vigorously opposed the efforts of the Calvinist-minded Hohenzollern rulers in Brandenburg-Prussia to find a compromise between the Lutheran and Reformed traditions on the Lord's Supper.

Löscher also had a reputation among Orthodox Lutherans as an opponent of Pietism. He founded a periodical devoted to reviews of religious literature, called *Unschuldige Nachrichten* (Innocent news), which appeared between 1701 and 1720.[146] Löscher intended it to be "not a so-called learned journal but an exercise in good thinking concerning such matters as may best contribute to the church at the present time."[147] The journal had two parts: one part offered a selection of passages from older works and Christian classics worthy of Christian consideration; the other consisted of reviews of books that had recently come on the market. These works were carefully scrutinized with a view to their orthodoxy, with the review identifying any "dangerous teachings" from the perspective of the Lutheran faith.[148] Many Pietist works received Löscher's critique in the periodical's pages.

Löscher and many other Orthodox theologians took seriously the need to combine Lutheran doctrine with heartfelt emotion and inward piety. They often added mystical texts to the theological scheme in order to express the new life that came with justification. Löscher composed works of mystical piety and devotion that encouraged the inward growth of the renewed Christian life. Orthodox doctrine, he believed, must enable and awaken a pious life.[149]

Löscher was consumed with efforts to mediate the stand-off between Pietism and Orthodoxy, convinced that Pietists and Orthodox Lutherans should work together in the common cause of church reform and in facing the threats of princely absolutism and Enlightenment Rationalism. He hoped to integrate within a renewed Orthodox Lutheranism the Pietist concerns for renewal of piety and a holy life, confident that Spener's reform program of 1675 was fully compatible with traditional Lutheran doctrine. In 1718 and 1721 he published *A Complete Setting Forth of the Truth and the Way to Peace in the Present Day Pietist Conflicts.* The major stumbling block in attaining his goal, he found, was the Pietists' veneration of Spener as the final authority. This was especially true after Spener's death in 1705. When Löscher put forward six points for discussion between Orthodox representatives from Dresden and Pietists from Halle, the plan was opposed from both sides. His Orthodox colleagues wanted the discussion points increased to sixty; the Halle representatives felt humiliated that their orthodoxy was even in question. On May 10 and 11, 1719, Löscher arrived in Merseburg for a private conversation with A. H. Francke. At the conclusion, Löscher hoped to arrange for future meetings. Instead, Francke presented him with a sealed letter in which he told

Löscher that Halle had the truth and that he, Löscher, was caught up in error; he would not be freed from his errors until he converted and was born again.[150] Löscher's hopes for Orthodox-Pietist cooperation in Christian renewal were shattered.

Although Orthodox reforms had much in common with Spener's *Pia Desideria*, there were at least two points of difference: Spener's promotion of house gatherings—the *collegia pietatis*—and his postmillennial hopes for better times found no resonance among the Orthodox.[151]

Conclusion

This chapter has found the setting and inspiration for German Pietism primarily in currents of radical discourse that persisted in small underground circles and in protest literature right into the eighteenth century. German Anabaptists, Spiritualists, mystics, and alchemists promoted a religion of inward renewal, transformation, and new birth that was taken up by the Pietists. Two main sources of renewal in seventeenth-century German Protestantism were Johann Arndt and Jakob Böhme and their disciples. These Spiritualist reformers were marked by disillusionment with church structures and concern for an inward Christianity of new birth and a holy life. Gottfried Arnold and Friedrich Christoph Oetinger are key instances of the connection between Spiritual alchemy and Pietism. Something different from Luther is going on among the Pietists; their theology and piety are distinct from those of sixteenth-century Reformers and Lutheran Orthodoxy.[152] Pietism can no longer be understood as a consistently Lutheran effort to take Luther's Reformation of *doctrine* a step further by adding reformation of *life*.

The differences between Pietism and Lutheran Orthodoxy, however, should not be exaggerated. Reforming energy and ideals are evident among many Orthodox Lutheran preachers after the Thirty Years War. Figures such as Johann Gerhard and Valentin Ernst Löscher taught the importance of combining Lutheran doctrine with heartfelt emotion and inward piety. In the early days of the Frankfurt collegium, Spener used books of devotion authored by two Orthodox Lutheran writers. And Pietist and Orthodox pastors alike read and treasured Johann Arndt's *Four Books of True Christianity*.

CHAPTER 2

The Thirty Years War, Seventeenth-Century Calvinism, and Reformed Pietism

A variety of factors in the social and political world of seventeenth-century Europe created the conditions for people of faith in German lands to seek out new forms of piety. Two major military events did much to shape the popular mood: the Thirty Years War and the Peace of Karlowitz. This seventeenth-century climate of devastation was also marked by hopes for Christian peace and unity and by forward-looking optimism. It is not surprising that, in such a setting, one should find among Germans a readiness to explore new forms of piety. This chapter shows how this readiness was nurtured by the works of English, French, and Dutch Calvinist writers who called for renewal not only of individual piety but of church and society as well. Later Pietist concerns for Christian renewal and new birth were part of this larger groundswell of renewal within European Protestantism that W. R. Ward has called "Early Evangelicalism."[1]

The Thirty Years War and the Peace of Karlowitz

Prior to the First World War, the Thirty Years War (1618–1648) was long considered "The Great War in Germany," and was so described in works by Karl Holl and Ricarda Huch.[2] Respondents to a 1962 survey in German Hesse rated the Thirty Years War and the accompanying plague as the greatest disaster in German history, greater than the two world wars. Although atrocities were not commonplace and the war's impact varied from region to region, it is generally agreed that the Thirty Years War was an economic disaster and that the population in German lands decreased by about one-third during those years.[3]

The war began with the defenestration of Prague on May 23, 1618. Protestant nobility and gentry in Bohemia, determined to elect a German Calvinist as their king, responded to pressures from Ferdinand, the Catholic Habsburg emperor in Vienna, by hurling two of his councilors from the castle window. The Protestant cause found support from the Danish Coalition under King Christian IV of Denmark and later from the Swedish king, Gustavus Adolphus (d. 1632). The conflict culminated in twelve years of general European war, with fighting mainly in Germany but also in France, Italy, and the Netherlands.[4] The continent was divided into two warring camps based on the "all-pervading ideology" of religion: the Protestant territories of northern Germany and Sweden versus the German empire under the Catholic house of Habsburg. Magdeburg and many other Protestant cities were destroyed, with a devastating loss of life and culture, including destruction of valuable church archives. Some suggest that, had Gustavus Adolphus not intervened, Lutheranism in central Europe would have been extinguished.[5] Many factors besides religion were at play: local and territorial, national and supranational, dynastic and democratic, economic and military.[6] Two Catholic dynasties, the French Bourbons and the Austrian Habsburgs, fought to gain hegemony in Europe. The Peace of Westphalia was finally signed on October 24, 1648.

The impact of the Thirty Years War was especially devastating in parts of Hesse, where Lutheran Darmstadt came into conflict with Reformed Kassel and the Wetterau territories. Upper Hesse lost 40 to 50 percent of its inhabitants and most of its livestock.[7] The seventeenth-century German literary classic *The Adventures of Simplicius Simplicissimus* reflects with stark realism the vivid experiences of its author, Johann Jakob von Grimmelshausen (1622–1676).[8] In 1634 his hometown of Gelnhausen, in Hesse, was sacked, and he spent the winter in the nearby fortress of Hanau. Captured by imperial troops in 1635, Grimmelshausen served in the Catholic Habsburg army, taking part in the siege of Magdeburg and

Defenestration of Prague in 1618. Two governors are seized and thrown from the window by Czech noblemen. Woodcut by Matthäus Merian the Elder.

the battle of Wittstock in 1636.[9] Grimmelshausen's description of the Battle of Wittstock reflects his firsthand experience.

> The dreadful noise of the guns, the clatter of harnesses, the clash of pikes and the cries of both attackers and wounded combined with the trumpets, drums and fifes to produce fearful music. You could see nothing but thick smoke and dust, which seemed to be trying to hide the horror of the dead and wounded. In the middle of it all you could hear the pitiful wails of the dying and the excited cheers of those who were still full of fight . . .
>
> The earth, whose usual task it is to cover the dead, was itself strewn with corpses, all with different mutilations: here were heads that had lost the bodies they belonged to and bodies lacking heads; some had their entrails hanging out in sickening fashion, others their skull smashed and the brain spattered over the ground; you could see dead bodies emptied of blood and living ones covered in the blood of others; there were shot-off arms with the fingers still moving, as if they wanted to get back into

> the fighting, while some men ran away without having shed a single drop of blood; there were severed legs lying around which had become much heavier than they were before; you could see mutilated soldiers begging to be put to death, others to be granted quarter and spared. In a word, it was a pitiful sight. The Swedish victors drove our defeated army from the field, splitting it up and scattering it completely with their swift pursuit.[10]

Besides the injuries and deaths, there was the devastation of crops, famine, and disease. Epidemics and migrations overtaxed the capacity of cities to meet the needs of the multitude of refugees. This all added up to an experience of human and natural devastation that was passed down in collective memory.[11]

The response to the Thirty Years War was at least fivefold. First, there was a desire among clergy and some political leaders to restore basic Christian morality to a society that had seen opposing sides commit the most horrible abuse and torture of fellow human beings. Ernst the Pious of Saxon-Gotha (1601–1675) instituted public catechism to instill repentance in his subjects and faith and piety in the coming generation. In 1640 he arranged for publication of a new edition of the Luther Bible with concise commentary. Each congregation in his territory was required to have a copy of the "Ernestine Bible." He also instituted universal education.[12]

Second, antiwar prophets arose, such as Paul Felgenhauer (1593–1677) in Bohemia, Ludwig Friedrich Gifftheil (1595–1661) in Württemberg,[13] and Christian Hoburg (1607–1675) in Lüneburg.[14] Felgenhauer led a restless existence, migrating through Bohemia, northern Germany, and the Netherlands and establishing separatist Philadelphian communities that practiced foot washing.[15] He was one of the most prolific and controversial authors of his day, conducting ongoing polemics with Lutheran Orthodox theologians. His writings sold like hotcakes.[16] Felgenhauer taught that all humankind possesses a spark of divine light, and on this basis he promoted a universal religion that would unite Jews, Christians, and all peoples and nations in love and in "one knowledge, faith, and religion."[17] Gifftheil berated church authorities for their obsession with confessional conflicts and condemned the war as unchristian and opposed to the will of God. He sent political authorities his plan for establishing a theocracy and instructions on how to proceed. Gifftheil's views found influential supporters, including the Brandenburg minister Lorenz Grammendorf in Berlin.[18] Hoburg's critique of confessional Lutheranism and plea for Christian love is found in his *Mirror of the Abuses Found among the Clergy in Christendom Today* (1644). And the poet Anna Hoyer (1584–1655) of Holstein, a Schwenckfeld sympathizer, wrote harsh religious and political satires against the Lutheran clergy and jurists of her day, at the same time celebrating the new birth and Christ's dwelling within.[19] These various seventeenth-century dissidents were united in condemning Protestant church leaders and calling for an end to confessional strife.[20]

Third, the Thirty Years War instilled a widespread desire for a Christianity marked by practical piety and cooperation among the three main religious confessions in Germany—Catholic, Lutheran, and Reformed—so that religious wars might never be repeated. Christians should be characterized by love and heartfelt faith, not disputation in defense of correct doctrine.[21] The legacy of this kind of German Lutheran thinking can be found in edifying tracts, hymns, prayers, and poems from the seventeenth century.

Fourth, the war left some profoundly disillusioned with religion and skeptical about ever arriving at religious certainty. One observes this thinking in Johann Christian Edelmann and his conviction that there was no religion on earth more violent than Christianity.[22]

Finally, one finds in postwar Lutheranism, for the first time, a concern for world improvement, social reform, and a sense of being God's chosen instrument to change the world through German churches and schools.[23]

There are echoes of many of these sentiments in Grimmelshausen's *Simplicissimus*. The Huntsman insists that he is neither Papist nor Protestant, but a simple believer in the articles of the Apostles' Creed. When the Reformed pastor inquires as to why he does not confess the Reformed faith of his parents, the Huntsman replies, "Which [Church] should I believe? Do you think it is easy for me to entrust my soul's salvation to one that the other two decry and accuse of false doctrine? . . . Which one should I join when each is screaming that the others are the work of the devil?"[24] The Catholics denounce Luther, and the Lutherans denounce the pope. The narrator concludes *Simplicissimus* with the reflection, "There is no better field of expertise than theology *if* you make use of it to love and serve God."[25] Grimmelshausen saw that Germany's future peace depended on church leaders overcoming their differences and recognizing the damage caused by divisions in matters of faith.

Seven years later, in *Pia Desideria*, Pietist patriarch Philipp Jakob Spener (1635–1705) called on pastors to redirect their energies away from controversy toward practical Christian love and unity. The lessons of the Thirty Years War are clearly reflected in the Pietist agenda. Pietism found its strongest early resonance in Frankfurt and neighboring regions where the loss of life and the economic impact of the war were most severe. In the Wetterau counties of central Germany, Pietist princes welcomed French Huguenots, Jews, alchemists, Calvinists, and Lutherans, who all worked together to rebuild their lives in a cooperative spirit. Economic hardship meant that princes and city councils prioritized immigrants' skills and ability, not their confession.

Another significant military and political event in the seventeenth century was the successful Habsburg campaign against the Turks, culminating in the Peace of Karlowitz in January 1699. From 1683 to 1697, the Austrian Habsburgs reclaimed Turkish Hungary. The Habsburg victory represented, for Europe, "the breakthrough of brilliant sunshine," replacing the dark mood of threat and fear represented by the Ottoman Turks.[26] An almost euphoric optimism spread throughout European lands. Stories of Turkish Muslims in eastern Europe converting to Christianity inspired in many a postmillennial confidence that a worldwide "conversion of the heathen" was under way.

The Inspiration of English Puritan Writers

In the aftermath of the Thirty Years War, one finds among German Christians a readiness to explore new forms of piety. Over the course of the seventeenth century, writings by English Puritans such as William Perkins, Richard Baxter, Lewis Bayly, and John Bunyan became available in German translation. In 1678 the Lutheran theologian Elias Veiel observed that "the book shops are full to overflowing with works translated out of the English." One researcher identified some seven hundred English religious works translated into German between 1600 and 1750.[27]

The devotional classic by Lewis Bayly (1565–1631), *The Practice of Piety: Directing a Christian How to Walk, That He May Please God*, met with great interest among German Lutherans, especially Pietists, judging by the number of German editions of the work.[28] Bayly's book was read and discussed at a Pietist gathering in the home of Philipp Jakob Spener in Frankfurt in the early 1670s. Something of the flavor of the book can be gathered from the way Bayly encouraged believers to spend more time in prayer. He suggested they consider the time they devoted to frivolous activities such as cards and dice and the "superstitious devotion" and many prayers of the Catholics and then decide how much time they owed to the true worship of God: "If thou hast spent divers hours at a vain ball or play; yea whole days and nights in carding and dicing, to please thy flesh, be ashamed to think that praying for a quarter of an hour is too long an exercise for the service of God."[29] Bayly's forcefulness and eloquence are evident in his meditations on "the Misery of a Man Not Reconciled to God in Christ":

> There [in hell] thy lascivious eyes will be afflicted with sights of ghastly spirits; thy curious ear affrighted with hideous noise of devils, and the weeping and gnashing of teeth of reprobates; thy dainty nose will be cloyed with noisome stench of sulphur; thy delicate taste pained with intolerable hunger; thy drunken throat will be parched with unquenchable thirst; thy conscience shall ever sting thee like an adder, when thou thinkest how often Christ by his preachers offered the remission of sins.

Bayly balanced this with a meditation on the blessings of the godly in paradise: "Here my meditation dazzles, and my pen falls out of my hand; the one being not able to conceive, nor the other to describe, that most excellent bliss, and eternal weight of glory."[30] *The Practice of Piety* offers meditations on hindrances to piety and how to read the Bible with profit, prayers for morning and evening, and prayers for the sick and the dying. Bayly's meditations on proper observance of the Sabbath were influential on both Spener and A. H. Francke.

One study distinguishes four phases in German reception of English devotional literature between 1595 and the early 1700s. In the first period, 1595–1630, the writings of William Perkins found a welcome within the German Reformed (Calvinist) Church.[31] In the second period, 1630–1660, translations of English works were printed in German towns, with Lutheran church approval. In this phase, the writings of Emanuel Sonthom, Lewis Bayly, Daniel Dyke, and Joseph Hall were most popular. In the third phase, 1660–1690, the number of German translations underwent a sharp increase as the writings of more than a hundred

English writers became available on the German market. It was during this phase that works by John Bunyan and Richard Baxter were translated and published in German. The physician Johannes Lange produced the first German translation of Bunyan's *Pilgrim's Progress* in 1685. In the fourth phase, after 1690, one finds a growing German interest in English sermons and moral tract literature, as well as in anti-deist writings.[32]

Gottfried Arnold included a complete German translation of Bunyan's autobiography *Grace Abounding* (*Die Gnade Gottes*) in his collection *The Life of the Believers: A Description of Well-Known Godly Persons of the Last 200 Years* (1701). Arnold found in Bunyan a heroic example of practical Christian holiness and a rebuke to defenders of established forms of religion in Germany. Arnold was impressed by the way Bunyan "sweetly set forth the inner path of his way to repentance."[33] Bunyan offered encouragement to believers who were despised by the world but beloved of God. His works were read by German Reformed Christians, and Pietists in the city of Halle made "frequent anonymous uses of Bunyan."[34] Bunyan was also popular in Berleburg, where Johann Friedrich Haug produced the famous *Berleburg Bible*, a commentary shaped by mystical and millenarian piety. In commenting on I Thessalonians 5:8, Haug observed, "We should not observe a lazy sobriety but a ready and armed one; armed with faith, hope, and love as the three chief virtues which are needed in our conflict. For it is these which are described in such edifying fashion in Bunyan's *The Pilgrim's Progress to Eternity*, as well as in his *Holy War*."[35]

It is unlikely, however, that English devotional works were the main influence in shaping the key features of Spener's reform: home gatherings of the godly designed for study of the scriptures and hopes for better times for the church, when conflicts would be replaced by love and unity. These notions are *not* prominent in the English writings. Nevertheless, English devotional books did form part of the tradition of piety in which Philipp Jakob Spener and August Hermann Francke were reared and provided them with the language of heartfelt devotion and self-denial. German readers could identify with the emphasis in English devotional literature on self-examination, repentance, sanctification, and growth in holiness. English authors typically laid down rules for daily life and for dealing with temptations as a pilgrim and stranger on earth who is seeking the way to heaven. The Calvinism of these English works was often modified by the Pietists to fit a Lutheran setting. The Calvinist teaching on "signs of election," for example, was changed to a discussion of "signs of new birth."[36]

The Influence of Jean de Labadie (1610–1674)

More influential among early German Pietists was the Frenchman Jean de Labadie. The nineteenth-century church historian Max Goebel insisted that "not Spener but Labadie was the true founder of Pietism in the Lutheran church; Spener was merely the more cautious and successful disciple of Labadie."[37] While Goebel may have exaggerated Labadie's importance, in recent decades there has been a tendency to ignore the Frenchman's role in the rise of Pietism.[38] Yet there are clear personal and ideological ties between Labadie and early Pietist figures. Both Philipp Jakob Spener and Theodor Undereyck heard Labadie's preaching in Geneva. Johann Jakob Schütz, Spener's associate, corresponded with two disciples of Labadie, Anna Maria van Schurman and Pierre Yvon.

Jean de Labadie was born on February 13, 1610, to aristocratic parents in southern France. At the age of seven, he joined his brothers in attending the Jesuit school in Bordeaux. Though short and sickly, he was highly gifted and marked by a restless and independent spirit. In 1639, after fourteen years in the Jesuit order, he left because of illness and tensions over his increasing independence of mind. Labadie spent the next ten years as a traveling preacher throughout southern France, convinced that God had called him to reform the church along the lines of the early apostolic churches. He worked to establish a true church of the reborn within the existing church by gathering conventicles of laypeople for Bible study and prayer. He lived in constant danger due to opposition from the Jesuits and the threat of arrest by soldiers of the king. On one occasion he escaped capture when a French woman hid him in a travel trunk.[39]

A spiritual nomad, Labadie lived a life of perpetual change and experimentation in religious matters. As his wanderings took him from France to Switzerland, the United Provinces, Germany, and Denmark, his religious identity changed as well, from Roman Catholic to Calvinist to separatist.[40] In 1650 he converted to the Reformed faith, although he continued to affirm Catholic views on confession, mystical communion with God, and the monastic life. He became a Reformed pastor and professor of theology, first in Montauban and then in Geneva, followed by three years in Middelburg (1666–1669). In Geneva, his students included Pierre Yvon, Pierre Dulignon, and Jean Menuret, all of whom became his close associates in the Labadist movement.

Labadie's distinctive goal and practice were to bring reform to the church by establishing a true church of the reborn within the existing church. Only those who had experienced a conversion and new birth and who lived a Christ-like life, separate from the world, could participate in the Lord's Supper. In his 1668 booklet *Manual of Piety*, he listed twelve marks of new birth: self-knowledge, conversion, hatred of the world, self-denial, eradication of all lust, complete devotion to God, mystical fellowship with God, life in the presence of God, inner cleansing, humility, childlike simplicity, and a quiet spirit. In Middelburg, Labadie invited reborn believers to meet together in homes to read scripture, to pray, and to grow in their faith.[41] He described these gatherings as follows:

> The leader offers a short address followed with a prayer. Then those gathered sing and a challenging passage of Scripture is read and introduced. Then the exercise of prophecy begins, with discussion concerning the Scripture text or especially important Christian truths, done concisely and clearly, in a way that is practical and not obscure. Anyone—meaning only the men, not women as among the Quakers—can speak and raise questions, ideas, objections, always keeping edification in view. Then follows a short summary and prayer (or silent prayer) and a blessing.[42]

Labadie encouraged pastors to establish such gatherings, because routine preaching produced so little fruit. In home meetings, the people would better understand the sermon and pastoral care would be much easier. Labadie soon had imitators, including Theodor Undereyck in Mülheim in 1665, Philipp Jakob Spener in Frankfurt in 1670, and Joachim Neander in Düsseldorf in 1674.[43] This communal practice became the distinguishing mark of both "Labadism" and "Pietism," continually attracting suspicions of separatism, sectarianism, Anabaptism, and Quakerism. Labadie's practice alienated him from other Reformed pastors, and in October 1668 he was removed from office and asked to leave Middelburg.

Labadie then moved to Amsterdam, where he founded a house community. His colleague Pierre Yvon described their fellowship to Anna Maria van Schurman (1607–1678) as follows:

> You know Labadie, my dear sister in the Lord, how he is full of the Holy Spirit. Since we arrived in Amsterdam, it is as if the Spirit had been poured upon him in still greater measure. Each morning we all gather together and he leads us in prayer and thanksgiving, and we have the morning meditation. Then each goes off to his own work and spiritual devotion. At the table we come together as brothers and sisters and eat with delight and inner joy. Then we sing a hymn to the glory of God and our dear Savior. The evening devotion consecrates our hearts so that we enjoy our evening meal with gratitude for God's gifts. If you could only witness it, you would never want to leave us again. Come and join us. Why do you delay? Be like Paula and follow our Jerome. It is a joy and blessing of soul to sit at his feet.[44]

After consulting with her mentor, Gisbertus Voetius, about the meaning of the reference to Paula and Jerome, van Schurman traveled to Amsterdam and joined Labadie's group.[45] The community grew quickly, attracting many former members of Reformed churches. Converts included the mayor of Amsterdam, Conrad von Beuningen (1622–1693), and six wealthy young women from noble families: Anna Maria van Schurman, Lucie von (Lucia de) Sommelsdyk from Friesland, Louise Huygens from Rhynsburg, Aemilie van der Haer from the Haag, Elisabeth Schlüter, and Wilhelmine von Buytendyk. These women joined Labadie's community against the bitter complaints of their parents and the men to whom they were engaged. Reformed clergy in Amsterdam became concerned, complaining that "the Labadists win over the best Christians and the churches are stripped of their pearls."[46]

In October 1670, Labadie set out from Amsterdam harbor with a group of fifty followers on a journey to Herford in Germany, to the estate of Princess Elisabeth von der Pfalz in Westphalia. When asked by Elisabeth to provide a declaration of their faith, Labadie confessed his adherence to the Reformed faith of the Heidelberg Catechism and the Synod of Dordt and to the teachings in Calvin's *Institutes*. Using its own printing press, the community put out numerous tracts, and in 1672 published a con-

Jean de Labadie

fession of faith entitled *Declaration or Clarification of the Pure Doctrine and Sound Faith of Jean de Labadie*. Labadie was affectionately called "Papa" and van Schurman "Mama" by community members.[47] After Labadie's death in February 1674, Pierre Yvon (1646–1707) took over the leadership. "Labadism" became associated with ascetic withdrawal from the world, mysticism, enthusiasm, separatism, and chiliasm (millennialism).[48]

The Labadists conformed to the Reformed faith except in the Labadist doctrine of the church, their strict observance of the sacraments, and their renunciation of normal family relations. Initially, the Labadist community demanded a life of celibacy for all members. But in Herford, one of the young women became pregnant and the father was found to be Pierre Yvon, Labadie's key associate. At the insistence of Princess Elisabeth, the celibacy issue was reevaluated. Yvon then married the young woman, Catharine Martini. The other leaders also married: Pierre Dulignon married Aemilie van der Haer, and the sixty-one-year-old Labadie married twenty-two-year-old Lucie von Sommelsdyk, the youngest and most beautiful of the women. Further marriages soon followed within the community. The offspring of these couples were raised communally as children of the Lord, the children calling the adults Aunt and Uncle. Each child was assigned a tutor or governess who oversaw the child's education and behavior.[49]

Constant opposition proved too much for some members of the community. One of Labadie's closest supporters was Francois Menuret, who along with Yvon traveled to numerous towns seeking supporters for Labadie. In July 1670, Menuret began acting erratically. He became violent and loud, barking like a dog and screaming blasphemies against God and Labadie. He died on August 10, 1670. A disillusioned member reported that Menuret was not remembered in communal prayers during his illness, and his name was excluded from later records.[50]

Labadie was a prolific author, with many of his writings translated from French into Dutch and German. His *Reformation of the Church by the Pastorate* consists of two letters that he wrote to sympathizers in 1667 and 1668. He offered a frank portrayal of the corruption of Christian Europe and "the need for a reformation in the entire Christian world." Christian behavior in church, at law courts, in the business world, and at home, he wrote, was "devoid of grace and piety" and marked by injustice and wickedness. Young people knew the catechism by heart but did not understand or practice it. Their parents read and heard the Bible but "without hearing in it the voice of God." Pastors preached and performed their duties badly, without zeal. "The Christian world is like a sick man," Labadie wrote, "who enjoys his illness and does not want anyone to interfere with it." He was confident, however, that a great renewal was close at hand, and he pointed to signs that "the reign of God is approaching." He found encouragement in the fact that "in different places a very large number of people who are as respected and learned as they are eminent and holy . . . agree in thinking that a great renewal is at hand."[51] Labadie proposed a concrete "Project for General Reformation of the Church," which began with pastors working for renewal within their flocks.

Labadie's millennial hopes were closely tied to the conversion of the

Jewish people and his conviction that they would have a place in the coming millennial age. His 1667 work on "the present condition of the Jews" offered a moderated response to the Jewish rabbi Sabbatai Sevi and his messianic claims. Like his friend Peter Serrarius (1600–1669), Labadie was impressed by the Jewish penitential revival but considered it to be an external affair and not a true renewal. Labadie remained reserved toward Sabbatai Sevi, suspecting he was an impostor, an instrument not of the Lord but of the devil.[52]

The separatism advocated by Labadie plunged the Dutch "Remonstrant Reformation" into a deep crisis, in which Reformed Pietism in Germany was included. The minutes of the Reformed Synod of the Lower Rhine attest to a strong disturbance within the churches on account of the separatist conventicle begun in 1670 by Heinrich Schlüter. Individual students of Jodocus van Lodenstein and Theodor Undereyck, such as Peter Kittelbach and Reiner Kopper, sympathized with Labadie and went over to the Labadists.

Jean de Labadie anticipated key features of Spener's reform program—the home gatherings of the godly for study of the scriptures and the hopes for better times for the church when conflicts would be replaced by love and unity. It is no great leap from Labadie's *Reformation of the Church by the Pastorate* to Spener's *Pia Desideria*, written just a few years later.

The Inspiration of the Dutch Further Reformation

Another influence on German Pietism was the seventeenth-century Dutch reform movement known as the Further Reformation or Second Reformation (*Nadere Reformatie*). The impact of Dutch reformers on both Lutheran and Reformed Pietists in Germany was significant. When one considers how many German theology students attended Dutch universities and the amount of English Puritan literature translated from Dutch into German,[53] it is evident that the spirit of the Dutch Further Reformation had a profound influence in German lands.

The father of the Dutch Further Reformation was Willem Teellinck (1579–1629). While a student in England, Teellinck encountered Puritanism and committed himself to working for similar reforms in the Netherlands. He wrote a report about his visit to Banbury, where family and public life were governed by daily devotion and the fear of God.[54] In 1608 he began promoting "the practice of piety" by gathering together like-minded associates and publishing a series of edifying writings. In 1627 Teellinck laid out the program of the Further Reformation in a work entitled *Necessary Exposition concerning the Present Sad State of God's People*.[55] The main cultural contribution of the Further Reformation lay in the production of books intended to encourage the practice of Reformed piety in families and in private devotions. The movement had an urban character, evident in a leadership consisting of Reformed clergymen from the cities and the participation of publishers and booksellers.[56]

A key figure in the Dutch Further Reformation was Gisbertus Voetius (1589–1676), along with his colleagues Johannes Hoornbeek, Johannes Teellinck, and Jodocus van Lodenstein. The movement reflected the Puritan concern for practical reform of daily life in church and society. A long list of sins was read out in Utrecht churches in March 1659, which included failure to observe the Sabbath and warnings to the rich not to love riches and luxury. Voetius denounced long hair in men, dancing, and smoking of tobacco. He called for theology students to lead exemplary lives, as those who would one day be leaders of congregations. He recommended a book that had profoundly affected him, the *Imitation of Christ* by Thomas à Kempis.[57]

The Further Reformation also emphasized renewal of the heart and the experiences of assurance and new birth.[58] Voetius encouraged gatherings of the godly, or conventicles, for strengthening of faith. His colleague van Lodenstein described the activities of the Utrecht conventicle as follows: "Periodically at least one hundred men and women, from differing stations of society, will meet together in order to pray, to sing, to encourage one another in the service of the Lord, thereby to stir up the fire [of the Spirit] within the Church."[59] These gatherings were widely criticized by Dutch Reformed pastors for undermining regular church services and for intermingling classes and genders.

The spirit of Dutch renewal was embodied above all in Jodocus van Lodenstein (1620–1677), probably the most influential member of the Dutch Further Reformation. If Willem Teellinck can be considered the Dutch Johann Arndt, then van Lodenstein was the Dutch Spener.[60]

> Van Lodenstein was a unique phenomenon in his day; a Dutch Reformed "secular" monastic, living in the world while stoutly resisting its

> appeal. He was an orthodox Calvinist in theology, but innovative and often unique in his practices . . . He never married, was abstemious with respect to food, little given to social niceties, and preached a life of Christian discipleship in which renunciation played a major role. He lived in a cloistered, monastic-like setting on his estate in Utrecht.[61]

Jodocus van Lodenstein was raised in a noble family in Delft. He studied theology under Voetius in Utrecht between December 1637 and April 1642 and spent two more years in Franeker, studying Hebrew and Aramaic. After serving parishes of two hundred in Zoetermeer and of twelve hundred in Sluis, in April 1653 he took up ministry in the prestigious Cathedral Church in Utrecht, a congregation of some ten and a half thousand people. His staff numbered twelve to fifteen pastors and included Johannes Teellinck and Voetius.[62] He was widely admired for his Puritan-style preaching and catechetical instruction.

Van Lodenstein became known for his "methodistic" piety and disciplined life. He generally awoke at 4:30 or 5:00 a.m. with thoughts of gratitude to God for his care through the night. Before beginning his day's work, he had a time of meditation that included a prayer of thanksgiving and Bible reading, usually three chapters a day. Throughout the day he spoke and thought of heavenly things. He lived humbly, eating cabbage and bread and mixing his wine with water. He thought it inappropriate for a pastor to know much about the various wines.[63] He ended the day with reflection on how he had used his time, repenting of his sins and expressing gratitude for God's grace in what he had done well. "Together with these spiritual disciplines went a great aversion to everything worldly," Carl Schroeder writes. "The world and sin were one essence for Lodenstein: dances and going to comedies he considered temptations to unchastity."[64] He was convinced that the church and the clerical calling had no other function than to deliver people from the sinful world and to bring them to Christ.[65]

Van Lodenstein kept a busy preaching and teaching schedule. He preached three or four times a week in various churches and at two Sunday morning services, followed by four hours of public catechism in the afternoon before a crowd of people who came to him with questions. On Tuesdays he held a one-hour class for new members. On Wednesday afternoons he held three more hours of catechism. The Friday class on practical spirituality was the largest class of the week and was attended by his fellow clergy. He emphasized training in spiritual habits and disciplines and called on his hearers to make faith more than just a belief in the truth.[66]

In his preaching and writing, van Lodenstein focused on sanctification and the practice of piety. His best known work, *Contemplation of Zion* (1674), takes the form of a dialogue between a pastor and two elders concerning the present condition of the church. Van Lodenstein saw the Reformation as incomplete, like a body without a soul.[67] He emphasized conversion of life as the proper end of Reformed doctrine. Christ's incarnation had the purpose of restoring the image of God in humankind. Van Lodenstein lamented that the Reformation had not retained Catholic monastic orders and the sacrament of confession; as a result, he thought, the emphasis on conversion of life had been lost. The late medieval Dutch piety of the Modern Devotion and the imitation-of-Christ tradition of à Kempis were in sore need of recovery.[68]

During the week, van Lodenstein hosted house gatherings in his garden, with the focus on singing and sharing experiences of faith. He also met regularly in the van Schurman home with a group known as the "Utrecht Circle." It included Anna Maria and her brother, the physician Johan Godschalk (1605–1664), along with various pastors and professors, comprising a Who's Who of Dutch theologians and reformers. The common topic of discussion was the work of reformation in the Dutch church and society. As Schroeder describes the meetings, "Even if there were present among the fellowship some of his most valued colleagues, be they preachers or professors, there was no conversation other than that of the state of the Church. They spoke of the study of and concern for the fostering of God's Zion."[69] Some theology students who attended went on to become Pietist leaders in Germany.

It was Johan Godschalk who introduced Jean de Labadie to the Netherlands, and to van Lodenstein and Anna Maria van Schurman in particular. Godschalk made a point of visiting Labadie in Geneva in 1662, to meet him and to experience the work of reform going on there. In a letter to his sister, he described Labadie as "an Ambrose in heart, a Chrysostom in eloquence, an Augustine in love, and a Bernard in fervor."[70] Anna Maria shared his letter and his enthusiasm for Labadie with the Utrecht Circle. At Anna Maria's invitation, Labadie spent eleven days in the van Schurman home in 1666. The members of the circle were not impressed by Labadie. Van Lodenstein approved of Labadie's emphasis on conversion and new birth, but rejected his separatism. In 1669, after her brother Johan had died (in 1664) and two other members of the circle were banned from the city, Anna Maria moved to Amsterdam to join Labadie's community.

In later life, van Lodenstein turned increasingly to mystical writers such as Bernard of Clairvaux, Johannes Tauler, and Thomas à Kempis. His constant theme was the importance of not only confessing the truth but personally experiencing Christ in one's soul. His spiritual verse and hymns, widely admired in his day, indicate a piety that was not afraid of honesty and self-disclosure.[71] Like Labadie, he called for renewal of the pastorate as the key step toward renewal of church and society. He is the source of the motto of Reformation churches, *ecclesia semper reformanda est*—the church must always be reforming.[72]

Reformed Pietism in Germany

Reformed Pietism in Germany began as a movement among the churches in Bremen and along the lower Rhine, under the direct influence of Dutch precedents—notably, Willem Teellinck, Gisbertus Voetius, Johannes Coccejus, and Labadie. Dutch works in German translation were far more influential than English Puritan writings among early German Reformed Pietists.

German Reformed Pietism owed its rise to the work of Theodor Undereyck; thanks to his disciples, the movement spread to various parts of the central and northern German empire. Undereyck's importance was nicely summed up in 1703 by his colleague Cornelius de Hase: "What Spener was to the Lutheran Church, Undereyck was to the Reformed Church."[73] The period of early Reformed Pietism, from 1660 to 1693, has been called "the era of Undereyck."[74] Before Schütz and Spener founded the collegium pietatis in Frankfurt in 1670, Undereyck was holding house conventicles among Reformed believers in Wesel, Mülheim, and Duisburg, with women participating as well as men. However, the terminology of "Pietism" was never as widely used among German Reformed Pietists as it was among the Lutherans.

THEODOR UNDEREYCK (1635–1693)

Theodor Undereyck was born in Duisburg on June 15, 1635, the son of Gerhard Undereyck, a prosperous merchant, and his wife, Sara—both exiles from the Netherlands. At just two years of age, Theodor Undereyck lost both his parents to the plague and was taken in and raised by an uncle. He pursued studies in philosophy and theology in Utrecht from 1654 to 1657. There he encountered Gisbertus Voetius, leader of the Nadere Reformatie, a movement that joined the Synod of Dort's strict teaching on predestination with passion for piety and renewal of life. Especially important for Undereyck was the influence of two Utrecht preachers, Jodocus van Lodenstein and Justus van den Bogaart (d. 1663). They helped to guide his spiritual life and became models for his own pastoral ministry. For the rest of his life, Undereyck expressed gratitude for van den Bogaart as "the instrument blessed by God in his conversion and new birth."[75]

During his short time at the University in Duisburg, Undereyck encountered the federal theology of Johannes Coccejus (1603–1669). Still too young for pastoral ministry, in April 1658 Undereyck went to Leiden to attend lectures by Coccejus and Johannes Hoornbeek. Coccejus called for renewal of both theology and church life. He sought to free the study of the scriptures from the dominance of Aristotelian, Ramist, and Cartesian ideas and methods, promoting instead "a more open, modern, and Biblically founded Christianity."[76] Undereyck absorbed three features of Coccejus's piety and thought. First, Coccejus taught that scholarship should lead to piety; biblical understanding should lead to biblical obedience.[77] Second, Coccejus understood Revelation and Song of Solomon in terms of seven historical periods of God's working in the world. Third, Coccejus affirmed that a new age was imminent, marked by the worldwide spread of the Gospel. He had a lifelong interest in biblical prophecy and problems relating to eschatology.[78] In the end, Undereyck drew upon both Voetius and Coccejus, refusing to align himself with either school.[79]

In May 1660 Undereyck was called to serve as minister in the Reformed church in Mülheim. There he married Margarete Hüls, daughter of a preacher in Wesel. As a gift, he gave his bride a copy of Thomas à Kempis's *Imitation of Christ*. The couple had three daughters. Undereyck's ministry was characterized by improved catechism instruction and strict church discipline. His preaching emphasized the need for new birth. He helped to institute regular visitations by pastors and elders in the homes of church members to determine who should be welcomed at the Lord's Table. Through the initiative of a layperson, Johann Backhaus, members gathered in a home after the Sunday service to discuss Undereyck's sermon.[80]

In 1668 Undereyck became court preacher to Countess Hedwig Sophie in Kassel. He dedicated his first book, *The Bride of Christ among the Daughters of Laodicea,* to the countess.[81] In the book he discusses "the living power of saving faith," considering the signs of true faith, hindrances to faith, and the means for promoting true faith. True faith, according to Undereyck, consists of union and fellowship with Christ through Word, sacrament, sorrow for sin, and avoidance of whatever might lead to temptation. He called for a disciplined Christian life, free of luxuries, games, and dancing. He taught that the chief means of grace, besides the Sunday sermon, was gathering in homes for Bible reading, prayer, singing, and mutual instruction and correction. He called these gatherings "house churches" or "little churches," the latter an expression used by Willem Teellinck.[82] Undereyck was the founder of German Pietist home gatherings.

After a couple of years in Kassel, Undereyck was called in April 1670 to be first preacher at the old and prestigious St. Martin's Church in Bremen, against the wishes of the city's clergy. The Bremen ministerium accused Undereyck of Labadism and sought to undermine his appointment, but the Bremen city council had the last word. Undereyck held this position until his death in 1693. In Bremen, Undereyck succeeded in planting a reform movement within the city's churches. He instituted an intense program of catechizing for young people preparing for their first communion, a model that other city churches took up in 1672. He aimed his preaching at the heart and conscience of his hearers, calling them to repentance. He saw many conversions; there were also reports of people being driven to despair and suicide by Undereyck's sermons.[83]

In April 1674 the Bremen ministerium attacked Undereyck for holding a conventicle in his home and for offering catechetical instruction, with the help of his wife, Margarete, and household servants. The conflict lasted four years, but Undereyck received the full support of the Bremen city council. In 1679 he submitted a plan for establishing a presbytery and implementing church discipline so that unbelievers would be prevented from attending the Lord's Supper and having their children baptized. Although the plan was not realized, he did achieve improvement in catechetical instruction among church members. Late 1680 saw a renewed attack by the ministerium on Underecyk and his wife for holding conventicles in their home. After church on Sundays, Undereyck met separately with men and women in the church parsonage. He discussed the Bible with the adults and held catechism with the young people. Margarete met with young girls on weekdays at noon. She also taught catechism to children after school and held discussions on the catechism with women servants in the afternoons, with the permission of their masters.[84]

Undereyck had a profound impact on a number of young theology students in Bremen. When he was first called to St. Martin's, Heinrich Horch, Johann Henrich Reitz, Conrad Mell, and "many other young men from Hesse" followed Undereyck to Bremen to pursue studies in theology.[85] Some went on to become Reformed Pietist leaders in various parts of northern Germany. Others found positions in Bremen churches through Undereyck's intervention, laying a foundation for Pietist ministry in Bremen for years to come. These men included Cornelius de Hase, who succeeded Undereyck at St. Martin's Church, Joachim Neander, Werner Köne (Undereyck's son-in-law), Gerhard Neckelmann, and Andreas Raukamp. Thanks to Undereyck and de Hase, Bremen became the center of German Reformed Pietism in the late seventeenth century; from there, it spread along the lower Rhine to Ostfriesland and beyond.[86]

GERHARD TERSTEEGEN (1697–1769)

Gerhard Tersteegen has been called "the most fascinating character in the whole history of religious revival."[87] A man of contradictions, Tersteegen's place within Protestantism is still a source of dispute. A Catholic interpreter called him a Carmelite in disguise, while a Protestant historian suggested that Tersteegen probably had never held a writing by Luther or Calvin in his hands.[88] One biographer observed that "through his ties with the French Quietists [especially Madame Guyon] he became a person who lived on the boundary between two religious worlds. He certainly cannot be reckoned as a legitimate representative of the Reformation; nor was he a Catholic . . . He lived on the border between two countries and partook of the spiritual-intellectual life of both."[89] Yet Tersteegen's oft-published *Spiritual Flower Garden of Ardent Souls* made him the most important figure in German Reformed Pietism and the third leading hymn writer in the history of German Protestantism, alongside Martin Luther and Paul Gerhard.

Tersteegen was born on November 26, 1697, in the lower Rhine city of Moers, the son of a merchant and the eighth of nine children. His father died in 1703, when Gerhard was not yet six years old. Gerhard attended the Latin school in Moers run by the Reformed church. There he studied the Heidelberg Catechism in Latin and read the New Testament in Greek. By the time he finished Latin school, he had mastered Latin, Greek, Hebrew, and French. In June 1715 his mother sent him to live with relatives in Mülheim so that he could enter an apprenticeship in business, following his two older brothers. But Tersteegen showed little interest in or aptitude for this line of work, and in 1719 he gave it up.[90]

In Mülheim, Tersteegen came into contact with a conventicle led by Wilhelm Hoffmann (1685–1746), a convert of Hochmann von Hochenau. Hoffmann was a mystical Quietist and disciple of the writings of Pierre Poiret and Madame Guyon. Hoffmann lost his chance of obtaining a Reformed pastorate when he refused to subscribe to the Heidelberg Catechism; instead, he assumed leadership of some separatist conventicles in the region. By 1717 Tersteegen was following Hoffmann's mystical Quietism and was no longer attending the Reformed church or taking the Lord's Supper. During a severe illness, Tersteegen prayed that God would grant him time to prepare for eternity. He immediately got better and committed himself to serving God. Tersteegen described his new direction in life thus: "[In 1717] God called me out of the world and bestowed on me the desire to belong completely to him and to follow him."[91] This marked his first conversion. After giving up his apprenticeship, he lived for five years in ascetic withdrawal and poverty, like Madame Guyon and the Spanish mystics, separating himself from family and friends. He persisted in this simple life despite coming into a rich inheritance when his mother died in 1721. Most of the inheritance he gave away to the poor.

In 1724 Tersteegen had a second, more dramatic experience of God's grace, a deep and abiding impression of the presence and nearness of God. He documented the experience on April 13 by signing a covenant in his own blood. "My Jesus! I sign myself over to you, my only Savior and Bridegroom, as your entire and eternal possession. I renounce from my heart all rights and powers over myself." The document closes with the words, "May your Spirit seal what your unworthy possession has written in all simplicity."[92] Madame Guyon had made a similar covenant in 1672, and other Catholic mystics did so as well. Tersteegen encouraged people he counseled to commit themselves to God using the terms of a betrothal or contract or monastic vow. For much of his life, the experience of God's presence would be the subject of his teaching, correspondence, and hymn writing.

In 1725 Tersteegen began assisting Wilhelm Hoffmann in various conventicles around Mülheim, serving as pastor and teacher. He undertook an extensive correspondence with people referred to him by Hoffmann, sometimes traveling to offer encouragement to Pietist gatherings along the Rhine and as far away as the Netherlands and the Wetterau. Tersteegen took a special interest in Heinrich Otterbeck in Heiligenhaus, pursuing a friendship by correspondence. In 1727 the Otterbeck family made their house available to a community of Tersteegen's disciples. In early 1732 Tersteegen drew up "Important Rules of Conduct for a Community of Brothers Living Together." His rules for their common life included work, meditation, and prayer, all done in silence. "Talkativeness," he wrote, "always disrupts Christian communities, dries up devotion, confuses minds, wastes time, and drives away the presence of God. God dwells only in silent souls [*Gott wohnet nur in stillen Seelen*]."[93]

Tersteegen also wrote tracts and longer works in both Dutch and German, publishing these anonymously to avoid the censors of the Reformed church. His literary activity consisted mainly of translating the works of mystical writers or selections from their writings, accompanied by his detailed introductions.[94] In 1727 Tersteegen put out a new translation of Jean de Labadie's *Manual of Piety* (1668); in March 1730 he published his translation of the *Imitation of Christ*. Thereafter, most of Tersteegen's translations were of works recommended by Pierre Poiret (1646–1719) in his *Select Library of the Mystics* (1708). Over a period of twenty years, between 1733 and 1753, Tersteegen completed a three-volume work of translation that he entitled *Select Biographies of Godly Souls*. The work recounted the lives of twenty-five saints as a source of inspiration and guidance in living the Christian life. These lives included Gregory Lopez and his practice of the prayer of the heart, Theresa of Avila as an example of the value of suffering, Brother Lawrence and John of the Cross on pastoral care, and Francis of Assisi on love of nature. Tersteegen was inspired by Gottfried Arnold's conviction that a history of true Christians was a far better church history than one taken up with theological disputations. Next to the Bible, wrote Arnold, it is the books of Catholic mystics that best describe "real, inward Christian faith and true godly learning." Tersteegen agreed, observing that Roman Catholic mystics were "more Reformed and Evangelical than most Protestants."[95]

The last years of Tersteegen's life were marked by sufferings engendered by the Seven Years War (1756–1763) and by his experience of inner darkness and loss of the sense of God's presence. He wrote, "I had thought long ago [that] I was at the goal of blessedness, that the beloved Master was already mine; now I see myself correctly for the first time lying in pain and suffering; it seems love can deceive a little."[96] Tersteegen was forced to rely on simple trust in God in the absence of his earlier enjoyment of the presence and nearness of God.

Today, Tersteegen is known to English-speaking Christians as a hymn writer, thanks to translations of his hymns by John Wesley, Emma Francis Bevan, Francis Elizabeth Cox, Catherine Winkworth, and others.[97] Tersteegen's best-selling book was the *Spiritual Flower Garden* (1729). The first edition included 28 hymns and 440 poems. Later editions grew to 122 spiritual songs and 1,200 poems and verses.[98] In his address To the Reader, Tersteegen wrote:

> God is your beginning. If you have him in essence,
> You have already read this book through to its end.
> If you seek him, read this on your way.
> If you are not one who seeks him, it will be of no use to you.[99]

John Wesley discovered the hymns of Tersteegen in a copy of the Moravian hymnal that he obtained either on his voyage to Georgia in 1735 or during his ministry there. Wesley translated four hymns by Tersteegen, including "God Himself Is with Us," "Thou Hidden Love of God," and "Lo, God Is Here, Let Us Adore!" The work of translating these hymns helped Wesley resolve his spiritual crisis.[100]

Tersteegen's most famous hymn is "God Himself Is with Us" (Gott ist gegenwärtig). Verse 1 reads:

God Himself is with us: Let us now adore Him,
And with awe appear before Him.
God is in His temple—All within keep silence,
And before Him bow with reverence.
Him alone, God we own,
To our Lord and Savior;
Praises sing forever![101]

Verses 5 through 7 of the German hymn include the elements of the three-fold mystical path of purgation, illumination, and union.[102] *Purgation:* "Make me pure of heart, so I may / Behold your glory / In spirit and in truth" (verse 7). The verse includes reference to Jesus's words in the Sermon on the Mount: "Blessed are the pure in heart, for they shall see God" (Matt. 5:8). One must become free of all images and imaginings and impurities. *Illumination:* "as the tender flowers open out their petals / And calmly welcome the sun's warmth, / so may I, calm in joy, / embrace your rays from heaven, / And allow you to do your work!" (verse 6). This illumination is a gift from God and can only be received as grace. *Union:* "Sea without bottom or end, wonder of all Wonders, / I settle down into you. / I in you, you in me, / May I disappear entirely, / And see and find only you!" (verse 5). Here is the goal of all contemplation: union with God.[103] These classic mystical themes run through the hymn in a somewhat random fashion.

Tersteegen's verses and hymns have had an enduring legacy, not only in Protestant worship but also in secular German culture. Frederick III made Tersteegen's hymn "Ich bete an die Macht der Liebe" (I beseech the power of love) the evening prayer of the Prussian Army. In modern times, the hymn has been used to mark the end of day in the German armed forces.[104]

Gerhard Goeters described Tersteegen's poetic gift, biblical language, and abundant imagery as representing "the best that German literature in the pre-classical period of sensibility has produced."[105] Ernest Stoeffler offered a fitting tribute to Tersteegen, calling him "perhaps the best loved spiritual advisor of his day, the writer of some of the most treasured hymns in Protestantism, and the author of edificatory books which have held their own in spite of the shifting moods of the modern intellectual climate."[106]

Conclusion

After the devastations of the Thirty Years War (1618–1648) and the defeat of the Ottoman Turks (1699), many European Christians were marked by desires for peace and unity and deepened Christian faith. In this climate, German Protestants explored new forms of piety in the works of English, French, and Dutch Calvinist writers who called for renewal of church and society and of individual piety. Reformed Pietism in Germany began in Mülheim and Bremen and among the churches of the lower Rhine, under the direct influence of Dutch precedents, notably Teellinck, Voetius, Coccejus, and Labadie. Theodor Undereyck held house conventicles among Reformed believers in Wesel, Mülheim, and Duisburg well before Schütz and Spener founded the collegium pietatis in Frankfurt in 1670. The period of early Reformed Pietism, from 1660 to 1693, has been called "the era of Undereyck," thanks to his influence and that of his disciples. Gerhard Tersteegen's *Spiritual Flower Garden* made him the most important figure in German Reformed Pietism; his hymns and mystical piety have earned him an enduring place in the history of Christian spirituality.

Part II

A Tale of Three Cities

CHAPTER 3

Beginnings of Lutheran Pietism in Frankfurt, 1670 to 1684

The beginnings of Lutheran Pietism are traditionally traced to events in Frankfurt, Germany, in the 1670s. Until recently, the main sources of information for these events have been the reminiscences of Philipp Jakob Spener. But these are problematic in one key respect: Spener makes no reference to Johann Jakob Schütz, even though there is evidence that Schütz played a prominent role. The reason is clear: Spener wished to put Pietist beginnings in the best possible light; the separation of Schütz and the Saalhof Pietists from the Lutheran church in Frankfurt was too painful and embarrassing.[1]

It seemed unlikely that letters and writings by other participants in these events would have survived the destruction of the Frankfurt Ministerial Archive during the Second World War.[2] However, in the late 1980s, a German scholar discovered papers and unpublished letters from the estate of Johann Jakob Schütz in a Frankfurt archive.[3] Thanks to this discovery, the chronology of events in the early days of Frankfurt Pietism can be reconstructed and the role of Schütz better understood.[4]

This chapter considers first the setting of early Pietism in late seventeenth-century Frankfurt; it then examines the work and ideals of Schütz, Spener, the Saalhof Pietists, and the early Pietist separatists.

Seventeenth-Century Frankfurt: The Setting of Early Pietism

Frankfurt was a free imperial city, meaning that the city council acted with a high degree of autonomy in managing the city's affairs, accountable only to the Habsburg Emperor. Local princes and bishops had no say in city matters. Frankfurt suffered greatly during the Thirty Years War, not because of direct attacks but due to food shortages, hunger, and disease. In the fall and winter of 1631, the city housed the soldiers of Sweden's King Gustavus Adolphus. From 1634 to 1637 Frankfurt was besieged by a host of refugees left homeless by the war, making shortages worse. In 1635 alone there were some seven thousand deaths in the city, out of a population of twenty thousand. Not until 1675 did the city's population return to its prewar numbers.[5]

The main business in Frankfurt was the trade fair, which took place twice a year, at Easter and in the fall, making it the leading trade city in the western German empire. There were four main industries: bookselling, silk, jewelry, and banking. Dutch refugees brought the silk and jewelry businesses with them. The Frankfurt book fair was the main center of the European book trade until the mid seventeenth century, attracting book handlers from Italy, France, Belgium, and the Netherlands. The fair's success was due to the city's ideal location, with links to the Rhine River and thereby to Strasbourg and Basel and connections to the south, as well as to Cologne and the north and northwest. The fair was held in the "book dealer quarter" of the city, on the banks of the Main River, facilitating easy transport of book barrels out to ships and then on to their destinations. The booksellers were lodged on the main street of the book quarter, enabling them to enjoy a lively exchange of business and conversation with paper dealers, book printers, and scholars.[6] In the late seventeenth century, Frankfurt lost priority of place to the Leipzig book fair. But it continued to have close contacts with at least fifteen Dutch book houses and was a key distribution center for radical sectarian literature.[7]

As a prosperous business town, Frankfurt attracted skilled workers from various parts of Europe, especially from the Netherlands, resulting in a broad mix of confessional backgrounds among its residents. The majority of the city's population was Lutheran, and this confession controlled the city council. The city also included about a thousand Reformed believers and two Reformed (Calvinist) churches just outside the city, along with some Roman Catholics and various other confessional minorities. There was a saying that nicely summed up this distribution: "The Roman Catholics have the churches, the Lutherans have the government, and the Reformed have the money."[8] Jewish residents made up more than 10 percent of the population, with a ghetto dating back to medieval times. The Frankfurt city council encouraged wealthy Jews to settle there. In the early modern period, Frankfurt, Prague, Worms, and Friedberg were among the few cities in the Holy Roman Empire that welcomed the presence of a Jewish community. Frankfurt, then, was a city in which various nationalities, confessions, and ideas mingled and engaged with one another. Between 1555 and 1685 it was a city of immigrants and minorities "to a degree unmatched by any other German city at that time."[9]

Well before Spener's arrival, Frankfurt's Reformed believers were marked by a desire for deepened personal piety and an appreciation for the writings of Spiritualist authors. Johann Arndt's main readership in the mid seventeenth century was mainly among the Reformed. The key figures in the Frankfurt nonconformist book trade were the Schwenckfeld sympathizer Matthäus Merian (1593–1650) and his son-in-law Christoph Leblon (1600–1665), both members of the Reformed church.[10] Merian put out eight titles by Christian Hoburg, all of them critical of church authorities.[11] Leblon printed works by Caspar Schwenckfeld and Johann Arndt, as well as a multitude of alchemical and Paracelsian works.[12] Christoph's brother Michael Leblon, who was tied in to Jakob Böhme study circles, passed along to Christoph valuable Böhme manuscripts. In May 1664 the city's preachers presented the city council with a list of forty-four titles of sectarian, heretical works that had been printed in Frankfurt, asking that countermeasures be taken, especially against Christoph Leblon. Copies of his printing of the Socinian New Testament were collected and burned.[13]

Frankfurt's radical religious subculture dated back to the 1620s. The city had long served as a gathering point for a variety of religious streams, groups, and personalities. Frankfurt nonconformists formed a network with those in other German cities, such as Tübingen and Nuremberg, and with nonconformists in various Dutch cities. In these circles, the works of Caspar Schwenckfeld, Johann Arndt, Christian Hoburg, and Jakob Böhme were read and exchanged. It was in this prosperous and religiously diverse setting in Frankfurt that Lutheran Pietism first took root.

The Conversion of Johann Jakob Schütz (1640–1690)

Johann Jakob Schütz was born on September 7, 1640, to Jacob Schütz (1587–1654) and his second wife, Margaretha (d. 1687). The Schütz family belonged to the upper echelon of Frankfurt society; Margaretha was from a prosperous business family in the city. Johann Jakob's father, Jacob, grew up in Tübingen, his father a Lutheran clergyman in Württemberg and his mother a daughter of the famous Tübingen theologian Jacob Andreae.[14] Jacob completed studies at Tübingen University in 1608, spent ten years traveling through the Netherlands and France, and returned to Tübingen to complete a law degree in 1619. Jacob Schütz's first wife and seven of his nine children died during the Thirty Years War. He married Margaretha in 1636, and in 1637 was appointed as one of four syndici in Frankfurt, a position that involved various diplomatic responsibilities on behalf of the city. Jacob and Margaretha were marked by a deep and disciplined piety, engaging in prayer and devotions in the morning and evening. Jacob read widely in the writings of church fathers such as Augustine, Ambrose, Cyprian, and Chrysostom.

Their son, Johann Jakob Schütz, began his studies in Jena in April 1657 and continued them in Tübingen in 1659, completing a law degree there in 1665. He spent a further two years gaining practical experience at the court in Speyer and pursuing educational travels. In October 1667 he returned to Frankfurt and took his oath as a lawyer. On October 3, 1680, the forty-year-old Schütz married Katharina Elisabeth Bartels (1652–1721). The Bartels family had left Antwerp in the sixteenth century during the Spanish Inquisition and had become one of the leading business and banking families in Frankfurt. They were also among the wealthiest, with an extravagant lifestyle that included a large staff of servants and a luxurious coach drawn by the best horses. The marriage meant a significant increase in Schütz's wealth and social status. The couple had five daughters, four surviving to adulthood. The second youngest, Maria Katharina Schütz

(1687–1742), became a leading Frankfurt separatist in the 1730s and was sought out by Pietist figures such as Count Nikolaus Ludwig von Zinzendorf and F. C. Oetinger.[15]

During his student years, Schütz set aside the Lutheran Orthodoxy of his youth; his increasing doubts about the truth of Christianity culminated in his espousing total atheism. After returning to Frankfurt in 1667, Schütz began reading the German mystic Johannes Tauler, along with works inspired by Johann Arndt. The newly arrived Lutheran superintendent, Philipp Jakob Spener, encouraged him in this endeavor and was impressed with his progress. Sometime in 1668 Schütz experienced a dramatic conversion from atheism to heartfelt personal faith, setting a new direction for his life. The key feature of Schütz's new orientation was his discovery of the Bible. As Deppermann describes, "Schütz did not simply fetch his Bible off the shelf; the key was the new way and method in which he began to read it. With help from Tauler he learned to pay attention to the way the Bible moved his soul and to how it spoke to his conscience; in a word, he brought his own experience to the reading of Scripture."[16] Schütz sought out those who shared his heartfelt zeal and devotion to the imitation of Christ, whether Quakers, Labadists, Reformed, or other fellow travelers. He had no patience for confessional rivalries.

After his conversion, Schütz nurtured his newly won faith through reading and various contacts. In his work as a lawyer in the city, he developed close ties with leading Reformed business figures, including the Merian family. In 1685 he acted on behalf of Maria Sibylla Merian (1647–1717), daughter of Matthäus Merian, to ensure that she retained her rightful property after her divorce from the Nuremberg painter Johannes Andreas Graff. In early 1686, accompanied by her mother and daughters, Maria Sibylla moved to Friesland to join the Labadist religious community, a move arranged through Schütz.[17] She and her family lived in a home owned by Cornelis van Sommelsdijk, the governor of Surinam. In 1699 Maria Sibylla sold her belongings and set sail for the Dutch colony with her younger daughter, Dorothea Maria, age twenty-one. There she studied and painted South American tropical flora and fauna. Two years later she returned to Amsterdam for health reasons, along with a native housemaid and containers of specimens.[18] An artist, naturalist, author, and

Labadist, Maria Sibylla is "possibly the best known of all early Radical Pietist figures."[19] She was the subject of exhibits in 1998 in Frankfurt and in 2008 in Los Angeles.

Schütz corresponded with Anna Maria van Schurman and Pierre Yvon, members of Jean de Labadie's community. He nurtured contacts with separatist groups in the Netherlands through Frankfurt businessman Jacob van de Walle. Schütz also pursued conversations with a circle of Kabbalist authors in the Sulzbach Court, including Christian Knorr von Rosenroth and Francis van Helmont, and came to share their belief in the soul's preexistence.[20]

Schütz's conversion was significant in inspiring Pietist beginnings in Frankfurt and was comparable to August Hermann Francke's conversion in its importance for the early Pietist movement. Schütz influenced a key feature of Spener's theology: while Orthodox Lutherans emphasized the role of *preaching* in the beginnings of faith, Spener followed Schütz in emphasizing the *reading of scripture* as the key to the Spirit's work.[21] It was through direct encounter with the Bible that seeking souls experienced the working of God's Spirit and came to faith.

Philipp Jakob Spener and the First Lutheran Pietist Conventicle, 1670–1674

Philipp Jakob Spener (1635–1705) was born on January 13, 1635, in Rappoltsweiler, Alsace; his father was a jurist and, later, Count of Rappoltstein. His early life was immersed in books, especially the English devotional writers Lewis Bayly and Emanuel Sonthom and Johann Arndt's *True Christianity*, which Spener considered the best book after the Bible.[22] At age sixteen, Spener began attending university in Strasbourg. In two years he completed his master's degree with a thesis on Thomas Hobbes. From 1654 to 1659 he studied in the theology faculty at Strasbourg. His professors included Johann Schmidt, Johann Conrad Dannhauer, and Sebastian Schmidt, men whom he would honor for the rest of his life. Johann Schmidt (1594–1658) shared Spener's esteem for Johann Arndt and English devotional writers; Spener later called Schmidt "my beloved father in Christ."[23] Sebastian Schmidt (1617–1696) taught that biblical exegesis should be free of dogmatic assumptions, a method Spener later followed and recommended to A. H. Francke and students in Leipzig.

Spener's fellow students in Strasbourg included later proponents of Orthodoxy such as Johann Benedict Carpzov and Johann Fecht, as well as later Pietists and lifelong friends such as Theophil Spizel and Johann Heinrich Horb, and mystical Spiritualists such as Friedrich Breckling and Johann Georg Gichtel.

From 1659 to 1662 Spener made academic trips (*Bildungsreisen*) that took him to Basel, where he continued his study of Hebrew, and to Geneva, where he was influenced by the preaching and mystical devotion of Jean de Labadie. In 1664 Spener received his doctorate from Strasbourg University for a thesis on Revelation 9:13–21. He examined fifty commentaries, including millenarian interpretations, and became doubtful about the traditional Lutheran teaching that the book's prophecies were already fulfilled and that the last judgment was not far off.[24] On the same day that he received his doctorate, he married twenty-year-old Susanne Ehrhardt, of noble background. They had eleven children.

In early 1666, at thirty-one years of age, Spener arrived in Frankfurt to assume the position of senior pastor, making him head of the city's twelve Lutheran clergymen. He won the post through the intervention of the pious nobleman Johann Vincenz Baur von Eyseneck (d. 1672) from the Saalhof estate. Spener and von Eyseneck had been friends while students in Geneva in 1660–1661.[25] Spener filled the role of senior pastor for the next twenty years. He sought to encourage among Frankfurt Lutherans a "true living faith" that went beyond outward churchly observance. He soon became frustrated in his efforts to bring renewal to Frankfurt churches through stricter Sabbath observance, enforcement of church discipline, and renewed catechism instruction.[26]

In the summer of 1670, however, Spener found cause for encouragement in a small group that began to meet in the study in his home. The initiative for the first Pietist conventicle lay not with Spener but with two men in his congregation who approached him that summer. Spener later recalled their desire for a social gathering where conversation was edifying and not focused on worldly matters.

> The men were discouraged that they never came away edified from the everyday conversations that they experienced but rather felt that any good in them was more and more suppressed. They longed to have some opportunity when godly-minded people could come together and confer

> with each other in simplicity and love. They hoped that in such conversations they might find what they had previously sought in vain.[27]

Spener reported that one of these men was a theology student, the other a jurist.[28] They have been identified, respectively, as Johannes Anton Dieffenbach (1642–1671) and Johann Jakob Schütz.[29] The group that met in Spener's study also included Johann Baur von Eyseneck and two brothers, both jurists: Zacharias Conrad Uffenbach (1639–1691) and Johann Christoph Uffenbach (1643–1684).

In August 1670 the six men (including Spener) began meeting on Sunday and Wednesday evenings in Spener's study. Spener opened with prayer and read a passage from a book of devotion. He summed up the passage and shared his reflections on the most important lessons it contained. Then the other members asked questions or offered their reflections. Finally, the conversation ranged widely over any other matters that came to mind. The spirit of the gatherings was "a free conversation among friends."[30] The only rules were that all should be done for edification, controversy should be avoided, and nothing should be discussed pertaining to anyone not present.

The books of devotion that Spener used in the early days included Lewis Bayly's *The Practice of Piety* (1610), Nikolaus Hunnius's *Epitome of Things to Be Believed* (1625), an outline of Orthodox Lutheran dogmatics, and Joachim Lütkemann's *Foretaste of God's Goodness* (1653). The last of these was chosen not by Spener but by Schütz; the book had been recommended to him by his friend Anna Sophia Hagemeister. Bayly's work offers meditations on hindrances to piety and on how to read the Bible with profit; prayers for morning and evening; meditations on how to keep the Sabbath; and prayers for the sick and dying. Hunnius's *Epitome* describes the life of regenerate believers in whom "all the powers of the body and soul have undergone an entire change." The believer's reason is awakened from ignorance to true knowledge of God, and his mind is renewed so that he walks in righteousness and holiness. In sum, "A man of this description is born again, and has become quite another man . . . his life and purposes have changed."[31] Lütkemann's work reflects a mystical Spiritualist emphasis on inward devotion and a Lutheran emphasis on the importance of the outer word as the means of grace. The book was clearly influenced by Johann Arndt's *True Christianity* and took its place alongside Arndt as one of the most widely read devotional books of the time. Lütkemann's spirit is reflected in his saying, "I would rather help one soul become godly than a hundred become learned."[32]

By December 1670, fifteen to twenty people were participating in the collegium in Spener's home, all men from families of prominent Frankfurt jurists and pastors. By 1675 there were fifty in attendance, and by 1677 close to a hundred, consisting of both men and women from all classes of society. The women sat in an adjoining room and kept silent. "There are quite a few Christian women who attend, married and unmarried," Spener wrote, "but they sit separate from the rest so they cannot be seen. But they can hear everything. It is not permitted for them to speak or ask questions. In this way we act according to the Apostolic ordinance in I Cor. 14 and I Tim. 2, even though we are only a house gathering."[33] Schütz noted two important features of this early Pietism: the language of "brother" and "sister" that members used in addressing each other and the notion of the priesthood of all believers. He wrote, "We are all one, and call one another brother or sister, for there is neither male nor female but we are all one in Christ Jesus . . . The surpassing value of our rebirth causes me to forget my natural birth, and so the brother according to the Spirit in Christ is far closer to me and dearer than any other."[34]

In September 1674 the Frankfurt gatherings underwent a significant change and reorientation away from discussion of devotional books to reading and study of the Bible. Some attribute the new direction to Schütz's reading of Jean de Labadie's *The Exercise of Prophecy* and *Reformation of the Church by the Pastorate* (1668) and Theodor Undereyck's *Bride of Christ* (1670). Labadie had recommended small gatherings, *collegia pietatis*, for theology students. Undereyck spoke of gatherings in homes for edification as "little churches" and supported the practice from I Corinthians 14:26: "When you come together, each one has a hymn, a lesson, a revelation . . . Let all things be done for building up." Deppermann finds these sources less likely as factors promoting change than Schütz's conversion in 1668 and his preference for reading the Bible above all other books.[35] But Deppermann leaves unexplained why Schütz waited until 1674 to make the innovation.

The Saalhof Pietists and Pietist Separatism in Frankfurt, 1675–1684

From the start, a different notion of church and Christian community was evident in the Pietist collegia. Hierarchical, state-supported structures, based on confessional unity, were minimized or set aside in favor of free associations of true believers, independent of confession and the state.[36] The collegium in Spener's home in Frankfurt, for example, included Reformed (Calvinist) believers as well as Lutherans.[37] Separatist conventicles, with no ties to state churches, soon developed in Frankfurt under Spener's very eyes. Spener's idea of the collegium as a small church within the church, under clerical leadership, became harder and harder to maintain.

By late 1675, private conventicles or collegia were being held in Frankfurt without Spener's supervision or knowledge, including one in the home of the physician Dr. Johann Kißner and his wife, Anna Elisabeth, and one hosted by Schütz for theology students.[38] Another gathering met under the direction of Maria Juliana Baur von Eyseneck (1641–1684) on her estate, called the Saalhof, on the banks of the Main River. When her husband, the nobleman Johann Vincenz Baur von Eyseneck, died in 1672, he left her with three young children, two sons and a daughter. She took on the education of her children, along with the eight-year-old niece of Johanna von Merlau. Von Eyseneck authored a commentary on Luther's *Small Catechism* to assist with her instruction. Spener praised Maria Juliana von Eyseneck as "a true Christian with many gifts."[39]

The Saalhof circle included the two women who led the group, Maria Juliana Baur von Eyseneck and Johanna Eleonora von Merlau, as well as Schütz, Christian Fende, some theology students, and a number of Frankfurt burghers of Reformed background. They met on Sunday afternoons to discuss the morning's sermon, as well as during the week for edifying conversation. A key factor in the rise of the Saalhof group was the frustration that Baur von Eyseneck and von Merlau experienced in Spener's collegium, where they had to sit separately from the men and keep silent. The two women sought a setting in which they could freely express their questions and opinions on matters of theology and biblical interpretation. In the less regulated meetings of the Saalhof circle, women played a prominent part.[40]

Johanna Eleonora von Merlau (1644–1724) was born in Frankfurt am Main into a family of Hesse nobility that had become impoverished during the Thirty Years War. After her mother's death, Johanna Eleonora served as court maiden to some noble families in Hesse and Saxony. She was repelled by the superficial pursuits that she observed in court life. On May 29, 1672, von Merlau met Schütz on a ship to Mainz. Their conversation lasted several hours, and she was deeply affected by his words. Schütz convinced her of his chiliastic hopes for the coming kingdom of Christ and of the need to follow Christ and his commands in simplicity.[41]

In early 1675, von Merlau moved back to Frankfurt. Soon after her arrival she began holding devotional times with young servant girls and offering instruction to young women in the Greek language so that they could read the New Testament in the original. Among her students was Spener's daughter. Over the next four years, von Merlau joined Schütz and Christian Fende as a leading figure among the Saalhof Pietists. On September 7, 1680, she married Johann Wilhelm Petersen, a Lutheran pastor and theologian, passing on to her husband the legacy of Frankfurt Pietism in which she had been nurtured by Schütz and Spener. Spener preached the sermon at their wedding.[42] The Petersens became the leading promoters in German lands of the Philadelphian eschatology of Jane Leade, including her teachings on the coming thousand-year kingdom and the restoration of all things to God's rule, including the devil and the fallen angels.

Johanna Eleonora Petersen published fifteen books, making her the most significant female Pietist author of her day. Many of these works were sharply critical of the divisions and low level of piety within state Lutheran churches.[43] Her 1689 autobiography belongs to the early phase of Pietist autobiographical writing, coming before those of Francke and Spener. In contrast to autobiographies by English Puritan women, Petersen's is not primarily a conversion story; the emphasis is, rather, on her growth in understanding and her conflicts with the authorities.[44] Drawing on her mastery of Greek and Hebrew, Petersen wrote some impressive works of biblical interpretation. Her 1696 commentary on John's *Apocalypse, Guide to a Thorough Understanding of the Holy Revelation of Jesus Christ,* is the most extensive presentation of her millenarian ideas. She later identified it as the most important of all her works.[45] In commenting on scripture, Petersen blazed new ground and surmounted a formidable barrier facing women writers in the early modern period. She broke from the tradition of women publishing their works anonymously; as a result, she attracted the attention and criticism of leading Lutheran theologians. Petersen's writings show her to be "an extremely intelligent, educated, and self-confident woman."[46]

In August 1677, the Quaker William Penn visited the Saalhof community and participated in its fellowship and worship. He observed that the Saalhof Pietists were a fragile, fearful, and suppressed community, a situation Penn called "the German sickness."[47] Penn explained to them his "Holy Experiment" and invited them to join other persecuted Christians in migrating to Pennsylvania. Johann Jakob Schütz and some friends established the Frankfurt Land Company, acquiring fifteen thousand acres of land in Pennsylvania. In April 1683 they appointed as administrator a young lawyer who had joined the Saalhof circle four years earlier, Franz Daniel Pastorius (1651–1720).[48] On June 10, 1683, Pastorius and nine others sailed from Deal in England on the ship *America*, arriving in Philadelphia on August 20. In October of that year, thirteen families, Mennonites and Quakers from Krefeld, followed Pastorius and joined him in establishing Germantown, the first permanent German settlement in North America.[49] Pastorius became a prolific author, producing legal guidelines for the colony as well as books of poetry and works on gardening and medicine. His largest work was an encyclopedia compiled for his sons, entitled *Bee-Hive*.[50] He assembled a personal library of 350 books and pamphlets, including works by Schütz, Spener, Labadie, Jakob Böhme, and Johann Arndt. In contrast to the Puritan settlers, Pastorius and his Mennonite and Quaker friends dealt kindly with the native peoples and found them peaceful and friendly in return. On February 18, 1688, Pastorius authored a protest, the first in North America, against the use of black slaves in America, arguing that a different skin color did not justify the theft and sale of human lives.[51]

For almost ten years, until the death of Maria Juliana Baur von Eyseneck in April 1684, the Saalhof Pietists were a vibrant center of Pietist gathering and conversation, attracting attention from both supporters and critics. Unhampered by clerical oversight or confessional theology, the Saalhof Pietists pursued a distinct path. They developed close ties with the Labadists, discussing the writings of Jean de Labadie and Anna Maria van Schurman at their meetings, and highly esteemed the works of Antoinette Bourignon.[52] Van Schurman's *Eukleria* (1673), in which she justified her decision to leave the Reformed church and join de Labadie's community, became the most widely read Labadist writing in Germany.[53] Schütz's ties to van Schurman and Bourignon were especially close, with a vigorous exchange of letters. The Saalhof Pietists were also marked by an eschatology, introduced by Schütz, that looked for the soon-to-come millennial kingdom of Christ.[54]

Complaints arose in Frankfurt in 1677 about the growth of the Saalhof circle and reports that students were preaching at the meetings. One theology student, Otto Richardi, was arrested for preaching on a street corner. That same year, Johanna Eleonora von Merlau was threatened with banishment from the city because of fears she would influence the Saalhof Pietists into separating from the established church.[55] There were growing fears that Frankfurt might be on the verge of giving up Evangelical Lutheranism in favor of a new form of religion—Pietism.[56]

The Saalhof Pietists eventually became a separatist conventicle, breaking ties with the Lutheran church in Frankfurt. Schütz became increasingly unhappy with Spener's collegium, lamenting that "there was no more heartfelt devotion to be found there; it was only displays of knowledge and learning." By the end of 1676 he no longer partook of the Lord's Supper, saying he could not, in good conscience, celebrate with those who were manifestly ungodly. Schütz was probably influenced on this point by the views of Caspar Schwenckfeld, Christian Hoburg, and van Schurman.[57] In 1682 Spener learned that Christian Fende (1651–1746) had denounced Lutheran worship as idolatry and expressed doubts about the Trinity. Forced to distance himself from the Saalhof radicals, Spener reported Fende to the Frankfurt ministerium and broke off fellowship with all who refused the Lord's Supper.[58] Schütz and his wife withdrew from public worship, and in March 1682 a large number of their Saalhof friends joined them in this decision, including von Eyseneck. Schütz defended their action in writing, arguing that love for fellow believers is best expressed in small communities, not in the large state church (*Volkskirche*). He called for those in whom Christ dwelt to "flee Babel" and to seek out a true fellowship of saints so that their growth as new creatures would not be hindered.[59]

The separatism of the Saalhof Pietists marked the end of Spener's hopes for the collegia as a means of bringing renewal to Frankfurt churches.[60] In 1682 he moved the collegium from his home to the Barfuß Church, where it devolved into a conversation between Spener and some theology students. When Spener took up a position in Dresden in 1686, he did not establish any collegia there.

Gatherings modeled on Spener's collegia took root in parts of southern, central, and northern Germany, exhibiting their own regional leadership and flavor. In 1695, a contemporary observed that Spener's Pietist gatherings could be found in seven German provinces and in twenty-five German cities. In Württemberg, the first conventicles appeared in 1684 under the leadership of Ludwig Brunnquell, a clergyman dismissed for his chiliastic preaching and his affection for the writings of Jakob Böhme. He was soon joined by other disillusioned pastors, students, and craftsmen, who quickly opted for separatism. A *Reskript* in 1743 institutionalized conventicles within the region's state churches under the oversight of clergy.[61]

In Schwarzenau in Wittgenstein, in 1708, some disciples of Hochmann von Hochenau formed the separatist community of New Baptists, under the leadership of Alexander Mack. These home gatherings practiced the sacraments and became an organized religious body, known in America as the Church of the Brethren. In Ysenburg in the Wetterau, in 1715, conventicles began meeting under the oversight of the Inspirationist leaders Eberhard Gruber and Johann Friedrich Rock.[62] The way for these various forms of separatist collegia had been prepared by Schütz and events in the Saalhof community in Frankfurt.

Early Pietist Literature on Behalf of Renewal and Reform

THE LITERARY CONTRIBUTION OF JOHANN JAKOB SCHÜTZ

In the fall of 1674, Johann Jakob Schütz published, anonymously, *A Christian Book of Reflection*, a small work of three chapters intended to provide practical guidance in living the Christian life. In chapter one, Schütz discussed purification of the conscience; in chapter two, sanctification of the desires; and in chapter three, union of the will with God. These themes reflect the mystical steps of purgation, illumination, and union found in the writings of Johannes Tauler. Schütz added an appendix, almost as long as the main body of the book, that included some hymns, a portrait of "a truly converted Christian," two passages from the writings of Tauler, and a concluding prayer. The book was highly successful, going through twenty editions over the next fifty years and being translated into French, Swedish, Finnish, and English.[63]

Early in 1677 Schütz published, under his own name, a 759-page volume of sixty-one chapters entitled *Christian Rules of Life*. Here Schütz revealed how far removed his thinking was from traditional Lutheran teaching. The book consists of a collection of Bible passages arranged thematically and without commentary. Spener expressed dissatisfaction with an earlier version of the work; he disliked the format and noted that Schütz had displaced the topics of Christian forgiveness and justification through Christ's righteousness in favor of an emphasis on Christian renewal and obedience. Schütz, however, proceeded with publication. The book presents the Christian life as consisting of following the laws of Christ by the power of the Spirit. Schütz the lawyer saw the New Testament as essentially a book of regulations. *Christian Rules of Life* was influenced by Schütz's reading of a work by the Dutch Hebraist Adam Boreel, who presented Jesus of Nazareth as "the lawgiver of all humankind." Schütz also read with appreciation various Dutch Arminian authors who rejected the doctrine of the Trinity.[64]

Less well known among Schütz's writings are the biographies he wrote for four members of the Saalhof Pietists on the occasion of their death: the physician Johann Kißner (1645–1678), the printer Conrad Pertsch (1646–1678), Maria Juliana Baur von Eyseneck, and the Frankfurt jurist Niclas Christoph von Hünefeld (1619–1685). Schütz emphasized their devoted study of the scriptures and their earnestness in following Christ and his commandments with simplicity. It is an indication of the prominence and respect that Schütz enjoyed among Frankfurt Pietists that he was asked to compose these life stories.[65]

Schütz also wrote five hymns, included in the appendix to his *Christian Book of Reflection*. The hymns appeared in many Protestant hymnbooks, but without identifying the author, since *A Christian Book of Reflection* was published anonymously. The most famous of Schütz's hymns is "Sei Lob und Ehr dem höchsten Gut," known to English-speakers as "Sing Praise to God Who Reigns Above."[66] Here are the first and fifth verses:

> 1. Sing praise to God who reigns above,
> The God of all creation,
> The God of power, the God of love,
> The God of our salvation;

With healing balm my soul He fills,
And every faithless murmur stills;
To God all praise and glory!

5. The Lord is never far away,
Throughout all grief distressing
An ever-present help and stay,
Our peace and joy and blessing.
As with a mother's tender hand,
He leads his own, his chosen band;
To God all praise and glory!

The hymn's eight verses appeal to God's fatherly and motherly care in time of need. It has been called "the gem of German hymns" and is still found in German hymnbooks.[67]

Schütz's greatest literary influence, however, came through his work in publishing and distributing vast amounts of mystical-Spiritualist literature, using a network of personal contacts, printers, and publishers. Especially productive in this regard were his ties with Heinrich Betke (1625–1708) of Amsterdam, the most important publisher of mystical-Spiritualist books at that time. Betke published works by Christian Hoburg, Friedrich Breckling, Johannes Tauler, and Jan Amos Comenius, as well as the writings of Jakob Böhme. The importance of Schütz's contribution to the rise and spread of the Pietist movement by way of literature distribution cannot be overstated.[68]

THE LITERARY CONTRIBUTION OF PHILIPP JAKOB SPENER

It was Philipp Jakob Spener, however, whose prolific writing inspired and set the tone for the growing Pietist movement throughout German lands, Scandinavia, and Eastern Europe. Spener exerted his influence through networking, letter writing (some six hundred letters per year), preaching, and publishing tracts and books, including large volumes of his sermons. His publications amount to some two hundred titles, making him the most widely read German author of his day.

Spener's most influential work was probably an eighty-page booklet that appeared in early 1675. His friend Johann David Zunner, a Frankfurt Publisher, invited Spener to contribute a foreword to a new edition of Johann Arndt's gospel sermons (*Evangelienpostille*).[69] At the Frankfurt book fair in March 1675, the new Arndt edition appeared, with Spener's "Foreword to the Reader." In the fall, the foreword was published on its own as a small, and more affordable, book entitled *Pia Desideria* (Pious longings), *or Heartfelt Desires for Improvement Pleasing to God of the True Evangelical Churches, including Some Christian Recommendations to That End.* The work includes words of commendation from Spener's two brothers-in-law, Johann Heinrich Horb and Joachim Stoll, and a new introduction addressed to Christian clergy. Spener explained that in former times, when pressing issues faced the church, a general council of church leaders would come together to discuss them. This no longer seemed practical, leaving the alternative of publishing his views on issues of concern and inviting input from other pastors. In 1678 he published a Latin translation of *Pia Desideria,* so that non-German pastors and theologians could read it.

The tone of Spener's *Pia Desideria* is "a mix of humility and confidence."[70] His humility is evident in words such as the following:

> I gladly admit my inadequacy, so that I would neither presume nor imagine that I have some special gift of understanding above that of other servants of God. Rather, I find daily within myself that in which I am lacking. Therefore I plead from the bottom of my heart that men who are more gifted and equipped with more light, understanding, and experience than I, may take this matter upon themselves and reflect on it in the fear of God, and when they find something important to recommend, that they would present it to the whole Christian Evangelical Church.[71]

Spener was respectful of his fellow clergy. In calling for greater use of the scriptures, for example, he assured his clerical colleagues that he by no means minimized the importance of preaching; he was a preacher himself, after all. But preaching was simply not sufficient to bring the renewal that was needed among Christian people.

Pia Desideria has three parts: a *critique of Christian behavior* in all three levels of society—rulers, clergy, and people; Spener's *vision of church renewal,* including the fall of the papacy and conversion of Jews and heathen to a renewed Christianity; and six practical *recommendations for reform.* Spener seems to follow a medical model of diagnosis, prognosis, and therapy. He often refers to the illness afflicting the body of Christ and the urgency of finding an effective medicine so that it might be restored.[72] The first part of the work sets forth the sickness that plagues the Christian church and society in Spener's time; the second offers hope of restoring the "patient" to health, based on God's promises; and the third offers a sixfold remedy based on renewed devotion to God's word and a life of Christian love. Also noteworthy is how the three parts of *Pia Desideria* set forth the Christian virtues of *love, hope, and faith*. The first section explains how German Christians fall short in demonstrating *Christian love* to their neighbor; this was a serious failing, because Christ said that Christians are known by their love. The middle section contains Spener's *hopes for the church*, based on God's promise of a better day. The final section offers means for restoring *true and living faith* by devoted reading and study of God's word.[73]

In part one, Spener recognizes the Lutheran church of his day as a true church, because of its purity of *doctrine*, but finds it to be less pure in the sphere of everyday *life*. He identifies the source of the problem in the traditional Lutheran church order, the *Dreiständeordnung*, or hierarchy of three classes in the church: the rulers, who cared for the outward order of the church; the clergy, who cared for its spiritual well-being; and the ordinary church members.[74] The main source of church corruption and decline lay in the first two orders: rulers made the church subject to their own political self-interest, and clergy lacked the illumination of the Spirit and a godly life. Among ordinary Christian people there was a notable lack of love of neighbor, widespread drunkenness, and insensitivity toward the poor. Spener describes the body of Christ as seriously ill, lying in a sick bed, in need of a physician and medications to treat the illness that had spread throughout the whole body.[75]

Part two of *Pia Desideria* assures readers that God has promised a better day for the church. Spener points to the promised future conversion of the Jews, in Romans 11:25, and the fall of the Roman Catholic Church, in Revelation 18:19. He hopes one day to see a church that includes the Jews and heathen, that worships God in unity of faith, and where believers encourage one another in living a holy life. Spener assures readers that he does not anticipate the arrival of a perfect world, a platonic republic; yet God surely had in mind a greater degree of perfection than was then in evidence among the churches. The church's goal should be to resemble the Christians of the early church. Tertullian wrote that people could easily identify the Christians because of their godly way of life.[76] Spener's hopes for better times departed dramatically from the traditional Lutheran expectation of God's imminent judgment. Spener's hopes found a ready audience, thanks to the widely spread mystical-Spiritualist writings of Jakob Böhme, Christian Hoburg, Friedrich Breckling, and Johann Georg Gichtel, all of whom proclaimed the future reign of Christ on earth.[77]

In part three, the six proposals for reform, Spener draws on Luther for the first two recommendations and Johann Arndt for the last four.[78] The first recommendation is Spener's plea "to bring the word of God more richly among us . . . The more richly the word dwells with us, the more we will bring faith and its fruits into being."[79] The prescribed pericopes, the Gospel preaching texts and other passages assigned for each Sunday in the church year, represent just a small portion of the whole Bible. The rest of the Bible, with all its edifying content, deserves people's attention as well. Spener suggests three means of introducing Christian people of all social classes to more of the Bible: (1) Bible reading in homes, as fathers read to their families and individuals read by themselves; (2) public reading in church of whole books of the Bible, accompanied by short summaries to help people understand; and (3) "apostolic gatherings" according to I Corinthians 14, where people meet at certain times of the week, outside church services, for mutual instruction and edification. Spener encourages laypeople to read the New Testament, especially, because it is easier for them to understand. He calls reading and study of God's word "the foremost means of improvement."[80]

Luther, too, had encouraged people to put reading of the scriptures above all other reading.[81] Yet in the sixteenth and seventeenth centuries, the Reformation remained largely a "catechism Reformation," with Luther's catechism serving as the lay Bible.[82] The ideal of Christians reading and knowing the Bible for themselves was taken seriously only with Spener's Pietism, made possible by more widespread literacy.

In his second recommendation, Spener calls for establishing "the spiritual priesthood," again looking to Luther for inspiration. This point follows from the first. It is a Christian's duty to study God's word and then to instruct, admonish, and encourage fellow believers according to its teaching. Anyone acquainted with Luther's writings, Spener states, knows of his idea that all believers are made priests by Christ and are called and enabled not only to offer prayers and good works but also to observe, care for, and admonish their Christian brothers and sisters. Spener insists that this point in no way undermines the pastoral office of his colleagues: "The orderly use of the spiritual priesthood does not harm the preaching office. Rather, one of the foremost reasons that the office is not all that it should be is because without the cooperation of the common Priesthood it is too weak; one man is not sufficient to care for so many."[83] According to Spener, the clerical monopoly of the Catholics, with spiritual offices belonging to clergy alone, was a mistake.

Spener's third recommendation is to teach people that Christian faith consists not of knowledge but of practice. Jesus taught that the true mark of his disciples was love. Awakening this kind of love among German Christians, toward each other and toward all people, represented the heart of Spener's reform efforts. Spener suggests having a confessor, a trusted Christian to whom one can give an account of one's life, of whether or not one has acted out of love toward one's neighbor. Spener supports this point with a passage from Arndt's *True Christianity*.[84]

The fourth point addresses a key issue for early modern German Protestants: how to deal with other confessions and with those who hold erroneous beliefs or do not believe at all. Spener suggests that disputation is not the only way to defend the truth; another is demonstrating the love of God toward unbelievers. Spener calls on readers to offer prayers to God on behalf of the erring brother so that he might come to the light and see the truth; to behave toward the brother with kindness and not hinder his coming to the truth; to take advantage of opportunities to demonstrate the truth in God's word with clarity and humility; and to behave with love as a neighbor and fellow creature of God. In *True Christianity*, Johann Arndt had insisted that pure doctrine and God's word are best defended not with argument but with a life of repentance and holiness.[85]

Spener's fifth, and longest, recommendation concerns reforming the education of pastors. For his other proposals to be effective, there must be pastors who are true Christians and able to guide others in the way. This required that universities be "gardens of the church" and "work stations of the Holy Spirit." Professors should demonstrate a life dead to the world and to personal reputation, seeking only the honor of God, and should be as concerned with students' way of life as with their mind. "Since theology is a practical science, everything should be directed towards the practice of Christian faith and life. Theology consists not in mere knowledge but in the heart and practice."[86] From their first year of study, theology students should strive to lead a life that would equip them to be examples to their flock. Spener offers two practical suggestions. First, theology students should read books by Johannes Tauler, Thomas à Kempis, and Johann Arndt, for they teach a theology of purity and simplicity. Second, they should meet in their own collegia, where they could learn how to apply their studies to their own edification and how to combat the lusts of the flesh and die to the world.[87]

The final recommendation for improving the churches relates to the sermon. Pastors should follow the example of Johann Arndt in their preaching. Their sermons should aim not to demonstrate their own learning but to encourage their hearers in faith and love. "Because our entire Christianity consists in the inner or new man, in faith and its fruits," sermons should aim to present the goodness of God and to encourage hearers to take the matter to heart and heed the Holy Spirit speaking within.[88]

FINDING PRECEDENTS FOR SPENER'S REFORM PROGRAM IN *PIA DESIDERIA*

There are at least five reform programs that anticipated features of Spener's *Pia Desideria* and possibly influenced Spener as he wrote: the *Twelve Strassburg Recommendations* (1636); Christian Hoburg's *Mirror of the Failings of the Clergy in the Churches Today* (1644); Friedrich Breckling's *Mirror of the Pastors* (1660); Theophil Großgebauer's *Watchcry in the Zion of Devastation* (1661); and Jean de Labadie's *The Reformation of the Church by the Pastorate* (1668).[89]

The greatest influence on Spener was Jean de Labadie's 1668 work on reform through the pastorate. Though it is difficult to determine the precise extent of Labadie's influence on Spener, there is convincing evidence that Spener not only had read *Reformation by the Pastorate* but had it by his side and used it as a model as he wrote *Pia Desideria*. In 1660 Spener encountered Labadie while in Geneva, heard him preach, and met with him personally. In 1667 Spener put out a German translation of Labadie's "The Practice of Christian Prayer and Meditation." Labadie was the first to call for "apostolic gatherings" according to I Corinthians 14, as a key means of church reform and renewal.[90] An anonymous tract of 1734, entitled "Labadie as the Source of Pietism," pointed to similarities between the two reformers, indicating that contemporaries already linked Spener to Labadie.[91]

At first glance, the two works appear very different: Labadie's *Reformation by the Pastorate* fills two volumes and is more than five hundred pages long; Spener's *Pia Desideria* is less than a third this length. Nevertheless, there are too many similarities to ignore. (1) The overall structure of the two works is similar. Like Labadie, Spener begins with a description of the miserable condition of the church, followed by a list of means for improvement. (2) Both men use the foreword to reflect on the ancient church's method of reform by calling an ecumenical synod or council; failing this, Labadie and Spener turn to circulating recommendations in writing for common discussion. (3) Both works begin with a reference to Jeremiah 9:1 and the prophet's lament for the sins of Israel.[92] (4) Both lament the sorry condition of the clergy, observing that most of them were not born again and were not true Christians. (5) Both regret the miserable condition of Christian people as a whole, noting widespread drunkenness and dishonest business practices and emphasizing that church attendance and the hearing of sermons is insufficient. (6) Both men derive encouragement from the presence of people of faith who look for the day when God will bring reformation to his Church. (7) Both men recommend use of *collegia pietatis*, gatherings of the faithful, for mutual encouragement. Both support the idea from I Corinthians 14 and refer to "the old manner of church gatherings" and the brotherly spirit of the gatherings.[93] (8) Both men demand that pastoral candidates be true Christians, called of God. Theology professors must demonstrate an exemplary Christian life, and not just oversee the studies of their students but admonish them in a Christian way of life. (9) Both encourage students to read the works of Christian mystics, such as Johannes Tauler and Thomas à Kempis. (10) Both use the expression *pious desires* to describe the spirit of their writing on behalf of reform.[94]

REACTIONS TO SPENER'S *PIA DESIDERIA*

Spener sent copies of *Pia Desideria* to leading pastors and theologians and to government officials, launching a vigorous discussion that lasted several years. By 1677 he had received more than a hundred letters of reply, most of them expressing enthusiastic support.[95] Ahasver Fritsch (1629–1701), chancellor in Schwarzburg-Rudolstadt, was hopeful about implementing the program in Thuringia. Other laypeople told Spener they were promoting his reforms in their home parishes. Some, such as Elias Veiel in Ulm, were opposed to the collegia pietatis and Spener's expectation of the conversion of the Jews and better times for the church. Spener's brother-in-law Joachim Stoll also expressed objections to these two points. He believed that he was living in the last hours before the final judgment of God.[96] Lutheran Orthodox preachers accused Spener of spreading his movement by strategically placing young theology students in pastorates throughout German lands. The accusation was just.

The theology faculty in Strasbourg was critical of Spener's views, asking for further proof of a future conversion of the Jews and arguing that by denying the governing authorities a role in church reform, he was effectively changing church-state relations as constituted by law. Spener sensed a more positive response from politicians than theologians. But Strasbourg proved the exception. In Kiel, Professor Christian Kortholt supported Spener and welcomed *Pia Desideria,* as did professors in Jena, Wittenberg, Leipzig, and Tübingen.[97] As of 1678, Spener had the support of the leading theologians in eight German universities. He took it as a sign of success that he had avoided public confrontation and conflict over *Pia Desideria.*

The initial expressions of support were mainly literary, rather than actual reforms. Spener observed in 1677 that "the response to my *Pia Desideria* is mainly words of approval; in most places it has not changed anything."[98] In a few imperial cities in upper Germany, where Spener had contacts, Pietist collegia were meeting. The movement also spread to small territories where sympathetic princes had ties to Spener, such as the counties of Hesse-Darmstadt, Solms-Laubach, Stolberg-Gedern, and Waldeck. But "the great wave of Pietist conventicle formation" throughout almost all of Protestant Germany appeared only after 1690 and the turn of century.[99] Gradually, *Pia Desideria* captured the imagination of reform-minded people, becoming the movement's programmatic statement—a Pietist manifesto.

The Contours of Spener's Thought

Spener has been called "the most important German Protestant theologian in the period between the Reformation and the Enlightenment" and "the most influential and controversial German Evangelical theologian of his day."[100] He has been placed alongside Luther, Schleiermacher, and Barth as one of the great thinkers in Protestant history.[101] Yet his thought has received nothing like the attention devoted to the other three men. There is still a good deal of confusion about various aspects of his theology, partly because Spener never wrote a systematic theology in the traditional sense. He was not an academic theologian and expressed dissatisfaction with traditional "school theology." He insisted that theology was no mere intellectual knowledge but the wisdom that came from faith that speaks to the whole person. Theology is rooted in the Bible, Spener thought, and its focus is on God's work of salvation in Christ that brings renewal to humanity.[102]

The main sources for understanding Spener's theology are his sermons and letters. Spener's Pietism, like English Puritanism, was a movement that valued preaching. Spener published large collections of sermons that discussed Lutheran doctrine, faith, and life, as well as individual sermons on topics such as the new birth, hopes for better times, true righteousness, and themes from Johann Arndt's *True Christianity*. Spener's shift of emphasis from the Gospels to preaching primarily from the Epistles was highly innovative. The published sermons were the most-read of Spener's works in his day and the source of his greatest influence. His sermons collected in *Evangelical Doctrines of the Faith* (1688) went through four editions and are the closest thing in Spener to a systematic theology.[103] Also important for understanding Spener's thought are his letters. Especially valuable are three collections of letters that Spener helped to compile in his later years: *Theological Reflections* (1702), *Theological Counsels and Judgments* (1708), and *Final Theological Reflections* (1711).[104] A complete edition of Spener's letters is planned and is well under way.[105]

Besides the Bible, there were several key influences on Spener's thought: Spener's professors in Strasbourg, Johann Arndt, and Martin Luther. Spener engaged with these resources critically and with an eye to the needs of the church of his own day.[106] The Strasbourg theologian Johann Conrad Dannhauer (1603–1666) had a profound effect on Spener.

Dannhauer was a popular preacher who had the common touch. He encouraged his students to meet in collegia for Bible study and was himself involved in collegia with both students and Strasbourg citizens. Spener practically memorized Dannhauer's systematic theology, using it throughout his life as a reference on theological matters. Spener claimed that he never departed from the Lutheran theology he learned from Dannhauer, except on one point: the issue of eschatology.[107] Johann Arndt was also a lifelong influence on Spener. Spener agreed with Arndt's concern for restoring the image of God in humankind to its original fullness, after its loss in the Fall. Spener moderated Arndt's Spiritualism and individualism, understanding him in "a churchly sense." Spener retained an important place for the church, preaching, and sacraments.[108]

Spener read Luther carefully while in Frankfurt, but not in a slavish way. Brecht observed that "Spener was not simply a student but a partner" of Luther in the task of reforming the church. The Luther that Spener discovered was a different Luther from the one Dannhauer had taught him. Four notions in Luther were especially significant for Spener: faith as a work of God and as a living and active thing that makes believers new; Luther's teaching on the spiritual priesthood; Luther's esteem for mystical writers such as Johannes Tauler; and Luther's description of a third form of Christian community besides the German and Latin Mass, comprising a close circle of earnest believers who met in homes and lived a consistent Christian life.[109]

Spener was the theologian of new birth: the ideas of new birth and the new man are key themes in *Pia Desideria*. He wrote, "The most important thing I have to say is this: that our whole Christian faith consists in the inward or new being, whose soul is faith and whose outworking are the fruits of life."[110] In Berlin, between 1691 and 1694, Spener preached sixty-six sermons on the subject. The stages of new birth include the stirring up of faith, justification and adoption, and the creation of a new man. The features of new birth include, first, passivity, for just as in human birth, conception begins outside ourselves, with God; second, inwardness, for the new birth takes place in the depths of the human heart; third, a great change in existence, as one is brought from spiritual death to new life; fourth, a new likeness to God, based on the believer sharing in the divine nature (2 Pet. 1:4); and finally, Christian perfection, the goal and fruit of new birth.[111]

An innovative, non-Lutheran feature in Spener's thought was his "hopes for better times for the church." Spener's teaching on the coming millennial kingdom became increasingly guarded in later years. In 1698 he said he could think of no Christian congregation for whom this doctrine was essential to its growth in faith. It was more important to preach the crucified Christ. Spener suggested that it was not necessary to teach all truths at all times. For the sake of Christian love and peace, it was often best to leave some things unsaid. "The Christian teacher should be the kind of father who brings forth from his treasure both old and new, and should do so at the right time, at the right place, when it is helpful."[112] The question resolved itself to the following: given the present situation among the churches, with such a lack of repentance and faith, was the truth of the millennium of such importance that it must be publicly promoted, knowing it would cause great commotion and offense among many pastors and bring damage to the church? His answer was no; it was not that important.

A recent study of Spener's eschatology considers the nature of his thinking on the end times, the opposition it stirred up, and the place of Spener's future hopes within his Pietist program and whether they belong to the *nota pietismi*—the essential marks of Pietism. The study shows that the first evidence of Spener's belief in hopes for better times for the church is in a letter to Johanna Eleonora Petersen in late 1674 and in *Pia Desideria* of early 1675.[113] Spener's eschatology was remarkably consistent over the course of his life. It was marked by his interest in a future *earthly* kingdom of Christ, his focus on the Christian church, resistance to any form of speculation, and affirmation of the biblical promises of a conversion of the Jews and the fall of Babel. Spener was careful to set himself apart from the teaching of the Petersens, even though he sometimes rose to their defense and called for more careful investigation of the matter.[114] The opposition to Spener's eschatology changed over time. In the late 1670s, he was accused of making an exegetical error in his understanding of Romans 11:25–32. In the 1690s, he was accused of teaching chiliasm, a future *earthly* kingdom of Christ, a doctrine expressly denounced in chapter 17 of the *Augsburg Confession*. He was also charged with creating a new sect.[115]

To those who suggested that the chiliastic doctrine was the central Pietist belief and the thousand-year kingdom the main focus of Pietist efforts, Spener responded by rejecting any identification of his reform program with his eschatology of hope for better times. His goal was not the millennial kingdom but a holy life among Christians. But Spener's arguments were tactical. He realized that the millennial teaching represented a theological insight that not all of his supporters could grasp; it could become a distraction if used by opponents to denounce Pietism as heretical. He was therefore increasingly reticent to discuss it. Nevertheless, it is clear that, for Spener himself, his eschatology and future hopes belonged to the *nota pietismi*—the central belief and motive of his reform program.[116]

Conclusion

The beginnings of the collegium pietatis in Frankfurt should be credited to Johann Jakob Schütz. He was the inspiration for and initiator of distinctive features of the Pietist movement: the meetings of the godly in private gatherings outside regular church services; the centrality of the Bible; the practice of the spiritual priesthood in mutual encouragement and admonition; and hopes for better times and the millenarian expectation of the coming reign of Christ on earth. Contemporaries occasionally referred to the Frankfurt Pietists as "Schützianer." It seems justified to conclude that "without Schütz, there would have been no Pietism."[117] Spener's role was not that of founder of the Frankfurt conventicle but rather of popularizer of notions he derived from Schütz.

Without Spener, however, Pietism would not have become a lasting and influential force within the German Lutheran church. Spener must be credited with formulating the theology and program that marked the early Pietist movement. Wallmann called Spener the "Father of Neo-Protestantism," because of the new understanding of church and Christian renewal that he injected into Protestant Christianity.[118] Much of Spener's theology lives on in Evangelical Protestantism in North America and England.

Women played a crucial role in the early Pietist movement, in networking and in hosting and leading Pietist meetings. This was true among the Saalhof Pietists, and the pattern continued as Pietist gatherings spread throughout German lands. The writings of Anna Maria van Schurman and Antoinette Bourignon influenced Schütz, Johanna Eleonora von Merlau, and other members of the Saalhof circle.

CHAPTER 4

Conventicles and Conflicts in Leipzig and the Second Wave, 1684 to 1694

The rise of German Pietism is the tale of two cities: not the London and Paris of Charles Dickens but the Frankfurt and Leipzig of Spener, Schütz, and Francke. It was after Spener won the support of Leipzig theology students and commoners that Pietism gained the momentum to become a popular reform movement and to spread throughout much of Germany.[1] The dispersal of Leipzig students in 1690 marked the "second wave" of Pietism as a radicalized social movement, coming between the beginnings in Frankfurt in the 1670s and 1680s and its full-fledged institutionalization in Halle in the late 1690s. Leipzig's importance in the rise of the early Pietist movement is captured nicely by the slogans "No Leipzig, no Pietism" and "Leipzig was the true place of origin of Pietism."[2]

Several lines of evidence point to the city's significance in the rise of German Pietism. First, theology students at Leipzig University were among Spener's earliest supporters. In July 1686, a nucleus of students joined the *collegium philobiblicum,* under the leadership of August Hermann Francke, to study the Bible in Greek and Hebrew. Seeing the potential among these students, Spener traveled from Dresden to attend their meetings and to offer suggestions on making the gatherings more than just an academic exercise. Second, the student movement caught on with the

Leipzig populace, who formed their own collegia, with women often assuming leadership of the meetings. In these *collegia biblica*, men and women from a variety of social backgrounds came together, debated scripture, and worked with Francke to build a vibrant Pietist network.[3] Third, in response to investigations by Saxon authorities, in 1690 the Leipzig students dispersed throughout northern Germany. Some followed Francke to Erfurt, others found their way to universities in Hamburg, Wittenberg, and Jena, while still others returned to their home communities. Wherever they went, they took their Pietist convictions with them. Finally, Pietist-Orthodox conflicts were decisively stamped by events in Leipzig. Events between 1686 and 1691 marked the transition from mainly positive acceptance of Spener's reform program to growing opposition from Spener's former supporters and from church and civic leaders.

This chapter follows the story of the unique convergence of students and commoners in Leipzig that created the movement and inspired the terminology of *Pietism*. Early Leipzig Pietism was dominated by students, women, and tradesmen; missing were the upper social classes.[4] The piety and religious practices of this transitional period were marked by an unbridled lay enthusiasm that was eventually moderated and disciplined by the Halle institutions under A. H. Francke.

Leipzig's Economic Boom

Leipzig suffered greatly during the Thirty Years War, more so than Frankfurt. It was attacked on five occasions, the first time in 1631, and three major battles were fought near the city. For eight years, from 1642 to 1650, the Swedish army was garrisoned in Leipzig. The traditional trade fairs almost shut down. Epidemics and food shortages resulted in many lives lost. The postwar population was only fourteen thousand, compared with a prewar number exceeding sixteen thousand. Recovery was hampered by severe floods in 1651, 1655, and 1661. By the 1680s, however, there were signs of economic recovery. Leipzig regained its position as a major trade and distribution center, second only to Hamburg. Its fairs, held three times a year, were larger and more successful than Frankfurt's, and it became the leading German city for book publishing.[5] All in all, Leipzig made an impressive economic recovery after the losses it suffered during the Thirty Years War.[6]

By the late seventeenth century, Leipzig was a city of some twenty thousand residents and the center of a flourishing Baroque culture. Like Frankfurt, as a center of trade and manufacture it was dominated by wealthy merchants and governing elites. It became known for its consumption, wealth, and architecture. Leading merchants built lavish homes with magnificent public gardens. Coffee and tobacco consumption were associated with social gatherings in homes and coffeehouses.[7] Through its university, law courts, and trade fairs, Leipzig exercised a significant impact on the society and culture of early modern Germany. Unlike Frankfurt, however, Leipzig was not a free imperial city; it was beholden to Dresden and the elector.

Churches, Pastors, Sermons, and Congregants in Late Seventeenth-Century Leipzig

Leipzig had two main *Pfarrkirchen* (parish churches), St. Thomas and St. Nicolai. The churches were restored after the war, and in 1684 a balcony was built in the St. Thomas Church for the use of the elector and his family when they visited Leipzig. Clerical vestments, donated by wealthy merchants and councilors, were made of silk, satin, and velvet and trimmed with gold and silver. Each church had a pastor, a Saturday preacher (*Sonnabendsprediger*), and three deacons; the number of clergy had not changed since the sixteenth century. Professors in the university's theology faculty also had clerical appointments in the churches and preached occasionally. Church services were held daily during the week and three times on Sundays and holy days: at 7 a.m., 9 a.m., and in the afternoon. Pastors were responsible for teaching, preaching, and the spiritual care of their people. With the growing population, pastors were increasingly overburdened and unable to care properly for the large parishes. In February 1688 Spener expressed alarm at what he was hearing about Saxon churches: "I hear of many places that have only one pastor, making it impossible for him to fulfill his pastoral duty before God."[8]

Pews were assigned, with Leipzig elites obtaining the best seating, close to the pulpit; artisans typically sat behind the pulpit, behind pillars, and farther back; the poor and those without a pew simply stood at the rear of the church. The wealthy sometimes had their own sections, called chapels, around the edge of the church and with their own private entrance, resembling the boxes in an opera house. St. Thomas Church had a balcony reserved for students. In the 1690s, the Leipzig city council created a partitioned area for professors and their sons that incorporated the first row of the student balcony. In response, students broke the lock and door, removed the partition, and threatened to disrupt services if they were restored.[9]

Sunday services were preceded by bells calling the people to worship. Lutheran services had three parts, each lasting about an hour: first, a service of hymns, scripture readings, and cantata; then the sermon; and finally, the Lord's Supper. The cantata was performed on alternate Sundays, before the sermon, and was based on the scriptural text for that day. People would arrive in the course of the first hour, many coming just before the sermon and leaving right after it. This behavior prompted Leipzig city councilors to suggest that the offering be collected during the sermon. This would disrupt the sermon, however, since the offering bags (*Klingelbeutel*) had bells attached to them, which jingled as the bags were passed along the pews.[10]

The sermon was the center of Lutheran and Reformed worship. The Leipzig city council made a point of hiring pastors who were good preachers and had a pleasing voice. The sermon typically began with the week's Gospel text, followed by an explanation of its meaning and practical implications for everyday life. Sermons often addressed current social and political events. In the late 1680s, Pietist and Orthodox preachers began to include attacks on each other in their sermons.[11]

The Leipzig city council had to address a variety of disturbances in the services, such as students throwing things from the balcony onto the women below and young people hiding behind the chapels and making noise. The elite classes often refused to stand for the reading of the Gospel.[12] It became common for leading families not to partake of communion in church, preferring to take private communion at home with the clergyman. Sunday observance became more and more lax. A. H. Francke noted that many began to leave church before the afternoon sermon was finished, heading out to various pursuits—shooting, dancing, games, and other amusements. In February 1670 a complaint was lodged with the elector that the Sunday market was growing steadily.[13]

Reception of Spener and *Pia Desideria* in Leipzig and Dresden

Spener's comments in *Pia Desideria* on the miserable level of Christian practice and devotion, made with Leipzig and Frankfurt in mind, found a positive response in Leipzig. His greatest supporters at Leipzig University were Jakob Thomasius and Johann Benedict Carpzov (1639–1699). Carpzov had been a fellow student with Spener at the University of Strasbourg. In a sermon in 1680, Carpzov encouraged students to pursue the living and active Christianity taught by Spener. Another Leipzig professor, Valentin Alberti, was in regular correspondence with Spener after *Pia Desideria* was published. Johannes Olearius, professor of theology, remained a lifelong friend of Spener, even when the rest of the Leipzig faculty finally came out against him. August Pfeiffer, professor of Hebrew in Leipzig, was also a Spener supporter. When Spener was called to Dresden in 1686 to be head court preacher to elector Johann Georg III, the Leipzig faculty sent him their greetings and best wishes.[14]

Spener's call to Dresden had overwhelming support among the Saxon authorities, both clerical and secular. His supporters included Carpzov's younger brother, Samuel Benedict Carpzov (1647–1707), the Dresden superintendent; Nicholas von Gersdorf, president of the elector's privy council, later to become the grandfather of Count von Zinzendorf; and Karl von Friesen, president of the consistory. Yet within a short time of Spener's arrival in Dresden, almost all of these people turned against him, along with most Lutheran clergymen in Germany. The reason can be found in events associated with August Hermann Francke and the Pietist movement in Leipzig, events that reached beyond university students to include Leipzig commoners as well.[15]

The Leipzig Collegium Philobiblicum and Francke's Conversion in Lüneburg, 1684–1687

August Hermann Francke (1663–1727) spent his childhood and youth in Gotha, the residence city of Duke Ernst the Pious (1601–1675). Francke's father served as councilor to the duke from 1666 to 1670. In his parents' home, Francke encountered the works of Johann Arndt and Puritan devotional writers. In 1679, at just sixteen years of age, he began attending the nearby University of Erfurt, studying Hebrew, geography, logic, and metaphysics. The more he studied, he recalled, the more concerned he became with worldly praise and honor: "I deviated far from the earlier good beginning in true Christianity which I had had in my childhood." Francke then spent three years at the University of Kiel, the city of his mother's brother. There he studied philosophy, metaphysics, ethics, physics, Latin eloquence and authors, and Aristotle's *Rhetoric*. In Kiel, Francke also began study of Orthodox Lutheran theology with Professor Christian Kortholt; this included exegetical and polemical theology and early church history. Francke later recalled, "I grasped my theology with my head, not my heart; it was more a dead science than a living knowledge."[16] In 1682 Francke moved to the University of Hamburg to continue his Hebrew studies with Esdras Edzard and to complete the theology curriculum.[17]

On Easter 1684, Francke arrived in Leipzig to study Hebrew and theology as a master's student. He also worked to improve his abilities in French, English, and Italian through daily conversation. He completed the master's degree and in the summer of 1685 presented his habilitation dissertation on Hebrew grammar and philology, earning him the right to hold university lectures. That fall, Francke offered lectures in oriental languages and biblical interpretation in the philosophy faculty, while continuing his theology studies.[18]

Leipzig University had a large number of *collegia*—academic seminars for master's students within all four faculties: philosophy, theology, law, and medicine. Because theology at Leipzig focused on dogmatics and homiletics, Professor Johann Benedict Carpzov suggested that Francke and his friend Paul Anton (1661–1730) form a collegium devoted to biblical interpretation.[19] In July 1686, Francke and Anton founded the *collegium philobiblicum* (see table 4.1). It met weekly, on Sunday afternoons, for what was essentially practice in biblical exegesis. They read and studied selected Bible passages in the original Hebrew and Greek. The whole exercise was conducted in Latin. When the group reached twelve participants, the collegium began meeting in the home of Professor Valentin Alberti.

When Spener learned of the collegium philobiblicum, he encouraged Anton and Francke to change the focus from an academic exercise to a devotional one, to engage with the kernel of scripture, not merely the shell.

Table 4.1. The Eight Founders of the Collegium Philobiblicum in Leipzig in 1686

Name	*Hometown or place of birth*	*Destination after Leipzig*
Paul Anton (1661–1730)	Hirschfelde	October 1689 to December 1692, served as superintendent of the Evangelical Church in Rochlitz; in 1695, became professor of theology in Halle
August Hermann Francke (1663–1727)	Lübeck and Gotha	Easter 1690, appointed deacon in the Augustine Church in Erfurt; in January 1692, called to St. George's Church in Glaucha, outside Halle
Andreas Friedel (b. 1658)	Schkeuditz	Became a leading Pietist separatist in Halberstadt and Kelbra
Polikarp Elias Huffland (1665–1714)	Tennstedt	In 1692, called to Stolp (now Slupsk), Farther Pomerania, as archdeacon, where he founded a school for poor children modeled on the Halle Foundations
Johann Christian Lange (1669–1756)	Leipzig	Lectured at Leipzig University, 1694–1697; separated himself from church and sacraments; in 1697, joined Gottfried Arnold in Giessen as philosophy professor; in 1716, became court preacher in Idstein
Johann Caspar Schade (1666–1698)	Kühndorf	Pursued studies in Leipzig, 1685–1687, and served as secretary to Francke; in December 1691, was ordained deacon at the St. Nicholas Church in Berlin
Clemens Thieme (1666–1732)	Zeitz	Ordained in 1690 and became chaplain to the Saxon Elector Johann Georg IV; in early 1692, became archdeacon in Wurzen
Ernst Christian Wartenberg (ca. 1665–1742)	Leipzig	Completed his Leipzig dissertation in 1689; in 1690, became sub-rector in Berlin

Spener also suggested they give the New Testament priority over the Old Testament.[20] When he visited Leipzig in April 1687, Spener again encouraged the group to aim at a living encounter with the Word, not merely historical understanding. This was the first meeting between Francke and Spener and marked the beginning of Francke's attempt to put Spener's suggestions into practice.

Francke's autobiography, or *Lebenslauf*, describes the long and arduous spiritual battle (*Bußkampf*) that led to his conversion and to a new mindset and way of life.[21] His reflections on his state of mind, with frequent references to *Gemüht* (soul, mind) and *Herz* (heart), form a prominent refrain throughout. The account has two acts: first, the story of his misery of heart and the things that stood in the way of his soul's peace with God, and second, the steps by which he came to find rest in God. In the first act, Francke described his misery of heart in terms of being caught up in worldliness and a worldly way of life. Worldliness included the "lusts of youth and the outward attraction of the world" that he experienced as a young man as well as pride in his academic accomplishments (7, 10). Even theological study contributed to his misery. He could define faith and new birth, but had no personal experience of them.

> My theology I understood in my head but not in my heart; it was more a dead science than a living acquaintance . . . I had no other notion of theological study than that a person should have in his head the theological discussions and theological books and be able to discuss them intelligently. I knew that theology was defined as a practical discipline but I was more concerned with the theory. (12)

Study and learning only increased his hypocrisy as a theology student: he could engage in theological discussions and partake in the sacraments, yet he had no ability to live the Christian life. Describing his condition as a twenty-four-year-old, he wrote, "I was little better than an unfruitful tree which bears many leaves but for the most part rotten fruit" (22; see also 1–13).

The second act of the *Lebenslauf* began with Francke's search for God in devotion and study, but this brought only further misery and doubt (13).[22] His study of the Bible was unsatisfying; it was scientific, not practical. The collegium philobiblicum in Leipzig was "the best and most valuable seminar" that he experienced in his university life, but it was more concerned "with the shell than with the kernel and heart of the matter" (18). While reading the Bible one day, the thought suddenly came to him: "Who knows whether the [Christian] Scriptures are God's word; when the Turks believe this of their *Qur'an* and the Jews likewise of their *Talmud,* who can say who is right?" (26).[23]

In October 1687, Francke moved to Lüneburg to pursue exegetical studies under Superintendent Kaspar Hermann Sandhagen. He found a room in the home of Sandhagen's brother, Deacon Gabriel Sandhagen, where he was able to spend time alone with God. Shortly after his arrival, Francke was invited to preach in St. John's Church in Lüneburg. He chose as his text John 20:31: "This is written that you might believe that Jesus is the Christ, and by faith have life in his name." Francke realized that he did not have the faith of which the text spoke. In resignation of heart, he was overcome by his misery.

> My whole life to that point came before my eyes, just as if one were to look out over a city from a high tower . . . Then my whole life, and everything I had done, said, and thought, was presented to me as so much sin and a great horror before God . . . This misery caused me many tears, something to which I was not normally prone. I fell to my knees and called upon him whom I still did not know. Then I prayed, if there really were a God, that he might take pity on me. (26, 27)

The next Sunday evening, Francke, in great anxiety of mind, fell to his knees in prayer and cried out to God to save him from his miserable condition. Under great duress, Francke experienced deliverance from the intellectual impasse at which he had arrived.

> Then the Lord, the living God, heard me from his throne as I knelt . . . For as someone might turn over their hand, so all my doubts vanished and I was assured in my heart of the grace of God in Christ Jesus. I could address God not only as God but as my Father. In an instant all my sadness and unrest of heart were taken away, and I was suddenly overwhelmed as if by a stream of joy, so that I praised and magnified God with a full heart, who had shown me such wonderful grace . . . When I had got down on my knees, I did not believe that there was a God; when I got up I would,

without any fear and doubt, have confirmed [it] with the spilling of my blood. (29)

Three days later, he preached his sermon with great joy of heart. Francke considered this to be his true conversion, one that "was not my work but God's work" (25, 31).

Francke's conversion experience highlights an innovation in Pietism. In contrast to Luther's discovery of God's forgiving grace in Christ through faith, and his recognition that the believer remains both saint and sinner in this life, Francke portrayed his conversion as a hard-won struggle (*Bußkampf*) from unbelief to belief, an experience not merely of forgiveness but of certainty, new birth, and new life. This marked a sharp deviation from the traditional Lutheran understanding, also found in Arndt and Spener, in which trials and doubts belong to the nature of faith and are seen as a test from God. Francke's model of a once-for-all, datable conversion experience was promoted in many Pietist circles, above all within Halle Pietism. But even in Halle, individuals such as Louise Charbonnet, who served for forty years as teacher and governess at the girls' school, never experienced the desired conversion.[24]

Revival in Leipzig, 1689–1690

Francke returned to Leipzig at the end of February 1689, after spending a year in Hamburg and two months in Dresden with Spener. The Francke who visited Spener in Dresden was a new man, "completely filled with a burning piety."[25] Back in Leipzig, Francke approached his teaching and academic work from a new perspective. "While once I had made an idol out of scholarship, I now saw faith as a mustard seed which is worth more than a hundred bushels of scholarship."[26] During Lent and summer of 1689, he lectured on Paul's Epistles, applying the devotional approach he had learned from Spener. Francke dropped the use of Latin, lecturing instead in the vernacular German in order to communicate more effectively. His new pedagogical method allowed for discussion at the end of each lecture. Francke was amazed at the response. He soon had more than three hundred students, filling the lecture hall. Leipzig citizens began attending the lectures as well.[27]

Francke had two close friends in the university, Paul Anton and Johann

Caspar Schade (1666–1698), who shared his conviction that theological education must move away from polemics and scholasticism toward nurturing students in the practice of prayer and the Christian life. The three men held lectures on biblical books in 1689, with students flocking to attend them; attendance dwindled in the classes of the other professors.[28] After hearing Francke and his two friends critique scholastic disputation and metaphysics, Pietist students began selling their philosophy books.[29]

The 1689 lectures of Francke, Anton, and Schade sparked a citywide revival, as the student awakening spread throughout the city. Leipzig theology students became the vanguard of Pietism as a popular movement, holding collegia for Bible study and prayer in the homes of burghers (commoners or citizens), with craftsmen and women attending. The student leaders were mostly young men in their late twenties from outside Leipzig.[30] The students became acquainted with Leipzig commoners through arrangements for room and board. Another occasion for contact was through visits that medicine and theology students made to the homes of the sick. It was common for burghers to send for students when they fell ill. Burghers and students also met in bookshops. Bookshop clerks often joined the students in attending the collegia. "At the table, at the sickbed, and in bookstores students recruited their acquaintances to come to *collegia*."[31] By July 1689, the terms *Pietism* and *Pietist* were again in the air, much to Spener's chagrin. Carpzov used the terms to criticize, Joachim Feller to praise, the movement.[32]

Those attending the Leipzig collegia came from a variety of occupations and classes. Most were Leipzig citizens who owned property. The greatest number were craftsmen: a baker and wife, a shoemaker and wife, a roper and son, two shopkeepers, a goldsmith, a book dealer, and a journeyman haberdasher—brother to a Leipzig student. Also attending collegia were the town grain registrar and the town mortuary registrar and his daughter. Among "sub-artisans" were a gardener, a guard, and a lace washer, Catharina Mey, who was married to an unemployed carpenter. Francke led a collegium in Mey's home and, at Francke's encouragement, Mey became the leading woman among the Leipzig Pietists.[33]

Tanya Kevorkian suggests that a certain psychological profile seemed to characterize members of the collegia. Many had experienced social alienation; others suffered from poor mental or physical health. At least two members of Leipzig collegia died shortly after the stressful investigations:

professor Joachim Feller committed suicide in 1691 and Johann Heinich, a Leipzig book dealer and one of Francke's most ardent supporters, died in December 1693 after suffering from mental derangement.[34]

Leipzig Interrogations in October 1689 and from March to August 1690

The Dresden court demanded a report of events surrounding the Pietist students and the lectures being held by Francke, Schade, and Anton. There were rumors that Francke advised students to avoid studying philosophy and that he wished to create a new sect, called Pietism, with a focus on renewal and holiness of life.[35] University authorities launched a preliminary investigation in October 1689, led by theology professor Johann Benedict Carpzov.[36] The questions put to Francke reflect students' complaints that Francke was teaching "new doctrines." Does he, Francke, see value in studying not only theology but philosophy as well? What is his opinion of philosophy? Does he consider it sufficient that students read only the Bible and lay aside their other books? Has he not publicly supported the collegia biblica? Has he not visited with some commoners in their homes and instructed them? What did he teach them? Who has appointed him to this work? Does he think that the people are not sufficiently instructed by the teachers and pastors set over them? What does Francke think of private revelations and inward illumination? Are such to be credited in matters of faith? Does he not actively seek to draw to himself students and common people so they might follow him and his teachings?[37]

Francke wrote an *Apologia* in his own defense and enlisted the support of professors Christian Thomasius and Joachim Feller. Francke explained that some students who could not afford to complete a full university program had approached him, seeking his advice on how best to pursue their theology studies. He had advised them not to spend valuable time in the philosophy faculty studying metaphysics and scholastic thought; instead, they should pursue biblical studies, especially Greek and Hebrew. Spener advised Francke to moderate his words, to distance himself from Thomasius, and to avoid open conflict with the Orthodox Lutherans.[38]

By early 1690, the meetings in homes were being led by commoners, with no students or clergy involved, attracting the attention and antagonism of the city council, theology faculty, and clergy. In early March

1690, the Leipzig theology faculty responded to the provocative writings of Francke and Thomasius. The faculty held the two men responsible for the unrest in the city and called for withdrawal of their right to teach and a ban on all conventicles in Leipzig.[39]

The Dresden authorities then took the investigation out of the university's hands and entrusted it to the Leipzig city council and consistory. On March 10, 1690, the Leipzig consistory published a *Konventikelverbot,* a ban forbidding any conventicle gatherings within the city limits. From March to August 1690, the consistory conducted an investigation directed against "those students who are called Pietists." Most of the student leaders and citizens who had been involved in collegia were called in for interrogation. This included eleven students and nineteen Leipzig citizens; of the latter, six were women and thirteen were men. In addition, four women and two men were brought forward as witnesses.[40] Among questions put to the students were the following: Does Mr. Francke teach that it is not necessary to spend time reading systematic theology? Does he not consider it far better and more pleasing to God when people offer prayers in their own words rather than praying from a prayer book or speaking the Lord's Prayer? Has Mr. Francke himself preached without any reflection beforehand? What method of preaching does he use? Does he think that a further Reformation is to be expected, beside the one by Luther? Has not Francke complained about the preachers in the Evangelical churches, that they do not properly carry out their office because they do not visit the people in their homes and admonish them to live a holy life?[41] One member of the collegium philobiblicum, Johann Christian Lange, was asked whether he had read any works by Jakob Böhme, Valentin Weigel, or Caspar Schwenckfeld.[42]

The beleaguered Pietist movement in Leipzig received new energy from a visit by Johann Wilhelm Petersen and his wife on May 5, 1690. Johanna Eleonora Petersen visited with Catharina Mey. That evening, Petersen preached a sermon in the home of August Frenzel, a pastry baker. His text was from Luke 14:25–30: "Whoever does not carry the cross and follow me cannot be my disciple." More than a hundred people, students and burghers, crowded the house, spilling out onto the street. The next day, the city council forced the Petersens to leave.[43]

The Dresden elector, Johann Georg, kept pressuring the Leipzig consistory to provide a consistent picture of events relating to the Pietist disturbances. Finally, in the fall of 1690, he directed the Leipzig authorities to act on the consistory's recommendations. Thomasius, Feller, and Francke were deprived of their teaching privileges. Pastoral candidates who had Pietist sympathies would no longer be eligible for pastoral positions, and Pietist students lost their scholarships. Schade and many of Francke's friends were banished from the city. Francke, by this time, had already left for Erfurt. Thomasius moved to Magdeburg to take up a position in the Brandenburg government. Feller, suffering from depression, committed suicide.[44] The Leipzig Pietist movement was reduced to an underground existence, with students and burghers gathering in secret conventicles. Most of the student supporters left the city and made their way to Erfurt, Wittenberg, or Jena, taking their Pietist convictions with them. In the coming years, the Leipzig conflicts would be repeated in cities and towns throughout the central and northern German empire.[45]

Francke in Erfurt, 1690–1691

During the Easter season in 1690, thanks to the intervention of senior Erfurt clergyman Joachim Justus Breithaupt, Francke was invited to apply for the position of deacon, or assistant pastor, at the Augustine Church in Erfurt. After a trial sermon and a theological examination before members of the Erfurt ministerium, Francke was appointed. In early June he was ordained to ministry in the Evangelical Church.[46] A number of Pietist students followed Francke from Leipzig to Erfurt.

In Erfurt, Francke continued to pursue opportunities for informal teaching outside regular church services. On Sundays, after the sermon, he met with young people and adults, examining them on the message. He was a regular dinner guest in homes and used the opportunity to distribute New Testaments and to instruct families in the Bible.[47] Francke continued to be popular with students. In his university lectures, he worked through Paul's Epistle to the Colossians and was warmly received. The students took Francke's message back to the homes where they boarded. Among these students was Francke's future son-in-law, Johann Anastasius Freylinghausen (1670–1739). Francke's influence spread beyond Erfurt, as he made regular visits to Pietist circles in Gotha, Jena, Quedlinburg, and Halberstadt. On these trips he encountered former Leipzig students and won over more students, pastors, and laypeople.[48]

In late 1690, the Erfurt city council launched a commission charged with investigating the presence and behavior of Pietists within the city. In January 1691, the commission called for a ban on all Pietist meetings in Erfurt. In June the Erfurt ministerium seconded the call for a ban and demanded that Francke be prohibited from giving public lectures and that students no longer be allowed to teach Pietist ideas to the families where they boarded. The city council acted on the recommendations, forbidding Francke to hold lectures, on pain of a fine of twenty *Reichstalern*. Erfurt citizens could no longer provide room and board to students. Despite protests from a number of city councilors and from members of the Augustine Church, on September 18, 1691, the city council dismissed Francke from his position as deacon and banned him from the city on grounds of inciting confessional and political discord. On September 27, Francke left Erfurt, returning to his hometown in nearby Gotha.[49]

Pietism during the "Second Wave," 1689–1694

Ryoko Mori speaks of the "second wave" of Pietism, occurring between 1689 and 1694. Between Pietist beginnings in Frankfurt in the 1670s and 1680s and the institutionalized Pietism in Halle in the late 1690s, Pietism took on the character of a radical social movement.[50] Spener's student disciples in Leipzig and elsewhere proved to be far more radical than the Pietist patriarch. Influenced by Johann Wilhelm and Johanna Eleonora Petersen, the students and their lay associates were marked by an unbridled enthusiasm and openness to visionary revelations and millenarian prophecies.[51] It was this movement that opponents had in mind in 1689 when they warned authorities of the dangerous "Pietists" in their midst.

ANDREAS ACHILLES (1656–1721)

A good example of second-wave Pietism is Andreas Achilles (1656–1721), a student friend of Francke's in Leipzig who became the charismatic leader of conventicles in Quedlinburg and Halberstadt.[52] A vicious literary attack compared these gatherings to events in Anabaptist Münster in the sixteenth century.[53] Achilles's professional life from 1690 to 1704 was marked by conflict, instability, and migration. A colleague in Halle eulogized him as a servant whom God "preserved through all kinds of sufferings and deemed worthy of the markings of Christ."[54]

Andreas Achilles was born on May 28, 1656, in Halberstadt, to Eberhard and Catharina Achilles; his father was a Halberstadt burgher and worked as a furrier.[55] Young Andreas attended school in Halberstadt before leaving home, in 1678, to study at the University of Leipzig. In 1685 he was awarded the master's degree; in 1687 he habilitated, qualifying as a university lecturer in philosophy. On January 10, 1690, Achilles returned to Halberstadt to preach a guest sermon; soon after, the city council, his patron, called him to serve as pastor in the Hospital Church of the Holy Spirit. During his ministry in Halberstadt, between January 1690 and January 1693, Achilles met with "very bitter sufferings" and conflicts with the other ministers, followed by a drawn-out and messy termination.[56] His fellow preachers challenged his ministry at the Hospital Church on three different occasions: in January 1690, when he first sought the pastoral position; in early 1692, when suspicions were raised about his behavior in conventicles; and in December 1692, resulting in his dismissal.

Achilles reported to the Brandenburg authorities, "You yourself know that my adversaries, from the beginning . . . have without cause opposed the presentation and choice of the patrons and foundation very vehemently. And for that reason have tried to portray as evil my teaching and behavior to the higher and lower authorities."[57] His fellow clergy in Halberstadt excluded him from the ministerial fraternity, not allowing him to preach or administer the sacraments in their churches and warning their parishioners and others against his teaching and company. Pastors denounced him by name from their pulpits, calling him perfectionist, enthusiast, Arian, and Montanist. Achilles asked the Brandenburg elector to put a stop to their opposition so that he could pursue his pastoral duties "without sighs."[58] Writing in his own defense, Achilles portrayed himself as a young pastor who never won acceptance from his older, more mature colleagues. They first tried to sabotage his appointment, and, when this failed, they determined to make his life as miserable as possible.

The Achilles *Lebenslauf*, or biography, suggests that he bore this opposition with "a humble heart overflowing with love for his enemies," preferring to suffer for the sake of righteousness rather than defend his innocence.[59] Court records, however, show that Achilles persistently sought to retain his position in Halberstadt, playing off the patrons—the city council and the Brandenburg elector, Frederick III (I) (1688–1713)—against the Halberstadt ministerium in a drawn-out court case that lasted from January to December 1693.[60]

In 1695 Achilles was appointed senior pastor in Dornum, East Friesland, where he served until his dismissal in 1703 or 1704. The remote region was a refuge and place of ministry for a significant number of German Pietist preachers who were forced out of their churches.[61] In Dornum, Achilles again endured opposition "for some years" and "there was no lack of sufferings and nastiness." The burdens of office began to affect his health; the biography refers to "his very sickly constitution and many bodily afflictions which consumed his life before his time under the burdens and cares of his office."[62]

Achilles was finally dismissed because of the conventicle he held in Dornum. "His distinction [between the mixed multitude and proven disciples of Christ] became a painful thorn in the eye to the contrary-minded in that time and place, and after bearing with it for some years, suddenly he was put out of office under a completely different pretext."[63] Achilles returned to Halberstadt for a brief time before moving to Halle in 1704, remaining there until his death in 1721.[64] Achilles never married.

Achilles experienced a deep measure of social alienation and homelessness in the world, marked by his dismissals and experience of opposition from the clerical class. Achilles found fulfillment through leading conventicles made up of a close circle of friends. While a student in Leipzig, Achilles had joined A. H. Francke in leading the collegium philobiblicum, the student circle devoted to study of scripture and to practical application of biblical teaching.[65] Later, in Quedlinburg, Achilles led conventicle gatherings in homes for scripture reading and mutual edification. In Halberstadt he quickly gained a considerable following, as "many ran after him." Achilles's most devoted disciple was Anna Margaretha Jahn, the unmarried daughter of Oswald Jahn, a citizen and shopkeeper in Halberstadt. From late 1691 to December 1692, Anna attended Achilles's sermons in the Hospital Church in preference to Pastor Wurtzler's preaching in the St. Moritz Church. Her charismatic revelations made her the dominant personality in the Halberstadt conventicle. Achilles himself submitted to her inspired messages. Wurtzler finally banned her from the Lord's Supper until she renounced her Pietist practices. After a brief period in which she submitted to Wurtzler's demands, she fell back into associating with her radical friends, "traveling about the land" with them.[66]

In Dornum as well, Achilles organized a small, exclusive group of communicants, something close to a conventicle.

> With great energy Achilles examined the communicants [in Dornum]. He planned to administer the Lord's Supper not to the mixed multitude of people, but to such souls as showed themselves in their life to be proven and tried disciples of Christ; such a distinction in the flock awoke in many souls a devotion and zeal to behave with seriousness as true and proven disciples of Christ, who sought to grow in faith, love and good works; so that the simplicity of the first Christians might again come into bloom.[67]

Achilles clearly found his primary ministry and source of affirmation not in the state churches but in the small conventicle gatherings of like-minded believers.[68]

Achilles's worldview was closely tied to his migratory life and conventicle experience. His conventicles in Quedlinburg and Halberstadt were characterized by an apocalyptic mindset. The gatherings were dominated by the eschatological pronouncements of women such as Anna Jahn, Katharina Reinecke, and others. These roving women prophets unleashed a wave of prophetic excitement in the fall of 1691 that caught up a host of Pietists, including Achilles.[69]

CHARACTERIZING THE PIETISM OF THE SECOND WAVE

The Pietism of the second wave was characterized by several features. First, it was above all a conventicle movement. These Pietists met regularly in each other's homes, where they read the Bible and devotional books, engaged in edifying conversation, and shared their understandings and experiences with one another. Conventicles in various cities in central and northern Germany formed a communication network, with members visiting and corresponding with one another.[70] Second, the conventicles were increasingly marked by displays of ecstasy and prophecy and claims to hearing the voice of God. The prophecies often included harsh denunciations of local authorities, especially clergy.[71] Third, there was a strong sense of individualism, with subjective claims to intimate and direct dealing with God. Fourth, the Pietists of the second wave saw themselves as more perfect and more sanctified than their neighbors, leading them to separate themselves from the ways and pleasures of "the world."[72] Fifth, the sense of God's direct working in their lives led these Pietists to close self-examination and to interpreting their feelings as the moving and speaking of God within them. Finally, members of the second wave included an unusually large number of individuals who had reason to be angry and frustrated with church and secular authorities. In many cases, their career paths had been blocked from traditional routes to success. In sum, the Pietism of the second wave took Spener's "church Pietism" of the collegia pietatis in a new and more radical direction.[73]

In the mid 1690s, second-wave Pietism began to change under the authoritarian and patriarchal discipline of the Halle foundations. Conventicles fell away as Francke and his colleagues came to see them as a threat to their control and oversight. The language of chiliasm and Christ's coming earthly kingdom was also minimized. Spener's ideal of the new Christian man and woman was transformed by Halle into a once-for-all, datable conversion experience of personal renewal and certainty of faith.[74]

Conclusion

Francke arrived in Leipzig as a conflicted young master's student. His dramatic conversion in October 1687 expressed itself in new approaches to Bible study and teaching that saw students flock to his classes at Leipzig University. The 1689 lectures of Francke, Anton, and Schade sparked a revival that spread throughout the city. Leipzig theology students formed the vanguard of Pietism as a popular movement, as they held collegia for Bible study and prayer in the homes of burghers. By July 1689, the terms *Pietism* and *Pietist* were again in the air. Spener's ideals of collegia pietatis, hopes for better times, and creation of the new man through new birth were radicalized by the Pietism of the second wave, as women prophets came to dominate Pietist conventicles.[75] In the late 1690s, the Pietism of Frankfurt, Leipzig, and Erfurt entered another phase under the influence of August Hermann Francke and his foundations in Halle.

CHAPTER 5

Halle Pietism and Universal Social Reform, 1695 to 1727

A third city played a prominent part in the story of German Pietism—namely, Halle. In Halle, August Hermann Francke's efforts to care for and educate poor children developed into a vast enterprise of schools, orphanage, publishing house, and medicine production, supported by an ambitious building program. Halle Pietism became a social reform movement, with the orphanage as its distinguishing mark. Even when the complex included Latin and German schools, print shop, bookshop, and pharmacy, the foundations were simply called "the orphanage," and Pietism was identified as an orphanage movement.[1]

In the past twenty years there has been lively scholarly interest in the social impact of German Pietism, with particular focus on the Halle Foundations of August Hermann Francke. The three-hundredth anniversary of the Halle orphanage in 1998 prompted renewed scholarly attention that shows no sign of abating.[2] Three innovative works deserve special mention.[3] One is Markus Meumann's book on orphans and orphanages in early modern society, which shows the importance of private initiatives in these programs, even in the age of Absolutism. Meumann calls the period from 1650 to 1750 "the age of orphanages" and observes that the orphanages included private foundations, communal foundations, and those under princely sovereignty.[4]

After the Thirty Years War, impoverished governments put a hold on building projects on behalf of the poor. But the last third of the seventeenth century saw a boom in the building of orphanages, unprecedented in number, geographic distribution, and confessional representation. A book by Thomas Kuhn offers an assessment of social engagement from the perspectives of German Pietism, the Enlightenment, and the nineteenth-century Awakening. He shows that in all three cases, faith and piety were conceived, articulated, and promoted from a social and diaconal perspective. "Religion was formulated predominantly with attention to its individual, social, and religious usefulness; dogmatic and theological emphases move into the background." Finally, Veronika Albrecht-Birkner's 2004 study draws on previously ignored archival sources to revise the traditional portrait of Francke's ministry in Glaucha, the backdrop to the orphanage project.[5] The present chapter draws especially on Albrecht-Birkner's valuable study.

The story of the social reforms and institutions associated with Halle Pietism is one of the most dramatic in Christian history. Against the background of early modern care of orphans, Francke's enterprise was unusual on several counts. First, there was the massive size of the building, based on careful planning and investigation of orphanages in the Netherlands. When construction began in 1698, it was met with both amazement and criticism. As Francke observed, "In this region people are not really accustomed to building orphanages."[6] Second, the enterprise was launched through a single individual, not by a territorial lord or local government, and with little capital in hand. Third, Francke's vision of social reform was centered on a philosophy of schools and education for the poor and a plan for "universal social reform."[7] His reform strategy aimed at educating a Pietist elite for schools, churches, and political positions. Halle Pietism was as much a school movement as it was an orphanage movement. Fourth, Francke's motivation and justification were rooted in his Pietist hopes for better times and a desire to practice Christian love. Fifth, the orphanage and its schools became "a powerhouse of the Pietist movement . . . a machine for the world-wide propagation of the distinct faith of the German Pietists."[8] The resources generated by the printing press and medicine production were used to fund missionary enterprises throughout the world. In coming years, orphanages and schools within and outside Germany were founded with Halle in mind.

The following account examines Francke's Halle Foundations, considering his early ministry in Glaucha, the founding of a school for poor children in 1695, Neubauer's investigation of Dutch models in 1697–1698, and aspects of the foundations from 1698 to 1727: Francke's report of 1704, the children in the orphanage, Francke's associates, his theology of work, and his pragmatism. A final consideration is the worldwide impact of Halle Pietism.

Francke's Early Ministry at St. George's Church in Glaucha

In 1690, Leipzig city authorities forced August Hermann Francke and Pietist students to leave the city, and in September 1691 Francke was likewise compelled to leave Erfurt, in both cases due to his association with conventicles. In early 1692 Francke was appointed pastor at St. George's Church in the city of Glaucha, which lay just outside Halle's southern city door and remained an independent municipality until 1817.[9] Francke preached his trial sermon in Glaucha on January 24, 1692, and finally moved into the parsonage on March 19. In the same year, he also became professor of Greek and Hebrew at the University of Halle.[10] He served in Glaucha until 1715, when he left to become pastor at St. Ulrich's Church in Halle.

Glaucha's economy had once depended on the land, but after the Thirty Years War it depended on a distillery, brandy production, fabric manufacture, and other handcrafts. Glaucha citizens also had the right to raise, slaughter, and sell their own cattle. Considering the lack of good land, Glaucha had a relatively strong and independent economy when compared with other regions at the time. Glaucha's population was severely affected by the Thirty Years War, falling from around two thousand before the war to less than a thousand after. By the second half of the seventeenth century the city population had grown to about twelve hundred, but was reduced to four hundred by the ravages of the plague in 1682. By the time Francke arrived, the population had grown to about five hundred people in 160 households.[11]

On April 27, 1700, Francke and his assistant, Johann Anastasius

Freylinghausen, submitted a lengthy report concerning their ministry at St. George's Church in Glaucha. Their report is largely responsible for the traditional portrait, passed down to the present day, of the lamentable social, economic, and spiritual conditions of the city and church when Francke arrived in 1692. In accordance with their prince's request, Francke and Freylinghausen addressed six questions: how the Word of God is proclaimed; how the sacraments are being administered, especially the practice of confession; how abuses and offenses are dealt with; what is being done to care for the needs of the poor; whether Francke and Freylinghausen have adequate assistance and resources for their ministry; and what blessing and fruit are evident from their ministry.[12] Francke wrote that he found the church in a "miserable condition," with no semblance of church discipline. "Everything lay in such a state of abuse, one could not cry enough tears for it."[13] The children, for example, were catechized for only an hour a week for three months of the year, adding up to just twelve hours of catechizing per year. They did not know how to behave in church and were a distraction to others.[14] In the city of Glaucha, thirty-seven of the two hundred dwellings were pubs, in which all manner of ungodly and heathen behavior occurred—a figure repeated by historians in almost every account of Francke's ministry. The portrait has been further embellished by unsupported claims that the city had no school.[15]

Unlike their predecessor, the report noted, Francke and Freylinghausen conducted catechism "almost daily" at the church, morning and evening. They preached from Bible passages that addressed people's needs, not just from assigned preaching texts, and they avoided use of foreign languages and rhetorical artistry in their sermons. Francke explained that he preached in the most simple and clear way possible "so that servants and maids and even small children can understand and grasp it," and so that "their hearts might receive Christ in faith."[16] During their eight years of ministry, they had witnessed many conversions and dramatic improvement in the city in every respect.

> Anyone who considers the abominations, disorderliness, and sins that were pursued in former times in this community, and then observes its present condition, cannot deny the blessing of God . . . The Word of the Lord is active and at work from morning to evening, both publicly and in private instruction and admonition, so that both old and young are deliv-

> ered from their ignorance. We hope that our future successors will have no small advantage, for we, on the other hand, [when we came] found nothing but great ignorance and blindness.[17]

Most of the pubs were now closed, and many of the former proprietors were sending their children to Francke's schools.

The background to Francke's negative portrait of the city in the report was his tense relationship with the church and citizens of Glaucha. Things had begun well for Francke. The Glaucha parishioners welcomed him enthusiastically in 1692, and when he faced opposition from two members in the first year, the majority campaigned successfully on his behalf to keep him in Glaucha. Jacob Vogler, a goldsmith and judge, and Elias Naumann, an innkeeper, had complained to the consistory on June 22, 1692, when Francke denied them absolution at confession and the right to receive the Lord's Supper. They brought wide-ranging accusations against Francke: in his sermons he taught that people "must be melancholy and sorrowful if they would experience the Spirit's inner leading and power"; he taught that there was no value in reading books—people should be content with holy thoughts; he held daily conventicles in the parsonage that were attended by young women and visitors from out of town; finally, on June 18 of that year, when Vogler and Naumann went to Francke for heartfelt confession, he refused them absolution because they would not promise to stop serving beer to guests on Sundays. Francke defended himself on each point, insisting that if Vogler and Naumann had been truly repentant, they would have agreed to stop sinning by serving drinks on Sundays. On July 7, the consistory brought down their decision, recommending that Vogler and Naumann be allowed to have another confessor. In a letter to Francke dated July 9, 1692, Spener expressed his "shock" over Francke's strictness in excluding an innkeeper from the Lord's Supper because he served people on Sundays.[18]

In the ensuing years, Francke's warm relationship with his church changed, and by 1695 was marked by increasing conflicts with parishioners over innovations that he introduced and decisions he made without consultation. After almost a year of controversy with the majority of his congregants, in December 1695 Francke succeeded in obtaining electoral approval to hire Johann Anastasius Freylinghausen (1670–1739) as his ministerial assistant. The congregation did not think they required two full-time clergy, suggesting that Francke felt overtaxed and in need of an assistant because of an overabundance of weekly church services and his frequent absences due to travel.[19] Another source of conflict was the choice of location for the new orphanage complex. Francke chose the most attractive piece of land in Glaucha, the Goldener Adler, a location that many citizens thought ideal for a new city hall. Francke attained his wish because of his ties to the court in Berlin. The Glaucha clergy enforced the decision with threat of excommunication, a threat applied against Johann Jakob Hensel, a judge who had acted as advocate for the Glaucha citizens.[20]

Meanwhile, Francke and Freylinghausen excluded a growing number of church members from the Lord's Supper. On October 27, 1704, forty of Francke's parishioners sent a petition to the Prussian king in which they complained that they and some already deceased church members had been denied the Lord's Supper, in some cases for a period of eight years.[21] Like the Labadists and Puritan and Reformed churches, Francke sought to exclude those who did not give evidence of new birth and true Christianity. This perfectionist ecclesiology was an enduring feature of Francke's thought and explains why many of his early associates decided to forsake church appointments and join separatist communities. Instead of gathering a separatist church, Francke used lengthy excommunications to exclude from the *Volkskirche* those whom he did not consider true Christians—an instance of separatism in reverse.[22]

The traditional portrait, Francke's portrait, of Glaucha as "a bad place" must be revised in the light of its many exaggerations and inconsistencies. The suggestion that Francke's predecessor, Johann Richter (1643–1699), was a complete failure, neglecting Christian discipline and instruction, is untrue. That Glaucha could be a place of misery and neglect and at the same time an attraction because of its amusements and pleasures is clearly problematic. Francke's portrayal of a depraved Glaucha served as a useful foil for his endeavors on behalf of social renewal.[23]

A School for Poor Children, 1695

August Hermann Francke's social reforms began with founding a school for poor children in Glaucha during Easter 1695. A gift of four thaler and sixteen groschen earlier that year inspired Francke to declare, in a joyous act of faith, "This is a fair sum of money. I will use it to begin a school for poor children." He "consulted not with flesh and blood but went ahead in faith."[24] In the summer of 1695, Georg Rudolf von Schweinitz of Magdeburg made his first generous gift to Francke, a sum of five hundred thaler, followed a few months later by another thousand. The first of von Schweinitz's gifts caught Francke completely by surprise; he interpreted the unsolicited bounty as a sign of God's blessing on his newly begun school for children from poor families. Francke used von Schweinitz's gifts to welcome a large number of poorer students to Halle and to provide them with support—up to twelve groschen per week.[25]

From the beginning, Francke was inspired not primarily by a vision of care of the needy but by a pedagogical philosophy that he described as "guiding the children to true godliness and Christian intelligence."[26] This philosophy was eventually realized in a school program with multiple educational institutions, including schools for orphans and the poor, a Latin school, and the exclusive Pädagogium Regium, an elector's school.[27] Francke's foundations in Halle were justly described as "a school city." The schools' reputation and progressive program attracted children from all over Europe. By the fall of 1706, 989 children were enrolled in the schools; of these, 122 were orphans.[28]

Neubauer's Investigation of Orphanages in the Netherlands, 1697–1698

During a visit to Hamburg, Francke became acquainted with the poor school and orphanage in the city and learned that they had been inspired by institutions in Holland. In April 1696, Francke contacted a physician in Kleve named Johannes Overbeck, requesting that he send him the regulations governing the houses for orphans and the poor in Amsterdam. Desiring more detailed information, in 1697 Francke sent his colleague and assistant Georg Heinrich Neubauer (1666–1727) on a trip to the Netherlands to investigate how the Dutch built, managed, and funded their orphanages and poorhouses.[29] Neubauer's trip took him to Hanover, Hamburg, Bremen, Ostfriesland, and finally the Netherlands, and included raising funds for an orphanage in Halle. The trip lasted a year, from June 2, 1697, to June 19, 1698. In every city orphanage and poor foundation that he visited, he sought to determine what might be useful in relation to building an orphanage in Halle.[30]

Neubauer went equipped with a list of "183 Questions" that he planned to raise in discussions with orphanage directors.[31] The questions go into great detail about construction of the orphanage building, financing, and the feeding and care of the children, revealing the priorities and care that lay behind the Halle Foundations. The questions cover seven main areas of concern: the children, the caregivers, the building, the main purpose of the orphanage, the costs, the duties of the house father and staff, and care of the children—feeding, clothing, and educating them. Here are some sample questions: How many boys and how many girls are in the orphanage? How old must they be in order to be accepted? Who is the director and what is his salary? How many caregivers are there per child? How big is the orphanage building in its length, breadth, and height? How many rooms are there? What is the floor made of, wood or plaster, and which material is most healthy for children? How many windows are there? How many children sleep in a room? Where is the toilet room and how is it furnished? Are there different toilets for each gender? Is there a dairy farm nearby, and how big is it? How many cows and horses are there? How big is the garden? What well or source of water is there? How much grain is needed to feed a child for a year? What can the children earn through their work in a year? What do the children wear? Do they have a change of clothing? How often do you wash their clothes? Where do the children wash? Who brings them the water? What do they use to brush their teeth? How do you prevent the children from getting scabies? How do you get rid of scabies among the children? Does each child have his or her own towel? How are they taught to fear God? How often are the children catechized? How many hours of schooling do the children have? What subjects are they taught? What work do the children do after school hours? How many kinds of punishment do you use when children misbehave?

Francke did well to look to the Netherlands. The Dutch model of orphan care had emerged in the early sixteenth century, inspired by humanist reformers and pedagogues. In place of the poor begging for their needs in the streets, a community chest was established to gather charitable resources from private gifts, foundations, and churches. The Dutch orphanages were highly selective, accepting only the children of citizens of the city. Modeled on the family household, the Dutch orphanage offered complete care of the child's physical needs and education for a productive adult life. These citizens' orphanages (*burgerweeshuizen*) were a source of local pride and were administered by leading citizens. They became large foundations, with substantial buildings and properties, sometimes on former monastic lands. Local magistrates provided them with sufficient resources from endowments, taxes, and door-to-door collections.[32]

In the mid seventeenth century, a new kind of orphanage was created, designed to accommodate all orphans of whatever background, including abandoned children. Local orphans were now recognized as wards of the city. These public orphanages were founded either by a city magistrate or by deacons from the Reformed church. They were supported from city and church subsidies, but not as richly as the more prestigious citizens' orphanages. The public orphanages were, like the citizens' orphanages, structured as a substitute family for the children. They, too, were a source of civic pride and were managed by a board of governors made up of well-to-do artisans. The orphans were housed in large buildings that were attractively decorated. The children were dressed in colorful uniforms similar to those of children in the citizens' orphanages. But their clothes were less expensive, their food more simple, and the conditions more crowded. The children worked at some form of textile manufacture such as spinning, knitting, lace-making, sewing, and weaving. Older children were apprenticed to a craftsman so they could learn a skill and be self-sufficient when they left the orphanage, around the age of twenty.[33] Some graduates joined the East India Company on expeditions to the Far East. Some orphan boys completed Latin school, studied theology at university with support from the city, and went on to become Reformed pastors.[34]

Religious observance and instruction were central to the care of Dutch orphans in the seventeenth century. There were five times of prayer in the day: when the children got up in the morning, at the three mealtimes, and when they went to bed. During meals, a passage was read aloud from the Bible, the catechism, or a book of devotion. Sometimes an older child would read. There was also singing of psalms and hymns. On Sunday mornings and afternoons the children attended church services, where special seating was reserved for them. Adolescent orphans were a frequent source of distraction in the service; they talked during the sermon or got up early to leave.[35] During the week, the school program included regular instruction in the Heidelberg Catechism, by a teacher, theology student, or pastor. Gisbertus Voetius, the famous Utrecht theologian, was known to take his turn in providing catechism instruction to orphans.[36] Most children made their confession of faith and were confirmed by the time they left the orphanage.

The directors of the Dutch orphanages, *Binnenväter* in German, lived in the orphanage along with their wives, the *Binnenmütter*, and children. These positions were not prestigious and attracted some dubious individuals, especially in the public orphanages. There are numerous cases of *Binnenväter* who had to be reprimanded or dismissed because of misappropriation of funds, drunkenness, incompetence, or sexually inappropriate behavior with the children. In two cases, the *Binnenväter* were sentenced to death for sexual abuse. But there were also pious *Binnenväter* who saw the position as an opportunity to provide religious instruction and moral direction to the children. Two such examples were Johannes Hoevenaar, who in 1686 became *Binnenvater* and schoolmaster at the city orphanage in Leeuwarden, and Johannes Eswijler (1633–1719), a German immigrant and lay pastor who was appointed *Binnenvater* at the citizens' orphanage in Hoorn in 1668 and served there for more than forty years. Eswijler's orphanage became a meeting place for pious believers in the area who identified with the Further Reformation (*Nadere Reformatie*). In 1685, Eswijler published a devotional book, *Solitary Meditations on the Essential Truths of the Gospel*, that was popular for years among Dutch conventicles. Francke's emissary, Neubauer, may have met with Eswijler.[37]

In Halle, Francke adopted a number of features of the Dutch orphanages. Following the Dutch model, Halle's orphanage was strictly for children. Halle's supporters took pride in seeing that the children were well-dressed, well-fed, and educated and prepared for life as adults.[38] But the Halle orphanage greatly surpassed the models observed by Neubauer. Although Dutch orphanages offered useful examples, the Further Reformation probably did *not* inspire Francke's initial desire to found an orphanage.[39]

The Francke Foundations in Halle, 1698–1727

The foundation stone for the Glaucha orphanage was laid on July 13, 1698. On September 19, the Brandenburg elector, Frederick III, signed the *Privilegium* that made the orphanage a public institution. The *Privilegium* brought with it significant financial benefits. Within the principality of Halberstadt and the Duchy of Magdeburg, the orphanage would receive 10 percent of all fines (so long as this did not amount to more than fifty thaler). All churches in these regions would contribute one thaler per year to the orphanage. Once a year, house-to-house collections would be made in all parts of the elector's lands. The orphanage was freed from paying taxes on its purchases of food, clothing, wool, and paper, and it was granted the right to produce its own baked goods, beer, and medicines, and to print, publish, and sell books.[40]

The Halle orphanage was dominated by its school program. The day began at 5 a.m. The children got up, washed, and had an hour of devotion that included singing, Bible reading, prayer, and catechism instruction. At 7 a.m. they carried out tasks relating to schoolwork or chores. After breakfast there was a schedule of classes in the different schools. In late afternoon the community came together for prayer. The Latin school was more rigorous than the German school, which had just two hours of instruction in the morning and two in the afternoon. The day ended with evening prayers and the child's reflection on his or her activities and behavior. Bedtime was at 9 p.m.[41]

The orphans were required to work outside school hours. This usually involved knitting stockings. In 1705, for example, thirty boys worked for two hours a day; another thirty boys worked for four hours. Thirty-two of the boys had a more demanding class schedule and so were free of work altogether. But unlike most orphanages at the time, the Halle orphanage was above all a center for schooling and education. The teachers met in conference to discuss children whose performance fell behind expectations. In these cases the issue became, "How long should they be allowed to remain in the house?" Teachers were expected to judge which orphans were not gifted for study. These children were told they would have to leave the orphanage when they turned sixteen. Of 204 orphan boys who lived in the Halle orphanage prior to 1700, 63 ran away and 4 were asked to leave.[42]

The orphans were supervised day and night. Preceptors lived with the children, managed their money, oversaw their cleanliness and hygiene, and censored their mail. They accompanied them to meals and assigned their food portions. Girls were supervised by the orphanage mother and had separate instruction from the boys. The orphanage was a pioneer in the field of modern hygiene. The children were made to brush their teeth and bathe and regularly received clean clothes and bedding.[43]

August Hermann Francke in Halle

The Halle orphanage and schools were a kind of Protestant monastery; every hour of the day was strictly regulated in a rhythm of prayer, study, and work. Passages from the Bible were read aloud during meals. Importance was given to the children's intercessory prayers for their benefactors. Francke reflected that the prayers of the orphans "were a true wall of protection for the city and land." Private gifts to the orphanage were often accompanied by a request for the prayers of the children on behalf of a specific need. This was carried out, as promised, at the daily morning and evening prayer times. Francke emphasized the Evangelical character of the Halle Foundations, noting that this was not a money-making scheme and that the prayers were in no way tied to the gifts. Only truly converted believers would benefit from the children's prayers.[44]

FRANCKE'S *SINCERE AND THOROUGH REPORT* OF 1704 (*DER GROSSE AUFSATZ*)

In 1704 Francke composed a 125-page report that he sent to supporters and friends. Entitled *A Sincere and Thorough Report concerning the Inward State and Importance of the Work of the Lord in Halle, in the Duchy of Magdeburg*, it became known simply as *The Great Project* (*Der Große Aufsatz*).[45] It has long been considered the most important literary reflection of the goals and vision of Halle Pietism—the Halle equivalent of Spener's *Pia Desideria*. Francke set out his plan for universal reform in Germany, Europe, and "all parts of the world" through reform of Christian education. The key lay in preparation of godly teachers and professors for schools and universities, who would see it as their duty to instill the love of Christ in the hearts of children and young people. Schools would then produce Christian leaders for all spheres of society who could advance spiritual and social renewal. Pastors so educated would no longer prepare their sermons from their brains and books, using heathen arts of oratory, but would preach out of duty to God and neighbor (9ff.).

Francke's report reflected on the growth of the Halle Foundations over the previous nine and a half years, offering a concise summary of the work of nine different Halle institutions. First, the Theological College for Oriental Studies (Collegium orientale), founded in 1702, consisted of twelve university students, many of them master's students, who were given free room and board in a designated house for four to six years. These were gifted individuals who wanted to perfect their knowledge of biblical languages and one day become professors. The demanding curriculum included mastery of Aramaic, Syriac, Arabic, Ethiopic, and Hebrew. Some also studied Turkish, Persian, and Chinese. This was all in addition to the regular program of theological study. Francke's successor in the collegium, Johann Heinrich Michaelis (1668–1738), oversaw an edition of the Hebrew Bible, completed in 1720.[46] Second, the Seminary for Teachers consisted of seventy-two theology students who devoted two hours a day to tutoring children in the orphanage. Third, the Special Table provided a midday meal for sixty-four poor university students. Fourth, the Pädagogium Regium offered advanced education for seventy gifted children and children of nobility; the school was funded by their parents and had no connection with the orphanage. Fifth, the orphanage proper, housed in a new building that cost twenty thousand Thaler, had, in 1704, a hundred boys and twenty girls. All children were carefully nurtured in the Christian faith. There were also facilities for a pharmacy, bookstore, and print shop (96–99). Francke was excited by the prospect of mass-producing a German Bible that even the poor could afford (159ff.). Sixth, eight different school programs were associated with the orphanage. The most gifted boys attended the Latin school and were prepared to go on to university. The others were taught reading, writing, reckoning, and music, and outside school hours engaged in spinning wool, carding, and sewing socks. The girls were taught similar subjects in their own school and engaged in women's handcrafts. In 1704, about 665 children attended these schools, 120 of them orphans. Seventh, there were two homes for widows, thanks to the gifts of benefactors. Eighth, a foundation was set up to collect alms from the congregation once every four Sundays and to distribute them to Glaucha's poor. Finally, a foundation distributed alms daily to any poor in the city and taught them catechism (100ff.).

In the *Sincere and Thorough Report,* Francke promoted the Halle Foundations as worthy of his readers' financial support: "I set forth these notions for the benefit of those who have been blessed by God with temporal wealth and who fear God as the giver of wealth, and who seek to use it so they may do good and be rich in good works and store up treasure in heaven" (60). No other cause was as worthy as the Halle Foundations, for God himself had begun the work and was directing the work—something one could not say with equal confidence of any other project (63ff.).

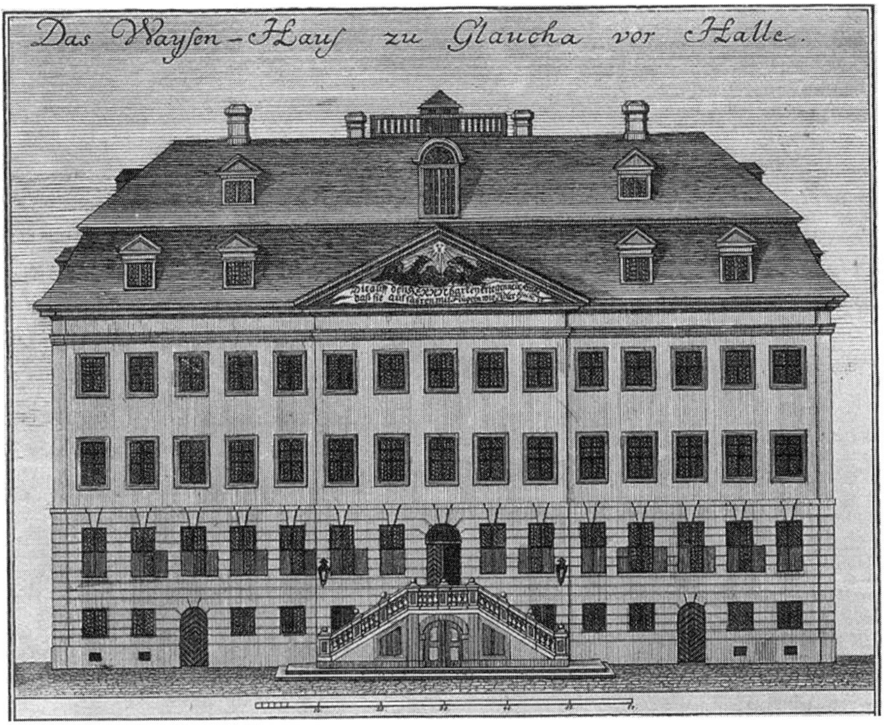

The Orphanage in Glaucha. Engraving by Gottfried August Gründler, 1749.

THE ORPHANS IN HALLE

Who were the orphan children who were housed in Halle? What were their ages and living conditions? What was the social background of children in the Halle orphanage during Francke's time? How did the children fare in later life? These questions can be answered, in large measure thanks to the survival of a key primary source: *The Album of Orphans in the Francke Foundations* for the years 1695–1749.[47] The album contains an abundance of information concerning the children and their education in the Halle orphanage and schools. The first inspector, Georg Heinrich Neubauer, provided written instructions on the information to be collected when a child was admitted.

> As soon as a child is received, the Inspector should inquire concerning his name, nationality, age, family connections, and the day on which he ar-

> rived, and write it all down in a book especially devoted to this purpose. Likewise, in the same book should be noted the date on which a child leaves the orphanage. In a special part of the book should be recorded, devotedly and accurately, how each child is behaving, what it is learning, and why the child left the orphanage. When a child dies in the orphanage, a short report should be made in another part of the book concerning his birth, life, Christian confession, illness, and death.[48]

Also noted in the album were the level of schooling the child had attained at the point of arrival and the class and educational program in which the child was then placed. The album contains information on all 2,152 orphan children in Halle from 1695 to 1749. In an average year there were a hundred boys and thirty girls living at the orphanage.

The average age of boys entering the orphanage was twelve and a half; for girls, the average was just under eleven. Prior to 1713, the orphanage admitted a large number of children between the ages of four and nine, but the number of young children dropped as time went on. The focus was on educating the children, not merely saving them from begging and putting them to work in some productive industry.[49] This is in stark contrast to most such institutions of the time, where it was not unusual for children to work seven, eight, or more hours a day and to leave the orphanage with minimal education and no craft.

The social spectrum of the orphans in Halle favored the upper reaches of society. In her study of the social background of the Halle orphans, Juliane Jacobi arranges the professions of the fathers into six social classes: (1) farm laborer, (2) nobility, (3) upper class (civic leaders and prominent middle-class positions such as jurists and professors), (4) middle class (small businessmen, lower officials, skilled craftsmen), (5) urban lower class (servants, day laborers, poor handworkers), and (6) clergy. More than 40 percent of both boys and girls at the orphanage came from middle-class families; about 10 percent came from the upper class. In the case of the boys, another 17 percent had fathers who were clergy or had studied theology; just 5 percent of girls came from the homes of clergy. Some 21 percent of the boys and 37 percent of the girls came from the urban lower class—a group comprising about 40 percent of the population at large in German lands at this time. Jacobi concludes that the orphans were "a highly select group."[50] In the period between 1695 and 1749, only three children from the city of Glaucha were received into the orphanage, suggesting it did little to address the needs of Glaucha's orphans.[51] Compared with other orphanages, the Halle orphanage was *not* really a model for the care and education of the poor.[52]

It seems clear that Francke's orphanage was engaged in "fostering gifted protégés" rather than caring for the poor. The orphanage aimed at educating a new generation of Pietist leaders who, in turn, could advance wide-ranging social reforms.

> The most important function of the orphanage was the selection of suitable children for the study of theology. The preparation and realization of a consistently Pietist program of theological study can be seen as the core of Francke's educational concept. Education had the goal of producing pious ministers for the Church . . . The orphans and theology students who came from the lower social class found themselves economically dependent upon the Foundations, so that realization of Francke's goal was relatively straightforward.[53]

Francke saw the children as potential converts and pastors who, when properly educated, would form the vanguard of worldwide Christian renewal and reform.[54]

The Halle orphanage attained a new level in the care of children, thanks to the excellent layout of the facility, the quality of care the children received, and the progressive educational methods used in the schools. But despite the improved conditions in Halle, during the first fifteen years of the orphanage's existence, more than 20 percent of the boys ran away, never to return. Over the whole period up to 1749, 10 percent of the boys ran away. Up to 1729, an average of 10 percent of the boys and girls in the orphanage died while in care. Part of this can be attributed to the epidemic of 1698–1699.[55]

There were many success stories of Halle orphans going on to become productive citizens and Christian leaders. One is the story of Anna Hedwig Petersin, the daughter of a pharmacist, who was received into the orphanage at twelve years of age. After a time, it was reported in the album that "she can read and has made a beginning in arithmetic and writing." She later worked in Francke's home, helping to care for his children. The album recorded that she married a furrier in Halle and "is doing well."[56]

An exceptional story is that of Johann Heinrich Schulze (1687–1744), the son of a poor tailor. He entered the Halle orphanage when one of his parents died. He attended the Latin school and soon demonstrated a gift for languages. After studying theology, he taught for a few years at the Halle Pädagogium. He then returned to university, and in 1717 he completed studies in medicine. He became a professor of medicine, chemistry, and Greek at universities in Altdorf and Halle. As a young man he published a Greek grammar that was widely used in schools. He also published a book of chemical experiments, a medical text on the illnesses of women and infants, and a work on the history of ancient coinage.[57]

FRANCKE'S COLLEAGUES IN HALLE

> [Francke's] work would not have been possible without the help of a large number of friends and supporters throughout all of Europe and the extraordinary contribution of a group of close associates, who today are seldom mentioned.[58]

For four years, from June 1701 to July 1705, Francke met at least weekly in conference with a close circle of ten fellow-workers that included Georg Heinrich Neubauer; Heinrich Julius Elers, director of the Halle press; and Christian Friedrich Richter, who oversaw the production of medicines in the pharmacy.[59]

Georg Heinrich Neubauer was a key figure in the early years. He and Francke met as students at the University of Leipzig; he then followed Francke to Erfurt and finally to Glaucha. In 1695, when Francke began to take in orphans and place them in homes, he made Neubauer the overseer and financial manager of the endeavor. In 1698 Francke put Neubauer in charge of overseeing the building of the orphanage, known as Reichenbach House. In accordance with Francke's wishes, Neubauer oversaw the building of a four-storey structure that avoided all unnecessary ornament, decoration, and artistry. This was soon followed by other structures. That same year, Neubauer became chief business manager of the foundations, and G. C. Müller replaced him as director of the orphanage.[60] Neubauer was unpretentious, multitalented, and hardworking. He never married.[61]

Francke met Heinrich Julius Elers (1667–1728) in Lüneburg in 1688; they also studied together in Leipzig. While working as a tutor in Arnstadt, from 1690 to 1694, Elers held conventicles and promoted the teaching of the coming thousand-year kingdom of Christ. He rejected marriage, believing it held no appeal for those who experienced intimate union with Christ. After being banned from Arnstadt in 1694 because of his separatism, Elers settled in Muskau, where he persisted in his separatist activities.[62] In 1697 he moved to Halle to continue his studies. But a sermon by Francke in June of that year, on the Christian's obligation to the poor, convinced Elers to give up on further study and to serve the needy. Without any business experience, he took on the work of building up the Halle bookstore and publishing enterprise. The first catalogue appeared in 1698, listing fifty-five of Francke's writings. The Halle press also published works by Spener, Petersen, and Arnold. By 1717 the catalogue contained three hundred titles by seventy authors.[63]

Like many of Francke's associates, Elers was marked by "fanatical devotion" to his work.[64] Francke boasted of Elers's success with the Halle publishing house: "The splendid publishing house has produced such a quantity of books, contained in the latest Catalogue, that one is amazed . . . It provides testimony that, in just a few years, God has done what other businesses could not accomplish in thirty or more years."[65] Elers attributed his success to the blessing of God. The profits were poured into the work of the Halle Foundations.[66] The publishing enterprise became the means of spreading Francke's vision throughout the German lands.

Christian Friedrich Richter (1676–1711) was the third of six children, four sons and two daughters, born to Anna Margaretha Döbler and Sigismund Richter, a prominent jurist and councilor in Promnitz. His mother's younger sister, Sidonia Sybilla Döbler, married an older brother of A. H. Francke. Richter began studies in Halle in 1694, pursuing theology at the encouragement of his parents. He also studied medicine and served briefly as the orphanage physician in 1697 and 1699. By 1700 the whole Richter family had settled in Halle and, thanks to Francke, had found positions in the Halle Foundations.[67] Richter's brother Sigismund became inspector of the Pädagogium in 1699, and Albrecht served as the orphanage physician until his death in 1699. The younger siblings attended the Halle schools.

Halle's successful production and trade in pharmaceuticals was due to Christian Friedrich Richter's initiative and leadership in heading the pharmacy. He and his younger brother Christian Sigismund engaged in extensive laboratory experiments, always beginning with prayer. Richter insisted on using the best and purest chemical ingredients, and he traveled to Amsterdam, Hamburg, Bremen, Berlin, and Venice to buy them in bulk at the best price. In December 1700, a man by the name of Burgstaller gave Francke a manuscript containing instructions on the preparation of a wonder drug derived from gold. Francke passed this on to the Richters, and in 1701 they produced a medicine that proved effective in treating spotted fever, the cause of many deaths in Halle.[68] The *essentia dulcis* was marketed widely and made a handsome profit for the Halle Foundations. From 1710 to 1720, sales of the medicine brought in nine thousand thaler per year, growing to thirty-six thousand per year by 1761. This profit not only covered the costs of the foundations but left a significant surplus.[69]

Richter was a talented and passionate individual. He composed twenty-five hymns and works of verse, eleven of which have been translated into English. In 1699 Richter contracted tuberculosis and thereafter was not a well man; he died of the disease twelve years later. His experience of physical suffering is portrayed in his hymn "God Whom I as Love Have Known."

> God whom I as love have known,
> Thou hast sickness laid on me,
> And these pains are sent of Thee,
> Under which I burn and moan;
> Let them burn away the sin,
> That too oft hath checked the love
> Wherewith Thou my heart wouldst move,
> When Thy Spirit works within!
>
> Suffering is the work now sent,
> Nothing I can do but lie
> Suffering as the hours go by;
> All my powers to this are bent.
> Suffering is my gain; I bow
> To my heavenly Father's will,
> And receive it hushed and still;
> Suffering is my worship now.[70]

Richter's medical condition may account for a letter he sent to Francke in 1700 in which he committed himself to God and the work in Halle and to a celibate life, signing it in his own blood. In 1707, when Richter married, he asked Francke to return the letter.[71] Richter published a successful medical text, *Brief and Clear Instruction on the Body and the Natural Life of Man* (1705), which was reprinted up to 1791.[72]

While a student in Halle and as Francke's colleague in the foundations, Richter had practically worshipped Francke. But after 1704, relations between the two men became more difficult.[73] At issue were the costs of Richter's chemical experiments, the price to be charged for the *essentia dulcis,* and the rights to it. Feeling pressure to ensure that his family was well cared for, Richter claimed the rights to the medicine for himself.[74] There developed a three-party dynamic among the Halle leadership: those supporting Francke, led by Neubauer; those supporting Richter; and Baron von Canstein, who remained independent. Neubauer begged Francke to dismiss the Richter brothers from their positions, but Francke refused. When Christian Friedrich Richter died in 1711, at thirty-five years of age, Neubauer saw it as God's judgment on a man who had interfered with God's work in Halle.[75]

Francke's closest associates in the university were the jurist Samuel Stryck (1640–1710) and the theologians Joachim Justus Breithaupt (1658–1732) and Paul Anton (1661–1730), a friend from Leipzig.[76] In 1694 Breithaupt published the first Pietist dogmatics with his *Theological Institutes*. Besides offering lectures in theology, both Breithaupt and Anton met with students in small collegia pietatis. During educational travels in 1713, Johann Albrecht Bengel spent three months in Halle. He reflected on the combined impact of Anton, Breithaupt, and Francke: "Who knows if ever again in all Christendom three such colleagues could be brought together as has been the case in Halle with Breithaupt, Anton, and Francke."[77]

There were close ties between the university and the Halle Foundations. The students were engaged as teachers at the Halle schools, even before they had completed their studies. And medical students worked in caring for the health needs of children in the orphanage and schools.[78]

FRANCKE'S THEOLOGY OF WORK, POVERTY, AND WEALTH

Francke was indebted to Dutch Calvinism not only for his social reforms but also for his theology of work. In addition to Dutch programs for care of orphans and the poor, Francke adopted features of Calvinist ethical theory.[79] In response to the question of how the believer can know that his conversion is true and from God, Francke emphasized the importance of "indubitable signs" that one is a child of God. These signs included a datable experience of conversion and daily evidences of the soul's rebirth. Francke differed from Spener in his emphasis on the Calvinist idea of fulfilling one's worldly vocation in a way that was pleasing to God. He went far beyond Johann Arndt's view that, for the Christian, work in the world is secondary to following Christ.[80] Francke offered six reasons why the Christian should be diligent in work: (1) God commands us to work (Gen. 3:19); (2) humanity is made to find fulfillment in work "just as the bird is made to fly"; (3) God has decreed that we work for our daily bread (2 Thess. 3:10–12); (4) work is a means of suppressing our aptitude for sin; idleness is the beginning of vice; (5) believers should not be a burden to others, especially not to unbelievers; (6) we should work so that we have the means to help the needy (Eph. 4:28). Francke saw the need for rest, but warned against too much free time.[81] The only activity he valued above work was prayer.

Like the Puritans, Francke was quick to take up the latest technical inventions if they had some practical benefit. Francke's idea of "Christian intelligence" (*die Klugheit der Gerechten*) included pursuing every economic and technical advantage that presented itself. The cleverness of the children of light was a Christian virtue, according to Ephesians 5:15–17.[82] Francke's own family found success in business and trade; his brother was a merchant in Venice.[83] In Pietism, then, one observes "the religious legitimation of individual activity in the social, political and economic sphere."[84] But Francke's Pietism differed from Dutch Calvinism and English Puritanism on one key point: his Pietist ethic was directed not so much toward encouraging capitalist activity as to encouraging education and educational activity.

Francke was clear about the duties of believers toward the poor. He preached a sermon on "awaking dead and cold hearts by means of the heart of the Lord Jesus which lives in love and is enflamed with compassion." When he published the sermon, Francke attached a list of "Twenty-four Reasons to Take Seriously Our Obligation toward the Poor." The reasons include God's emphatic command to show love and kindness toward the poor; the promises that God has given to those who practice love toward the poor; the blessing that God brings to the livelihood and business of those who show mercy; and the Word of Christ: as we give, so will be given to us (Luke 6:38).[85]

Francke joined Spener in emphasizing not just the duties of individual Christians toward the poor but the obligations of government: "Christian rulers should see that every poor person be sufficiently served that they are cared for and that grants be properly distributed. If the poor can work, they would be expected to do so; if not, they should be given as much as they need."[86] Francke pointed to the example of government-sponsored orphanages and poorhouses in various parts of the Netherlands.

FRANCKE'S PRAGMATISM: PIETISM AND THE PRUSSIAN STATE

The key to Francke's success in Halle lay in his "pragmatic reordering of social institutions," evident in the way he joined together educational programs and care for the poor.[87] Pietist social programs represented a convergence of ideals: rejection of idleness and demand for hard work, productivity, and self-discipline. Halle's schools promoted both godliness and Christian intelligence.

Francke's pragmatism was also evident in the way he pursued cooperation with pastors, wealthy individuals, and the Brandenburg government. The Halle Foundations benefited from a continual interplay of private initiatives with state support and influence. Christian statesmen and princes were key figures in Halle's success.[88] Francke nurtured a network of contacts with influential nobility such as the Wetterau counts, the prince of Ostfriesland, the king of Denmark, and especially the Prussian king, Frederick William I. Francke saw the state as the organ by which Pietist reforms could be implemented. The Halle idea of social foundations as a cooperative enterprise was replicated throughout the German empire and around the world.

Another instance of Francke's pragmatism was his creation of a successful patronage network that controlled appointments to the Prussian Army chaplaincy in a way that favored Halle graduates.[89] In 1713 the new Prussian king, Frederick William I, a Pietist sympathizer, gave Baron Carl Hildebrand von Canstein the right to nominate candidates for vacant chaplaincies.[90] Von Canstein typically put forward young men in their late twenties who had studied in Halle. Many had served as teachers in Francke's Pädagogium.[91] Halle graduates won key positions within the Prussian state and used their offices "to manipulate Frederick William and to block his agenda." Benjamin Marschke writes that "the Pietist faction exercised hegemony over several institutions of the state, and used their official power and influence to extend their patronage system, to check opposing factions, to expand further their role within the state and to expand the scope of the state."[92] This pattern of shrewd recruitment and placement of educators and pastors became a central pillar of Halle Pietism—as central a feature as the orphanage program. The Pietist network gradually lost its influence after Francke's death in 1727.

The Worldwide Impact of Halle Pietism

Up to 25 percent of orphanages founded between 1695 and 1806 in the old German empire were modeled on the Halle Foundations. This is evident in the way the orphanages combined the ideals of both education and piety, as well as in their economic structure. They often had personnel who had studied in Halle or had worked in the Halle Foundations.[93] Halle-inspired institutions could be found in every part of the empire, including Darmstadt, Langendorf in Saxon-Weißenfels, Esens in Ostfriesland, Züllichau in Silesia, Göttingen, Pyrmont, Stuttgart, and Potsdam.

The driving force in Darmstadt was the city preacher, Eberhard Philipp Zühl (1662–1730), a friend of both Spener and Francke. In 1698 he oversaw the building of the Darmstadt orphanage, along with printing press, book publishing business, and Latin school, in close imitation of the Halle Foundations. Zühl gained the support of Landgrave Ernst Ludwig, a Pietist-friendly prince and the grandson of Ernst the Pious of Saxon-Gotha.[94] Thanks to the landgrave, five thousand gulden in funding were raised to launch the Darmstadt orphanage. The ongoing needs of the orphanage were financed by setting up a manufacturing industry. All the teachers in the Darmstadt orphanage and schools were Halle graduates.

The orphanage foundation that most closely imitated Halle was in Esens, Ostfriesland. It, too, was a cooperative enterprise, in this case between Pastor Wilhelm Christian Schneider (1677–1725) and the Pietist Prince Georg Albrecht. Albrecht's court was the center of Pietist reform in Ostfriesland, and the prince was a regular and intimate correspondent with

Francke.[95] Pastor Schneider had been Francke's colleague in the Collegium orientale in Halle. In 1712 Schneider set up a school for poor children, with a director and teachers from Halle. Construction of the orphanage began on June 23, 1713, and by December it was completed, with accommodations for more than fifty children. The number of children attending the school outnumbered the orphans almost fourfold.[96]

In early 1716, Schneider published the booklet *The Blessed Footsteps of the Living God*, whose title and contents were a close imitation of Francke's 1701 *Footsteps*. Schneider's initial plan to start a school for poor children was followed closely by a plan to found an orphanage. The facade of the orphanage was decorated with two eagles and a verse from Psalms: "How precious is your goodness O God, that the children of men find refuge in the shadow of your wings" (Ps. 36:8). Schneider's efforts to replicate the Halle Foundations in Esens included his own founding legend of a gift of eight thaler that he took as guidance, or "leading," from God that he, too, should establish a school and orphanage. He also hoped to found a Latin school for gifted children, a printing press, and a publishing house.[97]

The orphanage in Esens, however, put greater emphasis on the children's work than on their education. The children spent between six and nine or more hours a day working in wool manufacture or other industries; school instruction remained at a very elementary level. The planned Pädagogium and book publishing enterprise never materialized. This was because, while Halle's orphanage and schools were shaped by the university setting and Francke's goal of universal social reform, Schneider's orphanage and schools were determined by the immediate need to care for the poor and to remove beggars from the streets.[98]

Francke's vision extended far beyond German lands. He saw Halle as providing the outline of a much greater work—establishing the knowledge of God throughout the world and "changing the world by changing people."[99] He believed the key lay in education, especially in the preparation of teachers. Francke published *The Footsteps of the Living God* in 1701 with this goal in view: to call others to follow in his footsteps and to bring about reforms in schools, orphanages, and universities. Francke derived satisfaction in seeing how "from near and far they seek out good and true laborers in the Lord's work, well-educated graduates [from Halle], for foreign enterprises."[100] Halle exercised a worldwide influence in two ways: through imitation of Halle institutions in other parts of the world and through students and teachers from Halle who took their experience with them to other countries, including England, Denmark, Hungary, Estonia, Siberia, and India.

The Protestant Danish mission in southeast India was led by two Halle graduates, Bartholomäus Ziegenbalg (1682–1719) and Heinrich Plütschau (1677–1747). In December 1707 they established a mission school for Tamil boys and girls in Tranquebar, using the curriculum and educational methods found in Halle. When sick, the children received medicines produced in the Halle apothecary. Because of the social support system in that part of India, there was little need for an orphanage. The missionaries focused instead on "planting the knowledge of God" and training native-born schoolteachers, pastors, and catechists. The Halle mission reports between 1710 and 1772 represent the first Protestant missions periodical, designed as an effective means of raising support from patrons.[101]

The Danish-Halle mission and exchanges between Halle and Denmark led to establishing an orphanage in Copenhagen in 1727. This foundation followed the Halle model and included a printing press. Copenhagen became a center for Pietist influence in Denmark. Under Christian VI (1699–1746), a form of state Pietism came to dominate the Danish court and society.[102]

In Slovakia, Mattias Bels (1684–1749) incorporated the curriculum and methods of the Halle schools and translated and published many of Francke's writings. During his university studies in Halle from 1704 to 1708, Bels had worked in Francke's schools and proved an exceptionally gifted teacher. Among his students was Francke's son, Gotthilf August. On his return to Slovakia, Bels became rector of the gymnasium (academic-oriented high school) in Neusohl and later in Bratislava. His schools became, in turn, models for the reform of education in Hungary and Estonia.[103]

Halle's influence also extended to England. The most famous Halle orphan, Georg Friedrich Händel (1685–1759), never lived in the orphanage. When it was being built, in 1698, Händel lived in Halle as a "half-orphan," his father having died a short time earlier. After 1711, Händel made his home in London. His financial support for the city's Foundling Hospital was probably inspired by the Halle orphanage. Händel would have observed the impressive growth of the Halle Foundations when he returned to Halle in 1719.[104] When the London Foundling Hospital was established in 1749, Händel composed a hymn for the occasion. Each year, until his death, he held a benefit performance of the *Messiah* and devoted the proceeds to the hospital. He donated an organ to the hospital chapel and served on the hospital's board of governors from 1750 until he died.[105]

The Halle legacy reached America as well. In 1737 two former Halle teachers, Johann Martin Boltzius and Israel Christian Gronau, established an orphanage in Ebenezer, Georgia. They received an ongoing supply of material resources and practical guidance from Halle.[106] The English preacher George Whitefield visited the Ebenezer orphanage in 1738 and was so impressed that he began collecting money to found his own. In 1740 he laid the foundation stone for the Bethesda orphanage in Savannah, Georgia. He sought to follow the Halle model of schools as a basis of universal reform.[107]

Conclusion

In August Hermann Francke one finds a unique combination of rationally founded initiatives and strategies and pious devotion to God's leading and providence. His ambitious projects aimed at nothing less than a second Reformation that would restructure the political and social world of his day from the ground up. The Francke Foundations in Halle were intended to be "the spiritual center for realizing God's kingdom on earth."[108] Francke was inspired not primarily by a vision of caring for the needy but by a pedagogical philosophy that he described as guiding the children "to true godliness and Christian intelligence." Francke's orphanage was engaged more in fostering gifted protégés than in caring for the poor. He saw the children as potential converts and pastors who, when properly educated, would form the vanguard of worldwide Christian renewal and reform.

Francke's efforts in social and educational reform owed their success to his pragmatism and cooperation with Absolutist regimes. An important factor in establishing Halle's social institutions was "winning over the lords," thereby obtaining the necessary permissions, privileges, oversight, and administrative approval. Francke used his influence to place Halle graduates in key positions within the Prussian state, creating a highly successful Pietist network.

Part III

The Social and Cultural Worlds of German Pietism

CHAPTER 6

Radical German Pietism in Europe and North America

The designation "Radical Pietism" goes back to Albrecht Ritschl in the 1880s. Since then, surveys of German Pietism have typically contrasted the Pietism of Spener and Francke with the Pietism of the Radicals. The category of Radical Pietism is used in Peter C. Erb's *Pietists: Selected Writings* and in Ernest Stoeffler's *German Pietism during the Eighteenth Century* to include figures such as Gottfried Arnold, Johann Konrad Dippel, Johann Wilhelm and Johanna Eleonora Petersen, Heinrich Horch, Hochmann von Hochenau, Gerhard Tersteegen, and Alexander Mack—people who were either separatist or heterodox, or both.[1]

In recent years, study of the Radicals has flourished, becoming a scholarly field unto itself. This chapter, therefore, begins with a brief survey of Radical Pietism research. This is followed by an overview of divergent expressions of Radical German Pietism, a proposed fourfold typology of various expressions of Radical Pietism, and portraits of three contrasting Radical Pietist figures: Johann Wilhelm Petersen, Johann Friedrich Rock, and Georg Conrad Beissel.

Radical Pietism Research up to the Early 1990s

The best point of entry for understanding Radical German Pietism is Hans Schneider's research survey and historical overview of Radical Pietism in the seventeenth and eighteenth centuries, now available in English translation. Schneider identified Pietism as a movement that began with Spener in the 1670s, observing that contemporaries saw something new in Spener and his student disciples that they identified as "Pietism" during the controversies in Leipzig in 1689 and 1690. Followers of Johann Arndt never formed a comparable group.[2]

Schneider argued for a close connection between Radical Pietists and Church Pietists. "The vast majority of the better-known Radicals," he writes, "had close personal ties to . . . the movement associated with Spener."[3] Both Spener and Francke maintained contact with Radical figures—Spener with the Petersens and Francke with Andreas Achilles and radical conventicles. The boundary between Church Pietists and the Radicals was porous, with individuals migrating back and forth between the two camps, often making it difficult to determine where an individual belongs. Following Johannes Wallmann, Schneider suggested that the two branches of Pietism began simultaneously in Frankfurt, with the radical Johann Jakob Schütz serving as a second founder of Pietism along with Philipp Jakob Spener. Both Schütz and Spener started conventicles and held to the new eschatology of hopes for better times.[4]

Schneider pointed to the literary achievements of the Radical Pietists. Gottfried Arnold's *Impartial History of the Churches and Heretics,* Johann Henrich Reitz's *History of the Re-born,* and books by Johann Wilhelm and Johanna Eleonora Petersen were bestsellers in the eighteenth century. Arnold's widely read histories make him "undoubtedly the most important representative of radical Pietism."[5] A classic expression of Radical Pietist biblical commentary is *The Berleburg Bible.* The German Inspirationists made a significant literary contribution through their practice of recording and publishing the words of their prophets, which became authoritative texts in their communities, alongside the Bible. A notable example is Ursula Meyer, from Bern, whose prophetic words were published and esteemed by her community long after her death. When the Inspirationists emigrated to Iowa, they took her printed prophecies with them. A host of Radical Pietist manuscript writings remain to be explored, including a vast correspondence located in Herrnhut, Halle, and local archives.[6]

Largely unexplored are the social origins of the Radicals. Hirsch's suggestion that they came mainly from the lower, uneducated classes seems misguided; many were lawyers, theologians, and doctors. Eva von Buttlar and the Callenberg sisters were of old, noble background. Many others were craftsmen and apprentices. Schneider called for study of the relation of Radical Pietists to state and society. Some upper-class Radical Pietists disregarded class distinctions and renounced their social status and wealth.[7]

Radical Pietism in Recent Scholarship

The vitality of Radical Pietism research in the past two decades is evident in a recent collection of essays, *Radical Pietism: Research Perspectives*.[8] The book offers a distillation of the latest research on key radical figures, such as Johann Georg Gichtel, Gottfried Arnold, Johann Wilhelm Petersen, Johann Friedrich Rock, and Eberhard Ludwig Gruber, and on social questions such as the roles of women among the Radicals, the practice of marriage and sexuality, and radical views on pacifism. Three of the essays deserve special consideration here, because they address issues touching on the field as a whole.

In his earlier survey of Radical Pietism research, Hans Schneider described the field as still largely unknown and unexplored territory.[9] More than twenty-five years later, in "Retrospect and Prospect," Schneider reports a much improved situation, with a host of articles and monographs appearing in the intervening years on the Ephrata Cloister, Conrad Bröske, the Eva Buttlar Society, Johann Konrad Dippel, Johann Georg Gichtel, Johann Wilhelm and Johanna Eleonora Petersen, Johann Jakob Schütz, and the Schwarzenau New Baptists. Several of these studies are in English.[10]

Schneider wonders whether Wallmann's three-fold characterization of Pietism—conventicles, hopes for better times, and biblical devotion—is comprehensive enough to include all Radical figures. For the Spiritualist Eberhard Ludwig Gruber (1665–1728), all forms of community, even conventicle meetings, were suspect. One finds no inclination toward "hopes for better times" in the Quietist Charles Hector de Marsay (1688–

1753). And sometimes biblical devotion also seems to be lacking. Some Spiritualist Radical Pietists were marked by their experience of the inner word, not study of the outer word. Among communities of the True Inspiration, the living prophetic word took priority over the word of scripture.[11]

Schneider grants that the notion of Radical Pietism is imprecise and multivalent, but this is true of many other historical concepts, such as "early modern" or "liberal." He suggests three criteria for identifying the Radicals: heterodoxy, separatism, and social nonconformity.[12] Important clues to a figure's Radical identity lie in the degree of conformity or deviation from a Reformation Lutheran or Reformed view of the church and in the self-understanding of these figures.

A priority in future research must be unearthing the wealth of material that these Radical Pietists produced, much of it still hidden away in public and private archives.[13] The promised critical edition of Hector de Marsay's autobiography will offer a rich and fascinating primary source.[14] Key figures still await much-deserved treatment, such as Joachim Lange, the prolific Halle Pietist; Andreas Groß, a central figure among Frankfurt separatists; and the anti-Trinitarians Christian Fende and Christoph Seebach.[15] The question of the traditions at work among the Radical Pietists is still an open one. Some studies point to the importance of Jakob Böhme's thought and writings for the Radicals; others highlight the Spiritualism of Caspar Schwenckfeld, Valentin Weigel, and Johann Arndt; still others note Labadie's importance. A key feature of the Radicals was their eclecticism.[16] Finally, a constellation of questions remains surrounding collective memory and identity, uses of history, forms of communication, social background, and notions of family, marriage, and gender in Radical Pietism.[17]

In his essay "Church and Radical Pietism—toward a Basic Distinction," Johannes Wallmann raises two questions for researchers of Radical Pietism. Are there significant gaps in the field that need to be addressed? And which form of Pietism had historical priority, Church Pietism or Radical Pietism? The most serious area of neglect, for Wallmann, is the lack of attention to Jean de Labadie (1610–1674) and the Labadists. Relying on newly discovered letters from the Amsterdam Labadist Anna Maria van Schurman to Johann Jakob Schütz, Wallmann argues for Labadie as the father of Frankfurt Pietism. It is surprising, therefore, that the new four-volume *History of Pietism* (published between 1993 and 2004) neglects Labadie almost entirely.[18] For Wallmann, the minimal mention of Labadie means that the key point of connection between Dutch and German Pietism is missing. It also serves to shift the weight of importance from Radical Pietism to Church Pietism during the movement's early years. Wallmann suggests that the artist, naturalist, and Labadist Maria Sibylla Merian (1647–1717), daughter of the Frankfurt publisher Matthäus Merian, is "possibly the best known of all early Radical Pietist figures."[19] She and her family were close friends of Schütz. Yet, Maria Sibylla Merian is also missing from the new *History of Pietism*.

On whether Church Pietism or Radical Pietism had historical priority, Emanuel Hirsch's view was that Church Pietism began with Spener and Radical Pietism with Jakob Böhme. They were two distinct movements, with Radical Pietism having the priority by about fifty years.[20] The new *History of Pietism* gives implicit priority to Church Pietism when it traces its beginnings back to Johann Arndt and suggests that Radical Pietism arose later as a deviation from Spener. But Wallmann sees Schütz as the source of key Pietist notions of separate meetings of the godly and the imminent reign of Christ on earth. Schütz was a Radical from the beginning, seeking to establish a community of true Christians drawn from all confessions, and whose faith was grounded solely in the Bible.[21] Schütz was profoundly influenced by non-Lutheran sources, especially the Labadists. Wallmann argues for at least the simultaneity of the two forms of Pietism in Frankfurt, and preferably the priority of Radical Pietism.[22]

Radical Pietism was the original form of Pietism in other regions as well. In the lower Rhine and Westphalia, the first Pietists were Labadists; in Württemberg, the early leaders were the Radical separatists Ludwig Brunnquell and Johann Jakob Zimmermann; in Bavaria, it was Radical Pietists who were most influential; in Bern, Radical Pietists played the most important roles at the beginning; in Denmark and Norway, the early leader was the Radical Otto Glüsing; in Sweden, Johann Konrad Dippel was a key influence; and it was the Frankfurt Land Company, under Schütz's leadership, that sent the first Pietists to Germantown, Pennsylvania. Wallmann concludes that in all of these places, Radical Pietism was the original, genuine form of Pietism.[23]

In his contribution "The Long-term Consequences of the German Churches' Exclusion of Radical Pietism," Hartmut Lehmann considers the implications of the decision of early modern German authorities to persecute those who followed their religious conscience. Lehmann asks a question that goes to the heart of the conflicts engendered by Pietism: "Why did there exist among Evangelical Christians in Germany in the centuries after the Reformation so little brotherly and sisterly love, so little tolerance, so little respect for other opinions and other forms of Christian life?" The question is all the more pressing when one contrasts Germany with the situation in Britain and North America. After the Glorious Revolution of 1688–1689, nonconformist religious groups in Britain were tolerated and able to grow and thrive alongside the established Anglican Church. This is illustrated by the rise of Methodism and the Quakers. By 1700, Britain had "a modified form of religious pluralism."[24] In the United States, constitutional separation of church and state and religious freedom were guaranteed by the First Amendment of 1791. This provision was gradually added to the various state constitutions as well, resulting in religious pluralism and denominationalism and a free and open market of competing religious services.[25]

In German lands after the Thirty Years War, church and state authorities focused on social disciplining and indoctrination, denouncing nonconformists as enemies of the state. Orthodox Protestant leaders controlled three spheres of influence into the eighteenth century: theological faculties at the leading universities, the majority of clergy and leadership positions, and territorial governments and city councils.[26] German authorities persecuted and expelled radical religious groups, forcing them to migrate to tolerant territories, or to wander from territory to territory in search of refuge and acceptance, or to emigrate to the New World. From the seventeenth to nineteenth centuries, German Radicals made their way first to Pennsylvania, then to the Midwestern states and other parts of North America, as well as to southern Russia, Australia, and Latin America. Even in the nineteenth century, the free churches in Germany were labeled "sects" and defamed for their "un-German" forms of religion imported from Britain and America. Yet Radical Pietists brought no disruption or threat to the German state and society; they wanted only to live a consistent Christian life and to prepare for the coming reign of Christ. Rather than *radical*, a better term for them would be *committed* or *consistent* Christians.[27]

Lehmann asks, "What might have happened if, in the Protestant territories of the old Reich in the decades before and after 1700, no decrees were issued forbidding private religious meetings?" It is likely that Germany would have witnessed a differentiation within the Evangelical churches and, eventually, religious pluralism. Because Germany failed to develop a free and open religious market, European Protestantism was deprived of a rich resource of earnest Christian people. Today, Germany and much of Europe are a destination for English and American Evangelical missionaries.[28]

Divergent Expressions of Radical Pietism in the Seventeenth and Eighteenth Centuries

The story of Radical Pietism is a diverse and colorful one, stretching over several generations. The early radicalism of Johann Jakob Schütz and the Saalhof community in Frankfurt was followed by a "second wave" that lasted from 1689 to 1694, characterized by unbridled enthusiasm, millenarian expectations, and conventicle gatherings in which women prophets proclaimed visionary revelations.[29] Pietist Spiritualists and separatist conventicles continued to thrive into the eighteenth century in territories such as Wittgenstein and Ysenburg, with some separatists migrating to the New World.

Radical Pietism in the seventeenth and eighteenth centuries was socially diverse, including a wide array of pastors, scholars, itinerant preachers, polemicists, male and female prophets, and many "bizarre figures and comical groups with foolish ideas."[30] Among its divergent religious expressions were German Philadelphians; Radical theologians such as Heinrich Horch, Samuel König, and Johann Konrad Dippel; separatists in Frankfurt, the Wetterau, and Wittgenstein; the Eva Buttlar Society; the Schwarzenau New Baptists; and the Community of True Inspiration.[31] For some, the language of inner transformation was central; for others, Philadelphian eschatology was central. Some lived by strict communal ethical standards; others followed the inner word of Christ.

These differences reflect the eclectic nature of Pietism and the various influences at work within it. Marcus Meier finds three main "streams of tradition" among Radical Pietists in the year 1700: the pure Spiritualism of the Quakers, the mystical Spiritualism of Johann Arndt and Jakob Böhme, and a third stream represented by Anabaptism and the Mennonites. Also influential were Philadelphians such as Jane Leade. Radical

Pietists with a Lutheran background tended toward forms of mystical Spiritualism; those with a Reformed background tended toward conventicle and sect formation inspired by Labadie, Theodor Undereyck, and the Anabaptists.[32]

Meier notes widely different understandings of baptism among Radical Pietists. The largest group, radicalized through contact with the mystical Spiritualism of Jakob Böhme and Johann Arndt, retained infant baptism as an outward sign. This group included Gottfried Arnold, Hochmann von Hochenau, and Horch. A second group of "pure Spiritualists" came under Quaker influence and took up a Spiritualist perspective that rejected all outward rituals such as baptism and the Lord's Supper. This group included Johann Konrad Dippel and Christoph Seebach. A third group, under Anabaptist influence, affirmed the biblical necessity of baptizing adult believers. This group included Alexander Mack and the Schwarzenau Brethren, who came from a Reformed (Calvinist) background and reinstituted the practice of believer's baptism in August 1708.[33]

Unfortunately, there is no taxonomy for categorizing the Radical Pietists, similar to the one created by George Williams for the sixteenth-century Radical Reformation. Using the ideal types of "sect" and "mystic," Williams distinguished Anabaptists, Spiritualists, and Evangelical Rationalists, with subcategories for each.[34] Such a device is sorely needed in the face of the bewildering variety of Radical Pietists.

A FOURFOLD TYPOLOGY OF EXPRESSIONS OF RADICAL PIETISM

To address this need for a way of categorizing the Radical Pietists, I propose a fourfold typology of the various programs for conversion and renewal within Radical Pietism: the *Spiritualist-Alchemist model*, the *Millennialist model*, the *Conventicle model*, and the *Sect model*. This typology reflects the sociological categories of mystic and sect, as well as differences based on theology and degrees of conformity to traditional Protestant churches.[35] Some Radicals stressed conversion and personal transformation; some stressed the end times and millennial expectations; others highlighted the experience of fellowship in the priesthood of all believers; still others focused on founding a new church with new offices and born-again membership. The first two models, the Spiritualist-Alchemist and the Millennialist, held their radical views in tension with conformity to traditional Lutheran or Reformed worship and sacraments. The last two, the Conventicle and Sect models, took their radical views a step further, renouncing ties to traditional churches and exploring new forms of community. These four models of Radical Pietism are summarized in table 6.1.

The Spiritualist-Alchemist model of Gottfried Arnold was marked by the inward hearing of God's word and the believer's transformation into the new man and new woman, without regard for boundaries of denomination or confession. The Millennialist model of Johann Wilhelm and Johanna Eleonora Petersen had two distinctive features: the imminent conversion of Muslims and Jews and the dawning of the Philadelphian age of Christian unity and peace. The Conventicle model of Johann Jakob Schütz and Johann Henrich Reitz is reflected in Reitz's conversion accounts in his *History of the Reborn*. Reitz highlighted "the special meetings and gatherings of the pious where they train each other, confer with each other, question each other, teach and admonish each other, comfort each other and discipline each other, and do so with brotherly unity, love, submission, patience and meekness."[36] The meetings were often dominated by women prophets who brought God's word of rebuke or comfort to the assembled hearers. Finally, the Sect model of the Schwarzenau New Baptists and the Moravians is marked by God's call to forsake family and world in order to serve and obey Christ in his community.[37] Church offices and sacraments were renewed according to God's calling and direction.

The advantage of this typology is that it identifies four distinct families or types of Radical Pietists, bringing some order to the diversity and variety among them and adding some nuance to our understanding of the radicals. These four models are comprehensive enough to account for the figures and groups in Hans Schneider's survey of Radical Pietism. Included in the Spiritualist-Alchemist model are itinerant preachers, prophets, and mystics such as Hochmann von Hochenau (1670–1721),[38] Charles Hector de Marsay, the theologian Johann Konrad Dippel, and prophetic loners such as Johannes Tennhardt, Johann Georg Rosenbach, and Johann Maximilian Daut. In the Millennialist model are German Philadelphian pastors such as Ludwig Christoph Schefer, Conrad Bröske, Johann Christian Lange, and Samuel König, all court preachers,[39] along with Radical theologians such as Heinrich Horch. In the Conventicle model are the communities of True Inspiration in the Wetterau, led by Eberhard Lud-

Table 6.1. Four Models of Radical German Pietism

	Spiritualist-Alchemist model	*Millennialist model*	*Conventicle model*	*Sect model*
Best examples	Gottfried Arnold Johann Konrad Dippel	Johanna Eleonora and Johann Wilhelm Petersen	Johann Jakob Schütz Johann Henrich Reitz Johann Friedrich Rock	The New Baptists of Schwarzenau Alexander Mack
Main influences	Caspar Schwenckfeld Johann Arndt Jakob Böhme Valentin Weigel Christian Hoburg	Jane Leade and English Philadelphians Thomas Beverley Joseph Mede and Heinrich Alsted	Jean de Labadie Anna Maria van Schurman Antoinette Bourignon Madame de Guyon Pierre Poiret Theodor Undereyck	Bohemian Brethren Anabaptists, Hutterites, Mennonites, Amish Johann Georg Gichtel
Key features	Inward renewal and new birth; Christian perfection; allegiance to the invisible church of the Spirit; the language of transformation found in Spiritual Alchemy	Critical of conflicts in Reformation churches; looks for the new Philadelphian age of Christian unity and peace	Priesthood of all believers; prominence of women and prophecy; low level of organization	Priesthood of all believers; prominence of women; higher level of organization
	Often conforming to Lutheran worship and sacraments	Often conforming to Lutheran or Reformed worship and sacraments	Separatist, denouncing the worship and practice of Reformation churches	Separatist, denouncing the worship and practice of Reformation churches

Other examples	Hochmann von Hochenau Charles Hector de Marsay Johann Tennhardt Christoph Seebach	Conrad Bröske Heinrich Horch Samuel König Johann Christian Lange Ludwig Christoph Schefer	Andreas Groß Andreas Achilles Gerhard Tersteegen Christian Fende Communities of True Inspiration: Eberhard Ludwig Gruber and Johann Adam Gruber Mother Eva Society Johann Otto Glüsing Johann Friedrich Haug	Georg Conrad Beissel The Ephrata Cloister Peter Becker Christopher Sauer Peter Miller Anna Nitschmann and the Moravians

wig Gruber and Johann Friedrich Rock, which grew to three hundred members, and the Mother Eva Society of Eva von Buttlar, which grew to about seventy members. The Sect model includes the New Baptists under Alexander Mack and the Ephrata Cloister in America.[40]

WHAT THE RADICALS SHARED IN COMMON

This system for classifying radical differences raises the question of what features the various radicals had in common. At least seven features characterized most Radical Pietist groups and figures. First is a strong resonance with the language of personal and cosmic renewal found in Jakob Böhme and Johann Arndt. One can find representatives from all four models who valued the life and writings of Böhme and Arndt. Second is a worldview shaped by the Philadelphian eschatology of Jane Leade and Thomas Beverley and their hopes for Christ's coming kingdom on earth and a new age of harmony, peace, and love.[41] Third is a migratory lifestyle and homelessness in the world. Radicals from all four types, such as Dippel, Horch, Rock, and Beissel, led a migratory life. A fourth feature is the eclecticism of the Radicals as they drew from mystical, alchemical, and Radical Reformation traditions.[42] A fifth common feature is that most Radicals felt free to critique the Reformation heritage and to downplay differences among confessional traditions.[43] A sixth is that many Radicals combined involvement in state churches with critique of those same churches, as they lived "between the paradigms" of confession and renewal. This was the German way of being radical in early modern times.[44] Finally, Radical Pietist groups were marked by women leaders and prophets. The Radical critique of tradition created a new openness to women's voices and involvement.

Some additional features characterized German Radicals who migrated to the New World. These include advocacy of the celibate life as a higher spiritual state; charismatic leaders whom the community held to be divinely inspired; an emphasis on active work rather than contemplation; and communal equality and sharing.[45] These qualities are exemplified in the Ephrata community in Pennsylvania, described later in this chapter.

Portraits of Three Radical Pietist Figures

The diversity among the Radicals can be seen in the life experiences of three contrasting figures: Johann Wilhelm Petersen, Johann Friedrich Rock, and Georg Conrad Beissel. Petersen and Rock represent the Millennialist and Conventicle models, respectively; Beissel represents the Sect model. The focus here is on their migratory and unsettled existence and their encounters with opposition and adversity.

JOHANN WILHELM PETERSEN (1649–1726): HIS MIGRATIONS AND SENSE OF CALLING

Johann Wilhelm Petersen and his wife, Johanna Eleonora Petersen (1644–1724), have been described as "the most fascinating manifestations of Pietist Radicalism."[46] The vast quantity of their writing sets them apart, even in a day of prolific authorship. Some 15 works have been attributed to Johanna and about 150 titles to her husband, who "flooded the German book market" with his tracts, pamphlets, and books. The couple's importance lies in their energetic promotion of views inspired by Jane Leade: a millennialist eschatology and the doctrine of God's final restoration of all things, including the devil and the fallen angels. The Petersens spoke of a threefold gospel: the *gospel of faith* preached by Christ and his disciples; the *gospel of the millennial kingdom,* which Jesus taught in a mystery; and the *eternal gospel* of universal salvation, which God would reveal at the end of time. So effective were the Petersens in bringing these teachings to public attention that Orthodox Lutheran theologians were provoked into vigorous response. The Petersens got a sympathetic hearing from their Brandenburg benefactor, Dodo von Knyphausen, and from numerous followers and admirers in Pietist conventicles throughout northern Germany.[47]

Johann Wilhelm Petersen's travels took him to the courts of Pietist counts and to "awakened circles" in numerous cities.[48] His journeys served to connect him with like-minded friends as far away as southern Germany.[49] Petersen's autobiographical account, *Das Leben Jo. Wilhelmi Petersen* (1717), is a key source for investigating the extent and occasion of his migrations and for examining his dealings with the authorities.[50] Pe-

Johann Wilhelm Petersen, 1717

tersen devoted some fifty pages to detailing his travels (*Das Leben*, 282–333).

Petersen's journeys fall into three parts: his journeys to Altdorf, Nuremberg, Herolsberg, and Württemberg; his trip to Silesia; and finally, his visits to Carlsbad, Zeitz, Halle, and Berlin. These travels reveal the extensive network of friends, acquaintances, and readers that Petersen had developed by the time he wrote his account, at sixty-eight years of age. Unfortunately, Petersen paid little attention to matters of chronology and dating.

A Pietist preacher and friend invited Petersen to travel with him to Nuremberg and Altdorf to visit "the good souls who awaited him" and offer them encouragement. Petersen traveled by postal wagon to Erlangen, where he preached on Jubilate Sunday, with the duke and duchess in attendance. The director of the gymnasium (academic-oriented high school) invited Petersen to stay and serve as inspector of the school, but Petersen declined. He then traveled to Altdorf, where he was invited to attend catechism in the home of Dr. Michael Lange. Lange invited Petersen to attend his public collegium devoted to Paul's Epistle to the Galatians. Lange discussed the biblical passage, noting its context and interpretation; he then invited Petersen, in the presence of other professors, to present his thoughts. Petersen then traveled to Nuremberg in the company of Professor Rötenbeck and was lodged at an inn at the expense of some friends in Nuremberg. A Mr. Winckler invited Petersen to attend a collegium devoted to the Sermon on the Mount. Petersen met over a meal with some preachers who were eager to discuss his views on the kingdom of Christ (282ff., 286–288).

Petersen next traveled to Herolsberg, near Nuremberg,[51] at the invitation of a local nobleman. He was introduced to some leading citizens, including three of the city's clergymen and a physician, Dr. Thomasius. Petersen felt wonderfully renewed in body, soul, and spirit, describing the visit as an experience he would never forget. He was eager to go to Stuttgart, in Württemberg, "where I well knew that there are many pious hearts among whom I could strengthen myself in the Lord." Accompanied on the trip by a Tübingen professor, Petersen took the opportunity to inquire about the customs and ways of the region and the court and to learn about the university. Petersen was impressed by the open-hearted Württembergers, "among whom Christ could work freely" (*Das Leben*, 288–290). He then traveled to Tübingen, where he met with Dr. Johann Wolfgang Jäger, a theology professor, who presented him with two expensive bottles of wine. He also visited Heilbronn and Rotenburg ob der Tauber. Petersen then hurried home, because his wife had written to inform him that he had guests who had traveled from England to speak with him (291, 293ff.).

A second series of trips took Petersen to Silesia. A young student who had visited the Petersens in Nieder-Dodeleben had moved to Silesia to take up the position of *Hofmeister* (court steward). The young man informed Petersen that some Silesians were eager to meet with him. Petersen described the trip as follows:

> I must tell of my trip to Silesia, in which there are many souls who have had opportunity to read my writings, to receive the truth, and to become children of the truth . . . A Hofmeister there wrote to me and told me of the request, from people of both upper and lower station, that I come and speak with them, and of their willingness to gladly pay my travel costs. (308)

Petersen traveled to Sorau (in Niederlausitz, Upper Silesia) in the company of Baron von Löwenstein, who offered the use of his carriage. Petersen instructed neighboring counts and countesses on the meaning of Paul's Epistle to the Romans 1–11. They invited him to preach on Sunday from the Gospel text John 10:12–16. Petersen then went to Breslau, where he was received by a baron and friends and addressed members of the leading families. He was well-loved and respected in Breslau, for he had previously preached and held *Beth-Stunden* (times of prayer and devotion) there. Baron von Löwenstein next accompanied Petersen to Jordans-Mühle and to the court of the count, where he preached at the count's invitation (308–314, 317–319). Finally, Petersen visited Lemberg where he met some Schwenkfelders. He spoke with them and "found much good in their souls." He was convinced that they should be tolerated and not persecuted, for "on the last day there will be a completely different kind of judgment than what we think it will be" (320–322). Petersen reflected on his experiences in Silesia: "I traveled to Silesia because it was the very time when the children there had such an uncommon eagerness for prayer. In the churches of the preachers there I observed wonderful things, such zeal in their devotions and service that I could not watch without being profoundly moved" (318–319). He then returned home to Thymer.[52]

The final series of travels began with his trip to Carlsbad (now in the Czech Republic). "As I am now relating how and when I made some of my journeys, which [people in] other places constantly invite me to undertake, I must now explain what happened when my wife and I drove to Carlsbad" (324). This was unlike Petersen's other trips. The driver of a postal coach on his way to Prague took the Petersens with him for about eight miles; he let them off at an inn and continued on to his destination. The Petersens conversed with the Jewish innkeepers, who listened with interest to the Petersens' views on the messiah. These hospitable owners successfully procured horses and a carriage so that the Petersens could continue on their way to Carlsbad.

The Petersens next set out for Zeitz at the invitation of a preacher who had written to say they were bidden to visit the ducal court; the duke, a learned and wise man, was eager to speak with them. Petersen also held conversations with the city preachers and superintendent in Zeitz (325ff.).[53] From there they traveled to Halle, at one time a frequent destination for the Petersens because of the blessing they experienced among the Halle Pietists. But Halle's Pietist leaders had spoken out against the teaching of the *Wiederbringung aller Dinge* (God's restoration of all things), and the Petersens felt increasingly estranged from the city.

A couple of factors account for Petersen's many travels. Most of these trips were at the invitation of people who sought his presence, instruction, and encouragement. Many of these people had read his books and knew of his reputation. Petersen visited their communities as an invited guest and was welcomed as a celebrity. He received gifts of wine, books, and free lodging, either in local inns or in castles and private homes.

Another factor was the Petersens' desire to spread the eternal gospel of the restoration of all things, the *Wiederbringung aller Dinge*. The Petersens were on a mission to spread this teaching as far and wide as possible (*Das Leben*, 297).[54] Petersen's account of his travels includes a ten-page *Excursus* in which he describes how he and his wife first encountered the teaching. In 1694 their Brandenburg benefactor, Baron von Knyphausen, received a book from England written by Jane Leade, entitled *Concerning the Eight Worlds*, which contained Leade's views on the universal restoration of all creation. The baron asked the Petersens to read it and to give their opinion. The Spirit of God showed them that Leade was right. "We came to understand that God is essentially love, and that his unending mercy would pour itself out on all his creation." Petersen was convinced that the eternal gospel would turn many from their atheism, from Papism, and from Reformed Calvinism and its doctrine of predestination (299, 304–307).

Petersen kept account of who accepted the teaching on the coming universal restoration and who did not. In Stuttgart, for example, he found a receptive audience for the doctrine in General Superintendent Johann Andreas Hochstetter (1637–1720), as well as some nobility and other leading citizens. Petersen mentioned the Inspirationist leader Eberhard Ludwig Gruber as one who accepted "the testimony to the truth" (290, 292). A Berlin councilor, Baron Paul von Fuchs (1640–1704), promoted Petersen's book on the subject, and Petersen's benefactor Baron von Knyphausen was an enthusiastic supporter of the teaching. Petersen worked the restoration teaching into his explanation of Romans before the counts and countesses in Silesia and found that "they were convinced" (296, 299, 313).

Many, however, spoke and wrote against the doctrine. Petersen was disappointed to learn that Pietists in Halle had decided to let it be known publicly that they were not in agreement with the teaching of the restoration of all things. Professor Johann Friedrich Mayer (1650–1712) of Hamburg and Greifswald was Petersen's most vigorous opponent, along with Ferdinand Helfreich Lichtscheid, provost in Berlin, whom Petersen called "*Licht-Scheuenden*"—"light-shunning" (327, 329).[55] Petersen continued to travel and speak, hoping for the day when others would realize the truth of the teaching and become his supporters rather than his enemies. "I hope a time will come when they [his enemies] will realize these truths that I have discovered by God's grace, and then prefer me" rather than oppose (*Das Leben*, 328, 301). Petersen was pleased that although Spener had not come out on behalf of the restoration of all things, at least he had promised Petersen that he would not write against it. As Peterson recorded, Spener said he, too, hoped that in the end, the whole world would be saved (330).

Another factor in Petersen's many travels was the example of the French prophets, or French Inspired, whom he admired and took as a model for his own migrations. Petersen pointed to the work of the French Inspired and their travels throughout German lands.

> The French Inspired . . . have traveled far and wide to kingdoms and principalities and to various cities, and have proclaimed the judgment of God. They have awakened some in Germany, although they sometimes have mixed in things which they should not have done . . . I have seen some of them in Halberstadt, and I credit two of the Inspired who visited me in Thymer as authentic witnesses of God. I warned them that they bear the treasure in earthen vessels and should not ruin it, but prove all things. (333)

Petersen was greatly impressed with the German Inspirationist Eberhard Ludwig Gruber and his 1716 tract, *On True and False Inspiration* (*Das Leben*, 334).[56]

Petersen's Dealings with the Authorities

Petersen never missed an opportunity to mention in his autobiography the invitations and hospitality he received at the hands of church and city officials as well as from the nobility, including counts, dukes, barons, and princes. In Stuttgart, Petersen was treated as though he were nobility himself. He was invited to a gathering of the *Land-Ständen* (estates general), which included numerous abbots and prelates. A princess invited him to her court.

> I obtained a gracious invitation to visit the court of an elderly princess when she was holding her prayer hour along with all her court . . . I have often spoken to her and other members of her retinue. She opened up her special chamber of rarities and showed me some amazing things, of which there were many. In sum, they showed me every honor that one could possibly show to a special person whom one loved. (*Das Leben*, 290)

Petersen was also introduced to some members of the Stuttgart *Geheimer Rat* (privy council), to General Superintendent Hochstetter, and to the senior pastor Weißmann and his son, who showed Petersen much kindness. The court's coach was made available to him for the journey to his next destination, Tübingen.

Petersen traveled through Silesia in the company of Baron von Löwenstein in the baron's own chaise. The baron accompanied Petersen to Jordans-Mühle and to the court of the count, where he preached at the count's invitation. In Halle, Petersen was welcomed into the home of privy councilor Hazeln, a regular meeting place for Pietist gatherings. Petersen was also a frequent visitor to the estates of J. E. von Naumeister, a friend of August Hermann Francke, and of Carl Christian von Goldstein (b. 1678). Von Goldstein had an interest in the writings of Gichtel and was a supporter of Halle's missionary efforts (317–320, 325–327).[57]

Petersen saw it as divine providence that he was able to win the favor of powerful people and thereby smooth the way for his teaching. Opponents frequently sought to convince the authorities that his teachings were dangerous. In 1701 Corvinus called the teachings a renewal of the errors of Münster. But when Petersen was with the Queen of Prussia and with Paul von Fuchs of the Berlin privy council, he had the opportunity to discuss theological matters. Von Fuchs stated that he could not believe that God's condemnation of sinners would last forever. When Petersen agreed and explained that this was precisely what he taught in his books, von Fuchs said he would gladly support Petersen's right to teach on these matters. Soon Petersen's *The Restoration of All Things* was available in every bookstore in Berlin (*Das Leben*, 294–297).

JOHANN FRIEDRICH ROCK (1678–1749): HIS MIGRATIONS AND PROPHETIC CONSCIOUSNESS

The Community of True Inspiration was truly "a peripatetic church." Its prophets and missionaries, notably Johann Friedrich Rock and his two assistants, traveled about on foot for months and years at a time. One missionary group from this community made its way across northern Germany to Berlin and on to Prague and Breslau, back to Saxony, Thuringia, and Württemberg, and then to Alsace and Switzerland. The community itself migrated from territory to territory, due to persecutions and expulsions, finally emigrating to North America and settling along the Iowa River.[58]

Johann Friedrich Rock was the migratory Pietist *par excellence*.[59] Between 1715 and 1742, Rock made at least ninety-four journeys to establish new communities and to encourage members of the Community of True Inspiration. Of these, forty-three were short trips within the Wittgenstein region; twenty-seven were to Württemberg to establish prayer communities in Calw, Stuttgart, Göppingen, and Heilbronn; the rest were to Switzerland, the Pfalz, Thuringia, and Saxony.[60] Rock and his fellow wandering prophets followed the example of the French prophets and their many missionary travels from France to England, the Netherlands, Germany, Poland, Sweden, and even Asia Minor. The French prophets were especially active in Berlin and Halle, where they formed conventicles in the early 1700s.[61]

Rock's two main autobiographical accounts are *Beginnings of the Journey of Humility of a Sinner on Earth in and by God's Grace* (1707) and *A Second*

Account of the Journey of Humility of a Sinner on Earth (1717), written when he was twenty-nine and thirty-nine years old, respectively.[62] In two short additional accounts in 1715 and 1726, Rock told the story of how he founded the Community of the Inspired.[63] He identified himself in these writings as *I.F.R.*, meaning "Johann Friedrich Rock" or "*In Fort-währendem Reisen*" (always on the road) or "*In Fried und Ruh*" (in peace and tranquility).[64]

Rock's *Beginnings of the Journey of Humility* (1707) is structured geographically by the cities he visited over the course of his life. He was born in a village in Ober-Welden, Württemberg, near Göppingen, where his father, Johann Heinrich Rock (1641–1693), served as a Lutheran preacher. Here Johann Friedrich learned the trade of harness maker. As a young man his work took him to the Catholic city of Rastadt, where he experienced his "first awakening" and sorrow for sin, while reading a devotional book. He then moved to Halle in Saxony, where he began attending church and was brought to a second awakening and repentance for his sins and vices. He found work in Berlin but did not intend to remain there long. While in Berlin he endured a period of illness that resulted in his decision to avoid bad company and to join a group of people known as "Pietists." Rock was impressed by their single-minded devotion to God. At his mother's urging, Rock returned home to Stuttgart. She and his brother soon came to share his faith.[65] The time frame for this period of his life is 1696–1702.[66]

The reason for these early travels seemed to be a youthful yearning for adventure: "I set out on my travels." Rock's narrative concluded with some hymns in which he used the imagery of journey and migration. He saw his travels as a spiritual pilgrimage that would lead him to eternal rest with God. "I will follow your word until you bring me to the heavenly gate." "I will not stop on my short pilgrim way until I am singing your faithfulness in eternity." "I will continue! I will forever praise you, till I arrive in that new city of God; transfigured I will behold you, three in one."[67]

Rock's *Second Account of the Journey of Humility* (1717) is likewise structured geographically.[68] Calling his life story "a journey of humiliation and degradation" (*Erniedrigungs-Lauff*), he recounted his "awakening, and manifold battle, conflict, and victory" during his first three years as leader of the Inspirationists, from 1715 to 1717 ("Zweyter Aufsatz," 19). The story repeats some events in his earlier account; these will not be repeated here. Rock returned home to his mother in Württemberg after being away for six years (1696–1702). From 1703 to 1707 he worked in a harness shop in Stuttgart. During this time he began to associate with a separatist group, attracting antagonism and persecution from both the preachers and the ruling authorities. In the summer of 1707, the magistrate imprisoned Rock for eighteen days, releasing him with a warning that he either attend the parish church or be banished. Rock reported, "We chose the latter" (26ff.).

Rock and his mother made their way to Ysenburg, where they lived from 1707 to 1715.[69] There a community of Inspirationists was established, under the leadership of Eberhard Ludwig Gruber. For two years Rock engaged with Gruber in discussion and debate and had his first encounters with prophetic speaking. In November 1714, at age thirty-six, Rock decided to join with Gruber; this marked the beginning of his itinerant career and speaking in God's name. "And so the Lord drew me to this work with the cords of his love; otherwise, I would never have been set aside for this, much less employed in traveling and speaking in the name of my God." At this point, Rock's own prophetic gift enters the account. He experienced the overpowering love, grace, and peace of God, shaking in his body and breaking out in shouts of joy, laughter, and praise ("Zweyter Aufsatz," 32). In 1715 God assured other members of the group that in his grace and mercy, he had entrusted his word to Rock, revealing his truth to Rock in his heart. In 1728, with Gruber's death, Rock assumed leadership of the Community of True Inspiration. Of some twelve women and men in the community who received the gift of prophecy, only Rock exercised the gift throughout his whole life, for more than thirty years (34, 36).[70]

The main body of Rock's second autobiography, the *Zweyter Aufsatz*, is a twenty-five page account of his prophetic journeys from 1715 to 1717 on behalf of communities of the Inspired; it is divided into shorter and longer journeys. At first, Rock made small trips of just a few hours to Büdingen, the Ronneburg castle, Gedern, Frankfurt, Himbach, Eschborn, Frankfurt again, Keltersbach, and Itzstein. These early trips were difficult, because the Inspirationists were still distrustful of Rock; they remembered a time when he had often opposed them. Rock was initially hesitant to admit God's call to speak in his name and reluctant to assume the mantle of "prophet." He later insisted that it was something he did not seek. He gradually came to see that "when God's gracious urging came, then I had to follow," or risk losing God's grace and favor. God assured him that it was a gift given to him for the benefit of his neighbor ("Zweyter Aufsatz," 38–43).

Rock wrote that he journeyed "always in fears . . . and frequently exhausted by various testings, battles, and temptations [*Anfechtungen*] from within and without; but the Lord always provided" just what he needed (43). When Rock traveled to Eschborn, he went with a Mr. Schwanfelder and Mr. Hagin. He avoided going with the prophet Ursula Mayer because he was always hesitant about journeying with women. He traveled with two community brothers to Birstein and Büdingen. Further travels took him to Vogelsberg, Frankfurt, Laubach, Göppingen, Düdelsheim, Stuttgart, Laubach, Oehringen, and Lindheim. In each of these places, God directed him to speak his word; this often involved delivering a message from God to a specific person. In Vogelsberg, Rock converted the pregnant wife of a believing miller; in Laubach, Rock was used to deliver Brother Becken from an illness due to his pride. In Düdelsheim, Rock visited a brother who was seriously ill in order to speak a word of God's grace to him. A short time later, the man was eating and feeling much better. In Laubach, God enabled Rock to reveal to a Mr. Reich his sin of unbelief, whereupon he converted. In Oehringen and Lindheim, Rock warned two preachers not to teach falsehood anymore; the Lindheim preacher died ten days later (48–51, 55ff.).

Rock's longer journeys began in Ulm, "a dark and gloomy region," which his brothers warned him against: "it will go badly for you there." In Ulm he found that the few people who had some knowledge of God were in a miserable condition, living in fear of the severity of the Ulm preachers and ruling authorities (56). Rock next traveled in rain and snow to Weissenburg am Sand, to Regensburg, to Schwäbisch Hall, and, reluctantly, again to Ulm. For six weeks, during terrible weather, he and his companions went from inn to inn, spending only one night with friends. In Ulm, Rock and his companions faced the enmity and threats of the city council, soldiers, and territorial lord, and were condemned to eight days in prison (59).

With trepidation Rock then set out for Augsburg and Memmingen. God directed him to stay overnight in the Black Eagle Inn in Memmingen, where Rock met and converted a dyer and his wife. After a time back in Schwarzenau, in Wittgenstein, Rock set out again for Memmingen, a trip of some forty to fifty miles. In Lindau they again encountered trouble with the authorities (61–63).[71]

The occasion for these many travels was Rock's sense of God's leading. One day he awoke feeling sick, with a severe headache. While sitting at the table and singing a hymn with his mother, Rock felt God's urging to make a trip. "I received the word, 'You must go to Eschborn.'" When he told his mother, she immediately protested: "You are sick and the weather is bad." (It was a few weeks before Easter, Rock explained.) But he set out anyway, and in a few hours he felt well again. He was in Eschborn for only a day when God told him, "You must go to Frankfurt." The message was confirmed for Rock by a brother among the Inspired in Eschborn. And so it went with Rock's migratory life. Rock described his experience of God's presence as lying in a sleep, in the castle of his heart, and feeling his heart warmed by God's love and made quiet, still, and peaceful. Such a peace could last for hours. He also described God's leading as soft movements "such as a child might feel in its mother's womb before it is born" ("Zweyter Aufsatz," 42–44).

Rock wished he could perform miracles and signs and wonders, like the apostles and prophets of old, when the preachers challenged him to prove his calling. But he had to learn to be satisfied with God's "small droplets of grace" and not to crave great things (40ff.). When a Stuttgart physician, Dr. Kayser, expressed doubts about Rock's prophetic gift, Rock's reply was emphatic: "Howl or write, scold or torment, By grace I am the child of God. Let the high priest think what he will. I bear in me the word of God." Near the end of his life, Rock reflected, "The Spirit, who proceeds from the Father and the Son, has been poured out in my heart; it is he who has driven me to testify. I have followed him now for twenty-four years, and he has become my guarantee and seal."[72]

Rock's Dealings with the Authorities

Rock's encounters and dealings with church and civic authorities form a regular refrain in his accounts. He referred to being "often persecuted and hunted up and down the country" by his enemies. His life was full of troubles, a valley of misery. For Rock, the authorities represented the devil and his spiritual enemies, because they opposed his prophetic words. One of Rock's great triumphs was in Keltersbach, where he converted the son of the *Schultheiss* (president of the city council).

> I felt moved to address a room full of all kinds of people as brands from hell and children of the devil. When they began to murmur among themselves and threaten to attack me, I had to go with my arms extended out against them. They intended to beat me, but no one could do anything because God protected me. Then the son of the Schultheiss was awakened and turned from his sins to God, and immediately began to experience the hatred of this world. ("Zweyter Aufsatz," 20, 43)

Rock recounted a meeting with the rector in Birstein who had knowledge of the truth. He also met the count, who was likewise sympathetic and a witness to God's grace (47). But these were unusual cases.

Rock experienced the opposition of the ruling authorities primarily in Ulm, Lindau, and Kassel. Fearful but determined, he returned to Ulm to support his brothers who suffered under persecution. Soon after Rock and his companions arrived at the inn, they were taken away by five soldiers to the city hall and thrown into prison, where they remained for eight days. Rock said that he never slept better in his life than he did in that prison. God made his heart a home of joy and love. In Lindau, God revealed to Rock that he should issue a testimony to the priests, the ruling authorities, and the whole city. Under the leading of God, Rock and his brother attended the Tuesday church service, and there they spoke a word of prophecy in the hearing of all. Soon after, they were visited in the inn by two soldiers, arrested, and thrown into prison. Rock interpreted the events in St. Paul's words: "we battled with the wild beasts." When he was interrogated by a council member, Rock's loving disposition won over the council member and he became their friend (59, 62ff.). In Kassel, Rock and his companions spent three and a half days in a terrible, stinking prison. They were then driven out into the cold by three to five soldiers who beat them with rods, until they came to Marburg and were placed in the main prison. There they suffered not only cursing and mockery but also severe beatings. Rock said it was the worst treatment he had ever received in all his travels (65).[73]

Petersen and Rock visited many of the same regions and cities, but their experiences and reception by the authorities were dramatically different. Petersen was welcomed as a celebrity and had a host of influential friends. Rock was persecuted, "hunted up and down the country," and imprisoned in four towns. One reason for the difference lies in their social stations. Petersen was a doctor of theology, a former pastor and superintendent, and a prolific author; Rock was a sattler, a harness maker. Another factor is the way they acted out their calling. Petersen was the edifying teacher and celebrity who proclaimed the good news of universal salvation and avoided denunciations of pastors and churches.[74] Rock was the inspired prophet who proclaimed the bad news of God's coming judgment.

RADICAL PIETISM IN AMERICA: GEORG CONRAD BEISSEL (1691–1768), FOUNDER OF EPHRATA, PENNSYLVANIA

Early modern German authorities followed a consistent policy of persecution and expulsion of members of radical religious groups who followed their conscience in matters of faith, denouncing them as enemies of the state. It is no surprise, therefore, that many of these earnest Christians chose the option of migrating to the New World.[75] Some three to five thousand members of Radical Pietist communities were among the hundred thousand Germans and Swiss who emigrated to North America between 1683 and 1800, for religious and economic reasons. The most significant numerically were the Moravians and New Baptists, or Dunkers. The German sects typically kept to themselves, settling in distinct enclaves throughout the Pennsylvania countryside.[76]

Representative of these Radical Pietist migrants is the story of Georg Conrad Beissel and the community he established in Pennsylvania. Historians have a rich collection of sources at their disposal for investigating the life of Beissel and the community at Ephrata. Two contemporary narrative accounts offer very different perspectives on Beissel. *The Ephrata Chronicle* of 1786, edited by Peter Miller, is the key source but tends toward hagiography.[77] Also valuable is the autobiography of Ezechiel Sangmeister (1724–1786), a disgruntled opponent of Beissel: *The Life and Conduct of Brother Ezechiel Sangmeister, a Longtime Resident of Ephrata.*[78] Beissel was an author in his own right, especially after 1742. He composed hymns, devotional writings, mystical proverbs and poems, letters, 67 *Spiritual Speeches (Geistliche Reden)*, and a major work entitled *A Dissertation on Man's Fall.*[79]

Georg Conrad Beissel was born on March 1, 1691, in Eberbach in the Palatinate, the tenth child of a baker. His father, Matthias Beusel, died before Conrad was born, and his mother died when he was just eight years old. The family was Reformed. Conrad grew up in circumstances of poverty and war. While still in his youth, he was apprenticed to a baker and spent time as a journeyman in Mannheim, Strasbourg, and Heidelberg.[80]

In the early eighteenth century there was intense Pietist activity in and around the city of Heidelberg, with itinerant preachers coming and going. One of these was Matthias Baumann, who separated from the Reformed church after a series of visions in June 1701. Other preachers included Johann Georg Rosenbach, Hochmann von Hochenau, and Alexander Mack. These Pietist circles were also exposed to the writings of Jakob Böhme and Jane Leade. After studying the Bible and the works of Böhme, Beissel experienced a conversion at a Pietist meeting in 1715. By this time, authorities were harassing and arresting Reformed Pietists out of concern for the large and growing number who were responding to the Pietist message. In 1718 Beissel was forced to leave Heidelberg. He found refuge with Jacob Schatz, a baker in Düdelsheim who belonged to the Community of True Inspiration.[81]

In 1720 Beissel and four friends sailed on the ship *Elizabeth and Hannah,* arriving in Boston in October of that year. He made his way to Philadelphia with the hope of joining Johannes Kelpius (1673–1708) and the hermit community Kelpius had started near Germantown, called the Woman in the Wilderness. Beissel arrived only to find the community had disbanded.[82] He spent the next year in Germantown as an apprentice to the weaver and New Baptist leader Peter Becker (1687–1758). Becker had emigrated to Pennsylvania from Krefeld the year before, along with twenty families of New Baptists.[83]

In 1722 Beissel moved to Conestoga, Pennsylvania, newly settled by Swiss and German Mennonites and other groups. For a year he lived in a cabin on Mill Creek as part of a communal household with some other young men. In November 1724, Peter Becker arrived in Conestoga during a preaching mission through the Pennsylvania countryside. In the ensuing revival, Beissel and six others were baptized by Becker. The fledgling Dunker congregation in Conestoga chose Beissel as its leader, reflecting the love and admiration the sectarians felt toward him. He quickly established principles that would guide his future religious life: he observed the Sabbath on Saturday, the seventh day, and he upheld celibacy as superior to marriage. Beissel's teachings brought conflict with the other Dunkers, and in 1725 Beissel and some supporters established a community on the farm of Rudolf Nägele, a former Mennonite whom Beissel had baptized. In December 1728, Beissel "reenacted" the baptism he and six others had received from Becker, marking their definitive break from Becker and the Dunkers.[84]

In February 1732, Beissel withdrew to a solitary life in a cabin on Cocalico Creek, in what is now Lancaster County, Pennsylvania. Soon joined by members of his former congregation, he established the Ephrata community, or Ephrata Cloister.[85] Beissel organized the Order of Spiritual Virgins for single women and the Zionitic Brotherhood for single men. Over the next ten years, the community continued to grow through Beissel's evangelistic efforts; two of his converts were sons of Alexander Mack, leader of the New Baptists. This period saw a building boom, with construction of monastic houses for sisters (Kedar and Sharon) and brothers (Zion and Bethany), houses for families, and chapels. At its peak in 1755, the Ephrata community numbered three to four hundred residents, comprising celibate men and women and some families. The community owned all the land within a radius of three to four miles. Members farmed and built an industrial center with sawmill, paper mill, oil mill, fulling mill, tannery, and weaving enterprises. Beissel died on July 6, 1768, his last years marred by illness and conflicts over his successor and ownership of the cloister's land. When the last nun died, in 1813, Ephrata was reorganized as the German Seventh-Day Baptist Church.[86]

The principles guiding the religious life of Ephrata can be found in Beissel's *Maxims* and *Rules of the Solitary Life*. The themes of poverty, humility, and acceptance of adversity are prominent. "In all your doings carry yourself as poor and as a possessor of nothing in this world." "A solitary life, which is separated from the world and creatures, ought to be your greatest treasure, for we can easily forfeit our fortune in this world."[87] "Everything which presents itself to you, be it small or great, prosperous or lean, severe or mild, should not cause you to be moved by too great a joy nor too great a sorrow; rather, balance." "In all things be careful and thoughtful, and dwell only on those things which benefit your salvation and peace." "At all times listen rather than speak, for the ears of the wise are attentive; but the fool's heart is on his tongue."[88]

Beissel gradually introduced distinctive rituals and dress to Ephrata. Between 1735 and 1740 he required that celibate members wear common clothing as a symbol of unity. It consisted of a long white habit with wide sleeves and pointed monk's hood for men and a similar habit with rounded hood for women. In 1740 Beissel appointed a date when the celibate brothers would read vows of eternal chastity and receive the tonsure, a symbol of betrothal to Christ/Sophia. On the same day, the sisters also read vows and had their hair cut short. Beissel established ascetic rituals for the celibates that included fasting, reduced sleep, and frequent times of prayer. Other practices included baptism of believers by threefold immersion, foot washing and the love feast, the Eucharist, and the holy kiss.[89]

The Ephrata community inherited the love feast celebration from Alexander Mack and the Schwarzenau New Baptists, who based it on New Testament accounts of the Last Supper and the early Christian practice of love feasts described by Gottfried Arnold. The love feast looked forward to the great wedding banquet of the Lamb at the last judgment, described in Revelation 19. The ritual consisted of foot washing, a common meal, and celebration of the Eucharist. The meal was preceded by a sermon by Beissel, calling for self-examination and repentance, in accordance with I Corinthians 11. The love feasts could last several hours, sometimes going past midnight. They were held regularly, averaging sixteen times a year, according to Sangmeister. They were also held to mark special occasions, such as the consecration of a new building or the death of a member of the community. The love feast reinforced an awareness of God's covenantal presence and the sense of a common identity that marked the Ephrata community as distinct from other colonial Christians.[90]

Another unique feature of Ephrata was the understanding of gender. Beissel taught a notion he derived from Jakob Böhme, that God possessed a perfect balance of male and female attributes, with Sophia representing the female dimension of God. God created the first humans in his image, with both genders, but this duality was lost at the Fall in the Garden of Eden. The mystical language of Ephrata spoke of spiritual rebirth through marriage with heavenly Sophia, whereby men and women regained their missing female and male qualities.[91] An attitude of submission in interpersonal relationships was upheld for men as well as for women. The community encouraged women to live a celibate life as Sisters of Sharon, free from the rule of husbands and fathers. The sisters experienced a degree of autonomy that included their own living and worship space, their own leaders, and some economic independence. Around 1736, Maria Eicher (1710–1784) became prioress of the sisters, serving for more than twenty-five years. She was called "Mother" and women's "Director," corresponding to Beissel's titles of "Father" and "Superintendent," and was second only to Beissel in the power she held within the community.[92]

This unusual mystical group had an exceptionally vibrant cultural life. The Ephrata community became famous for its handcrafts, including embroidery, *Fraktur* calligraphy, painting, and spinning and weaving. Beissel was an outstanding musician and hymn writer, composing more than a thousand hymns, of which 441 were printed. The Ephrata Cloister established one of the earliest German print shops in the New World in 1745. The shop produced forty-three German books, including the entire *Martyrs' Mirror* in 1748 at the request of some Mennonites. The *Martyrs' Mirror* was the largest book published in the American colonies before the Revolution—a folio volume of 1,482 pages in fine calf binding. A long tradition says that fourteen of the cloister's brothers worked on it for three years: six in the paper mill, four as typesetters, and four as printers. Peter Miller, prior of the cloister, translated it from Dutch into German. Beissel directed and coordinated the undertaking. The German edition of the *Martyrs' Mirror* has been called "the most precious German book that was published in the eighteenth century in the German language in America."[93] W. R. Ward's words capture the unique world that was Ephrata: "The Ephrata community [was] an extraordinary centre of music and cultural achievement, of spiritual sweetness and practical help to neighbors, of spiritual impulses which issued in revival, of theosophy, alchemy and magic."[94]

Beissel's piety was an eclectic blend of Jakob Böhme's theology of new birth, Radical Pietist devotion and love, the visions of the Inspirationists, the teachings of Peter Becker and the Dunkers, and the practices of the Mennonites. "Many groups influenced Beissel, but he never embraced any fully."[95] Like Böhme, Beissel used mystical language imbued with symbols from alchemy, astrology, and magic to communicate the truths of spiritual rebirth and union with God. A contemporary called Beissel "a spiritual alchemist" who brought forth the gold of faith. He was a man of "lively imagination, great energy and inspiring eloquence, especially when the Spirit came upon him."[96]

A summary of Beissel's beliefs is found in his *Dissertation on Man's Fall*, first published in 1765. The work reveals how deeply rooted his beliefs concerning God, sin, and salvation were in the thought and writings of Böhme. Beissel understood the believer's spiritual rebirth in terms of two conversions: the first conversion is an awakening to sin and condemnation; the second is a mystical death to the Law and new life in the Spirit. For Beissel, the true church is marked by the Spirit of prophecy, as opposed to the "Babel churches" in Europe where the Holy Spirit and prophecy have been lost. The true church is also marked by suffering. "We must pass through many tribulations into the kingdom of God" (Acts 14:22). Like Johann Georg Gichtel, Jane Leade, and the Petersens, Beissel saw reborn believers as priests of Melchizedek commissioned to lead others to faith and forgiveness through their prayers.[97]

The themes of migration and adversity are prominent for Beissel, just as they are for Petersen and Rock. "The *motifs* of homelessness, orphanhood, and pilgrimage permeate Ephrata's spirituality," Bach writes. "Beissel often called himself one 'who possesses nothing' and [who was] 'on pilgrimage to silent eternity.' These phrases reflect the social conditions that he and some followers experienced."[98] Beissel's was a migratory, unsettled, and conflicted existence—both in Europe and in North America.

Conclusion

Radical Pietism was the original, more genuine form of Pietism. As this chapter shows, in Frankfurt, the Rhine-Westphalia region, Württemberg, Bavaria, Bern, Denmark, Norway, and Sweden, it was Pietist Radicals who played the most important roles in the early days of the movement. Radical German Pietists displayed a colorful variety; their notions of renewal and strategies for attaining it included a wide range of possibilities. I have proposed a fourfold typology for understanding the various expressions of Radical Pietism. A key feature of the Radicals was their eclecticism. Another was the freedom with which they critiqued and departed from the Reformation heritage and downplayed confessional boundaries.[99]

Compared with Orthodox Lutherans, the Radicals were marked by a new relation to time and space, evident in their eschatology and homelessness. They were a migratory and often socially disruptive lot, frequently experiencing opposition and exile. In Georg Conrad Beissel one observes a Radical Pietist whose religious views "were rooted in the Old World yet were impossible to realize there."[100] This was true of Petersen and Rock as well. But of the three, only Beissel migrated to America, where he created a community of the reborn with a vibrant culture.

The story of Radical German Pietism continues into the present day in various Evangelical and Believers' church denominations. This form of Christianity is marked by emphases such as a regenerate life of discipleship, church discipline, world mission, pacifism, and ecumenism.[101] Groups with Radical Pietist roots include the North American Baptist Conference (German Baptists), the Moravian Church, the Church of the Brethren,[102] the Mennonite Brethren, the Evangelical United Brethren, Brethren in Christ, the Evangelical Free Church, the Baptist General Conference (Swedish Baptists), and the Evangelical Covenant Church.[103] Germany's loss in the seventeenth and eighteenth centuries has been America's gain.

CHAPTER 7

Pietism and Gender

In her review of a 2007 work on Pietism and gender, Jeannine Kunert refers to the book as "a shaft of light on the horizon for those who have an interest in new perspectives, questions, and methods in Pietism research."[1] The past twenty years have seen growing interest in new methods of investigating early modern German Pietism, including increased use of gender as a category of analysis.[2] But there are still obstacles to overcome before a gender perspective is fully integrated into the field of Pietism research and the shaft of light becomes a noonday sun.

Gender studies includes at least three tasks: (1) examining how womanhood is understood in a society and identifying the contribution of women to that society; (2) examining how manliness is constructed and what this implies in a particular society; and (3) considering how the "gender order" in a society works as an instrument of power. A gender approach in Pietism studies asks questions such as: How can the sources be read to give us information not only about men but also about women? What contribution did women make to the culture of communication within Pietism? What factors went into the notion of manliness among Pietist pastors and leaders? How was male dominance "produced and secured" in Pietist groups?[3]

Recent groundbreaking work has focused on constructions of masculinity among Moravians in the eighteenth century.[4] In Moravian communities, single men and single women lived separately from each other in "choirs," residing in communal houses based on gender and marital status. Paul Peucker has found source materials that point to instances of same-sex intimacy among both men and women. He notes that "instructions for choir helpers from 1785 contained detailed information on how to deal with the sexual development of choir members and also touched upon the subject of homosexual acts."[5] The case of Christian David Nitschmann (b. 1744) makes it clear that although eighteenth-century Moravians believed homosexual acts to be sinful, they were not considered to be worse than other lustful acts, and if the sinner repented, he was forgiven and received back into fellowship.[6]

The erotic language of the *Song of Songs* infused Moravian literature. The single brothers portrayed their union with Christ the Bridegroom as a male-male relationship. The recently discovered manuscript of a Moravian hymnbook includes love songs to Jesus Christ, with references to him as husband, groom, darling, and "sidehole," referring to Christ's wounded side. In September 1748, the single brothers of the Moravian congregation at Ebersdorf in Thuringia composed a poem to celebrate the birthday of Christian Renatus, son of Count Nikolaus Ludwig von Zinzendorf. The hymn describes Christ making love to Christian Renatus. The birthday poem includes the lines:

O dear Lord Jesus Christ!
Kiss, kiss, O kiss me please,
Pass through me nuptially.
Make me hot through and through
O hole! O Kyrie Eleis[on].

In March 1750, Johannes von Watteville, Zinzendorf's son-in-law, visited Herrnhaag and Marienborn on a mission to end such excesses. The notion of Christ the Bridegroom who wished to embrace the brothers as they embraced each other was no longer acceptable. Peucker concludes, "the homoerotic devoutness that existed among Moravian men during the mid-eighteenth century remains truly remarkable."[7]

To this point, however, gender research on Pietism has focused mainly on the first task mentioned above: examining how womanhood was understood in Pietism and identifying the contributions of women to the movement. In the past two decades, women's contributions to the work and discourse of Pietist renewal have become more clear. Women, in large measure, made up the rank and file of Pietist conventicles and networks.[8] Though they held no official office and had no formal theological education, women played prominent roles in the formative phase of the Pietist movement. The most obvious instance of this is Johanna Eleonora Petersen (née von Merlau). This intelligent and independent woman was a well-known author in her day, her influence possibly outstripping that of her talented husband. And she was not alone.[9]

But there is still a "gender gap" in the field of Pietism research. Much work remains to be done in situating Pietist women as agents, leaders, and authors within their social setting in a way that illumines their gender roles and spheres of influence.[10] Questions remain to be addressed, such as: What opportunities did Pietist conventicles and networks offer to women, and how did women take advantage of these opportunities? Also needing research is the phenomenon of Pietist marriages that crossed accepted social boundaries, especially noblewomen marrying middle-class men. What views on marriage did these women have? How are we to understand the choice made by many Pietists, both men and women, to live a celibate life?[11]

A major barrier to incorporating a gender perspective into Pietism research is the traditional approach still used by many church historians—an approach that is biographical and theological. This is illustrated by Johannes Wallmann and his conviction that "the history of Pietism is essentially the history of individual leaders and tradition-building figures."[12] Over the past two hundred years, histories of Pietism have given the impression that the movement consists of the stories of pious men and their accomplishments.[13] The gender approach consistently critiques this one-sided history of Pietism and its focus on male heroes. Gender historians show how the contribution of women agents has been downplayed or ignored altogether in traditional Pietism scholarship.[14] Mirjam de Baar observes that a chapter on women in volume 4 of the *History of Pietism* (2004) only confirms the continued marginalization of women in its approach.[15]

This chapter examines the issue of gender and German Pietism from several angles: the growth of new research perspectives, questions, and methods; the place of women in early Frankfurt Pietism; women as leaders of Pietist networks and conventicles; women as ecstatic prophets; Spener's view of women; women as subjects of collective biography; and women in critiques of Pietism.

New Perspectives, Questions, and Methods in Pietism Research

Gender scholars are finding that Pietist networks and conventicles gave women "new opportunities to say 'I,'. . . and therefore new ways to gain self-confidence."[16] Women gained freedom to read and interpret the Bible and to raise their voice as prophets with a message from God. Women found the courage to write of their faith experience in diaries and memoirs and found a ready audience for their writing. Women took leadership roles within households and Pietist gatherings. They pursued theological discussions with men and corresponded with Pietist leaders.

At a conference in Basel in June 2005, participants delivered papers on the culture of memory in Pietism from the perspective of gender history. Papers discussed biography, tradition building, and the role of archives in preserving the memory of Pietist women. This gathering is just one example of new initiatives promoting gender historical study of Pietism among German scholars so that gender becomes an unavoidable category in future research.[17]

A leading figure in these initiatives is Ulrike Gleixner, whose writing leads the way in promoting the use of gender in the study of Pietism. Gleixner observes that when one applies the questions of historical anthropology to Pietist beginnings, the importance of women to the genesis of the movement becomes readily apparent. Gleixner has highlighted the experiences of middle-class Pietist women in Württemberg and their cultivation of collective memory around female ancestors. Württemberg Pietist Charlotte Zeller created a voluminous history of pious female family members, beginning in the 1860s. Pietist women collected letters and possessions and wrote biographical accounts in an attempt to reinsert women into the history of Pietism.[18] It was household practices, including singing, Bible reading, letter writing, and informal gatherings, that shaped Pietist culture.[19] Religion, women, and the household played a central role in this culture, representing "the last great Protestant attempt to reorganize the totality of life under Christian claims."[20]

Gleixner's leadership in the field of gender research is complemented by a growing number of scholars whose work is helping to address the gender gap in Pietism studies. A sampling of this scholarship reveals how the picture of women's contributions to the Pietist movement is gaining in clarity and detail.

Women in Early Frankfurt Pietism

Four women played significant roles in early Pietism in Frankfurt: Anna Elisabeth Kißner, Johanna Eleonora von Merlau, Maria Juliana Baur von Eyseneck, and Katharina Elisabeth (Bartels) Schütz.[21]

Anna Elisabeth Kißner (1652–1730) was the daughter of a Frankfurt businessman and was named for her mother. In August 1672 she married the Frankfurt physician Johann Kißner (1645–1678). Her husband died just six years later, leaving her with two children, a boy and a girl; she lived as a widow for the next fifty-two years.[22] Kißner continued to command great respect and influence and belonged to the elite of Frankfurt society. Her uncle served as Frankfurt's mayor, and from 1698 her brother was a member of the city council.

Anna Elisabeth Kißner was first mentioned by Spener in a letter in 1677. When a rumor circulated that Kißner had preached at a women's meeting, Spener defended her as a pious and intelligent woman who was incapable of anything foolish or improper. He said that she and her husband were exemplary for the house church they held with their servants. Nevertheless, church authorities pursued an investigation of Kißner and her family in 1677, and again in 1686. In a letter to a friend and fellow Spener supporter, Countess Benigna von Solms-Laubach, Kißner revealed something of her views and her criticisms of the Lutheran church. She identified with the children of God who must suffer persecution from church officials and their spirit of Babel and educated wisdom. She looked for God's coming judgment on them and the arrival of Christ's millennial kingdom.[23] On most points her theology was close to Spener's.

Kißner and Spener maintained an active correspondence after Spener left Frankfurt in 1686, up to his death in 1705. Taege-Bizer writes that Kißner continued to serve Spener "as counselor, fellow-worker, coordinator of Spener's circle of friends, and reliable informant of church and political happenings that impacted the Pietist movement."[24] Kißner communicated news of Spener's most recent publications to his friends in Frankfurt. She also passed on funds from Spener to those in need in Frankfurt and to refugees in neighboring cities. In his letters to her, Spener shared his concerns about various radical manifestations among the Pietists and his opinions on Pietist theological writings that appeared in print. In 1687 she contributed an appendix to his book *Nature and Grace,* in which she assembled relevant passages from the writings of the medieval mystics Thomas à Kempis and Johannes Tauler. Spener's esteem for Anna Elisabeth Kißner and her contribution to the Pietist community is evident in a letter he wrote from Dresden that year: "My esteemed sister, I just wish you could spend a quarter or half a year here with me. I am sure that you could offer me more assistance in my office than you or anyone else could believe."[25]

The other three women represent a more radical expression of Frankfurt Pietism. They were more severe in their criticism of the churches and belonged to the group of Saalhof Pietists who finally separated entirely from the Lutheran church in Frankfurt.

An account of the life of Maria Juliana Baur von Eyseneck (1641–1684) was composed at her death, in April 1684, by Johann Jakob Schütz.[26] Schütz observed that her piety was based on her decision to renounce all human wisdom and to depend solely on God and follow his voice within. "She was a source of irritation in the eyes of the mighty but a shining and burning light of Christian love, humility, and innocence among those who follow Christ in simplicity of heart."[27]

In 1675 the widowed Maria Juliana Baur von Eyseneck and Johanna Eleonora von Merlau established a school for girls on the Saalhof estate. There were about twelve girls in all, including von Eyseneck's own children, a niece of von Merlau, the daughter of Spener, and some others. The study plan included instruction in the Bible, Greek, and practical subjects such as sewing, as well as regular times of prayer. Beginning in 1675, von Eyseneck and von Merlau also hosted a gathering for Bible study and discussion in which both women and men took part. And in 1677 the women began hosting an academic circle for theology students on Sunday evenings. In contrast to Spener's collegia, women were full participants in these gatherings.[28]

Baur von Eyseneck twice entertained William Penn as a house guest in August 1677. Penn was impressed with the Saalhof group of Pietists that met on her estate. She responded enthusiastically to Penn's invitation to buy land and settle in Pennsylvania with other persecuted believers. She and Christian Fende were packed and ready to leave in November 1682 but held back at the last minute, to the disappointment of Franz Daniel Pastorius, who left without them. Her last words to her children before her death, in April 1684, reveal her desire to imitate Christ and forsake the world: "Do not love the world or what is in the world. It is God's truth: whoever wishes to be a friend of the world must be the enemy of God. Do not say, 'My social position requires this,' when Christ has forbidden it. What is your position? You come from dirt, as all do, kings and beggars."[29]

Katharina Elisabeth (Bartels) Schütz (1652–1721), the wife of Johann Jakob Schütz, came from a wealthy Frankfurt business and banking family. She was an active member of the Saalhof group of Frankfurt Pietists, along with her husband, Johann Jakob Schütz, Maria Juliana Baur von Eyseneck, and Johanna Eleonora von Merlau. She married Schütz in October 1680 and joined him in 1682 in separating from the Lutheran church and its sacraments. She later withheld their daughters from confirmation.[30] When her husband died in 1690, Katharina Elisabeth Schütz took over leadership of the Frankfurt Land Company, formed after William Penn's visit to the Saalhof in 1677. This included responsibility for the company's property in Pennsylvania. When she decided not to emigrate, she left the land to some Pietists in Holstein, led by the Hamburg separatist George Müller, to assist in their emigration.[31]

Katharina Elisabeth Schütz held the Philadelphian hope that Christ would soon establish his church of love and peace and end the divisions that plagued Christendom at the time. The English Philadelphians included her name in their catalogue of German friends.[32] The Lutheran ministers in Frankfurt considered her to be "much more stubborn than her husband."[33] This firmness of mind can be found in her ancestors as well, several of whom were burned at the stake in the Netherlands during the Spanish Inquisition. In 1696 and 1700 Schütz was investigated by the Frankfurt clergy. The records reveal her antagonism toward the church and strong sense of spiritual independence. When the clergy inquired as to which confession she identified with, she replied, "God's church and that of the Apostles." She rejected their offer of instruction, insisting that her anointing in the Spirit provided all the instruction that she required.

Her independence antagonized her examiners, who accused her of "devilish pride."[34] She maintained her separation from the Lutheran church to the end of her life.

Johann Jakob and Katharina Elisabeth Schütz had five daughters, the oldest of whom, Margarete Elisabeth, was not yet nine years old when her father died.[35] Margarete Elisabeth (1681–1744) married Johann Jacob Metting, who served in the court of Countess Hedwig Sophia of Sayn-Wittgenstein. The couple became involved with radical Pietists in Berleburg. The second-youngest daughter, Maria Katharina Schütz (1687–1742), became a leading Frankfurt separatist. She used her wealth to support various Radical Pietists in Bad Homburg; before her death she set up a foundation devoted to aiding "the needy and oppressed members of Christ."[36]

Women as Leaders of Pietist Networks and Conventicles

Women played important and leading roles in Pietist networks and conventicles. They were joined by theology students who had turned away from a career in ministry and clergy who had been ejected from their positions.[37] Two examples of women leaders from the early days of Pietism are Anna Maria van Schurman (1607–1678) and Antoinette Bourignon (1616–1680). The two women maintained an extensive correspondence with men and women in the Netherlands and beyond. Their letters are a key source for demonstrating how well-connected they were to various religious networks and their role in leading and teaching Lutheran Pietist men and women in Frankfurt.

Close contacts developed between the Frankfurt Pietists and Anna Maria van Schurman, as well as between the Pietists and the circle around Antoinette Bourignon. "With books and letters to the Frankfurt Jurist Johann Jakob Schütz and Johanna Eleonora von Merlau, van Schurman instructed the leaders of this educated circle . . . ," de Baar writes. "And between the representatives of early Frankfurt Pietism and Bourignon there existed much closer connections than was assumed recently by [Andreas] Deppermann."[38] Yet neither woman has been taken seriously as a formative influence on early Lutheran Pietism. Either they are dismissed as heretics or hysterics or their influence is restricted to Reformed Pietism or Radical Pietism, as distinct from Lutheran Pietism or Church Pietism.

But these lines of division, reflective of polemics at the time, do not fairly reflect the exchanges of books, letters, and ideas going on in the name of religious renewal within Pietist networks.[39]

Born in Cologne in 1607 into a noble family, Anna Maria van Schurman lived most of her life in Utrecht in the Netherlands. Privately educated, she proved a gifted linguist in both ancient and modern languages. From 1636 onward she moved in humanist literary circles, "corresponding with learned women and men all over Europe in Latin, French, Greek and even Hebrew, and achieved international renown for her defence of a woman's right to engage in scholarly pursuits."[40] Van Schurman's best-known work is the *Eukleria*, or *The Better Part*, of 1673, the title referring to Jesus's commendation of Mary for choosing to sit and learn at his feet (Luke 10:41–42).[41] Van Schurman's objective in the book was to explain her decision a few years earlier to join Jean de Labadie's community. She wrote in Latin, because her primary audience was theologians—the "great men" whose disapproval of her choice she hoped to change. The book includes autobiographical sections on her childhood and youth, her education and entry into the academic world, her attraction to Labadie's teachings in 1662, her identification with his community in 1669, and the fortunes of Labadie's house communities in Amsterdam, Herford, and Altona. The *Eukleria* is reminiscent of Augustine's *Confessions* and humanist autobiography. It contains van Schurman's reflections on theological topics and her belief that Labadie's house church was a close imitation of the early church. She offers an impressive defense of Labadist thinking, using scholastic logic and drawing on hundreds of literary citations from the Bible, classical literature, Augustine, and Calvin. It is likely that "she seized upon the genre of the autobiography in order to be able to advance a number of views about learning, theology and the church on her own authority."[42] The *Eukleria* became the most widely read Labadist writing within Germany.[43]

Johann Jakob Schütz initiated contact with Anna Maria van Schurman in 1674, resulting in an extensive correspondence that continued until van Schurman's death in 1678.[44] The letters discuss the true Christian way and the path to union with God. Schütz emphasized self-denial as taught by the medieval mystic Johannes Tauler, while van Schurman put the emphasis on serving God in daily life in expectation of Christ's imminent return to earth. In response to Schütz's request, van Schurman provided a description of Labadist beliefs and practices and encouraged the Frankfurt Pietists to read Labadie's writings. She especially recommended Labadie's treatise on the prophecy meeting (1668) as useful guidance for their own conventicle. Labadie encouraged apostolic gatherings, according to I Corinthians 14, where laypeople could read and interpret the Bible together.[45] In 1674, Johanna Eleonora von Merlau wrote to van Schurman after reading *Eukleria*. It may have been advice from van Schurman that prompted von Merlau to leave the Holstein court and move to Frankfurt. It is likely that the move toward separation among the Saalhof Pietists can be traced to Labadist influence, especially that of van Schurman.[46] In these exchanges, van Schurman acted as a spiritual counselor and guide to the Frankfurters, sharing advice in response to their questions.

Antoinette Bourignon was born in 1616 in Lille, in the Spanish Catholic Netherlands, into the family of a wealthy businessman. From childhood, she sensed that she was called by God to a special mission. After a vision in 1635 in which St. Augustine appeared to her, she believed her calling was to reestablish true Christianity on earth before God's soon-to-come final judgment. The next year she ran away from home to escape the marriage arranged by her father. In 1653 she established a home for poor girls in Lille, using money inherited from her mother. During her stay in Amsterdam between 1667 and 1671, Bourignon, a Roman Catholic, met up with Calvinists, Lutherans, Arminians, Mennonites, Quakers, Socinians, Cartesians, and Jews and had contact with Jan Comenius, Jean de Labadie, and Anna Maria van Schurman. This encounter with the many divisions within Christendom made a deep impression on Bourignon. The Spirit of God speaking within her replaced the Bible as the source of revelation. She rejected all outward forms of worship and sacraments and all traditions of piety and theology, in favor of direct encounters with God.[47]

Bourignon began a program of writing and correspondence to win people to true Christianity, rooted in the imitation of Christ's life and teachings.[48] Between 1668 and 1680 she wrote hundreds of letters, some poems, two autobiographies, polemical tracts, and biblical commentaries in French, Dutch, and German.[49] Her writings were often in response to questions she received from her readers, relating to submission to God, the Bible, doctrinal issues, and the church. An international network of people looked to her for inspiration and direction. In 1679 Johanna Eleonora von Merlau translated two of Bourignon's works into German; they were published two years later in Amsterdam as *Licht der Welt* (Light of the world). Pierre Poiret, a disciple of Bourignon, undertook to compile an edition of her collected works. In 1686 the Amsterdam publisher Wetstein put out a nineteen-volume collection of her writings. Poiret also wrote an influential biography of Bourignon.[50] Her popularity in German lands can be credited in part to Gottfried Arnold's *Impartial History of Churches and Heretics,* which includes long excerpts from her writings.[51] Bourignon's collected writings appeared in a new German edition in 1717, with the title *Geistliche Schrifften* (Spiritual writings).

The close contacts between Bourignon and the Frankfurt Pietists have scarcely been acknowledged. Indeed, she has been almost completely forgotten in German scholarship.[52] Yet Bourignon was read and highly esteemed by Schütz, Johanna Eleonora von Merlau, Jacob van de Walle (1631–1694), and Johann Peter Scheffer (ca. 1650–1719). Van de Walle, a successful Frankfurt businessman, was skeptical at first of Bourignon's teachings, but he was won over by her letter of December 1676 in response to his concerns.[53] In a later letter, in January 1677, Bourignon asked van de Walle to pass on "to all friends of the truth" in Frankfurt her wishes for a good year. That year, Scheffer, a theology student from Darmstadt, began corresponding with Bourignon and even traveled to Ostfriesland to visit her and her disciples. Johann Jakob Schütz was a devoted reader of Bourignon's writings and in 1677 asked Scheffer to bring back two or three of her works with him from Rotterdam. Von Merlau likewise became a regular correspondent with Bourignon. In October 1678, however, Bourignon expressed her disappointment with the Saalhof circle; they were "too wise in their own eyes" to receive the simple Gospel, and they still found value in public worship and preaching, practices she dismissed as useless before God.

Both van Schurman and Bourignon exercised leading and teaching roles in their exchanges with Lutheran Pietist men and women in Frankfurt. Van Schurman acted as a spiritual counselor and guide, sharing advice in response to their questions. The Frankfurters also corresponded with Bourignon and avidly read her works. Her writings and letters found a wide readership in Pietist circles in Germany and Switzerland. She called herself "the Mother of true Christians" and "Mother of true believers," and she truly was for the Saalhof Pietists in Frankfurt.[54] Mirjam de Baar argues that the Pietists' use of letters as a means of personal instruction and

Antoinette Bourignon, 1686. Engraving made for the edition of her collected works (1686), from a drawing by Pierre Poiret.

spiritual encouragement on the path to Christian perfection can be traced to the influence of Antoinette Bourignon.[55]

Women as Ecstatic Prophets

In the early 1690s, women prophets and ecstatics were prominent in the separatist conventicles that began to spring up in central Germany, in Erfurt, Gotha, Quedlinburg, Halberstadt, and Halle.[56] The women themselves did not leave any writings behind, due to their lack of education. But there are testimonies from contemporaries, records of church interrogations, theological discussions of women and prophecy, polemical denunciations of the women, defenses of the women, and court records. In December 1691, some letters were exchanged among Pietist associates of these women and published in the book *Actual News of Three Enthusiastic Maidens*.[57] Also valuable are the sympathetic eye-witness reports about Anna Maria Schuchart's ecstasies, written by thirty-year-old Johann Baptist Crophius in November 1692. Crophius became known as "the Pietist Judas" after he converted to Catholicism in 1694.[58]

These women prophets had several characteristics in common. They were mainly uneducated and from the lower social class—a circumstance that was seen as confirmation of their special calling as a humble instrument of God. Their social status was reflected in their message, which usually contained a condemnation of the powerful and mighty. Most of these women prophets were unmarried and childless. Unhampered by family cares, they were free to pursue their religious calling. Their role as prophet was sometimes accompanied by bodily signs such as illness or stigmata.[59] The women received their prophetic revelations in a state of ecstasy, their body sometimes frenzied, sometimes completely rigid. During this ecstatic experience, they saw or heard something that was denied to others. The revelations received by Pietist women contained new insight into the meaning of scripture, usually interpretations that confirmed Pietist teachings on Christ's coming millennial kingdom. Finally, the women prophets typically belonged to a network of Pietist fellow believers. In this setting, they found affirmation and were assured of the truth of their worldview.[60]

The stories of three women prophets can be reconstructed in some detail: Anna Maria Schuchart in Erfurt, Magdalena Elrichs (b. 1667) in Quedlinburg, and Agnes Gräfner, the wandering prophet. Anna Maria

Schuchart has been especially well researched.[61] Little is known of her early life, just that she was born in Rossel, near Frankenhausen, and that her father was a bricklayer. She could neither read nor write. She arrived in Erfurt in early 1691 and worked as a maid in the home of the jurist Johann Gottfried Schmaltz, a devoted Pietist and friend of Augustus Hermann Francke. Shortly after her conversion, in early November of that year, Schuchart had her first ecstatic experience. Prior to this she had no interest in Christian things; she did not even learn the catechism and disliked listening to sermons. In the vision, God showed her the torment of the damned and the joy of the redeemed. God also showed her which of her neighbors were godly and which would be condemned. She fell into a pleasant sleep and heard God say, "Be of good comfort, my daughter, your sins are forgiven."[62]

On December 17, 1691, around 6 p.m., Schuchart again fell into ecstasy, and during a half-hour period she recited more than two hundred rhymed verses, as God held her in his arms. Although she normally spoke a Thuringian dialect, she recited the verses in high German. She was later unable to remember what she had recited. One observer said that in the verses, she thanked God for converting her and asked God that he might convert the ungodly, preserve the godly, and give her strength to resist the world's temptations.[63] An eyewitness, a smith, reported what he observed during Schuchart's ecstatic experience while visiting in Leipzig.

> When I saw her in ecstasy, she lay down as if dead, completely rigid. After lying like this for a while, she began to move and to speak. In her speaking she made unusual gestures depending upon what she was speaking about. When she spoke of the downfall of Babel, she stood in an awful, terrifying manner that made my skin shiver. But when she spoke of help from Zion or the hope of better times, I cannot describe the joy that she expressed. It was as if she would burst for joy.[64]

Schuchart began to receive visions almost daily, often five times a day.

In January 1692 her messages became more harsh, as she spoke of God's imminent final judgment: "Make yourself ready, the judgment day is not far off."[65] She condemned Erfurt for its treatment of A. H. Francke and warned that the city would face God's punishment shortly. God showed her a great pit that held some Erfurt clergymen who had opposed the Pietists. Schuchart began singing while in ecstasy, sometimes for up to two hours. Some witnesses noted that at such times her voice was much more beautiful than usual. Sometimes she cried out, "That is delicious," later explaining that she had eaten heavenly food and had heavenly water to drink. After an illness in late February 1692, her ecstasies temporarily ceased. But in a letter of March 11, 1692, an observer wrote that she once again sang some "unknown hymns."[66]

In May of that year, some friends encouraged Schuchart to work at home and be more quiet, observing that "she would rather be with people than stay home and work . . . for she is by nature a great talker."[67] One eyewitness said that he had seen Schuchart, in her ecstasy, grasp the hand of someone standing nearby, pull him to herself, and hold him with both arms so tightly to her body that he could not get free. The person had to remain like this until Schuchart finally released him. What most impressed Johann Baptist Crophius from his interactions with Schuchart in Erfurt was her ability to reveal to him the innermost secrets of his heart. She also did this with complete strangers.[68]

In the fall of 1692, Schuchart moved to Halle and was welcomed by A. H. Francke. In October, Francke reported to Spener that while Schuchart and he were praying together she fell into ecstasy. She recited rhymed verses, which he found deeply moving.[69] On October 23, 1692, at an afternoon prayer gathering, drops of blood began to form on her left hand; when they were wiped away, more blood appeared. That evening, witnesses observed drops of blood on her forehead while she was in ecstasy. This happened again a month later. Francke became unhappy with the tumult that soon surrounded Schuchart and asked her to leave the city. The sources indicate that in the summer of 1694, she migrated to Pennsylvania with a group of radical Pietists led by Johannes Kelpius. There she continued her prophetic activities as "the Erfurt Prophetess."[70]

Magdalena Elrichs was born into a poor family in Quedlinburg in 1667.[71] In 1691 she was serving as a maid in the home of Johann Heinrich Sprögel, the Lutheran pastor in Quedlinburg. Sprögel reported that when he first met her, she was a bad sort and knew almost nothing of the Christian faith. Sprögel repeatedly warned her of God's judgment and her coming damnation if she did not change her ways. After a conversion experience, Elrichs changed completely. On Wednesday, December 9, 1691, at age twenty-four, she had her first experience of ecstasy during a worship service. During the sermon, she fell into a trance and could not be roused.

She was sitting still with her eyes open and staring up into heaven. An hour later, after the service had ended, she regained consciousness and began to move. Tears flowed down her face, but she appeared happy. She explained to Sprögel that she had seen Jesus with a host of angels, and he had shone beautifully. The experience was repeated in the following weeks, several times a day. During these ecstasies she sat with hands folded and eyes looking heavenward. She answered questions and showed a remarkable knowledge of the Bible, although she had never studied it.[72]

On the evening of Monday, December 14, a group arrived in Quedlinburg from Halberstadt, in the company of their prophet, Catharina Reinecke. Reinecke worked as a maid in the home of the Halberstadt high commissioner, Johannes Prätorius. She experienced a conversion in late November 1691. Like Elrichs, she was often sickly and bed-ridden. Reinecke and Elrichs shared repeated experiences of rapture before a crowd of three hundred onlookers. A short time later, Elrichs was overcome by weakness and unable to do her work in Sprögel's home. The pastor brought in two physicians to examine her, but they could find no illness. In an effort to determine the source of her ecstatic experiences, three doctors and two clergymen examined her, but they were unable to agree on their findings. One physician thought the source of her ecstasies lay in hysteria; the others attributed it to supernatural causes. In the course of the year 1692, the ecstasies became less frequent. On November 5, 1699, Elrichs delivered a baby out of wedlock. She was banned from her hometown of Quedlinburg and went to live with her sister in Ermsleben and worked as a wet nurse. Her ecstasies further diminished and eventually stopped.[73]

Agnes Gräfner grew up in Leipzig in a middle-class family and was able to read and write. In Leipzig she made the acquaintance of A. H. Francke and joined in a collegium that he organized in the city. In 1690 she followed Francke to Erfurt, after the Pietists were banished from Leipzig. By the summer of 1692, she was living in Halle. Francke described her to Spener as "a pious, God-fearing person, who has never had a bad name, but is often sickly." In the fall of 1692 Gräfner visited friends in Gotha. During a communal Bible reading, she had a vision of Christ and cried out, "I see the Lord Jesus and the holy angels. The Lord is King, the Lord is King, the Lord is King."[74] One witness later testified that Gräfner was suspended in the air above them and the whole room shook.

In early 1693 Gräfner moved to Quedlinburg, where she lived in the home of Pastor Sprögel. On April 29, 1693, in a state of ecstasy, she prophesied that in seven days the city would be destroyed. Several of her friends promptly left the city. When Spener and Francke heard about the prophecy, they became concerned that her outbursts would bring shame on other Pietists. But Francke was more accepting of Gräfner than was Spener. This was probably because Francke's mother, Anna, who lived in Gotha, often used Gräfner as an intermediary to deliver letters to her son, since Gräfner was a frequent traveler between Gotha and Halle.[75]

Philipp Jakob Spener's Writings on Women

Pietism held a conflicting message for women: on the one hand, it called for reform, proclaimed the priesthood of all believers, and offered encouragement to women to be agents of their own spiritual development; on the other hand, the thinking of Pietist leaders differed little from traditional views on women and their submission to men. Niekus-Moore writes, "Here was the possibility of new birth and new self-understanding which demanded a new life style; yet women did not have power over their own way of life and their sense of calling was monitored and controlled by society more than with men."[76]

Philipp Jakob Spener vacillated on what roles and involvements were open to women. In "The Spiritual Priesthood" of 1677, he encouraged women to read and interpret the Bible. They had every right to discourse about the Bible and to instruct and edify fellow believers. For Spener, this was not a problem so long as it was restricted to informal conversations with friends and family in a private setting. He spoke positively about the growing number of families who held devotions in the home, in which women participated along with men.

> There are godly fathers and mothers who have been moved by God to call together their children, servants, and friends daily or at appointed times. They read aloud a chapter from the New Testament that they have chosen as suited for edification and admonish them to put it into practice. In some homes there are women whom God has blessed with understanding and who speak to their families in their house church meeting.[77]

Spener supported these efforts among Pietist women in Frankfurt. He observed that they worked harder than other women to fulfill their duties to their families and also have time to pursue their spiritual activities and interests. Yet, in what is surely a contradiction, Spener did not allow women to speak at the gatherings in his home in Frankfurt. It could be that he was increasingly concerned about criticisms and accusations that the Pietists allowed women to preach.

Spener held traditional assumptions about women and their inherent weakness, their obligation to silence in public, and their subordination to their husband in all things. Spener wrote a letter to his daughter "on the necessary duties of a pastor's wife," encouraging her to make their home as pleasant as possible for her husband. There is no mention of her involvement in collegia pietatis. Spener's relations with his own wife were likewise traditional; there was nothing conspicuous about his wife's roles or behavior. This led one biographer to comment, "The one non-Pietist thing about Spener was his wife." This was true of the wives of many other Pietist leaders as well. "They combined traditional roles with the new tasks of Pietism under male oversight."[78] Spener's thinking about women and marriage followed closely from Luther's. Marriage and sexuality were regarded as good, and women were no longer considered tools of the devil. But the wife was still subject to her husband as part of God's intended order.

Spener's position in restricting women from any form of public ministry was also little different from Luther's. However, unlike Luther, Spener encouraged nonpublic activity by women in private gatherings. He supported women writers, such as Johanna Eleonora Petersen, and the publication of their writings.[79] Spener also approved of noblewomen using their influence and resources to support the Pietist movement. In a letter to a noblewoman, Sophie Elisabeth von Holstein-Sonderburg, in which Spener discussed the role of a nobleman's wife, he said nothing about weakness and obedience. He encouraged her to have a positive influence on her husband's rule. And in numerous instances where Pietist noblewomen offered financial and political support to the Pietist cause, Spener welcomed it and praised them for it.[80]

Philipp Jakob Spener had deep reservations about women prophets, from their first appearance in the early 1690s—more so than did A. H. Francke. Spener was open, in principle, to the possibility of ecstatic experiences and direct revelations from God, but he was quick to submit them to careful scrutiny, since the Bible warned of false prophets who would appear in the last days. Under Spener's influence, Francke eventually rejected the authority of ecstatic experiences and the chiliastic message they contained.[81]

Women in Pietist Collective Biography

In the late seventeenth century, there arose among middle-class Pietists "a biographical culture" that preserved the memory of male and female family members and their piety after their death. This practice of preserving and passing down (*Tradierung*) the memory of family piety became an essential element of middle-class Pietist culture. The portraits of family members took the form of either a brief life history (*Lebenslauf*) or a report on their last hours and final passing (*Letzte- Stunden-Berichte*). Women were usually responsible for collecting and preserving the necessary documents, such as diaries, letters, and autobiographies. Up to the early nineteenth century, this biographical legacy included both men and women of various social backgrounds.[82]

This biographical culture was also expressed in published literary form in collective biographies. The four most influential collections of Pietist life histories are filled with the stories of women: *The History of the Reborn* (1698–1701) by Johann Henrich Reitz; the *Impartial History of Churches and Heretics* (1699, 1700) and *The Life of Those Who Believe* (1701), both by Gottfried Arnold; and *The Final Hours* (1733) by Count Erdmann Heinrich Henckel.[83] In these works, women are prominent as spiritual leaders whose experiences differed in important ways from those of men. These accounts make it clear that the house church gathering, the vision, and the life story, with a mixing of the mystical and the everyday, were typical of Pietist women's spirituality.[84]

In his *History of the Reborn*, Johann Henrich Reitz (1655–1720) sought to document, above all, the Christianity of the conventicle, women, and the unlearned. In the first part, Reitz assembled thirty-five autobiographical accounts, mostly of English Puritan women, translating the accounts from English into German.

> Here now, Christian reader, I set before you in our German tongue histories of the reborn, most of them unlearned, and most of them English

> women (except for the last two), who conferred with each other, [showing] how they in their gatherings sought to tell and recount for each other, to the praise of God and the edifying of their neighbor, how God had drawn, wonderfully led and converted them, also how and what He had worked in them, what kind of conflict, temptation and experience they had had, in what condition their souls had been and were now, what testings of faith and ground for hope they had.[85]

Women figured significantly in Reitz's *History.* He believed that there were more women than men among the reborn, since women were generally more tender and submissive and more sensitive to God's leading.[86]

In all, Reitz's five-part *History of the Reborn* includes fifty-four stories of women and fifty-four stories of men.[87] He explains the principles of selection that he used as follows:

> Most of those included [in Part I] are unlearned, anonymous women, identified by the first letter of their name. The stories of the anxieties and hurts of their rebirth are described, and the following [experience] of peace and joy. But in the two following Parts we will include men and women of various classes, great and small, lords and servants, learned and unlearned, nobility and commoner, with their names and a description of their Christian life and blessed death. If someone knows of a worthy example, we would ask them to communicate it [to us] to the glory of God and edification of others.[88]

Women hold a significant place in Reitz's four-part history. He gave the priority to documenting women's experience that Arnold gave to documenting the experience of heretics.

In Gottfried Arnold's *Impartial History of Churches and Heretics,* the true Christians are found among the marginalized and persecuted throughout history. He pays tribute to figures such as Caspar Schwenckfeld, David Joris, and Jakob Böhme.[89] Arnold cites a work by Friedrich Breckling (1629–1711) in which Breckling observed that "the best witnesses to the truth, like the prophets, are largely unknown to the world. Included here are those whose writings or persons became known to me when, after much traveling about, I discovered these anonymous [secret, hidden] friends of God and [their message of] truth."[90] Breckling included some sixty *godly women* who "have testified to the truth, or suffered much, or been wonderfully gifted, illumined and led by God, just as the men listed above."[91] For Breckling and Arnold, these women were among the heroes in Christian history. Johann Heinrich Feustking observed that Arnold presented a host of women prophets, at least four dozen, as witnesses to the truth, women who were gifted and inspired by God.[92]

Gottfried Arnold included the complete works of Anna Vetter in his *Impartial History*, along with comments by her anonymous editor defending women as spiritual leaders and visionaries and their right to speak in church. Vetter felt called by God to preach, and on several occasions she sought to enter the pulpit. The *Impartial History* includes letters that Vetter addressed to the cities of Nuremberg and Ansbach in which she compared the cities to a woman guilty of adultery and condemned their neglect of the poor. The *Impartial History* also includes her autobiography of 1663, in which her story is interspersed with ten visions.[93] Vetter described her experience of childhood poverty during the Thirty Years War. During her first ten years of marriage she gave birth to seven children. At age thirty she became seriously ill and almost died. During this time, she was mistreated by her husband and gave birth to a daughter, who died. It was at this point that her visions began.

In one vision, Vetter was walking through a garden with God or angels in human form and wearing white robes and a golden crown. In another, she was present when Christ turned the water into wine at a wedding celebration and invited her to dance with him. The most dramatic vision brings together her life story and religious zeal into one account, joining the abstract and the personal. In this vision, she saw a pregnant woman who was ready to deliver but unable to give birth to the child. Both mother and child were about to die. But Anna helped the mother and she delivered a baby boy, whom Anna then presented to God. In the birthing process, Anna felt as much pain as the mother. This baby represented all the lost people in the city of Nuremberg who must be born again from above. These details present Anna's sense of mission in the world: to visit cities, to preach and prophesy, and to endure opposition until the church was reborn.[94]

In *The Final Hours* (1733), Count Erdmann Heinrich Henckel (1681–1752) provided fifty-four accounts of pious deaths, including twenty-seven stories of adult women and three of young girls. The majority of the adult women came from a noble background.[95] Henckel's choice of figures was determined by their connection to Halle Pietism. "While Reitz and Arnold present 'witnesses to the truth' from the Catholic church, and from a variety of confessions and countries," Ulrike Witt writes, "Henckel limits his selection to people who are connected to churchly Pietism, above all Halle Pietism."[96] Only two of the fifty-four persons in the book had no Pietist connection, but their death-bed conversion made them attractive for Henckel's purpose nonetheless.

Protestant funeral sermons traditionally praised women who combined the attributes of Mary and Martha: on the one hand, piety, devotion to Christ, and interest in spiritual things; on the other, hard work in a spirit of service to others. But for Henckel, these ideals were distinct and exclusive; women pursued one or the other. Of the twenty-seven women in Henckel's accounts, eighteen were married. This reflects his conviction that it was a minority of women, widows and the unmarried, who could pursue Mary as the ideal. More typical were women who endured bodily and spiritual trials, such as illness or the death of a child. Such trials were a test from God, intended to instill a desire to prepare for death.[97]

Women in Critiques of Pietism: Johann Heinrich Feustking's *Gynaeceum Haeretico Fanaticum* (1704)

In 1704 a work appeared that, while focused on a critique of Pietism and its women supporters, was much more ambitious: Feustking's *Gynaeceum Haeretico Fanaticum*, or *A Collection of Heretical-fanatical Women*, subtitled *History and Description of False Prophetesses, Female Quakers, Schwärmer, and Other Sectarian and Enthusiastic Women through Which the Church of God Has Been Disturbed*.[98] Johann Heinrich Feustking (1672–1713) was an Orthodox Lutheran theologian who earned his doctor of theology degree at Wittenberg University in 1698.[99] In the late 1690s Feustking joined Lutheran Orthodox leaders in claiming that abundant resources for renewal were already present in the Lutheran church, through proclamation of the Word in preaching and the sacraments. They denounced Spener and the Pietists for stirring up unrest and divisions in the churches and for giving over leadership to women. Feustking asked rhetorically, "How has this Pietism arisen in our churches except through the testimonies, raptures and enthusiasm of women such as von Asseburg and Johanna von Merlau?

How has it spread to Erfurt, Quedlinburg and Halberstadt except through frenzied young women? And how does it now maintain itself but through all kinds of suspect writings by these women?"[100] Feustking directed his antagonism toward three individuals in particular: Gottfried Arnold, Johanna Eleonora Petersen, and her husband, Johann Wilhelm Petersen.[101] All three had written in defense of women visionaries and their role in bringing Christian renewal. Feustking saw Arnold's history as an effort not only to exalt women but to undermine the very foundation of the Lutheran church in its clergy and theologians.[102]

The *Gynaeceum Haeretico Fanaticum* consists of three parts: *Vorbericht,* or preliminary report (128 pages); *Historie und Beschreibung,* or history proper of heretical women (550 pages); and *Anhang,* an appendix devoted to a refutation of Gottfried Arnold's *Impartial History* (86 pages).[103] In the *Vorbericht,* Feustking establishes his basic conviction that in every age of church history, the devil's strategy has been to use women to deceive and damage the church. Reflecting on his own day, he wrote, "From Luther's time up to the present hour, any reasonable man can see that false teachers rely too much upon inspired prophetesses and women teachers and gloss over their blasphemous thoughts and erroneous ideas." These fanatics and heavenly prophets typically used a threefold net: a fictitious piety; simplicity of doctrine learned in the school of the Spirit; and the science of divine mysteries.[104] In the *Anhang,* Feustking argues that Arnold's defense of women prophets amounted to placing their revelations above the Bible. Arnold was encouraging Christians to "set aside the holy scriptures and henceforth establish their faith upon the inspired teachings of women."[105]

In the main historical section of the book, Feustking presents the stories of 170 women, arranged alphabetically, with articles ranging from a half-page to thirty pages in length. The work is an encyclopedia of female heresy and fanaticism, from Old Testament women guilty of leading their husbands and the Hebrew people into idolatry up to women of the eighteenth century who disrupted the faithful.[106] Feustking's focus is on the seventeenth century, with twenty-eight accounts of English Quaker women and thirty-four accounts of mostly German Pietist women. His main sources of information were Gottfried Arnold's *Impartial History,* the *Magdeburg Centuries* overseen by Matthias Flacius Illyricus (published 1559–1574), Caesar Baronius's *Annals of the Church* (1588–1607), the writings of the Dutch theologian Gisbertus Voetius, and Orthodox Lutheran histories.[107]

Feustking observed that, from the beginning, Pietism arose because of women and their deceitful influence on men. Pietist women typically exercised their influence through ecstatic revelations and through writing.[108] Johann Wilhelm Petersen, for example, was led astray not only by his wife but also by the woman prophet Rosemunda Juliana von Asseburg. Likewise, August Hermann Francke was influenced by enthusiastic women such as the Halberstadt Catharine (Catharina Reinecke), the Quedlinburg Magdalene (Magdalena Elrichs),[109] and the Erfurt Lise (Anna Maria Schuchart). In Quedlinburg, Magdalena Elrichs (Schultz) deceived Pastor Sprögel, claiming that on December 9, 1691, in a state of rapture, she was in the presence of Christ and he spoke with her. In 1698, Christina Regina Bader, the daughter of a Württemberg preacher, made up stories of divine visitations and appearances of a shining angel. Her father believed her stories and wrote an account of them. These men provide proof of how "wives and maidens can deceive the wise."[110]

This kind of gullibility, Feustking observed, was also evident in Gottfried Arnold, who presented a host of women prophets—at least four dozen—as witnesses to the truth, who were gifted and inspired by God. Arnold's only sources in defense of the women were Friedrich Breckling, Christian Thomasius, and Peter Poiret. It was obvious to Feustking that in most cases, the prophetic words of these women were pure fabrications, did not arise from divine inspiration, and did not come to pass. Feustking said he was justifiably skeptical of their teachings concerning the thousand-year kingdom, the final salvation of all, and the need for universal cleansing and reform of the church, and of their criticism of the clergy.[111] He was likewise skeptical of the writings of the English Philadelphian Jane Leade, which Arnold praised as wholesome and full of divine instruction. Feustking found her writings to be full of the mystical teaching of the inner light and the Christ within; they were founded not on the Bible but on Jakob Böhme.[112]

Feustking's *Gynaeceum Haeretico Fanaticum* is a highly polemical history and should be used with caution. He instrumentalizes Pietist women who stepped out of traditional roles but ignores the many who followed traditional Lutheran expectations for women.[113] Nevertheless, Feustking's book is a valuable source for assessing the place of women in Pietism because of what it tells us about women prophets and authors, their writings and their readers.[114] The book provides concrete evidence of women's important contributions to the movement.

Conclusion

The gender gap in German Pietism research is being addressed, and the picture of women's contributions to the Pietist movement is gaining in clarity and detail. Women in the movement found ample room to exercise their gifts in innovative ways that went beyond the Reformation ideal of pastor's wife. Pietist women expressed their spirituality through involvement in house church gatherings, through visions, and by composing their life story. The correspondence of Anna Maria van Schurman and Antoinette Bourignon reveals their extensive influence on early Lutheran Pietism. They were spiritual leaders in their own right, building up an international network that crossed confessional lines. Inspired by Antoinette Bourignon, letters became the means of personal instruction and spiritual encouragement on the path to Christian perfection among the Pietists. The flood of anti-Pietist polemical literature, in which women were often the focus of attention, proves the public impact of women's new roles and activities within Pietism.[115] Pietism initiated a discussion about women's roles and opened opportunities for women in a way that drew the attention of contemporaries.

A key factor in restoring the place of women in the Pietist story has been the integration of Radical Pietism into Pietism research. In the twentieth century, German Pietism was often portrayed as a socially, economically, and politically engaged movement with Evangelical Lutheran roots. Its mystical features were downplayed and women's involvements and experiences excluded. In recent years, mystical and radical influences within Pietism are being taken more seriously, and women are finding their rightful prominence in the story.[116]

CHAPTER 8

Pietism and the Bible

The Pietist Bible movement represented a significant innovation, a move away from the "catechism Christianity" of Luther and the Reformation.[1] Pietism played the decisive role in promoting popular Bible reading and literacy in German lands in the eighteenth century. But there was more at stake in Pietist engagement with the Bible: Pietists recognized the need for a revision of the Luther Bible and for alternative translations, and converted these realizations into action.[2] For the first time, German versions other than Luther's became available, making it possible for German Christians to read a variety of translations. Within a period of thirty-six years, from 1703 to 1739, more new German Bible translations appeared than had been produced in the previous two centuries.[3] The credit for this work belongs not to the Halle Pietists but to "the Radical Pietist underground."[4] Orthodox Lutherans saw the flood of new Bibles as disturbing evidence of a departure from Luther and the true church.[5]

Martin Brecht pointed to Pietist engagement with the Bible as a key feature of Pietist culture. "Apart from certain enthusiastic circles and Radical Pietist figures, Pietism's high regard for the Bible as a source of revelation and normative authority surpassed even that of the Reformation and Lutheran Orthodoxy . . . This high regard revealed itself in persistent efforts to understand and interpret the Bible. The language of the Pietists was constantly saturated with it. In Pietist educational institutions considerable attention was devoted to study of biblical passages. All things considered, the Bible contributed to Pietist culture in many respects."[6]

Thanks largely to the work of the Pietists, the eighteenth century is rightly considered "the century of the Bible." It was a century marked by efforts to recover the original documents, to produce critical editions and new translations (see table 8.1), and to publish works of biblical interpretation and commentary.[7] This chapter unfolds the character of Pietism as a Bible movement. After a brief overview of Pietist engagement with the Bible, it examines three notable examples of Pietist editions, translations, and commentaries: Johann Otto Glüsing's *Biblia Pentapla* of 1710, Johann Friedrich Haug's *Berleburg Bible* of 1726–1742, and Johann Albrecht Bengel's Greek New Testament of 1734 and his commentary *Gnomon Novi Testamenti* of 1742.

Pietism as a Bible Movement

Philipp Jakob Spener's recommendations in *Pia Desideria* in 1675 begin with the plea to "bring the Word of God more richly among us," with special emphasis on lay Bible reading in the home and in small gatherings—*collegia pietatis*. "The more richly the Word dwells with us, the more we will bring faith and its fruits into being." Spener considered diligent reading of God's Word to be "the foremost means of improvement."[8] In his Sunday sermons, he ranged beyond the prescribed Gospel texts, focusing on the Epistles of Paul and their ethical teachings. He encouraged his congregation to bring a Bible with them to church services so they could look up the passages he cited in the sermon. He called on theology students to form collegia where they could read and discuss the Bible with a view to practical edification rather than mere historical interpretation. Many students in Leipzig, including August Hermann Francke, learned and followed Spener's method of Bible study.

The Bible movement continued in Halle Pietism. In 1694 Francke published a popular guide, entitled "Simple Instruction as to How One Should Read the Holy Scriptures to Their Edification," in which he emphasized that the prerequisites for understanding the Bible are the experience of new birth and God's Spirit within.[9] In April 1708, Francke published an edition of the Luther Bible with an introduction in which he offered readers both warning and encouragement.

Table 8.1. German Pietist Bible Translations and Editions

Year(s)	*Bible edition: Language and features*	*Translator/editor*	*Place of publication*
1703, 1738	New Testament: German translation	Johann Henrich Reitz	Offenbach am Main
1703	New Testament: highly literal German translation	Caspar Ernst Triller	Amsterdam
1704	New Testament: Luther's German translation "greatly corrected and improved"	Johann Reinhard Hedinger	Stuttgart
1705–1706, 1739	Wisdom Books of the Old Testament Apocrypha: German translation with commentary	Gottfried Arnold	Halle Foundations
1710–1712	*Biblia Pentapla*, Old and New Testaments: five German translations in parallel columns (3 vols.)	Johann Otto Glüsing	Wandesbeck, Schiffbeck, and Hamburg
1711	Old and New Testaments: Luther's German Bible revised and explained	Heinrich Georg Neuß	Halberstadt
1712, 1733	*Marburg Bible*, Old and New Testaments: German translation with commentary (1 vol.)	Heinrich Horch	Marburg
1720	*Michaelis Bible*: edition of the Hebrew Old Testament	Johann Heinrich Michaelis	Halle Foundations
1726–1742	*Berleburg Bible*, Old and New Testaments: German translation with commentary (8 vols.); serving Philadelphian Radical Pietist communities	Johann Friedrich Haug	Berleburg
1727	*Ebersdorff Bible*: A much revised version of the Luther Bible	Johann Andreas Rothe and Count Ludwig von Zinzendorf	Ebersdorff

1732	New Testament: literal German translation	Johann Jakob Junckherrot	Offenbach am Main
1733–1736	Gospels, Acts of the Apostles, Epistles: free German translation for the Philadelphian community in Stuttgart	Johann Kayser (Timotheus Philadelphus)	Stuttgart
1734	Edition of the Greek New Testament	Johann Albrecht Bengel	Tübingen
1739	Book of Revelation: free German translation	Johann Kayser	Stuttgart
1739; revised in 1741, 1744, and 1746	New Testament: free German translation	Count Ludwig von Zinzendorf	Büdingen
1753	New Testament: German translation done "with deep respect, with fear and trembling"	Johann Albrecht Bengel	Stuttgart

> Whoever does not read the holy Scriptures in the fear of God and to his true conversion and further edification and improvement in faith and love, but rather reads it out of mere habit or curiosity or quarrelsomeness, or for any other ungodly reason, and does not read it for the purpose for which it was written . . . that person desecrates God's Word and robs himself of all the usefulness that he could derive from holy Scripture and remains under the judgment of God . . .
>
> I wish with all my heart that every reader of the Bible might read the holy Scripture, and read it repeatedly, with great and abundant benefit for the daily quickening and strengthening of his soul . . . and might grasp Jesus Christ, the kernel of Scripture, in true faith, and taste him sweetly in his heart, and become one heart and soul and spirit with him, and live and triumph with him eternally.[10]

In 1710, thanks to the initiative of Baron Carl Hildebrand von Canstein in Berlin, Halle began producing Bibles at a more affordable price. Heinrich Elers, director of the press, rejoiced that "not even the poor can say that they cannot obtain a Bible because of the cost."[11] Between 1711 and 1719, more than a hundred thousand New Testaments and eighty thousand Bibles were printed in Halle. In its first hundred years, the Canstein Bible Society published two million Bibles and more than a million New Testaments.

Although they respected Luther's German Bible, Spener and Francke recognized the need for a new and improved translation that took into account the latest scholarly advances. Spener noted passages in Luther's translation that could have been rendered "better, clearer, more accurately, and more in consonance with the original text." Francke observed that in Luther's version "there are still, here and there, many incorrect and unclear translations."[12] In 1695 Francke launched a monthly publication, *Observationes biblicae* (Biblical observations), whose purpose was to critique the Luther Bible and to point out its faulty readings and translations. Francke's periodical met with vigorous criticism from scandalized Orthodox Lutherans. Halle's commitment to biblical scholarship was mixed, however. The Halle press continued to print and sell unrevised Luther Bibles at a handsome profit. The Hebrew Bible produced in 1720 by the Collegium orientale, under Johann Heinrich Michaelis, was criticized for paying inadequate attention to reconstructing the best text.[13]

There was energetic engagement with biblical interpretation and translation among the Radical Pietists. Heinrich Horch's *Mystical and Prophetical Bible,* also known as the *Marburg Bible* (1712),[14] and the more ambitious *Berleburg Bible* (1726–1742) are two notable examples. Horch, a former theology professor at the Reformed Academy in Herborn, put out a revised edition of the Luther Bible with introduction and commentary. He emphasized that the Bible's message must be grasped by a purified heart in faith, not merely with the mind and mouth. He approached scripture as an eschatological puzzle that, as he understood it, pointed to the early eighteenth century as the time when the church of Philadelphia would be realized on earth and believers would be of one heart and mind.[15] In the same spirit was the eight-volume *Berleburg Bible,* whose commentary reflected the mystical and millenarian ideas of the Philadelphian sympathizers who worked on it, as well as the views of the French Quietist Madame de Guyon. The *Berleburg Bible* represents a "storehouse of Radical Pietist Biblical understanding."[16]

Use of the Bible by Count Nikolaus Ludwig von Zinzendorf and the Moravians is exemplified by the *Losungen* (Watchwords), a book of readings for each day of the year. On May 3, 1728, Zinzendorf began the practice of distributing to his congregation, when they gathered for the evening song service, a Bible text and a hymn verse for reflection, discussion, and memorization on the following day. It became customary to choose the readings "by lot" (*Los*) for the coming year. Even today, the *Losungen* continues to be a popular book of devotion and is published in fifty languages.[17] The Moravian tendency to see the Bible as a "treasure chest," full of gems that one could draw on for guidance on every occasion, was criticized by Bengel, who advocated a coherent literary and historical approach.[18]

Bengel's approach to the Bible was marked by application of his linguistic gifts in Hebrew and Greek. In 1734 Bengel produced an edition of the Greek New Testament, the fruit of his efforts to find the best original Greek text. In 1742 he published a commentary on the Greek New Testament, the *Gnomon Novi Testamenti.* This is considered "the supreme achievement of Pietist Biblical interpretation" and has been translated into several modern languages.[19] Bengel had a consuming interest in biblical chronology and salvation history; he calculated that the end of the age and the arrival of Christ's thousand-year kingdom would take place on June 18, 1836.

Jonathan Sheehan recently pointed to the cultural significance of Pietist engagement with the Bible. The Pietists participated in a paradigm shift in the eighteenth century, whereby "the Bible was transformed from a work of theology to a work of culture."[20] Pietist biblical scholars treated the Bible as a document, while Pietist translators produced "not a single authoritative text but a panoply of Bibles."[21] Through their scholarship and translation, these Protestants created the Enlightenment Bible. Four scholarly techniques or practices helped to move the Bible away from theology toward culture: philology, pedagogy, poetry, and history. "It was Germany that provided the most productive laboratory for the Enlightenment Bible," Sheehan writes. "It was in Germany that the philological sciences teamed up most effectively and explicitly with the zealous efforts of religious reformers to keep the Bible fresh and relevant to the modern age."[22] Pietism played an important part in this process. The Pietists were convinced that, besides spiritual renewal, German Christians needed an improved translation of the German Bible that was "unstained by devotion to party and doctrine."[23]

Sheehan's argument for a Pietist contribution to the Enlightenment Bible reflects the new historiography that sees Enlightenment in Britain and Germany as occurring *within* Protestantism, not against it.[24] The Enlightenment was concerned with reshaping rather than attacking religion.[25] The new "media-driven" concept of the Enlightenment is one marked not by philosophical hostility to religion but by salons, reading circles, scholarship and scholarly techniques, book reviews, journals, newspapers, translations, and encyclopedias.[26] In Pietist hands, these Enlightenment media helped to create new religious cultures, practices, and Bibles.

The *Biblia Pentapla* of Johann Otto Glüsing, 1710–1712

A key figure in the Radical Pietist network was Johann Otto Glüsing, who belonged to a group of Spiritualists, Böhmists, and separatists in Altona. Because of its remarkable tolerance, Altona was also a center for Mennonites, Spinozists, and Jews.[27] Glüsing expressed the ideal of Christian tolerance and unity by producing a new kind of Bible, the *Biblia Pentapla,* with five different German translations arranged in parallel columns, including a Jewish translation of the Hebrew Bible. At a time when German Christians were divided by which Bible translation they preferred,

Glüsing's *Biblia Pentapla* served as an "ecumenical bridge" among believers; German Christians could read their chosen version and compare it with the others.

JOHANN OTTO GLÜSING (1675–1727)

Johann Otto Glüsing studied theology in Jena from 1696 to 1700. Following his studies, he traveled to Copenhagen and took a position as a private tutor. He gained a reputation as a gifted individual with extensive knowledge of church history. Glüsing and his friend Christian Funch, from Halle, began holding a conventicle in Copenhagen that soon moved in a separatist direction, with members no longer attending church or sacraments. This conventicle represents the beginnings of Pietism in Denmark and Norway.[28] Glüsing soon attracted the animosity of Copenhagen's ministers. In 1706 he published a satire of the Lutheran clergy in which he denounced them as "false apostles."[29] By the time a ban on Pietist gatherings was published on October 2, 1706, Glüsing had left to take up a tutoring position in Christiania (Oslo).[30] He once again organized conventicles and published separatist Pietist tracts. He condemned the Lutheran churches as the kingdom of Antichrist, upheld standards of Christian perfection, and proclaimed the coming thousand-year kingdom of Christ. The Lutheran provost in Christiania, Jakob Lodberg, opposed Glüsing,[31] describing him as follows:

> He is neither of our faith, nor a Papist, nor Reformed, but holds a teaching which consists of the most extreme kind of heresy and spreads it abroad. He never makes use of the Sacrament for fear that he might be stained by people with whom a true Christian should not associate. He disdains the coming together of Christians in church, despises Baptism, and finds it laughable that we baptize infants. He also mocks the sufficiency of Christ and the idea of eternal punishment in Hell. He believes that one can achieve perfection and no longer sin and thinks that the Christendom of the present day is the kingdom of Antichrist and will soon perish with the coming of the thousand year kingdom.[32]

Glüsing attracted a significant number of disciples as his influence spread to neighboring towns. Opposed by Orthodox Lutherans as an "arch

Quaker," he was finally banished from the kingdom by royal decree on December 11, 1706. Glüsing moved to Hamburg with his Danish bride, residing there from March 1707 until February 1708 and again forming a small circle of disciples. In 1707 he published a book in which he denounced Orthodox Lutherans as Pharisees and insisted that the only worship pleasing to God was by those who had experienced a heartfelt conversion to Jesus.[33]

From 1708 to 1713 Glüsing lived in Altona, where he joined followers of Johann Georg Gichtel (1638–1710). After Gichtel's death, Glüsing headed up the society of "Angel-brothers." It was in Altona, from 1710 to 1712, that he edited the *Biblia Pentapla*, publishing it anonymously. In 1712 his wife died, leaving him with two small daughters. After the fire of January 1713, which left Altona and Glüsing's personal library in ashes, he moved to Hamburg, residing there until 1726. He met regularly in homes with a circle of disciples. He supported himself as a clockmaker but found time for extensive publication, mainly producing works of translation. In 1715 Glüsing reprinted Gichtel's 1682 edition of Jakob Böhme's collected works, along with a hundred-page biography of Böhme. Glüsing's further publications included excerpts from the works of Gottfried Arnold and, in 1718, a selection of Böhme's writings entitled *Christosophia*. In 1723 he published his own translation of the writings of the Apostolic Fathers.[34] All of these publications were printed by his friend Hermann Heinrich Holle, who worked as a printer of Radical Pietist literature in Hamburg and in nearby Wandesbeck and Schiffbeck. Banished from Hamburg in February 1726, Glüsing spent his last days in Altona.[35]

THE *BIBLIA PENTAPLA*: FIVEFOLD GERMAN INTERPRETATION

The title page of the *Biblia Pentapla* reads as follows:

> *The Books of the Holy Scripture of the Old and New Testament according to Five-fold German Interpretation: I. The Roman Catholic by Caspar Ulenberg II. The Evangelical-Lutheran by Martin Luther III. The Evangelical-Reformed by Johann Piscator IV. The Jewish Old Testament of Joseph Athiae, and the New, in the New Testament by Johann Henrich Reitz V. The Dutch by the Decree of*

the Sovereign General States. Each with their own Forewords and Parallels, with short Summaries and useful Indices.

The New Testament volume of the *Pentapla* appeared in 1710 and included a map of the Holy Land, an index of people and places in the Bible, and a timeline of world history from the creation in 4004 BC up to the death of the Apostle John.[36] The two Old Testament volumes were published in 1711 and 1712. Altogether, the three volumes comprised forty-five hundred pages.[37]

The first column of the *Biblia Pentapla* contains the Catholic translation by Caspar Ulenberg (1549–1617), known as the Mainz Bible, published in 1630. The second column has the most widely used Protestant version, the Luther Bible. In the third column is the first post-Reformation Reformed translation, by Johannes Piscator (1546–1625), published in 1602. The fourth column holds the transcription into Latin letters of a Yiddish translation of the Hebrew Bible by Josel (Joseph) ben Alexander von Witzenhausen, published in Amsterdam by Joseph Athia in 1679;[38] for the New Testament, the translation is by the Reformed separatist Johann Henrich Reitz. This last version attracted the most criticism. The last column of the *Pentapla* contains the untranslated Dutch version commissioned by the Synod of Dordrecht in 1618, first published in 1636 and known as the Dutch States Bible. The *Pentapla* is thus a virtual "archive" of German New Testaments.[39]

The *Biblia Pentapla*'s anonymous editor, Glüsing, had an anonymous associate, Gottfried Arnold. Only recently has Arnold's contribution to the *Pentapla* been determined with precision. Arnold provided translation with commentary of the Wisdom books of the Old Testament Apocrypha (*Wisdom of Solomon* and *Jesus Sirach*) and of the Apostolic Fathers. Glüsing's foreword refers merely to the "new translation" of these works provided by the *Pentapla*, without mentioning Arnold by name. Arnold wished to remain anonymous because of the public controversy surrounding his translation of the Wisdom books in 1705–1706, in which he argued that the early church had treated the works as canonical. For the writings of the Apostolic Fathers included in the New Testament volume, Glüsing used Arnold's translation of the letters of Barnabas and Clement and a revision of Arnold's version of the letters of Polycarp and Ignatius of Antioch.[40]

The translations in the *Biblia Pentapla* represented, in Glüsing's words, "the five most distinguished, best known, and most useful German translations of the whole Bible."[41] He believed that Christian readers would find the *Pentapla* a useful aid (*Hülfsmittel*) to Biblical understanding. If one translation should miss the proper meaning of the Hebrew or Greek text, one could consult the others and find the correct interpretation. Even where a translation was correct, the similar or slightly varying renderings of the other four versions would help to further clarify the meaning. Some might object that an uneducated person had no way of knowing which of the various translations was the correct one, to which Glüsing replied that all Christians were able to test the spirits and determine which were from God and according to the faith (1 John 4:1). The *Pentapla* would help Christians become acquainted with the insights and beliefs of the different confessions and groups, leading to greater Christian peace and unity. Glüsing hoped that "this fivefold joint Bible translation might be to the praise of the one true God, to the growth of true Christianity, to the establishing of Christian love and unity, and to the increase of the Christian faith."[42]

In his "preliminary comment" (*Allgemeiner Vorbericht*), Glüsing explained that the Jewish translation was the one published "in the German language with Hebrew letters" in 1670 (actually, 1679),[43] and then in a revised edition with Latin letters in 1686, by Joseph Athia, "a famous Jewish printer in Amsterdam." The translator was Josel Witzenhausen, who consulted the most famous rabbinic commentators. Glüsing acknowledged that the Jewish translation erred in its understanding of messianic passages, but he believed that, apart from this, it was useful and shed valuable light on the Hebrew text. The commentary by Witzenhausen provided insight into the theology of the Jews. Glüsing observed that Christian teachers, both past and present, had not been ashamed to consult rabbis, for whom Hebrew is the mother tongue. Origen of Alexandria, for example, made use of the translation work of Aquila and Symmachus, both of whom were Jews.[44]

The Yiddish translation of the Hebrew Bible has a fascinating history. It was mainly the work of two men, a publisher and a translator. The publisher was Joseph Athia (1635–1700), who founded his Amsterdam press in 1658. It soon became the most respected printing establishment in the city.[45] Athia decided to make a name for his press by producing a scholarly edition of the Hebrew Bible, for which Johannes Leusden, professor of Hebrew in Utrecht, provided the editorial oversight.[46] The Bible appeared in 1661 and is considered among "the most beautiful specimens of Hebrew presswork" and the first Hebrew Bible with numbered chapters and verses. Athia was granted membership in the Amsterdam Printers' Guild, the first Jew ever to achieve this status in the Dutch republic.[47] In the second edition, of 1667, he paid tribute to the memory of his father, Abraham Athia, who had been burned as a Marano at an *auto da fé* in Cordova on June 29, 1665.[48] For this edition, Athia was rewarded with a gold medal and chain from the estates general of the Netherlands.[49]

Athia's next project was a German translation of the Hebrew Bible, true to the Hebrew and in good, readable German. The translator would be his learned typesetter, Josel ben Alexander von Witzenhausen (1610–1686). Born in Witzenhausen in north Hesse, Josel had worked as a printer in Amsterdam since 1644.[50] When the German Bible was completed in 1679, Athia took pride in the result: "I spared no cost, using only the most choice paper, good ink, beautiful new type, the best workers, and the translator himself did the type-setting with care, so that everything was as attractive as possible."[51] The Bible would be an aid to Jews in the diaspora, especially uneducated Jews, women, and children, who did not have sufficient command of Hebrew to follow the liturgy.[52] Athia prayed that "the reward earned by my saintly father and the merit of this glorious book [might] abide until the last day and for all eternity."[53]

Glüsing's decision to include in the *Pentapla* the first complete Jewish translation of the Hebrew Bible into German is not surprising. The Radical Pietists' literal approach to Bible translation and their expectation of the millennial kingdom were reflected in Witzenhausen's own approach and outlook. Witzenhausen's translation was "entirely true to the letter" of the Hebrew original, down to the comma; he hoped his Yiddish-German translation would enable European Jews to better observe the Law, thereby hastening the coming of the messiah and the Jews' return to Israel out of exile.[54]

The inclusion of the New Testament translation by Johann Henrich Reitz (1655–1720) in the *Biblia Pentapla* was also controversial. First published in 1703, Reitz's translation went through eight editions by 1738.[55]

Glüsing praised Reitz as a translator who had been baptized by the Holy Spirit. Reitz believed that only a literal version preserved the Holy Spirit's words and inspiration. A proper translation should retain "the same expressions and words that the Holy Spirit used and, as far as possible, [should] translate word for word."[56] The result was a Bible that sounded "strange, awkward, and new." This approach was very different from that of Martin Luther, who had sought to produce a German text that rang true and was readily understood by German readers: "One must first inquire of the mother in her house, the children in the alleys, the common man at the market, and observe them in conversation, how they speak, and then translate. Only then will they understand it."[57] Reitz, however, rejoiced in his version's strangeness and unfamiliarity. "God's words are always hard for natural men who neither can grasp them nor confine their reason to the school and simplicity of Christ."[58]

It is ironic that the Radical Pietists, who often mocked scholars, should make use of scholarly tools such as the Greek text, footnotes, and alternative readings to promote a literal and universal Bible. They sought to make available in translation "all of the possible variants in the original." For example, in a footnote to 2 Peter 1:19—"And we have the firmer prophetic word"—Reitz added the variant: "thus we have something firmer than the prophetic word."[59] Such a reading favored the enthusiasm of prophets and radicals. In a footnote to 1 John 5:7, Reitz observed that the verse had been left out in Luther's New Testament translation of 1523 and that it "was also missing in many old Greek exemplars, in some Latin, in the Syrian, Arabic, and Moorish translations."[60] Whereas Lutheran Orthodoxy believed that the insights of scholarship should be the preserve of the learned, Reitz made them available to everyone. He put scholarly issues on the public stage. Valentin Löscher, an Orthodox Lutheran polemicist, thought Reitz's translation and notes would confuse the common reader and undermine their faith.

MICHAEL BERNS'S CRITIQUE OF THE *BIBLIA PENTAPLA*

Soon after the *Pentapla*'s New Testament volume appeared in 1710, Michael Berns, an Orthodox Lutheran pastor in Wandesbeck, wrote a sixty-eight-page critique entitled *Discovery of the Abominable Things Which the So-called New Christians Have in Mind with Their Biblia Pentapla, Newly*

Printed in Wandesbeck. Composed for All Honest Christians and Godly Souls for Their Warning and Protection.[61] In the foreword, Berns emphasized that he had had nothing to do with publication of the *Biblia Pentapla;* in fact, he had warned his congregation against it.[62] Berns knew Glüsing and the publisher Holle personally, and he denounced their work in the strongest terms, calling the *Pentapla* "poison from hell" and Glüsing and Reitz "slaves of the devil."[63]

Berns's critique offers insight into the features of Glüsing's *Biblia Pentapla* that Orthodox Lutherans found disturbing. Berns lamented that the *Pentapla* was published with the purpose of undermining the authority of the Bible by creating a Babel of confusion out of it. The various versions it included demonstrated Glüsing's complete indifference to religious matters. Berns was disgusted, for example, that the *Pentapla* should include a Jewish version of the Old Testament and a new translation of the New Testament by Reitz. In place of the original Hebrew and Greek text, they had set up the authority of their own mind and spirit.[64]

Berns had some further concerns.[65] According to the *Pentapla,* it was incidental that the New Testament was first written in Greek; this was simply the language used by Christian people at the time. The Holy Spirit no longer had any special attachment to Greek when it came to communicating God's Word but spoke to all nations in their own language by means of God's chosen witnesses, truly converted believers. For the Pietists, the foundational text (*Grund-Text*) was the light of the Holy Spirit in the soul of believers, not the Greek text. The language in which the Bible was expressed was merely a copy and form (*Abdruck und Abbildung*) of the Spirit's original speaking. Berns was amazed that the Pietists could ground their hope of eternal salvation on their own inward understanding and consider this to be God's Word. For Berns, the only sure and saving Word was the Word that Christ spoke to the disciples (John 17:14). "The written Word in Holy Scripture, whether of Moses, the Prophets, or the Evangelists and Apostles, is the Word of God. It abides forever and is the only imperishable seed by which we are born again."[66]

Concerning different translations of the Bible, Berns said that the Pietists judged a translation by the piety of the translator and whether he had been baptized by the Holy Spirit. Berns surmised that the Pietists had doubts as to whether Luther was sufficiently illumined to be a competent translator. "Does this blessed and holy work of Luther deserve such an ugly slander? Can they say this with a clear conscience?" If they did believe that Luther's version was translated by a man sanctified by God, then why print so many other translations alongside it? And why include a translation by a Jew, an enemy of Christ, who misunderstood the Old Testament references to the messiah and the Trinity?[67] A year later, Berns continued his denunciation, insisting that no honest person would benefit from reading the *Biblia Pentapla*: the Jewish version and Reitz's New Testament were "of the devil," and whatever was useful in the Catholic and Reformed versions was based on Luther's translation. Luther's version did "not need the help" of godless Pietists and Jews.[68]

Berns's *Discovery* (*Entdeckung*) reflects on the implications of the Pietist view that God's Word in the Bible is a mere "copy and form" of the inward light, the true foundational text. The Pietists say, Berns wrote, that the new covenant in Christ's blood is sealed in the hearts of believers, not with ink and paper. This covenant is "not an outward Gospel set down in apostolic writings; rather, the Light in the heart and conscience reveals itself as the true Messiah in word and deed." Berns reflected, "as goes the foundational text, so goes the Gospel."[69] The Pietists taught a completely different Gospel than the one found in the Apostolic writings. They twisted the letters of the Bible so that everything they derived from it, including the name of Christ, was misinterpreted; only the letter remained, and this they used to clothe their horrible teaching. There was nothing in their Gospel concerning the blood of Christ that cleanses from sin; yet without Christ's blood there is no forgiveness (I John 1:7). Their inward light had its source in the devil.[70]

SIGNIFICANCE OF THE *BIBLIA PENTAPLA*

This German polyglot Bible and its editor, Johann Otto Glüsing, are a unique and early example of Pietist engagement with the Bible. Four features of the *Biblia Pentapla* set it apart in its day. First, it employed the ancient polyglot approach, going back to Origen's *Hexapla*, by providing five German versions in parallel columns. Second, the *Pentapla* published, for the first time, a Jewish translation into German (with Yiddish overtones) and gave it equal place alongside the Christian versions. Third, in pursuit of the Philadelphian program of religious harmony, the editor and publisher dared to ignore imperial censorship laws, thereby opening a door to religious toleration and ecumenical-mindedness in the German empire.[71] Finally, by including Apocryphal works and the writings of the Apostolic Fathers, the *Pentapla* pushed the limits of the Protestant biblical canon. These achievements were only possible under cover of anonymity.[72]

The Radical Pietist spirit of the *Biblia Pentapla* is evident in several respects: its publication in the tolerant city of Altona; its goal of promoting Christian love and unity; the decision to include Reitz's New Testament translation; the inclusion of Arnold's translation of writings devoted to "Sophia"; and the conviction that salvation comes through reading and study of scripture. The Enlightenment character of the *Pentapla* is evident in its encyclopedic comprehensiveness, its recognition of multiple translation possibilities, and its ideal of tolerance and ecumenical-mindedness.[73] To sum up: "The *Biblia Pentapla* is an exemplary Radical Pietist edition of the Bible whose program reached beyond the provincialism of the day in religious matters and demonstrated the implications of early Enlightenment toleration."[74]

The *Berleburg Bible*, 1726–1742

The *Berleburg Bible* has been called "the most important literary work of Radical Pietism" next to Gottfried Arnold's *Impartial History of Churches and Heretics*.[75] The first volume was published in Berleburg in 1726, followed by seven more volumes over the next sixteen years, comprising eight thousand folio pages in all. Its approach differed from that of the *Biblia Pentapla*: instead of providing an archive of German Bible translations, it offered "a veritable encyclopedia of biblical interpretation" in the German vernacular. It includes geographic, historical, genealogical, theological, anthropological, and linguistic information pertinent to understanding the biblical text and setting. A typical page of the *Berleburg Bible* has a small passage of biblical text at the top and, underneath, two columns of commentary in small print, with references to "Hebrew and rabbinic literature, the cabala, travel diaries, lexica . . ."[76]

Pietist engagement with the Bible was a hazardous and fragile project. Whereas England had become a "post-confessional nation" after 1689, the Holy Roman Empire remained a patchwork of 250 territories and principalities in which religion was unevenly distributed according to the inclinations of political sovereigns. State boundaries remained "barriers to religious diversity" in some cases and opportunities for heterodoxy in others.[77] The Berleburg Bible depended on the tolerant princes who ruled in eighteenth century Sayn-Wittgenstein.

BERLEBURG AND SCHWARZENAU IN SAYN-WITTGENSTEIN

In the early eighteenth century, several hundred Radical Pietists settled in the counties of Sayn-Wittgenstein, thanks to the toleration and support of the counts. Countess Hedwig Sophia (1669–1738) ruled the northern county from her palace in Berleburg, while Count Henrich Albrecht (1658–1723) ruled the southern county from his palace in Laasphe.[78] Both were Reformed Calvinists and Pietist sympathizers who offered refuge to separatists and radicals.[79] In 1700 a group of Philadelphian separatists led by Hochmann von Hochenau (1670–1721), Samuel König (1671–1750), and Johann Henrich Reitz (1655–1720) settled in Berleburg and were welcomed by the countess, often eating at her table. The three men preached daily in public and in the court.[80] During Easter 1700 there were reports of services being held in Berleburg Castle by Hochmann von Hochenau in which participants experienced trance and ecstasy. Some fell to the ground; others were overcome by fits of holy laughter.[81] The tumult attracted growing concern among neighboring counts, including Count Rudolf zur Lippe-Brake (1664–1707), brother of the countess. Opposed to such Pietist enthusiasm, he swore he would drive out "all so-called Pietists and Quakers" from the principality and called a special session of the Imperial Court in Wetzlar to deal with the matter.[82] The result was that Hochmann was brutally whipped and briefly imprisoned in July 1700, and then banned from Berleburg.[83] Many Pietist separatists, including Hochmann, found refuge in the village of Schwarzenau on the Eder River, a few kilometers from Berleburg. When Ludwig Christoph Schefer became Berleburg's new first preacher in September 1701, many hoped that calm and order would once again prevail.

Count Henrich Albrecht was impressed by the ecstatic manifestations that he witnessed in Berleburg over Easter. He wrote to his brother in Berlin that if the opposing counts could just hear Hochmann speak, "they would believe, repent, and change their lives, and support this work of God."[84] The count and his family adopted a Philadelphian chiliastic worldview, expecting the imminent arrival of Christ's millennial kingdom. Count Albrecht welcomed members of the Philadelphians, Inspirationists, and New Baptists to his territory, took part in Pietist meetings, and invited their preachers to speak in his court in Laasphe and at his summer residence in Schwarzenau. In nearby Hüttenthal, an ever-growing number of Pietists found refuge and built primitive accommodations. In January 1704, Hochmann founded an experimental fellowship devoted to the practice of community of goods.[85] He spent his last years living a simple life in Hüttenthal.

> In Schwarzenau Hochmann built a lonely little house for himself on a quiet slope with a glorious view and beautiful fruit trees. There he lived as a hermit with a servant and few conveniences, with simple clothing and nourishment, happy in the Savior. He stayed in touch with his many friends, spread widely about, partly by their visits in summer and partly by correspondence. He called this place his hut, which was just a few paces long and wide and consisted of only one room and a kitchen.[86]

Several factors account for the region's appeal to these Pietists: they knew they had a secure refuge and, in the count, an energetic spokesman and advocate; the land was undeveloped and had lost population during the Thirty Years War; the region appealed to the settlers' desire to live a life of simplicity and withdrawal, like the first Christians; and there was no church in the area, so Pietist separatists could live undisturbed by overzealous church pastors and overseers.[87]

By 1710 some three hundred separatists were living near Schwarzenau. Three of Count Albrecht's sisters joined the Pietists there, living in humble conditions that stood in sharp contrast to life at the court.[88] A group under the leadership of Alexander Mack (1679–1735) settled in Schwarzenau in 1706. In the summer of 1708, eight adults were baptized by immersion, marking the founding of a group that observers called the Schwarzenau New Baptists, later known as the Church of the Brethren. They remained on the count's lands until 1720, eventually migrating to Pennsylvania.[89] In 1714 a group of Inspirationists under Johann Friedrich Rock settled in the region as well. To his critics, Count Henrich Albrecht replied, "If other rulers in Hamburg, Altona, Cleve, in the Pfalz, Neuwied, Ostfriesland, and other territories tolerate the Anabaptists, then I too have the right to do so."[90]

In the northern county of Sayn-Wittgenstein-Berleburg, Casimir (1687–1741) was not yet seven years old when his father, Count Ludwig Franz, died, leaving his mother, Hedwig Sophia, to raise him and four younger siblings. Guardianship of Casimir was shared by his mother and his uncle, Count Rudolf zur Lippe-Brake. After a brief period of study in Marburg and Giessen, Casimir fulfilled his mother's wishes by going to Halle in 1705 to study under August Hermann Francke. The countess maintained a regular correspondence with Francke and the jurist Samuel Stryck concerning her son's progress.[91] In 1707 Casimir traveled to England on his *Kavalierstour* ("Cavalier's tour"—an educational trip customary for the children of nobility) and attended gatherings of the Philadelphians in London. He was deeply moved by their example of Christian love.

In 1712 Count Casimir assumed office in Berleburg. Under his rule, "the spirit of true piety of Spener, Francke, and others, again found a residence and home." The county became the focus of Philadelphian hopes and remained so for several decades. The count welcomed refugees from all over Germany, France, and Switzerland, from a great variety of religious backgrounds.[92] He believed that Christianity consisted of heartfelt repentance and living faith. At daily devotions, Casimir invited a family member to read aloud from a Pietist sermon or devotional work. His favorite authors included Johannes Tauler, Christian Scriver, Johann Arndt, Gottfried Arnold, Jane Leade, Pierre Poiret, François Fenelon, August Hermann Francke, and, especially, Madame Guyon. From 1724 until shortly before his death, Casimir kept a diary in which he reflected on his inward spiritual life. The diary is a valuable source for understanding the count's policy and piety.[93]

Casimir often visited the separatists in the southern county, in Schwarzenau and Homrighausen, and was moved by the simplicity of their devotion. He recorded his thoughts after visits in March 1724 and April 1726.

> O Lord, grant us grace that we might likewise go about in the simplicity, humility, and fear of God of those who are dwelling here . . . I drove with my gracious mother and my dear wife to Schwarzenau to spend some time there . . . I found in the huts and rooms of the pious ones whom I visited a close approximation of those in the early church who served God in their day in true faith, in great renunciation of the world, denial

> of their flesh, and withdrawal. Lord, give me more zeal and earnestness to follow Jesus in the denial of the world and the crucifying of my lusts and desires.[94]

Count Casimir remained loyal to the Reformed church, however, attending its services and taking notes on the sermons. He was a patron of the arts, retaining the services of painters, sculptors, and musicians, and had an impressive library of writings by the Protestant Reformers.[95] Notations in the margins of his books reveal that he read widely and deeply.

In the 1720s and 1730s, Berleburg was the center of the growing Philadelphian movement; Philadelphians had also settled in Offenbach, Elberfeld, Ronsdorf, and various parts of western Germany and Switzerland. Key figures in Berleburg were Hochmann von Hochenau; Hector de Marsay; the Inspirationist Johann Friedrich Rock; Johann Christian Seitz, a separatist from Beyreuth; and the count's physician, Samuel Carl, who arrived in 1724. The author Heinrich Jung-Stilling reported that "in all of church history, there has been no period in which the expectation of the Lord's coming was so strong and universal as in the first half of the eighteenth century. The Halle awakenings took the lead; then followed the restoration of the *Brüdergemeinde* by Zinzendorf; then the mystical Philadelphian society in Berleburg, whose fruit was the *Berleburg Bible*."[96] Seitz, who devoted twenty years to studying the prophecies in scripture, assured the Berleburg community that it should expect Christ's return in the year 1736. Those who doubted him he rebuked as unbelievers. This tolerant setting and vibrant Philadelphian mood provided the context and editorial perspective of the *Berleburg Bible*.

KEY FIGURES INVOLVED IN PUBLISHING THE *BERLEBURG BIBLE*

With the arrival of the Strasbourg printer Johann Friedrich Haug (1680–1753) in 1720, Berleburg soon became the leading publishing center for Radical Pietist literature. Works printed in Berleburg typically used the name "Philadelphia" to identify their place of publication.[97] Under the inspiration of Ludwig Christoph Schefer (1669–1731), the court preacher, the press's most ambitious publication project was the eight-volume *Berleburg Bible*. Count Casimir served as an enthusiastic promoter of the project and contributed a translation from French into German of Madame Guyon's twelve-volume biblical commentary. Her comments were integrated throughout the *Berleburg Bible*. Casimir invited others to come to Berleburg and assist with the work, offering to cover the costs of their travel and lodging. Chief among those who accepted his offer were Johann Christian Edelmann; Tobias Eisler, a jurist from Nuremberg; Christoph Seebach, from Thuringia; and Johann Konrad Dippel.[98] The two individuals responsible for overseeing production of the *Berleburg Bible* were Schefer and Haug.

Ludwig Christoph Schefer was born in Marburg on October 28, 1669, to Anna Catharina Pauli and Johann Ludwig Schefer, his father serving as an envoy for the Count of Wittgenstein and Berleburg. In March 1684 Schefer began studies in theology and biblical Hebrew at Philipps University in Marburg. In September 1701 he became Berleburg's new inspector, court preacher, and member of the consistorial council.[99] Previous preachers, Johann Henrich Reitz and Hochmann von Hochenau, had been dismissed by Count Rudolf zur Lippe-Brake because of their chiliastic preaching and the disorderly conduct they inspired. It is unlikely that Schefer adhered to Philadelphian ideas at the time of his appointment. In May 1702 Schefer married Louise Susanne Mieg, daughter of a Reformed theology professor in Heidelberg who was a friend of Spener. They had five children. As Casimir's court preacher, Schefer became the count's closest and most valued colleague.[100]

In 1712 Schefer and Heinrich Horch published the *Marburg Bible*, a version of the Luther Bible with Philadelphian-minded commentary that served as a precursor to the *Berleburg Bible*.[101] By this time, Schefer was a Philadelphian sympathizer and a strong supporter of the various groups that had settled in the Wittgenstein region. Under the Reformed Count Casimir, Schefer offered catechism and confirmation instruction and even baptized the children of various Berleburg separatists.[102] In 1722 the count appointed him inspector of the newly founded Berleburg Orphanage. After 1725 Schefer worked closely with Haug in producing the first four volumes of the *Berleburg Bible*, but he died before the project was complete.

Johann Friedrich Haug was born in Strasbourg in 1680, the son of David Haug, who worked as a printer in the city.[103] Johann Friedrich studied theology at the university in Strasbourg, reading deeply in the Church Fathers and in Luther's German Bible. He was exposed to the Philadelphian ideas of Gottfried Arnold, such as his denunciation of the churches as Babel, and began attending conventicles in homes throughout the city. Haug's early sermons, which reflect Philadelphian views, brought him to the attention of church authorities in Strasbourg. He gained a reputation for being stubborn, brash, and arrogant. Initially accepted into the preacher seminar in 1704, Haug was suspended and denied ordination after a sermon in which he described the majority of clergy as false office-holders and a sign of the end times. In January 1705 he was imprisoned briefly for his participation in small devotional gatherings, and was then expelled from the city. His friend Andreas Groß suggested they seek refuge in Wittgenstein, something Haug did not do until much later.[104] In February 1707 he wrote a work in his own defense in which he insisted on his freedom of conscience in rejecting the Lutheran symbol books, emphasized the need for new birth, and confessed his belief in Christ's imminent millennial kingdom on earth. By 1714 Haug was living in Idstein, where he worked in the small printing establishment of the Pietist Erdmann Andreas Lyce.[105] The firm was marked, however, by "a perpetual struggle for existence," frequent idleness, and mismanagement.[106]

In 1720 Johann Friedrich Haug turned up in Berleburg, and in June of that year he married Charlotte von Rauchbar of Marburg. In 1723 his father and younger brother Johann Jacob (1690–1756) arrived in Berleburg. In April 1725 Count Casimir appointed Johann Friedrich director of the printing press and publisher of the newly planned *Berleburg Bible*. Haug would receive free lodging, use of the garden, and free firewood for as long as he served in the position. He could appoint his own assistants.[107] The *Berleburg Bible* occupied Haug for the next seventeen years. He expressed joy and amazement when it was finally completed: "Finally, with God's help, the publication of this Bible has been completed. Many were full of doubt and despair that this day would ever come. The Bible is even better than we imagined. It is a miracle that we have reached this point. But God has stood by us and helped us right to the end."[108] The *Berleburg Bible* offered a new German translation from the Greek, supplemented by interpretative commentary intended to clarify the mystical and spiritual meaning of the text. The title of the Bible reads:

The Holy Scripture of the Old and New Testaments, newly revised and translated according to the original text: including a clarification of the literal sense as well as of the chief symbols and prophecies of Christ and his kingdom, together with some teachings which are directed to the condition of the churches in our last times; also included is an explanation of the inner condition of the spiritual life or the ways and workings of God in the soul for its purification and illumination and union with him.

The Bible was directed to awakened Christians in all parts of Christendom. It was prepared in the expectation that the Philadelphian church age would soon arrive, even though "in our day only a small bit of Philadelphia [is] evident."[109]

The title page of the first volume, devoted to the Pentateuch, shows an open doorway between two columns. Over the doorway, two cherubs hold a crown, and between them is written: "The Philadelphian Church." Below that is a verse from Revelation 3:7–13: "See, I have put an open door before you and no one can shut it, for you have kept my word and not denied my name."[110] The open doorway provides a view of the heavenly Jerusalem. The second volume contains the Old Testament historical books, from Joshua to Esther; the third volume, the poetical books, from Job to Song of Solomon; and the fourth volume, the prophets. The high point of volume 3 is reached with the Song of Solomon, which is interpreted eschatologically as portraying the union of Christ with his church. It is divided into seven parts that correspond to the seven ages of church history in Revelation 1–3. The Berleburg commentary on Song of Solomon 6:9 to 7:14 relates the passage to the Philadelphian church age, Christ's millennial reign on earth.

Volume 5 is devoted to the Gospels, volume 6 to the Acts of the Apostles and the writings of Paul, volume 7 to the other New Testament Epistles and the Book of Revelation, and volume 8 to the Apocryphal writings and the works of the Apostolic Fathers—suggesting the influence of the *Biblia Pentapla*. The commentary on Revelation 10:9 ("The angel said to me, 'Take the scroll and eat; it will be bitter to your stomach, but sweet as honey in your mouth'") includes the following poem:

This book one should not read but eat:
For the one who reads, to him it is easy to forget what he has grasped;
But the one who takes it into himself, into his flesh and blood,
He obtains the power of the book, and has become one with it.

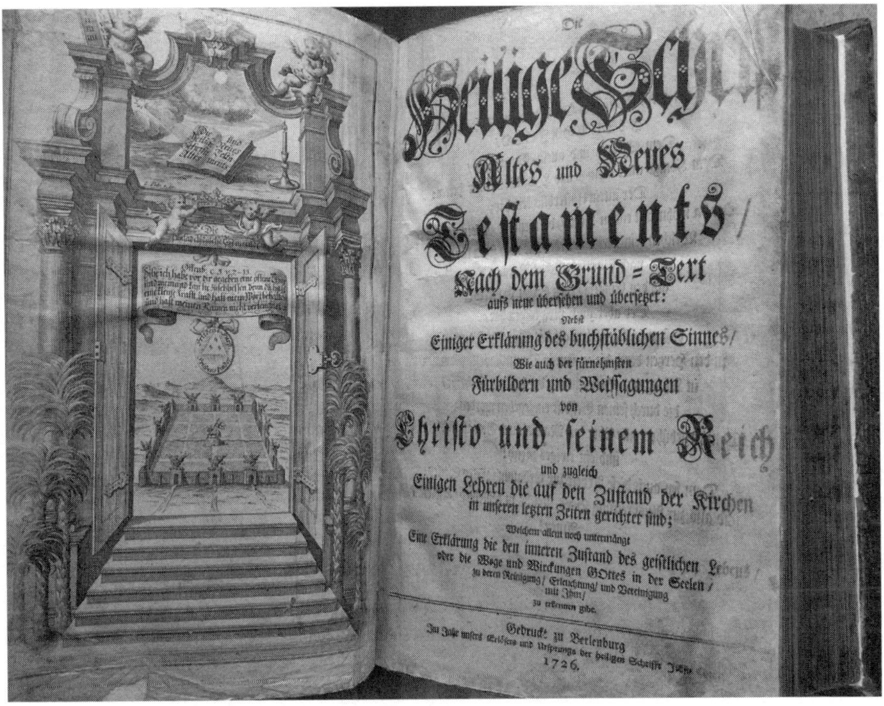

Title Page of the *Berleburg Bible* (1726). Sepher-Verlag Herborn, http://sepher.de/berleburger-bibel-erstausgabe-komplett/

If you know how to recite the matter historically,
It is still only an outward thing; you must bear it within.
It is not a matter of the letter, images only put to death:
The meaning that brings spirit and life, that has the nature of Spirit;
That penetrates through and through and has a living essence,
That speaks without words, and restores the sick:
From it come prophecy, understanding, and a pure Spirit,
Which through a pure vessel can then flow out pure upon others.[111]

SIGNIFICANCE OF THE *BERLEBURG BIBLE*

The *Berleburg Bible* represents an eclectic gathering of heterodox traditions, along with the traditional fourfold exegesis of the medieval church that included the literal, moral, allegorical, and mystical meanings.[112] Its commentary draws on sources such as Johann Arndt, Gottfried Arnold, Jakob Böhme, Friedrich Breckling, the Secret Wisdom of the Jews, Luther, the Rosicrucians, the Talmud, Paracelsus, and, especially, the commentaries of Madame Jeanne-Marie Guyon (1648–1717).[113]

> The scattered intellectual inheritance of Radical Pietism, the *Sophia* speculation of Jakob Böhme, the critique of forensic justification, the emphasis on new birth and mystical union with God, the expectation of the 1,000 year kingdom, the restoration of all things, and above all the idea of the final coming together of the Philadelphian church of Revelation 3, are all brought together in the *Berleburg Bible* as a Radical Pietist biblical theology.[114]

Like the *Biblia Pentapla*, the *Berleburg Bible* was more likely to confuse readers than to help them in understanding the Bible. The annotations frequently contradict one another, leaving the reader unsure of what the commentary intended. This is illustrated by the comments on Exodus 32:15, where Moses descends the mountain with two tablets containing the Ten Commandments. On the question of how the commandments were distributed on the two tablets, the commentary notes that Philo and Josephus argued for five on each tablet; others, such as Augustine, argued for three and seven; Athanasius and Ambrose argued for four and six. In the end, Haug dismisses the discussion as unimportant compared with obeying the commandments, however they were inscribed.[115]

The *Berleburg Bible* shared significant features with Pierre Bayle's *Dictionnaire historique et critique* (1697), a model of Enlightenment skepticism. The two works have similar modes of presentation, accumulating and organizing vast amounts of information. Both offer "a simple aggregation of materials," each as significant as the others, with no effort to distinguish the important from the less important. Rarely does the information lead to a conclusion.[116] Both works provide a virtual library of information at one's fingertips. The only order is provided by the alphabet (Bayle) or the succession of biblical books (*Berleburg Bible*). Such projects required a team of researchers under an editor. The editor of the *Berleburg Bible*, Johann Friedrich Haug, was assisted by many others.[117]

The significance of the *Berleburg Bible* lies in its combination of an encyclopedic format and separatist, Philadelphian ideas. It used the media of the Enlightenment, including the techniques of collection, presentation, and organization, to repackage the Bible in service to a religious aim. The Radical Pietists advanced their attack on Orthodox Protestant theology by means of a vernacular Bible that made scholarly information easily available and left confessional theology behind. Translation had become a weapon against theology.[118]

Johann Albrecht Bengel and the *Gnomon Novi Testamenti*, 1742

Johann Albrecht Bengel embodied two features of the early Pietism of Spener and Francke: a passion for the Bible and eschatological hope. In Bengel's own words:

> The scripture preserves the church; the church guards the scripture. When the church is strong, the scripture shines; when it is sick, its relation to scripture has worsened. The condition of the church is directly related to its engagement with the scripture.[119]

Bengel's great gifts to Protestantism were his work in textual criticism and biblical interpretation. His *Gnomon Novi Testamenti* has been called "the supreme achievement of Pietist biblical interpretation."[120] "What Halle Pietism accomplished for the Hebrew Old Testament, Württemberg Pietism, through Johann Albrecht Bengel, did for the New Testament."[121] Bengel would set the direction for German scholarship for centuries to come.

JOHANN ALBRECHT BENGEL (1687–1752)

Bengel was born on June 24, 1687, in the village of Winnenden near Stuttgart, where his father, Albrecht Bengel, served as second preacher in the Lutheran church. As a child, Johann Albrecht met with great tragedy and loss. His father died in 1693 when the boy was not yet six years old. That same year, the family lost house and property when the troops of Louis XIV plundered and torched Winnenden and other Swabian cities and villages. Bengel was taken into the home of his father's friend David Spindler, a theologian and teacher in a Latin school. In 1699 Spindler obtained a position in the Stuttgart gymnasium (academic-oriented high school), which had a reputation for providing the best education in the empire. There Bengel gained a good grounding in classical languages, French and Italian, sciences, and history.[122] During his ten years with Spindler, Bengel was also exposed to separatist, chiliastic thinking. The teacher was a devoted reader of works by Jakob Böhme and Gottfried Arnold and he was fascinated by the Book of Revelation. Spindler refrained from taking the Lord's Supper, and his home was a regular meeting place for Radical Pietists. In 1710 Spindler was dismissed by the Stuttgart consistory for espousing separatism and chiliasm.[123] Spindler's interests and fate may explain Bengel's attraction to chiliasm but rejection of separatism.

In 1703 Bengel began studies at Tübingen University as a scholarship student. During his first two years, he became disturbed when he encountered variant textual readings in Greek New Testament manuscripts. He finally came to see that, like the church, the transmission of the biblical text was subject to human weakness and error, but this did not prevent scripture from having its saving effect. He was surprised that more alternative readings had not arisen and observed that those that did exist "do not in the least disturb the ground of our faith."[124] In 1704 he earned his master's degree for taking part in a disputation entitled "On the Price of Redemption," passing at the top of his class. Bengel studied theology for the next three years and was especially influenced by the Pietist professor Andreas Adam Hochstetter, a disciple of Spener and promoter of conventicles, and by the anti-Pietist professor Johann Wolfgang Jäger, an advocate of a renewed Lutheran Orthodoxy and an opponent of chiliasm, conventicles, and mysticism. Bengel assisted Jäger in preliminary research and writing for a book on church history; he assisted Hochstetter by making final corrections to an edition of the German Bible and writing the foreword and summaries for each biblical book. In January 1707 Bengel took part in a disputation under Jäger on the theme "Concerning Mystical Theology," focusing on Pierre Poiret and Madame Guyon.[125] Bengel spent much of the next six years working as a tutor (*Repentent*) in Tübingen.

Bengel's educational travels, from March to September 1713, took him to some twenty-three German cities, including three months in Halle. He visited Latin and German schools in these cities, Lutheran, Reformed, and Catholic, comparing their methods of instruction and their results and

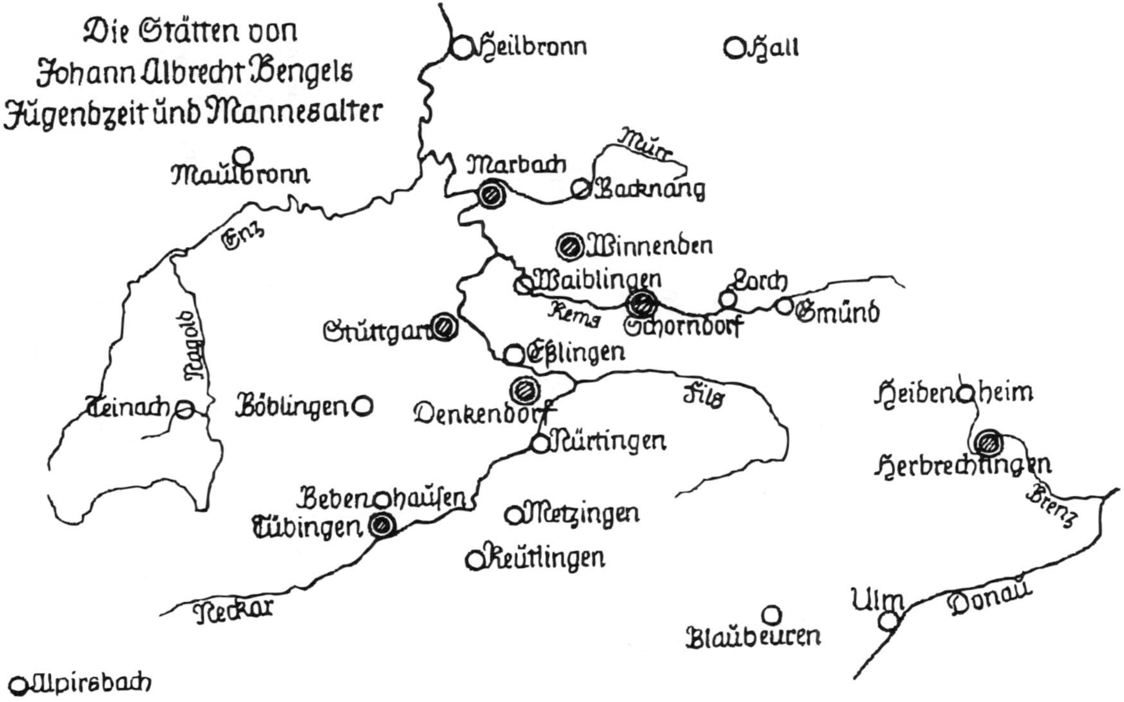

Cities in the Life of Johann Albrecht Bengel. Courtesy of Calwer Verlag

recording his impressions in a diary. Bengel was impressed by the Halle Foundations: "Till now I was a Christian alone, by myself, but here I am learning to consider the meaning of Christian community and the fellowship of the saints."[126] In Leipzig he met the wandering separatist mystic Johannes Tennhardt (1661–1720), and in Frankfurt he attended services in a synagogue.[127]

An early biographer of Bengel observed that "in vain does one seek in his life story a point at which one can say, here is his awakening to goodness."[128] Bengel never experienced a new birth of the Halle variety, with a long battle through to life-changing repentance, and he rejected the strict conversion piety advocated by Francke. From early childhood, he made use of every opportunity to hear and learn God's Word and to commit to memory prayers, hymns, and passages of scripture. His favorite reading included devotional writings by Johann Arndt, Johann Gerhard, and Spener.[129]

In early December 1713, Bengel took up the position of preceptor at the newly constructed school in the Denkendorf Cloister, near Esslingen, teaching boys fourteen to eighteen years of age who were preparing for university study in Tübingen.[130] For twenty-eight years he taught Latin, Greek, and Hebrew, as well as history, mathematics, and logic.[131] His inaugural lecture was entitled "On the Most Certain Method for Arriving at True Learning: Devotion to Piety." Godliness is both the means and goal of all true education, Bengel said. The primary source for learning and teaching is the Bible; then come conscience, experience in the world, and books. Bengel's guiding maxims or principles as a teacher were the honor of God, constant self-examination, and fulfilling one's calling as the servant of God. He embodied these principles in his own life.[132] Bengel nurtured his spiritual life with the simple truths of the catechism and the virtues of faith, hope, love, gentleness, and humility.[133] Because of a reticence to act without clear guidance from God, Bengel did not respond to offers of university professorships in Tübingen and Giessen.[134]

In his final years, Bengel served in church and state administrative posts. He was elected to the Württemberg *Landtag* (state assembly) in 1747, and in 1749 he was made a member of the Stuttgart consistory, overseeing church affairs in the region. Like Spener, he promoted a more strict practice of church discipline and objected to state interference in church affairs. But he avoided direct criticism of the authorities. He counseled the Stuttgart court preacher Johann Christian Storr, a former pupil, against confrontation with his lord over plans for a carnival. It is largely due to Bengel that Württemberg Pietism avoided radical separatism and worked instead for renewal from within the state church.[135]

BENGEL'S GREEK NEW TESTAMENT AND *GNOMON NOVI TESTAMENTI*

In the midst of his busy teaching schedule, Bengel's main academic interest and occupation remained the Bible, including work on a new critical edition of the Greek New Testament and an exegetical commentary based on this text. Bengel accepted Spener's recommendation that biblical scholars follow the grammatical-historical method of biblical theology in place of the dogmatic method of scholastic theology.[136]

The impulse for the Greek edition came from Bengel's experience as an undergraduate at Tübingen and from his work as a teacher in the Cloister School in Denkendorf, where in a two-year period he and his pupils read through the entire Greek New Testament. He assembled more than thirty versions of the Greek Testament, with the purpose of reconstructing the oldest, original text. In comparing and deciding among textual variants, Bengel formulated a rule still followed by scholars today: the more difficult reading is to be preferred to the easier one. Ancient copyists were more likely, consciously or unconsciously, to harmonize passages than to introduce a more difficult, alternative reading. Bengel divided the Greek manuscripts into two families: the Asiatic or Byzantine, centered in Constantinople, and the African, centered in Alexandria.[137] In 1734 his Greek New Testament appeared in two editions, one with a critical apparatus for scholars and one without apparatus for the use of students and pastors.

Bengel completed his German translation of the New Testament in 1740 but held it back, possibly due to controversy surrounding efforts to improve on Luther's version. In 1752 he finally gave the translation to a Stuttgart publisher, and he was reading the page proofs when he died on November 2, 1752.[138] His German New Testament appeared in 1753. Bengel aimed to produce an alternative to Luther's translation that was true to the Greek: "a German text, upon which I might found and build my German interpretation of the New Testament and not always have to say about the Luther translation: 'In Greek it actually says such and such.'"[139] He realized, however, that Luther's translation would remain the preeminent and most popular German version.

Bengel's best known book is the *Gnomon* (Pointer), published in 1742,[140] the product of twenty years of intense work. It consists of a new Latin translation of the New Testament with commentary, also in Latin. Named for the pointer on a sundial,[141] Bengel's *Gnomon* contains concise explanations, or pointers, on matters of philology, exegesis, literary structure, figures of speech, and practical edification to assist pastors with their sermon preparation. For example, he highlights the presence of "ancient rhetorical forms in the New Testament, in particular its Hebraisms."[142] Bengel believed that conciseness was a virtue and that "the true interpretation is more frequently buried than assisted by a multitude of conflicting opinions."[143] On this point, Bengel makes a significant departure from the philosophy of the *Biblia Pentapla* and the *Berleburg Bible*.

In the preface to the *Gnomon*, Bengel offered twenty-seven admonitions (*Monita*) or guidelines for assessing New Testament manuscript evidence. He suggested that "more witnesses are to be preferred to fewer," but more importantly, "witnesses who differ in country, age, and language, are to be preferred to those who are closely connected with each other." Most important of all, "ancient [Greek] witnesses are to be preferred to modern ones." Then there is the principle of preferring the more difficult reading to the simpler one: "A reading which does not allure by too great facility, but shines with its own native dignity of truth, is always to be preferred to those which may be supposed to owe their origin to either the carelessness or the injudicious care of copyists." He concluded with five principal criteria for determining a disputed text: the antiquity of the witnesses, the diversity of their extraction, and their multitude; the apparent origin of the corrupt reading; and the native color of the genuine one. "When these criteria all concur, no doubt can exist, except in the mind of a skeptic."[144]

An interesting example of Bengel's reasoning can be found in his comments on I John 5:6–9. He acknowledged that the majority of Greek manuscripts do not include verse 8: "And there are three who testify in heaven: the Father, the Word, and the Holy Spirit; and these three are one." But Bengel defended the authenticity of the verse.

> The Greek manuscripts in which the letters of John are contained are neither so numerous nor so ancient that they must stand in the way of

> [including] the verse concerning the three witnesses in heaven . . . This verse rests upon the Latin version, and that almost exclusively. But this version is the most ancient and at the same time the most correct, which, through the centuries, the church fathers in Africa, in Spain, in France and Italy continually use as their basis. And finally, this verse is demanded by the context of the whole letter as well as by the preceding and following verses as the indispensable mid-point and summary of the whole letter.[145]

For Bengel, rhetorical analysis of the passage in favor of the Trinitarian clause trumped the meager historical witness for the verse in available Greek manuscripts.

Bengel's *Gnomon* was a great success, with generations of German pastors turning to it as a helpful guide. John Wesley translated the *Gnomon* into English, relying on it heavily for his *Explanatory Notes on the New Testament* (1754). Wesley called Bengel "that Great Light of the Christian World."[146] Bengel's words of advice for Bible study have become classics in the Christian tradition: "Apply yourself wholly to the text, and apply the text wholly to yourself"; "Bring nothing into the text, but take everything from it and leave behind nothing that is in it."[147] Many have resonated with his Bible metaphor: "the Bible is a letter that my God has written for me, according to which I should align my life and by which God will direct me."[148] Bengel's legacy was an emphasis on the original Greek text, philological commentary, new translation, and pious edification. In this he helped set the direction for German scholarship for centuries to come.

Conclusion

Thanks in large measure to the work of the Pietists, the eighteenth century was the century of the Bible, marked by efforts to recover the original documents, to produce critical editions and new translations, and to publish works of biblical interpretation and commentary. Over a period of thirty-six years, the Pietists produced more Bible translations than appeared during all of the sixteenth and seventeenth centuries. Pietist figures such as Glüsing, Haug, and Bengel advanced their renewal of Orthodox Protestant theology by means of a vernacular Bible and commentary that made scholarly information easily available, leaving traditional confessional theology behind. Only recently have the *Biblia Pentapla* and its editor, Glüsing, begun to receive the recognition they deserve as a unique and early example of Pietist engagement with the Bible alongside the *Berleburg Bible* and the work of Bengel.

The Enlightenment character of the *Biblia Pentapla* is evident in its goal of encyclopedic comprehensiveness, its recognition of multiple translation possibilities, and its ideal of tolerance and ecumenical-mindedness. The significance of the *Berleburg Bible* lies in its combination of an encyclopedic format and a separatist, Philadelphian theology. It uses the media of the Enlightenment, including techniques of collection, presentation, and organization, to repackage the Bible in service to a religious aim. Bengel's rules for Biblical scholarship and devotional Bible study have become classics in the Christian tradition. He set the direction for future generations, so that by the 1760s, Germany had become the center of European biblical scholarship and manuscript study.[149]

CHAPTER 9

Pietism, World Christianity, and Missions to South India and Labrador

Neither in Martin Luther's time nor in the age of Lutheran Orthodoxy did Protestants make any concerted effort to fulfill Christ's great commission, to go into all the world and preach the Gospel. In fact, "in Lutheran Orthodoxy the abiding validity of the missionary obligation was expressly denied."[1] It was considered the sole privilege of the first-century Apostles, and a task they had completed. As St. Paul said, "Have they not heard? Indeed they have; for their voice has gone out to all the earth" (Rom. 10:18). In seventeenth-century Protestantism one finds, for the first time, widespread, concerted appeals for Christian mission to the Jews and heathen. These calls were expressed not only in sermons and theological treatises but also in mission agencies founded by Anglicans, Congregationalists, Dutch Reformed members of the Further Reformation, and German leaders such as Ernst the Pious and Gottfried Wilhelm Leibniz.

The new thinking did not result in immediate Protestant missionary activity, however. The new beginning had to wait until the eighteenth century and the mission efforts of the Halle Foundations and the Moravians. Even among the Pietists, it took an outward push to move them from theological conviction to practical missionary engagement—specifically, the initiative of the Pietist king of Denmark, Frederick IV, who in 1705 asked Halle for missionaries to send to his Danish colonies in India and the Caribbean. Bartholomäus Ziegenbalg and Heinrich Plütschau arrived in Tranquebar, India, in July 1706.[2] When the English Baptist missionary William Carey, often called the "father of the modern missionary movement," arrived in Calcutta in 1793, Lutheran Christianity in India was nearly a century old.[3]

The Halle Foundations, under Augustus Hermann Francke, and the Moravian Brotherhood, under Count Zinzendorf, took very different approaches to the missionary enterprise. In Halle, mission remained one of many initiatives whose focus was primarily on German and European Christians; for the Moravians, mission was the central priority of their community. This difference in priority carried over to differences in the preparation of missionaries, methods of evangelism, and practical work in the field. Halle sent university-educated pastors and theologians, whereas Herrnhut missionaries were generally uneducated craftsmen who had felt the call of God. The difference in training was reflected in different methods of evangelization. Halle missionaries to Tranquebar relied on preaching, catechism, and the building of schools. The missionaries lived together in a house, rarely venturing into the countryside to visit the people. In contrast, Moravian missionaries sought out every opportunity for contact with the indigenous people whom they hoped to convert. They lived and worked among the people every day and earned their living by practicing a trade.[4]

The vast majority of eighteenth-century missionaries and mission agencies were German. Five German mission societies and support agencies came into being in the eighteenth and early nineteenth centuries. The first was the Danish-Halle Mission society, which sent Ziegenbalg and Plütschau to India in November 1705. In the early nineteenth century, the legacy of the Danish-Halle mission was taken over by the Leipzig Evangelical Lutheran Mission Society.[5] The second society was the Herrnhut Mission. When Count Zinzendorf visited the Danish court in 1731 and met a former slave from the Danish-held island of St. Thomas in the Caribbean, he committed himself to organizing his own mission to the Caribbean islands. In August 1732, Leonhard Dober and David Nitschmann were sent to St. Thomas. The third agency was the Evangelical Mission Society in Basel, "the mother of modern German Missionary Endeavor," which sent out its first missionaries to Armenia in 1821 and to Africa in 1827. Its roots lay in Württemberg and the *Deutsche Christenthumsgesellschaft* (German Christian Society) founded by Johann August Urlsperger (1728–1806) in Basel in 1780.[6] A fourth society, the Rhine Mission Society, was established in 1828 in Wuppertal, bringing together several smaller groups: the Barmen Mission of 1815 and mission societies in Elberfeld (Wuppertal), Cologne, and Wesel. The Rhine Mission sent its first missionaries to South Africa in 1829 and to Borneo in 1834. The fifth early German mission society was founded in Berlin in 1824 through the efforts of ten prominent Christian laymen, along with Johannes Jänicke, pastor of the Bohemian-Lutheran Church in Berlin. Its first missionaries set out for South Africa in 1834.[7]

The societies in Basel, Wuppertal, and Berlin were the creation of prominent lay business people. Initially, these societies raised funds for existing mission efforts; only later did they become sending agencies, preparing their own candidates and overseeing their own missionary endeavors. All three were nonconfessional organizations, bringing together mission-minded leaders and missionaries from various Protestant Christian backgrounds.[8]

Some of these mission societies established schools for prospective missionaries. In 1800 Jänicke set up the first German mission school in Berlin, starting with seven students. By the time of Jänicke's death in 1827, the school had sent out some eighty workers into various mission fields. In August 1816 the Basel Mission School opened its doors, with seven students under the leadership of Christoph Blumhardt. It provided missionaries and pastors to the London Missionary Society and to missions in America, Brazil, Australia, and Russia.[9] The Basel school had an ambitious educational program that clearly aimed at professionalization of the missionary calling. Subjects of study included the following:

> the Latin, Greek, Hebrew, Arabic (or Sanskrit), and English languages, as well as arithmetic, geometry, geography, along with natural science subjects, German language, world history, study of the Old and New Testaments in the original languages, church history, Christian faith and life, the history of the heathen religions, acquaintance with the heathen peoples and the science of mission. Additionally, music, singing, painting, and the fundamentals of business are cultivated. Practice in preach-

ing and catechizing take place at the mission school and in the local city school.[10]

In contrast, Moravian missionaries received training that focused on the practical needs of missionaries in the field. The guidelines in August Gottlieb Spangenberg's "Instruction for Brothers and Sisters Who Serve the Gospel among the Heathen" (1784) remained in effect until the early twentieth century.

The remarkable vitality of German Pietism is nowhere more evident than in this drive to make Christianity a world religion. Pietists' conviction that Christianity was a religion for the world led to astonishing efforts to plant the faith in cultures worldwide. Yet, until recently, the story of German missions has been largely ignored in German scholarship.[11] In this chapter, two early Pietist mission efforts are examined: the Halle mission to Tranquebar from 1706 to 1733, and the Moravian mission to Labrador between 1752 and 1795.

The Danish-Halle Mission to Tranquebar, India, 1706–1733

SOURCES ON THE TRANQUEBAR MISSION

Thanks in large measure to the prolific writing of Bartholomäus Ziegenbalg, the sources reflecting the European side of the early Tranquebar mission are many.[12] He wrote two accounts of the mission to the Indians in Tranquebar,[13] composed studies on aspects of Hindu religion and Malabar culture,[14] and wrote many letters.[15] A. H. Francke began publishing the diaries, letters, and other information sent back to Halle by missionaries in southeast India. The nine volumes of *Halle Reports* (*Hallesche Berichte*), preserved in the Halle Foundations archive, cover the period from 1710 to 1772.[16] Especially valuable are two collections of letters, originally written on palm leaves, in which Tamils answer questions posed to them by Ziegenbalg and Johann Ernst Gründler. The letters, ninety-nine in all, were published in the *Halle Reports* in 1714 and 1717 and became known as the "Malabar Correspondence."[17] Europeans were fascinated by these reports and the information they held concerning language, literature, religion, and culture in south India. Johann Wolfgang von Goethe, for example, was a devoted reader of the *Halle Reports*.[18] The Halle archive also holds eighteenth-century palm-leaf writings in Tamil by Ziegenbalg that await transcription and interpretation.[19] Benjamin Schultze's diaries are another rich source of information on eighteenth-century south Indian society and religion. Key figures in the mission to south India, such as Schultze, Christoph Theodosius Walther, Christoph Samuel John, Johann Philipp Fabricius, and Christian Friedrich Schwartz, still await source-based biographical studies.[20]

Arno Lehmann, editor of Ziegenbalg's letters, cast some doubt on the reliability of the *Halle Reports*, pointing to the strict censorship that Francke exercised over the journals and reports of missionaries, and his insistence on removing anything "odious." Heike Liebau points out, however, that there has never been a careful investigation of Halle's editing of these documents. Her own experience has been that Halle's published reports rarely depart in any significant way from the manuscript originals of the missionaries.[21]

Recently, there have been efforts to investigate interactions and negotiations between the missionaries and the local Indian peoples, considering the nature of their intercultural encounters. New studies are examining the mission from the perspective of the Indian mission associates who worked alongside the Europeans and the influence they exerted on the Europeans. What was the self-understanding and identity of these Indian nationals? And how did they go about creating an indigenous Indian Christianity? A rich collection of sources bears witness to the work and experience of these Indian mission workers, including their reports, letters, and life stories (*Lebensbeschreibungen*).[22]

BARTHOLOMÄUS ZIEGENBALG (1682–1719) AND HEINRICH PLÜTSCHAU (1677–1747)

When King Frederick IV of Denmark (1671–1730) decided to launch a mission to his Danish colonies in India and the Caribbean, his court preacher, the Pietist Franz Julius Lütkens (1650–1712), was unable to find anyone suitable in Denmark. Lütkens asked his friend Joachim Lange (1670–1744), rector of the Friedrich Werder gymnasium in Berlin and assistant pastor of the New Church in the city, if he could recommend candidates for a mission to the Danish colonies. Lange wrote to two of his former pupils, now Halle theology students, Bartholomäus Ziegenbalg and

Heinrich Plütschau, and asked them to consider the missionary calling. Lange met with the two men on October 1, 1705, to discuss the matter. Ziegenbalg at first held back on account of his youth, lack of a university degree, and ill health. But when Plütschau, five years older, expressed his willingness to go, Ziegenbalg decided to join him on the mission expedition. On October 7, Ziegenbalg wrote a letter to A. H. Francke, informing him of their decision. This was the first Francke knew of the matter.[23]

Ziegenbalg and Plütschau were ordained in Copenhagen on November 11, 1705, and commissioned by the king to conduct a mission among the people living in and around Tranquebar (in Tamil, *Tarangambadi*, "village of singing waves") for a three-year term. Tranquebar was a seaport city controlled by the Danish East India Company. Danish traders had dominated the region since 1620, building an impressive fortress and designing the city according to European standards. The king assured Ziegenbalg and Plütschau of his protection and said he would instruct the governor to do all he could to support the missionaries in their work.[24]

The son of a Saxon grain trader, Bartholomäus Ziegenbalg attended a gymnasium in Görlitz, once the home of Jakob Böhme, and the Friedrich Werder gymnasium in Berlin, under Rector Lange.[25] In 1703 Ziegenbalg went to Halle to study under Francke. His health was delicate, possibly a severe case of hypochondria, and he never completed his university studies. Heinrich Plütschau, from Mecklenburg, also attended the gymnasium in Berlin, under Lange. He began theology studies in Halle in 1702 and served as a tutor in the Halle schools. While under Lange's influence, he had felt called to mission work; when the opportunity to join the mission to Tranquebar came along, he gladly took it.

After seven months on ship, Ziegenbalg and Plütschau arrived in Tranquebar, on the Coromandel Coast of southeastern India, on July 9, 1706. By the late seventeenth century, the city had six to seven thousand people. Of these, 250 were Europeans, mostly Portuguese. The vast majority were Tamil Hindus; in addition, there were 840 Muslim Tamils as well as some Catholics and Protestants.[26] The larger Tranquebar Colony comprised some fifteen villages, encompassed some thirty-two square kilometers, and had a population of ten to fifteen thousand people.[27] Ziegenbalg wrote, "The Inhabitants are partly white Europeans, partly white tawny Portuguese, and partly yellow Moors; but for the most part, black-brown Tamils."[28] Tranquebar was ethnically and religiously pluralistic, with

Buddhism, Jainism, Hinduism, Christianity, and Islam all part of its history. Ziegenbalg found that Tamil society allowed room for individuality and personal ambition. He felt a deep sympathy and respect for Tamil culture, possibly due to his rural upbringing in Lusatia.

Ziegenbalg and Plütschau immediately devoted themselves to learning the Tamil language. Ziegenbalg offered the use of his house to the seventy-year-old Tamil schoolmaster named Kanabadi, and in September 1706 the school moved in. Ziegenbalg sat among the children as Kanabadi taught them to draw Tamil characters in the sand.[29] But the schoolmaster knew no German and so could not explain the meanings of words. Ziegenbalg then sought the help of Aleppa (1660–1730), a leading figure in the Tamil community and chief interpreter for the Danish East India Company, who was fluent in German, Dutch, Danish, Portuguese, and Tamil. Ziegenbalg offered him a salary and lodging, which Aleppa accepted. With his help, Ziegenbalg made rapid progress in the Tamil language.[30] "In less than a year," a biographer notes, "Ziegenbalg spoke Tamil so masterfully that the Indians listened to him breathlessly. He only needed to appear in the street or in a field, when at once hundreds of Tamilians gathered around him and impulsively showed him their respect and love because he spoke their language."[31]

By April 1707 Ziegenbalg was preaching in Tamil, and soon after he translated the Danish Lutheran worship service into Tamil. He established a small Lutheran church in the Tamil quarter of Tranquebar, and on August 14, 1707, the "New Jerusalem Church" was dedicated. By October 1707 the missionaries had baptized forty Tamil- and Portuguese-speaking Indian converts.[32] In December of that year, the Danish-Halle mission established a school for boys that met in Ziegenbalg's home, as well as a school for girls, the first girls' school in India. Ziegenbalg described the religious setting in Tranquebar as of 1709: "In the city there are three Christian churches, the Danish which is called Zion, ours which is called Jerusalem, and the Catholic. The Moors or Mahomedans have a large Church and the Malabar heathen [Hindus] have five large pagodas [temples]."[33]

Plütschau assumed leadership of the Portuguese community in Tranquebar. Tranquebar had been a Portuguese port since the sixteenth century, and the Portuguese language was the *lingua franca* of the region. In 1711 Plütschau returned home due to ill health. There he authored a cat-

Bartholomäus Ziegenbalg, 1715

echism for the Portuguese school in Tranquebar and for a short time gave instruction in the Tamil language to mission candidates in Halle.[34]

Ziegenbalg's closest associate in Tranquebar was Johann Ernst Gründler (1677–1720), who arrived on July 20, 1709, with the second group of Danish-Halle missionaries.[35] Gründler had studied in Leipzig and Wittenberg, completing his master's degree, and in 1701 began work as a teacher at the Halle orphanage. Inspired by reports of the mission work in south India, Gründler decided to join the mission. On the voyage to India he studied the Tamil grammar sent to him by Ziegenbalg, and devoted several months to further mastery of the language after his arrival. By the end of September 1709, Gründler had reorganized the schools according to the model used in Halle, setting up separate classes according to age and providing instruction in weaving, knitting, and sewing for the girls.[36] Gründler, in contrast to Ziegenbalg, was a skilled diplomat in dealing with the European colonial authorities.

Ziegenbalg soon came into conflict with Johan Sigismund Hassius, the Danish governor, who had not been informed of the Danish-Halle mission and was surprised by the missionaries' arrival. Hassius became concerned over Ziegenbalg's conventicle gatherings and efforts to convert the Europeans who were working in Tranquebar. The governor perceived the mission as a threat to his rule and to the business interests of the Danish East India Company. "I consider Ziegenbalg to be a Thomas Müntzer who is intent on stirring up rebellion."[37] Hassius imprisoned Ziegenbalg in a dungeon in the century-old fortress, from November 19, 1708, to March 26, 1709. Christian Ludwig, a German soldier, provided Ziegenbalg with pen and paper, enabling him to compose two manuscripts on "the God-pleasing Pastor" and "the God-pleasing Christian." They contain Ziegenbalg's reflections on the writings and ideas of Johann Arndt and Gottfried Arnold.[38]

By this time, the missionaries found themselves in a precarious position and in desperate need of funds. In 1710 they found the support they needed—from the London Society for Promoting Christian Knowledge, an Anglican educational organization. A. H. Francke was a corresponding member of the society and on close terms with the London group. Unable to find Englishmen to send to India, the society took on support of the two Halle missionaries and even recognized their Lutheran ordination. On October 14, 1714, Ziegenbalg wrote a letter to England, rejoicing that "God has awakened and encouraged the blessed English nation to support the work of the Lord" in India.[39]

Ziegenbalg rose to prominence because of his leadership abilities and impressive linguistic gifts. His translation of the Tamil New Testament, completed in March 1711, appeared in 1713–1715, along with a Tamil hymnbook and a translation of Luther's *Small Catechism*. These were printed on a press sent by the London Society in 1712, using fonts from Halle.[40] In 1716 Ziegenbalg produced a Tamil grammar, based on an earlier existing grammar, which offers impressive testimony to his involvement with the Tamil people and his grasp of the colloquial Tamil that they spoke.[41] The grammar provides insight into the sociocultural, religious, and linguistic fabric of the Tamil people in Tranquebar. Ziegenbalg became convinced that "the Tamil language deserves to be included by the learned in Europe among the Oriental languages that are worth learning."[42]

In an effort to grasp the essentials of Tamil culture, Ziegenbalg gathered a library of Tamil literature. With the help of the interpreter Aleppa, he obtained many Tamil books, including palm-leaf manuscripts. Ziegenbalg approached Brahmin widows in Tranquebar, offering to buy their books. "When they understand that I am using their books against them to prove the absurdity of their religion," Ziegenbalg wrote, "they become a little mean and avoid giving them to me. Everybody keeps their books bundled up and well hidden so whenever I ask for books they are in a position to pretend they do not have any. Still, with money and a little tact one can get almost anything from them, however precious."[43] By August 1708, Ziegenbalg had collected and read 112 Tamil works on theology, philosophy, ethics, rhetoric, poetry, politics, medicine, mathematics, and music. He provided reviews of these books in 1708 in a work he entitled *Catalogue of Tamil Books*.[44] By 1709 he had collected more than three hundred Tamil works, mostly Hindu, Muslim, and Jain writings. His collection included all the major works of Tamil literature.

Ziegenbalg translated three Tamil collections of "wise sayings." One was a book of rules of behavior that was used with young schoolchildren. This was the first translation from Tamil into a European language. He also completed a study of Hindu gods and sent the manuscript to A. H. Francke in Halle. In reply, Francke reminded Ziegenbalg that his mission was not to "spread this heathenish nonsense in Europe" and suggested he stick to the business of conversion. As a result, the study was not published until 1867.[45] Ziegenbalg also discovered the works of Civavaakiyar, a popular fourteenth-century Tamil siddhar poet and spiritual alchemist who taught a yoga that aimed at finding Sivam (Shiva), the highest good within. Some verses of a Civavaakiyar poem read as follows:

Oh dumb people who wander and run around the town, the land and the forest, suffering,
The highest of the highest is spread everywhere in the earth and the sky.
Know that the highest is directly within you, remain with that feeling!
Oh poor people who seek to bathe yourself in the sacred waters . . .
After it is clear to you that the sacred waters are within you,
That the sacred five syllables [Civam] are the sacred waters itself, there is nothing more.
Civam is indeed inside and you and you yourself can know and feel him.
("Conversations in Tarangambadi," 264)[46]

It struck Ziegenbalg that the renewal project of the Tamil siddhars bore some similarity to the Pietist ideals of the German missionaries. Indeed, Ziegenbalg noted that the "natural moral behavior" instilled by writers such as Civavaakiyar often put Christians to shame (262–264).

Many Tamils at the time, both Muslim and Hindu, had a sense that the world was in turmoil, that "everything is confused." An old man observed that "there are so many different opinions about the nature of God and the names for God, a person does not know what to choose" (261). Muslims and Hindus had a prophecy that change was coming, brought by men from God; unity of belief would one day be restored to all humankind. A Muslim holy man visited Ziegenbalg and lamented the impiety he observed among Christians, Muslims, and Hindus. He and Ziegenbalg agreed that renewal must begin with improvement in one's own life.

Ziegenbalg found the Tamil people to be intelligent and forthright: "Truly the Malabarians are a witty and sagacious people, and will need to be managed with a great deal of wisdom. Our school-master argues with us daily . . . He is confident that sooner or later we shall all turn Malabarians, abandon Christianity, and adopt the Tamil point of view" (257). On one occasion, a Tamil gentleman said to Ziegenbalg, "We accept such teaching with gratitude and are eager to hear more, but you should let us speak more and assure us that you will not get angry if we object to something you say" (265).[47] In March 1714, a local Tamil merchant told the missionaries that Tranquebar was a happy, well-ordered society, and he objected to Europeans criticizing their religion. The Tamils observed the bad behavior of members of the Danish trading company and suggested the missionaries begin their preaching among their fellow Europeans. They told Ziegenbalg, "We can tell by the way Christians live that their religion is not good. If only those make it to heaven who stick to the straight and narrow path that you have described, then not very many of you Christians will attain salvation. Every day we see things with our own eyes that are disgusting to us; surely God will be even more disgusted by such things" (261). The *Halle Reports* frequently commented on the bad behavior of local European Christians and lamented the detrimental effect on the mission effort. Tamils also found the Europeans offensive for cultural reasons: the Europeans ate beef, drank alcohol, used their left hand to eat after defecating, mistreated their animals, and had poor hygiene (258).

TAMIL MISSION ASSOCIATES

From the beginning, it was part of the Pietist mission strategy to involve local Indians directly in the mission work. A diary entry of May 28, 1707, reports on the appointment of a Tamil catechist whose duties included helping new catechumens learn Luther's catechism by heart and explaining to them the meaning of the words, visiting the catechumens in their homes and seeking to overcome their prejudice against Christian missionaries, and meeting with non-Christians to convince them of the errors of their religion and the truth of Christian teaching.[48] The Indian workers had to be Christian converts, be skilled in their native language, literature, and culture, and have the trust and respect of their own people. Members of a family often served as catechists for three generations and more. One source for candidates was the mission school, where missionaries could observe and identify young men and women in whom they recognized potential for service.[49]

When Plütschau returned to Europe in September 1711, he took along a fifteen-year-old Tamil boy named Timothy Kudiyan, so that the boy could pursue theological studies in Halle. Timothy proved a great advertisement for the mission and attracted considerable donations. He did not, however, find success in his studies and returned to India in 1720 to work as a bookbinder. On his trip back to Europe in October 1714, Ziegenbalg took with him fourteen-year-old Peter Malaiappen as a conversation partner so that he could practice the Tamil language. Peter was bright and, during the two-year furlough, was able to master German. The boy served as an object lesson for Ziegenbalg's mission reports in Halle, London, and Copenhagen. On July 26, 1715, Peter spoke before the Danish royal family in Copenhagen, greatly impressing the king. Peter later assisted Benjamin Schultze in completing a translation of the Bible into Tamil.[50]

Ziegenbalg returned to India with his new wife, Maria Dorothea, arriving in Tranquebar on September 1, 1716.[51] He devoted himself to training Tamil pastors and catechists so that they could spread the Christian faith among their own people. On October 30, 1716, the seminary program was launched, enrolling eight graduates of the Tamil school for boys. The curriculum placed emphasis on theological subjects, the biblical languages, Hebrew and Greek, and Bible exegesis. Rhetoric and impromptu public speaking were required, with students gaining practice before school classes and in churches. The catechists were expected to be skilled debaters and defenders of the Christian faith. Those serving as interpreters for the missionaries had to gain facility in German and Danish.[52]

On average, there were four or five Indian workers for every missionary of European origin. These included Indian preachers, catechists, teachers, and translators. By 1731 the following Tamil mission associates were working alongside the six European missionaries in Tranquebar: six local catechists, nine helpers for the catechists, and six teachers in the schools (four men and two women). Support workers included two Indian bookbinders and two assistants, a watchman, a house servant, a woman to do handwork, a nurse, a water-bearer, and a washerwoman. By 1776 the Tamil mission associates included three preachers, two catechists, fourteen catechist assistants, eight teachers, and two prayer leaders (*Vorbeter*). The mission associates were salaried; the support workers were often Hindu Tamils who were paid for their services.[53]

Among Tamil mission associates, the country preachers (*Landprediger*) had the place of honor. Having passed the seminary program and further examination by the missionaries, they were formally called and ordained by the church as country preachers. As national mission workers, they remained under the oversight of the European missionaries. The country preachers were responsible for speaking in church and in public, dispensing the sacraments, exercising discipline over their congregants, overseeing the catechists, celebrating weddings and funerals, and generally exercising leadership in the territorial churches. The first Tamil preacher was a young man named Aaron (1698–1745); he was ordained in 1733. The catechists were responsible for instructing the baptized and unbaptized in the Christian faith and teaching catechism classes. The catechists used a manual of questions and answers, published in 1731, called *The Order of Salvation*. They also visited the sick, oversaw distribution of alms to the poor, organized funerals and weddings, and assisted in the churches. The most outstanding early catechist was Rajanayakkan (1700–1771). He assisted Christoph Theodosius Walther (1699–1741) in writing the first history of Christianity in the Tamil language, published in 1735.[54]

The teachers in mission schools required competency in religion, languages, and other subjects, as well as in methods of pedagogy. These Tamil mission associates often served as leaders in the community and as mediators between the people and the missionaries. Prayer leaders, like teachers, included both men and women. They were responsible for organizing worship and bible study within a region that had no church, repeating the sermon of the missionary or national preacher. Women prayer leaders provided pastoral care to women.[55] In the 1740s, Indian associates began contributing to the literature in the *Halle Reports*. By the 1780s, the diaries and travel reports of Indian workers occupied as much space in the *Reports* as those of the European missionaries.[56]

By the time the Danish trade colony was turned over to the British in 1845, more than fifty missionaries, mainly German, had served among the Tamil people, with several hundred Indian workers serving alongside the missionaries in spreading the Christian message to their own people.[57] It is clear that the Danish-Halle mission did not remain a European undertaking but quickly became a cross-cultural project with significant involvement of indigenous agents. Tamil workers brought their own abilities, interests, and expectations, which often changed the strategies of the European missionaries. The cooperative work of Tamil and European agents, who were so dependent on one another, was marked by dialogue and bargaining. There is still much to learn about the biographies, motives, self-understanding, and strategies of the Tamil colleagues of European missionaries. Their many letters, reports, translations, and other writings await investigation.[58]

Aaron, the First Tamil Country Preacher, Ordained in 1733. Courtesy of the Archive and Library of the Francke Foundations

ZIEGENBALG'S LEGACY

Ziegenbalg died in February 1719 at the age of thirty-six, leaving behind a Lutheran church in Tranquebar with some 350 members.[59] In September of that year, his successor, Benjamin Schultze (1689–1760), arrived in Tranquebar to carry on the work that Ziegenbalg and Plütschau had begun. Schultze, who remained in India until 1742, represented a new era in the history of the Tranquebar mission.[60] Like Ziegenbalg, he picked up the language quickly and within months was preaching in Tamil.[61] He wrote of the Malabar language, "At first we thought this language to be very wrong because of the word order. It differs from all other oriental and occidental languages known to us. But if one understands the construction, there is no language more clear, more regular and more graceful than this one."[62] Thanks to Schultze, the translation of the Old Testament into Tamil was finally completed in 1726. In that year he moved to Madras, a change prompted by his uncooperative and prickly personality and conflicts with the other missionaries. In Madras, Schultze encountered other Indian languages, leading to his work on a Telugu-English dictionary, accompanied by an introduction to the Telugu culture in that region, which was never published. His Telugu grammar, completed in 1728, was translated into English and became a text for new missionaries.[63] He also produced a four-language dictionary in English, Telugu, Tamil, and Latin. The legacy of Ziegenbalg and Schultze was not just the establishment of churches; they also served as "key figures in the transmission of knowledge of the Indian languages and culture, both within India and between India and Europe."[64]

The continuing impact of the Halle mission in Tranquebar is apparent from a conference that took place from July 3 to 9, 2006, at the Lutheran Theological College in Tranquebar (now known as Tarangambadi). More than three hundred delegates, church leaders, and academics met to honor the three-hundredth anniversary of the arrival of Ziegenbalg in India as the first Lutheran missionary. In a plenary address, the Hindu scholar Professor S. P. Thyagarajan spoke of Ziegenbalg's *Weitsicht* (broad perspective) that enabled him to bring European and Indian cultures into contact with each other. Through his translations, Ziegenbalg helped to bring India's rich cultural heritage to Europeans. He contributed to social harmony and the strengthening of civil society. Dr. Ramachandran

Nagaswamy pointed to Ziegenbalg's openness to the Indian context, as evidenced by his effort to master the Tamil language and to acquaint westerners with the rich Tamil culture and literature. Daniel Jeyaraj noted the contribution of Ziegenbalg to the academic discipline of Indology. Missionaries such as Ziegenbalg enriched the local culture and tradition. The success of his mission lay in the way he worked so closely with the Indian people and was able to articulate their deepest hopes and fears.[65] Stephen Neill was surely right when he observed that with Ziegenbalg, "a new epoch in the history of the Christian mission had begun."[66]

The Moravian Mission to Labrador, 1752–1795

Study of the Moravian mission to Labrador is greatly assisted by the Moravians' meticulous record keeping from the day they arrived. They produced reports and diaries, as well as maps and landscapes of their surroundings. The Moravian archive in Bethlehem, Pennsylvania, holds letters, minutes, reports, community news, and statistics of conversions and baptisms for the early mission stations in Nain, Okak, and Hopedale.[67] A recent study of early Moravian mission settlements in Labrador makes use of the journals and diaries of Johann Christian Erhardt, Jens Haven, and Christian Drachardt. Also valuable are Haven's and Drachardt's letters and reports.[68]

COUNT NIKOLAUS LUDWIG VON ZINZENDORF (1700–1760): COUNT WITHOUT BORDERS

The Moravian devotion to mission and to meticulous records is due largely to the founder of the renewed Moravian Church, Count Nikolaus Ludwig von Zinzendorf.[69] While a pupil at the Pädagogium Regium in Halle, Zinzendorf met Ziegenbalg, Plütschau, and Gründler and the Tamil boy Timothy. Zinzendorf later credited his missionary zeal to his encounter with these missionaries and to his reading of the *Halle Reports*.[70] Under his leadership, Moravian missionary endeavors became legendary. "By the time Count Zinzendorf died in 1760," Rollmann writes, "226 missionaries had been sent to Greenland, North America, the Danish West Indies, Antigua, Suriname, and Berbice (Guyana), where they had 7,000 people under their care and had baptized 3,000."[71] The number of Moravian missionaries soon far outstripped the number sent by Halle. For Zinzendorf's renewed Moravian Church, worldwide mission was essential to its identity and to Moravians' calling as children of God. Zinzendorf himself would spend years abroad, visiting various Moravian mission fields.

Zinzendorf has been described as "one of the most colorful and intriguing figures of eighteenth-century Pietism,"[72] and indeed, in Christian history.

> Nikolaus Ludwig von Zinzendorf . . . is without doubt one of the most original figures in all of church history, and also one of the most controversial. Already in his own lifetime, opinions on him were divided: his followers called him tenderly "dear Papa" (*Papachen*), submitted to his authority . . . and saw in him a "true prince of God"; but his opponents untiringly cautioned others against this "false apostle," denounced him as a heretic unparalleled in the history of the church, or poured their scorn upon this "most laughable spiritual Don Quixote."[73]

His creative energy and his social behavior in crossing traditional social boundaries were unusual for his time.[74] W. R. Ward observed that the "central biographical problem" of Zinzendorf's life was "his universal ability to make a splendid first impression, and his universal inability to cooperate for long with men of independent mind." Ward illustrated this by reference to the in-fighting between Halle and Herrnhut, a conflict that "formed the context of Zinzendorf's greatest failure (in America) and his greatest success (in the Baltic)."[75] There are diverging interpretations of Zinzendorf's theology, due to his lack of theological training and his refusal to write a systematic theology.[76] The wealth of research devoted to Zinzendorf makes him the most discussed German religious figure of the eighteenth century. This interest can be attributed to his personality, his controversial piety, and his impact on German culture.[77]

Zinzendorf had a remarkable family and upbringing. He was born in Dresden on May 26, 1700, to a family of old Austrian nobility that had emigrated on account of their Protestant faith. His parents, Georg Ludwig and Charlotte Justine, were influential supporters and admirers of Philipp Jakob Spener, the Pietist patriarch. After Georg Ludwig died in July 1700, Charlotte Justine remarried and the child was sent to live with his maternal grandmother, Henriette Katharina von Gersdorf (1648–1726) on her estate near Zittau. It was here that Spener, just a year before his death, met the four-year-old Zinzendorf. Henriette Katharina was "one of the most educated women of her time, a German Anna Maria van Schurman."[78] The theologian Abraham Calov praised her knowledge of biblical languages, and she was widely admired for her religious poetry and verse. She corresponded with the philosopher Leibniz, with prominent Lutheran theologians, and with Pietist leaders such as Spener and Francke. Henriette Katharina read widely, including works by radical religious thinkers such as Jakob Böhme and Jane Leade, who advocated creation of a unified, loving community of true believers who set aside their denominational differences. She used her wealth to support oppressed Pietist individuals such as Johann Wilhelm Petersen. Zinzendorf said of Henriette, "I received my principles from her. If it weren't for her, the movement would never have come about. She saw no great difference among Catholic, Lutheran, and Reformed religion; whoever had a heart for faith and came to her in need was her neighbor."[79]

At age ten, Zinzendorf was sent to one of the famous schools of the Halle Foundations. He spent six years in Halle, forming lifelong friendships and imbibing its entrepreneurial spirit. The Halle experience included regular mission reports and encounters with missionaries, laying the groundwork for Zinzendorf's lifelong interest in missions.[80] Zinzendorf hoped to study theology at university, but his family directed him to study law at Wittenberg University as preparation for following his father in serving at the court in Dresden. Zinzendorf continued to read widely on theological subjects, however, especially the works of Luther and Spener. In 1734 he was ordained by the Lutheran church in Tübingen.

In 1719–1720 Zinzendorf embarked on an educational trip—*Bildungsreise*, or *Kavalierstour*—an experience that stamped him for life. He visited leading church figures in Holland and Paris. His dealings with Reformed and Catholic Christians in these places "confirmed his views about a cross-confessional religion of the heart." In describing his experiences and his sense of discovery, the young count sounds almost like a modern university student.

> I came to know all kinds of religious groups, and found that they had more to say for themselves than I had heard . . . Cardinal Noailles and some bishops sought to make me a Catholic. I grew fond of them, but

> their plan did not succeed. Nevertheless, I became so familiar with the Catholics that I gained a better idea of the honest souls that there are among them. From this time on, I determined to discover the best in all religions and . . . to attain a better and more benign understanding of their teachings and what might be removed as a hindrance to godliness. For I knew that the Lord must have his own among all kinds of people. I returned from my travels with the conviction not to allow myself to engage in any [religious] favoritism, for I saw that those [Pietists] in Halle and Wittenberg were also human and fallible. This notion helped in promoting the kingdom of God on my estate, but it alienated the Halle Pietists from me somewhat.[81]

After returning from his travels, Zinzendorf sent the Jansenist Cardinal Noailles a book of Pietist devotion—Arndt's *Wahres Christenthum*. The two men continued to exchange letters until the cardinal's death. In the fall of 1721, Zinzendorf began his service in Dresden as legal counselor in the court of the elector of Saxony. On Sundays, Zinzendorf welcomed into his home a "Philadelphian" gathering of Pietists, separatists, and devotees of Jakob Böhme and offered them edifying discourses.[82]

In 1722, three important events occurred: Zinzendorf married Erdmuth Dorothea, Countess von Reuß-Ebersdorf (1700–1756); he purchased his grandmother's estate in Berthelsdorf in Upper Lusatia, near the Czech border of today, hoping to establish "Halle-style" institutions, beginning with an orphanage; and in the summer, he began welcoming religious refugees to his Berthelsdorf estate.[83] These refugee groups were under threat of persecution by the Catholic Habsburg Emperor Charles VI (d. 1740),[84] who sought to enforce the 1648 decree of the Peace of Westphalia that only three official faiths should be tolerated in the German empire: Lutheran, Reformed, and Catholic.[85] The refugees included Moravians, Schwenkfelders, and other Protestant groups.[86] The Moravians were German-speaking Christians from villages in Moravia, led by the carpenter Christian David (1691–1751), a Pietist convert from Catholicism. They were descendants of the old Unity of the Brethren (*Unitas Fratrum*), deriving from the Hussite movement.[87]

On June 17, 1722, Christian David felled the first tree for building a house for the refugees in Berthelsdorf. W. R. Ward observed that "this handful of refugees brought by David to Berthelsdorf in 1722 were to leave an indelible mark on the history of Protestantism."[88] Five years later, in April 1727, there were two hundred and twenty settlers on Zinzendorf's estate, about two-thirds of these Moravians; by 1734 the number had grown to between six and seven hundred. The Schwenkfelders came from Silesia and were the spiritual descendants of the Silesian nobleman Caspar Schwenckfeld von Ossig (1489–1561). The other groups came from various parts of Germany and included Pietists, separatists, Lutherans, and Calvinists (Reformed). The vast majority of these settlers were craftsmen; it was a community of artisans and handworkers. In 1724 they began to call the settlement "Herrnhut," meaning "God's protection" or "the Lord's watch."[89]

Inevitably, tensions and divisions arose among the diverse Herrnhut settlers, forcing Zinzendorf to return to his estate. Wallmann observed:

> There were Moravian families who were still committed to the old brethren traditions. They had no interest in joining the neighboring Lutheran Church in Berthelsdorf. A separatist refugee from Ebersdorf called the Lutheran Church "Babel." Christian David finally left the Herrnhut community. When the Lutheran pastor Johann Andreas Rothe could no longer manage the quarrels and divisions, Zinzendorf took leave of his Dresden post to devote himself entirely to working among the Herrnhuters. Through his intensive efforts with individual members, through the imaginativeness of his ideas, and not least through the charisma of his personality, he was able in a short time to bring about peace among the settlers, indeed, to make them a close community . . . a cross-confessional brotherhood.[90]

On May 12, 1727, Zinzendorf delivered a constitution to the Herrnhut community, "Principle Things Required and Forbidden" (*Herrschaftlichen Geboten und Verboten*); in addition, on July 4 he presented "Statutes of Brotherly Union," consisting of forty-two articles governing their communal life. Herrnhut would be a community free of outside princely interference, ruled by elders. Zinzendorf created a series of offices for the laity: elder, teacher, encourager, and nurse to the sick. Their life together should be according to the pattern of the first Christians and express Christian freedom before God. The Herrnhuters must commit themselves to the Philadelphian ideal of "constant love toward all brethren and children of

God in all Religions."[91] The statutes were signed by almost all in the Herrnhut community.

Under Zinzendorf, a renewal of the old Moravian Brethren came about, resulting in a new kind of community marked by at least three features. First, the community was shaped by his close relations with the ruling princes. His marriage to Erdmuth Dorothea, Countess of Ebersdorf, was advantageous. "Marriage into the house of Ebersdorf appeared to confirm Zinzendorf's connexion with that network of Imperial counts which sustained the Pietist enterprise," Ward observed.[92] Second, the community was marked by Zinzendorf's increasing rivalry with Halle Pietism. And third, Zinzendorf made the community a missionary movement.[93] He had a global vision that was ahead of his time and is rightly described as "a pioneer of world mission."[94]

JOHANN CHRISTIAN ERHARDT (1718–1752)

The first Moravian mission efforts were to the slaves in the West Indies in 1732 and to the Inuit in Greenland in 1733. In 1747 and 1749, Johann Christian Erhardt, a German mariner and Moravian convert, visited Greenland. He spent time among the missionaries and Inuit people there and became interested in the Inuit across the strait, in British North America. After reading *A Voyage to Hudson's Bay* by Captain Henry Ellis, Erhardt became convinced of the need for a mission among the Inuit in Labrador.[95] On May 20, 1750, he wrote a letter to Bishop Johannes von Watteville in Herrnhaag, suggesting an exploratory venture. The bishop and count Zinzendorf approved the endeavor.[96] Erhardt then struck an agreement with the English Moravian businessman Claude Nisbet and his associates, John Grace and William Bell, to pursue a combined mission and trade voyage to Labrador. Four missionaries were appointed for the trip: Matthäus Kunz, Georg Wenzeslaus Golkowsky, Johann Christian Krumm, and Christian Friedrich Post, all with mission experience. Erhardt would serve as the trade agent.

On May 18, 1752, Erhardt, the missionaries, and a crew set out from London on the ship *Hope*. It was a dangerous journey, taking them through fog and ice fields. Sailing northward along the Labrador coast, they dropped anchor on July 31, 1752, in a bay Erhardt named Nisbet Harbor. On eight occasions, the nearby Inuit came to their ship on kayaks to trade.

Erhardt obtained 1,322 pounds of fish in exchange for knives, sabers, and sewing accessories. In August the Europeans built a small settlement near a stream. It consisted of a log house, twenty-two feet long and sixteen feet wide, and gardens around the house. Erhardt traded whalebone, seal-skins, and oil with some Inuit who camped nearby.[97]

On September 5, Erhardt and the crew sailed northward in search of further trade, leaving the missionaries to spend the winter in the settlement. According to Erhardt's last diary entry, on September 12, Inuit men in two kayaks came on board the ship and persuaded them to visit a nearby island where they had fish to trade. The next day, Erhardt and six crew members visited the island. They were never seen again. Days later, the remaining crew returned to Nisbet Harbor, picked up the missionaries, and returned to England, arriving in Deal on November 24. A search party in the following year found and identified the men's dismembered bodies on the island of Manneriktok. They also found the ruins of the log house.[98]

EXPLORATORY JOURNEYS AND EARLY SUCCESS

The Moravians undertook further exploratory journeys in 1764, 1765, and 1770, thanks to the initiative of Jens Haven, a Danish carpenter. Haven learned to speak the Inuit language while in Greenland. On an exploratory voyage in the summer of 1764, he established contact with Inuit in Quirpont and found immediate acceptance as a friend because he knew their language. The following year, the Inuit said to Haven and Christian Drachardt, "Come and build here, but bring no Kablunak (Europeans) with you, but only people who are like us and you, namely Inuit." On September 12, 1765, Haven and Drachardt spent the night among the Inuit for the first time, sleeping in the tent of a witchdoctor named Segullia. They even observed his shamanic dance.[99] That the Moravians should sleep among them without weapons at hand was taken by the Inuit as proof of their good intentions.[100] The witchdoctor was clever enough to demand payment for lodging them overnight.

In 1770 some Moravian ship-owners in London bought a vessel for the use of Haven and other missionaries.[101] The 1770 voyage included eighteen persons in all: three Danish Moravian brothers, three German Moravians, four English Moravians who were sailors, five more sailors, Captain Mugford, a helmsman, and a first mate. In Labrador they met up with an Eskimo woman named Mikak and her husband, Tuglavina, who joined them on ship and showed them the way to Esquimaux Bay. Here the Moravians had rights to a hundred thousand acres of land; in 1771 they built a permanent settlement, to which they gave the biblical name "Nain."[102] Two further mission stations were established, one north of Nain on Okak, the island where Jens and Mary Haven settled in 1776, and one south of Nain in Hopedale, where Moravian missionaries settled in 1782.[103]

The success of the late eighteenth-century Moravian mission in Labrador was due to several factors. Because of their experience living in Greenland, both Jens Haven and Christian Drachardt knew the Inuit language and were well versed in the dress, customs, morals, and religion of the Inuit people. Because the Moravian missionaries knew the Inuit language and customs and behaved differently from European traders, the Inuit welcomed their presence among them. The Moravians were careful to seek permission from the Inuit before taking up residence on their lands.[104] Also, the Inuit woman Mikak played a key role in the success of the Moravian mission in Labrador; the first Labrador mission station would not have been founded without her help. In what follows, the contributions of Jens Haven and Mikak to the Labrador mission are considered in more detail.

JENS HAVEN (1724–1796)

Three Danes are associated with the early Moravian settlement in Nain and the Labrador mission: the carpenter Jens Haven, the theologically educated Christian Larsen Drachardt (1711–1778), and the physician Christoph Brasen (1738–1774). It was Haven who had the courage in 1764, twelve years after the death of Erhardt and his companions, to undertake renewed contact with the Labrador Inuit. But it was Brasen, an ordained deacon, not the difficult Haven or the aging Drachardt, who led the 1771 missionary expedition that established Nain and who served as the mission's first superintendent. He was often called on to use his medical expertise in this remote settlement. In the summer of 1774, Brasen and three other missionaries and crew, nine in all, journeyed northward up the Labrador coast, hoping to establish a second mission settlement. On the return trip on September 14, in snow and cold, a gale came up from the

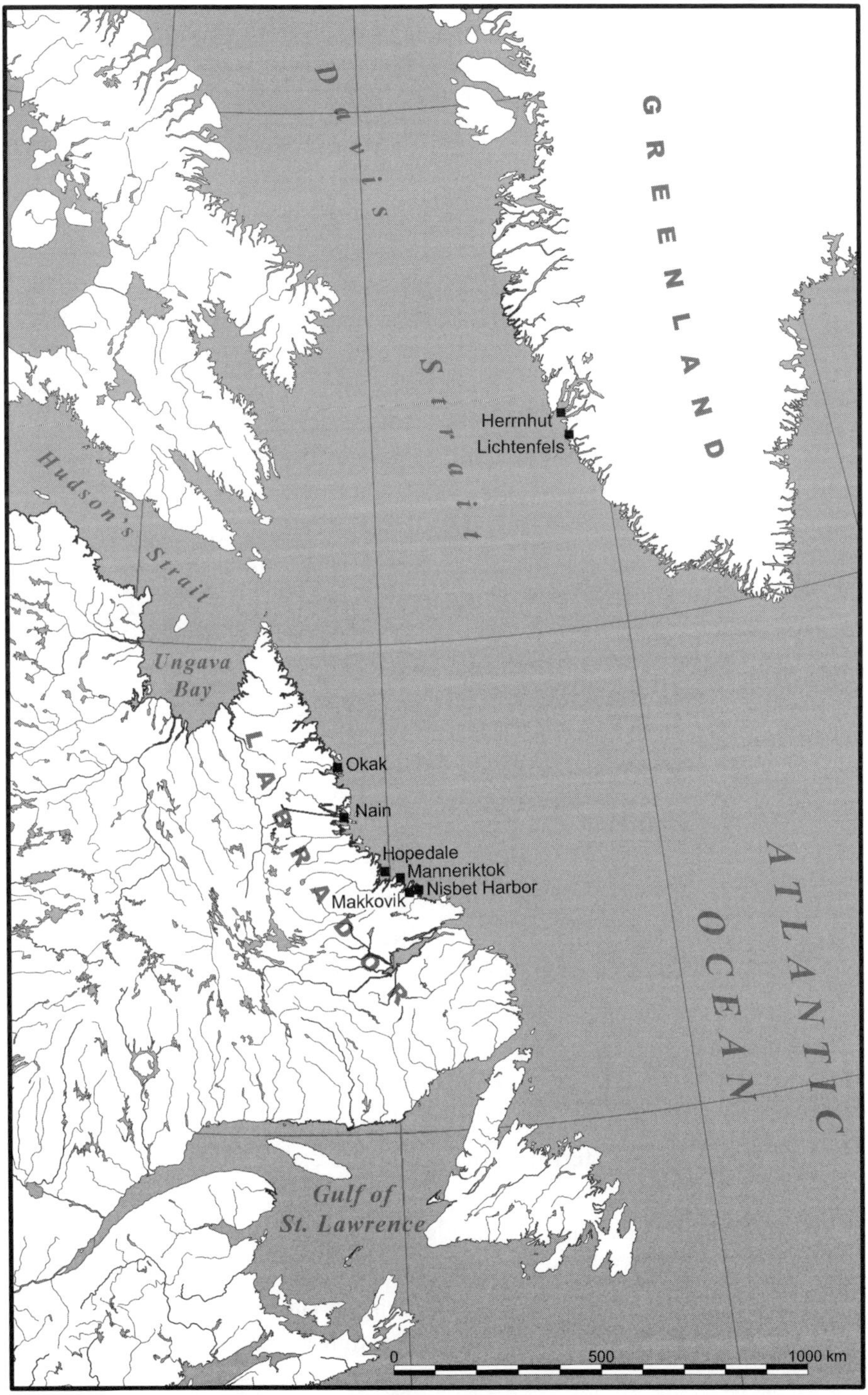

Eighteenth-Century Moravian Mission to Labrador.

northeast and their ship, the *Jersey Packet*, suffered shipwreck on the rocks about ten miles from Nain. Brasen and Gottfried Lehman drowned in attempting to reach the shore. Haven and the others survived.[105]

Jens Haven is justly recognized in Moravian tradition as "the trailblazer of the mission in Labrador and builder of the first three mission stations." He was born on June 23, 1724, in Wust, a small village in Jutland, Denmark, where his father was a farmer. As a young man, he was working in the field one day when lightning struck near him and threw him, unconscious, to the ground. Coming to himself, he begged God for his life and asked for help to become a new man. Later, on hearing of the Herrnhuters, Haven moved to Copenhagen with the hope of joining their community. There he became an apprentice to a cabinetmaker who was a Herrnhut brother (Moravian). Haven soon joined up with the Moravians in the city. In 1748 he traveled with other Moravian brothers to Herrnhut in Germany. He was accepted into the community there and worked for several years as a printer. After he heard of the death of Erhardt in Labrador in 1752, there grew in him a desire to go to Labrador and take the Gospel to the Inuit.[106]

Haven's first assignment, however, was to go on a mission to Greenland, along with his brother Peter and Matthäus Stach. Zinzendorf sent Haven off with the words, "Go my child, learn the language of Greenland, and the Savior will provide." They set out on March 15, 1758, and settled in a place they called Lichtenfels, building a mission house there. Haven quickly felt at home and mastered the language. He would have spent the rest of his life in Greenland but for a dream he had in 1762, in which a voice said, "This is not your destination; you are to make my name known to a people that has not yet heard of me." He fell back to sleep and heard the same voice two more times, awaking each time. On the third occasion, the voice added that he was to proclaim the Gospel *to the people of Labrador*. He took it as the Lord's confirmation of his call to Labrador. In January 1763, he returned to Herrnhut and put before Bishop Johannes von Watteville and the elders his desire to go to Labrador. They put the question to the lot: should he return to Greenland? The lot answered no. When the possibility of Labrador was put to the lot, the answer was positive. During his future mission work in Labrador, whenever Haven was in doubt about how to proceed, he consulted the lot and found assurance of the Lord's leading.[107]

Haven immediately made his way to London and, after finding support among English Moravian businessmen, as Erhardt had done, undertook a series of exploratory voyages to Labrador in 1764, 1765, and 1770. On April 11, 1771, he married Mary Butterworth, a Moravian woman from Yorkshire. A month later, Jens and Mary set sail for Labrador, arriving in Nain on August 9, 1771. In 1774 and again in the summer of 1775, Haven made trips with Steffen Jensen up the Labrador coast, hoping to establish a second mission station. In Okak, 150 miles north of Nain, they bought land from the Inuit and began construction of a mission house in 1776. It was still unfinished when Jens, his wife Mary, and their infant son moved in. Haven immediately began to instruct the Inuit in the rudiments of the Christian faith, often preaching four or five times in a day. The first Inuit baptism took place on February 19, 1776, and the new church was dedicated the same day.[108] Haven considered this the happiest year of his life. "I could preach the Gospel to the Esquimaux with a cheerful heart," he wrote, "and the Lord blessed my weak testimony of His death and love to sinners, so that several of them became concerned to obtain deliverance from sin and everlasting life, and most were sober and attentive hearers."[109]

In the fall of 1777, Haven and his wife made a return trip to England with their two small children. At the Moravian love feast in London in November, the Haven family attended in "Esquimaux Dress."[110] After visiting Niesky and Herrnhut, in Germany, they returned to Labrador by way of England, though the seas were especially dangerous and "swarmed with privateers" because of the American Revolutionary War.[111] Jens and Mary continued their mission work among the Inuit in Okak from August 1778 to September 1781. By the end of this time, they had baptized thirty-eight Inuit and the church had grown to fifty members.[112]

Jens and Mary then moved to Hopedale, about 150 miles south of Nain, founding a mission station there in 1782. Haven's exceptional ability in communicating with the Inuit in their own language led to further success in evangelism. In 1784 he baptized seventeen Inuit converts. Although short in stature, Jens Haven was marked by uncommon physical strength, endurance, and tenacity. However, by this time he was sixty years old, and he and his wife were worn out. After applying to the Moravian elders to be released from their missionary service, they left Hopedale in August 1784 and retired to Herrnhut. Haven returned to his carpentry work. His eyesight began to fail, and for the last six years of his life he was totally blind. He died in Herrnhut in 1796.[113]

The work of the Moravians among the Inuit continued to thrive after Jens and Mary Haven returned to Europe, although not without setbacks and difficulties. By the year 1800 there were 110 baptized converts and 228 persons in the care of the missionaries at the three stations. In 1804, Haven's successors witnessed a great revival and awakening among Inuit believers. It began in Hopedale and by February 1805 had reached Nain. Revival spread to Okak through letters that the missionaries received from their colleagues and from some of the Eskimos at Hopedale, which they shared with the congregation. "In the course of ten years the number of Eskimoes under the care of the brethren at the three stations was doubled, amounting to 457, of whom 265 belonged to the classes of communicants, baptized, and candidates for baptism."[114] In 1871 the Inuit Bible translation was completed, and the Inuit people were given the scriptures in their own language.[115]

MIKAK AND TUGLAVINA

If there was one person who proved essential to the success of the early mission in Labrador, it was the Inuit woman Mikak (ca. 1740–1795). It is hard to imagine the first mission station being established without her. She proved a great help to the missionaries in at least three ways. First, during her visit to London in 1768–1769, she promoted the work of the Moravian missionaries among the English authorities. Second, in 1770 she and her family went on board the *Jersey Packet* to show the way to Esquimaux Bay, where, in 1771, the Moravians built the permanent settlement that they called Nain. Third, after being instructed in the Christian faith by Drachardt, Mikak began passing on what she had learned to her people. She was known within the Labrador mission as the "first fruits" among the Inuit in accepting the Christian faith.[116]

Mikak was an impressive and charismatic person. Europeans found her captivating; Haven called her "the great lady."[117] She was among the first Inuit to stand out as a distinct individual in the historical encounter between Europeans and Labrador's aboriginal people. One scholar observed that "our best opportunity to examine the Inuit encounter with the Moravians in particular and Europeans in general is through the life of the Inuit woman Mikak."[118] She held tremendous influence among her own people as well.

Mikak was born around 1740, the daughter of the Inuk chief Nerkingoak. In 1762 she married the son of an Inuk chief; after he died, she married Tuglavina in 1770. While on an exploratory expedition in September 1765, Jens Haven and Christian Larsen Drachardt were forced by bad weather to spend a night with the Inuit. They slept in the tent of the witchdoctor Segullia, who was the brother of Tuglavina. It was on this occasion that they met Mikak.[119] She learned the names of the missionaries and memorized a prayer that Drachardt taught her. In August 1767, the Inuit attacked Nicholas Darby's fishing station at Cape Charles, stealing their boats and killing three of Darby's men. Men from Fort York responded by pursuing the Inuit, killing twenty Inuit men and taking five women and six children to Fort York and keeping them in the blockhouse. Mikak and her son were among them. A naval officer at the garrison, Captain Francis Lucas, noticed how quickly she picked up English words. He helped her to learn English; she taught him some Inuit.[120]

On Lucas's recommendation, the governor of Newfoundland, Hugh Palliser, arranged in fall of 1768 for Mikak and her six-year-old son, Tutak (Tootac), to accompany Lucas back to England.[121] In London Mikak became a celebrity, impressing the English with her intelligence, charisma, and language ability. She was lavished with gifts, including a gold crown, the king's medal, and a dress with gold lace from the Princess of Wales. The artist John Russell painted her portrait with her son, Tutak, at her elbow.

While in London, Mikak stayed with Francis Lucas. Jens Haven visited her several times, seeking her help in persuading the English authorities to allow the Moravians to set up a mission in Labrador. Haven reflected on these visits:

> [In 1768] the well-known Esquimaux woman, Mikak, was brought from Labrador to London. She rejoiced exceedingly to find in me one who could speak her language, and earnestly begged that I would return with her and help her poor countrymen, who were almost ruined, many of them having been shot in an affray which happened between them and the English. Her repeated applications were of great use in putting forward the business of the projected Mission, for she was noticed by many persons of rank and influence, and her request attended to.[122]

John Russell's 1769 portrait of Mikak and Her Son Tutak

Haven told her of Christ as the way of salvation, and she seemed to understand, promising him, "I shall certainly get to know the Lord because I want to get to the eternal joy." She then turned on Lucas and rebuked him: "Oh, you miserable person! You know God and you live worse than the Inuit. I do not believe that you know God."[123] In the spring of 1769, Mikak returned to Labrador with Lucas.[124]

It is a measure of Mikak's success in promoting the work of the Moravian missionaries with her royal patrons that Haven and Drachardt gained the right to negotiate for land when they returned to Labrador in the summer of 1770. On July 16, they met up again with Mikak and her husband, Tuglavina, a man of influence, intelligence, and a "turbulent spirit." Mikak and Tuglavina accompanied the missionaries on ship, guiding them through the narrow channels to Esquimaux Bay, the site for their first mission post (Nain). Drachardt held a preaching service for Mikak and Tuglavina twice daily on ship, from July 18 to August 1. When they landed at Esquimaux Bay, Mikak encouraged the three hundred Inuit living there to come and hear Drachardt speak. In August 1771, fourteen Moravian missionaries arrived in Labrador to establish the settlement in Nain, including Jens Haven and his new wife, Mary, under the leadership of the surgeon Christoph Brasen.[125] Mikak was the key to the Moravians' successful interaction with the Inuit. "Although Haven and Drachardt could communicate in Inuktitut, it is . . . unlikely that they could have integrated themselves quite as readily without Mikak's efforts as interlocutor and ambassador."[126]

After 1773, relations between Mikak and the Moravians became strained. The Moravians felt that Mikak's experience in England had made her proud and ungodly: "Her presents are now spoild & good for nothing; & she Herself is far from being happier by what she received in England. She is prouder, more wretched and miserable than she was before, less contented with the station she must however submit to & less fit to enjoy for the future what other Eskimaux call Enjoyment of Life."[127] Mikak and Tuglavina were unhappy when the Moravians refused to offer Tuglavina a sail in exchange for whale fins. The couple traveled north and inland for the caribou-hunting season and lived near the Nain islands in the winter, where they could hunt seals and sea birds. The missionaries feared that if the Inuit lived too far from Nain they would fall back into their old ways, exchanging spouses and relying on shamans for healing and prosperity. By April 1773 Mikak was unwell and unhappy over Tuglavina's decision to leave her and take her sister as his wife. Mikak began living with her sister's husband, Pualo. For the first five years of her marriage with Pualo, Mikak was distant toward the Moravians, avoiding the mission settlement and showing no interest in converting or being baptized.

In April 1779, she and Pualo indicated their desire to receive instruction so they could be baptized.[128] Mikak, her son Palliser, and Pualo became candidates for baptism in January 1781. Only the men were chosen for baptism, however, not Mikak. Pualo was given the name Abraham and Palliser the name Jonathan. But their chaotic life continued.

> [By summer of 1785], several Inuit had died, including five of the nineteen baptized Inuit who had gone south; Nerkingoak, Mikak's father, had ordered the death of a woman in order that she might keep her dead brother company; Pualo shot a young man by the name of Sirkoak because he had partnered with Mikak, but Sirkoak survived after receiving treatment when he reached Nain; Pualo may have died of an infection at this time; two Inuit men were shot dead "for the sake of their wives" by Tuglavina and another Inuk called Adlucock; one woman hanged herself; and many wives were stolen.[129]

In the fall of 1795, Mikak arrived in Nain critically ill. In the final ten days of her life, she welcomed the advice and care the Moravians offered her and was finally baptized. She died on October 1, 1795, at fifty-five years of age.[130] Mikak was a woman marked by intelligence and generosity. She was respectful toward the Moravians and their teachings, all the while remaining her own person.

THE MORAVIAN LEGACY IN LABRADOR

To this day, the majority of those living on the north coast of Labrador are Moravian, testimony to the impact of eighteenth-century Moravian missionaries in the region. In 2002 the Moravian 250 exhibit was created, and a commemorative volume—*Labrador through Moravian Eyes: 250 Years of Art, Photographs & Records*—was compiled, to honor the Moravian missionaries who first arrived in Labrador in 1752.[131] About 250 photographs and pieces of art were included in the traveling exhibit, accompanied by a narrative that placed the images within the context of Labrador history. The exhibit was first displayed in St. John's, Newfoundland, from August 21 to September 8, 2002. Earlier, from August 8 to 10, an academic symposium was held in the communities of Makkovik and Hopedale, with the theme "From Nisbet Harbour to Nain: The Early Moravian Exploration of Labrador." Papers addressed Inuit life in eighteenth-century Labrador, the archaeology of the Makkovik area, the first Moravian exploration of 1752, preparations for the first permanent settlement of Moravians at Nain in 1771, and the contribution of the Moravians to the history and culture of Labrador's north coast.[132] All of this confirms the importance of the Moravian missionary legacy in Labrador.

Conclusion

The remarkable vitality of German Pietism is nowhere more evident than in the drive to make Christianity a world religion. The conviction that Christianity was a religion for the world led to astonishing endeavors to plant the faith in distant cultures. The early Pietist mission efforts to south India and Labrador were cooperative German-Danish enterprises. Two key figures in this endeavor, Ziegenbalg and Haven, left a missionary legacy that is apparent to this day. With Ziegenbalg, "a new epoch" in the history of Christian missions was launched.[133] The legacy of the Danish-Halle mission to south India includes the establishment of churches and transmission of knowledge about Indian languages and cultures throughout India and Europe. The legacy of Haven and the Labrador mission is three extant Moravian communities, in Nain, Hopedale, and Makkovik, home to the Inuit and white settlers of northern Labrador. Another legacy of the Moravian mission was a missionary awakening among eighteenth-century British Evangelicals. The Labrador mission prompted revival of the Society for the Furtherance of the Gospel and led, in turn, to the founding of the Baptist, London, and Church mission societies. These societies looked to the Moravians as a model and adopted the Moravian approach to preaching and to sending uneducated craftsmen into the field.[134]

Part IV

Pietism and Modernity

CHAPTER 10

The Contribution of German Pietism to the Modern World

In parts I and II of this book, the emphasis is on ways in which past events, traditions, institutions, and thinkers conditioned and influenced early Pietism in Bremen, Frankfurt, Leipzig, and Halle. Among these influences were the Thirty Years War; English, French, and Dutch Calvinism; and German Radicalism, including mystics, Spiritualists, alchemists, and Anabaptists. Whole dissertations have been devoted to showing how one or more of these traditions shaped the beginnings of Pietism.[1] The Spiritualism of Caspar Schwenckfeld, the spiritual alchemy of Johann Arndt and Jakob Böhme, and the conventicle piety of Jean de Labadie contributed greatly to the thought world of German Pietists.

Part III, on the social and cultural worlds of Pietism, has a different orientation. In this section, the emphasis is on how German Pietism departed from past precedents and brought about innovations that look distinctly modern. The Pietists rode the wave of cultural change, helping to create new traditions with an enduring impact. Some ways in which Pietism initiated departures from the past and helped stimulate modern trends become clear from a brief review of chapters 6 to 9. Pietism's contribution to the modern world is also apparent from its place in recent scholarly narratives about the rise of modern culture and religion in the West.

Social and Cultural Change in German Pietism: Paths to Modernity

Many of the features that characterized the Radical Pietists had a dual aspect of departure and innovation; they questioned old confessional certainties and demonstrated an eclectic openness to new truths from various sources. The Pietists' Spiritualist-alchemical language of personal renewal and new birth and their Philadelphian hopes of "better times" for church and society represent an innovation within Lutheran and Reformed churches. Pietist optimism and perfectionism challenged the pessimism of Luther and his expectation of God's coming judgment. The Pietist outlook bears comparison with the modern worldview, found in the French and American revolutions, that society and human existence can be shaped and improved to accord with values of justice and human dignity. Radical Pietist perfectionism challenged the traditional Lutheran understanding, also found in Arndt and Spener, that trials and doubts belong to the nature of faith and are a test from God. Not surprisingly, the Pietists' promotion of teachings not found in Luther was like a red flag to Orthodox Lutheran theologians.

One cannot consider Radical German Pietism without raising the issue of religious toleration in the German empire. German society at this time was out of step with the state-supported tolerance and pluralism in the Netherlands and England. The Radical Pietists rejected not only the old forms of religion but also the social order that was committed to preserving that religion. The faith, practice, and writings of these Pietists helped to undermine Christendom as a unitary system of belief and practice and to promote a modern society marked by individualism, diversity, pluralism, and tolerance. In the eighteenth century, the Radicals were forced to migrate to small counties with tolerant Reformed princes—in Berleburg in Wittgenstein, and in counties in the Wetterau such as Ysenburg-Büdingen. They followed a migratory lifestyle and experienced homelessness in the world—features Peter Berger identifies as the marks of modern consciousness.[2] Many emigrated and joined the early settlers of the New World. A prominent example of migratory Pietists is the Community of True Inspiration, truly "a peripatetic church." Inspirationist prophets and missionaries, notably Johann Friedrich Rock and his two assistants, traveled about on foot for months and years at a time. The community itself migrated from territory to territory due to persecutions and expulsions, finally emigrating to North America and settling along the Iowa River.[3]

Pietist affirmation of women and women's voices was another modern innovation. Chapter 7 shows how Pietism initiated a discussion about women's roles and opened opportunities for women in a way that drew the attention of contemporaries. Pietist women found freedom to express their spirituality in house church gatherings, in visions, and in writing their life stories. New social networks and informal gatherings in homes, along with new literary genres such as the memoir and autobiography, provided cultural space and opportunities for women's self-expression. Here is the beginning of a long trajectory of activism on behalf of women's rights that leads directly into the twenty-first century.

Chapter 8 considers how Pietists in the eighteenth century participated in a paradigm shift in which the Bible was liberated from theology and became "an instrument of culture."[4] This Enlightenment Bible was a Protestant creation, through scholarship and translation. In Pietist hands, Enlightenment techniques helped create new religious cultures, practices, and Bibles. The Pietists provided German Christians with alternative translations of the German Bible that were "unstained by devotion to party and doctrine."[5] In Germany, the philological sciences joined with Pietist efforts to make the Bible "fresh and relevant to the modern age."[6]

Chapter 9 notes how the legacy of the Danish-Halle mission included not only establishing new churches but also preserving and transmitting knowledge about south Indian languages and cultures throughout India and Europe. Ziegenbalg's translations helped transmit India's rich cultural heritage to Europeans, bringing European and Indian cultures into contact with each other as never before. Pietist missionaries helped make Protestantism more open, culturally aware, and worldly-wise—features that western Christians would do well to take to heart.

German Pietism in Scholarly Narratives on the Rise of Modern Culture and Religion

Pietism's contribution to the modern world is also apparent in scholarly narratives about the rise of modern culture and religion in the West. In recent years, the impact of German Pietism has been discussed in terms of two scholarly narratives: the *Enlightenment-secularization narrative* and the *evangelical-believers' church narrative.* In the Enlightenment-secularization narrative, Pietist individualism and subjectivism join with modern science and the Enlightenment in contributing to the dismantling of centuries-old certainties and hierarchies.[7] Both Pietists and Enlightenment Rationalists breathed the spirit of modernity.[8] Both spoke of renewal of the heart, the conscience, and the senses.[9] In the evangelical-believers' church narrative, Pietism is included in the story of the triumph of lay, experiential Christianity over state churches in England, Europe, and North America.[10] Pietism prepared the way for the Wesleys, Methodism, and American Revivalism.

> With the Pietists the whole direction of the modern age announced itself: personal experience and action became the chief values. These became more important than doctrinal formulations and systems and polemical debates about truths of the faith. Life not doctrine was the Pietist slogan . . . The ground of the Reformation has been left behind. The justification of the sinner through Jesus Christ was no longer sufficient; new birth was demanded and welcomed as a greater human event with tangible results.[11]

Both of these narratives agree that there is something distinctly modern about Pietism.

GERMAN PIETISM AND THE ENLIGHTENMENT-SECULARIZATION NARRATIVE

One of the most incisive accounts of the rise of secular societies in the West is by Canadian philosopher Charles Taylor in his book *A Secular Age* (2007). Taylor offers valuable insights into the complex factors that have given rise to secularism in the West. He also explains the continuing strength of religious faith in our day and why many secularization theorists, who have prophesied the demise of religion, are wrong. Taylor asks why, in our Western society, it was virtually impossible not to believe in God in, say, the year 1500, whereas in 2000, many of us find this not only easy but even inescapable? In 1500, there were three modes of "God's felt presence in the world": a sense of God's providence in ordering natural events; a society in which the gatherings of guild, city council, and parish were "interwoven with ritual and worship"; and a sense of living in an enchanted world filled with spiritual forces for good and evil. By contrast, in our day "a purely self-sufficient humanism has come to be a widely available option" for the first time in history. While our ancestors lived with faith naively, we must live it reflectively. It is this cultural shift that Taylor calls the coming of "a secular age."[12]

Taylor points to two main engines of secularization that helped undermine the enchanted world of our ancestors: first, the late-medieval drive to reform and remake European society, culminating in Protestant movements such as the Reformation, Pietism, and Methodism; second, the appeal of modern science. The Protestant Reformation was the main engine of disenchantment, especially in its Calvinist expression. Calvin rejected the sacramental religion of Roman Catholicism, the elements of magic in the old religion, in a way that Luther did not. Calvinist Reform also focused on the reordering of society through three levels of order building: a disciplined personal life, a well-ordered society, and the right inner attitude. In Calvinism one finds increasing criticism of popular culture and rejection of accommodation to Carnival.[13]

Pietism played an important role in this cultural shift. In the seventeenth and eighteenth centuries there arose "a new Christianity of personal commitment." In German Pietism and English Methodism, the stress was on feeling, emotion, and a living faith, reflecting the logic of Enlightenment "subjectification." Given the options of Protestant Orthodoxy and complete unbelief, many chose a third way—subjective religious experience. Pietism and early Evangelicalism helped undermine features of traditional religion and were in turn affected by a world that had lost its sense of enchantment and of God's providence.[14] Pietists and Methodists found themselves in a situation that was intellectually and spiritually unstable, resulting in melancholy and doubt. Reform, disenchantment, and personal religion went together. My own research into Pietist autobiography has largely confirmed this picture of subjectivity and melancholy among the Pietists. The autobiographies of Adam Bernd (1676–1748) and Johann Georg Hamann (1730–1788) reflect enthusiasm for self-representation, a world in which the experience of God's presence has begun to fade, and a deep-seated melancholy and *angst*.[15]

But Pietism not only contributed to the dismantling of the old; it contributed to the Enlightenment culture that characterized the new. Recent studies are showing that Pietism and Enlightenment "both contributed substantially to the development and formation of modern society."[16] Albrecht Beutel speaks of "the early Enlightenment character of Pietism" (*Der frühaufklärerische Charackter des Pietismus*),[17] arguing that Pietism made a substantial contribution to the new age of Enlightenment. Beutel appeals to five lines of evidence in support of his point.

First, in its effort to win people to the cause of Christian renewal, Pietism participated in creating new communication strategies. It used such modern communication forms as tracts and journals, as well as letters, open discussions and debates, and even the rumor mill.[18] One could add to this Pietist literary forms such as the monthly reports created by the Danish-Halle missionaries and the autobiographies that became so popular as Pietists testified to God's grace and leading in their life.

Second, the Pietists created alternative social networks, societies, and friendship circles. One thinks of the collegia pietatis in Frankfurt, some hosted and led by women, and the collegium biblicum in Leipzig, which began as a student society but soon spread among the citizens and included meetings in homes.

Third, Pietism undermined the theological and philosophical systems of the day, promoting instead a pragmatism in service to individual experiences and perceptions of truth. One thinks here of Gottfried Arnold and Friedrich Christoph Oetinger, who found in alchemy and Rosicrucianism the resources for a renewal of both theology and medicine. It has been observed that "one of the characteristics of all the protests against systematic Orthodoxy was eclecticism."[19]

Fourth, Pietism played a significant role in shaping modern individualism through a piety "authorized by one's own religious experience,"[20] resulting in a pluralizing of religion and the growth of religious toleration.[21] The story of Pietism is in large part the story of personal discovery, new experiences of God, and new truths about God, gained either through Bible study or through ecstatic experience.

Finally, Pietism promoted a Christianity of active engagement in the world, reflected in various forms of social and political reform. The modern character of Pietism is especially evident in its social programs and efforts to address poverty and the plight of orphans. A recent study of social engagement from the perspectives of German Pietism, Enlightenment, and the nineteenth-century Awakening shows that in all three cases, faith and piety were conceived, articulated, and promoted from a social and diaconal perspective. "Religion was formulated predominantly with attention to its individual, social, and religious usefulness; dogmatic and theological emphases move into the background."[22] Francke's ambitious projects aimed at nothing less than a second Reformation that would restructure the political and social world of his day from the ground up. Francke's Halle Foundations were intended to be the means for reforming all human relations—becoming "the spiritual center for realizing God's kingdom on earth."[23] Some see in Halle Pietism the first inklings of the modern welfare state. Both Francke and Spener were bold in calling on governing authorities to take responsibility for the poor and disadvantaged in society.

GERMAN PIETISM AND EARLY EVANGELICALISM IN ENGLAND AND NORTH AMERICA

French scholar Michel Godfroid observed that "to write the history of Pietism means nothing less and nothing more than to write the history of Protestants in the modern age—meaning the last three centuries."[24] There is an element of truth in this. Pietism initiated a departure from traditional Reformation Protestantism by introducing a new paradigm that was marked by the experience of renewal and new birth, conventicle gatherings for mutual encouragement, successful mission to the world, and the millennial reign of Christ on earth. These features of the Pietist paradigm live on in the Evangelical Christianity found in North America and England in the past three centuries.

It is largely thanks to W. R. Ward that the Evangelical debt to German Pietism is now more widely recognized. In his three books on the history of early Evangelicalism, Ward single-handedly reoriented the story of Evangelicalism away from the North Atlantic to Central Europe, showing the largely German roots of Evangelical religion.[25] Evangelicalism is no longer simply "an Anglo-American story," beginning with the 1738 conversion of John Wesley at Aldersgate. Ward gave central place in the Evangelical story to Johann Arndt, Jakob Böhme, and Pierre Poiret. Pietists read Luther through the lenses of these radical Spiritualists, resulting in a very different kind of Protestant religion, one that found an enthusiastic following in the German empire, the Netherlands, France,

England, and North America. The ideals of religious renewal crossed national boundaries; one misses this cross-pollination if one's attention is focused on just a national or linguistic field of study, as has often been the case in scholarship on Evangelicalism.

Ward's history of early Evangelicalism includes a volume devoted to the Evangelical mind. There he highlighted the "radical underworld" of Paracelsian, alchemical, kabbalistic, and theosophical religion that was the meat and potatoes of leading German Pietists.[26] Oetinger and Arnold, for example, doubted one could be a theologian without mastery of this esoteric world of thought. Pietists and Evangelicals understood human nature and the natural world in terms of correspondences and notions of macrocosm and microcosm.[27] The impact of Pietism as a social and intellectual force can be traced not only in the thousands of Pietist emigrants to the New World but also in Evangelical and Revivalist religion that flourished in eighteenth- and nineteenth-century England and North America.

Stephen Stein has argued that German Pietism deserves a larger place in accounts of American religious history. This adjustment would provide a much-needed corrective to the tendency to focus too much on New England and too much on English-speaking immigrants. The story of Pietism in North America provides the necessary historical context for the Great Awakenings and the ecstatic phenomena that appeared among the converted.[28]

An especially important contribution of German Pietism to modern Evangelicalism is the many Pietist hymns that have been translated into English and continue to be sung right up to the present day. These hymns are marked by a deep sense of God's presence and closeness with the believer. John Wesley personally translated thirty-three German hymns, most of them by Gerhard Tersteegen and other Pietists, including Gottfried Arnold, Christian Friedrich Richter, Freylinghausen, and Zinzendorf. Wesley's last words on earth were a paraphrase of Tersteegen's greatest hymn, *God Himself Is with Us*, as he confessed, "The best of all is, God is with us!"[29] After Wesley, Pietist hymns continued to find their way into English hymnbooks and to become a valued part of Evangelical worship, thanks to the translation work of Frances Cox, Catherine Winkworth, and others.[30]

Conclusion

Pietist individualism and subjectivism, along with modern science and Enlightenment, contributed to the dismantling of centuries-old certainties and hierarchies. Pietism embodied the final departure from the medieval worldview and its threefold sense of God's presence in the world—in providence, in the natural order, and in social orders of ritual and worship. In its place, Pietism created new kinds of religious community in a setting of pluralism and individualism. In the eighteenth century, German Pietism offered Europeans a third way besides the options of traditional Orthodoxy and unbelief. Pietism, along with capitalism, confessionalization, modern science, and the Enlightenment, was one of the movements that helped usher in our modern age.

CONCLUSION

Reflecting on the Cultural and Religious Legacy of German Pietism

Every society, born and issued forth from a religious matrix, must confront the relation that it keeps with its archeology . . . The study of religion is tantamount to reflecting on what its contents have become in our societies.
—Michel de Certeau, The Writing of History

This book reflects the new understanding of Pietism's beginnings, achievements, and cultural significance that has been gained over the past thirty-five years. Pietism is no longer viewed as a consistently Lutheran effort to take the Reformation a step further by adding reformation of *life* to Luther's reformation of *doctrine*. Pietism is seen, rather, as an eclectic mix of biblical devotion and notions found in Caspar Schwenckfeld, the Anabaptists, Paracelsus, Jean de Labadie, Johann Arndt, Jakob Böhme, and the English Philadelphians. Radical Pietism, not Church Pietism, was the original, more genuine form of Pietism. Along with capitalism, confessionalization, modern science, and the Enlightenment, Pietism helped to undermine traditional social and theological norms and to usher in our modern age. The Pietists inspired programs to care for the poor and the orphan, new Bible translations, new social networks, new experiential literature such as the autobiography and memoir, and worldwide mission. German Pietist hymns, translated into English and still sung today, represent an important Pietist contribution to modern Evangelicalism.

German Pietism introduced a new paradigm to Protestant Christianity, one that still exercises a strong appeal among North American Christians. Pietism reconceived traditional Reformation Protestantism of Luther and Calvin in terms of personal renewal and new birth, conventicle gatherings for Bible study and mutual encouragement, social activism and postmillennialism, and ecumenical cooperation—all in contrast to the confessional and polemical Protestantism that gave rise to the Thirty Years War. The genius of Pietism lay in the adjectives it employed: *true* Christianity; *heartfelt, living* faith; a *living* knowledge of God; the *inward* Christ and the *inner* Word. Another set of adjectives expressed Pietist hopes for renewal of humanity and a better future for the church: the *new* man, *born-again* Christianity, the *coming Philadelphian* church. Born-again laypeople became agents of their own spirituality, reading the Bible for themselves and teaching and encouraging one another in non-church settings. The Pietists paid a huge price for their innovations: while renewal movements were blossoming in England, the Netherlands, and North America, German Pietists were fragile, fearful, and suppressed, a situation William Penn called "the German sickness."[1]

Some hard questions remain about the legacy of German Pietism. Historians have long been divided on this point: for some, the Pietist story represents something valuable and worth preserving; for others, it is a cautionary tale of wrong choices and failed ideals. In this conclusion, I consider what the historical study of German Pietism indicates about its cultural and religious legacy and the nature of its impact in the world of today.

The Cultural Achievements of German Pietism

It is no coincidence that the century of Pietism was also the century of the Bible and the century of orphanages. Pietists were cultural leaders on both counts. They can be credited with intellectual innovation in their work of Bible translation and commentary, offering alternatives to the Luther

Bible. They established some of the first Bible societies, publishing and distributing affordable Bibles and New Testaments. The Pietists can also be credited with social innovation and compassion in their efforts to address problems of poverty and the many orphans who were left vulnerable within German society. Pietist orphanages and programs for the education of young people set new standards and were widely copied in Europe and North America. It is also significant that the Pietist century was the century when women gained a sense of agency and began to express their voice in speaking and writing as never before. And it was Pietists who laid the foundations for the academic disciplines of Indology and linguistics, with their work in translating Tamil literature and producing grammars of south Indian languages.

When the cultural legacy of the Pietists is compared with widely accepted attitudes of that time, the Pietists appear as innovators and leaders in anticipating understandings, practices, and institutions that we now think of as valued components of a modern worldview and modern society. Such modern features include Pietist individualism, religious independence, social activism, openness to new cultures, literary innovation and creativity, and ecumenical cooperation.

The Dark Side of German Pietism

But there is also a dark side to German Pietism. An honest appraisal must include not only the positive achievements and intentions of the Pietists but also the disruptive and destructive real-life consequences of their beliefs, experiences, and actions.[2] These cannot simply be dismissed as aberrations of "true Pietism"; they belong to the warp and woof of the movement and are reflective of inherent problems in the Pietist paradigm of conversion and renewal.

THE PIETIST LEGACY OF DIVISIVENESS, CONFLICT, AND SELF-DECEPTION

Pietism began as a response to the divisive and polemical Protestantism of the seventeenth century. Yet the Pietists themselves left a trail of division and conflict. In 1682, the Saalhof Pietists in Frankfurt became a thorn in Philipp Jakob Spener's side, with their separatism and refusal to attend church services and sacraments. They divided the Christian world into those who were born again and those who were not, into those with living faith and those with nominal faith. This spiritual elitism marked Pietism from the beginning and left its members open to pride, presumption, overconfidence, and dramatic falls from grace.

Pietism in Halle is a story of unrelenting interpersonal tension and conflict. By 1695, August Hermann Francke's relationship with his church and the city of Glaucha was marked by increasing conflicts over decisions he made that antagonized parishioners and city leaders. He hired Johann Anastasius Freylinghausen as his pastoral assistant, against the church's wishes. Francke decided on a parcel of land on which to construct the orphanage, despite vehement opposition from community leaders who envisioned a city hall on this choice location. Francke's relations with a close colleague in the Halle Foundations, Christian Friedrich Richter, deteriorated until they became embittered and beyond repair. Francke had a falling out with his wife, Anna, over the marriage he arranged for their daughter, Sophia; for some months, Francke and Anna lived apart.

Francke's judgmentalism and strict application of church discipline became a source of concern to Spener. In a letter to Francke dated July 9, 1692, Spener expressed shock over Francke's strictness in excluding an innkeeper from the Lord's Supper because he served people on Sundays.[3] On October 27, 1704, forty of Francke's parishioners sent a petition to the Prussian king, complaining that they and some already-deceased members had repeatedly been denied the Lord's Supper—in some cases for eight years. A perfectionist ecclesiology was an enduring feature of Francke's thought and explains why many of his early associates decided to forsake church appointments and join separatist communities.[4]

The theme of division and conflict can be found among the Radical Pietists as well. They fell into conflict not only with church and civic authorities but also with each other. Alexander Mack and his mentor Hochmann von Hochenau lived in close proximity in Schwarzenau for years without speaking to each other. In an instance of "what goes around comes around," Mack's disciple Georg Conrad Beissel refused Mack's repeated efforts to bring about a reconciliation. A source of many conflicts lay in charismatic leaders who refused to cooperate with each other. One historian identified the central problem in Count Zinzendorf's personality as "his universal *ability* to make a splendid first impression and his universal *inability* to cooperate for long with men of independent mind."[5] This inability contributed to the continual in-fighting between Halle and Herrnhut and to competition for hegemony.

The enhanced subjectivity of the Pietists could easily become a liability, as seen in the extreme behavior of Pietist prophets during the "second wave." Pietist experiences of ecstatic prophecy and "divine leading" often resulted in deranged and immoral behaviors that Pietists themselves had difficulty controlling.[6] A dramatic example is the case of Anna Margaretha Jahn, a prophet in the Halberstadt conventicle of Andreas Achilles. Anna Jahn's prophecy on December 22, 1692, three days after the death of Halberstadt pastor Johann Wurtzler, included the threat of God's judgment upon him and her promise to raise him from the dead if the text of her prophecy were placed on his corpse. Jahn brought scandal and infamy upon Pietism, from which it never fully recovered.[7] The Pietists' religion of inward renewal and Spirit-inspired prophecy often left them unable to distinguish God's leading from their own inclinations and passions. They were unable to exercise a healthy self-criticism, much less accept correction from others.

PIETIST TENDENCIES TOWARD HERO WORSHIP AND ANTI-INTELLECTUALISM

The story of Pietism, whether Church Pietism or Radical Pietism, is inconceivable without dominant leaders, or "patriarchs," who exercised quasi-divine status in guiding the mind and conscience of Pietist laypeople.[8] As the Pietism of the "second wave" receded after 1694, Pietist laity found their religious freedom and independence greatly diminished. The triumph of Halle Pietism was the triumph of a hierarchical organization, with Francke as the head, that devalued conventicles and placed restrictions on the initiative and freedom of lay leaders, especially women.

Radical Pietists of the Spiritualist, conventicle, and sect varieties were dominated by prophetic figures such as Hochmann von Hochenau, Eberhard Ludwig Gruber, Johann Friedrich Rock, Alexander Mack, and Georg Conrad Beissel. In exercising their Christian freedom to follow the Spirit, Radical Pietist groups and churches almost invariably granted unfettered authority to charismatic leaders. The authority exercised by these leaders replaced more traditional and stable authorities such as creeds, confessions, and established church hierarchies. Radical Pietist religion exchanged one form of authority for another. The Pietist model, however, left Christian laypeople more vulnerable, subject to the whims and weaknesses of individual leaders.[9]

Another unresolved issue in German Pietism was the place of reason in born-again Christianity. The tendency to link exaltation of the Spirit with rejection of reason was evident in Pietist leaders such as A. H. Francke and the Inspirationist prophet J. F. Rock. Francke's interrogation in Leipzig focused on concerns about the place of reason and philosophy in his Pietist religion. Francke later rebuked Bartholomäus Ziegenbalg for his studies of south Indian religion and culture, encouraging him to focus on conversions. Similarly, a contemporary expressed amazement that Rock could be so much against reason.

By the mid eighteenth century, there was already a growing number of people who had been nurtured in the Pietist fold only to turn their back on it in frustration at the irrationality of Pietist leaders and the gullibility of their followers. Two notable examples of disillusionment are Johann Christian Edelmann and Karl Philipp Moritz. Edelmann's autobiography (1753) contains a harsh indictment of Pietism, after his encounters and experiences with dozens of forms of misguided, pious self-denial and "holy foolishness." Edelmann observed that the Inspirationists "accepted every pronouncement of their prophets as the infallible word of God."[10] He reflected that if this community had made greater use of reason, they would not have been so easily deceived by their leaders. He compared Pietist leaders to murderers who sought to rob him of God's gifts and leave him half dead. Through reading Spinoza, Edelmann came to see reason and understanding as gifts from the Creator, designed for human happiness.[11]

Moritz's *Anton Reiser* (1785), an early German novel, is stamped with autobiographical content and represents his "testimony of religious crisis."[12] Moritz portrays the Pietist environment in which he was raised as one that suppressed all natural joy in life; not one person from the world of Pietism is portrayed in a positive light. A Christianity that denigrates reason undermines its own integrity and threatens its viability in the next generation.

Contested Visions of Historical Pietism

The two sides of the Pietist legacy, one positive and one decidedly not, must be taken seriously. Modern-day descendants of the Pietists, however, tend to be defensive when faced with the failings noted above, and their portrayals of Pietism are often highly selective. Dale Brown's *Understanding Pietism* responds to those who accuse Pietism of subjectivism, individualism, mysticism, legalism, perfectionism, and otherworldliness. Brown addresses these charges by examining the theology of the early Pietist movement, "looking at its founders and their intentions." On this basis, he concludes that it would be unfair to accuse the Pietists of individualistic excesses and perfectionism, although Pietism "embodied potential weaknesses."[13] More recently, Roger Olson follows a similar strategy in responding to an Evangelical critic who accused Pietism of departing from "a doctrinally full and sound faith."[14] Olson is convinced that "for the most part, those deleterious effects are based on distortions of true, historical Pietism." He writes, "To Pietism's Evangelical critics I say—please go back and read original Pietist sources."[15] By recourse to history, Brown and Olson mean a return to a near-pristine beginning as reflected in the stated intentions and ideals of theological spokesmen. Such a strategy is lamentably inadequate when it ignores the contrary evidence of Pietist behaviors, conflicts, and failings in the real world.

One is reminded of Harold Bender's efforts to recover historical Anabaptism. In "The Anabaptist Vision," he portrayed Anabaptism in terms of a life of discipleship, a new concept of the church with membership based on conversion and commitment to holy living, and an ethic of love and nonresistance.[16] Scholars have since moderated Bender's picture in favor of a more realistic portrayal of Anabaptism that includes nonpacifist beginnings among former participants in the Peasants' War, instances of hypocrisy and immorality, leadership conflicts, and regional diversity.

Such realism and honesty are also needed in confronting the history of Pietism. The strategy of returning to "true historical Pietism" is problematic when it ignores or minimizes the dark side of the Pietist legacy. It is time for heirs of the Pietists to grapple with the significant failings inherent in the Pietist tradition. Again, the Anabaptist tradition is instructive. Modern Mennonites have shown an impressive openness to confronting the historical record of their tradition, even when it is less than edifying. Arnold Snyder has led the way in urging Mennonites to engage with their tradition in a dialogical fashion. Reflection on issues and practices in the tradition can lead to either of two responses: acceptance of inherited tradition or reevaluation and change.[17] It is this kind of open and honest engagement that this book seeks to encourage. The view of historical German Pietism presented here is both more dynamic and more messy than one finds in most accounts. But it is also more authentic.

APPENDIX A

Sources in Translation

The source translations in this appendix and in appendix B are designed to accompany the historical overview of German Pietism provided in this book. To my mind, these sources are an essential resource for students and professors, for two reasons. The first is that most of the documents are unavailable in English anywhere else. There are still too few English translations of the writings of German Spiritualists and Pietists. The second reason is pedagogical. An encounter with primary sources from the age of the Pietists invariably enhances students' learning and engagement with the material. The translations are my own, unless otherwise indicated.

Chapter 1. German Radicalism and Orthodox Lutheran Reform

PARACELSUS, "CREDO"[1]

Wherever I went I diligently investigated and sought after the tested and reliable arts of medicine. I went not only to the doctors, but also to barbers, bathkeepers, learned physicians, women, and magicians who pursue the art of healing. I went to alchemists, to monasteries, to nobles and common folk, to the experts and the simple . . . I have often reflected that medicine is an uncertain and haphazard art, curing one and killing ten . . . It is an art tested in need, useful to all the sick and beneficial in restoring their health. This is my vow: to perfect my medical art and never to swerve from it so long as God grants me my office, and to oppose all false medicine and teachings. Then, to love the sick, each and all of them, more than if my own body were at stake . . . I will let Luther defend his cause, and I will defend my cause, and I will defeat those of my colleagues who turn against me.

OPORINUS'S LETTER TO THE COLOGNE PHYSICIANS, NOVEMBER 26, 1565[2]

Background

Paracelsus's reputation has suffered because of the recollections of Johannes Oporinus (1507–1568), who served as Paracelsus's secretary in Basel during the two-year period from 1527 to 1528. In a letter, Oporinus portrayed Paracelsus as a debauched drunk. But several factors help mitigate his comments. First, Oporinus later regretted his remarks, insisting that they had been "lured out of him" and published against his will. Second, Oporinus remained a great promoter of Paracelsus and was instrumental in the preservation and eventual publication of his works.[3] Third, the recollections of Oporinus relate to Paracelsus's brief period in Basel and Alsace—a low point for Paracelsus. Widely varying dates have been assigned to the letter, from 1555 to 1565. The latter date was confirmed by discovery of a manuscript at the Duke August Library in Wolfenbüttel.[4]

Text of Oporinus's Letter[5]

I was able to perceive nothing of piety or erudition in him [Paracelsus] beyond a marvelous quickness and ease in preparing medicines. During the two years that I lived with him, his days and nights were given over to drunkenness and dissipation, so that it was hardly possible to discover him sober from one hour to the next, especially after he had left Basel [and was living] in Alsace where he was celebrated by all the leading peasants as a second Esclapius. Every night he dared to surpass the peasants in downing full bottles of wine. He would then stick his finger down his throat to free himself of his dissipation, and indulge in drinking again, as if he had not even swallowed one drop . . . During the entire time that I lived with him, he never undressed at night—which I ascribed to drunkenness. Most of the time, indeed unless he was not drunk, he would come home in the wee hours of the night to retire and would hurl himself into bed with his clothes on and his sword at his side, which he boasted had belonged to an executioner. He would often rise in the middle of the night and run mad through the room with his sword drawn, and with frequent blows would assault both the floor and the walls, so that I often was afraid that he would cut off my head. Meanwhile, if he returned home especially drunk, he made a point of dictating to me something of his philosophy, which seemed so beautifully coherent that the most sober person would not have been able to do better. I then set to work at translating this dictation into Latin as well as I could. It is these writings, some translated by me into Latin, some by others, that were later printed. He always had a fire going in his little corner stove so that he could cook up some kind of alkali, or sublimated oil, or an arsenol, or crocus martis or a wonderful Oppoteldoch and I know not what kind of brew . . . Sometimes he claimed that he could prophesy something and would claim to have knowledge of whatever kind of wonder drug. He had no interest in women; I do not believe he ever spent any time with one. He loved to spend money and often burned his way through all he had, so I knew he had not even a penny left. But then the very next day he would show me that his money bag was almost full, leaving me to wonder where he had gotten the money. In his cures, even of extremely bad ulcers, he achieved wonders. He would require or consider no special diet, but rather would drink with his patients, day and night, and thus cure them on a full stomach. He used, in treating all kinds of illnesses, a powdered precipitate, theriak or Mithridat or the juice from cherries or plum brandy in pill form for purging purposes. With his Laudanum pills, which resembled mouse excrement and which he would use as a sacred medicine in imprecise number in treating the most serious illnesses, he boasted that he could raise the dead. This he has in fact proven to me on several occasions when I was with him.

I never heard or saw him pray, and he had no interest in the church's sacraments. Nor did he pay much attention to the Evangelical teaching which at this time had been spread about and was earnestly promoted by our preachers. He threatened that one day he would set Luther and the Pope straight, just as he had done with Galen and Hippocrates. Indeed, no one who had been writing about Holy Scripture up to that point, whether ancient or more recent authors, had correctly drawn out the true kernel of scripture, but only the rind and skin of it.

JAKOB BÖHME ON WRITING *Aurora* (1612)[6]

I am amazed how many in Silesia have obtained my writing, for I myself no longer have a copy. But I see God's hand in this and understand that the book has become known not only in Silesia but also in other lands without my foreknowledge. My own thought was to keep it solely for myself for the rest of my life, for I wrote it just for me.[7]

Author's Foreword to Aurora

Christ the Messiah, by nature a man, went about in this world in great simplicity, like one of us, although he was really a prince and king. Likewise his apostles were all poor and despised fishermen. Christ thanked his heavenly Father that He had hidden himself from the clever and wise in this world and revealed himself to children.

In the same way, I can say or praise or write nothing of myself except that I am a simple man, a poor sinner, and must pray every day, "Lord, forgive my debts!" But although I have not climbed to heaven, heaven itself has been revealed in my spirit, so that I in the Spirit might understand the works and creation of God (*Aurora*, 71–73).

Selections from Aurora, *Chapters 2 and 11*

This is a short introduction and guide, how one should think about God and nature. In future I will describe the true foundation and depth of things, what God is and how in the being of God all things are contained. This is hidden from the world, for one cannot grasp it with reason. But because God wishes to reveal himself in simplicity in this last age, I follow his urging and will. I am merely a small spark [*Fünklein*]. Amen . . . (93)

You should not think that I might have ascended into heaven and have seen this with my fleshly eyes. O no. I am like you, and have no greater light in my outward being than you. I am as much a sinner and mortal being as you are, and must scratch and fight with the devil every day and every hour. Sometimes I win, sometimes he does. But God's strength helps me and he loses the battle . . . Because of our ruin in the fall, God's birth in us does not always well up. (216–217)

JAKOB BÖHME DESCRIBES HIS EXPERIENCE OF THE LIGHT OF GOD, *Aurora* (1612)

Selections from Aurora, *Chapter* 19

People have always thought that Heaven is many hundreds and thousands of miles from this earth and that God dwells in this heaven. Some astronomers have even dared to investigate and measure the heavens and they have discovered some amazing things.

I myself thought, before I gained new insight in a revelation from God, that Heaven was high above the stars, and that God dwelt there in his essential being and ruled over this world merely by the power of his Holy Spirit . . . (360)

But thanks to a hard blow from the Spirit, I fell into a deep melancholy and sadness as I beheld the great depths of this world, the sun and the stars, and the clouds with the rain and snow, and I considered in my spirit the whole creation of this world.

I considered the small spark of light that is humanity, and wondered what God thinks of us over against the great expanse of the heavens and earth.

For I found that there was good and evil in all things, in the elements . . . as well as in men and animals, and that in this world things went as well for the godless as for the godly, and that primitive peoples seemed to have the most prosperous land and that good fortune seemed to be on them more than on the godly.

And so I became even more melancholy and very troubled, and my beloved books offered me no comfort . . .

In my great distress I lifted my soul to God, with all my heart and soul and all my hopes and imaginings, knowing little or nothing of who He was, purposing to wrestle with the God of love and mercy and not to give up until He blessed me . . . (361)

But as I in my zeal raged against God and the portals of hell, just when I thought I had no more strength to continue, my spirit broke through to the inmost birth of God's being and I was embraced with love, just as a bridegroom would his dear bride.

Such a spiritual triumph I cannot adequately describe in writing or speech. It cannot be compared with anything else, except life being born out of death, a resurrection from the dead.

In this divine light my spirit came to recognize God in everything and in all creatures, even plants and grass—who He is and how He is and what His will is. In this light I grew in my ability to describe the being of God.

But because I could not immediately grasp the deep birthings of God in their essence and handle them with my reason, twelve years went by before I gained a true understanding . . . (362)

From this light I now have my insight, and along with it my will and motivation, and so I will write of this knowledge according to my gifts and God willing . . .

I have not written this for my own praise but for the reader's comfort, should he perhaps desire to wander with me on my narrow path. But he should not easily be discouraged if he encounters the portals of hell and the anger of God and comes under critical gaze.

The true heaven is everywhere, even in the place where you are now standing and going. When your spirit grasps the inmost birth of God, then you are in heaven . . . If one is not born of God, then he cannot accept this . . . (363–364)

Now this is the business and intention of my writing, to explain how the earth and the elements come to life again and how the outward birth gives birth anew. Secondly, it is the question and subject matter of this book to consider when the judgment of God will come. The Spirit answers, that at the end of this fallen age, after the resurrection of the dead, the earth will be cleansed and no longer be the devil's possession. The inmost birth will hold the devil fast and make him its footstool, and he will for eternity no longer attack nor disturb it. God's anger will be assuaged and be no longer, and the devils must again become holy angels and live in heaven.

You should not think that the Godhead is a being which is only in the heavens above and that our soul, when it leaves our body, travels many hundreds of miles to heaven above. Rather, the soul is set in the inmost birth; there it is with God and in God and with all the holy angels; and it can travel up or down, for it is not held back by anything. For where else would the soul of man rather be than with its king and redeemer Jesus Christ? For in God far and near is one thing, and everywhere he is Father, Son and Holy Spirit. (368–369)

JAKOB BÖHME ON JEWS, TURKS, AND THE HEATHEN, *Aurora* (1612)

Because everything lives in God, why should the weed praise itself over the wheat? Do you think God recognizes persons or names? Who was our common father? Was it not Adam? And so you, why do you boast that you are a Christian and know the light? Do you think the name makes you holy? Just wait, and you will see a multitude of Jews, Turks, and heathen enter heaven before you because they have trimmed their lamps well. What advantage do Christians have? Much, for they know the way of life and know how they should get up from the fall. But if they stay lying down, they will be cast in the pit and be condemned with all godless heathen . . .

God does not have regard for a person's name or birth. The one who journeys in the love of God, he goes in the light. And the light is the heart of God. There is only one God. If you just remove the covering from your eyes, then you will see and recognize all your brothers, whether Christians, Jews, Turks, or heathen. Or do you think that God is only the God of the Christians? Do not the heathen also live in God? Whoever does right, he is loved by God. Acts 10:35. (208–209)

ZACHARIAS THEOBALD, *The Old and New Schwärmer* (1701)[8]

Zacharias Theobald wrote a history of heresy in rhyme, devoting a stanza to Jakob Böhme.

For such a time has Jacob Böhme come,
Whom many enthusiasts rank foremost in piety.
But in the history of heresy, no one has ever seen such confused nonsense
As one finds in the vile writings of this foul shoemaker.
What Valentinian, Cerdon, and Marcion thought up,
And the confused piles of rubbish made by the Manicheans,
Turns up again in this man. Still, the man is much beloved,
Although there are many hundreds of proofs of his false beliefs.

JANE LEADE, *A Revelation of the Everlasting Gospel-Message* (1697)[9]

Part I. Introductory

I. Having put out a Treatise, call'd *ENOCHIAN WALKS*, in 1694 and . . . specified the *Universal* Restoration of all *Mankind*, with the *fallen Angels*; upon the which many Objections were raised, as well from the Illuminated, and Regenerated, as Unenlightened and Unregenerated: Which point being not so fully cleared up in that Discourse, as might satisfy the Objectors, I found my self obliged to give further Narrative concerning this Matter, from the deepest ground of Revelation, that opened it self in me.

II. For I may truly say, I received it not from the Wisdom of Men, or according to tradition, but From the pure Manifestation of the *Love*, that did break open its *Deeps* in me. For albeit I had heard of such a Notion, yet I did altogether disregard it; and would not entertain any belief concerning such a Latitude as this, that should extend so far, as to recover the *whole* lapsed Creation, till I had an apparent Vision opened unto me. Wherein my Spirit was carried out to behold several Regions, wherein I saw the Dead numerously and variously in their Confinements, being in dark Centers, as bewailing and bemoaning their State, that they had while in the Body, misspent their time, and lost their opportunity of taking hold of the redeeming Love of Christ. Then my Spirit passed through these, and was carried beyond them into a *Light*-Orb and Principle, where I saw the Throne of CHRIST in his Kingly and Priestly Office, interceding and pleading before the Father the validity of his *Redeeming* Blood. And right against this Throne, I saw ADAM the first, with his EVE placed together, as rejoicing in hope, that the Mediatorship of Christ would be of that Power and Force, as to release their off-spring out of all Woes, and Miseries, both in Bodies of time and out of time: and Further I saw numerous Spirits, as bright Flames flying as it were swiftly into this Principle, being set free from the confinements they were in. Whereupon, I being as a naked Spirit there, did query: *What these were?* And the LORD himself pronounced this Word. "These are those, for which my Blood was shed, tho long involved and shut up as in the *Second* Death, having passed through many Agonies and Anguishes: yet now see, how they are set free, and come here to be cloathed with new and bright Bodies." Whereupon I saw *ADAM* and *EVE* rise up with exulting Joy, saying: Thus shall our whole Offspring restored be, and come in by degrees: At which Word I addressed my self to *ADAM*, saying: *How can this be, that all should be restored from the beginning of the World to the end, that in Diabolical Spirits did live and rebel?* And it was answered me: "The *Second ADAM*, the *Lord from Heaven* is more than sufficient to repair that Breach, that was made by *Me*. Therefore doubt thou not, but Salvation shall gain the Victory: for Love's Kingdom will swallow up all Kingdoms that under the *Diabolical* Reign have been." This was an amazing Vision that made me consider and weigh well, what was meant hereby, I being left still in some Doubt.

III. Then it was thus further revealed, by *CHRIST* the Lord himself, who drew up my Spirit very near unto him, saying these words, "Dost thou marvel at this full and perfect Redemption by me of all Creatures in Humanity, What wilt thou say, if the Love of the immense Deity shall open yet more wonderfully and deep, so as to reach the Fall of *Lucifer* and his Hierarchy, that they too may reduced be to their first primary Glory and Excellency." At which I was cast into a silent Wonderment, saying in my self: *Lord, who has comprehended, or fathomed what the immense Love of a God may bring forth?* So returning again into my bodily Sense, I began then to entertain a certain Belief hereof, and searched the Scriptures, what I could find to make this out.

IV. Then were Opened to me several Scriptures, concerning the Restoration of *Mankind*, as that to the *Rom.* V, v.14,11,19,21. Which were very Emphatical to that purpose: with 1 *Cor.* XV, v.22. *As in Adam All die, so in Christ shall ALL be made alive*, and that 1 *Tim.* II, v.6. where it is said, that he was *given a Ransom for ALL, to be testified in due time*. So that these Scriptures, with several others, did a little confirm me . . .

Part II. Of the Extent of the Love of GOD to Man

VIII. Now whereas it is charged, that Redemption is to reach no further, than to such a Number as do receive and believe in Christ while in the Body, that then, if they fail of it here, they are destinated to an everlasting Damnation; this I deny as to that Eternity of Punishment which is by them meant. Because those Scriptures mentioned for the Confirmation of the *Never-ceasing* Torments, are properly to be understood but for *Ages of Time*. Which indeed may be long and tedious enough, according as the height of their Transgressions have been here: So will they find that Worm of their accusing Conscience cannot cease, till the determinated time, when the celestial Love-fire shall break forth to extinguish it. For it has been little understood or known what the Purgation Work will be, and how much is to be done in other Regions and Worlds: because it hath pleased the Father of Lights to reserve and conceal, what hath, is and shall be agitated there in these invisible Regions.

IX. Therefore let none be so Rash as to judge, that nothing more is to be known, than what has been reported of: for God doth not bring forth or reveal his Counsel, and the whole Extent of his Mind, all in one Age, no not in several Ages: As for instance, what he did reveal in the Patriarchs' days, and the first Ages of Time, had their Cessation and Period, and so as occasion was, new Prophecies and Revelations did succeed, till after Christ's time. Now we are not to think that there was a stop, as if no more Discovery should be made, of what is further needful to be known. Of the which many Witnesses both *dead* and *living* are, that have further and new Discoveries, relating to the Restoration . . .

X. Now as to that dreadful Sentence, that many do pass for all Eternities, It is very much to the Impeachment and Violation both of the Justice and Truth of God, which is not to be violated: for God gave that Eternity of *Life* and *Being*, from *Himself* into the Creature. And tho' Sin, as an Accident did happen, being awakened by the subtle Introducement of the Serpent, and so became a *limited* Transgression; which did admit, that such should reject in their Life-time, that Grace that brings Salvation; yet this is but after the Similitude of the Sin, under the *Old* Law and Covenant; for in the *New*, God undertakes to blot out all Transgressions and Sin, and to be a *Law of Life* written within. And this stands firm, while the other Covenant is nullified. So that to assert this is very Injurious to the *Grace of GOD*: for tho' he may punish for the Sin of *Unbelief* (which is the grand Iniquity), and chasten and rebuke; yet it is reckoned but as *for a Moment*, if you compare it with the *many* Circles of *Eternity*, because it is but *just* with God, to save and recover what is of his *own*; which can never be Annihilated: And that is the *Breath* of his Life, and the *Essence* of his own Being.

XI. And then it would be also exceedingly lessening of the Love Benignity in the Manifestation of the great Gift *Christ JESUS*, that he should be so very weak and incapable to repay, save and recover, what was lost by the Transgression of the first *ADAM* . . .

XVIII. All that I have now to request of the doubtful, that cannot receive these sayings is: that they would be still, and quietly wait, till the Central-Love within their own Souls shall open and spring. For I my self was *averse* to the taking in of this Universal Doctrine: But was always taught by Divine *Wisdom*, not to oppose, what I could not reach, or comprehend. So I did let it rest for some Years after the *Vision* of it: and being well acquainted and walking in fellowship, with a very Worthy Person, that had this Sentiment in her, who did often excite me, to look into it, and own it for a foundational Truth, and so to be a Publisher of it; I could no way concur by persuasion from any Creature, till the Light, Life and Spirit of Christ so strongly set upon me, that I could not forbear to give some Glances of it. Now I did expect no less, when ever I published it, but that it would blow up some zealous angry Flames upon me, as being contrary to the common Doctrines preached. But I knew well the Foundation and Ground I stood upon, that tho' uncouth, and like a strange Visage, it should appear to many, yet the Glory, Beauty and Strength of the *JEHOVAH*-Love would as Fire drink up all the Floods, that from the foaming Sea should be cast out upon it. So wait I in hope something of this to see before the Day of my Life shall expire. The joy of which to see, will be Trumpeted forth among the *Angelical* Quires.

Chapter 2. The Thirty Years War, Seventeenth-Century Calvinism, and Reformed Pietism

LEWIS BAYLY, *The Practice of Piety* (1610)[10]

Something of the tone and flavor of Bayly's book can be found in the way he encouraged believers to spend more time in prayer.

If thou hast spent divers hours at a vain ball or play; yea whole days and nights in carding and dicing, to please thy flesh, be ashamed to think that praying for a quarter of an hour is too long an exercise for the service of God . . .

Consider, that if the papists, in their blind superstition, do in an unknown, and therefore unedifying tongue mutter over upon their beads every morning and evening so many scores of Ave-maries, paternosters, and idolatrous prayers, how shall they, in their superstitious devotion, rise up in judgment against thee, professing thyself to be a true worshipper of Christ? (88)

Bayly's forcefulness and eloquence are evident in his meditations on "the Misery of a Man not Reconciled to God in Christ."

There [in hell] thy lascivious eyes will be afflicted with sights of ghastly spirits; thy curious ear affrighted with hideous noise of devils, and the weeping and gnashing of teeth of reprobates; thy dainty nose will be cloyed with noisome stench of sulphur; thy delicate taste pained with intolerable hunger; thy drunken throat will be parched with unquenchable thirst; thy conscience shall ever sting thee like an adder, when thou thinkest how often Christ by his preachers offered the remission of sins . . .

In these hellish torments there shall be no order, but horror; no voice, but of blasphemers and howlers; no noise, but of tortures and tortured; no society, but of the devil and his angels; there shall be punishment without pity; misery without mercy; sorrow without succor; crying without comfort; mischief without measure; torment without ease. (47–48)

Bayly then offers a meditation on "the Blessings of the Godly in Paradise."

Oh, what joy will it be to thy soul, which was wont to see nothing but misery and sinners, now to behold the face of the God of glory! yea, to see Christ welcoming thee, as soon as thou art presented before him by the holy angels, with "Well done, and welcome good and faithful servant, enter into thy Master's joy" . . .

Here my meditation dazzles, and my pen falls out of my hand; the one being not able to conceive, nor the other to describe, that most excellent bliss, and eternal weight of glory, whereof all the afflictions of this present life are not worthy, which all the elect shall with the blessed Trinity enjoy, from that time that they shall be received with Christ as joint-heirs (Rom. viii. 17) into that everlasting kingdom of joy. (52, 58)

GERHARD TERSTEEGEN'S COVENANT WITH CHRIST (*Verschreibung*), SIGNED IN HIS OWN BLOOD (1724)[11]

Meinem Jesu!

Ich verschreibe mich dir, meinem einigen Heylan [de] und bräutigam Christo Jesu, zu deinem völligen und ewigen Eigenthum. Ich entsage von Hertzen allem recht und macht, so mir der satan über mich selbst mit unrecht mögte gegeben haben. Von diesem Abend an, als an welchem du mein blutbräutigam, mein Goël, durch deinen todeskampf, ringen, und blutschwitzen im Garten Getsemane mich zum Eigenthum und braut dir erkauffet, die pforten der Höllen zersprenget, und das liebvolle Hertze deines Vatters mir eröfnet hast.

Von diesem abend an sey dir mein Hertz und gantze Liebe auf ewig zum schuldigen danck ergeben und aufgeopfert! Von nun an biß in ewigkeit, *Nicht mein, sondern dein wille geschehe!* befehle, Herrsche, und regiere in mir! ich gebe dir vollmacht über mich! Und verspreche, mit deiner Hülffe und beystand, eher dieses mein blut biß auf den letzten tropfen vergiessen zu lassen, als mit willen und wissen, inwendig oder auswendig, dir untreu oder ungehorsam zu werden. Siehe, da hast du mich gantz, süsser seelenfreund! in keuscher jungfräulicher liebe dir stets anzuhangen. Dein Geist weiche nicht von mir; und dein

My Jesus!

I sign myself over to you, my only Saviour and Bridegroom Jesus Christ, as your entire and eternal possession. I renounce from my heart all rights and powers over myself such as Satan may have wrongly bestowed on me. From this evening on, on which You my Bridegroom in blood through your battle to the death, your wrestling and sweating of blood in the Garden of Gethsemane have purchased me as your possession and bride, and burst open the portals of hell, and opened for me the loving heart of your Father.

From this evening on, may my heart and whole life be surrendered and offered to you forever as the thanks I owe! From now on into eternity, "let not my will but yours be done!" Command, rule, and govern in me! I give you full power over me! And promise, with your help and assistance, to pour out my blood to the last drop before I willingly and knowingly become inwardly or outwardly untrue or disobedient to you. See, now I am yours completely, my sweet soul-friend! as I hold on to you always in chaste, virgin love. May your Spirit not leave my side; and may

todes kampf unterstütze mich! ja,
Amen. Dein Geist versiegele es,
was in einfalt geschrieben dein
unwürdiges Eigenthum
Gerh. Tersteegen.
Anno 1724.

your victory over death support
me! Amen. May your Spirit seal
what your unworthy possession has
written in all simplicity.
Gerhard Tersteegen.
In the year 1724

Source: Gustav Adolf Benrath, "Der Mystiker Gerhard Tersteegen als Prediger und Seelsorger," *Monatshefte für Evangelische Kirchengeschichte des Rheinlandes* 58 (2009), 81–98, esp. 85.

GERHARD TERSTEEGEN'S HYMN, "GOD HIMSELF IS WITH US" (1729)[12]

1

Gott ist gegenwärtig; lasset uns anbeten,
Und in Ehrfurcht vor ihn treten!
Gott ist in der Mitte; alles in uns schweige
Und sich innigst vor ihm beuge!
Wer ihn kennt, Wer ihn nennt,
Schlagt die Augen nieder.
Kommt, ergebt euch wieder!

God Himself is with us: Let us now adore Him,
And with awe appear before Him.
God is in His temple, all within keep silence,
And before Him bow with reverence.
Him alone, God we own,
To our Lord and Savior;
Praises sing forever!

2

Gott ist gegenwärtig, dem die Cherubinen
Tag und Nacht gebücket dienen;
„Heilig, heilig!" singen alle Engelchören,
Wenn sie dieses Wesen ehren.
Herr, vernimm Unsre Stimm',
Da auch wir Geringen
Unser Opfer bringen!

God Himself is with us, Whom angelic legions Serve with awe in heav'nly regions;
"Holy, holy, holy," sing the hosts of heaven,
Praise to God be ever given.
Bow Thine ear to us here:
Hear, O Lord, the praises
That Thy church now raises!

3

Wir entsagen willig allen Eitelkeiten,
Aller Erdenlust und Freuden;
Da liegt unser Wille, Seele, Leib und Leben
Dir zum Eigentum ergeben.
Du allein Sollst es sein,
Unser Gott und Herre,
Dir gebührt die Ehre.

We gladly renounce all vanities,
All earthly lust and joys;
Here lie our will, soul, body and life
yielded to you as your possession.
You alone we claim,
Our God and Lord,
To you are due the glory.

4

Majestätisch Wesen, möcht' ich recht dich preisen
Und im Geist dir Dienst erweisen!
Möcht' ich wie die Engel immer vor dir stehen
Und dich gegenwärtig sehen!
Laß mich dir Für und für
Trachten zu gefallen,
Liebster Gott, in allen!

O majestic Being, I would praise you duly
and in spirit render service to you!
Like the holy angels who behold Thy glory,
May I ceaselessly adore Thee!
And in all, great and small,
Seek to do most nearly
What Thou lovest dearly!

5

Luft, die alles füllet, drin wir immer schweben,
Aller Dinge Grund und Leben.
Meer ohn' Grund und Ende, Wunder aller Wunder,
Ich senk mich in dich hinunter.
Ich in dir, Du in mir,
Laß mich ganz verschwinden,
Dich nur sehn und finden!

Air that fills everything, in which we ever hover,
Ground and life of all things.
Sea without bottom or end, wonder of all Wonders,
I settle down into you.
I in you, you in me,
May I disappear entirely,
And see and find only you!

6

Du durchdringest alles; laß dein schönstes Lichte,
Herr, berühren mein Gesichte!
Wie die zarten Blumen willig sich entfalten
Und der Sonne stille halten,
Laß mich so Still und froh
Deine Strahlen fassen
Und dich wirken lassen!

Let your glorious light, Lord, permeating all things,
reach my face and eyes to touch them;
as the tender flowers open out their petals,
And calmly welcome the sun's warmth,
so may I, calm in joy,
embrace your rays from heaven,
And allow you to do your work!

7	
Mache mich einfältig, innig, abgeschieden,	Make me to be simple, ardent, withdrawn,
Sanfte und im stillen Frieden,	Gentle and in quiet peace,
Mach mich reines Herzens, daß ich deine Klarheit	Make me pure of heart, so I may
	Behold your glory
Schauen mag in Geist und Wahrheit.	In spirit and truth.
Laß mein Herz Überwärts	Let my heart rise up
Wie ein Adler schweben	And hover like an eagle
Und in dir nur leben!	And live only in you!
8	
Herr, komm in mir wohnen, laß mein' Geist auf Erden	Lord, make me your dwelling,
	let my heart and spirit
Dir ein Heiligtum noch werden;	become for you an earthly temple:
Komm, du nahes Wesen, dich in mir verkläre,	Come, you who are ever near, glorify yourself in me,
Daß ich dich stets lieb' und ehre!	So I will always praise and love you!
Wo ich geh', Sitz und steh',	Where'er I may be,
Laß mich dich erblicken	there may I perceive you,
Und vor dir mich bücken!	and ever bow before you!

W. WECK'S LETTER TO J. E. TESCHEMACHER: "WORDS IN PRAISE OF GERHARD TERSTEEGEN"[13]

Dear Brother!

Here I have provided for you in haste a little sketch of what I think and believe concerning the beloved Tersteegen . . . It is a beautiful work to praise the saints in God and God in his saints.

Now I wish to speak in praise of the dear man Gerhard Tersteegen whom God in these last days has set up as a light in the church and adorned with his grace and gifts.

First of all, he is a man and at the same time a child who is strong in faith and active in love in many ways.

A man who leads a withdrawn, quiet life, despising the world, a true disciple and lover of Jesus Christ and his inner, hidden, crucified life.

A very friendly, patient, clever, learned, experienced, and trustworthy man.

A man of great dignity, virtue, modesty, childlike humility and calm [*Gelassenheit*].

A man who leads a life of calm and suffering in love and service to God, and at the same time is active in serving his neighbors in all kinds of ways, both outwardly and inwardly.

A man who has not only an open heart but also an open purse, kitchen, and pantry.

A man who knows the proper medicines for both bodily and spiritual afflictions and freely dispenses them.

A man who has presented, both orally and in writing, many powerful, spiritual matters and expressed himself clearly, knowledgeably, and simply, and served many with his gracious gift in word and deed in the midst of his own ongoing afflictions.

A man who willingly spent all he had in the service of God and his neighbor and as a spiritual priest offered prayers and petitions on behalf of all his fellows, both in secret and in public, as circumstance and opportunity allowed.

A man who with great effort sought out many costly pearls [of wisdom] and strung them on a lovely band and presented them unsoiled to eager souls and thereby has strengthened and quickened many souls in their quiet ways.

A man who possesses great endurance and shows impartial love towards all.

A man who knows the straight way to Jesus, who strengthens the weak, encourages the comfortless, instructs those who are in error, feeds the hungry, gives drink to the thirsty, clothes the naked, and in fulfilling his Christian duty nevertheless considers himself poor and unprofitable, despising the praise of others and giving God the glory.

A man who is considered by all to be salt of the earth, a pillar of the world, and a light and spiritual Bishop in the church of God, and who, like King Saul, "is head and shoulders above everyone else" among the children of Israel and Judah (I Samuel 9:2).

A man whose remembrance will abide thanks to his valuable writings, which testify that he was of a high and noble spirit, who did not concern himself with lowly matters and controversies but with the truth and treated his adversaries with love and mercy.

Finally, a man who regarded himself as a poor, frail, yet justified sinner, who hoped for salvation solely because of God's grace and for the sake of Jesus Christ and his precious suffering and death.

A man who lives in Christ and Christ in him, forever. Amen!

Chapter 3. Beginnings of Lutheran Pietism in Frankfurt, 1670 to 1684

CHRISTIAN FENDE'S LETTER OF 1680

Background

Christian Fende, in a letter dated in 1680, denounced Lutheran worship as idolatry. The letter played an important role in the beginnings of Pietist separatism. Only part of the letter is available, due to destruction of the Frankfurt Preacher Archive in the Second World War.

Text of Fende's Letter[14]
Frankfurt a.M. 1680

Christian Fende to Justus Dozem in Cologne:

. . . Concerning the Christian question, What has caused me and my family no longer to take communion? I answer in brief, that from their communion nothing remains . . . but [I abide] in the secret place of the Spirit, where the true union of the members with Christ their head and with the life-giving Spirit takes place (I Cor. 15:45). Concerning the outward communion, at this time I find no reason for myself to think about it and to engage with it. But when various ones among us come together and are of one mind, then it would not be difficult to devote ourselves to the institution. But my knowledge of the truth will not permit me in good conscience to associate any longer with the people of the world and their ways. For I am assured that their celebration is not a communion with Christ and his body and that they are not celebrating the Lord's Table. What they bring forth among them in terms of life, honor and favoring of persons are proof enough. The essential matter of the sacrament I reckon among the most potent errors that God can send, for they believe in a lie. For this idol is really the common form of all the various sects. How can Christ and Belial, lies and truth, idols and worship of God have communion and fellowship? Finally, it would be a great hypocrisy because I know for certain that if the leaders, teachers, and defenders of the world's communion knew what I think of their communion, they would certainly not allow me to partake of it. But as long as I disguise my feelings by going along, I keep it from them and commit a deception and falsehood toward them. But a person should not commit evil that good may come of it. Christ's command is, Keep yourself from lying (Matt. 23:27–33).

PASTORIUS'S LETTER OF PROTEST AGAINST SLAVERY, 1688

On February 18, 1688, Franz Daniel Pastorius authored a protest against the use of black slaves in America. It is the first such protest ever written in America.[15]

This is to ye Monthly Meeting held at Richard Worrell's.

These are the reasons why we are against the traffick of men-body, as followeth. Is there any that would be done or handled at this manner? viz. to be sold or made a slave for all the time of his life? How fearful and faint-hearted are many on sea, when they see a strange vessel, being afraid it should be a Turk, and they should be taken and sold for slaves into Turkey. Now what is this better done, as Turks doe? Yea, rather is it worse for them, which say they are Christians; for we hear that ye most part of such negers are brought hither against their will and consent, and that many of them are stolen. Now, tho they are black, we can not conceive there is more liberty to have them slaves, as it is to have other white ones. There is a saying, that we shall doe to all men like as we will be done ourselves; making no difference of what generation, descent or colour they are. And those who steal or robb men, and those who buy or purchase them, are they not all alike? Here is liberty of conscience, which is right and reasonable; here ought to be likewise liberty of ye body, except of evil-doers, which is an other case. But to bring men hither, or to robb and sell them against their will, we stand against.

In Europe there are many oppressed for conscience sake; and here there are those oppressed which are of a black colour. And we who know that men must not comitt adultery, some doe committ adultery in others, separating wives from their husbands and giving them to others; and some sell the children of these poor creatures to other men. Ah! doe consider well this thing, you who doe it, if you would be done at this manner? and if it is done according to Christianity? You surpass Holland and Germany in this thing. This makes an ill report in all those countries of Europe, where they hear off that ye Quakers doe here handel men like they handel there ye cattle. And for that reason some have no mind or inclination to come hither. And who shall maintain this your cause, or pleid for it? Truly we can not do so, except you shall inform us better hereof, that Christians have liberty to practise these things. Pray, what thing in the world can be done worse towards us, than if men should robb or steal us away, and sell us for slaves to strange countries; separating housbands from their wives and children. Being now this is not done in the manner we would be done at, therefore we contradict and are against this traffic of men-body. And we who profess that it is not lawful to steal, must, likewise avoid to purchase such things as are stolen, but rather help to stop this robbing and stealing if possible. And such men ought to be delivered out of ye hands of ye robbers and set free as well as in Europe. Then is Pennsylvania to have a good report, instead it hath now a bad one for this sake in other countries. Especially whereas ye Europeans are desirous to know in what manner ye Quakers doe rule in their province; and most of them doe look upon us with an envious eye. But if this is done well, what shall we say is done evil?

If once these slaves (which they say are so wicked and stubborn men) should joint themselves, fight for their freedom and handel their masters and mastrisses as they did handel them before; will these masters and mastrisses take the sword at hand and warr against these poor slaves, licke, we are able to believe, some will not refuse to doe; or have these negers not as much right to fight for their freedom, as you have to keep them slaves?

Now consider well this thing, if it is good or bad? And in case you find it to be good to handel these blacks at that manner, we desire and require you hereby lovingly, that you may inform us herein, which at this time never was done, viz., that Christians have such a liberty to do so. To the end we shall be satisfied in this point, and satisfie likewise our good friends and acquaintances in our natif country, to whose it is a terror or fairful thing that men should be handeld so in Pennsylvania.

This is from our meeting at Germantown, held ye 18 of the 2 month, 1688, to be delivered to the Monthly Meeting at Richard Worrel's.

Garret henderich
derick up de graeff
Francis daniell Pastorius
Abraham up Den graef

JOHANN JAKOB SCHÜTZ, "SING PRAISE TO GOD WHO REIGNS ABOVE" (1675)

This is Johann Jakob Schütz's most popular hymn; translated by Frances Elizabeth Cox (1812–1897).[16]

1. *Sing praise to God who reigns above,*
   The God of all creation,
   The God of power, the God of love,
   The God of our salvation;
   With healing balm my soul He fills,
   And every faithless murmur stills;
   To God all praise and glory!

2. *The angel host, O King of kings,*
   Thy praise for ever telling,
   In earth and sky all living things
   Beneath thy shadow dwelling,
   Adore the wisdom which could span,
   And power which formed creation's plan;
   To God all praise and glory!

3. *What God's almighty power hath made*
   His gracious mercy keepeth;
   By morning glow or evening shade,
   His watchful eye ne'er sleepeth:
   Within the Kingdom of his might,
   Lo! all is just and all is right:
   To God all praise and glory!

4. *I cried to God in my distress—*
   In mercy, hear my calling!
   My Saviour saw my helplessness,
   And kept my feet from falling;
   For this, Lord, thanks and praise to Thee!
   Praise God, I say, praise God with me!
   To God all praise and glory!

5. *The Lord is never far away,*
   Throughout all grief distressing
   An ever-present help and stay,
   Our peace and joy and blessing.
   As with a mother's tender hand,
   He leads his own, his chosen band;
   To God all praise and glory!

6. *When every earthly hope has flown*
From sorrow's sons and daughters,
Our Father from his heavenly throne
Beholds the troubled waters;
And at his Word the storm is stayed
Which made his children's hearts afraid;
To God all praise and glory!

7. *Then all my toilsome way along*
I sing aloud Thy praises,
That all may hear the grateful song
My voice unwearied raises:
Be joyful in the Lord, my heart!
Both soul and body bear your part!
To God all praise and glory!

8. *O ye who name Christ's holy name*
Give God all praise and glory;
Let all who know God's power proclaim
Aloud the wondrous story!
Cast each false idol from its throne,
And worship God, and God alone!
To God all praise and glory.

Johann J. Schütz, 1675
tr. Frances E. Cox, 1864; alt.
Tune: MIT FREUDEN ZART (8.7.8.7.8.8.7.)
Bohemian Brethren *Kirchengesang,* 1566

PHILIPP JAKOB SPENER, *Pia Desideria* (1675)

Philipp Jakob Spener cited the words of Martin Luther, encouraging people to put reading of the scriptures above all other reading.

I would be happy to see that all my books were put away or should perish, for I shudder to see how in the churches people are now occupied with collecting a great many books besides the Scriptures...The result is not only that they neglect to study the Scripture but also that the pure knowledge of God's Word is lost. That is the reason that I am beginning to translate the Bible into German, because I hope that study and reading of the Scriptures will increase. Whoever wishes to have books written by me should not allow them to hinder him from studying the Scriptures themselves.[17]

Spener contrasts two kinds of preaching, one that edifies and one that does not.

The sixth means for improving the Christian churches . . . is that sermons should be arranged so that they attain their goal of encouraging faith and its fruits in the hearers. But many godly people find no small deficiency in many sermons. There are some preachers who, in most of their sermons, are mainly concerned to show how educated they are. They introduce various foreign languages into the sermon even though not one person in the congregation knows a word of them. They are more concerned that all the parts of the sermon follow the laws of rhetoric than that their hearers might find profit for life and death. But this should not be, because the pulpit is not the place for showing off one's skill and magnificence, but for preaching the Word of the Lord in simplicity and power. Preaching should be the means for making the people holy, so that everything is designed towards this end.[18]

JOHANNA ELEONORA PETERSEN, *Autobiography* (1718)[19]

But when I had spent six years with dear Lady Bauer, the most high God ordained that my dear husband, who had seen me some years before in Frankfurt and become acquainted with me, got the idea of marrying me and gave a certain person in Lübeck the duty of speaking with me. Which he did only after a considerable period of time, through lack of opportunity . . .

My brother-in-law, who was from Dorffeld, court tutor in the Hanau court, was much against it, but my blessed father answered him very Christianly . . . His daughter was not suitable for a man of the world, and she was not marrying outside her social class in an irresponsible way. That everyone knew . . . On this point they must remain silent, and my blessed father uttered his consent.

Afterwards my dear husband travelled to Frankfurt and our wedding was performed on the 7th of September 1680 by D. Spener, in the presence of the princess of Philippseck, my blessed Father and some prominent people, about 30 people in all, and everything went so Christianly and well that all were pleased . . .[20]

Besides these, in my married condition the following additional mysteries have been opened up to me. In the year 1685 I received, first of all, the unlocking of the holy *Revelation* of Jesus Christ, which I never had thought about, but always passed by this great book, thinking that I could understand nothing of it. But when, quite early, I entered my small room and took my Bible in hand to find a short passage for myself, immediately there came before my eyes the words of the *Apoc. 1:3*: "Blessed is the one who reads and those who hear the words of the prophecy, and keep what is written there, for the time is near." These words went deep into my heart, as I thought, "You have ignored the book of the holy *Revelation* and passed it by, and yet there are such great matters within it." And although immediately an apology arose within me, that I should have passed it by because I did not understand the contents, there then came into my mind that there were indeed great promises in this book and also great threats, yet my faithful God would grant me the grace to learn to understand it.

In such consideration I fell down before God, imploring him with inward sighs to open the eyes of my understanding so that I might recognize in it his most holy will and find myself to be a true doer of his word. When I arose from prayer, I took up the blessed book to read it but hadn't the least notion that right away something would be opened up to me. But when I began to read I began to feel as if my heart were completely suffused with the light of God, and I understood everything that I read and so many passages of Scripture became clear to me, and in agreement with the holy *Revelation*. And when I consulted it, I understood [its meaning] right away. On account of this I was very moved and humbled before God, that he should cause such grace to happen to me, his humble maid. I took a piece of paper and wrote out the passages which agreed with what I had found in the *Apocalypse*, thinking, it might slip away from my memory.

And when I had written this out, I took it to my dear husband and said to him: Look what our dear Lord has revealed to me in his holy *Revelation*. He took the page in his hand to read it, and was amazed at it, and offered me his own page of writing, with the ink still wet and just written by him that very hour, and in which all the fundamental points were to be found that were on my own page. He then said to me: The Lord has surely revealed to you the same thing as he did to me . . . We then decided to show each other, over a period of some time, what the Lord would further reveal to us. So then it happened that when I showed him something that the Lord had revealed to me, then he showed me how the same thing had already been revealed to him. When he brought something to me, I [likewise] had already received it. Then we remembered the vision in a dream which I had had in 1662, when I was 18 years old, in which I saw in the heavens the number 1685 in large golden figures. The first two numbers flew quickly into the clouds, but the other two numbers, the 85, remained standing there. On my right I saw a man standing who pointed to the number and said to me, "Look, at this time great things will begin to occur, and something will be revealed to you." And so it actually came true. For in the year 1685 began the great unrest and persecution in France, and in the same year the blessed thousand year kingdom was revealed to me in the holy *Revelation* of Jesus Christ.[21]

Chapter 4. Conventicles and Conflicts in Leipzig and the Second Wave, 1684 to 1694

"ARTICLES ON WHICH MR. AUGUST HERMAN FRANCKE IS TO BE INTERROGATED" (1689)[22]

1. What is his full name and where is he from?
2. Who was his father and where did he live?
3. How long has Mr. Francke lived in Leipzig?
4. How does he pay his expenses at the University?
5. What Professors did he have at the University?
6. Whether he puts emphasis upon the study of philosophy besides theological study?
7. What does he think about such philosophical study?
8. Whether he considers it necessary for a theology student to busy himself with systematic theology and to study theology from this source?
9. Whether he thinks it enough that one only read the Bible and put aside other books?

10. Whether he has read the writings of Molinos and what he has learned from these writings?[23]
11. Whether he has not up till now spoken publicly in support of *Collegia Biblica*?
12. Who has given him the authority and right that he should be involved in such *Collegia* and should determine the moral and practical benefit that derives from them?
13. Whether he has not up till now been visiting certain commoners in their homes and instructing them?
14. For what reason has he done this and what has he taught them?
15. Who called him to this work and authorized it?
16. Whether he thinks that the people were not sufficiently instructed by their ordained teachers and pastors?
17. What is his opinion of God's Word?
18. Whether the Word of God has an inherent power to convert the people?
19. What is his opinion of revelations and inner illuminations?
20. Whether such pronouncements on matters of faith are to be accepted?
21. Whether the manner of teaching that is practised by our preachers is pleasing to him or not?
22. Whether he preached in the Leipzig prison and what he preached about?
23. Who spoke to him about this?
24. What is his opinion in general of the Articles of Faith, concerning which he must set down a brief confession?
25. Whether he would also add his approval from the heart to the Symbol Books?
26. Whether he does not discuss theology under the pretext of a *Collegii Philosophici* dealing with the affections?
27. Whether he has had any pastors from the countryside as hearers in his meetings? Who are they and where do they live?
28. Whether he does not intentionally seek to draw to himself students and commoners who would follow his teaching?
29. What is the real intent of his new teaching?
30. How and by what means did he arrive at such notions?

Chapter 5. Halle Pietism and Universal Social Reform, 1695 to 1727

FRANCKE AND FREYLINGHAUSEN'S REPORT ON THEIR MINISTRY AT ST. GEORGE'S CHURCH IN GLAUCHA, APRIL 27, 1700[24]

Background

On April 27, 1700, Francke and his assistant, Johann Anastasius Freylinghausen, composed a lengthy report concerning their ministry at St. George's Church in Glaucha. In accordance with their prince's request, they addressed six questions: how the Word of God is proclaimed; how the sacraments are being administered, especially the practice of confession; how abuses and offenses are dealt with; what is being done to care for the needs of the poor; whether Francke and Freylinghausen have adequate assistance and resources for their ministry; and what blessing and fruit are evident from their ministry (28–29).[25] The following selections are from the report's discussion of their preaching and teaching, administration of the sacraments, and care of the poor in Glaucha.

Text of the Report

How the Word of God Is Proclaimed

In our preaching we have no other purpose than building up our hearers in their faith in God, especially those who are unconverted and unrepentant, of whom unfortunately there is a great crowd, that their eyes may be opened, that they might turn from darkness to light and from the power of Satan to God, to receive forgiveness of sins and the inheritance belonging to those who are saved . . . We seek, for our part, to avoid everything in our presentation which might hinder attaining this goal. Therefore we do not tie ourselves to certain annual preaching texts but we keep in mind on every occasion what would be for the edifying of the Church. We keep away from foreign languages, speaking in the most simple and clear way possible so that servants and maids and even small children can understand and grasp it. Still less do we seek in our sermons to impress others with our artistry and wisdom, or to tickle people's ears by relating all kinds of stories and worldly things. Rather, we simply keep to God's Word and strive to teach the spiritual sense of it to the people in a simple and clear way of speaking. "We preach Christ, how He is made for us to be wisdom and righteousness and sanctification and redemption," so that their hearts may receive Christ in faith . . .

We make a proper distinction between Law and Gospel, considering not only what pertains to divine doctrine and truth but also to the application. Experience teaches us what damage can arise when the pure are not set apart from the impure, but the whole audience treated as if they were all children of God and fellow believers . . . (31–32)

Concerning the manner of home visitation, we are careful to inform the father of the house the day before our visit, so that he can bring his family together at the appointed time. In order to determine the spiritual condition of the household, we begin by examining the children, asking the parents about their behavior, and admonishing them. We then proceed to the father and mother of the home, touching on those things which may indicate a need for spiritual renewal. We use the opportunity to ask the parents whether they send their children to school and to prayer times, and whether they ask their children what they are learning in school or have heard in the sermon or prayer time. We inquire if there is a Bible in the house and if they take time to read it. We ask if they have other books, especially Johann Arndt's *True Christianity*. We ask how they spend Sundays and especially the time after the sermon . . . (50)

Finally, I would also like to mention the visitation of the sick, for one must deal with them according to God's Word. Just as a physician must be guided in his prescriptions according to the various conditions of his patients, so we in our care of souls must have regard for the particular state of each one. If they are spiritually sick, we must refer them to the physician Jesus Christ. If they are completely dead in sins, then we seek to awaken their conscience. We do not offer comfort to them too quickly, but neither do we neglect it, so that the word of repentance is received with gentleness. From the following list of questions I would like it to be observed how the sick should be treated . . . (52–53)[26]

1. How long have they been sick?
2. Where do they think that their illness originated?
3. What medicines have they used?
4. Who do they think might be able to offer them help? . . .
6. Do they recognize their need of God's spiritual help? . . .
8. Do they think that spiritual counsel could be of help to their soul? . . .
12. Do they recognize that they have led a bad and sinful life?
13. In what ways in particular has their life been sinful? . . .
15. Do they think that God, on account of the sins by which they have transgressed against their baptismal covenant, would be justified in excluding them from his grace and damning them? . . .
17. Do they believe that a loving God may have sent them the illness so that they might come to true conversion? . . .
19. Or do they think that by their illness they can atone for their sins and be reconciled to God? . . .
25. Do they think this [reconciliation] is such an easy thing that they can do it on their own without the Holy Spirit's help and working within them? . . .
32. Do they think that their prayer would help them even if they knowingly continued to sin? . . .
34. Do they intend to improve their sinful life, should God grant them their health again? . . .
37. But should it be God's will for them to die, would they be agreeable to this?
38. Why would they be willing to die? . . .
41. Would they like to leave something from their possessions to the poor? . . .
45. Do they believe that it will go well for their soul after they die? . . .
48. Do they believe that their body will rise again on the last day? (53–55)

How the Sacraments Are Being Administered

For some years now we have instituted the practice of instructing each and every child as to what belongs to the worthy use of the Lord's Supper. Each one is warned that he should not come to the Lord's Supper or to Confession if he is not in a state of repentance and faith . . .

We do not automatically allow the children to partake of the Lord's Table, as parents often expect, but rather we take time to instruct them properly, a half year and longer, and devote much effort and energy to this so we can find out which ones do not turn their hearts to God but continue in the lusts of youth. We inform the parents concerning this, so that they first determine whether the children are truly converted to God, and if so, that they learn to comply with [the demands of] the Lord's Supper. (58–59)

What Is Being Done to Care for the Needs of the Poor

To go into detail on this point would require much time. We would therefore refer to the publication of 1697, "Historical Information as to how provision for the poor in Glaucha has led to establishing the Foundations . . ." There one will find the following points among others:

(1) God has blessed us with an Orphanage, which began in simple trust in the grace of God. The number of children who are cared for there has grown greatly over time.

(2) Connected with this is a dining facility in which poor and needy students are fed twice a day. The number of students and orphans, along with the staff, is sometimes over 250.

(3) In the past year a home for widows has been founded thanks to a benefactor. At the present time there are four widows living there . . . Every two years they receive a completely new set of clothing and each year a new pair of shoes . . . A theology student comes by morning and evening to hold a prayer time with them and to explain a chapter from the Bible. A young woman is also available to attend to them when they are well or sick and keeps the house and rooms clean. For this she receives, besides free bed and lodging, 12 Gröschen per week and use of the garden.

(4) There is a program for all who come to us from outside, to give them two hours a day of instruction in the Christian faith and some financial help. This is made possible by the newly established Alms-office at the Church . . . The number of poor who came to us from outside in the past year was over 7,000.

(5) There is a program for the poor in Glaucha which provides for one hour of instruction each day and financial help. Each month a collection is held in the Church which is then distributed among the poor. (68–70)

CHRISTIAN FRIEDRICH RICHTER, "GOD WHOM I AS LOVE HAVE KNOWN" (1714)

This hymn by Christian Friedrich Richter was included in Freylinghausen's *Neues geistreiches Gesang-Buch* (1714), hymn no. 647, in seven stanzas.[27]

1. *God whom I as love have known,*
Thou hast sickness laid on me,
And these pains are sent of Thee,
Under which I burn and moan;
Let them burn away the sin,
That too oft hath checked the love
Wherewith Thou my heart wouldst move,
When Thy Spirit works within!

2. *In my weakness be Thou strong,*
Be Thou sweet when I am sad,
Let me still in Thee be glad,
Though my pains be keen and long.
All that plagues my body now,
All that wasteth me away,
Pressing on me night and day,
Love ordains, for Love art Thou!

3. *Suffering is the work now sent,*
Nothing I can do but lie
Suffering as the hours go by;
All my powers to this are bent.
Suffering is my gain; I bow
To my heavenly Father's will,
And receive it hushed and still;
Suffering is my worship now.

4. *God! I take it from Thy hand*
As a sign of love, I know
Thou wouldst perfect me through woe,
Till I pure before Thee stand.
All refreshment, all the food
Given me for the body's need,
Comes from Thee, who lov'st indeed,
Comes from Thee, for Thou art good.

5. *Let my soul beneath her load*
Faint not, through the o'er wearied flesh;
Let her hourly drink afresh
Love and peace from Thee, my God.
Let the body's pain and smart
Hinder not her flight to Thee,
Nor the calm Thou givest me;
Keep Thou up the sinking heart.

6. *Grant me never to complain,*
Make me to Thy will resigned,
With a quiet, humble mind,
Cheerful on my bed of pain.
In the flesh who suffers thus,
Shall be purified from sin,
And the soul renewed within;
Therefore pain is laid on us.

7. *I commend to Thee my life,*
And my body to the cross;
Never let me think it loss
That I thus am freed from strife—
Wholly Thine; my faith is sure
Whether life or death be mine,
I am safe if I am Thine;
For 'tis Love that makes me pure.

AUGUST HERMANN FRANCKE, "TWENTY-FOUR REASONS TO TAKE SERIOUSLY OUR OBLIGATION TOWARD THE POOR" (UNDATED)[28]

The 24 reasons are: the inexpressible love and mercy of God; the love of our Lord Jesus Christ; the indescribable patience which God has shown us in Christ; the love God has shown in sparing us the wars, pestilence, and other plagues that have come to other lands; the abundant love of God in proclaiming his whole counsel to us for our salvation; the pleasure God takes in showing mercy; the earnest and emphatic command of God to show love and kindness towards the poor; the glorious promises that God has given to those who practice love towards the poor; the blessing that God brings to our livelihood and business when we show mercy; the Word of Christ: as we give, so will be given to us (Luke 6:38); the description of the last judgment (Matthew 25:12); the horrible image that a loveless heart has in the eyes of God; the beautiful image that a loving heart has in the eyes of God; the quickening that we ourselves receive if we act in heartfelt love towards our neighbor; the necessity of following after Christ; the beautiful example left behind by believers who showed love towards the poor and needy according to the witness of Scripture; the temptation of the good things that God grants to us; the increase of faith that we receive through the exercise of love; the wonderful example of Christ in feeding the 5,000 and the 4,000; the Lord's rebuke of his disciples when they did not understand his deeds (Mark 8:17); the uncertainty of how long we will live; the sign which Christ gives of his true disciples in John 13:35: hereby will everyone know that you are my disciple, if you have love for one another; the gift of love which God has awakened at the present time in so many; the imminent, still-to-come judgment of God.

Chapter 6. Radical German Pietism in Europe and North America

GOTTFRIED ARNOLD, *The Mystery of the Divine Sophia* (1700)

She (Sophia) did not cease to speak to each child of Adam internally in their heart. It is nothing other than a soft and living breath and inner word in the soul which comes to the soul unlooked for. In this first seeking, Sophia's proposal is nothing other than a divine call to obedience . . . The sweet beams of her love are also in the very first kiss and are experienced as so piercing that they set the soul-spirit in an indescribable joy. One can then lay consoled on her breast and drink to satisfaction, and all her pure powers are open to draw one into a paradisiacal love-play in her.[29]

GOTTFRIED WINTER'S LETTER DESCRIBING THE FELLOWSHIP OF MOTHER EVA VON BUTTLAR, 1703

Background

In the fall of 1699, the Philadelphian followers of Heinrich Horch, and the radical Pietist movement as a whole, were looking for the return of Christ and the dawning of the "golden age" with the turn of the century. When this failed to happen, they speculated as to why. Among the reasons given for this failure were the following: the condition of the world; the too small number of truly born-again Christians; and the incomplete conversion of the Jews. In January 1700, in Allendorf an der Werra, not far from Eschwege, these Pietists established an official Philadelphian Society that was recognized by the London Philadelphian movement. For them, the society represented the core of the true fellowship of Jesus Christ and would prepare for the return of Christ.[30]

The Allendorf Society established a communal living arrangement in the home of a Mr. Gille, an apothecary in Allendorf.[31] Living in the house were Eva von Buttlar (1670–1721), the leader of the group; Justus Gottfried Winter, a twenty-four-year-old theology student; five young noblewomen, the Callenberg sisters from Rothwesten, near Kassel: Charlotte, Anna Sidonia, Anna Dorothea, Juliane, and Klara Elisabeth; and for a short time, Catharine Uckermann, with her young children, and Philipp Stirn. According to source testimonies provided by Christian Thomasius, "there can be no doubt that in Allendorf not only did the 'love kiss' serve as a bond of unity and sign of the covenant, but that there took place among the members sexual intercourse as well as female circumcision [*Verschneidung*]."[32] Eva von Buttlar was honored by the others as "the heavenly Sophia."[33]

In March 1703 the group moved to Laasphe, the residence of the Count of Sayn-Wittgenstein.[34] Through the efforts of an influential member of the Allendorf Society, the group managed to lease a farm in Saßmannshausen bei Laasphe. Von Buttlar now guided her followers in honoring her as the third person in the divine Trinity, which in the flesh included the theology student Justus Gottfried Winter, who embodied the Father; the medical student Johann Georg Appenfeller, who embodied the Son; and Eva.[35] Temme notes that "the history of the Eva Society is not as closely tied to any other place or region as it is to the Land of Wittgenstein . . . the group lived here openly and freely for two years . . . Here for the first time they were confronted with a territory which was not antagonistic toward radical Pietism, but on the contrary had welcomed them. It was the first time that the group resided in a purely rural setting, leaving the city and city culture far behind . . . Laasphe had only about 700 inhabitants in 1680."[36] Wallmann noted that, "Here they were supported by other separatist Pietists such as Dr. Vergenius who defended the community before the court [*Kammergericht*], saying he found 'nothing out of order among them.'"[37]

Gottfried Winter's 1703 letter is especially significant for his attempt to justify the group's unusual communal life. Temme notes, "His letter is an answer to several letters that two onetime members of the society, the two young sisters from Callenberg, had written to their two older sisters, to persuade them to leave the society of Mother Eva. The two younger sisters, in several letters directed to the group to which they shortly before had themselves belonged, and which are no longer extant, had accused the group of 'incest, adultery, prostitution, idolatry, murder, magic and the most frightening things.' In his answer, Winter in no way evades these accusations; rather, he justifies their unusual communal life as well as the promiscuous sexual relations, the honoring of Eva von Buttlar, and the so-called circumcision of women. These details are a sure foundation for the evaluation of all the other materials. Comparison shows that in essential points, the accusations of 'the outside world' against the life of the Society correspond to how it is represented in the self-testimonies."[38]

Text of Winter's Letter[39]

You do know, and are convinced along with me, that God is incomprehensible and his ways past finding out, and therefore cannot be understood by the natural man and by those who stand in their own strength. Now you will say: Yes! that is so. The ways of God are incomprehensible, but these are obviously the works of the flesh.

I respond: you are making no distinction between the flesh, which is evil lust from which all sins arise, and the flesh of the Son of Man. You think that all mingling [or intercourse, *Vermischung*] which happens in the flesh is fleshly. No indeed, for there is also a bodily intercourse which is Christian, namely when I have intercourse with the flesh of the Son of Man, whose flesh I cannot summon from heaven, but find among his members whose flesh is crucified with its lusts and desires; they no longer live but Christ lives in them. This intercourse is not of the flesh but of the Spirit, as the Savior testifies when he speaks concerning the nature of his flesh: "the words which I speak, they are spirit and life." At which all his disciples and bystanders became annoyed and said: "How can he give us his flesh to eat?" Now I ask this of you. For we must eat his flesh, otherwise we have no life in ourselves. I find no other explanation, being so convinced by God's anointing, that when I join myself to the flesh of Christ, and practice this union by faith, that there are no longer two but only one flesh; that I am flesh of his flesh, and bone of his bone, and that nothing can separate us from each other. This happens through the marriage bond of love, of which the apostle says, when he speaks of marriage: The secret is great, but I speak of Christ and the Church, of which the bond of union is the holy intercourse from which two become one flesh. Now this holy intercourse is neither fleshly nor sinful but of God, and pleasing to him; for them it is like that given to the first humans, and begotten of God. But what is from God, that is holy and good.

This holy intercourse and becoming one was quickly corrupted, and further darkened and hidden, so that one could hardly find any trace of it any more. So that now one neither desires to believe nor can believe that such union can come about without lust and sin. Why? All flesh has corrupted its way and the whole world lies in wickedness, and no one wishes anymore to allow the Spirit of God to punish him. Because now these holy ways have become so darkened, so that those in fleshly marriages experience nothing more of it; should it for this reason not be of God, or not be considered right and holy for his children? May it never be so. In this as in other things, God will yet demonstrate his power, according to his holy will. Therefore the godly secret of the true marriage of Christ and his members will become evident to all the world, of which the height and depth, breadth and length, no one can fathom, but only the one to whom God reveals it and leads to it.

REPORT OF THE INVESTIGATION OF THE EVA BUTTLAR SOCIETY (OCTOBER 1705)[40]

All the suspected persons were arrested, seven in number, and taken to prison. Immediately an inquiry was pursued, and a painful proceeding was undertaken. In the course of this proceeding there came up a variety of things which were godless, careless, irritating, and never-before-heard-of things . . . (16)

(1) Did W[inter] present himself as the first person of the Godhead? and J[ohann Georg Appenfeller] as God the Son, and the Mother Eva as the third person of the Godhead? They have at all times stayed together, sitting beside each other on a throne, being worshipped by the other simple folk on bended knee; sleeping together in a bed as we ourselves observed, noting that the bed used by Mother Eva was about half again as wide as an ordinary bed.

(2) There have come to our attention so many prostitutions and lustful things of such an ugly and bestial kind, that one hesitates to write about such things.

(3) From the case of Adam and the fleshly cravings he had soon after the creation to mingle with the animals, from this amazing imaginings arose, as the second appendix proves.

(4) The circumcision of the women came up at various times, as some of the women recounted . . . how they were laid on a bed . . ."

(5) The people confessed that they banished the soul of a Mr. . . . into an ox, and that of a great gentleman into a rooster.

In the course of the inquisition, great effort was devoted to bring the people being examined to the proper belief.

When one asked them, whether they prostituted themselves with each other, and committed adultery, they utterly denied it.

When Mother Eva was asked whether Winter and J[ohann Georg Appenfeller] had laid in a bed with her? She admitted it.

Did he not lie on her body? She responded, Yes.

Whether he did not have intercourse with her? Yes.

Whether this was not to engage in prostitution [*Hurerey*]? No.

Did she feel any lust in this practice? She responded no.

Would Winter and J[ohann Georg Appenfeller] have had lust in this practice? She did not know. She felt nothing at the time for she mingled not in the flesh but in the spirit.

When they were in the process of bringing the proceeding to an end, all the prisoners bolted, and after they made the watchman drunk, escaped with the help of their fellow believers. They ran after them, and again captured Mother Eva ... They were all publicly condemned on the 14 May, 1705. (16–18)

HOCHMANN VON HOCHENAU'S LETTER TO THE COUNTESS OF LIPPE, DECEMBER 21, 1702[41]

Background

Ernst Christoph Hochmann von Hochenau grew up in Nuremberg and began his studies in Altdorf and Giessen. In early February of 1693, he arrived in Halle to study law at Halle University. He also attended the theology lectures of Joachim Justus Breithaupt. In early March of that year, Hochmann experienced the conversion that he describes in this letter.

Text of Hochmann's Letter

I must confess that, sad to say, I formerly went about for a long period of time in great spiritual blindness, yet supposed myself to be one of the Lord's chosen. But when God in his grace opened my eyes and brought me from darkness into his wonderful light, only then could I see that I was on the broad way, along with the great worldly crowd, that leads to damnation. And because in this divine light I now considered with compassion the great ruin of my fellowmen, the love of Christ constrained me to point out [to others] the great ruin of our fallen human nature.

HOCHMANN VON HOCHENAU, "DETMOLD CONFESSION OF FAITH" (1702)[42]

Background

This confession has been called the surest testimony of Hochmann's personal beliefs. Hochmann spent five months imprisoned in the Detmold Castle. Before granting his release, the Count of Lippe-Detmold demanded he compose a confession of his faith. After Hochmann had written out his beliefs on six points, the count insisted that he also record his convictions on the matter of marriage. Hochmann presented the teaching of the mystics concerning the creation of the androgynous being, the fall into sin, and the view of marriage taught by Weigel, Pordage, Leade, and Arnold.

Text of Hochmann's Confession

(1) Concerning water Baptism, I believe that Christ instituted it solely for adults and not for children, because one can find not one iota of an express command concerning it [infant baptism] in the whole of sacred scripture. Faith and baptism belong together.

(2) Concerning the Lord's Supper, I believe that it is only for the chosen disciples of Christ who follow Christ Jesus in deed and truth and renounce all worldly things. The covenant of Christ is much abused and his anger against the church greatly provoked when the godless children of the world are admitted to the love-feast of the Lord, as unfortunately happens in our day.

(3) Concerning Christian Perfection, I believe that although I have been con-

ceived and born of sinful seed, through Christ I can be not only justified but also completely sanctified so that no sin whatsoever can remain in me, if only I attain to the complete spiritual man in Christ. But I do not boast as yet that I have attained this perfection, but I strive for it with Paul in all seriousness and zeal. Therefore I have devoted myself to God and the Lamb to serve them completely, so that I desire nothing more in this age than to expend all my powers in the service of God and the Gospel of Christ, for which purpose God has set me apart and chosen me out of many thousands.

(4) Concerning Spiritual Office, I believe that Christ, who is the head of the Church, is the only one who can appoint a teacher and preacher and give them the ability, and no human authority.

(5) Concerning the Ruling Authorities, I believe they are divinely ordained in the realm of nature and are his servant, to which I gladly submit myself in all civil and outward matters, according to the teaching of Paul in Romans 13:1–7. But, in matters which go against the word of God and my own conscience or Christian freedom, along with all other Evangelicals I grant it no power (Acts 5:29), but rather, if something should be laid on me that goes against God and conscience, I suffer all unjust authority. I ask God that he would not hold it against the authority but rather convert it.

(6) Concerning the Restoration of All Things, here I wish only to introduce very briefly the fundamental point, that just as in Adam all have fallen, so also through Christ the second Adam all must be restored. If this were not so, it would necessarily follow that Christ was not powerful enough to restore the human race, which had been lost through Adam. On this point it can be seen from Romans chapter 5 how the restoration through the mediation of Jesus Christ is much stronger and more powerful than the fall through Adam could ever be.

(7) Concerning Marriage, according to God's word I see five kinds of marriage:

1. a completely bestial marriage;
2. an honorable marriage, but still completely heathen and impure;
3. a Christian marriage;
4. a virginal marriage;
5. the marriage with Christ Jesus the chaste lamb.

This fifth and perfect degree of marriage is where a soul becomes engaged exclusively to the lamb and recognizes only Jesus as its true husband. The souls which, like a bride, have been engaged and offered themselves up to Christ will attain the highest degree of glory in the kingdom of Christ (Psalm 45:10, 17; 48: 11, 12; Song of Solomon 6:8, 9).

According to the human condition, so are the marriages.

ALEXANDER MACK'S "OPEN LETTER," 1708

Background[43]

"By the spring of 1708 all those who would be the founding members of the New Baptists had arrived in Schwarzenau. In their meetings the question of baptism repeatedly arose. They had all been baptized as infants, yet they did not recognize their own baptisms as legitimate. Rather swiftly they were moving from Pietism to Anabaptism (rebaptism) represented by the Dutch Collegiants and the Mennonites. In the early summer of that year two 'foreign Brethren' arrived in Schwarzenau. They strongly urged the Pietists there to be baptized by immersion. Quite likely these were Collegiants whose own practice was immersion, and who encouraged adult baptism.

"On July 4th, Mack and another Schwarzenau Pietist carefully composed a letter to Hochmann at Nüremberg requesting his counsel concerning a service of baptism for adults. Writing from prison on July 24th, Hochmann gave his approval for such a ceremony if it followed true repentance and faith. Although he himself did not believe that water baptism was essential, he felt that if God were leading some of his children to be immersed in flowing water as Christ himself had been immersed, he would have no objection. Believing that Hochmann had approved their plans for a baptismal service, the little group of eight decided to proceed with a public baptismal service in the Eder River which flowed through Schwarzenau.

"Yet two pressing problems remained. First, what kind of Baptism? The English Baptists immersed once backwards. The Collegiants immersed once forward. After studying some church histories, this group came to the conclusion that the person being baptized should be immersed three times forward in the 'name of the Father, and of the Son, and of the Holy Spirit.' From their study of church history they were convinced that 'trine immersion' had been the practice of the early Christian Church. The second problem was 'Who should do the baptizing?' The group wanted Alexander Mack to officiate. Being a very modest and humble man, Mack did not want any one person to go down in history as the founder of their group and refused. He urged the group to cast lots for one of the others to do the baptizing, with the understanding that that person's name should remain secret.

"Early one morning in August, 1708, eight persons gathered at the bank of the Eder River to establish, in Alexander Mack, Jr.'s words, 'a covenant of good conscience with God.' One of the group read from Luke 14 about 'counting the cost,' which Hochmann had suggested. Mack was the first one baptized, after which he baptized the others. Following the baptisms the little group had prayers and sang favorite hymns.

"Mack was now the minister not of a group of separatists or a miscellaneous collection of Christians disenchanted with established religion, but of a congregation, a church, the 'New Baptists' or 'Schwarzenau Baptists' as they called themselves."

Text of Mack's Letter[44]

To All Those Beloved Called in Christ Jesus. Greetings!

Under the providence of God, in Christ Jesus the beloved, I announce and make known to the brethren beloved in God the wonderful divine ordinance which has revealed itself among brethren through their manifest confession about the true baptism.

According to the Holy Scriptures, Jesus Christ, our Savior, received this true baptism from John the Baptist. When John refused [to baptize Jesus] our dear Savior said, "... For thus it is fitting for us to fulfill all righteousness" [Matthew 3:15].

I must first describe the beginning, when all of us, in varying numbers of years ago, expressed to several brethren: "You men, dear brethren. We must be baptized according to the teachings of Jesus Christ and the apostles." However, when this was opposed, it was passed over, but was not completely erased from our hearts. At various times I had an occasion to admit or realize before God and my conscience that it would still occur, and I was assured of it in my heart. In the past two years the other brethren were moved in their consciences that they must be baptized, but none of us knew of the others' concern. Quite by accident, when two foreign brethren visited us, that which was in our hearts was revealed. Our inner joy increased and we were strengthened in the Lord not to be negligent, and to come together in the fear of the Lord. Each one revealed and opened the depths of his heart. As we found that we all agreed with one spirit in this high calling, we have decided to announce this to our beloved brethren through an open letter. This is to see whether they also find themselves convinced in their hearts to help confirm this high calling to the pride and glory of our savior Jesus Christ, and to follow the Creator and Fulfiller of our faith. We drew lots [to determine who would write the letter], and the lot has fallen on the most unworthy.

Concerning baptism, Christ, the first-born, is our forerunner, of whom the apostles and many thousands testified with their blood that Jesus Christ was the Son of the living God. Now Jesus did not only teach, but also acted and commanded, saying to His disciples: "Go, therefore and make disciples of all nations, baptizing them in the name of the Father and of the Son and of the Holy Spirit, teaching them to observe all that I have commanded you." Dear brethren! What is then better than being obedient and not despising the commandments of the Lord Jesus Christ, the King of all Glory? This, especially as we have left all sects because of the misuses concerning infant baptism, communion, and church system, and unanimously profess that these are rather man's statutes and commandments, and therefore do not baptize our children, and testify that we were not really baptized ...

In the second chapter of the Acts of the Apostles, it says that the multitude was so convinced by the sermon of Peter that they spoke, "Brethren, what shall we do?" And Peter said to them, "Repent, and be baptized everyone of you in the name of Jesus Christ ..." Now the apostles remained single-mindedly obedient ... and baptized those who had shown themselves repentant.

So then, if some more brethren wish to begin this high act of baptism with us out of brotherly unity according to the teachings of Christ and the apostles, we announce in humbleness that we are interceding together in prayer and fasting with God. We will choose him whom the Lord gives as the baptizer as God will reveal to us. If we then begin in the footsteps of the Lord Jesus to live according to His commandment, then we can also hold communion together according to the commandment of Christ and His apostles in the fear of the Lord . . .

Summer 1708.

JOHANN CHRISTOPH SAUER'S LETTER DESCRIBING THE SEA VOYAGE FROM EUROPE AND CONDITIONS IN PHILADELPHIA, 1724[45]

Background[46]

"Johann Christoph Sauer (Christopher Sower), the writer of the following letter, was born 1693 in Laasphe, a village not far from Marburg, Germany. He came to America in 1724 with his wife and their infant son, Christopher (born 1721)."

In the spring of 1725, the family met up with Beissel; and in 1732, Sauer's wife, Maria Christina, joined the Ephrata community. Sauer and his son had moved to Germantown. Maria Christina returned to her husband in 1745. Christopher the elder died in 1758.

"Sauer was a pharmacist by trade, but is best known for his publishing activities. In 1738 he received a printing outfit from Germany and began at once to print in German for his fellow countrymen in America. Altogether he published over two hundred works in German and English, most of them of a religious nature. His son Christopher became the well-known Bishop of the Church of the Brethren, in Germantown."

Text of Sauer's Letter

Germantown, Dec. 1, 1724.

Dear brothers and friends,

Since I left all of you, dear friends, and promised to write how we arrived here in America and how we lived, many have desired in addition that I should report somewhat more in detail on the quality of this country. Since it is not possible to make a special report to each one, many may make shift with one account.

During this voyage, of six weeks and three days, we lacked only the necessary east wind, and were obliged to sail with nothing but tack and head-winds, and it was wonderful that the sailors knew so exactly in what part of the sea they were. It is 1100 leagues from England to this coast, and yet the head-helmsman, though he is a young man and had never made this voyage before, hit it within three hours when we should see land. Because we had a strong wind, we got, however, a distance of twenty-three leagues to the left side of the river called Delaware. God, however, sent us a south wind which carried us in one day into the river.

Now we were still 100 miles from the boundary of Pennsylvania and instead of taking eight to ten days, as many do in getting up the river, we, with an extraordinarily good wind, arrived at Philadelphia Sunday noon, October first, and while they were casting anchor in the river they fired twenty-two guns. Then a great crowd of people came running to see the new comers. Then people came and brought apples to divide among the people [passengers], others brought fresh bread and the like, and when I went ashore a man came up to me and asked whether I was free and did not owe anything. I said I did not owe the captain anything, but I had to pay something to a Palatine for brandy. The man went to get twenty Florins with which I was to pay and make my start.

For the rest we have nearly all been ill and those who had been well on shipboard have become ill here, also people with the strongest constitutions. Those however who come here weakly and sickly generally grow strong again and live to old age, the doctors say. Because they make a change of sky and earth, water and air, food and drink, they generally grow strong and their whole constitution changes. Because one may hold here as much property as one wishes, also pay for it when one desires, everybody hurries to take up some property. One may choose where one pleases. The farther one goes, the better it is. This continent, as may be seen on the map, is almost as large as the other three continents together and has south of New England, say Spain, Virginia, Negro-land, Pennsylvania; north of New England, New Holland, the borders of York, New France, unto the region lying beyond us, which cannot be inhabited on account of the cold. The farther the Germans and English cultivate this country, the farther the Indians retreat. They are our nearest neighbors and quite agreeable and peaceable. They would rather harm their own kind than a German; they have very simple clothing. They do not gather more than they expect to eat.

As for the savages, they are dark yellow, believe that there is a God who has created everything and are very much afraid to commit a sin. They believe God does not like it and is looking on. If one has committed a fornication, they stone him to death by the roadside right away and anyone who within 20 years passes by where the malefactor lies, seeks a rock and increases the pile to show the All-seeing that he has a horror of such uncleanliness. They also believe that, when they are dead, and have lived such a life that the Pure One was not pleased with it, they will go to the North where it is very cold; in that land there is a bad ruler who torments them and lets them suffer from the cold. On the other hand the good go to the South where it is nice and warm, and a good ruler receives them kindly. They think more of a hen that is laying eggs than of some ducats. They make baskets and brooms and bring them here or to Philadelphia and accept blue blankets and red stockings, knives, etc., in exchange. The wise know full well the meaning of the godhead and call God in their language "Acs" and speak of him with fear, saying that the Acs sees it. Other simple minded ones say that the Acs at first made only one man and woman. At that time the garden in which he placed them was only small. But now that men had become many, the garden also has grown larger; and similar simple-minded talk. They are putting most Europeans to shame by their behavior.

The Pennsylvania borders lie between other well-settled countries, most of them belonging to the King of England. This country also is pretty well settled and is said to have over 100,000 inhabitants, consisting of French, Welsh, Swedes, Dutch and Germans. There are some companies in this country that have bought it of William Penn, to whom the king and his heirs have granted it. Here may one select a piece [of land] where one desires, near or far. All inhabitants of this country are free to live quietly and piously by themselves and everybody may believe what he chooses . . .

And if you, dear friends, should be expelled from a place and God should desire to lead you here, cling then firmly to the arm of God, as children are wont to do, and do not worry, for where a father goes, who has plenty of everything, the children may easily follow. In all your doings let this be your touch-stone, whether your heart is earthly. Seek only heavenly things, otherwise earthly things may flee away, or you may have to leave them. May God guide you according to His will! I greet you all and remain,

Yours affectionately,
Joh. Christoph Sauer
Germantown, 2 leagues from Philadelphia, Dec. 1, 1724.

Chapter 7. Pietism and Gender

ANNA MARIA VAN SCHURMAN, *Eukleria, Choosing the Better Part* (1673)[47]

Since for some years now I have looked with sorrowful eyes at the almost total deflection and defection of Christianity from its origin . . . and since I am left without any hope of its restitution through that common path on which the churchmen of our age walk (most of whom are themselves in need of Reformation), who could fairly blame me for having chosen for myself and joyfully welcomed pastors who are reformed and divinely instructed toward the goal of reforming deformed Christians? And when the wonderful providence and goodness of God, so worthy of devotion, showed me the correct and direct path to the true practice of the original life of the gospel through the singular Mr. Jean de la Badie, who is well practiced in the ways of the Lord and a faithful servant of the Lord, and his partners in grace, who likewise follow in the footprints of Christ, both in teaching and in working and suffering, how could anyone justly reproach me for following them as the best teachers and leaders? Or [deny] that I am also supported by the company of many faithful who all with the same mind and zeal look to Jesus the guide and perfecter of our faith, as we strive toward our heavenly homeland, aiming for the same and only goal of all, namely the glorification of our God and of Jesus Christ the king of glory?

. . . I shall not deny that I felt some small sparks of genuine piety in my heart from a tender age; during the whole later course of my life these could easily be seen at times to glow and even to break out in flames. One instance among others that comes to mind was when I was a little girl of scarcely four years. While collecting herbs with the maid whose chore this was, I sat down on the bank of a certain stream. When she suggested it, I recited from memory the response to the first question of the *Heidelberg Catechism*. At the words "that I am not my own but belong to my most faithful Savior Jesus Christ," my heart was filled with such a great and sweet joy and an intimate feeling of the love of Christ that all the subsequent years have not been able to remove the living memory of that moment.

. . . I found that the life of Christians is alone the most excellent image of the life of Christ, but it is not within easy reach in these times. When I saw the most vivid outline of this in our pastors, I believed their living examples had to replace for me the mechanisms of all the arts.

. . . If teachers are truly taught by God and are instructed and led by the strength of his Spirit, three books are more than sufficient for them, namely the book of Scripture, the book of Nature, and the book of inward grace, in order to know God and themselves thoroughly. In this knowledge all true wisdom is located. Those who lack this inward teacher can only borrow a kind of barren and false knowledge from a human school, which the Apostle elegantly calls "the form of knowledge" (Romans 2:20).[48]

JOHANNA ELEONORA PETERSEN, *Guide to a Thorough Understanding of the Holy Revelation of Jesus Christ Which He Sent to His Servant and Apostle John by the Angel, and Its Complete Fulfillment in the Last Days to Which We Draw Near* (1696)[49]

Some may be doubtful that this kind of writing should be produced by me since I am a woman. I can only say this, since I have not sought my own honor, let the judgment fall where it may. Whoever does not wish to accept that this writing represents a gift which I received from the Lord, is free to do so. It is enough that I know what the Lord has given to me . . .

Some will throw up to me the words of Paul in I Corinthians 14:34 and I Timothy 2:12, that it is not proper for a woman to teach in the church of God. But they should know that these words do not apply to me. I respect what the Holy Spirit has testified through Paul . . . But I also know that in Christ Jesus, in the distribution of grace and the Spirit, there is neither male nor female, Galatians 3:28, and that the grace and gift of God must not be quenched or suppressed. So while I know how to govern myself with proper submission in the Church of God, I also know that I must not hide the gift I received from God under a bushel but use it to His honor and to the benefit of my neighbor.

. . . At that time there will be a true holy catholic church that will praise God the Father of our Lord Jesus Christ with one voice and in the unity of the Spirit. Now we see that everything is split and divided into so many sects and religions. Each desires to serve God in its own particular way: the one believes and teaches about God and Christ in this fashion, the other in another, as if there were many kinds of Gods and Christs. But in that kingdom there will be one flock and one shepherd. John 10: 16.

In these seven churches in Asia [in Revelation 2 and 3], there is a prophetic representation of seven great churches and ages of the New Testament church. This includes times of humiliation and of victory for New Testament believers in the cross of Christ's kingdom, until the time of their rise and reward in the kingdom of Christ's glory, when the seven churches come to an end and the Lord will be honored in the great assembly. Then is the time of strife and conquering past and believers will reign with Christ on his throne, and the converts from the people of Israel will reign with Christ on earth after the downfall of the kingdom of Anti-Christ.

In the seven churches one finds an exact and concise sketch of all church history as it has unfolded over time and according to the prophetic word of Scripture will yet unfold. [50]

Chapter 8. Pietism and the Bible

AUGUST HERMANN FRANCKE, FOREWORD TO THE GERMAN BIBLE OF 1708[51]

Just as the readers of the Bible are extremely varied, so also some receive no benefit from their reading, others a little benefit, but others great and glorious benefits ... Those who receive great and glorious benefits from their reading of the Bible are those:

1. who read the holy Scriptures not merely for the sake of knowledge but so they might learn from God's Word how they can truly convert to God, become a friend of God, unite themselves rightly with the heart of God, believe rightly and live rightly, and die a godly death.

2. who consider that it is not the Word of men but of God, and that holy men of God have spoken as they were moved by the Holy Spirit. 2 Pet. 2:21.

3. who call upon God the Lord as they read the Bible, recognizing in humility their natural blindness and who pray with David: "Open my eyes, that I might behold the wonders in Thy Law." Ps. 119:18.

4. who are not easily deterred if in their reading of holy Scripture they encounter something extremely difficult and dark, but rather they read everything with appropriate attentiveness ... until God bestows on them more light into his Word ... It becomes more and more easy [to understand] the holy Scripture, just as if one were digging in a goldmine and probing ever deeper into its depths.

5. who treat nothing in holy Scripture as unimportant and who consider not just the outward account, but rather in everything that they read they direct their mind to finding proper food and nourishment for their soul and to using this in their spiritual life, just as bodily food assists in our natural life and provides the body with new power and strength each day.

6. who make Christ their main goal in reading the Bible, because he is the main goal of the whole Bible. "Everything that is written in the sacred Scriptures points to Christ," Augustine said.

So if a person begins to read the holy Scripture according to these rules and foundations of truth, and continues in them, God the Lord will not deny him his grace and help, so that he will soon come to know what an abundant benefit he may receive from it for his soul.

THE *Berleburg Bible*, VOL. 6 (1737)

A selection from the commentary on the Acts of the Apostles 11:26, "And it was in Antioch that the disciples were first called 'Christians.'"[52]

"What and Who Is a Christian?"

One who believes on the Lord Christ and publicly confesses, with his life, that he follows Christ's teaching and takes it to be true.

One who has put on Christ, Galatians 3:27, so that people observe in his whole way of life nothing other than Christ. He no longer lives by his own wisdom, Gal. 2:20, nor works by his own power, and no longer loves his own will. He finds all his joy in being occupied with him and finds all his honors and blessings in his title as a child of God and partaker of Christ.

One who is pervaded within by the truth of the Gospel, finds daily nourishment in it, lives by faith, and finds his strength, his comfort, and his light for all the circumstances of life in the word of God.

One who sees God in all things and all things in God.

One who prays without ceasing, 1 Thessalonians 5:17, and who stands in constant longing after God, his sole and highest good.

One who eats the flesh of Christ and drinks his blood as his spiritual nourishment. John 6.

One who allows himself to be brought by baptism to the death of the old man, and who rises again each day to new life. Romans 6.

One who, out of love for God, loves his neighbor as himself.

One who desires with deepest longing that all men be saved.

One who renounces his own affections and crucifies his flesh together with all its lusts and desires. Galatians 5:24.

One who is full of compassion and heartfelt love towards the poor, and who finds joy in helping them.

One who seeks to follow God in every area of his life [since it] belongs to him. Ephesians 5:1.

One who considers Christ as his pattern and example, and devotes himself, by constant imitation, to becoming more like his image.

One who loves what Christ loves: namely, a quiet life, poverty, obedience, and suffering.

One who despises the world as the enemy of Christ, and rejects the world's caresses, for the world is crucified to him. Galatians 6:14.

One who loves God with a whole heart and with all his strength.

One who lives with the body on earth, but with the mind and heart is in heaven.

One who needs nothing apart from God, speaks most gladly concerning him, and longs to be his child and for complete union and revelation. Romans 8.

One who is free and clear of all things in this world, and sets all his hope in God alone.

One who in every situation has determined to prefer faith to the senses, eternity to time, and God to the creature.

One who lives on earth as a foreigner and pilgrim, and despises and rejects everything that could hold him back from coming closer to his fatherland.

One who directs all his effort that he might become rich and adorned in virtues.

One who considers all things to be rubbish in comparison to Christ, and who seeks no other honor than to please him.

One who has the utmost abhorrence of sin.

One who seeks every day of his life to purify himself of the infirmity that still clings to us.

One who constantly mistrusts himself, and is therefore constantly on his guard so that he is not taken captive by the enemy, and carefully avoids every occasion for sin.

One who walks in the presence of God, and does everything with passionate love toward him.

One who, because he believes that God sees him at all times and is attentive to him, remains in constant fear of him, yet in such a way that his love for God is greater than his fear.

One who seeks to deny himself in all things, and does violence to himself in order to seize the kingdom of heaven.

One who bears his cross daily, following after Christ and the way he has gone.

One who makes use of the present life and this age in order [to] prepare himself for the future and eternal age; death he sees as gain.

In short, the one who lives in the Lord, also dies in the Lord.

JOHANN ALBRECHT BENGEL, PREFACE TO THE *Gnomon* (1742): BENGEL'S "MONITA"

Background

The "Gnomon" is the part of a sundial that casts the shadow. Bengel wrote: "I have given the name *Gnomon* . . . to these explanatory notes in the sense of a pointer or indicator, as of a sundial. The intention is briefly to point out the full force of words and sentences in the New Testament." In the preface to the *Gnomon*, Bengel provides a list of twenty-seven "Admonitions" (*Monita*) that represent a summary of his critical principles.[53]

Text of Bengel's "Monita"

1. By far the greatest part of the Sacred Text (thank God) labors under no important variety of reading.
2. This part contains the whole scheme of salvation, fully established.
3. Every various reading may and ought to be referred to these portions as a standard, and judged by them.
4. The text and various readings of the New Testament are found in Manuscripts, and in Books printed from Manuscripts, whether Greek, Latin, Graeco-Latin . . . Syriac, etc., Latinizing Greek, or other languages; in the direct quotations of Irenaeus, etc., according as Divine Providence dispenses its bounty to each generation. We include all these under the title of *Codices*, sometimes used comprehensively.
5. These codices, however, have been diffused through Churches of all ages

and countries, and approach so near to the original autographs, that, taken together, in all the multitude of their varieties, they exhibit the genuine text.

6. No *conjecture* is ever to be regarded. It is safer to bracket any portion of the text which may seem inexplicable.
7. The whole body of codices form the standard by which each separately is to be judged.
8. *Greek* manuscripts, so ancient as to date before the varieties of readings themselves, are very few: the rest are very numerous.
9. Although versions and fathers are of little weight where they differ from the Greek Manuscripts of the New Testament, where the Greek manuscripts vary, those have the greatest authority with which versions and fathers agree.
10. The text of the Latin Vulgate, where supported by the consent of the Latin Fathers, or even of other competent witnesses, deserves the utmost consideration on account of its high antiquity, in which it stands alone.
11. The *Number* of witnesses who support each reading of every passage ought to be carefully examined: and to that end, in so doing, we should separate those codices which contain only the *Gospels*, from those which contain the *Acts* and the *Epistles*, with or without the *Apocalypse*, or those which contain that book alone; those which are *entire*, from those which have been mutilated; those which have been collated for the *edition* of Stephens from those which have been collated for the Complutensian, or the Elzevir, or any obscure edition; those which are known to have been *carefully collated*, as, for instance, the Alexandrine, from those which are not known to have been carefully collated, or which are known to have been carelessly collated, as for instance the Vatican manuscript, which otherwise would scarcely have an equal.
12. And so, in fine, *more* witnesses are to be preferred to fewer; and, which is more important, witnesses which *differ* in country, age, and language, to those which are closely connected with each other; and, most important of all, *ancient* witnesses to modern ones. For, since the original autographs (which were in Greek) can alone claim to be the Fountain-head, the highest value belongs to those streams which are least removed from it; that is, to the most ancient codices in Greek, Latin, etc.
13. A reading which does not allure by too great facility, but shines by its native dignity, is always to be preferred to that which may fairly be supposed to owe its origin to either the carelessness or the injudicious care of copyists.
14. Thus, a corrupted text is often betrayed by *alliteration*, *parallelism*, a modification for the beginning or end of a church lesson. The recurrence of the same words suggests an omission; too great facility, a gloss. Where various readings are many, the *middle* reading is the best.
15. There are, therefore, *five* principal means of judging the Text. The *Antiquity* of witnesses, the *Diversity* of their extraction, and their *Multitude*; the *Origin* of the *corrupt* reading, and the *Native* appearance of the *genuine*.

16. Where these concur, none can doubt but a sceptic.
17. When, however, it happens that some of these favor one reading, and some another, the critic may be drawn now in this, now in that direction; or, even should he decide, others may be slow to agree with him. When one man has a keener eye than another, either in body or mind, discussion is vain. One man can force no view on another, nor take the views of another from him, unless, indeed, the original autograph Scriptures some day come to light . . .
21. It would be highly desirable to produce an edition of the Greek Testament, in which the text itself should in every instance clearly exhibit the genuine reading, and leave not a single passage in dispute. Our age, however, cannot attain this; and the more nearly any one of us has approached to primitive genuineness, the less does he obtain the assent of the multitude.
22. I have determined, therefore, in the meanwhile (until a fuller measure of light be vouchsafed to the Church), to construct as genuine a text as possible by a judicious selection from approved *editions*. In the *Apocalypse alone* I have introduced some readings here and there from *manuscripts*, and I have frequently stated the reason.[54]

Chapter 9. Pietism, World Christianity, and the Missions to South India and Labrador

BARTHOLOMÄUS ZIEGENBALG'S LETTER DESCRIBING HIS LEARNING OF THE TAMIL LANGUAGE, AUGUST 22, 1708,

From seven to eight [in the morning] I repeat all the Malabari words and phrases I have already written down. From eight to twelve I read some Malabari books I have not read before in the presence of an old poet and one of my Malabari scribes. The poet has to explain the stories to me and if a verse is particularly difficult and obscure he will explain this too. The scribe has to take down all the word and phrases I have not read before in any other book. In the beginning I had also an interpreter with me by the name of Alepla but this is no longer necessary . . . From three to five I again read Malabari books. At this time I always choose just one author and study him properly; after I have done so I take another author and start all over again . . . From seven to eight one of my Malabari scribes reads aloud to me because I find it very difficult to read by artificial light. On this occasion I always choose a book written in such a style as I would like to imitate in my speech and in my writing. I sometimes made my scribe read one and the same book a hundred times until in the end there was no word and no phrase I did not know thoroughly. This method has helped me to gain a certain facility in this language.[55]

BARTHOLOMÄUS ZIEGENBALG, *Catalogue of Tamil bBooks* (1708)

A book called *Mudirei* is a moral book full of beautiful similes taken from nature. Like all these books it shows that even after the fall of man these heathens had the Law written in their hearts. This fact manifests itself again and again in their literature and I can truly say that I have found a much higher level of morality in their books and their speeches than was common amongst the Greek and Roman heathens. Therefore, if we lead a pious and virtuous life amongst them, they are in full agreement with us Christians and they love those who devote themselves to virtue. But if one tells them about Christ, the importance of baptism and other things necessary for salvation, then they will not argue, but at the same time they will refuse to accept one's words, saying that a man who leads a good life will reach a good place after this death. It is extremely difficult to contradict their faulty way of reasoning and show them the necessity of having faith in Christ . . . Just as the Bible tells us that even amongst those who believed Jesus' words only a few agreed to be baptized, though this was the aim of his sermon, in the same way there are many Malabaris who have a high opinion of our Christian religion but only a few of them will agree to be baptized.[56]

BARTHOLOMÄUS ZIEGENBALG'S LETTER, WRITTEN IN TRANQUEBAR, TO JOACHIM LANGE IN BERLIN, OCTOBER 10, 1709[57]

The Malabars are a very clever and intelligent people and so can only be converted with a great deal of wisdom. In matters of faith they have a close analogy to what we Christians may claim to have. They are certainly more strongly convinced of the future life than are many Christians. They have a great number of books which they claim they have received from their gods just as Christians claim for the Holy Scriptures. These books contain amusing stories about their gods and matters concerning the future world, so that our Word of God seems to them quite tiresome by comparison. They lead a very quiet, honorable, and virtuous life in which they, by mere natural human strength, outdo us Christians tenfold. They have a great reverence for their gods, so that when I recently in my translation [of the Bible] came to the passage about how we can become God's friends and children, the schoolmaster denied it and instead asserted that God wishes us to kiss his feet. They recognize only one divine essence but in such a way that it expresses itself in many forms, establishing many gods both in heaven and on earth.

Yesterday we went for a walk a short ways inland and came across a pagoda in which the wife of their great god Shiva is worshipped as a goddess. There were an abundance of porcelain images of her standing about. Full of godly zeal, we knocked some of them down and broke off the heads of some, in order to show these poor people that these were just powerless and vain idols who could do nothing to help themselves nor those who served them. To this a teacher answered us, saying that these were not gods but only God's soldiers. We finally convinced him to admit that this was foolishness. Then he said that simple people need to contemplate images such as these in order to be directed to future things. We have often seen thousands of such images in one place. But even if one can convince them that serving such idols is false . . . nevertheless they have an abhorrence of Christianity because of the annoying life of Christians. They believe that there is no more irritating and evil people in the world than Christians.

THE MALABAR CORRESPONDENCE (1714, 1717)[58]

Background

Bartholomäus Ziegenbalg and Johann Ernst Gründler pursued a dialogue by correspondence with the Tamils in their own language. The two missionaries posed questions concerning the culture and religion of the Tranquebar region, to which the Tamils responded. These written responses, originally recorded on palm leaves, were then translated into German, sent to Halle, and published in the *Halle Reports* in 1714 and 1717.

Selections from the Malabar Correspondence

Question from Ziegenbalg/Gründler: What opinion do the Malabars have of the Christian religion and law?

Answer by the Tamils: The Christian religion is disdained by us because Christians slaughter and eat cattle, because they do not cleanse themselves after they have gone to the bathroom, because they drink strong drinks, and because, when someone dies, they do not take steps to assist the soul of the deceased in reaching the place of the blessed. Also, when they marry they do not perform the appropriate works of celebration.

Question: Why do the Malabars refuse to give place to the Christian religion?

Answer: God has created many classes of persons. When we observe that the Christians do not respect such distinctions of class, but make all one, and also that they do not take note of the great difference that exists between men and women, but bring all together without distinction into one great assembly, it is displeasing to us . . . (53–55)

Question: In the laws of the Malabars, what things are condemned as sinful and what things commanded as virtues or good works?

Answer: Condemned in our laws are all sins such as the following:

1. Murder and manslaughter, 2. Adultery and fornication, 3. Taking away someone's livelihood so that he can no longer reside in his homeland, 4. Animosity and malicious counsel, 5. Betrayal of one's benefactor, 6. Bearing false witness, 7. Swearing a falsehood on oath, 8. Lying, 9. Refusing to show kindness to others after one has received acts of kindness, 10. Despising and blaspheming the gods, 11. Slaughtering and killing the creatures and animals of the earth . . . (65)

Question: How did sin come into the world?

Answer: In the beginning, when the human race was created, both sin and virtue came into being. For God created both at once. For since among men the two principles of anger and patience have their departure and entrance, so sin and virtue have been present from our first parents right up to the present day.

Question: How and in what manner can a bad person become a good and pious person?

Answer: When those who are evil receive instruction from wise and pious persons, become their disciples, allow themselves to be disciplined and mastered by them, and follow after them in the way in which they go, then are they able, with good fortune, to attain to the good way of life and be changed from evil persons to pious and good ones . . . (71–72)

Question: Do the Malabars worship one God or many gods?
Answer: We all know and confess that there is only one God. But the gods which we honor beneath him are many in number. For example, five gods are the five faces of Shiva, and two others are the sons of Shiva. It is only the names that are manifold and changeable. Among all of these, there is only one highest being who created all the rest. This is prescribed in our law and in our ancient stories. There are some among us who pray only to God, the highest being, and worship this God alone. (140–142)[59]

EPITAPH ON THE LIFE OF MIKAK (1740–1795) IN MORAVIAN *Periodical Accounts*, 1790–96[60]

About the time that the brethren were consulting how to begin a mission on the coast of Labrador . . . a skirmish took place in 1768, between the English and some Esquimaux, who came, as was supposed, with hostile intentions, to annoy the former. Some were killed, but a woman called Mikak, with her son, and a boy of the name Karpik, were taken prisoners and brought to England. Sir Hugh Palliser, then Governor of Newfoundland, presented Karpik to the brethren, by whom he was sent to Fulneck in Yorkshire, to be instructed, hoping that if it pleased God to convert his heart, he might be of use in the Mission on his return to Labrador. However, after showing very promising dispositions, he fell sick of the small-pox and departed this life in the faith of Christ, under the care of that venerable Missionary, Christian Lawrence Drachart.

Mikak was introduced to many persons of high rank in London and returned, loaded with presents, in 1770, where she rendered essential services to the Missionaries on their first arrival in 1771. She was then married to the noted Tuglavina, now William, and accompanied the brethren to the place where they first settled. She even became an attentive hearer of the Gospel, expressed a desire to be converted, and was admitted to the class of candidates for baptism in 1782. But in 1783 she went with others to the South, where she mostly resided. Thus she lost the advantage of hearing the Gospel, and indeed seemed indifferent about it.

The last ten days of her life she spent at Nain. Immediately on her arrival, being very ill, she sent to brother Burghardt to request assistance and advice. He found her extremely weak, hardly able to speak, and apparently without hopes of recovery. However, after giving her some medicine, he took occasion to speak seriously with her concerning the state of her soul, advising her to turn as a repenting sinner to the Lord Jesus Christ, who will surely receive poor prodigals if with all their hearts they confess their deviations. He also reminded her of the promises she made formerly, to devote her whole heart to him. She assented to the truths of all he said, and exclaimed; "Ah, I have behaved very badly, and am grieved on that account, but what shall I do! I cannot find Jesus again!" Brother Burghardt encouraged her not to desist from crying to Him for mercy, for he came to seek and save the lost, and would not cast her out. In the following days she seemed to receive these admonitions with eagerness, and declared, that she had not forgotten what she had heard of her Savior in former days, nor what she had promised him when she became a candidate for baptism. She departed this life, October 1st, 1795, and was buried in our burying ground. We trust in our Savior's mercy, that he has also found this poor straying sheep.

Conclusion. Reflecting on the Cultural and Religious Legacy of German Pietism

JOHANN CHRISTIAN EDELMANN, *Autobiography (Selbstbiographie)* (1753)[61]

Background

Johann Christian Edelmann composed his *Selbstbiographie* between 1749 and 1753, during his period of exile in Berlin. The tolerant Friedrich II granted him welcome on condition that he publish no more books.[62] The autobiography was finally published in Berlin in 1849, a century after Edelmann wrote it.

Selections from Edelmann's Autobiography [63]

I was baptized shortly after my birth, and the miserable old devil (with or without horns, I didn't know) was cast out of me using the customary formalities . . . Whether he really heeded the command of the cleric I cannot be sure; it is sufficient that my dear parents believed firmly and without question that he had left. But I now know that he had never been in me, and that the whole comedy with which they still today seek to drive him out of innocent children is just a laughable game of deception . . . (6)

I came across the story of a certain Frenchman who fell seriously ill. For a time he endured the attention of some learned medical doctors, but without any improvement whatever. Finally he visited a gentleman whom the others dismissed as ignorant and unlearned. But this man cured the Frenchman. One of the medical doctors visited the Frenchman and asked if he were not ashamed to have put himself in the hands of someone who knew neither Greek nor Latin. The Frenchman replied: "My dear sir, he cured me in French." I [writes Edelmann] have likewise cured my countrymen in German, for none of those who know Hebrew and Greek have been of any help to them. I well know that these learned people are not a little bothered by this and have sought to make me despised and hated as the greatest of fools.

[As a young man] my intention was to study theology. My superstitious mindset at that time had some benefit, for it kept me away from dissolute company into which I might easily have fallen and provided the opportunity for me to apply myself to my studies. Everything has its time and season, and it is certain that the Freedom to which God called me after many long years I would not have put to good use at that wild time of life . . . (37–39)

I finally became discontented with my life as a student and longed to set out to see the world. But I did not have the means to fulfill this desire. And my father still hoped to make a pastor of me . . . (47–49)

What a huge influence this blind faith has upon us, that flowed into us with our mother's milk! By the grace of God I was finally delivered from it. I wish to relate out of my own experience into what troubled circumstances a tortured mind can fall . . . (109)

I spent most of my money on books. My Orthodox comrades could not understand why I bought books mainly by so-called Heretics, forbidden by the authorities, while they purchased books of sermons (*Postills*), funeral sermons, and Bible commentaries. But I avoided stepping beyond the limits of the Christian religion. If I came across something that seemed to oppose the Christian religion in some way, then I either ignored it or allowed myself to be intimidated and avoided considering the words of the infamous Deists, Naturalists, and Atheists.

In a word, I was still about three quarters Lutheran, but with this qualification, that I identified more with the Pietists and separatists than with the Orthodox. During my first six months in Dresden, I prayed, fasted, went to confession, took the sacrament, and did everything that one could ask of a true Church Christian. Except that with all these so-called means of grace, my human nature remained unchanged. My purpose was still to become a true Christian, to live as the first Christians had lived. In fact, I was foolish to think in this way. For by this standard, I was really not a Christian at all. But I assumed that others had attained this goal, and I longed to meet them and follow their example. I hoped to find such people among the Herrnhuters led by Count von Zinzendorf . . . I observed the obvious hypocrisy in the way the Count treated his Lutheran neighbors in Bertholsdorf. For the Herrnhuters attended services there on Sunday, but would allow none of these Lutherans to partake in the services in Herrnhut. After a meager meal, I noticed that much better food was served at the Count's table . . . (138–141, 145–146.)

How rash and empty are our thoughts when they turn their back on reason and follow a fanatical path. For then reason, the true guide of our affairs, is not attended to when it comes forward and shows us how to avoid a path that leads to ruin. My faithful reader should know that I had already begun to write the book *Innocent Truths*, whose story now follows. I knew that I would never become a pastor, but realized that I was unprepared for anything else. But I determined to rely on God's grace and to remain faithful to the truth until my death. To avoid idleness, I kept busy with the translation of the Italian Opera *Fabricio*, rendering it into good German verse.

But God directed me to another task. One morning, as I lay awake in bed enjoying my rest a little longer, thinking about I know not what, it was as if someone spoke to me in a clear voice: write *Innocent Truths*. This unexpected and unusual train of thought made a strong impression on my mind so that I got out of bed and went to my writing table, not knowing what I should write. I decided first to work on the title, which I put down as, *Conversations in the realm of the truth*. I then wrote the first part of it concerning the relative unimportance of the world Religions.

However it may have come about, and whatever my thinking was in launching my writing career, one thing is certain: this was the foundation for all my intellectual and material happiness in later life. If I had not heeded it, I would not have come to know the dear friends who have cared for and supported me in my dangerous work and destitute circumstances. I did not have any idea how and by what means I could get my work published. And when I completed four parts of it, and sent them to some people, I did not know for some time whether they had received them, and if they had received them, whether they considered them worth publishing. I had to persist in my work and endure many hard trials before I was assured of God's plan for me . . . (157–158)

In the matter of my increase in understanding, God dealt with me slowly and in stages. Reason, understanding, and perception are the gifts which my creator has entrusted to me for my happiness. But before I knew how to make proper use of these invaluable blessings, I fell among murderers who sought to rob me of them completely and to leave me half dead. But the lover of my soul helped me after a hard struggle . . . as my best friend. (436–437)

APPENDIX B

Translation of Georg Heinrich Neubauer's "183 Questions" (1697)[1]

Georg Heinrich Neubauer visited the Netherlands from June 2, 1697, to June 19, 1698, with the goal of observing orphan and poor foundations in various cities to determine what might be useful in relation to building the orphanage in Halle. In preparation for his trip, Neubauer prepared "183 Questions" that he planned to raise with the governors of the orphanages he visited. The questions were divided into seven main categories: concerning the children, the caregivers, the building, the ultimate goal, the costs, the duties of the house father and staff, and care of the children. These questions are a valuable historical source for revealing the practical concerns that were uppermost in Neubauer's mind as he and Francke prepared to build an orphanage in Halle.

The translation begins with the following heading that Neubauer placed over the pages of questions.

"The purpose of my trip, in service to the Orphanage in Halle, should be to consider carefully the establishments for orphans and the poor in various places, as well as to raise funds. In addition, it is no less important to investigate facilities for education, health, spinning, and manufacture, as well as other enterprises for the good of the poor and of human society generally, and anything else that is useful in each city should be noted in passing."[2]

Concerning the Children [*Von den Kindern*]

1. How many children are there from each region?
2. Do you have a certain number [of orphans], beyond which you will accept no more?
3. How many boys and how many girls are in the orphanage?

4. Are there some children in the orphanage whose parents left behind some goods when they passed away, and what do you do with these goods?
5. If you take in children from off the street who are full of lice and vermin, do you integrate them right away with the other children? And can you do so without the danger of infecting the other children?
6. How old must children be in order to be accepted into the orphanage?
7. How long do you keep children in the orphanage?
8. How many children did you have at the beginning?
9. Up to this point in time, how many children have you raised?
10. How many varieties of children do you have? E.g., foundlings, illegitimate children, orphans, children from poor families (whom the parents cannot care for) etc. How do the costs vary for these varieties of children?

Concerning the Caregivers [*Von den Pflegern*]

1. Who brought this work into being?
2. Who is supporting it financially up till now?
3. Who is the supervisor [*Aufseher*]? etc. Who appoints him?
4. Who is responsible for the work? What is his salary?
5. How many and what kinds of servants, farmhands, and maids are required?
6. How many teachers are there?
7. What kinds of Privileges [from the authorities] did the founders obtain in advance?
8. What provisions are in place for appointing their successors?
9. If the orphanage was founded by private individuals, how did they begin the undertaking and how did they manage to obtain the necessary Privileges from the authorities?
10. How many people are there [on staff] per child?
11. How many sorts of offices are there?
12. Who appoints [people to] these positions and according to what procedure?
13. What is the role of the preacher in the orphanage?
14. In what does the salary consist, in money, food, etc. or something else? How much exactly is the salary?
15. Must the orphanage staff support their wife and children from their salary or do [family members] share in the meals and other provisions of the orphanage?

Various Other Concerns [*Observationes variae*]

1. Is there some kind of printed orphanage regulation available?
2. If there is, arrange to make a copy or excerpt of it.
3. Take the head of the orphanage to a place where he can be questioned about his work and can explain the by-laws of the orphanage without being interrupted. It would be good to do this at an especially arranged mealtime.

4. Whatever I cannot myself receive in this way, can either be obtained from a third party or from information about the foundation and its operation.

Concerning the Building [*Von dem Gebäude*]

1. Where is the orphanage building situated, and why was this location chosen? Was it for the sake of the [children's] health?
2. How big is the orphanage building in its length, breadth, and height?
3. How many rooms are there?
4. How big are the rooms and how big is each separate room? How are the rooms connected to each other? What sources of light and fresh air are there? How many windows and stoves are there and how big are they? How many rooms are used for the children's mealtimes and instruction and work? Can these activities all be done in one room, or is there a separate room for each?
5. How wide and long would a room be in which fifty children are living?
6. How are tables and beds arranged, and the hooks on which they hang their clothing and hats?
7. If there are a hundred or more children, are they housed in one room or more? Which of these two arrangements has been found to be the best?
8. What is the floor made of, wood or plaster, and which material is most healthy for the children?
9. How many windows are there?
10. How many air vents are there, and how big are they, for taking away the smell that comes from so many children living together?
11. How high are the rooms?
12. How big are the stoves [for heat]?
13. How many apartments, rooms, and chambers does the head of the orphanage, along with his servants, require for living and sleeping? Where in the building are these located?
14. Where does the teacher reside?
15. Where is the sick room situated and how is it furnished?
16. Does the orphanage have a room where they can take in strangers and beggars for a night?
17. How big are the bedrooms? E.g. can one room sleep fifty people? Where are [the bedrooms] situated?
18. Where is the kitchen situated? How big is it? How big is the herd of cattle?
19. How big is the cellar? Where is it located?
20. Where is the pantry and how big is it?
21. Where is the storage room for dry foods, flour, and other foods, and how big is it? . . .
23. Can the upper story be used for storage as well? Or is it needed for hanging the laundry after it is washed? Where do they hang the laundry? . . .
25. Where is the toilet room and how is it furnished? Are there different rooms for each gender? How wide and deep is it?

26. Does it have a drain, or do you have to carry [the waste] out? And how often is this done? And in what manner?
27. How big is it? How many seats are there relative to the number of orphans?
28. How do you minimize the strong smell?
29. Is something deposited in the refuse so it can be burned up? What is deposited?
30. How do you make sure that the seats stay clean and are not fouled by the children?
31. Where do you allow the children to retire when they have to go at night? Are there night seats for this purpose, and how does this seem to work?
32. How big is the place at the orphanage where the children have their recreation time?
33. If there is a dairy farm nearby, how big is it?
34. How big is the barn in proportion to the acreage?
35. How many cows and horses are there in proportion to the acreage?
36. How many and how big are the stalls?
37. What poultry do they have?
38. Does the director of the orphanage have to oversee the dairy farm or does it have a special administrator?
39. How many workers are needed for the dairy farm?
40. How big is the garden?
41. What do you grow in it?
42. Who looks after the garden, the head of the orphanage or someone else?
43. How do they alternate sowing and planting so that they can have a crop more than once a year?
44. What wells or source of water is there?
45. Is it situated near the kitchen, and can the water easily be run to the herd? How is that done?

Concerning All Kinds of Necessary Matters [*Von allerhand nötigen Dingen*]

1. Do you burn oil or use candles?
2. How many candles or lamps are there in a room and where are they secured?
3. Who lights them?
4. What is the most advantageous form of lighting?
5. Who starts the fire?
6. Is one person enough to tend the fire and keep the stove stoked?

Concerning the Ultimate Goal of the Orphanage [*Vom Endzweck*]

1. How far along do you bring the children?
2. What employment do you find for the boys?
3. What for the girls?
4. To what age do you allow them to stay in the orphanage?
5. What do you seek to teach the girls in particular? Cooking, managing a

household, spinning, sewing? And how do you teach them the first two items?

6. Do you have enterprises in the orphanage so the boys can learn to be cabinetmakers, woodworkers, blacksmiths, shoemakers, and so on?
7. Are they later accepted by the guilds?

Concerning the Costs [*Von den Kosten*]

1. At the start, how much capital was invested in the orphanage foundation?
2. How is it invested, in arable land, meadows, or something else? Is some invested in a bank? Or is some loaned to individuals? What interest do they pay?
3. How is the capital gradually increased?
4. How much is consumed annually? . . .
6. Do you have arable land nearby that provides you with grain for bread, drink, cattle, milk, vegetables, butter, and cheese? Or do you buy these things? What is the best practice?
7. How many cattle are slaughtered each year?
8. How much grain do you need to feed a child for a year?
9. Do you require the capital to increase in order to increase the number of children?
10. What can the children earn through their work in a year? What part of the expenses of their upkeep can they cover?
11. Are there bequests that yield an annual income? Or from which the children can be fed for a time?
12. How are the bequests invested securely?

Concerning the Duties of the Head of the Orphanage and of the Servants
[*Von des Waysen-Vaters und Gesindes Verrichtungen*]

1. How does he manage the orphanage? By personal oversight or through a deputy?
2. What else does he do? How often must he give an accounting? Who does the audit? Can we see the account?
3. Who awakens them in the morning? How early do they rise in winter? How early in summer?
4. Who leads them in prayer? The head of the orphanage or the preceptor?
5. When does he give them their morning bread? What does he give them?
6. Does he oversee their work and whatever else they do?
7. What do the maids do?
8. What do the servants do?
9. How does the head of the orphanage spend his day?
10. How do the maids and servants spend their day?

Concerning the Feeding, Clothing, Cleaning, Education, and Work of the Children
[*Von der Kinder Speisung, Kleydung, Reinigung, Aufferziehung und Arbeit*]

1. What do the children get to eat each day? What is on the menu?
2. Who prepares the meals? Can the orphanage mother and a maid do it or do you need to appoint a cook?
3. Who brings the food to the table? The oldest children or the servants?
4. Who serves the children at the table? Does the orphanage father do it or the servants? Do they cut up the food for the smaller children and divide the food among them and cut up the bread and so forth? What measure is used for allotting the food so it is done equally? How is it supplied?
5. Who supervises the prayer and the meal? Is something read at the table or is something edifying recited to the children?
6. Who cleans up after meals, the children or staff?
7. At what time do the children eat in the morning? at mid-day? in the evening? What do you do with any food that is left over?
8. At what time do the head of the orphanage and the servants eat? What advantage do they have in food selection?
9. Do you all eat together or do the servants eat on their own?
10. Do the children receive specific portions to eat or are they given as much as they want?
11. What dishes and utensils do the children use in eating and drinking? Are they made from pottery, tin, or wood? Do they have a knife and other utensils for eating? Do you go to a butcher and other craftsmen when you buy food and clothing? Do you buy at a good price?
12. How many children sit at a table?
13. What dishes are used in cooking? Are they made from pottery, iron, or copper? Which of these are best?
14. What do the children wear? From what material and fabric are they made?
15. How often do they receive a change of clothing?
16. Do they have two sets of clothes?
17. How many tailors are required for the number of children?
18. How many individuals are needed to make and repair the shoes?
19. Once they have finished making new clothes, are these people kept busy in repairing the old? Does this keep them busy until new clothes and shoes are required? Or do they work constantly at keeping new clothes in stock for the future?
20. Do you get fabric and leather at a good price?
21. How many shirts, scarves, and handkerchiefs does each child have?
22. Does each child have his own specially marked laundry or is he given any old shirt that fits him at the end of the week?
23. If it is the latter, how do you keep track of what clothing a particular child has?

24. Do you keep track of what clothing each child deserves? Must a shirt be torn before it is replaced?
25. Do the children all receive new clothes at the same time, or do you think it better to wait till a child has torn a piece of clothing before he receives another?
26. How do you prevent the children from sharing handkerchiefs?
27. How often do you have to make new shirts to replace those that are always wearing out?
28. How often do you wash their clothes? Who does the wash? Is there a special person designated to do it?
29. How many pillows do you give each child for the bed?
30. Do the pillows have a covering?
31. How expensive are they per yard?
32. How many pounds of feathers are there in a pillow?
33. What under-bed is laid on the mattress: feathers, or straw, or some other material?
34. How do you prevent children from wetting the bed? If they do, how do you dry it out?
35. How do you prevent lice and flees and bedbugs and the like from coming into the beds and clothing? And when they come, how do you get rid of them?
36. How often is the bedroom swept out?
37. How often are the other rooms swept out?
38. Who sleeps with the girls?
39. Who sleeps with the boys?
40. Where do the children get dressed and undressed in winter? In the cold room?
41. When do you comb their hair? Where do the children wash? Who brings them the water? What do they use to brush their teeth?
42. How often in a week is their hair combed?
43. How many people are needed to do the combing and brushing in proportion to the number of children?
44. How many hours do the staff spend on this each day?
45. How many children's hair can you brush in an hour?
46. How often do you do it?
47. Do the children comb each other's hair?
48. How do you deal with bad knots in the hair?
49. How do you prevent a child who has bad scabs from infecting the others?
50. When and where do you try to rid their clothes of bugs and vermin?
51. How do you prevent children from getting scabies?
52. How do you get rid of scabies among the children?
53. How do you prevent it from spreading? Does each child have their own towel?

54. What else do you do to keep the children clean? Do you bathe them sometimes, or just wash their feet? Are there people who help with bathing them?
55. Do you have your own pharmacy, surgeon, and doctor?
56. Are there enough sick children to keep a doctor and surgeon busy?
57. Are they diligent in visiting the sick children?
58. Are the sick children given a special diet?
59. Are they waited on, and are there staff especially assigned to this duty?
60. What do these people do when there are no sick children?
61. How are the children brought up to fear God?
62. How often are the children catechized? Observe their method of instruction.
63. What subjects are they taught?
64. How many hours of schooling do the children have each day?
65. In your orphanage, are the children ever left alone? Do boys and girls learn and eat together, or are they kept separate?
66. What work do the children do after school hours?
67. Do the children work while being instructed? How is the children's work put to the best advantage?
68. If they work at sewing, how quickly can a child complete a pair of stockings?
69. Do the children get a break from work and a change in their task? How often and how long?
70. What do they do during the break?
71. Do they sometimes go for a walk?
72. Who accompanies the children?
73. How many kinds of punishment do you have for when children misbehave?
74. How do you check on the new children who are taken into the orphanage from a background of poverty?

APPENDIX C

Discussion Questions

These discussion questions address issues that arise in the book chapters and in the translated sources in appendixes A and B. The questions are a resource for students, helping them to reflect on and internalize the materials in each chapter. Many of the questions are suitable topics for term papers. They are also a resource for professors for guiding class or small group discussions.

Introduction. Issues in Defining and Describing the Pietist Movement

1. Why must each generation study Christian history afresh? How might the study of German Pietism benefit Christians and churches today?
2. Michel Godfroid observed that "to write the history of Pietism is to write the history of modern Protestantism."[1] How does the study of German Pietism illumine our understanding of modern-day Protestantism and Evangelicalism?
3. Why should church history consider not only the intentions and ideals of Christian movements but also their actions and results?
4. Compare the "working definition of Pietism" used in this book with the definitions provided by Wallmann, Lehmann, van Lieburg, and Gierl. Which do you prefer and why?
5. Carl Mirbt (1860–1929) observed that "the full historical understanding of Pietism will only come about when it is no longer treated as merely a phenomenon of church history or theology but is investigated from every possible point of view."[2] Why do you think it has taken so long for this kind of comprehensive study of Pietism to happen?

Chapter 1. German Radicalism and Orthodox Lutheran Reform

1. Heinrich Bornkamm and Emanuel Hirsch found key features of the modern spirit in sixteenth- and seventeenth-century Spiritualism: the dissolution of a historical-objective religion of faith; dismissal of the Lutheran view of God and justification; a religion of spiritual inwardness; and the call for religious tolerance and freedom of conscience.[3] To what extent do these features accurately represent Spiritualism, and to what extent do they represent the modern mind and spirit?
2. Ute Gause said that Paracelsus "united in himself Reformation, Spiritualist, humanist, and early church elements which he combined with his background in natural philosophy. From these elements he built up a unique and independent theology."[4] Is this variety of influences a strength or a weakness in Paracelsus's thought? To what degree do these elements reappear in German Pietism? Discuss.
3. In a review of Schneider's book on Johann Arndt, Johannes Zachhuber observed, "The source criticism and biographical investigations of Schneider result in a picture of Arndt as a man who was more strongly indebted to the ideas of nature philosophy and hermeticism than previously thought . . . Schneider must face a key interpretive question: what does this historical reconstruction mean for our overall conception of Arndt as a theologian, for his historical context, his reception and his immense influence? The answer is always the same: when all is said and done, Arndt is not really a Lutheran at all. Arndt is advocating a theology which stands in fundamental opposition to that of the Reformer Martin Luther."[5] What are the implications of Schneider's view of Arndt for our understanding of German Pietism?
4. Jakob Böhme wrote, "God does not have regard for a person's name or birth. The one who journeys in the love of God, he goes in the light. And the light is the heart of God. There is only one God. If you just remove the covering from your eyes, then you will see and recognize all your brothers, whether Christians, Jews, Turks, or heathen. Or do you think that God is only the God of the Christians? Do not the heathen also live in God? Whoever does right, he is loved by God. Acts 10:35."[6] How do Böhme's background and experience contribute to such a view?
5. "Rarely in European intellectual history has a book exercised such a profound and continuing impact as Böhme's *Aurora*."[7] How might one account for the appeal of Böhme's book?
6. Anselm Steiger suggests that there has been too little effort to understand the Orthodox Lutheran faith from which the radicals deviated. Research into seventeenth-century radical movements far exceeds research into Lutheran Orthodoxy, due to "sympathy for the persecuted and oppressed in a previous time."[8] Do North American church historians tend to favor dissidents and the persecuted in their research and writing? If so, to what extent, and why?

Chapter 2. The Thirty Years War, Seventeenth-Century Calvinism, and Reformed Pietism

1. Why is the background of the Thirty Years War (1618–1648) important for understanding the goals and ideals of the Pietists?
2. Jodocus van Lodenstein called on his hearers to make faith more than just belief in the truth; he emphasized conversion of life as the proper end of Reformed doctrine.[9] Carl Schroeder suggests that Lodenstein represents a tradition of "born-again Christianity" within Dutch Calvinism. Agree? Explain.
3. What do you make of Tersteegen's 1724 covenant with Christ, signed in his own blood, in which he writes, "I renounce from my heart all rights and powers over myself"? Is this a model for Christians today? Why or why not?
4. What do W. Weck's "Words in Praise of Gerhard Tersteegen" tell us about the ideals of Reformed Pietism?
5. The last years of Tersteegen's life were marked by his experience of inner darkness and loss of a sense of God's presence. He wrote, "I had thought long ago I was at the goal of blessedness, that the beloved Master was already mine; now I see myself correctly for the first time lying in pain and suffering; it seems love can deceive a little."[10] What do you think he meant by this?

Chapter 3. Beginnings of Lutheran Pietism in Frankfurt, 1670 to 1684

1. Who was truer to Pietist ideals, the separatist Schütz or the church Pietist Spener?
2. Compare the attitude and approach of the German Pietist Pastorius to Native Americans and the issue of slavery with that of the English Puritans.
3. Spener wrote in *Pia Desideria*, "The pulpit is not the place for showing off one's skill and magnificence, but for preaching the Word of the Lord in simplicity and power. Preaching should be the means for making the people holy, so that everything is designed towards this end." Why is it problematic to take Spener's words as an accurate reflection of Orthodox Lutheran preaching generally?
4. Although they addressed theological questions, neither Spener nor Count Zinzendorf wrote works that we would call systematic theology. Spener was opposed to traditional "school theology" and Zinzendorf was opposed to systems of thought and "enjoyed speaking in paradoxes and with imprecision."[11] Why did they have this perspective on theology? Does it reflect an anti-intellectualism within Pietism?
5. Carter Lindberg observed that "Spener's 'hope for better times' has been transmuted in the American context into a self-righteous nationalistic identification with the Kingdom of God, and the mission to all peoples has been secularized into a triumphalistic crusade to impose American interests on the world . . . Pietism in America has become decadent."[12] Discuss.

Chapter 4. Conventicles and Conflicts in Leipzig and the Second Wave, 1684 to 1694

1. Discuss the evidence for the statements "No Leipzig, no Pietism" (Tanya Kevorkian in *Baroque Piety*) and "Leipzig was the true place of origin of Pietism" (Claudia Wustmann in *Die "begeisterten Mägde"*).
2. Early Leipzig Pietism was dominated by students, women, and tradesmen; missing were the upper social classes. Why was this the case?
3. Francke portrayed his conversion as a hard-won struggle (*Bußkampf*) from unbelief to belief, an experience not merely of forgiveness but of certainty, new birth, and new life. Compare Francke's understanding of what it means to be a Christian with Luther's understanding.

Chapter 5. Halle Pietism and Universal Social Reform, 1695 to 1727

1. "It was August Hermann Francke, not Spener, in whom the Pietist potential to change the world was realized . . . Over against the more contemplative Spener is Francke, the man of action, the systematizer and organizer of the Pietist movement. In him the movement of social reform, growing since the Thirty Years War, reached its peak and advanced in a comprehensive attack upon the 'world' and its failings."[13] Discuss whether this is a fair comparison of the two Pietist leaders, Spener and Francke.
2. Francke's *Der Große Aufsatz* (The Great Project, 1704) has been called the Halle equivalent of Spener's *Pia Desideria* (1675). What similarities and differences do you find in these two programmatic writings?
3. Whose side do you take in the conflict between Francke and Richter, and why?
4. What changes marked Francke's development between 1687 and 1698, from the idealistic young convert who was part of the radicalized "second wave" of Pietism to the Francke who served as pastor and head of the Halle Foundations? How do you account for these changes?
5. Are social engagement and the founding of social institutions an *essential* feature of German Pietism or are they only typical of some forms of Pietism in some places?[14] Discuss.
6. What does Neubauer's "183 Questions" tell us about the Halle approach to caring for orphans? Is there anything that surprises you about these questions? Anything left out?
7. Discuss the contrasts Juliane Dittrich-Jacobi draws between Pietist and Puritan expressions of the Protestant ethic: "The Christian religion responded to the disintegration of feudal society with religious legitimation of individual activity in the social, political, and economic sphere. Lutheran Pietism, which according to Max Weber in the *Protestant Ethic* represents a parallel to English Puritanism, differs in its Halle variety on one important point from Pu-

ritanism: the Pietist ethic does not so much promote capitalist work activity but rather encourages an interest in education and educational activity."[15]

8. Frederick Herzog argues that Francke's politicizing of Pietism and "uncritical alliance with the secular realm of government" led to a loss of spiritual vitality.[16] Discuss.

Chapter 6. Radical German Pietism in Europe and North America

1. Discuss points of agreement and disagreement between Hochmann von Hochenau, a Spiritualist, and Alexander Mack, minister of a new congregation known as the "Schwarzenau Baptists." (See appendix A in preparing your answer.)
2. Willi Temme expressed amazement "that in the context of Pietism, which laid such weight upon strict custom and morals, a group could arise like the followers of Mother Eva, which so blatantly ignored the norms and standards of a pious way of life."[17] How might one account for the rise of a group such as the Eva von Buttlar Society within radical German Pietism? (See appendix A in preparing your answer.)
3. Explain and evaluate Johannes Wallmann's argument that Radical Pietism was the original, more genuine form of Pietism.
4. Georg Conrad Beissel "created a unique synthesis of religious thought and practice from the Old World embodied in a singular religious community in the New World."[18] Discuss.
5. The leader of a disgruntled Ephrata faction, Ezechiel Sangmeister, portrayed Beissel in his later years as overindulging in food, drink, and sex. Jeff Bach calls the account into question, observing that in his seventies, Beissel was too frail for such a lascivious way of life.[19] What other factors might call Sangmeister's account into question?
6. Jeff Bach suggests that Sangmeister's account "is a necessary critical voice to accompany the *Chronicon*" of Peter Miller, which overpraised Beissel.[20] Describe Bach's approach to weighing and interpreting these historical sources.

Chapter 7. Pietism and Gender

1. This chapter discusses women in early Frankfurt Pietism, women as leaders of Pietist networks and conventicles, and women as ecstatic prophets. Which of these represents women's most important contribution to Pietism? Why?
2. "The ideal Pietist woman was the religiously active, exemplary housewife, devoted to Bible reading, prayer, and attendance at worship and devotional gatherings, but not to the neglect of her household duties. She was responsible for the instruction of her children and stood by the side of her husband as his help and support."[21] Spener observed that Pietist women worked harder than other women in order to fulfill their duties to their families and still have

time to pursue their spiritual activities and interests. Discuss the Pietist ideal for women: was it liberating and modern or backward and restrictive?

3. Feustking argues that Pietism arose because of women and their deceitful influence on men: "From Luther's time up to the present hour, any reasonable man can see that false teachers rely too much upon inspired prophetesses and women teachers and gloss over their blasphemous thoughts and erroneous ideas."[22] Was Feustking right about the role of women in the early Pietist movement? Discuss.

Chapter 8. Pietism and the Bible

1. Over a period of thirty-six years, the network of Radical Pietists "produced more new Bible translations than ever seen during the sixteenth and seventeenth centuries."[23] "For the first time there arose translations besides Luther's which made it possible for Christians to read a variety of German translations."[24] Why did the Pietists produce so many translations? Why did sixteenth- and seventeenth-century Lutherans produce so few?
2. The radical Pietist Johann Henrich Reitz preferred literal, word-for-word biblical translation over literary elegance, whereas Luther was more concerned to produce a translation in everyday, spoken German that could be easily understood by people in the street. Which translation philosophy makes the most sense to you? Why?
3. Because of problems with financing the printing of the *Berleburg Bible*, Count Casimir instituted a lottery. Publishers were put under contract to sell tickets, collect the income, and award a free Bible to the winner. The proceeds went toward the costs of producing the Bible.[25] Discuss the pros and cons of this Pietist business approach.
4. Bengel wrote, "The scripture preserves the church; the church guards the scripture. When the church is strong, the scripture shines; when it is sick, its relation to the scripture has worsened. The condition of the church is directly related to its engagement with the scripture."[26] Give evidence from Christianity, past and present, to support or refute Bengel's observation.
5. In a letter to a student, dated February 24, 1721, Bengel wrote, "Concerning the differing readings in the New Testament, I would have more to say to you than this letter could contain . . . Christ and his church present themselves to the eyes of the world in the guise of weakness and lowliness: it is the same with his word. I find this entirely appropriate to the character of Christ and his word. If the holy scriptures, which were so often copied and so often passed through error-prone human hands, should be without any deficiency, it would be such a great miracle that faith in scripture would no longer be faith. On the contrary, I am amazed that many more alternate readings have not arisen and that those that do exist do not in the least disturb the ground of our faith. So you can confidently banish this doubt which also

once tormented me so terribly."[27] How convincing is Bengel's explanation of the variant readings among the Greek texts?

6. "More so than Pietism of the Halle type or the Zinzendorf blend, Württemberg Pietism [found in F. C. Oetinger and Bengel] presented a well-balanced outlook."[28] Discuss.

Chapter 9. Pietism, World Christianity, and Missions to South India and Labrador

1. The legacy of the Halle missionaries was not only the establishment of churches; they also served as "key figures in the transmission of knowledge of the Indian languages and culture, both within India and between India and Europe."[29] Why did Ziegenbalg and Schultze consider it so important to learn the language and culture of south India?
2. Francke wrote to Ziegenbalg in December 1715, "If, indeed, I . . . did not consider it necessary to publish this book [Ziegenbalg's *Genealogy of the South Indian Deities*] because in printing new and strange things we have to look not to idle curiosity but rather to the glorification of God's name and the real benefit of the Church, which I cannot hope to achieve through the publication of the writing in question—nevertheless I could not by any means find fault with the great efforts which you for your part have expended on the accurate study of the heathen theology."[30] Evaluate Francke's reasoning in deciding not to publish Ziegenbalg's book on Hindu religion.
3. In January 1763, Jens Haven expressed to Moravian Bishop Johannes von Watteville and the elders his desire to go to Labrador. They put the question to the lot: should he return to Greenland? The lot answered no. When the question of his going to Labrador was put to the lot, the answer was yes.[31] Discuss the pros and cons of Moravian use of the lot.
4. "Although Haven and Drachardt could communicate in *Inuktitut*, it is uncertain and even unlikely that they could have integrated themselves quite as readily without Mikak's efforts as interlocutor and ambassador."[32] Discuss the role of Mikak in the success of the early Moravian mission to Labrador.

Chapter 10. The Contribution of German Pietism to the Modern World

1. In chapters 6 to 9, which Pietist innovations strike you as most important and as having the most enduring impact in modern times?
2. As stated in chapter 10, "Pietism not only contributed to the dismantling of the old; it contributed to the Enlightenment culture that characterized the new." Discuss.
3. Karl Barth wrote, "In both the Pietist and the [Enlightenment] Rationalist we are dealing with the modern man and the modern citizen with the same perspective: that in every situation Christianity must serve the improvement of life."[33] Discuss.

Conclusion. Reflecting on the Cultural and Religious Legacy of German Pietism

1. "The genius of Pietism lay in the adjectives it employed." Discuss.
2. What does historical study of the real-life consequences of Pietist beliefs, experiences, and actions reveal about the Pietist legacy? Why is study of the theology and intentions of Pietism's leading spokesmen an insufficient basis for judging its legacy?
3. The conclusion observes that "in exercising their Christian freedom to follow the Spirit, Radical Pietist groups and churches almost invariably granted unfettered authority to charismatic leaders . . . The Pietist model . . . left Christian laypeople more vulnerable, subject to the whims and weaknesses of individual leaders." Discuss.

APPENDIX D

Student Members of the Leipzig Circle of Pietists in the Late 1680s

Name	*Hometown*	*Destination after Leipzig*
Andreas Achilles (1656–1721)	Halberstadt	In 1690, appointed pastor at the Hospital Church of the Holy Spirit in Halberstadt; 1695–1703, pastor in Dornum
*Paul Anton (1661–1730)	Hirschfelde	October 1689 to December 1692, served as superintendent of the Evangelical Church in Rochlitz; in 1695 became professor of theology in Halle
Johann Christoph Bielefeld (1664–1727)	Delitzsch	In 1692 became court preacher in Darmstadt; in May 1693, professor of theology in Giessen
Paul Blebel	Bialogard, Pomerania	Moved to Stolp (now Slupsk), along with numerous other Leipzig Pietists; later studied medicine and joined the Mennonites in Danzig
Georg Braun	Tennstedt	Moved with Francke to Erfurt in 1690, where he experienced a conversion

Name	*Hometown*	*Destination after Leipzig*
Andreas Care	Bialogard, Pomerania	Returned to Pomerania in 1690; suffered severe doubts and anxieties; married a woman of nobility in Stolp, Eastern Pomerania
Martin Ebert	Unknown	Moved to Stolp, along with numerous other Leipzig Pietists
Gottfried Edelmann	Marck Liese	Unknown
Heinrich Julius Elers (1667–1728)	Bardowick bei Lüneburg	Easter 1690, followed Francke to Erfurt; that autumn, became chaplain to a Pietist baroness in Arnstadt; in 1697, became head of Halle's bookstore and printing enterprise
Gotthard Fonne	Revel (now Tallinn), Livonia	Unknown
*August Hermann Francke (1663–1727)	Lübeck and Gotha	Easter 1690, appointed deacon in the Augustine Church in Erfurt; in January 1692, called to St. George's Church in Glaucha, outside Halle
Johann Anastasius Freylinghausen (1670–1739)	Gandersheim	Easter 1690, accompanied Francke to Erfurt; went to Glaucha in 1692, and in December 1695 became Francke's pastoral assistant
*Andreas Friedel (b. 1658)	Schkeuditz	Became a leading Pietist separatist in Halberstadt and Kelbra
Christian Gaulicke	Unknown	Studied medicine
Paul Christian Hilscher	Waldingen	Unknown
*Polikarp Elias Huffland (1665–1714)	Tennstedt	In 1692, called to Stolp as archdeacon, where he founded a school for poor children, modeled on the Halle Foundations
Johann Conrad Keßler	Gotha	Went to Gotha as a tutor in 1691; had an ecstatic religious experience in 1692

Name	*Hometown*	*Destination after Leipzig*
Daniel Köhler (d. 1729)	Tangermünde	In 1689, became a tutor in Stolp
Joachim Lange (1670–1744)	Gardelegen	Followed Francke to Erfurt; in 1709, joined the theology faculty in Halle
*Johann Christian Lange (1669–1756)	Leipzig	Lectured at Leipzig university, 1694–1697; separated himself from church and sacraments; in 1697, joined Gottfried Arnold in Giessen as philosophy professor; in 1716, became court preacher in Idstein
Georg Andreas Meißner	Schönebeck	Easter 1690, accompanied Francke to Erfurt
Georg Heinrich Neubauer (1666–1727)	Desdorf, Halberstadt	Followed Francke to Erfurt in 1690, then to Glaucha in 1692; in 1698, oversaw construction of the orphanage and became chief business manager of the Halle Foundations
*Johann Matthias Sauerbier	Unknown	Unknown
Johann Caspar Schade (1666–1698)	Kühndorf	Pursued studies in Leipzig, 1685–1687, and served as secretary to Francke; in December 1691, was ordained deacon at the St. Nicholas Church in Berlin
Johann Andreas Schilling (1665–1750)	Chostnick	Easter 1690, accompanied Francke to Erfurt; joined Gottfried Arnold in Giessen in 1697
Johann Georg Schilling	Pössneck	Tutor in Böhlitz bei Leipzig; later, a promoter of separatist teachings, rejecting church, baptism, and the Lord's Supper
Johann Eusebius Schmidt (1670–1745)	Hohenfelden	Easter 1690, accompanied Francke to Erfurt

Name	*Hometown*	*Destination after Leipzig*
Johann Heinrich Schröder	Springe am Deister	Easter 1690, accompanied Francke to Erfurt; in February 1692, experienced a dramatic conversion in Halle
Friedrich Christian Seebach	Tennstedt	Moved with Francke to Erfurt, where he experienced a conversion; later, moved to Halle
Gebhard Levin Semler (1665–1737)	Loburg bei Jerichow	Easter 1690, accompanied Francke to Erfurt; in 1691, became a tutor in the home of Adelheid Sybille Schwarz in Lübeck; moved to Halberstadt in 1692
Christian Friedrich Sinner	Leipzig	Published *Prisca Decora Philosophorum Iuvenibus* (Leipzig, 1694)
Ludwig Joachim Stolle	Alsace	Defended two disputations for his master's in philosophy in Leipzig, in 1688 and 1689
*Clemens Thieme (1666–1732)	Zeitz	Ordained in 1690 and became chaplain to the Saxon Elector Johann Georg IV; in early 1692, became archdeacon in Wurzen
Justinus Töllner (1656–1718)	Gera	Pastor in Panitzsch bei Leipzig, 1682–1696; in 1697, became inspector of the Halle orphanage
*Ernst Christian Wartenberg (ca. 1665–1742)	Leipzig	Completed his Leipzig dissertation in 1689; in 1690, became subrector in Berlin
Heinrich Westphal	Bardowick bei Lüneburg	Easter 1690, accompanied Francke to Erfurt; returned to Bardowick in 1691
Johann Hieronimus Wiegleb (1664–1730)	Pferdingsleben bei Gotha	Easter 1690, accompanied Francke to Erfurt; went to Gotha in the early 1690s to become co-rector of the gymnasium; led conventicles in Gotha that saw ecstatic occurrences; in 1701, joined Francke in Glaucha

Name	*Hometown*	*Destination after Leipzig*
Paul Otto Zießler (1660–1732)	Rochlitz, Dresden	In early 1690s, served as school rector in Tennstedt

Sources: Ryoko Mori, *Begeisterung und Ernüchterung in christlicher Vollkommenheit* (Tübingen: Max Niemeyer Verlag, 2004), 15–37, 45–49; Veronika Albrecht-Birkner, "Die radikale Phase des frühen August Hermann Francke," in W. Breul, ed., *Der radikale Pietismus: Perspektiven der Forschung* (Göttingen: Vandenhoeck & Ruprecht, 2010), 60ff., 81–84; Erhard Peschke, ed., *August Hermann Francke: Streitschriften* (Berlin: de Gruyter, 1981), 25ff.; Hans Leube, *Orthodoxie und Pietismus* (Bielefeld: Luther-Verlag, 1975); databank of the Archive of the Francke Foundations in Halle.

*One of the eight founders of the collegium philobiblicum in Leipzig in 1686

Notes

Foreword

1. F. Ernest Stoeffler, *The Rise of Evangelical Pietism* (Leiden: E. J. Brill, 1965, 1971).

2. See Martin Brecht et al., eds., *Der Pietismus vom siebzehnten bis zum frühen achtzehnten Jahrhundert* (Göttingen: Vandenhoeck & Ruprecht, 1993); Martin Brecht and Klaus Deppermann, eds., *Der Pietismus im achtzehnten Jahrhundert* (Göttingen: Vandenhoeck & Ruprecht, 1995); Ulrich Gäbler, ed., *Der Pietismus im neunzehnten und zwanzigsten Jahrhundert* (Göttingen: Vandenhoeck & Ruprecht, 2000); Hartmut Lehmann, ed., *Glaubenswelt und Lebenswelten des Pietismus* (Göttingen: Vandenhoeck & Ruprecht, 2004).

3. See the series "Arbeiten zur Geschichte des Pietismus," beginning in 1967, vols. 1–16 (Bielefeld: Luther-Verlag), vols. 17–58 (Göttingen: Vandenhoeck & Ruprecht); and the series "Kleine Texte des Pietismus," beginning in 1999, vols. 1–13 as of 2012 (Leipzig: Evangelische Verlagsanstalt).

4. Note in particular the framework of W. R. Ward, *The Protestant Evangelical Awakening* (Cambridge: Cambridge University Press, 1992, 2002), and the essay collection of Carter Lindberg, ed., *The Pietist Theologians* (Oxford: Blackwell, 2005).

Introduction. Issues in Defining and Describing the Pietist Movement

1. Aaron Spencer Fogleman, *Hopeful Journeys: German Immigration, Settlement, and Political Culture in Colonial America, 1717–1775* (Philadelphia: University of Pennsylvania Press, 1996), 1–11, 101–107, 177–179. Fogleman notes that radical Pietist dissenting groups included Church of the Brethren, German Baptist Brethren, and Moravians. They tended to migrate in groups, settle in distinct communities, and quickly organize church congregations. See also Marianne S. Wokeck, "The

Flow and the Composition of German Immigration to Philadelphia, 1683–1776," *Pennsylvania Magazine of History and Biography* 105 (1981): 249–278; Marianne S. Wokeck, "German Settlements in the British North American Colonies: A Patchwork of Cultural Assimilation and Persistence," in Hartmut Lehmann et al., eds., *In Search of Peace and Prosperity: New German Settlements in Eighteenth-Century Europe and America* (University Park: Penn State University Press, 2000), 91–216. As of 2000, German was the largest reported ancestry in the United States, at 15.2%, with English and Scottish (combined) at 10.4%. See U.S. Census Statistics, www.census.gov/prod/2004pubs/c2kbr–35.pdf.

2. F. Ernest Stoeffler, *The Rise of Evangelical Pietism* (Leiden: E. J. Brill, 1965, 1971); F. Ernest Stoeffler, *German Pietism during the Eighteenth Century* (Leiden: E. J. Brill, 1973); Dale Brown, *Understanding Pietism* (Nappanee, IN: Evangel Publishing House, 1978, 1996); Emilie Griffin and Peter C. Erb, eds., *The Pietists: Selected Writings* (New York: HarperCollins, 2006); Carter Lindberg, ed., *The Pietist Theologians* (Oxford: Blackwell, 2005).

3. See Martin Schmidt, "Review of F. Ernest Stoeffler, *The Rise of Evangelical Pietism* and *German Pietism during the Eighteenth Century*," *Pietismus und Neuzeit* 3 (1976), 145; Martin Schmidt, *Der Pietismus als theologische Erscheinung* (Göttingen: Vandenhoeck & Ruprecht, 1984), 71. Schmidt called Stoeffler's books the "standard works" on the subject in English. He pointed to Stoeffler's qualifications: his acquaintance with Swabian Pietism and equal facility in German and English, thanks to his upbringing in Heilbronn, Germany, and his migration to Pennsylvania as a young man, with his parents. Schmidt, "Review of Stoeffler," 146.

4. In the first volume, Stoeffler offers detailed portraits of early Puritans such as John Bradford and William Perkins and of various promoters of a godly life such as Lewis Bayly, Jeremy and Daniel Dyke, Joseph Hall, John and Thomas Goodwin, Richard Baxter, and John Bunyan. For Stoeffler, Dutch figures such as Willem Teellinck and Gisbertus Voetius provided the essential foundation for German Pietism. Stoeffler concludes the volume by introducing Johann Arndt, Philipp Jakob Spener, and early Lutheran Pietism.

5. Stoeffler's second volume discusses A. H. Francke in Halle, Bengel and Oetinger in Württemberg, Zinzendorf and the Moravians, Radical Pietism and migrations to Pennsylvania, and F. A. Lampe and Conrad Mell, and concludes with the "new Pietism" of Johann Heinrich Jung-Stilling. For the review, see Schmidt, "Review of Stoeffler," 148.

6. On the interdisciplinary work of a new generation of Pietism scholars, see Douglas H. Shantz, ed., *The Brill Companion to German Pietism* (Leiden: Brill, forthcoming). For a survey of Pietism scholarship, see Jonathan Strom, "Problems and Promises of Pietism Research," *Church History* 71, no. 3 (2002): 536–554.

7. The four volumes of *History of Pietism* [*Geschichte des Pietismus*], edited by Martin Brecht, Klaus Deppermann, Ulrich Gäbler, and Hartmut Lehmann, were published in 1993, 1995, 2000, and 2004 by Vandenhoeck & Ruprecht in Göttingen. Completion of the final volume was marked by a celebration in Berlin on January

20, 2004. See Paul Raabe, "Rede zur Vollendung der *Geschichte des Pietismus*," *Pietismus und Neuzeit* 31 (2005): 218–224.

8. In her review of Ulrike Gleixner and Erika Hebeisen, eds., *Gendering Tradition: Erinnerungskultur und Geschlecht im Pietismus* (Stuttgart: Didymos-Verlag, 2007), Jeannine Kunert notes a consistent theme in the book: the critique of a one-sided history of Pietism that focuses on male heroes. See H-Soz-u-Kult, Sept. 4, 2008, http://hsozkult.geschichte.hu-berlin.de/rezensionen/2008-3-134. On gender and Pietism, see Ulrike Gleixner, "How to Incorporate Gender in Lutheran Pietism Research: Narratives and Counter-narratives," in Jonathan Strom, Hartmut Lehmann, and James Van Horn Melton, eds., *Pietism in Germany and North America: 1680–1820* (Farnham, UK: Ashgate, 2009); Gleixner and Hebeisen, *Gendering Tradition*.

9. Andreas Deppermann, *Johann Jakob Schütz und die Anfänge des Pietismus* (Tübingen: Mohr Siebeck, 2002), 352–354. Schütz was the inspiration for distinctive features of the Pietist movement: the meetings of the godly outside regular church services; the centrality of the Bible; the practice of the spiritual priesthood in mutual encouragement and admonition; and hopes for better times with the postmillenarian expectation of the imminent reign of Christ on earth. There is now little sympathy for Stoeffler's suggestion that "the father of Lutheran Pietism is not Spener but Johann Arndt." Stoeffler, *Rise of Evangelical Pietism*, 202–203.

10. Johannes Wallmann, "Was ist Pietismus?," *Pietismus und Neuzeit* 20 (1994): 24–26. Wallmann contrasts Luther's *sola scriptura* (only scripture) with Spener's *tota scriptura* (all of scripture). New research also highlights the vitality of Protestant Orthodoxy and its concern to bring reform to preaching and piety. Stoeffler's portrayal of Orthodoxy in terms of dead religiosity, ethical insensitivity, and irrelevant preaching seems especially dated. Stoeffler, *Rise of Evangelical Pietism*, 182–187. There is little sympathy for Stoeffler's decision to speak broadly of "Pietism among the English Puritans." See Hartmut Lehmann, "Einführung," in *Glaubenswelt und Lebenswelten* (Göttingen: Vandenhoeck & Ruprecht, 2004), 11.

11. The Enlightenment took shape around "a new constellation of formal and technical practices and institutions," as a media-driven movement. See Jonathan Sheehan, "Enlightenment, Religion, and the Enigma of Secularization: A Review Essay," *American Historical Review* 108, no. 4 (2003): 1075, 1076, www.history cooperative.org/journals/ahr/108.4/sheehan.html; J. Sheehan, *The Enlightenment Bible: Translation, Scholarship, Culture* (Princeton: Princeton University Press, 2005).

12. Mary Noll Venables, "Pietist Fruits from Orthodox Seeds: The Case of Ernst the Pious," in Fred van Lieburg, ed., *Confessionalism and Pietism: Religious Reform in Early Modern Europe* (Mainz: Verlag Philipp von Zabern, 2006), 92.

13. For recent discussions of the issue of definition, see Strom, Lehmann, and Van Horn Melton, eds., *Pietism in Germany and North America, 1680–1820*, 3–5 and chaps. 1–4.

14. Wallmann, "Was ist Pietismus?," 18.

15. Johannes Wallmann, *Der Pietismus* (Göttingen: Vandenhoeck & Ruprecht, 2005), 26.

16. Ibid., 22–26.

17. Wallmann, "Was ist Pietismus?," 13. Government edicts prohibited Pietist conventicles. Lutheran Orthodox pastors objected to conventicles because of the threat of separatism that would undermine the state churches. For the Orthodox, Luther's heritage was best preserved through the confessions, beliefs, structures, and traditions that had grown up in the century and a half since Luther's time. On early use of the term *Pietists*, see also Martin Brecht, "Einleitung," in Martin Brecht et al., eds., *Der Pietismus vom siebzehnten bis zum frühen achtzehnten Jahrhundert* (Göttingen: Vandenhoeck & Ruprecht, 1993), 4.

18. Hartmut Lehmann, "Engerer, Weiterer und Erweiterter Pietismusbegriff," *Pietismus und Neuzeit* 29 (2003): 30–33, 36.

19. Hartmut Lehmann, "Zur Definition des 'Pietismus,'" in Martin Greschat, ed., *Zur Neueren Pietismusforschung* (Darmstadt: Wissenschaftliche Buchgesellschaft, 1977), 83–89.

20. Fred van Lieburg, "Conceptualizing Religious Reform Movements in Early Modern Europe," in van Lieburg, *Confessionalism and Pietism*, 9.

21. See Fred van Lieburg, "Wege der niederländischen Pietismusforschung: Traditionsaneignung, Identitätspolitik und Erinnerungskultur," *Pietismus und Neuzeit* 37 (2011): 211–253, esp. 212, 247, 251–253. See also Fred van Lieburg, "Bible Reading and Pietism in the Dutch Reformed Tradition," in M. Lamberigts and A. A. den Hollander, eds., *Lay Bibles in Europe, 1450–1800* (Louvain: Peeters, 2006), 223–244.

22. Strom, "Problems and Promises of Pietism Research," 541.

23. Martin Gierl, *Pietismus und Aufklärung: Theologische Polemik und die Kommunikationsreform der Wissenschaft am Ende des 17. Jahrhunderts* (Göttingen: Vandenhoeck & Ruprecht, 1997), 259.

24. Ibid., 266, 280.

25. Ibid., 42–48, 193–195. See also Martin Gierl, "Im Netz der Theologen," *Zeitschrift für Historische Forschung* 32, no. 3 (2005): 485–486.

26. Carter Lindberg accepts Wallmann's definition of Pietism but sets it in close relation to English Puritanism and Evangelicalism. Lindberg, *Pietist Theologians*, 15n21.

27. See Martin Brecht, "Einleitung," in Martin Brecht et al., eds., *Der Pietismus vom siebzehnten bis zum frühen achtzehnten Jahrhundert* (Göttingen: Vandenhoeck & Ruprecht, 1993), 1, 2. An example of the distinctive nature of the nineteenth-century German awakenings is the Diaconal movement under the leadership of Theodor Fliedner (1800–1864). "On the 30th of May 1836 [Fliedner] founded the Rhine-Westphalia Diaconal Association in Düsseldorf along with a few other men. On the 13th of October of that year there followed the opening of the first diaconal foundation in Kaiserswerth. Today there are more than 60 mother houses with 9,000 sisters." Georg Fliedner, *Theodor Fliedner, Durch Gottes Gnade Erneurer des*

apostolischen Diakonissen-Amtes in der evangelischen Kirche. Kurzer Abriß seines Lebens und Wirkens (Kaiserswerth: Verlag der Diakonissen-Anstalt, 1892), 5. (All translations are my own, unless otherwise indicated.) See also Norbert Friedrich, *Der Kaiserswerther: Wie Theodor Fliedner den Frauen einen Beruf gab* (Berlin: Wichern-Verlag, 2010).

28. van Lieburg, "Conceptualizing Religious Reform Movements," 2–3.

29. Wallmann, *Der Pietismus*, 27. Wallmann sees the biographical method as the best approach because it opens up features of Pietist theology and piety—the most important aspects for church history. But church historians such as Bernd Moeller, writing on Reformation in the cities, or Luise Schorn-Schütte, on clergy as a social class, give priority to both theology and social setting.

30. Hedwig Richter's review of Wallmann's revised *Pietism Handbook* laments that in his hands, "the little garden of Pietism has been nicely set apart from the work of the rest of the academic world." Hedwig Richter, "Review of Wallmann, Johannes," *Der Pietismus: Ein Handbuch*, H-Soz-u-Kult, H-Net Reviews, July 2006, www.h-net.org/reviews/showrev.php?id=21276.

31. Benjamin Marschke, *Absolutely Pietist: Patronage, Factionalism, and State-Building in the Early Eighteenth-Century Prussian Army Chaplaincy* (Tübingen: Max Niemeyer Verlag, 2005); Tanya Kevorkian, *Baroque Piety: Religion, Society, and Music in Leipzig, 1650–1750* (Aldershot, UK: Ashgate, 2007); Ulrike Gleixner, *Pietismus und Bürgertum: Eine historische Anthropologie der Frömmigkeit* (Göttingen: Vandenhoeck & Ruprecht, 2005); Gleixner and Hebeisen, *Gendering Tradition*.

32. Margaret R. Miles, "Becoming Answerable for What We See: 1999 AAR Presidential Address," *Journal of the American Academy of Religion* 68, no. 3 (2000): 471–485.

33. Martin Brecht, "Einleitung," in Brecht et al., *Der Pietismus vom siebzehnten bis zum frühen achtzehnten Jahrhundert*, 8.

34. Martin Schmidt, "Epochen der Pietismusforschung," in Kurt Aland, ed., *Der Pietismus als Theologische Erscheinung* (Göttingen: Vandenhoeck & Ruprecht, 1984), 37. Schmidt writes, "It should not surprise us that a rich source material, found in theological writings, books of devotion, confessions of faith, letters, diaries, poetry and hymns, offers itself for all manner of scholarly consideration and investigation" (37).

35. Johannes Wallmann, "Überlegungen und Vorschläge zu einer Edition des Spenerschen Briefwechsels, zunächst aus der Frankfurter Zeit (1666–1686)," *Pietismus und Neuzeit* 11 (1985): 345–353. The researcher quoted in the text is Spener biographer Paul Grünberg. Volume 3 of his Spener biography consists of a Spener bibliography of primary and secondary sources. Paul Grünberg, *Spener-Bibliographie: Systematisches und Chronologisches Verzeichnis der gesamten Spener-Literatur* (Göttingen: Vandenhoeck & Ruprecht, 1906; reprint, Hildesheim: Georg Olms Verlag, 1988).

36. In 1996, Johannes Wallmann announced the plan for a complete edition of Spener's letters in three series: letters from the Frankfurt period, 1666–1686;

from the Dresden period, 1686–1691; and from the Berlin period, 1691–1705. A final volume will include letters from Spener's Alsace period up to 1666. As of 2012, most of Spener's Frankfurt letters and many of the Dresden letters have been published. See Johannes Wallmann, "Vorwort," in *Philipp Jakob Spener: Briefe aus der Frankfurter Zeit 1666–1686*, vol. 2, *1675–1676* (Tübingen: Mohr Siebeck 1996), v.

37. Paul Raabe and Almut Pfeiffer, eds., *August Hermann Francke 1663–1727: Bibliographie seiner Schriften* (Tübingen: Max-Niemeyer Verlag, 2001); Schmidt, "Epochen der Pietismusforschung," 34–35.

38. Erich Beyreuther and Gerhard Meyer, "Vorwort," in *Nikolaus Ludwig von Zinzendorf Hauptschriften*, vol. 1, *Schriften des jüngeren Zinzendorf* (Hildesheim: Georg Olms, 1962), vi–viii. Dietrich Meyer pointed out that less than 40% of Zinzendorf's works were ever printed, meaning that a reprint edition leaves out most of his writings. See Dietrich Meyer, "Zum Programm einer zehnbändigen Zinzendorf-Ausgabe," *Pietismus und Neuzeit* 12 (1986): 145–161.

39. In an appendix to the second edition of his autobiography, Petersen reported sixty-seven printed books and more than a hundred works in manuscript, ready for publication. See J. W. Petersen, *Lebens-Beschreibung Jo. Wilhelmi Petersen, Die zweyte Edition, auffs neue mit Fleiß übersehen . . . Auch am Ende dieser meiner Lebens-Beschreibung ein Catalogus aller meiner gedruckten und noch ungedruckten Schriften angefüget* (Frankfurt, 1719), 397–402.

Chapter 1. German Radicalism and Orthodox Lutheran Reform

1. Karl Barth said of the eighteenth century, "This century not only had its philosophers, its historians and students of nature, its school masters and journalists, but also its mystics and inspired and Pietists, its Rosicrucians and illuminated, as well as its alchemists . . . and its Swedenborg." Karl Barth, *Die Protestantische Theologie im 19. Jahrhundert: Ihre Vorgeschichte und ihre Geschichte* (Zurich: Theologischer Verlag Zürich, 1947), 18.

2. See Wilhelm Kühlmann, "Frühaufklärung und chiliastischer Spiritualismus—Friedrich Brecklings Briefe an Christian Thomasius," in Friedrich Vollhardt, ed., *Christian Thomasius: Neue Forschungen* (Tübingen: Niemeyer, 1997), 179, 183; Andreas Deppermann, *Johann Jakob Schütz und die Anfänge des Pietismus* (Tübingen: Mohr Siebeck, 2002), 7. Deppermann speaks of an underground stream that continued into the eighteenth century: "Despite being suppressed by the established churches, their questions and theological examples were an abiding presence, being passed on underground. Anabaptist groups and above all the disciples of Schwenckfeld continued on in small circles within the churches right into the eighteenth century, exercising a clandestine influence through distribution of literature [and] whose ultimate significance is hard to determine . . . The medical and philosophical ideas of Paracelsus, including his criticisms of the churches, were kept alive in the seventeenth century in small but influential circles." Deppermann, *Johann Jakob Schütz*, 7.

3. Martin Schmidt, *Der Pietismus als theologische Erscheinung* (Göttingen: Vandenhoeck & Ruprecht, 1984), 27. Heinrich Bornkamm and Emanuel Hirsch traced a line of intellectual influence from Schwenckfeld to Pietism. They found the origins of the modern spirit in sixteenth- and seventeenth-century Spiritualism: the dissolution of a historical-objective religion of faith, destruction of the Lutheran view of God and justification, a religion of spiritual inwardness, and the call for religious tolerance and freedom of conscience. See Heinrich Bornkamm, *Mystik, Spiritualismus und die Anfänge des Pietismus im Luthertum* (Giessen: Alfred Töpelmann, 1926), 16, 18. See also Hans Schneider, *German Radical Pietism* (Lanham, MD: Scarecrow Press, 2007), 191n15.

4. Caroline Gritschke, *"Via Media": Spiritualistische Lebenswelten und Konfessionalisierung: Das süddeutsche Schwenckfeldertum im 16. und 17. Jahrhundert* (Berlin: Akademie Verlag, 2006), 118n233.

5. Crautwald was a Christian humanist, skilled in Latin, Greek, and Hebrew, and influenced by Reuchlin and Erasmus. He studied at the University of Cracow. In 1523, Duke Friedrich II appointed Crautwald lector at the Liegnitz Cathedral, a position that involved giving public lectures on the Bible. See Douglas H. Shantz, *Crautwald and Erasmus: A Study in Humanism and Radical Reform in Sixteenth Century Silesia* (Baden-Baden: Valentin Koerner, 1992), 17–26.

6. Shantz, *Crautwald and Erasmus*, 138; see also 29–30, 79–80, 88. The Schwenkfelders took to heart Augustine's comment on John 6: "Believe and you have already eaten."

7. *Corpus Schwenckfeldianorum* (Leipzig: Breitkopf & Härtel, 1911), 2:329–333. See also Shantz, *Crautwald and Erasmus*, 31, 67.

8. Valentin Crautwald, "Epistola Ministri (1534)," *Corpus Schwenckfeldianorum*, 6:200–230; Valentin Crautwald, "Ein kürz Außlegung Der Offenbarünge Johannis (ca. 1536)," *Corpus Schwenckfeldianorum*, 19:264–374. Crautwald's humanism and reading of Joachim of Fiore shaped the Schwenkfeldian optimistic strain. Shantz, *Crautwald and Erasmus*, 163–175.

9. This view was expressed by Gregor Tag in 1549. See Crautwald, "Ein kürz Außlegung Der Offenbarünge Johannis," 260–263, 318; Shantz, *Crautwald and Erasmus*, 57n153, 168.

10. Gritschke, *"Via Media,"* 83, 89, 128–145, 384. Schwenckfeld wrote hundreds of letters to friends in southern Germany. Letters were also essential to later Pietist networks.

11. See Horst Weigelt, *Spiritualistische Tradition im Protestantismus: Die Geschichte des Schwenckfeldertums in Schlesien* (Berlin: Walter de Gruyter, 1973), 229–232, 254–260. On Schwenckfeld's appeal to women, see Gritschke, *"Via Media"*; Emmet McLaughlin, *The Freedom of Spirit* (Baden-Baden: Valentin Koerner, 1996), 229–230.

12. "In the first generation of Pietists, Caspar Schwenckfeld, Friedrich Breckling and Jakob Böhme were rated highly." Klaus Deppermann, "August Hermann Francke," in Martin Greschat, ed., *Orthodoxie und Pietismus* (Stuttgart: Kohlhammer, 1982), 248.

13. Fritz Heyer, *Der Kirchenbegriff der Schwärmer* (Leipzig: M. Heinsius Nachfolger, 1939), 27–45. According to Eberhard H. Pältz, "Schwenckfeld's idea that a new Pentecost would inaugurate the gathering together of the scattered members of Christ's body took on new life in Böhme and his circle of followers." See Eberhard H. Pältz, "Zu Jakob Boehmes Sicht der Welt- und Kirchengeschichte," *Pietismus und Neuzeit* 6 (1980): 145–146n36.

14. Johannes Wallmann, *Der Pietismus* (Göttingen: Vandenhoeck & Ruprecht, 2005), 45. See also Peter C. Erb, "Christian Hoburg und die schwenckfeldischen Wurzeln des Pietismus: Einige bisher unveröffentlichte Briefe," *Jahrbuch für Schlesische Kirchengeschichte* 56 (1977): 92–126.

15. Martin Brecht, "Die deutschen Spiritualisten des 17. Jahrhunderts," in Martin Brecht et al., eds., *Der Pietismus vom siebzehnten bis zum frühen achtzehnten Jahrhundert* (Göttingen: Vandenhoeck & Ruprecht, 1993), 225; Wallmann, *Der Pietismus*, 45.

16. Arnold credited Hoburg's writings with "bringing to light many witnesses to the truth." Gottfried Arnold, *Unpartheyische Kirchen- und Ketzer-Historie, Vom Anfang des neuen Testaments Biß auf das Jahr Christi 1688, Vierter Theil* (Frankfurt am Main: Thomas Fritschens, 1729), 1093.

17. W. R. Ward, *Early Evangelicalism: A Global Intellectual History, 1670–1789* (Cambridge: Cambridge University Press, 2006), 24, 50; C. Scott Dixon, "Faith and History on the Eve of Enlightenment: Ernst Salomon Cyprian, Gottfried Arnold, and the *History of Heretics*," *Journal of Ecclesiastical History* 57, no. 1 (2006): 47–51.

18. For Caspar Schwenckfeld and the Schwenkfelders, see Gottfried Arnold, *Unpartheyische Kirchen- und Ketzer-Historie*, pt. 2, 703–726, and pt. 4, 466–499, 1275–1298 (82 pages). For David Joris, see ibid., pt. 2, 750–778, and pt. 4, 534–737, 1185–1189 (238 pages). See also Douglas H. Shantz, "David Joris, Pietist Saint: The Appeal to Joris in the Writings of Christian Hoburg, Gottfried Arnold and Johann Wilhelm Petersen," *Mennonite Quarterly Review* 78 (July 2004): 415–432.

19. For Arnold's approach to history and his views on toleration, see Markus Sturn, "'daß man wol an fremden und vorigen schaden klug werden möchte': Aspekte einer pragmatischen Historiographie bei Gottfried Arnold" (doctoral diss., Faculty of Historical and Cultural Research, University of Vienna, 2007); Douglas H. Shantz, "'Back to the Sources': Gottfried Arnold, Johann Henrich Reitz, and the Distinctive Program and Practice of Pietist Historical Writing," in C. Arnold Snyder, ed., *Commoners and Community* (Kitchener, ON: Pandora Press, 2002), 75–99; Andrea Heizmann, "Kirchengeschichte als Ketzergeschichte: religiöse Toleranz bei Gottfried Arnold" (master's thesis, Konstanz University, 1993).

20. Astrid von Schlachta, "Anabaptism, Pietism and Modernity: Relationships, Changes, Paths," in Fred van Lieburg and Daniel Lindmark, eds., *Pietism, Revivalism, and Modernity, 1650–1850* (Newcastle upon Tyne, UK: Cambridge Scholars, 2008), 1–22; Marcus Meier, *Die Schwarzenauer Neutäufer: Genese einer Gemeinde-*

bildung zwischen Pietismus und Täufertum (Göttingen: Vandenhoeck & Ruprecht, 2008), 48–52, 107–122, 136–137.

21. Karen-Claire Voss, "Spiritual Alchemy: Interpreting Representative Texts and Images," in R. van den Broek and W. J. Hanegraaff, eds., *Gnosis and Hermeticism from Antiquity to Modern Times* (Albany: State University of New York Press, 1998).

22. Christopher McIntosh, *The Rose Cross and the Age of Reason: Eighteenth-Century Rosicrucianism in Central Europe and Its Relationship to the Enlightenment* (Leiden: Brill, 1997), 30–31.

23. See Hanspeter Marti's review of Erb's *Pietists, Protestants, and Mysticism* in *Pietismus und Neuzeit* 18 (1992): 203–206. See also Peter C. Erb's "Introduction," in *Johann Arndt, True Christianity* (New York: Paulist Press, 1979), 17; *Pietists, Protestants, and Mysticism: The Use of Late Medieval Spiritual Texts in the Work of Gottfried Arnold (1666–1714)* (Metuchen, NJ: Scarecrow Press, 1989), 2–5; and "Defining 'Radical Pietism': The Case of Gottfried Arnold," *Consensus* 16, no. 2 (1990): 32–33, 42–43.

24. Erich Beyreuther, *Geschichte des Pietismus* (Stuttgart: J. F. Steinkopf, 1978), 32.

25. Ward, *Early Evangelicalism*, 4, 11–24.

26. Christa Habrich, "Alchemie und Chemie in der pietistischen Tradition," in Hans-Georg Kemper und Hans Schneider, eds., *Goethe und der Pietismus* (Tübingen: Max Niemeyer Verlag, 2001), 59. Habrich notes that, whereas church Pietists tended more toward medicinal alchemy, the radicals were more inclined toward hermetic-mystical alchemy and natural magic.

27. The group is at the Interdisciplinary Center for Study of the Enlightenment in Halle. See the IZEA website, "Teilprojekt 1, Esoterik—Pietismus—Frühaufklärung: Halle um 1700," www.izea.uni-halle.de/cms/index.php?id=143.

28. See Douglas H. Shantz, "The Origin of Pietist Notions of New Birth and the New Man: Alchemy and Alchemists in Gottfried Arnold and Johann Henrich Reitz," in Christian T. Collins Winn, ed., *The Pietist Impulse in Christianity* (Eugene, OR: Pickwick, 2011), 29–41; Monika Neugebauer-Wölk, "Esoterik und Christentum vor 1800: Prolegomena zu einer Bestimmung Ihrer Differenz," *Aries* 3, no. 2 (2003): 148–149.

29. Habrich, "Alchemie und Chemie in der pietistischen Tradition," 74–76. On Oetinger's ties to alchemy and hermeticism, see the recently published thesis of Ulrike Kummer, *Autobiographie und Pietismus: Friedrich Christoph Oetingers Genealogie der reellen Gedancken eines Gottes-Gelehrten. Untersuchungen und Edition* (Frankfurt am Main: Peter Lang, 2010). Kummer provides the most recent, most authoritative edition of Oetinger's autobiography, as does Dieter Ising. Friedrich Christoph Oetinger, *Genealogie der reellen Gedancken eines Gottes-Gelehrten: Eine Selbstbiographie*, ed. Dieter Ising (Leipzig: Evangelische Verlagsanstalt, 2010).

30. Michael D. Doan, "Paracelsus on *Erfahrung* and the Wisdom of Praxis," *Analecta Hermeneutica* 1 (2009): 176.

31. Voss, "Spiritual Alchemy"; Neugebauer-Wölk, "Esoterik und Christentum vor 1800," 137–143.

32. Jolande Jacobi, "Paracelsus: His Life and Work," in Jolande Jacobi, ed., *Paracelsus: Selected Writings*, 2nd ed., trans. Norbert Guterman (Princeton: Princeton University Press, 1957), xlii.

33. Udo Benzenhöfer, *Paracelsus* (Hamburg: Rowohlt, 1997), 31. Details of Paracelsus's university studies, possibly in Basel and Vienna, cannot be confirmed. See Charles Webster, *Paracelsus: Medicine, Magic, and Mission at the End of Time* (New Haven: Yale University Press, 2008), 10, 40–41.

34. Benzenhöfer, *Paracelsus*, 31–32; Andrew Weeks, *Paracelsus: Speculative Theory and the Crisis of the Early Reformation* (Albany: State University of New York Press, 1997), ix, 6.

35. Basilio de Telepnef, "Wanderwege des Paracelsus von 1512–1525," in *Nova Acta Paracelsica* (Basel: Verlag Birkhäuser, 1946), 147, 161–162. Telepnef provides a *Zeittafel* (timeline) and map of Paracelsus's travels between 1512 and 1524.

36. Paracelsus, "Credo," in Jacobi, *Paracelsus: Selected Writings*, 4–5.

37. Jacobi, "Paracelsus: His Life and Work," lxiv.

38. Gottfried Arnold, *Unpartheyische Kirchen- und Ketzer-Historie, Von Anfang des Neuen Testaments Biß auf das Jahr Christi 1688* (Frankfurt am Main: Thomas Fritschens, 1729; reprint, Hildesheim: Georg Olms Verlag, 1999), pt. 2, 778; Jacobi, *Paracelsus: Selected Writings*, 264; Webster, *Paracelsus*, 41, 225.

39. Margaret J. Osler, *Reconfiguring the World: Nature, God, and Human Understanding from the Middle Ages to Early Modern Europe* (Baltimore: Johns Hopkins University Press, 2010), 120.

40. See Webster, *Paracelsus*, 248; Jacobi, "Paracelsus: His Life and Work," xxix, lxii; Benzenhöfer, *Paracelsus*, 8.

41. Paracelsus, "The Book Concerning the Tincture of the Philosophers" and "The Aurora of the Philosophers," in Arthur Edward Waite, ed., *The Hermetic and Alchemical Writings of Paracelsus* (Central, Hong Kong: Forgotten Books Reprint, 2007), 36, 62–67.

42. Paracelsus, "The Prologue," in *Of the Supreme Mysteries of Nature. Of the Spirits of the Planets. Occult Philosophy. The Magical, Sympathetical and Antipathetical Cure of Wounds and Diseases. The Mysteries of the Twelve Signs of the Zodiack*, trans. R. Turner (London: N. Brook and J. Harison, 1656).

43. Paracelsus, "Alchemical Catechism," in Waite, *Hermetic and Alchemical Writings of Paracelsus*, 110, 119–123, 128; Webster, *Paracelsus*, 136–137, 149.

44. Paracelsus, "Of the Secrets of Alchymy; Discovered in the Nature of the Planets," in *The Archidoxes of Magic*, trans. Robert Turner (London: Nath. Brooke, 1655), 21–22; Jacobi, "Paracelsus: His Life and Work," xlvi.

45. Jacobi, "Paracelsus: His Life and Work," xlvii; Benzenhöfer, *Paracelsus*, 67.

46. Weeks, *Paracelsus*, 4, 13.

47. Ibid., 7–8, 19–21, 50–51, 234–239, 251, 255n44.

48. Ibid., xi, 249.

49. By 1986, Kurt Goldammer had published six volumes of a planned fourteen-volume edition before his work came to a stop. His six volumes included Par-

acelsus's writings on the Old Testament, with a commentary on the Psalter, and several tracts on social ethics, matrimony, baptism, penitence, and dogmatics. But half of Paracelsus's theological writings, a fourth of the complete works, remained scattered in manuscript form around the world.

50. The de Gruyter website states, "The new Paracelsus edition brings to completion the total corpus of Paracelsus' writing, providing an eight volume edition of his theological writings." Vol. 1 is *Vita beata—Vom seligen Leben*, ed. Urs Leo Gantenbein (Stuttgart: Walter de Gruyter, 2008); vol. 2, Paracelsus's interpretation of Matthew's Gospel; vol. 3, further interpretation of Matthew's Gospel, along with commentary on the Gospels of Mark and John; vol. 4, further comments on Matthew; vol. 5, writings on the Virgin Mary and on selected New Testament epistles; vol. 6, sermons on the Gospels and the antichrist; vol. 7, sermons on Christ's miracles of healing and other themes; vol. 8, tracts on the Lord's Supper and new birth. See www.paracelsus.uzh.ch/theologica/theol_e.html.

51. Webster, *Paracelsus*, xi, 71–78, 161; Ute Gause, *Paracelsus (1493–1541): Genese und Entfaltung seiner frühen Theologie* (Tübingen: Mohr Siebeck, 1993), 118–144.

52. Webster, *Paracelsus*, 169, 171, 181, 249; Jacobi, *Paracelsus: Selected Writings*, 195–196. On the religious basis of Paracelsus's thought, see also Jacobi, "Paracelsus: His Life and Work," xlvii–li.

53. Webster, *Paracelsus*, 187, 188; see also 178–182, 184–199, 202–203, 247. Webster writes, "Paracelsus subscribed to a generalized separatist point of view, placing his confidence in the ideal of a loose federation of lay-dominated congregations of believers, tolerant of adult baptism and adopting an interpretation of the Lord's Supper that was confined to dissenting circles . . . He was extremely close to the spiritualist Anabaptists in his basic religious and secular outlook" (247, 197).

54. Ibid., 179, 204–208.

55. Urs Leo Gantenbein, "Paracelsus als Theologe," in Albrecht Classen, ed., *Paracelsus im Kontext der Wissenschaften seiner Zeit: Kultur- und mentalitätsgeschichtliche Annäherungen* (Berlin: De Gruyter, 2010), 70–72, 75, 85, 88–89.

56. A fifteen-volume edition of Weigel's writings is under way, edited by Horst Pfefferl under the auspices of the Mainz Academy for Science and Literature. See Horst Pfefferl, "Die Valentin Weigel-Ausgabe bei der Mainzer Akademie," *Akademie-Journal* 1 (2001): 38–42.

57. Carlos Gilly, *Johann Valentin Andreae: Die Manifeste der Rosenkreuzerbruderschaft* 1586–1986 (Amsterdam: Bibliotheca Philosophica Hermetica, 1986), 46–51, 94–98. Schwenkfelder physicians tended to be supporters of Paracelsus's teachings. See Gritschke, "*Via Media*," 118, 368, 420; Deppermann, *Johann Jakob Schütz*, 7.

58. Hugh Trevor-Roper, "Paracelsianism Made Political, 1600–1650," in Ole Peter Grell, ed., *Paracelsus: The Man and His Reputation, His Ideas, and Their Transformation* (Leiden: Brill, 1998), 123, 126, 132. See also Douglas H. Shantz, *Between Sardis and Philadelphia: The Life and World of Pietist Court Preacher Conrad Bröske*

(Leiden: Brill, 2008), 122–123; Neil Kamil, *Fortress of the Soul: Violence, Metaphysics, and Material Life in the Huguenots' New World, 1517–1751* (Baltimore: Johns Hopkins University Press, 2005), esp. chap. 8, "The Art of the Earth."

59. Martin Brecht, "Das Aufkommen der neuen Frömmigkeitsbewegung in Deutschland," in Brecht et al., *Der Pietismus vom siebzehnten bis zum frühen achtzehnten Jahrhundert,* 150. See Werner Anetsberger, *Tröstende Lehre: Die Theologie Johann Arndts in seinen Predigtwerken* (Munich: Herbert Utz Verlag, 2001), 13.

60. Wallmann, *Der Pietismus,* 35.

61. Hans Schneider, *Der fremde Arndt: Studien zu Leben, Werk und Wirkung Johann Arndts (1555–1621)* (Göttingen: Vandenhoeck & Ruprecht, 2006), 123–124, 133–134. See also Hans Schneider, "Der Braunschweiger Pfarrer Johann Arndt," in Hans Otte and Hans Schneider, eds., *Frömmigkeit oder Theologie: Johann Arndt und die Vier Bücher vom wahren Christentum* (Göttingen: Vandenhoeck & Ruprecht, 2007), 15–16.

62. Schneider, "Der Braunschweiger Pfarrer Johann Arndt," 15.

63. Schneider, *Der fremde Arndt,* 181.

64. Ibid., 214; see also 141–142.

65. Schneider, "Der Braunschweiger Pfarrer Johann Arndt," 21; Brecht, "Das Aufkommen der neuen Frömmigkeitsbewegung," 132.

66. Wilhelm Koepp, *Johann Arndt: Eine Untersuchung über die Mystik im Luthertum* (Berlin: Trowitzsch & Sohn, 1912; reprint, Aalen: Scientia-Verlag 1973), 24.

67. Johann Arndt, *Von wahrem Christenthumb, heilsamer Busse, wahrem Glauben, heyligem Leben und Wandel der rechten wahren Christen. Das erste Buch. Durch Johannem Arndt Dienern der Kirchen Christi zu S. Marten in Braunschweig* (Frankfurt am Main: Nicolao Hoffmann, 1605); a copy is located in the Herzog August Bibliothek in Wolfenbüttel: Th 82.

68. Ibid., 10–12, 283.

69. Johann Anselm Steiger, "Bemerkungen des Herausgebers," in *Johann Arndt, Von wahrem Christenthumb: Die Urausgabe des ersten Buches (1605)* (Hildesheim: Georg Olms Verlag, 2005), 354–359, 368–369. In the second edition of 1606, Arndt provided, for the first time, a brief overview of the four books that he had in mind for the work.

70. Wallmann, *Der Pietismus,* 36–37; Brecht, "Das Aufkommen der neuen Frömmigkeitsbewegung," 143–144. The tracts were entitled "Concerning True Faith and a Holy Life"; "On the Union of Believers with Christ Jesus Their Head"; "On the Holy Trinity"; and "Apologetic Repetition."

71. Brecht, "Das Aufkommen der neuen Frömmigkeitsbewegung," 134–138. In Book I, Arndt explains how the image of God, lost in the Fall, is restored in the new birth. The image consists of "the conformity of the human soul in its understanding, mind, disposition, will, and all inner and outer powers with God and the holy Trinity and the divine virtues and characteristics." Book II presents Christ as the physician of the soul and the model of humility, love, patience, and hope. Arndt focuses on prayer as the believer's connection with Christ. Book III, the Book of Conscience,

speaks of the reign of God within the heart of the believer. Love for God overcomes love of the world, leading to the pouring out of the Spirit. In Book IV, Arndt considers the work of God in creation, often using ideas he found in Paracelsus.

72. Schneider, *Der fremde Arndt*, 209–210, 235; Wallmann, *Der Pietismus*, 39. Arndt left untranslated many Latin passages and references.

73. See Udo Sträter, *Meditation und Kirchenreform in der lutherischen Kirche des 17. Jahrhunderts* (Tübingen: Mohr Siebeck, 1995), 38–39. In Book III, Arndt sets aside the methods belonging to a classic introduction to the practice of meditation; instead, he calls for readers to withdraw from the business of the day and to seek God in the depths of their heart in humble submission.

74. Wallmann, *Der Pietismus*, 37; Schneider, *Der fremde Arndt*, 204; Brecht, "Das Aufkommen der neuen Frömmigkeitsbewegung in Deutschland," 138–139.

75. Schneider, *Der fremde Arndt*, 37–38, 197–200, 210. Arndt lifted the thirty-fourth chapter, on prayer, from an unpublished work by Valentin Weigel. There is need for careful study of Arndt's sources and the manner in which he used them.

76. Friedrich Vollhardt, "Die Theosophie Jacob Böhmes und die orthodoxe Kritik," in Wilfried Härle and Barbara Mahlmann-Bauer, eds., *Prädestination und Willensfreiheit: Festschrift für Theodor Mahlmann zum 75. Geburtstag* (Leipzig: Evangelische Verlagsanstalt, 2009), 168–169. Book metaphors, referring to the book within and Christ the book of life, can also be found in the writings of Valentin Weigel and Sebastian Franck and their critique of learning that depends on the dead letter. Johann Valentin Andreae and Jan Amos Comenius spoke of the books of nature, conscience, and scripture. Beyreuther, *Geschichte des Pietismus*, 52.

77. Werner Anetsberger, "Tröstende Lehre: Die Theologie Johann Arndts in seinen Predigtwerken" (doctoral diss., Neuendettelsau University, 1999).

78. Schneider, *Der fremde Arndt*, 7, 144–147, 155. The title *Der fremde Arndt* translates as "the strange," "foreign," or "unknown Arndt."

79. Hermann Geyer, *Verborgene Weisheit: Johann Arndts "Vier Bücher vom wahren Christentum" als Programm einer spiritualistisch-hermetischen Theologie*, 3 parts (Berlin: Walter de Gruyter, 2001).

80. See Anne-Charlott Trepp, "Hermetismus oder zur Pluralisierung von Religiositäts- und Wissensformen in der Frühen Neuzeit: Einleitende Bemerkungen," in Anne-Charlott Trepp and Hartmut Lehmann, eds., *Antike Weisheit und kulturelle Praxis: Hermetismus in der Frühen Neuzeit* (Göttingen: Vandenhoeck & Ruprecht, 2001), 11.

81. Carlos Gilly, "Hermes oder Luther," in Otte and Schneider, *Frömmigkeit oder Theologie*, 198.

82. Schneider, *Der fremde Arndt*, 242–244. See also Schneider, "Der Braunschweiger Pfarrer Johann Arndt," 23. Arndt appealed to Luke 17:21 and John 4:23 as texts to prove this point. Luke 17:21: "The kingdom of God is not ushered in with visible signs. The kingdom of God is within you." John 4:23: "The time is coming . . . when true worshipers will worship the Father in spirit and in truth."

83. Schneider, "Der Braunschweiger Pfarrer Johann Arndt," 24–25.

84. Gerhard gave two reasons for Arndt's "inappropriate and dangerous" language in the *Four Books of True Christianity*: Arndt's lack of theological education and his overreliance on writings by Paracelsus and Weigel. See Schneider, *Der fremde Arndt*, 65–66, 117, 200.

85. Brecht, "Das Aufkommen der neuen Frömmigkeitsbewegung," 139; Wallmann, *Der Pietismus*, 40.

86. Schneider, *Der fremde Arndt*, 197.

87. Wallmann, *Der Pietismus*, 40; Ward, *Early Evangelicalism*, 8.

88. Hartmut Lehmann, *Das Zeitalter des Absolutismus: Gottesgnadentum und Kriegsnot* (Stuttgart: Kohlhammer, 1980), 116. "From the first edition in the year 1605 to the year 1740, Arndt's work appeared in ninety-five German editions and an additional twenty-eight times in translation (six Latin editions, five in English, four in Dutch, three each in Danish, Swedish, and French, and two editions in Czech, as well as one Russian and one Icelandic edition), adding up to 123 editions in 135 years" (116). This leaves out a Yiddish translation in the 1730s, undertaken by the Halle Jewish mission under Johann Heinrich Callenberg. See Schmidt, *Der Pietismus als theologische Erscheinung*, 26.

89. F. Ernest Stoeffler, "Johann Arndt," in Greschat, ed., *Orthodoxie und Pietismus*, 49; Wallmann, *Der Pietismus*, 40. See also Geoffrey G. Nuttall, "Continental Pietism and the Evangelical Movement in Britain," in J. Van den Berg and J. P. Van Dooren, eds., *Pietismus und Reveil* (Leiden: Brill, 1978), 208–209.

90. Steiger, "Bemerkungen des Herausgebers," 369–374, 393–397.

91. Martin Brecht, *Johann Valentin Andreae: Eine Biographie* (Göttingen: Vandenhoeck & Ruprecht, 2008), 143–145, 173–176. Andreae dedicated his utopian fantasy *Christianopolis* (1619) to Johann Arndt.

92. Heinrich Varenius, *Christliche, Schrifftmässige, wolgegründete Rettunge der Vier Bücher vom wahren Christenthumb, des seligen umb die Kirche Christi wolverdienten recht Lutherischen Evangelischen Theologi H. Johannis Arndten* [A Christian, moderate, and well-grounded defense of the Four Books of True Christianity by the blessed Lutheran evangelical theologian and true servant of the church of Christ Mr. Johann Arndt] (Lüneburg: Stern Verlag, 1624). See also Steiger, "Bemerkungen des Herausgebers," 393–394; Martin Brecht, "Die Aufnahme von Arndts *Vier Bücher von wahrem Christentum* im deutschen Luthertum," in Otte and Schneider, *Frömmigkeit oder Theologie*, 247–248, 258–259.

93. Leigh T. I. Penman, "The Unanticipated Millennium: Orthodoxy, Heterodoxy and Chiliastic Error in Paul Egard's *Posaune der göttlichen Gnade und Liechtes* (1623)," *Pietismus und Neuzeit* 35 (2009): 13–14. Egard was the first Lutheran to interpret Revelation 20 as teaching a future millennial age.

94. Brecht, "Die Aufnahme von Arndts *Vier Bücher von wahrem Christentum*," 243, 249; Wallmann, *Der Pietismus*, 43–45.

95. Brecht, "Die deutschen Spiritualisten des 17. Jahrhunderts," 228. See also Hoburg's *Praxis Arndiana, das ist: Hertzens Seufftzer über die 4 Bücher wahren Christenthumbs S. Johann Arnds* (1642) and *Arndus Redivivus, Das ist Arndischer Wegweiser zum*

Himmelreich (1677). In *Mirror of the Failings of the Clergy* and *The Unknown Christ,* Hoburg insisted that the churches and pastors of his day had no knowledge of the true Christ; they followed instead their own lies and ignorance.

96. Friedrich Breckling, *Autobiographie: Ein frühneuzeitliches Ego-Dokument im Spannungsfeld von Spiritualismus, radikalem Pietismus und Theosophie,* ed. Johann Anselm Steiger (Tübingen: Max Niemeyer Verlag, 2005), 132. Breckling met up with Hoburg in Amsterdam in 1655 and became his disciple.

97. Brecht, "Die deutschen Spiritualisten des 17. Jahrhunderts," 228, 231–232. In Zwolle in 1667, Breckling had sexual relations with a female servant whom he promised to marry. The maid protested when Breckling proposed to another young woman living in his home. Gichtel and Breckling parted ways over the matter.

98. Friedrich Breckling, *Catalogus testium veritatis post Lutherum* (1700). For the list, see Gottfried Arnold, *Kirchen- und Ketzer-Historie, Vierter Theil, Bestehend in allerhand nöthigen Documenten, Tractaten und Zeugnissen, Acten und Geschichten von vielen Religions-Streitigkeiten* (Frankfurt am Main: Thomas Fritschens sel. Erben, 1729), 1089–1110, esp. 1108. The last two pages he devoted to sixty godly women, who "have testified to the truth, or suffered much, or been wonderfully gifted, illumined and led by God."

99. Johannes Wallmann, "Johann Arndt," in Carter Lindberg, ed., *The Pietist Theologians: An Introduction to Theology in the Seventeenth and Eighteenth Centuries* (Oxford: Blackwell, 2005), 35; Johannes Wallmann, "Was ist Pietismus?," *Pietismus und Neuzeit* 20 (1994): 22.

100. Beyreuther, *Geschichte des Pietismus,* 26–28; Christa Habrich, "Alchemie und Chemie in der pietistischen Tradition," in Hans-Georg Kemper und Hans Schneider, eds., *Goethe und der Pietismus* (Tübingen: Max Niemeyer Verlag, 2001), 53–54. See also Gerhard Wehr, *Jakob Böhme: Ursprung, Wirkung, Textauswahl* (Wiesbaden: marixverlag, 2010), 75–108.

101. Brecht, "Die deutschen Spiritualisten des 17. Jahrhunderts," 207; Gerhard Wehr, *Jakob Böhme, mit Selbstzeugnissen und Bilddokumenten* (Hamburg: Rowohlt, 1971), 15. Unfortunately, no portrait of Böhme was made in his lifetime.

102. Johann Henrich Reitz, *Historie der Wiedergebohrnen,* pt. 2, 82–84; Vollhardt, "Die Theosophie Jacob Böhmes," 168n4. The field into which Böhme wandered was called the Neiss-Thor and, in early editions of his works, was indicated on a map of Görlitz.

103. Jakob Böhme, *Aurora, oder Morgenröte im Aufgang,* ed. Gerhard Wehr (Frankfurt: Insel Verlag, 1992), 362.

104. Vollhardt, "Die Theosophie Jacob Böhmes," 168–169. Book metaphors referring to the book within and to Christ the book of life can also be found in the writings of Valentin Weigel and Sebastian Franck.

105. "Sendbrief 55, An Joachim Morsius von Lübeck, April 20, 1624," in Jakob Böhme, *Theosophische Sendbriefe,* ed. Gerhard Wehr (Frankfurt: Insel Verlag, 1996), 388. See also Pältz, "Zu Jakob Boehmes Sicht der Welt- und Kirchengeschichte," 158n90.

106. "Im Wasser lebt der Fisch, die Pflanzen in der Erden, / Der Vogel in der Luft, die Sonn im Firmament, / Der Salamander muss mit Feur erhalten werden; / Und Gottes Herz ist Jakob Boehmens Element." Wehr, *Jakob Böhme: Ursprung, Wirkung*, 71.

107. Andrew Weeks, *Boehme: An Intellectual Biography of the Seventeenth-Century Philosopher and Mystic* (Albany: State University of New York Press, 1991), 29–30; Pierre Deghaye, "Oetinger und Boehme: Von der verborgenen Gottheit bis zum offenbaren Gott," in Sabine Holtz, Gerhard Betsch, and Eberhard Zwink, eds., *Mathesis, Naturphilosophie und Arkanwissenschaft im Umkreis Friedrich Christoph Oetingers (1702–1782)* (Stuttgart: Franz Steiner, 2005), 187.

108. Wehr, *Jakob Böhme, mit Selbstzeugnissen*, 24, 59–64, 70. Böhme's original handwritten copy was found in 1934. See selected translations from *Aurora* in appendix A.

109. Gerhard Wehr, "Jakob Böhme und sein Erstlingswerk: Einführung," in Böhme, *Aurora, oder Morgenröte im Aufgang*, 11. See also Böhme, *Aurora, oder Morgenröte im Aufgang*, 69–70

110. Brecht, "Die deutschen Spiritualisten des 17. Jahrhunderts," 210; Wehr, *Jakob Böhme, mit Selbstzeugnissen*, 24.

111. Jakob Böhme, "Sendbrief 54, Schriftliche Verantwortung an den Ehrbaren Rat zu Görlitz, April 3, 1624," in Böhme, *Theosophische Sendbriefe*, 384–385.

112. Hans Lassen Martensen, *Jakob Boehme: His Life and Teaching*, trans. T. Rhys Evans (London: Hodder & Stoughton, 1885), 13.

113. Wehr, *Jakob Böhme, mit Selbstzeugnissen*, 24, 26.

114. Böhme's friends included Hans Siegismund von Schweinichen, Caspar von Fürstenau, Karl Ender von Sercha, Dr. Balthasar Walter, Dr. Gottfried Freudenhammer zu Grossen-Glogau, and Dr. Johann Daniel Koschwitz. Abraham von Sommerfeld was a close friend and disciple. See Ferdinand van Ingen, "Jakob Böhmes Schrift Von der Gnadenwahl," in Härle and Mahlmann-Bauer, *Prädestination und Willensfreiheit*, 180. For a modern edition of Böhme's letters, see Böhme, *Theosophische Sendbriefe*.

115. Brecht, "Die deutschen Spiritualisten des 17. Jahrhunderts," 212.

116. "Unser Heil im Leben: Jesus Christus in uns!" See Böhme, *Aurora, oder Morgenröte im Aufgang*, 269, 316. See also Eberhard H. Pältz, "Jacob Böhmes Gedanken über die Erneuerung des wahren Christentums," *Pietismus und Neuzeit* 4 (1977/1978): 96–104.

117. Jakob Böhme, *A Compendium of Repentance* (1623), www.passtheword.org/Jacob-Boehme/compend-repentnc.htm. See the use of the Sophia metaphor in Gottfried Arnold, *The Mystery of the Divine Sophia* (1700) in a selection translated in appendix A.

118. Weeks, *Boehme*, 150–153.

119. Schmidt, *Der Pietismus als theologische Erscheinung*, 92.

120. Böhme, *Aurora, oder Morgenröte im Aufgang*, 219. See also ibid., 15, 372, 376; Beyreuther, *Geschichte des Pietismus*, 26.

121. Pältz, "Zu Jakob Böhmes Sicht der Welt- und Kirchengeschichte," 145–146n36. Pältz writes, "Schwenckfeld's idea that a new Pentecost would inaugurate the gathering together of the scattered members of Christ's body gained new life in Böhme and his circle of followers" (145–146n36).

122. Ibid., 133–146. The seven ages of history are prefigured in the blessing of Jacob in Genesis 49. The fate of Jacob's six sons, from Zebulon to Naphthali, portrays the fall; Joseph, a type of Christ, portrays the reintegration. Ibid., 143, 145.

123. Deghaye, "Oetinger und Boehme," 186, 189; Brecht, "Die deutschen Spiritualisten des 17. Jahrhunderts," 208–210.

124. See Ariel Hessayon, "'The Teutonicks Writings': Translating Jacob Boehme into English and Welsh," *Esoterica* 9 (2007): 132, 140–150, 160; Brecht, "Die deutschen Spiritualisten des 17. Jahrhunderts," 213–214, 235.

125. Leade's writing on the second Noah's Ark was influenced by Böhme's exposition of Genesis in *Mysterium Magnum*. See Julie Hirst, "The Divine Ark: Jane Lead's Vision of the Second Noah's Ark," *Esoterica* 6 (2004): 16–25.

126. Wallmann, *Der Pietismus*, 170–172; Hans Schneider, *German Radical Pietism*, trans. Gerald MacDonald (Lanham, MD: Scarecrow Press, 2007), 6, 23–25. See also Julie Hirst, *Jane Leade: Biography of a Seventeenth-Century Mystic* (Aldershot, UK: Ashgate, 2005), 9–10, 50–51.

127. See Deppermann, *Johann Jakob Schütz*, 243–244, 341–342, 347; Willem Heijting, "Hendrick Beets (1625?–1708), Publisher to the German Adherents of Jacob Böhme in Amsterdam," *Quaerendo* 3 (1973): 250–280. Beets, or Betke, published Böhme's works in Amsterdam between 1658 and 1678.

128. Wehr, *Jakob Böhme, mit Selbstzeugnissen*, 69. The first complete edition of Böhme's works was published in Dutch by the Amsterdam businessman Abraham van Beyerlandt (d. 1648).

129. Beyreuther, *Geschichte des Pietismus*, 27; Douglas H. Shantz, "Politics, Prophecy and Pietism in the Halberstadt Conventicle," in Fred van Lieburg, ed., *Confessionalism and Pietism* (Mainz: Verlag Philipp von Zabern, 2006), 129–147.

130. Athina Lexutt, in Otte and Schneider, *Frömmigkeit oder Theologie*, 114, 127.

131. This view is represented by Hans Leube, *Die Reformideen in der deutschen lutherischen Kirche zur Zeit der Orthodoxie* (Leipzig: Dörffling & Franke, 1924); and Kurt Aland, *Spener Studien* (Berlin: De Gruyter, 1943). Leube noted that there was no Orthodox controversy over Arndt's *The Four Books of True Christianity*. See Johannes Wallmann, "Pietismus und Orthodoxie," in Martin Greschat, ed., *Zur neueren Pietismusforschung* (Darmstadt: Wissenschaftliche Buchgesellschaft, 1977), 57–59.

132. Deppermann, *Johann Jakob Schütz*, 84–86; Johannes Wallmann, *Philipp Jakob Spener und die Anfänge des Pietismus*, 2nd ed. (Tübingen: J. C. B. Mohr, 1986), 279. Lütkemann (1608–1655) was a former rector of Rostock University.

133. Beyreuther, *Geschichte des Pietismus*, 126. Beyreuther called Nikolaus Hunnius "one of the most influential and original among early Orthodox Lutheran theologians." Nikolaus Hunnius (1585–1643) was the son of Egidius Hunnius (1550–

1603), the founder of Lutheran Orthodoxy in Wittenberg. See Markus Matthias, *Theologie und Konfession: Der Beitrag von Ägidius Hunnius (1550–1603) zur Entstehung einer lutherischen Religionskultur* (Leipzig: Evangelische Verlagsanstalt, 2004).

134. Johann Anselm Steiger, "Einleitung," in *Melancholie, Diätetik und Trost: Konzepte der Melancholie-Therapie im 16. und 17. Jahrhundert* (Heidelberg: Manutius Verlag, 1996).

135. Johann Anselm Steiger, "Versuchung—orthodox und heterodox: *Tentatio* bei Luther und dem mystischen Spiritualisten Christian Hoburg," in Rainer Hering, ed., *Gottes Wort ins Leben werwandeln: Festschrift für Inge Mager zum 65. Geburtstag* (Hanover: Landeskirchliches Archiv Hannover, 2005), 224–225. In the *Johann-Gerhard-Archiv,* Steiger produced, in six volumes, the first critical edition of the works of Johann Gerhard. Steiger also edited and published a bibliography of Gerhard's writings, *Bibliographia Gerhardiana: 1601–2002* (Stuttgart: frommann-holzboog, 2003), and published a reconstruction of the library of Gerhard and his son Johann Ernst (1621–1668) in the two-volume *Bibliotheca Gerhardiana.*

136. See Udo Sträter, ed., *Pietas in der Lutherischen Orthodoxie* (Wittenberg: Hans Lufft, 1998); Jonathan Strom, *Orthodoxy and Reform: The Clergy in Seventeenth Century Rostock* (Tübingen: Mohr Siebeck, 1999).

137. For the nine-volume systematic theology, see Johann Gerhard, *Loci Theologici* (1610–1622). Richard Dinda has recently translated (from the Latin) Gerhard's "Preface" and "Commonplace I on Scripture." Johann Gerhard, *Theological Commonplaces: On the Nature of Theology and Holy Scripture,* trans. Richard J. Dinda (St. Louis, MO: Concordia, 2006).

138. Johann Anselm Steiger, "Johann Gerhard: Ein Kirchenvater der lutherischen Orthodoxie," in Peter Walter and Martin H. Jung, eds., *Theologen des 17. und 18. Jahrhunderts* (Darmstadt: Wissenschaftliche Buchgesellschaft, 2003), 54; Jörg Baur, "Johann Gerhard," in Greschat, *Orthodoxie und Pietismus,* 99. There is an English translation of the 1723 biography by Erdmann Fischer: *The Life of John Gerhard by Erdmann Fischer,* trans. Richard Dinda and Elmer Hohle (Malone, TX: Repristination Press, 1999).

139. See Brecht, "Das Aufkommen der neuen Frömmigkeitsbewegung," 131, 143; Schneider, *Der fremde Arndt,* 140–141. In 1603, Gerhard was so ill that he composed his last testament and confession of faith. For the text, see Johann Anselm Steiger, *Johann Gerhard: Studien zu Theologie und Frömmigkeit des Kirchenvaters der lutherischen Orthodoxie* (Stuttgart: frommann-holzboog, 1997), 164–172.

140. Inge Mager, "Johann Arndts mystisch vertiefte Seelsorge, insbesondere Johann Gerhard gegenüber," in Martin Tamcke, ed., *Mystik-Metapher-Bild: Beiträge des VII. Makarios-Symposiums* (Göttingen: Universitätsverlag, 2008), 86. This article is based on Mager's lecture on June 16, 2007, at a colloquium sponsored by the Johann Arndt Gesellschaft in Ballenstedt.

141. Steiger, "Johann Gerhard," 54.

142. Wallmann, *Der Pietismus,* 31; Beyreuther, *Geschichte des Pietismus,* 18. Steiger's 2003 study gives prominence to Gerhard as a devotional writer and pastor. See Steiger, "Johann Gerhard," 54–69.

143. Sträter, *Meditation und Kirchenreform*, 43. The first English translation appeared within five years of the Latin first edition. Modern English translations of the work include Johann Gerhard, *Sacred Meditations*, trans. C. W. Heisler (Philadelphia: Lutheran Publication Society, 1896; reprint, Malone, TX: Repristination Press, 1998); and Johann Gerhard, *Sacred Meditations*, trans. Wade R. Johnston (Saginaw, MI: Magdeburg Press, 2008).

144. Baur, "Johann Gerhard," 105–107.

145. Martin Greschat, "Valentin Ernst Löscher," in Greschat, *Orthodoxie und Pietismus*, 287.

146. The publication appeared monthly in 1701, weekly in 1702, and then fifteen times a year for the rest of its publication life, up to 1720. See Martin Greschat, *Zwischen Tradition und Neuem Anfang: Valentin Ernst Löscher und der Ausgang der lutherischen Orthodoxie* (Witten: Luther-Verlag, 1971), 80–190, 280–288.

147. Valentin Ernst Löscher, *Unschuldige Nachrichten von Alten und Neuen Theologischen Sachen Zur heiligen Sontags Ubung verfertiget Von einigen Dienern des Göttl. Wortes. Erster und Andrer Sontag 1702* (Leipzig: Großischen Erben, 1702), 5–9.

148. Valentin Ernest Löscher, Pastor and Superint. Jüterbog, "Vorrede," in *Unschuldige Nachrichten von Alten und Neuen Theologischen Sachen Zur heiligen Sontags Ubung verfertiget Von einigen Dienern des Göttl. Wortes, 1. January 1701* (Leipzig: Großischen Erben, 1701), 9.

149. Greschat, "Valentin Ernst Löscher," 293–294.

150. Ibid., 289, 297, 298.

151. Wallmann, *Der Pietismus*, 85.

152. Deppermann, *Johann Jakob Schütz*, 4. A persistent question is whether German Pietism should be seen as a "foreign movement" inspired by radical sources outside the Lutheran tradition.

Chapter 2. The Thirty Years War, Seventeenth-Century Calvinism, and Reformed Pietism

1. W. R. Ward, *Early Evangelicalism: A Global Intellectual History, 1670–1789* (Cambridge: Cambridge University Press, 2006).

2. Karl Holl, *Die Bedeutung der großen Kriege für das religiöse und kirchliche Leben innerhalb des deutschen Protestantismus* (Tübingen: Mohr, 1917); Ricarda Huch, *Der große Krieg in Deutschland*, 3 vols. (Leipzig: Insel Verlag, 1912–1914). After the First World War, Huch's book was retitled, *Der Dreißigjährige Krieg* (Leipzig: Insel Verlag, 1937).

3. Geoff Mortimer, *Eyewitness Accounts of the Thirty Years War* (New York: Palgrave, 2002), 2.

4. Ibid., 5–9.

5. Hartmut Lehmann, "Lutheranism in the Seventeenth Century," in Ronnie Po-Chia Hsia, ed., *The Cambridge History of Christianity*, vol. 6, *Reform and Expansion, 1500–1660* (Cambridge: Cambridge University Press, 2007), 65–66.

6. Gerhard Benecke, ed., *Germany in the Thirty Years War* (London: Edward Arnold, 1984), 1–2.

7. Christof Dipper, *Deutsche Geschichte, 1648–1789* (Frankfurt am Main: Suhrkamp, 1991), 3:270.

8. Mike Mitchell, "Introduction," in Johann Jakob Christoffel von Grimmelshausen, *Simplicissimus*, trans. Mike Mitchell (Sawtry, UK: Dedalus, 1999), 9–11. Mitchell notes, "There is much that is autobiographical about this story" (10). J. V. Polisensky observed that although *Simplicissimus* is not a treatise on economics or politics, it responds to the issues of the time and "must belong to any final assessment of the period." J. V. Polisensky, *The Thirty Years War*, trans. Robert Evans (London: New English Library, 1971), 263.

9. von Grimmelshausen, *Simplicissimus*, 428–429, 434. First published in 1668, *Simplicissimus* is a kind of German *Pilgrim's Progress*, or regress, recounting the narrator's early piety and loss of his parents at age twelve, his conscription into the army during the war, the horrors and follies he witnessed, his accumulation of great wealth, and his final withdrawal to the life of a hermit. "When I went out into the world after my father's death, I was simple and pure, upright and honest, truthful, humble, unassuming, moderate, chaste, bashful, pious and God-fearing. But I quickly became malicious, false, deceitful, arrogant, restless and, above all, completely ungodly and all without needing anyone to teach me. I always had an eye to the present and my immediate advantage, never thinking of the future, much less that a time will come when I will see God face to face and have to account for myself . . . Therefore, O world, O unclean world, I protest that you shall have no part of me; and I for my part want no part of you. For you know what I have resolved, namely, 'I have put an end to cares; hope and fortune, farewell!' I have abandoned the world and become a hermit once more. God grant us His grace so that we all come to that which we most desire, namely a blessed END."

10. Ibid., 176–177.

11. Hans Medick, "The Thirty Years' War as Experience and Memory: Contemporary Perceptions of a Macro-Historical Event," in Lynne Tatlock, ed., *Enduring Loss in Early Modern Germany: Cross Disciplinary Perspectives* (Leiden: Brill, 2010), 25–49; Dipper, *Deutsche Geschichte 1648–1789*, 266.

12. Erich Beyreuther, *Geschichte des Pietismus* (Stuttgart: J. F. Steinkopf Verlag, 1978), 124–126. See also Mary Noll Venables, "Pietist Fruits from Orthodox Seeds: The Case of Ernst the Pious," in Fred van Lieburg, ed., *Confessionalism and Pietism: Religious Reform in Early Modern Europe* (Mainz: Philipp von Zabern, 2006), 95–104; Andreas Klinger, *Der Gothaer Fürstenstaat: Herrschaft, Konfession und Dynastie unter Herzog Ernst dem Frommen* (Husum: Matthiesen, 2002); Veronika Albrecht-Birkner, *Reformation des Lebens: Die Reformen Herzog Ernsts des Frommen von Sachsen-Gotha und ihre Auswirkungen auf Frömmigkeit, Schule und Alltag im ländlichen Raum (1640–1675)* (Leipzig: Evangelische Verlagsanstalt, 2002). Albrecht-Birkner is critical of Ernst's actual achievements: "The measures were in many respects unsuccessful. Many remained ineffective and had to be continually resur-

rected. Others, because of their criminalizing of people who evaded the reforms, had consequences for individuals and the whole population which are not consistent with the idea of progress." Albrecht-Birkner, *Reformation des Lebens*, 526.

13. See Horst Weigelt, "Ludwig Friedrich Gifftheil und die Schwenckfelder in Schlesien," in Bernd Jaspert and Rudolf Mohr, eds., *Traditio—Krisis—Renovatio aus theologischer Sicht* (Marburg: Elwert, 1976), 273–283; Friedrich Fritz, "Friedrich Gifftheil," *Blätter für württembergische Kirchengeschichte* (new series) 44 (1940): 90–105; Ernst Eylenstein, "Ludwig Friedrich Gifftheil: Zum mystischen Separatismus des 17. Jahrhunderts in Deutschland," *Zeitschrift für Kirchengeschichte* 41 (1922): 1–62.

14. See Martin Schmidt, *Wiedergeburt und Neuer Mensch* (Witten: Luther Verlag, 1969), 162. Christian Hoburg, *Spiegel der Misbräuche beym Predig-Ampt im heutigen Christenthumb* (1644), 43ff., 355.

15. See Paul Felgenhauer, *TauffSpiegel: Das ist Eine Schrifft oder Rede von der Tauffe und ihren Geheymnussen, fürnemlich an die Wiedertäuffer geschrieben* (Amsterdam, 1651), 155–156.

16. Wolters credits Felgenhauer with more than one hundred titles and ninety publications. See Ernst G. Wolters, "Paul Felgenhauers Leben und Wirken," *Jahrbuch der Gesellshaft für Niedersächsische Kirchengeschichte* 54 (1956): 63–84; 55 (1957): 54–94. See also Lutz Greisiger, "Chiliasten und 'Judentzer'—Eschatologie und Judenmission im protestantischen Deutschland des 17. und 18. Jahrhunderts," *Jewish History Quarterly* (2006), 555–559.

17. Greisiger, "Chiliasten und 'Judentzer,'" 557–558. In 1654, Paul Felgenhauer published *Harmonia Fidei et Religionis, Harmony des Glaubens, Das ist: Vereinigung deß Glaubens zur Seligkeit an Gott und seinem Sohn. Das ist: Deutliche warhafftige und unwiedersprechliche Darzeigung und Unterweisung, wie und auff was weise all Menschen, beydes Christen, Juden, Türcken und Heyden, gar gewiß leichte und bald, zu Einerley Erkenntnis, Glauben und Religion zur Seeligkeit an Gott und seinem Sohn gelanden können* [Harmony of faith and religion . . . That is: Clear, true, and irrefutable Demonstration and Instruction, how and in what way all people, Christians, Jews, Turks, and heathen, most certainly, easily, and speedily, can arrive at one form of understanding, faith, and religion for salvation in God and his Son] (Amsterdam, 1654).

18. Martin Brecht, "Die deutschen Spiritualisten des 17. Jahrhunderts," in Martin Brecht et al., eds., *Der Pietismus vom siebzehnten bis zum frühen achtzehnten Jahrhundert* (Göttingen: Vandenhoeck & Ruprecht, 1993), 218–219; Andreas Deppermann, *Johann Jakob Schütz und die Anfänge des Pietismus* (Tübingen: Mohr Siebeck, 2002), 8, 18.

19. On Anna Hoyer, see Cornelia Niekus Moore, "Anna Ovena Hoyers (1584–1655)," in Kerstin Merkel and Heide Wunder, eds., *Deutsche Frauen der Frühen Neuzeit: Dichterinnen, Malerinnen, Mäzeninnen* (Darmstadt: Primus Verlag, 2000), 65–76; C. N. Moore, "Anna Hoyers' Posaunenschall: Hymns of an Empire at War and a Kingdom Come," *Daphnis* 13 (1984): 343–362.

20. Caroline Gritschke, *"Via Media": Spiritualistische Lebenswelten und Konfes-*

sionalisierung. Das süddeutsche Schwenckfeldertum im 16. und 17. Jahrhundert (Berlin: Akademie Verlag, 2006), 371n47, 372, 376–377.

21. Karl Barth observed, "The Christian of the eighteenth century . . . was moved by the outcome of the awful religious and political battles that reached their high point in the Thirty Years War. Those battles and accompanying moral barbarism he wished never to see repeated, nor the idea of Christian belief that had caused them." Karl Barth, *Die Protestantische Theologie im 19. Jahrhundert: Ihre Vorgeschichte und ihre Geschichte* (Zurich: Theologischer Verlag Zürich, 1947), 72.

22. Christians spoke much of love, Edelmann noted, but in fact "there is no more hateful and hostile religion in the world than the Christian faith." Christians used the most extreme measures in dealing with enemies of Christ. See *Johann Christian Edelmann Selbstbiographie*, a facsimile reprint of the 1849 Berlin edition of Carl Rudolph Wilhelm Klose (Stuttgart: Frommann-Holzboog Verlag, 1976), 133.

23. Lehmann, "Lutheranism in the Seventeenth Century," 71; Carl Hinrichs, *Preußentum und Pietismus: Der Pietismus in Brandenburg-Preußen als religiös-soziale Reformbewegung* (Göttingen: Vandenhoeck & Ruprecht, 1971), 8ff.

24. von Grimmelshausen, *Simplicissimus*, 262.

25. Ibid., 414. See Hans Jakob Christoffel von Grimmelshausen, *Der Abenteuerliche Simplicissimus Teutsch* (Munich: Deutscher Taschenbuch Verlag, 1975). "Ich fand aber . . . daß kein besser Kunst sei, als die Theologia, wenn man vermittelst derselbigen Gott liebet und ihm dienet!" *Der Abenteuerliche Simplicissimus*, 458.

26. John G. Gagliardo, *Germany under the Old Regime, 1600–1790* (London: Longman, 1991), 251.

27. The quotation from Veiel was noted by August Tholuck in his history *Das kirchliche Leben des siebzehnten Jahrhunderts*, pt. 2 (Berlin, 1862), 20. See W. R. Ward, *The Protestant Evangelical Awakening* (Cambridge: Cambridge University Press, 1992), 12.

28. Bayly's work was first published in 1610. The first German translation appeared in Basel in 1628. See Jan van de Kamp, "Die Einführung der christlichen Disziplinierung des Alltags in die deutsche evangelische Erbauungsliteratur durch Lewis Baylys *Praxis Pietatis* (1628)," *Pietismus und Neuzeit* 37 (2011): 11–19; Deppermann, *Johann Jakob Schütz*, 84n131.

29. Lewis Bayly, *The Practice of Piety: Directing a Christian How to Walk, That He May Please God* (London: Hamilton, Adams, and Co., 1842), 102, www.ccel.org/ccel/bayly/piety.pdf.

30. Ibid., 54, 69.

31. See Udo Sträter, *Sonthom, Bayly, Dyke und Hall: Studien zur Rezeption der englischen Erbauungsliteratur in Deutschland im 17. Jahrhundert* (Tübingen: J. C. B. Mohr, 1987), 5, 11, 113. Sträter provided case studies examining the reception of four English works: Sonthom's *Güldenes Kleinod*, Bayly's *Praxis Pietatis*, Dyke's *Mystery of Selfe-Deceiving*, and Hall's *Arte of Divine Meditation*.

32. Sträter, *Sonthom, Bayly, Dyke und Hall*, 16, 21–23.

33. Gottfried Arnold, *Das Leben der Gläubigen Oder Beschreibung solcher Gottseligen*

Personen welche in denen letzten 200. Jahren sonderlich bekandt worden, ausgefertigt von Gottfried Arnold (Halle: Orphanage Publishing House, 1701), 829. *Das Leben der Gläubigen* was published a year after Arnold's more famous work, *Unpartheyische Kirchen- und Ketzerhistorie* (1699–1700), in which Bunyan did not appear.

34. Auguste Sann, *Bunyan in Deutschland: Studien zur literarischen Wechselbeziehung zwischen England und dem deutschen Pietismus* (Giessen: Wilhelm Schmitz Verlag, 1951), 51. The orphanage library has first editions of almost all German translations of Bunyan. Ibid., 15.

35. Ibid., 52.

36. Sträter, *Sonthom, Bayly, Dyke und Hall*, 114–115, 121–123. See also Peter Damrau, *The Reception of English Puritan Literature in Germany* (Leeds, UK: Maney, 2006), 1–10, 190–193.

37. Max Goebel, *Geschichte des christlichen Lebens in der rheinisch-westphälischen evangelischen Kirche* (Koblenz: Karl Bädeker, 1852), 2:184.

38. Johannes Wallmann, *Der Pietismus* (Göttingen: Vandenhoeck & Ruprecht, 2005), 59.

39. Goebel, *Geschichte des christlichen Lebens*, 2:186, 193–196.

40. T. J. Saxby, *The Quest for the New Jerusalem, Jean De Labadie, and the Labadists, 1610–1744* (Dordrecht: Martinus Nijhoff, 1987), vii.

41. Goebel, *Geschichte des christlichen Lebens*, 2:193–194, 206, 215.

42. Ibid., 208–209.

43. Ibid., 210–211. See also Wallmann, *Der Pietismus*, 85, 141.

44. Goebel, *Geschichte des christlichen Lebens*, 2:231.

45. In 1673, van Schurman published the *Eukleria*, in which she justified her decision to leave the Reformed church and join de Labadie's community. See Anna Maria van Schurman, *Whether a Christian Woman Should Be Educated and Other Writings from Her Intellectual Circle*, trans. Joyce L. Irwin (Chicago: University of Chicago Press, 1999). For a recent study of van Schurman, see Pieta van Beek, *The First Female University Student: Anna Maria van Schurman (1636)* (Utrecht: Igitur, Utrecht Publishing & Archiving Services, 2010).

46. Goebel, *Geschichte des christlichen Lebens*, 2:234–238; Saxby, *Quest for the New Jerusalem*, 178, 181–182, 203–206.

47. Goebel, *Geschichte des christlichen Lebens*, 2:236, 238, 242; Saxby, *Quest for the New Jerusalem*, 195, 214.

48. Johannes van den Berg, "Die Frömmigkeitsbestrebungen in den Niederlanden," in Brecht et al., *Der Pietismus vom siebzehnten bis zum frühen achtzehnten Jahrhundert*, 100–103, 105.

49. Goebel, *Geschichte des christlichen Lebens*, 2:243–245; Saxby, *Quest for the New Jerusalem*, 211–213, 248–249.

50. Saxby, *Quest for the New Jerusalem*, 161, 168, 186–187.

51. Jean de Labadie, "The Reformation of the Church by the Pastorate, 1667," in Frederick Herzog, *European Pietism Reviewed* (San Jose: Pickwick, 2003), 58–63, 66–67, 73–75.

52. Ernestine van der Wall, "A Precursor of Christ or a Jewish Impostor? Petrus Serrarius and Jean de Labadie on the Jewish Messianic Movement around Sabbatai Sevi," *Pietismus und Neuzeit* 14 (1988): 109, 120–122.

53. Willem Jan op 't Hof, "Die nähere Reformation und der Niederländische reformierte Pietismus und ihr Verhältnis zum deutschen Pietismus," *Dutch Review of Church History* 78 (1998): 161–183.

54. Fred van Lieburg, "Niederländische Waisenhäuser und reformierter Pietismus im 17. Jahrhundert," in Udo Sträter and Josef N. Neumann, eds., *Waisenhäuser in der Frühen Neuzeit* (Tübingen: Max Niemeyer Verlag, 2003), 171.

55. Books by Teellinck in English translation include Willem Teellinck, *The Path of True Godliness*, trans. Annemie Godbehere, ed. Joel R. Beeke (Grand Rapids, MI: Reformation Heritage Books, 2006); and Willem Teellinck, *North Star*, trans. Annemie Godbehere, ed. Joel R. Beeke (Grand Rapids, MI: Baker Book House, 2002).

56. Fred van Lieburg noted "the higher social-cultural level of Reformed clergymen in the cities as well as the presence of publishers and booksellers." Fred van Lieburg, "From Pure Church to Pious Culture: The Further Reformation in the Seventeenth-Century Dutch Republic," in Fred Graham, ed., *Later Calvinism: International Perspectives* (Kirksville, MO: Sixteenth Century Journal Publishers, 1994), 419; see also 422–424.

57. van den Berg, "Die Frömmigkeitsbestrebungen in den Niederlanden," 78, 82–87.

58. See Gisbertus Voetius and Johannes Hoornbeeck, *Spiritual Desertion*, trans. John Vriend and Harry Boonstra (Grand Rapids, MI: Baker, 2003).

59. van den Berg, "Die Frömmigkeitsbestrebungen in den Niederlanden," 84. Voetius authored a tract entitled "On the Private Meetings of the Christians."

60. van Lieburg, "Niederländische Waisenhäuser und reformierter Pietismus," 180. Albrecht Ritschl called van Lodenstein "the first Pietist," and Max Goebel considered him "the Dutch Spener." See van den Berg, "Die Frömmigkeitsbestrebungen in den Niederlanden," 59.

61. John Boldt, "Review of Carl J. Schroeder, *In Quest of Pentecost: Jodocus van Lodenstein and the Dutch Second Reformation* (Lanham, MD: University Press of America, 2001)," *Bulletin of the Institute for Reformed Theology* 4, no. 2 (2004): 8.

62. Schroeder, *Jodocus van Lodenstein*, 31, 37–38.

63. Johann Henrich Reitz, *IV. Theil der Historie Der Wiedergebohrnen* (1716), 24.

64. Schroeder, *Jodocus van Lodenstein*, 41–43.

65. Reitz, *IV. Theil der Historie Der Wiedergebohrnen*, 31.

66. Schroeder, *Jodocus van Lodenstein*, 44.

67. van den Berg, "Die Frömmigkeitsbestrebungen in den Niederlanden," 84–85.

68. Iain Maclean, "The First Pietist: Jodocus van Lodenstein," in John Leith, ed., *Calvin Studies VI* (Davidson, NC: Calvin Colloquium, 1993), 15–34. See also Iain Maclean's translations of *Tien Predicatie* by Jodocus van Lodenstein in William

Stacy Johnson and John H. Leith, eds., *Reformed Reader: A Sourcebook in Christian Theology* (Louisville, KY: Westminster, 1993), 1:296–297, 322–324.

69. Schroeder, *Jodocus van Lodenstein*, 54–56.

70. Ibid., 56.

71. van den Berg, "Die Frömmigkeitsbestrebungen in den Niederlanden," 85; Rudolf Th. M. van Dijk, "Lodensteyn, Jodocus van," *Biographisch-Bibliographisches Kirchenlexikon* 5 (1993): 160–163.

72. The motto first appeared in Jodocus van Lodenstein, *Beschouwinge van Zion* [Contemplation of Zion] (Amsterdam, 1674). See Michael Bush, "Calvin and the *Reformanda* Sayings," in Herman J. Selderhuis, ed., *Calvinus sacrarum literarum interpres: Papers of the International Congress on Calvin Research* (Göttingen: Vandenhoeck & Ruprecht, 2008), 286.

73. Wallmann, *Der Pietismus*, 53.

74. Johann Friedrich Gerhard Goeters, "Der reformierte Pietismus in Deutschland 1650–1690," in Martin Brecht et al., eds., *Der Pietismus vom siebzehnten bis zum frühen achtzehnten Jahrhundert* (Göttingen: Vandenhoeck & Ruprecht, 1993), 241–242.

75. Wallmann, *Der Pietismus*, 50; Goeters, "Der reformierte Pietismus in Deutschland," 244. On Undereyck's life and thought, see Do-Hong Jou, *Theodor Undereyck und die Anfänge des reformierten Pietismus* (Bochum: Brockmeyer, 1994), a doctoral dissertation in the Faculty of Evangelical Theology of the Ruhr-Universität Bochum, presented in the summer semester of 1993, under Johannes Wallmann's supervision.

76. Heiner Faulenbach, *Weg und Ziel der Erkenntnis Christi: Eine Untersuchung zur Theologie des Johannes Coccejus* (Neukirchen: Neukirchener Verlag, 1973), 133, 139.

77. Heiner Faulenbach, "Coccejus, Johannes (1603–1669)," in Gerhard Krause and Gerhard Müller, eds., *Theologische Realenzyklopädie* (Berlin: Walter de Gruyter, 1981), 8:138, 139.

78. Gottlob Schrenk, *Gottesreich und Bund im Älteren Protestantismus Vornehmlich bei Johannes Coccejus* (Darmstadt: Wissenschaftliche Buchgesellschaft, 1967), 4. For a critique of Schrenk, especially his view of Coccejus's influence on Pietism, see Willem J. van Asselt, *The Federal Theology of Johannes Coccejus (1603–1669)* (Leiden: Brill, 2001).

79. Goeters, "Der reformierte Pietismus in Deutschland," 246. See Jürgen Moltmann, "Geschichtstheologie und pietistisches Menschenbild bei Johann Coccejus und Theodor Undereyck," *Evangelische Theologie* 19 (1959): 343–361.

80. Johann Friedrich Gerhard Goeters, "Der reformierte Pietismus in Bremen und am Niederrhein im 18. Jahrhundert," in Martin Brecht and Klaus Deppermann, eds., *Der Pietismus im achtzehnten Jahrhundert* (Göttingen: Vandenhoeck & Ruprecht, 1995), 2: 398; Goeters, "Der reformierte Pietismus in Deutschland," 246–247.

81. Theodor Undereyck, *Christi Braut unter den Töchtern zu Laodicea* (Hanau, 1670).

82. Goeters, "Der reformierte Pietismus in Deutschland," 247–249. Undereyck cited works by Willem Teellinck, William Perkins, and Richard Baxter, as well as Johann Arndt's *True Christianity*.

83. Goeters, "Der reformierte Pietismus in Deutschland," 254; Wallmann, *Der Pietismus*, 51.

84. Wallmann, *Der Pietismus*, 52; Goeters, "Der reformierte Pietismus in Deutschland," 255, 272–273.

85. C. W. H. Hochhuth, *Heinrich Horch und die phsiladelphischen Gemeinden in Hessen* (Gütersloh: Verlag von C. Bertelsmann, 1876), 2.

86. Goeters, "Der reformierte Pietismus in Deutschland," 255–256; Wallmann, *Der Pietismus*, 54.–256.

87. W. R. Ward, *The Protestant Evangelical Awakening* (Cambridge: Cambridge University Press, 1992), 230. See also Goeters, "Der reformierte Pietismus in Bremen und am Niederrhein," 390–391.

88. Ward, *Protestant Evangelical Awakening*, 232; Wallmann, *Der Pietismus*, 65. The Protestant historian referred to in the text is Johannes Wallmann.

89. Cornelis Pieter van Andel, *Gerhard Tersteegen: Leben und Werk—sein Platz in der Kirchengeschichte*, trans. Arthur Klein (Neukirchen-Vluyn: Neukirchener Verlag, 1973), 265–266. See also Jürgen Moltmann, "Grundzüge mystischer Theologie bei Gerhard Tersteegen," *Evangelische Theologie* 16 (1956): 205–224.

90. Goeters, "Der reformierte Pietismus in Bremen und am Niederrhein," 391–392; Wallmann, *Der Pietismus*, 61.

91. Goeters, "Der reformierte Pietismus in Bremen und am Niederrhein," 392. See also Hansgünter Ludewig, "Gerhard Tersteegen (1697–1769)," in Carter Lindberg, ed., *The Pietist Theologians* (Oxford: Blackwell, 2005), 191–192.

92. Gustav Adolf Benrath, "Der Mystiker Gerhard Tersteegen als Prediger und Seelsorger," *Monatshefte für Evangelische Kirchengeschichte des Rheinlandes* 58 (2009): 85. See also Ludewig, "Gerhard Tersteegen," 194. The original of Tersteegen's blood-signed covenant has been preserved and is located in the Landeskirchenarchiv in Düsseldorf. Benrath's article includes a photocopy.

93. Gerhard Tersteegen, "Important Rules of Conduct for a Community of Brothers Living Together" (1732), reprinted in Winfried Zeller, "The Protestant Attitude to Monasticism, with Special Reference to Gerhard Tersteegen," *Downside Review* 93, no. 312 (1975): 188–192. Zeller provides an English translation of Tersteegen's "Important Rules of Conduct." See also Dietrich Meyer, ed., *Gerhard Tersteegen: Eine Auswahl aus seinen Werken* (Giessen: Brunnen Verlag, 1997), 35–43; Goeters, "Der reformierte Pietismus in Bremen und am Niederrhein," 403.

94. George Ella observed, "Hundreds of Tersteegen's works are extant and many letters from his pen have been rediscovered recently. Tersteegen's fine house in the center of Mülheim has been preserved and is now a museum depicting his life and background. A number of Tersteegen's artifacts and documents are placed under the care of the Mülheim Historical Society and its members assist in the care of the

Tersteegen Museum and City Archives and serve as guides for visitors." George M. Ella, "Gerhard Tersteegen," *Leben, Journal of Reformation Life* 3, no. 4 (2007): 16.

95. Goeters, "Der reformierte Pietismus in Bremen und am Niederrhein," 396. See also Ludewig, "Gerhard Tersteegen," 196–197.

96. Ludewig, "Gerhard Tersteegen," 203.

97. "Gerhard Tersteegen is best known to English-speaking Christians through his hymns translated by Emma Francis Bevan, Francis Elizabeth Cox, William Delamotte, Sarah Findlater (with her sister Jane Borthwick), Melanchthon Woolsey Stryker, John Wesley and Catherine Winkworth." Ella, "Gerhard Tersteegen," 15.

98. Ludewig, "Gerhard Tersteegen," 190, 193. A modern edition is Gerhard Tersteegen, *Geistliches Blumengärtlein inniger Seelen mit der frommen Lotterie und einem kurzen Lebenslauf des Verfassers* (Stuttgart: J. F. Steinkopf Verlag, 17th ed. 1988).

99. Gerhard Tersteegen, "From Spiritual Flower Garden," in Peter C. Erb, ed., *Pietists: Selected Writings* (New York: Paulist Press, 1983), 249.

100. J. Steven O'Malley, "Pietistic Influence on John Wesley: Wesley and Gerhard Tersteegen," *Wesleyan Theological Journal* 31, no. 2 (1996): 49, 50, 65. See also Kenneth J. Collins, "John Wesley's Critical Appropriation of Early German Pietism," *Wesleyan Theological Journal* 27 (1992): 57–92; Paul S. Wagner, "John Wesley and the German Pietist Heritage: The Development of Hymnody" (ThD diss., Toronto School of Theology, University of Toronto, 2004).

101. *The Lutheran Hymnal* (St. Louis, MO: Concordia, 1941), hymn no. 4, "God Himself Is Present," trans. ca. 1826 by Frederick W. Foster.

102. See appendix A for a translation of the eight verses of the hymn.

103. Manfred Rompf, "Gerhard Tersteegen als evangelisch-reformierter Mystiker" (lecture presented at Rengsdorf, Westerwald, Herbst, 2004), www.ekir.de/essen/PDF%20Meditation%20Teerstegen.pdf.

104. Werner Thiede, "Mystik im Zentrum: Gerhard Tersteegen," *Evangelisches Sonntagsblatt aus Bayern* 32 (Aug. 13, 2006): 6.

105. Goeters, "Der reformierte Pietismus in Bremen und am Niederrhein," 391.

106. Ernest Stoeffler, *German Pietism in the Eighteenth Century* (Leiden: Brill, 1973), 191.

Chapter 3. Beginnings of Lutheran Pietism in Frankfurt, 1670 to 1684

1. Wallmann writes, "In [Spener's] numerous reminiscences of the Frankfurt *Collegium pietatis*, which were foundational for Pietist historians, Spener did not mention the name of Johann Jakob Schütz. Spener was concerned to provide an unsuspicious portrait of Pietist beginnings. Schütz remains one of the darkest figures in the history of Pietism. Although Schütz is regularly mentioned in contemporary sources alongside Spener, at times even before him, Schütz quickly fell into oblivion after his separation from the church." Johannes Wallmann, *Der Pietismus* (Göttingen: Vandenhoeck & Ruprecht, 2005), 138n4.

2. Johannes Wallmann, *Philipp Jakob Spener und die Anfänge des Pietismus*, 2nd ed. (Tübingen: J. C. B. Mohr, 1986), 271n30. Wallmann's pessimism arose from the fact that the Frankfurt Ministerial Archive was largely destroyed during the Second World War, an archive described by those who had used it as both unbelievably rich in early modern sources and extremely disorganized. See Werner Bellardi, "Foreword," in *Die Vorstufen der Collegia pietatis bei Philipp Jakob Spener* (reprint, Giessen: Brunnen-Verlag GmbH, 1994).

3. Andreas Deppermann, *Johann Jakob Schütz und die Anfänge des Pietismus* (Tübingen: Mohr Siebeck, 2002), 4–5. Marburg church historian Hans Schneider discovered the Schütz papers in the Archive of the Senckenberg Library in Frankfurt. The estate contains letters and other handwritten sources from Schütz. Schneider informed me in January 2010 that in recent years these sources have gone missing.

4. Deppermann, *Johann Jakob Schütz*, 4n17, 368–369. Johannes Wallmann and Markus Matthias made selective use of the Schütz sources. Andreas Deppermann was the first to make thorough and critical use of these sources and to demonstrate Schütz's importance and the formation of his theological views.

5. Ibid., 31–32.

6. Christiane Duschl, *Der "Catalogus librorum" des Stuttgarter Buchhändlers Johann Gottfried Zubrodt: eine Untersuchung über die Meßkataloge der Fasten- und der Herbstmesse 1677* (Essay for the Diploma in the History of Library and Information Studies in the Library Science Program of the Stuttgart Academy for Media Studies, Stuttgart, Oct. 2002), 9. "The great [Frankfurt] fair was a place of financial, intellectual, and cultural exchange" (9).

7. Deppermann, *Johann Jakob Schütz*, 28, 32–33; Reinhard Wittmann, *Geschichte des deutschen Buchhandels: ein Überblick* (Munich: Beck, 1991), 77, 86. After 1680, Leipzig saw an economic recovery and became the leading city for the book business. See Martin Gierl, *Pietismus und Aufklärung: Theologische Polemik und die Kommunikationsreform der Wissenschaft am Ende des 17. Jahrhunderts* (Göttingen: Vandenhoeck & Ruprecht, 1997), 358.

8. Wallmann, *Philipp Jakob Spener und die Anfänge des Pietismus*, 199.

9. Deppermann, *Johann Jakob Schütz*, 33. For a study of the Jewish community in Frankfurt, see Cilli Kasper-Holtkotte, *Die jüdische Gemeinde von Frankfurt/Main in der frühen Neuzeit: Familien, Netzwerke und Konflikte eines jüdischen Zentrums* (Berlin: de Gruyter 2010). Kasper-Holtkotte focuses on families that dominated the social, economic, and political affairs of the Frankfurt Jewish community. The author includes 280 pages of sources from the Frankfurt City Archive and the Hessian State Archives in Marburg and Darmstadt, dating mainly from 1528 to 1712.

10. Deppermann, *Johann Jakob Schütz*, 28–29, 142–144. Several nonconformist leaders in Frankfurt had Schwenkfelder ties.

11. The symbol of the Merian firm was a stork with a snake in its beak, above the Latin motto *Pietas Contenta Lucratur*, "industrious piety pays." See Ingrid D. Rowland, "The Flowering Genius of Maria Sibylla Merian," *New York Review of Book*, Apr. 9, 2009.

12. See, for example, *Zehen lehr- vnd geist-reiche Predigten: Von den zehen grausamen vnd schröcklichen egyptischen Plagen* (Frankfurt am Main: Christoff le Blon, 1657).

13. Deppermann, *Johann Jakob Schütz*, 13–18, 22, 25–28.

14. Ibid., 36–40.

15. Ibid., 217–219. Maria Katharina Schütz is mentioned in the autobiographies of Edelmann and Oetinger and in reports by Zinzendorf. See Hans Schneider, "Der radikale Pietismus im 17. Jahrhundert," in Martin Brecht, ed., *Der Pietismus vom 17. bis zum frühen 18. Jahrhundert* (Göttingen: Vandenhoeck & Ruprecht, 1993), 425n76.

16. Deppermann, *Johann Jakob Schütz*, 65, 66.

17. Ibid., 146–150. Maria Sibylla's husband, the Nuremberg painter Johannes Andreas Graff, told Schütz in a letter that he believed his wife had tried to have him poisoned.

18. Rowland, "Flowering Genius of Maria Sibylla Merian." Maria Sibylla Merian became famous as a painter, her observations revolutionizing botany and zoology. Her best-known book was on the insects of Surinam. Maria Sibylla Merian, *Das Insektenbuch: Metamorphosis Insectorum Surinamensium* (Amsterdam, 1705; reprint, Frankfurt am Main: Insel Verlag, 1991).

19. J. Wallmann, "Kirchlicher und radikaler Pietismus: Zu einer kirchengeschichtlichen Grundunterscheidung," in Wolfgang Breul, ed., *Der radikale Pietismus: Perspektiven der Forschung* (Göttingen: Vandenhoeck & Ruprecht, 2010), 29–30. See the catalogues for the 2008 exhibit at the J. Paul Getty Museum in Los Angeles and for the 1998 exhibit in Frankfurt: Ella Reitsma, *Maria Sibylla Merian and Daughters: Women of Art and Science, June 10–August 31, 2008* (Los Angeles: Getty Publications, 2008); and Kurt Wettengl, ed., *Maria Sibylla Merian: 1647–1717: Künstlerin und Naturforscherin*, publication for the Exhibition in the Historical Museum in Frankfurt, December 18, 1997, to March 1, 1998 (Frankfurt am Main: Historisches Museum, 1997; new edition, Ostfildern: Hatje Cantz Verlag, 2002). Merian receives lengthy treatment in Natalie Zemon Davis, *Women on the Margins: Three Seventeenth-Century Lives* (Cambridge, MA: Harvard University Press, 1995), 140–202. Davis mistakenly identifies the Calvinist Merian family as Lutheran (157).

20. Wallmann, *Der Pietismus*, 139–143. Schütz also read works by the Cambridge Neo-Platonist Henry More.

21. Deppermann, *Johann Jakob Schütz*, 56–60, 67–68. In contrast to Francke's, Schütz's conversion was a process over time that was rooted in reading and reflection rather than a sudden experience after prayer.

22. Wallmann, *Philipp Jakob Spener und die Anfänge des Pietismus*, 48, 65.

23. Ibid., 70–71, 95–96. Johann Schmidt died while Spener was still a student.

24. Wallmann, *Der Pietismus*, 73–74.

25. Ruth Albrecht, *Johanna Eleonora Petersen: Theologische Schriftstellerin des frühen Pietismus* (Göttingen: Vandenhoeck & Ruprecht, 2005), 58. When Baur von Eyse-

neck died in 1672, Spener praised him as a true friend whose favorite reading was the word of God and Johann Arndt's *True Christianity.*

26. Wallmann, *Der Pietismus,* 74–75. Spener found traditional Lutheran Orthodox methods to be futile.

27. Philipp Jakob Spener, "Bericht über die Motivation der Anreger der *Collegia pietatis,*" in Ph. J. Spener, *Schriften,* ed. Erich Beyreuther and Dietrich Blaufuß (New York: Olms Verlag, 1979), 1:44–46.

28. Wallmann, *Philipp Jakob Spener und die Anfänge des Pietismus,* 264–289. K. James Stein makes errors at key points in recounting the details of the early collegium in Frankfurt. He fails to identify the theology student and does not give Schütz proper credit. See Johannes Wallmann, "Review of K. James Stein, *Philipp Jakob Spener: Pietist Patriarch* (Chicago: Covenant Press, 1986)," *Pietismus und Neuzeit* 15 (1989): 243–244.

29. Wallmann, *Philipp Jakob Spener und die Anfänge des Pietismus,* 276; Deppermann, *Johann Jakob Schütz,* 82–83. Dieffenbach died in March 1671 after a three-month illness.

30. Wallmann, *Philipp Jakob Spener und die Anfänge des Pietismus,* 278.

31. Nicolaus Hunnius, *Epitome Credendorum,* trans. Paul Edward Gottheil (Nuremberg: U. E. Sebald, 1847), 166–168. The *Epitome Credendorum* went through nineteen editions and was translated into Dutch, Swedish, Polish, and Latin. See Theodor Mahlmann, "Hunnius, Nikolaus," in Gerhard Krause and Gerhard Müller, eds., *Theologische Realenzyklopädie* (Berlin: Walter de Gruyter, 1986), 15:707.

32. Friedrich A. G. Tholuck, *Lebenszeugen der lutherischen Kirche aller Stände vor und nach der Zeit des dreißigjährigen Krieges* (1859), 379.

33. Jutta Taege-Bizer, "Weibsbilder im Pietismus," in Leonore Siegele-Wenschkewitz, ed., *Frauen Gestalten Geschichte. Im Spannungsfeld von Religion und Geschlecht* (Hanover: Lutherisches Verlagshaus, 1998), 118; Martin Brecht, "Philipp Jakob Spener, sein Programm und dessen Auswirkungen," in Martin Brecht et al., eds., *Der Pietismus vom siebzehnten bis zum frühen achtzehnten Jahrhundert* (Göttingen: Vandenhoeck & Ruprecht 1993), 297–298. See also Wallmann, *Der Pietismus,* 78.

34. Deppermann, *Johann Jakob Schütz,* 88. Letters between Schütz and Anna Sophia Hagemeister reveal features of early Pietist gatherings.

35. Ibid., 101–103. A letter from Anna Maria van Schurman, dated April 1675, contains the only indication of Schütz reading works by Labadie. Van Schurman noted that Schütz had not yet confirmed receiving the books.

36. Martin Greschat, *Christentumsgeschichte II: Von der Reformation bis zur Gegenwart* (Stuttgart: Verlag W. Kohlhammer, 1997), 94.

37. Johann Henrich Reitz, compiler of the *History of the Reborn,* attended Spener's collegium in Frankfurt in the early 1680s. See Douglas H. Shantz, "'Back to the Sources': Gottfried Arnold, Johann Henrich Reitz, and the Distinctive Program and Practice of Pietist Historical Writing," in C. Arnold Snyder, ed., *Commoners and Community* (Kitchener, ON: Pandora Press, 2002), 79.

38. Deppermann, *Johann Jakob Schütz*, 122.

39. Albrecht, *Johanna Eleonora Petersen*, 58–65. On Maria Juliana von Eyseneck's book, see Maria Juliana Baur von Eyseneck, *Biblischer Lehrgang im Christenthum mit Zugrundelegung des kleinen Katechismus Luthers*, ed. G. M. G. Bauer, with introductory foreword by Harms (Kiel: Schwers 1850).

40. See Albrecht, *Johanna Eleonora Petersen*, 65–69; Deppermann, *Johann Jakob Schütz*, 105–106; Wallmann, *Der Pietismus*, 96–98, 141–142.

41. Deppermann, *Johann Jakob Schütz*, 108–118. Deppermann notes, "Schütz's influence on the . . . Frankfurt Pietists is most evident in the case of Johanna Eleonora von Merlau."

42. Albrecht, *Johanna Eleonora Petersen*, 82–83.

43. For a gender study of Johanna Eleonora Petersen in English, see Ruth Albrecht, "Johanna Eleonora Petersen in the Context of Women's and Gender Studies," in Jonathan Strom, Hartmut Lehmann, and James Van Horn Melton, eds., *Pietism in Germany and North America, 1680–1820* (Farnham, UK: Ashgate, 2009), 71–84.

44. Albrecht, *Johanna Eleonora Petersen*, 337.

45. Ibid., 136–137, 245, 256–264.

46. Prisca Guglielmetti, "Nachwort," in Johanna Eleonora Petersen, *Leben, von ihr selbst mit eigener Hand aufgesetzet Autobiographie (1718)*, ed. Prisca Guglielmetti (Leipzig: Evangelische Verlagsanstalt, 2003), 91, 92.

47. Klaus Deppermann, "Pennsylvanien als Asyl des frühen deutschen Pietismus," *Pietismus und Neuzeit* 10 (1984): 192. Separatist Pietists migrated to regions with tolerant princes and/or city authorities, such as the Wetterau, Wittgenstein, Württemberg, or the New World.

48. Rudiger Mack, "Franz Daniel Pastorius—sein Einsatz für die Quäker," *Pietismus und Neuzeit* 15 (1989): 132–171. After legal studies in Strasbourg and Basel, Pastorius arrived in Frankfurt in April 1679 and joined the Saalhof community. He found lodging with Schütz and Fende.

49. Wallmann, *Der Pietismus*, 142, 145; Marion Dexter Learned, *The Life of Francis Daniel Pastorius, the Founder of Germantown* (Philadelphia: William J. Campbell, 1908), 85–89, 109, 116–117, www.archive.org/details/lifeoffrancisdan01lear.

50. Patrick M. Erben, " 'Honey-Combs' and 'Paper-Hives': Positioning Francis Daniel Pastorius's Manuscript Writings in Early Pennsylvania," *Early American Literature* 37, no. 2 (2002): 157–194.

51. Andreas Deppermann, *Johann Jakob Schütz*, 328–335; Klaus Deppermann, "Pennsylvanien als Asyl des frühen deutschen Pietismus," *Pietismus und Neuzeit* 10 (1984): 201, 205.

52. The influence of Anna Maria van Schurman and Antoinette Bourignon is discussed further in chapter 7.

53. Mirjam de Baar, "Internationale und interkonfessionelle Netzwerke: Zur frühen lutherisch pietistischen Rezeption von Anna Maria van Schurman und An-

toinette Bourignon," in Ulrike Gleixner and Erika Hebeisen, eds., *Gendering Tradition: Erinnerungskultur und Geschlecht im Pietismus* (Korb: Didymos-Verlag, 2007), 85–101, esp. 93. See Anna Maria van Schurman, *Whether a Christian Woman Should Be Educated and Other Writings from Her Intellectual Circle*, trans. Joyce L. Irwin (Chicago: University of Chicago Press, 1999).

54. Albrecht, *Johanna Eleonora Petersen*, 65–69.

55. Wallmann, *Der Pietismus*, 96; Deppermann, "Pennsylvanien als Asyl des frühen deutschen Pietismus," 192–193, 195–197.

56. Max Goebel, *Geschichte des christlichen Lebens in der rheinisch-westphälischen evangelischen Kirche* (Koblenz: Karl Bädeker, 1852), 2:561. See also Deppermann, *Johann Jakob Schütz*, 98.

57. Deppermann, *Johann Jakob Schütz*, 100, 107, 182–183, 188–189. The sixteenth-century Schwenkfelders practiced *Stillstand*, a suspension of sacramental observance until, through a program of catechism, churches consisted of reborn believers and the proper church order and leadership were established by Christ. See Douglas H. Shantz, *Crautwald and Erasmus: A Study in Humanism and Radical Reform in Sixteenth Century Silesia* (Baden-Baden: Valentin Koerner, 1992), 31, 67.

58. Deppermann, *Johann Jakob Schütz*, 123–125, 187–189. Fende's comments are in a letter dated in 1680 and reprinted in Johannes Wallmann, ed., *Philipp Jakob Spener: Briefe aus der Frankfurter Zeit, 1666–1686*, vol. 4, *1679–1680* (Tübingen: Mohr Siebeck, 2005), vi, 792–793. Fende came to Frankfurt in 1676 as a member of an imperial commission from Vienna. Schütz took Fende into his home, where he experienced a conversion. He became a Frankfurt citizen in 1679. The Frankfurt ministerium interrogated Fende in September 1683, and he left the city shortly after. Thomas Habegger, in Halle, is writing a dissertation on Fende: "Christian Fende: Ein radikaler Pietist und sein Wirken—mit besonderer Berücksichtigung kabbalistischer Einflüsse."

59. Deppermann, *Johann Jakob Schütz*, 190–205. In the fall of 1684, Schütz published anonymously his *Discourse on Whether God's Chosen Are Obligated to Belong to a Great Church and Religion of the Present Day*. A Frankfurt pastor published a critique in 1685, to which Schütz replied in a second edition of the work that same year. See also Wallmann, *Der Pietismus*, 142.

60. Wallmann, *Der Pietismus*, 99.

61. Greschat, *Christentumsgeschichte II*, 94–95; Wallmann, *Der Pietismus*, 128.

62. Hartmut Lehmann, *Pietismus und weltliche Ordnung in Württemberg vom 17. bis zum 20. Jahrhundert* (Stuttgart: Kohlhammer, 1969), 28–29, 93–94; Wallmann, *Der Pietismus*, 176–179, 206–207.

63. Deppermann, *Johann Jakob Schütz*, 158–163, 166–167; Brecht, "Philipp Jakob Spener, sein Programm," 296.

64. Deppermann, *Johann Jakob Schütz*, 172–180.

65. Ibid., 120–123.

66. Frances Elizabeth Cox, *Hymns from the German* (London: Rivingtons, 1864), 234–238. See appendix A for the complete hymn.

67. Deppermann, *Johann Jakob Schütz*, 168–171.

68. Ibid., 243–244, 336–351. See Willem Heijting, "Hendrick Beets (1625?–1708), Publisher to the German Adherents of Jacob Böhme in Amsterdam," *Quaerendo* 3 (1973): 250–280. Beets, or Betke, published a large number of Böhme's works in Amsterdam between 1658 and 1678.

69. Martin Brecht, "Philipp Jakob Spener, sein Programm und dessen Auswirkungen," in Martin Brecht et al., eds., *Der Pietismus vom siebzehnten bis zum frühen achtzehnten Jahrhundert* (Göttingen: Vandenhoeck & Ruprecht, 1993), 302. It is a common error to assume that Spener's foreword appeared in an edition of Arndt's *True Christianity*. Hartmut Lehmann makes this mistake in *Pietismus und weltliche Ordnung in Württemberg*, 28. More recently, Hartmut Krüger makes the same mistake in *Frauen im Pietismus: Ihr Dienst—ihr Verantwortung—ihr Einfluss* (Marburg: Francke, 2005), 44.

70. Klaus vom Orde, "Philipp Jakob Speners *Pia Desideria*: Glaube, Liebe und Hoffnung als Leitworte für die Hoffnung auf Gemeindeerneuerung," *Theologische Beiträge* 36, no. 6 (2005): 328.

71. Philipp Jakob Spener, *Pia Desideria: Deutsch-Lateinische Studienausgabe*, ed. Beate Köster (Giessen: Brunnen Verlag, 2005), 106.

72. Ibid., 6, 16, 106; Greschat, *Christentumsgeschichte II*, 95.

73. vom Orde, "Philipp Jakob Speners *Pia Desideria*," 327–341.

74. Wallmann, *Der Pietismus*, 80, 82, 84.

75. Spener, *Pia Desideria*, 6. See also Martin Schmidt, *Wiedergeburt und neuer Mensch* (Witten: Luther Verlag, 1969), 132.

76. Spener, *Pia Desideria*, 90, 92, 96–100.

77. Wallmann, *Philipp Jakob Spener und die Anfänge des Pietismus*, 341.

78. Wallmann, *Der Pietismus*, 84. For the prehistory of Spener's six recommendations, see Hans Leube, "Die Reformideen in der deutschen lutherischen Kirche zur Zeit der Orthodoxie (1924)," reprinted in Hans Leube, *Orthodoxie und Pietismus: Gesammelte Studien*, ed. Dietrich Blaufuß (Bielefeld: Luther-Verlag, 1975).

79. Spener, *Pia Desideria*, 108, 110.

80. Ibid., 112, 114, 116.

81. Ibid., 116, 118. See appendix A for the full quotation of Luther's words.

82. Wallmann, *Der Pietismus*, 26.

83. Spener, *Pia Desideria*, 122.

84. Ibid., 124, 126. Spener referred readers to Arndt's *True Christianity*, chaps. 22ff.

85. Spener, *Pia Desideria*, 128, 130, 132.

86. Ibid., 140, 142.

87. Ibid., 146, 152–156.

88. Ibid., 160, 162.

89. On the topic of influences on Spener's *Pia Desideria*: Erich Beyreuther points to the *Strassburg Recommendations*; Martin Schmidt highlights Hoburg's *Mirror*; Johannes Wallmann notes Breckling's *Mirror of the Pastors*; Carl Hinrichs and Martin

Schmidt point to Großgebauer's *Watchcry;* and Kurt Dietrich Schmidt and Wallmann point to Labadie's work.

90. Brecht, "Philipp Jakob Spener, sein Programm," 283; Wallmann, *Der Pietismus,* 85, 141. Wallmann argues that the idea for apostolic gatherings was passed on to Spener by Schütz. Such gatherings are not found in the Lutheran tradition.

91. Kurt Dietrich Schmidt, "Labadie u. Spener: Literarkritischer Vergleich der *Pia Desideria* Speners mit Labadies Schriften »La reformation de l'église par le pastorat« u. »L'exercice profétique,«" *Zeitschrift für KirchenGeschichte* (new series) 9, no. 46 (1927): 566–567n2. Schmidt suggests Sebastian Edzard, pastor in Hamburg, as the likely author of the 1734 tract.

92. Schmidt, "Labadie u. Spener," 568–570, 583.

93. Ibid., 571–577.

94. Ibid., 580–583.

95. Wallmann, *Der Pietismus,* 88–90. Spener received positive responses from pastors in Worms, Nuremberg, Darmstadt, Rothenburg ob der Tauber, Rostock, Brandenburg, and Gotha, and from Johann Fischer in Riga.

96. Brecht, "Philipp Jakob Spener, sein Programm," 311–313. See also Detlef Ignasiak, "Hoher Staatsbeamter und kritischer Schriftsteller: Der Lebensweg des Rudolstädter Kanzlers Ahasverus Fritsch," in Jürgen John, ed., *Kleinstaaten und Kultur in Thüringen vom 16. bis 20. Jahrhundert* (Weimar: Frommann-Holzboog Verlag, 1994), 139–159. Spener's supporters also included the Dresden court preachers Martin Geier (1614–1680) and his successor, Johann Andreas Lucius (1625–1686).

97. Brecht, "Philipp Jakob Spener, sein Programm," 313–315. Professors offering early support for Spener included Friedemann Bechmann in Jena, Abraham Calov in Wittenberg, Johann Benedict Carpzov in Leipzig, and Balthasar Raith in Tübingen.

98. Wallmann, *Der Pietismus,* 91.

99. Ibid., 128, 94. See also Ryoko Mori, *Begeisterung und Ernüchterung in christlicher Vollkommenheit* (Tübingen: Max Niemeyer Verlag, 2004).

100. Johannes Wallmann, "Vorwort," in Johannes Wallmann, ed., *Philipp Jakob Spener, Briefe aus der Frankfurter Zeit 1666–1686,* vol. 1, 1666–1674 (Tübingen: J. C. B. Mohr, 1992), v; Brecht, "Philipp Jakob Spener, sein Programm," 371, 373.

101. Martin Schmidt, "Der Pietismus als theologische Erscheinung," in Martin Schmidt, *Der Pietismus als Theologische Erscheinung: Gesammelte Studien zur Geschichte des Pietismus,* ed. K. Aland (Göttingen: Vandenhoeck & Ruprecht, 1984), 2:16–17.

102. Brecht observed that "the details of Spener's theology have by no means been adequately researched." Brecht, "Philipp Jakob Spener, sein Programm," 371, 373.

103. Wallmann, *Philipp Jakob Spener und die Anfänge des Pietismus,* 206; Johannes Wallmann, "Überlegungen und Vorschläge zu einer Edition des Spenerschen Briefwechsels, zunächst aus der Frankfurter Zeit (1666–1686)," *Pietismus und Neuzeit* 11 (1985): 346. Another systematic statement of Spener's thought is the 1677

"Simple Explanation of Christian Doctrine," based on Luther's *Small Catechism*. Spener's ethics can be found in a sermon collection entitled *Duties Belonging to an Evangelical Life* (1692).

104. Carl Hildebrand von Canstein completed these collections of Spener's letters after Spener's death. Together they include more than twenty-three hundred letters. Emanuel Hirsch observed that "one gets to know Spener, both as a man and as a theologian, solely from his many letters, words of advice, and opinions." Wallmann, "Vorwort," in *Philipp Jakob Spener, Briefe aus der Frankfurter Zeit 1666–1686*, 1:v.

105. In 1996, Wallmann announced the plan for a scholarly edition of all Spener's letters in three series (see the Introduction, n. 36 above). See Wallmann, "Vorwort," in *Philipp Jakob Spener, Briefe aus der Frankfurter Zeit 1666–1686*, 2:v.

106. Brecht, "Philipp Jakob Spener, sein Programm," 372–373. Brecht writes, "From the traditions passed down to him, above all Lutheran Orthodoxy, Arndt, and Luther, Spener developed the contours of his own theology suited to the church and the demands of the time. He wanted to retain a connection with tradition, but also to correct its deficiencies. Spener did not establish a theological school . . . but he created the basis upon which the next generation of Pietists could pursue theology within the church" (373).

107. Wallmann, *Der Pietismus*, 71; Hans Leube, "Die Geschichte der pietistischen Bewegung in Leipzig (1921)," in *Orthodoxie und Pietismus: Gesammelte Studien* (Bielefeld: Luther-Verlag, 1975), 167.

108. Brecht, "Philipp Jakob Spener, sein Programm," 374. See Wallmann, "Review of K. James Stein, *Philipp Jakob Spener: Pietist Patriarch*," 242–243. James Stein discusses Spener's thought under three headings: the new man, the new church, and the new world. See Stein, *Philipp Jakob Spener*, 183–255.

109. Brecht, "Philipp Jakob Spener, sein Programm," 373. Also see Wallmann, *Philipp Jakob Spener und die Anfänge des Pietismus*, 256–261. Luther discussed this third kind of Christian community in the foreword to the German Mass, in 1526.

110. Spener, *Pia Desideria*, 162.

111. Erhard Peschke, "Speners Wiedergeburtslehre und ihr Verhältnis zu Franckes Lehre von der Bekehrung," in Bernd Jaspert and Rudolf Mohr, eds., *Traditio—Krisis—Renovatio aus theologischer Sicht: Festschrift Winfried Zeller zum 65. Geburtstag* (Marburg: N. G. Elwert Verlag, 1976), 213–215; Schmidt, "Der Pietismus als theologische Erscheinung," 17–18.

112. Philipp Jakob Spener, *Letzte Theologische Bedencken und andere Brieffliche Antworten 1711*, pts. 1 and 2, ed. Dietrich Blaufuß and Peter Schicketanz (Hildesheim: Georg Olms Verlag, 1987), 17–22. Spener in no way despised the Petersens' doctrine of a coming millennial age; he saw much to recommend it and did not believe that those who taught it were mistaken. But neither could he give it complete approval.

113. Heike Krauter-Dierolf, *Die Eschatologie Philipp Jakob Speners: Der Streit mit der lutherischen Orthodoxie um die "Hoffnung besserer Zeiten"* (Tübingen: Mohr Siebeck, 2005), 79.

114. Ibid., 143–144.
115. Ibid., 330, 335, 336.
116. Ibid., 331–332, 339–340.
117. Deppermann, *Johann Jakob Schütz*, 125, 352, 354.
118. See Martin Friedrich, "Speners Leben, Werk und Bedeutung," in Dorothea Wendebourg, ed., *Philipp Jakob Spener—Leben, Werk, Bedeutung: Bilanz der Forschung nach 300 Jahren* (Tübingen: Max Niemeyer Verlag, 2007), 11.

Chapter 4. Conventicles and Conflicts in Leipzig and the Second Wave, 1684 to 1694

1. Martin Brecht, "August Hermann Francke und der Hallische Pietismus," in Martin Brecht et al., eds., *Der Pietismus vom siebzehnten bis zum frühen achtzehnten Jahrhundert* (Göttingen: Vandenhoeck & Ruprecht, 1993), 440.
2. See Tanya Kevorkian, *Baroque Piety: Religion, Society, and Music in Leipzig, 1650–1750* (Aldershot, UK: Ashgate, 2007); Claudia Wustmann, *Die "begeisterten Mägde": Mitteldeutsche Prophetinnen im Radikalpietismus am Ende des 17. Jahrhunderts* (Leipzig: Edition Kirchhof & Franke, 2008). Two key works on early Pietist conflicts in Leipzig are Hans Leube, "Die Geschichte der pietistischen Bewegung in Leipzig" (PhD diss., Leipzig University, 1921), reprinted in Hans Leube, *Orthodoxie und Pietismus: Gesammelte Studien*, ed. Dietrich Blaufuß (Bielefeld: Luther-Verlag, 1975); and Tanya Kevorkian, *Baroque Piety*.
3. Kevorkian, *Baroque Piety*, 169, 191.
4. Johannes Wallmann, "Erfurt und der Pietismus im 17. Jahrhundert," in Johannes Wallmann, *Theologie und Frömmigkeit im Zeitalter des Barock: Gesammelte Aufsätze* (Tübingen: Mohr Siebeck, 1995), 345.
5. Kevorkian, *Baroque Piety*, 19–20; Reinhard Wittmann, *Geschichte des deutschen Buchhandels: ein Überblick* (Munich: Beck, 1991); Martin Gierl, *Pietismus und Aufklärung: Theologische Polemik und die Kommunikationsreform der Wissenschaft am Ende des 17. Jahrhunderts* (Göttingen: Vandenhoeck & Ruprecht, 1997), 358.
6. George Stauffer, "Leipzig: A Cosmopolitan Trade Centre," in George Buelow, ed., *The Late Baroque Era: From the 1680s to 1740* (Englewood Cliffs, NJ: Prentice Hall, 1993), 254–295.
7. Kevorkian, *Baroque Piety*, 16, 18, 20–24.
8. Leube, "Die Geschichte der pietistischen Bewegung in Leipzig," 161–163.
9. Kevorkian, *Baroque Piety*, 30–33, 47.
10. Ibid., 31–33, 39, 47.
11. Ibid., 47–50.
12. Ibid., 33–34, 39–40.
13. Leube, "Die Geschichte der pietistischen Bewegung in Leipzig," 164.
14. Ibid., 166–168; Martin Brecht, "Philipp Jakob Spener, sein Programm und dessen Auswirkungen," in Brecht et al., *Der Pietismus vom siebzehnten bis zum frühen achtzehnten Jahrhundert*, 330.

15. Ibid., 168–170; Brecht, "Philipp Jakob Spener, sein Programm," 332. On Dresden Court Preachers, see Wolfgang Sommer, *Die lutherischen Hofprediger in Dresden: Grundzüge ihrer Geschichte und Verkündigung im Kurfürstentum Sachsen* (Stuttgart: Franz Steiner Verlag, 2006).

16. August Hermann Francke, "Herrn M. August Hermann Franckens vormahls Diaconi zu Erffurt . . . Lebenslauff (1691)," in Markus Matthias, ed., *Lebensläufe August Hermann Franckens* (Leipzig: Evangelische Verlagsanstalt, 1999), 9–12.

17. Brecht, "August Hermann Francke und der Hallische Pietismus," 440–441.

18. Ibid., 441–442; Johannes Wallmann, *Der Pietismus* (Göttingen: Vandenhoeck & Ruprecht, 2005), 106.

19. Kevorkian, *Baroque Piety*, 152.

20. Wallmann, *Der Pietismus*, 107.

21. Page numbers in the text refer to Francke, "Herrn M. August Hermann Franckens . . . Lebenslauff."

22. Francke writes, "Then I began anew to seek God with sincerity. But my search consisted more in outward things than inward. I would sing and pray often, read much in the Scriptures and other religious books, went often to church, repented of my outward sins and came with tears to confession, but my heart remained convinced that honors, wealth and a good life were not really sins." Ibid., 13.

23. One also finds this kind of question in the Puritan John Bunyan, reflecting the growing climate of religious diversity and skepticism.

24. Brecht, "August Hermann Francke und der Hallische Pietismus," 444–446; Wallmann, *Der Pietismus*, 108–110. On Louise Charbonnet, see Ulrike Witt, *Bekehrung, Bildung und Biographie: Frauen im Umkreis des Halleschen Pietismus* (Tübingen: Max Niemeyer Verlag, 1996), 184–194.

25. Martin Schmidt, *Pietismus* (Stuttgart: Verlag W. Kohlhammer, 1972), 65. The words in the text are Spener's.

26. Francke, "Herrn M. August Hermann Franckens . . . Lebenslauff," 31; Wallmann, *Der Pietismus*, 111.

27. Kevorkian, *Baroque Piety*, 152.

28. Wallmann, *Der Pietismus*, 111; Schmidt, *Pietismus*, 65.

29. Brecht, "Philipp Jakob Spener, sein Programm," 335. One student who sold his philosophy books was Johann Christian Lange. See Leube, "Die Geschichte der pietistischen Bewegung in Leipzig," 182–183.

30. Kevorkian, *Baroque Piety*, 152, 154, 163; Brecht, "August Hermann Francke und der Hallische Pietismus," 448. Two of the students were north Germans who had come to Leipzig to study at the urging of Francke; two were cousins. Many of the Pietist students remained close friends for the rest of their lives. Several, including Andreas Achilles, eventually joined Francke in Halle.

31. Kevorkian, *Baroque Piety*, 151, 154.

32. Brecht, "Philipp Jakob Spener, sein Programm," 336.

33. Kevorkian, *Baroque Piety*, 152–154. The interrogation protocols of fall 1689

and winter 1690 reveal much about the social makeup of the collegia and the network that united the participants.

34. Ibid., 152–154; Brecht, "Philipp Jakob Spener, sein Programm," 337. Just a few months earlier, in March 1693, Heinich had corresponded with Francke, assuring him of the warm regards of his Leipzig friends. Kevorkian, *Baroque Piety*, 180.

35. Jacob Ander Sohn Holsati [Christian Thomasius], *Sendschreiben auß Hamburg an einen vornehmen Freund von denen Leipzigischen Collegiis Biblicis, und daher so genanten Pietisten* (Hamburg, Sept. 20, 1690).

36. W. R. Ward, *The Protestant Evangelical Awakening* (Cambridge: Cambridge University Press, 1992), 59. There was a personal side to Carpzov's opposition to Spener. Carpzov had lost out to Spener in 1686 in the competition for the Saxon court chaplaincy.

37. *Gerichtliches Leipziger Protocoll in Sachen die so genandten Pietisten betreffend; samt. Hn. Christian Thomasii berühmten J.C. Rechtlichem Bedencken darüber; und zu Ende beygefügter Apologi oder Defensions-Schrifft Hr. M. Augusti Hermanni Franckens an Ihro Chur-Fürstl. Durchl. zu Sachsen; . . . von einem vornehmen Freund communicirt und herauß gegebenen* (1692).

38. Brecht, "Philipp Jakob Spener, sein Programm," 336–337, 448.

39. Kevorkian, *Baroque Piety*, 157–158, 161.

40. Ibid., 157–167, esp. 158.

41. *Gerichtliches Leipziger Protocoll in Sachen die so genandten Pietisten betreffend* (1692).

42. Karl Gottfried Goebel, *Johann Christian Lange (1669–1756): Seine Stellung zwischen Pietismus und Aufklärung* (Darmstadt: Verlag der Hessischen Kirchengeschichtlichen Vereinigung, 2004), 60.

43. Goebel, *Johann Christian Lange*, 61; Leube, "Die Geschichte der pietistischen Bewegung in Leipzig," 211, 237; Kevorkian, *Baroque Piety*, 179. Hans Schneider sees Johann Wilhelm Petersen as "an important link between Spener and Pietist enthusiasm." Hans Schneider, *German Radical Pietism*, trans. Gerald T. MacDonald (Lanham, MD: Scarecrow Press, 2007), 22.

44. Kevorkian, *Baroque Piety*, 153, 160–161.

45. Brecht, "August Hermann Francke und der Hallische Pietismus," 448, 449.

46. Ibid., 449.

47. Schmidt, *Pietismus*, 66.

48. Brecht, "August Hermann Francke und der Hallische Pietismus," 450.

49. Ibid., 451–452; Wallmann, *Der Pietismus*, 113.

50. Ryoko Mori, *Begeisterung und Ernüchterung in christlicher Vollkommenheit: Pietistische Selbst- und Weltwahrnehmungen im ausgehenden 17. Jahrhundert* (Tübingen: Max Niemeyer Verlag, 2004), 1.

51. Brecht, "Philipp Jakob Spener, sein Programm," 338.

52. The best source on Achilles is the "Curriculum Vitae" (*Lebens-Lauff*), a twelve-page manuscript composed by a colleague in Halle in August 1721, shortly

after Achilles died. See "Curriculum Vitae von M. Andreas Achilles," Archive of the Franckesche Stiftungen in Halle, AFSt/H D 90, 966–977.

53. *Ausführliche Beschreibung des Unfugs Welchen Die Pietisten zu Halberstadt im Monat Decembri 1692 umb die Heilige Weyhnachts-Zeit gestifftet* (1693), foreword, 3–5. See Hans Schneider, "Der radikale Pietismus im 17. Jahrhundert," in Brecht et al., *Der Pietismus vom siebzehnten bis zum frühen achtzehnten Jahrhundert*, 401, 426. Schneider suggested that the *Ausführliche Beschreibung* represented "one of the earliest and most comprehensive literary attacks on the Pietist movement. Spener and Francke felt obligated to reply to it" (401).

54. "Curriculum Vitae von M. Andreas Achilles," 977.

55. Ibid., 966. "Wie denn sein lieber Vater gewesen . . . Meister Eberhard Achilles, Bürger und Kürschner."

56. Ibid., 968, 969. The "Curriculum Vitae" suggests that Achilles had a positive impact on his parishioners, out of all proportion to the length of tenure of his ministry.

57. "Vorstellung pro informando . . . M. Achilles," sub dato den 14. Martii 1692 (written submission by Achilles to the Brandenburg authorities), Landesarchiv Magdeburg Rep. A 13, no. 870, vol. I, fol. l. 121v.

58. Ibid., fol. 121v, 123.

59. "Curriculum Vitae von M. Andreas Achilles," 974.

60. *Ausführliche Beschreibung*, 172. The Halle and Magdeburg Archives hold numerous archival sources, many of them court records, relating to Achilles's extended controversies in Leipzig, Quedlinburg, and Halberstadt.

61. Manfred Jakubowski-Tiessen, "Der Pietismus in Niedersachsen," in Martin Brecht and Klaus Deppermann eds., *Der Pietismus im achtzehnten Jahrhundert* (Göttingen: Vandenhoeck & Ruprecht, 1995), 440.

62. "Curriculum Vitae von M. Andreas Achilles," 969.

63. Ibid., 969, 970.

64. Ibid., 971.

65. Ibid., 967, 968.

66. *Ausführliche Beschreibung*, 120–123.

67. "Curriculum Vitae von M. Andreas Achilles," 970.

68. The *Lebens-Lauff* glosses over Achilles's conversion to radical Pietist spirituality while in Leipzig, as well as his involvement in conventicles in Quedlinburg and Halberstadt.

69. See Hans Schneider, "Die unerfüllte Zukunft: Apokalyptische Erwartungen im radikalen Pietismus um 1700," in Manfred Jakubowski-Tiessen, ed., *Jahrhundertwenden. Endzeit- und Zukunftsvorstellungen vom 15. bis zum 20. Jahrhundert* (Göttingen: Vandenhoeck & Ruprecht, 1999); Schneider, "Radikal Pietismus im 17. Jahrhundert," 401.

70. Kevorkian, *Baroque Piety*, 169–175.

71. Mori, *Begeisterung und Ernüchterung*, 1–2.

72. Kevorkian, *Baroque Piety*, 179–182.
73. Mori, *Begeisterung und Ernüchterung*, 2, 251–252.
74. Ibid., 2, 260.
75. Ibid., 2.

Chapter 5. Halle Pietism and Universal Social Reform, 1695 to 1727

1. Udo Sträter, "Soziales," in Hartmut Lehman, ed., *Glaubenswelt und Lebenswelten* (Göttingen: Vandenhoeck & Ruprecht, 2004), 617–619. See Carl Hinrichs, *Preußentum und Pietismus: Der Pietismus in Brandenburg-Preußen als religiös-soziale Reformbewegung* (Göttingen: Vandenhoeck & Ruprecht, 1971).

2. See, for example, Paul Raabe, ed., *Vier Thaler und sechzehn Groschen: August Hermann Francke, der Stifter und sein Werk* (Halle: Verlag der Franckeschen Stiftungen, 1998); Udo Sträter and Josef N. Neumann, eds., *Waisenhäuser in der Frühen Neuzeit* (Tübingen: Max Niemeyer Verlag, 2003); Claus Veltmann and Jochen Birkenmeier, eds., *Kinder, Krätze, Karitas: Waisenhäuser in der Frühen Neuzeit* (Halle: Verlag der Franckeschen Stiftungen, 2009).

3. Markus Meumann, *Findelkinder, Waisenhäuser, Kindsmord: Unversorgte Kinder in der frühneuzeitlichen Gesellschaft* (Munich: Oldenbourg Verlag, 1995); Thomas K. Kuhn, *Religion und neuzeitliche Gesellschaft: Studien zum sozialen und diakonischen Handeln in Pietismus, Aufklärung und Erweckungsbewegung* (Tübingen: Mohr Siebeck, 2003); Veronika Albrecht-Birkner, *Francke in Glaucha: Kehrseiten eines Klischees (1692–1704)* (Tübingen: Max Niemeyer Verlag, 2004).

4. Markus Meumann, "Unversorgte Kinder, Armenfürsorge und Waisenhausgründungen im 17. und 18. Jahrhundert," in Sträter and Neumann, *Waisenhäuser in der Frühen Neuzeit*, 8.

5. Kuhn, *Religion und neuzeitliche Gesellschaft*, 341; Albrecht-Birkner, *Francke in Glaucha*, 1–2, 115–116.

6. A. H. Francke, "Die Fußstapfen des noch lebenden und waltenden liebreichen und getreuen Gottes" (1701), in E. Peschke, ed., *August Hermann Francke, Werke in Auswahl* (Berlin: Luther-Verlag, 1969), 39.

7. Udo Sträter, "Vorwort," in Sträter and Neumann, *Waisenhäuser in der Frühen Neuzeit*, viii.

8. Joke Spaans, "Early Modern Orphanages between Civic Pride and Social Discipline: Francke's Use of Dutch Models," in Sträter and Neumann, *Waisenhäuser in der frühen Neuzeit*, 183. Also see Sträter, "Soziales," 628–629.

9. Albrecht-Birkner, *Francke in Glaucha*, 10.

10. Ibid., 3, 18–19. Francke initially taught in the philosophy faculty in Halle; he did not join the theology faculty until 1698. See Udo Sträter, "Drei Kollegen, als zu Halle Breithaupt, Anton und Francke," in Ralf-Thorsten Speler, ed., *Die Universität zu Halle und Franckens Stiftungen* (Halle: Martin Luther-Universität Halle-Wittenberg, 1998), 27.

11. Albrecht-Birkner, *Francke in Glaucha*, 11–12, 34.

12. The report was first published in 1863. August Hermann Francke, Letter of April 27, 1700, in Gustav Kramer, ed., *Vier Briefe August Hermann Franckes. Zur zweiten Säcularfeier seines Geburtstags* (Halle: Verlag der Buchhandlung des Waisenhauses, 1863), 28–76. See also G. Kramer, *August Hermann Francke: Ein Lebensbild* (Halle, 1880), 1:205–210. In the forty-nine-page report, thirty-eight pages are devoted to the first two questions: how God's word is proclaimed and how the sacraments are administered.

13. Francke, Letter of April 27, 1700, 61.

14. Ibid., 35, 74–75.

15. Martin Brecht, "August Hermann Francke und der Hallische Pietismus," in Martin Brecht et al., eds., *Der Pietismus vom siebzehnten bis zum frühen achtzehnten Jahrhundert* (Göttingen: Vandenhoeck & Ruprecht 1993), 456.

16. Francke, Letter of April 27, 1700, 31–32, 35.

17. Ibid., 74.

18. Albrecht-Birkner, *Francke in Glaucha*, 19–28.

19. Ibid., 30–31, 33–34.

20. Ibid., 90–91, 113, 116.

21. Ibid., 90–98, 105–110.

22. Veronika Albrecht-Birkner and Udo Sträter, "Die radikale Phase des frühen August Hermann Francke," in Wolfgang Breul, ed., *Der radikale Pietismus: Perspektiven der Forschung* (Göttingen: Vandenhoeck & Ruprecht, 2010), 61–63, 71, 80.

23. Albrecht-Birkner, *Francke in Glaucha*, 6–8, 16, 112.

24. Francke, "Die Fußstapfen des noch lebenden Gottes," 33, 55. The thaler was a silver coin used in Prussia until 1857. The name lives on in our English word *dollar*. The Groschen, the "fat penny" or large (*gros*) penny, arose in the thirteenth century. The German expression, "Jetzt ist bei mir der Groschen gefallen!" is equivalent to the English "Now the penny drops" or "Now I get it." See Helmut Caspar, *Vom Taler zum Euro: Die Berliner, ihr Geld und ihre Münze*, 2nd ed. (Berlin: Berlin Story Verlag, 2006).

25. D. Gustav Kramer, *August Hermann Francke: Ein Lebensbild* (Halle: Verlag der Buchhandlung des Waisenhauses, 1880), 169–170; Peschke, *August Hermann Francke*, 34, 57n3.

26. Udo Sträter, "Das Waisenhaus zu Glaucha vor Halle," in Veltmann and Birkenmeier, *Kinder, Krätze, Karitas*, 78. Sträter writes, "Behind the rapid growth of the foundations into a school-city, there stood not primarily a vision of care for the needy, but a theologically founded and pedagogically elaborated philosophy of nurture and education, 'guiding the children to true godliness and Christian intelligence.' " ["Hinter dem rapiden Wachstum der Anstalten zu einer Schulstadt stand nicht in erster Linie ein Versorgungs- sondern ein theologisch begründetes und pädagogisch umgesetztes Erziehungs- und Ausbildungskonzept, 'die Kinder zur wahren Gottseligkeit und Christlichen Klugheit anzuführen.' "] (78).

27. Ernst Bartz, *Die Wirtschaftsethik August Hermann Franckes* (Harburg-Wilhelmsburg: Wilhelm G. Frenk, 1934), 66ff.

28. Sträter, "Das Waisenhaus zu Glaucha," 77; Claus Veltmann and Jochen Birkenmeier, "Das Hallesche Waisenhaus von August Hermann Francke," in Veltmann and Birkenmeier, *Kinder, Krätze, Karitas,* 175.

29. Meumann, "Unversorgte Kinder," 2.

30. Bartz, *Die Wirtschaftsethik August Hermann Franckes,* 68, 83.

31. Ibid., 83–91. See appendix B for my translation of the "183 Questions."

32. Joke Spaans, "Dutch Orphanages in the Golden Age," in Veltmann and Birkenmeier, *Kinder, Krätze, Karitas,* 67–70.

33. Ibid., 72–74. See also Joke Spaans, "Early Modern Orphanages between Civic Pride and Social Discipline: Francke's Use of Dutch Models," in Sträter and Neumann, *Waisenhäuser in der Frühen Neuzeit,* 193–194.

34. Fred van Lieburg, "Niederländische Waisenhäuser und reformierter Pietismus im 17. Jahrhundert," in Sträter and Neumann, *Waisenhäuser in der Frühen Neuzeit,* 179–180.

35. Ibid., 174–175.

36. A. C. Duker, *Gisbertus Voetius* (Leiden: Brill, 1914), 3:141–142.

37. van Lieburg, "Niederländische Waisenhäuser," 175–178, 181; Joris van Eijnatten, *Liberty and Concord in the United Provinces: Religious Toleration and the Public in the Eighteenth-Century Netherlands* (Leiden: Brill, 2003), 57.

38. Spaans, "Early Modern Orphanages," 195–196.

39. This is the argument in Sträter, "Soziales," 640n13.

40. Bartz, *Die Wirtschaftsethik August Hermann Franckes,* 66–67.

41. Sträter, "Das Waisenhaus zu Glaucha," 78–79.

42. Ibid., 81–84.

43. Carter Lindberg, "The Lutheran Tradition," in Ronald L. Numbers and Darrel W. Amundsen, eds., *Caring and Curing: Health and Medicine in the Western Religious Traditions,* 2nd ed. (Baltimore: Johns Hopkins University Press, 1998), 185–188.

44. Sträter, "Das Waisenhaus zu Glaucha," 79–81. Francke explained in 1711 that the Halle Foundations were free of any papal superstition and were a source of prosperity to the region, not a burden.

45. Pages in the text refer to Otto Podczeck, ed., *August Hermann Franckes Schrift über eine Reform des Erziehungs- und Bildungswesens als Ausgangspunkt einer geistlichen und sozialen Neuordnung der Evangelischen Kirche des 18. Jahrhunderts: Der Grosse Aufsatz* (Berlin: Akademie-Verlag, 1962).

46. Brecht, "August Hermann Francke und der Hallische Pietismus," 519–520.

47. Juliane Jacobi and Thomas J. Müller-Bahlke, eds., *"Man hatte von ihm gute Hoffnung": Das Waisenalbum der Franckeschen Stiftungen 1695–1749* (Tübingen: Verlag der Franckeschen Stiftungen zu Halle, 1998).

48. Juliane Jacobi, " 'Man hatte von ihm gute Hoffnung': Die soziale Kontur der Halleschen Waisenkinder," in Sträter and Neumann, *Waisenhäuser in der Frühen Neuzeit,* 53, 54.

49. Ibid., 60–61, 66–69. The boys remained in the orphanage for about three and a half years, the girls for almost four years. But for 30% of cases the information is incomplete.

50. Ibid., 56–57. The profession of the child's father is noted in the album in almost every case.

51. Albrecht-Birkner, *Francke in Glaucha,* 13–14.

52. Jacobi, "'Man hatte von ihm gute Hoffnung,'" 63–64.

53. Juliane Dittrich-Jacobi, "Pietismus und Pädagogik im Konstitutionsprozeß der bürgerlichen Gesellschaft: Historisch-systematische Untersuchung der Pädagogik August Hermann Franckes (1663–1727)" (PhD diss., Faculty for Pedagogy, Philosophy, and Psychology, Bielefeld University, Apr. 1976), 130. A significant number of orphans and schoolboys went on to study theology, as expected, but later returned to the university to pursue their own interests, often to study medicine.

54. Claus Veltmann and Jochen Birkenmeier, "Einführung," in Veltmann and Birkenmeier, *Kinder, Krätze, Karitas,* 10; Ben Marschke, "Review of Sträter and Neumann, eds., *Waisenhäuser in der Frühen Neuzeit,*" *Pietismus und Neuzeit* 31 (2005): 232.

55. Jacobi, "'Man hatte von ihm gute Hoffnung,'" 61–62. See Jürgen Helm, "'Kein Bürger tractiret seine Kinder so': Das kranke Kind in den Anstalten des Halleschen Waisenhauses," in Joseph N. Neumann and Udo Sträter, eds., *Das Kind in Pietismus und Aufklärung* (Tübingen: Mohr Siebeck, 2000).

56. Jacobi, "'Man hatte von ihm gute Hoffnung,'" 54.

57. Veltmann and Birkenmeier, "Das Hallesche Waisenhaus von August Hermann Francke," 190–191.

58. Eckhard Altmann, *Christian Friedrich Richter (1676–1711): Arzt, Apotheker und Liederdichter des Halleschen Pietismus* (Witten: Luther-Verlag, 1972), 7. See also Gustav Knuth, *A. H. Franckes Mitarbeiter an seinen Stiftungen* (Halle: Waisenhaus, 1898), 18–54, 85–99.

59. Altmann, *Christian Friedrich Richter,* 29n73. This group of associates included Heinrich Julius Elers, director of the Halle press; Georg Heinrich Neubauer; Christian Friedrich Richter; Sigismund Richter; Justinus Töllner (1656–1718), who taught at the Latin and German schools; Johann Albert Fabricius; Hieronymus Freyer (1675–1747), who taught at the Pädagogium regium and became inspector in 1705; and Huth, Kock, and Eckebrecht. Other valued colleagues were Johann Anastasius Freylinghausen, Carl Hildebrand von Canstein, and Daniel Herrnschmid (1675–1723); Herrnschmid became assistant director of the orphanage and Pädagogium in 1716.

60. Bartz, *Die Wirtschaftsethik August Hermann Franckes,* 73, 77; Thomas J. Müller-Bahlke, "Die frühen Verwaltungsstrukturen der Franckeschen Stiftungen," in Sträter and Neumann, *Waisenhäuser in der Frühen Neuzeit,* 42–44.

61. In his last testament, Neubauer wrote, "I wish to be buried in complete silence. I want no songs, words of thanks, or sermon of remembrance. I was born in

1666 in Desdorf in Halberstädt. When I die, this is enough of my life story. What little I own of books, clothes, bed, linen, and tools, I leave to my elderly ninety-three-year-old Mother." Bartz, *Die Wirtschaftsethik August Hermann Franckes,* 73.

62. Albrecht-Birkner and Sträter, "Die radikale Phase des frühen August Hermann Francke," 82.

63. Brecht, "August Hermann Francke und der Hallische Pietismus," 484–485. See the catalogue of Halle publications up to the time of Elers's death: Brigitte Klosterberg and Anke Mies, eds., *Der Verlag der Buchhandlung des Waisenhauses zu Halle: Bibliographie der Drucke 1698–1728* (Tübingen: Max Niemeyer Verlag, 2009).

64. Brecht, "August Hermann Francke und der Hallische Pietismus," 485.

65. Podczeck, *Der Grosse Aufsatz,* 149.

66. See Joachim Böhme, "Heinrich Julius Elers und die wirtschaftlichen Projekte des Hallischen Pietismus," *Jahrbuch für die Geschichte Mittel- und Ostdeutschlands* 8 (1959): 121–186.

67. Altmann, *Christian Friedrich Richter,* 17, 20–23, 33–37. Richter finally completed his medical degree in 1706. His weak constitution may account for his medical interests.

68. Ibid., 45–49, 53–54, 85–86, 93.

69. Bartz, *Die Wirtschaftsethik August Hermann Franckes,* 73–76. The *Essentia dulcis* brought in 9,000 thaler per year from 1710 to 1720; 1,500 thaler per year from 1720 to 1730; 20,500 thaler per year from 1730 to 1740. By 1761 it was bringing in 36,000 thaler per year.

70. *Lyra Germanica: Hymns for the Sundays and Chief-Festivals of the Christian Year, First Series,* trans. Catherine Winkworth (London: Longman, Brown, Green and Longmans, 1855), 236–238. See also "Richter, Christian Friedrich," in John D. Julian, ed., *A Dictionary of Hymnology: Origin and History of Christian Hymns and Hymnwriters of All Ages and Nations* (London: John Murray, 1907), 2:959, 960.

71. Altmann, *Christian Friedrich Richter,* 37–38; Brecht, "August Hermann Francke und der Hallische Pietismus," 488.

72. Altmann, *Christian Friedrich Richter,* 216–217.

73. Ibid., 88, 92, 95–96.

74. Ibid., 100, 104–105.

75. Ibid., 23, 31, 117.

76. Sträter, "Drei Kollegen," 26–27, 30. Other great names would follow at the university, such as Joachim Lange (1670–1744), who joined the Halle faculty in 1709 and produced a host of works defending Halle Pietism against Orthodox figures such as Valentin Ernst Löscher and against Enlightenment thinkers such as Christian Thomasius. Lange published an eight-volume biblical commentary, *Biblical Light and Law* (1726–1738). In 1723, Johann Jakob Rambach (1693–1735) joined the faculty as theology professor, and he assumed Francke's chair when Francke died in 1727. Johannes Wallmann, *Der Pietismus* (Göttingen: Vanden-

hoeck & Ruprecht, 2005), 124–127. See portraits of the theologians at Halle University in 1775 in Brecht, "August Hermann Francke und der Hallische Pietismus," 455.

77. Wallmann, *Der Pietismus*, 125. In a letter to his mother, dated June 17, 1713, Bengel wrote, "What pleases me most is the harmony among these men, which they seek to maintain through communal prayer." See Johann Christian Friedrich Burk, *Dr. Johann Albrecht Bengel's Leben und Wirken meißt nach handscriftlichen Materialien* (Stuttgart: Johann Friedrich Steinkopf, 1831), 32.

78. Sträter, "Drei Kollegen," 36.

79. Bartz, *Die Wirtschaftsethik August Hermann Franckes*, 67.

80. Ibid., 18–21, 46–47.

81. Ibid., 39–42. Francke wrote, "A person cannot exist without rest, but it should be limited to the minimum."

82. Ibid., 33–34, 46, 50.

83. Renate Wilson, "Replication Reconsidered: Imitations, Models, and the Seeds of Modern Philanthropy," in Sträter and Neumann, *Waisenhäuser in der frühen Neuzeit*, 202.

84. Dittrich-Jacobi, "Pietismus und Pädagogik," 129.

85. Bartz, *Die Wirtschaftsethik August Hermann Franckes*, 55–56. See appendix A for a complete list of Francke's twenty-four reasons.

86. Ibid., 56.

87. Sträter, "Soziales," 638.

88. This includes statesmen such as Ludwig Veit von Seckendorf, the Rudolstädt chancellor Ahasver Fritsch, Enno Rudolph Brenneysen in Ostfriesland, and Otto Heinrich Becker in Waldeck.

89. Benjamin Marschke, "Halle Pietism and the Prussian State: Infiltration, Dissent, and Subversion," in Jonathan Strom, Hartmut Lehmann, and James Van Horn Melton, eds., *Pietism in Germany and North America, 1680–1820* (Farnham, UK: Ashgate, 2009), 219–220.

90. This authority was also granted to the Berlin chaplain Lampertus Gedicke.

91. Peter G. Wallace, "Review of Benjamin Marschke, *Absolutely Pietist: Patronage, Factionalism, and State Building in the Early Eighteenth-Century Prussian Army Chaplaincy* (Tübingen: Max Niemeyer Verlag, 2005)," *Central European History* 41, no. 2 (2008): 300–301.

92. Marschke, "Halle Pietism and the Prussian State," 228, 218–219.

93. Antje Fasshauer, "Ausstrahlung des Halleschen Waisenhauses ins Alte Reich," in Veltmann and Birkenmeier, *Kinder Krätze, Karitas*, 98. Of 220 orphanages founded between 1695 and 1806, 50 looked to Halle for inspiration.

94. Sträter, "Soziales," 632–633.

95. Udo Sträter, "Wilhelm Christian Schneider und das Waisenhaus in Esens," in Sträter and Neumann, *Waisenhäuser in der Frühen Neuzeit*, 73–74.

96. Sträter, "Soziales," 633; Sträter, "Wilhelm Christian Schneider," 80–81, 85.

97. Sträter, "Wilhelm Christian Schneider," 75–79, 92.

98. Ibid., 86–87, 90–93.

99. Ibid., 93.

100. Jochen Birkenmeier, "Die weltweite Ausstrahlung des Halleschen Waisenhauses," in Veltmann and Birkenmeier, *Kinder, Krätze, Karitas,* 101, 103–104

101. Ibid., 104–105 The Halle Reports are available online at www.francke-halle.de/main/index2.php?cf=3_1_3_3_2.

102. Birkenmeier, "Die weltweite Ausstrahlung des Halleschen Waisenhauses," 105.

103. Ibid., 106–107. See also Daniel Vesely, "Mattiaas Bel und der Einfluß des hallischen Pietismus auf Kirche und Schulwesen der Slowakei," in Johannes Wallmann and Udo Sträter, eds., *Halle und Osteuropa: Zur europäischen Ausstrahlung des hallischen Pietismus* (Tübingen: Max Niemeyer Verlag, 1998), 243–261.

104. Dorothea Schröder, *Georg Friedrich Händel* (Munich: Verlag C. H. Beck, 2008), 18–19, 70.

105. Birkenmeier, "Die weltweite Ausstrahlung des Halleschen Waisenhauses," 108–109; Veltmann and Birkenmeier, "Die Ausstrahlung des Halleschen Waisenhauses," 198–200. For recent scholarship on Handel's religion, see Ruth Smith, "Messiah," in Annette Landgraf and David Vickers, eds., *The Cambridge Handel Encyclopedia* (Cambridge: Cambridge University Press, 2009).

106. Wilson, "Replication Reconsidered," 203–210. See Hans-Jürgen Grabbe, ed., *Halle Pietism, Colonial North America, and the Young United States* (Stuttgart: Franz Steiner Verlag, 2008). The articles in this collection were first presented at a conference in 2002. The authors draw on a variety of methods and sources to illustrate the "full panoply of Halle-inspired activities" (9).

107. Birkenmeier, "Die weltweite Ausstrahlung des Halleschen Waisenhauses," 105–107. See Edward J. Cashin, *Beloved Bethesda: A History of George Whitefield's Home for Boys 1740–2000* (Macon, GA: Mercer University Press, 2001).

108. Kuhn, *Religion und neuzeitliche Gesellschaft,* 10–11.

Chapter 6. Radical German Pietism in Europe and North America

1. Albrecht Ritschl, *Geschichte des Pietismus in der lutherischen Kirche des 17. und 18. Jahrhunderts* (Bonn: Adolph Marcus, 1880–1886), 2:323, 339, 349, 353, 364, 424, 426, 552, 588; Peter C. Erb, ed., *Pietists: Selected Writings* (New York: Paulist Press, 1983); F. Ernest Stoeffler, *German Pietism during the Eighteenth Century* (Leiden: E. J. Brill, 1973).

2. Hans Schneider, *German Radical Pietism,* trans. Gerald T. MacDonald (Lanham, MD: Scarecrow Press, 2007), 19, 20, 184. This book contains Schneider's surveys of Radical Pietism research from the journal *Pietismus und Neuzeit* in 1982 and 1983 and his chapters from vols. 1 and 2 of *History of Pietism,* published in 1993 and 1995. Martin Brecht, Klaus Deppermann, Ulrich Gäbler, and Hartmut Lehmann, eds., *History of Pietism [Geschichte des Pietismus],* vols. 1–4 (Göttingen: Van-

denhoeck & Ruprecht (1993, 1995, 2000, and 2004). Also valuable are Schneider's collected essays, some of them in English, on figures such as Gottfried Arnold, Ernst Christoph Hochmann von Hochenau, Eberhard Ludwig Gruber, and Alexander Mack. See Hans Schneider, *Gesammelte Aufsätze I. Der Radikale Pietismus*, ed. Wolfgang Breul and Lothar Vogel (Leipzig: Evangelische Verlagsanstalt, 2011).

3. Schneider, *German Radical Pietism*, 184. Radical Reformed Pietists, such as Heinrich Horch and Johann Henrich Reitz, had ties to the Reformed Church Pietist Theodor Undereyck.

4. Ibid., 188–190.

5. Ibid., 29. See also Schneider, 151–152, 160. For Hanspeter Marti's Arnold scholarship and an edition of Gottfried Arnold's autobiographical *Offenhertzige Bekäntniß* (1698), see Antje Mißfeldt, ed., *Gottfried Arnold: Radikaler Pietist und Gelehrter. Jubiläumsgabe von und für Dietrich Blaufuß und Hanspeter Marti* (Cologne: Böhlau, 2011). For a bibliography of Arnold research, see Dietrich Blaufuß and Friedrich Niewöhner, eds., *Gottfried Arnold (1666–1714): Mit einer Bibliographie der Arnold-Literatur ab 1714* (Wiesbaden: Harrassowitz, 1995).

6. Schneider, *German Radical Pietism*, 120, 204–205. See also Isabelle Noth, *Ekstatischer Pietismus: Die Inspirationsgemeinden und ihre Prophetin Ursula Meyer (1682–1743)* (Göttingen: Vandenhoeck & Ruprecht, 2005).

7. Schneider, *German Radical Pietism*, 205–207. See Emanuel Hirsch, *Geschichte der neuern evangelischen Theologie im Zusammenhang mit den allgemeinen Bewegungen des europäischen Denkens* (Gütersloh: Gerd Mohn, 1951), 2:405–406.

8. Wolfgang Breul, Marcus Meier, and Lothar Vogel, eds., *Der radikale Pietismus: Perspektiven der Forschung* (Göttingen: Vandenhoeck & Ruprecht, 2010). The book consists of twenty-five papers from a conference held at Philipps University in Marburg in March 2007.

9. Hans Schneider, "Der radikale Pietismus in der neueren Forschung," *Pietismus und Neuzeit* 9 (1983): 150.

10. Hans Schneider, "Rückblick und Ausblick," in Breul et al., *Der radikale Pietismus*: 454. Monographs in English include Jeff Bach, *Voices of the Turtledoves: The Sacred World of Ephrata* (University Park: University of Pennsylvania Press, 2003); Marcus Meier, *The Origin of the Schwarzenau Brethren* (Philadelphia: Brethren Encyclopedia, 2008); and Douglas H. Shantz, *Between Sardis and Philadelphia: The Life and World of Pietist Court Preacher Conrad Bröske* (Leiden: Brill, 2008).

11. Schneider, "Rückblick und Ausblick," 455–456.

12. Ibid., 458–459. See also Hans Schneider, "Separatisten/Separatismus," *Die Theologische Realenzyklopädie* 31 (1999): 153–160.

13. Schneider, "Rückblick und Ausblick," 460. Schneider is preparing a Radical Pietism bibliography of primary and secondary sources. See Schneider, *German Radical Pietism*, 73n16.

14. Schneider, "Rückblick und Ausblick," 466. A thirty-two-page selection from Marsay's German autobiography is available in Jost Klammer, *Der Perner von Arfeld* (Bad Berleburg-Arfeld: Selbstverlag, 1983), 84–115.

15. Schneider, *German Radical Pietism*, 129, 132. Groß settled in Frankfurt in 1710, becoming "the most influential figure among the separatists in Frankfurt." Thomas Habegger, in Halle, is writing a dissertation on Fende entitled "Christian Fende (1651–1746): Ein radikaler Pietist und sein Wirken—mit besonderer Berücksichtigung kabbalistischer Einflüsse."

16. Schneider, *German Radical Pietism*, 158.

17. Schneider, "Rückblick und Ausblick," 463–466.

18. Johannes Wallmann, "Kirchlicher und radikaler Pietismus: Zu einer kirchengeschichtlichen Grundunterscheidung," in Breul et al., *Der radikale Pietismus*, 22, 24–28. Hans Schneider follows Wallmann in seeing Labadie as the key source for both Lutheran and Reformed Pietism in German lands. In 1911, Wilhelm Goeters traced the beginnings of Pietism in the Reformed churches of the Netherlands to Jean de Labadie and his emphasis on conventicles and gatherings of the godly outside regular church services.

19. Wallmann, "Kirchlicher und radikaler Pietismus," 29–30. See the website of the J. Paul Getty Museum regarding an exhibit at the Getty Center in Los Angeles: "Maria Sibylla Merian (1647–1717) and Daughters: Women of Art and Science, June 10–August 31, 2008," www.getty.edu/art/exhibitions/merian.

20. Wallmann, "Kirchlicher und radikaler Pietismus," 30–31.

21. See Andreas Deppermann, *Johann Jakob Schütz und die Anfänge des Pietismus* (Tübingen: Mohr Siebeck, 2002). Wallmann calls the work of Andreas Deppermann on Schütz "the foundational book on the beginnings of Radical Pietism within Lutheranism." Johannes Wallmann, *Der Pietismus* (Göttingen: Vandenhoeck & Ruprecht, 2005), 138n4.

22. Wallmann, "Kirchlicher und radikaler Pietismus," 35–36. Hans Schneider also sees Johann Jakob Schütz as the founder of Frankfurt Pietism; Radical Pietism thus preceded Church Pietism. See Schneider, "Rückblick und Ausblick," 456–457.

23. Wallmann, "Kirchlicher und radikaler Pietismus," 37–38.

24. Hartmut Lehmann, "Die langfristigen Folgen der kirchlichen Ausgrenzung des radikalen Pietismus," in Breul et al., *Der radikale Pietismus*, 46, 47–48. See also John Coffey, *Persecution and Toleration in Protestant England, 1558–1689* (London: Longman, 2000).

25. On constitutional separation of church and state in the United States, see Thomas J. Curry, *The First Freedoms: Church and State in America to the Passage of the First Amendment* (New York: Oxford University Press, 1986); William G. McLoughlin, *New England Dissent, 1630–1833: The Baptists and the Separation of Church and State* (Cambridge, MA: Harvard University Press, 1971). Also see Sidney E. Mead's classic book *The Lively Experiment: The Shaping of Christianity in America* (New York: Harper and Row, 1963).

26. Hartmut Lehmann, "Continental Protestant Europe," in Stewart J. Brown and Timothy Tackett, eds., *The Cambridge History of Christianity*, vol. 7, *Enlightenment, Reawakening, and Revolution, 1660–1815* (Cambridge: Cambridge University Press, 2006), 41.

27. Lehmann, "Die langfristigen Folgen," 46–50, 52, 54.

28. Ibid., 48, 54.

29. Ryoko Mori, *Begeisterung und Ernüchterung in christlicher Vollkommenheit: Pietistische Selbst- und Weltwahrnehmungen im ausgehenden 17. Jahrhundert* (Tübingen: Max Niemeyer Verlag, 2004), 1; Claudia Wustmann, *Die "begeisterten Mägde": Mitteldeutsche Prophetinnen im Radikalpietismus am Ende des 17. Jahrhunderts* (Leipzig: Edition Kirchhof & Franke, 2008), 17–18.

30. Schneider, "Rückblick und Ausblick," 451.

31. Schneider, *German Radical Pietism*, 79–99, 105–133, 207.

32. Marcus Meier, *Die Schwarzenauer Neutäufer: Genese einer Gemeindebildung zwischen Pietismus und Täufertum* (Göttingen: Vandenhoeck & Ruprecht, 2008), 176–178, 267.

33. Ibid., 139–140, 174–178.

34. Williams drew on Max Weber and Ernst Troeltsch. "With the fresh understanding of the inner nature of a true Sect derived from Max Weber and with Alfred Hegler's clarification of the difference between a Sectarian and a Spiritualist, Ernst Troeltsch worked out his tripartite scheme in which the Spiritualists are a third distinct type co-ordinate with the Sect type and the Church type." George H. Williams, "Introduction," in *Spiritual and Anabaptist Writers* (Philadelphia: Westminster Press, 1957), 26–28. See also Ernst Troeltsch, *The Social Teachings of the Christian Churches* (New York: Macmillan, 1931), 1:378.

35. Hans Schneider sees the Schwarzenau Brethren as a sectarian form of Radical Pietism and the Spiritualists and "separatist loners" as examples of the mystic type. See Schneider, *German Radical Pietism*, 207.

36. Johann Henrich Reitz, "Vorrede an den Christlichen Leser," *I. Theil der Historie Der Wiedergebohrnen*, ed. Hans-Jürgen Schrader (Tübingen: Max Niemeyer, 1982 reprint).

37. Alexander Mack explained in his letter of 1708, "If we begin in the footsteps of the Lord Jesus to live according to His commandment, then we can also hold communion together in the fear of the Lord." See Alexander Mack, *Complete Writings of Alexander Mack, Sr.*, ed. W. R. Eberly (Winona Lake, IN: BMH Books, 1991), 9–12.

38. Hochmann von Hochenau "stood opposed to the community of the New Baptists that arose from the ranks of former Spiritualists." Schneider, *German Radical Pietism*, 92.

39. Ibid., 117–118. Samuel König, court preacher to Count Ernst Casimir of Ysenburg-Büdingen from 1711 to 1715, "never surrendered his basic Philadelphian and chiliastic convictions" (82).

40. Ibid., 105–106, 107–108, 121–124.

41. For background on Johann Arndt, Jakob Böhme, Jane Leade, and the Philadelphians, see chapter 1.

42. Karl Gottfried Goebel describes Johann Christian Lange in Idstein as an eclectic thinker who developed a theology rooted in experiment and experience. For Goebel, Lange was a trailblazer of the German Enlightenment. See Karl Gottfried Goebel, *Johann Christian Lange (1669–1756): Seine Stellung zwischen Pietismus und*

Aufklärung (Darmstadt: Verlag der Hessischen Kirchengeschichtlichen Vereinigung, 2004), 325, 331.

43. Hans Schneider notes the Radicals' "detached treatment" of the Reformation heritage and "relativizing of confessional boundaries." Schneider, *German Radical Pietism*, 158–159.

44. See Shantz, *Between Sardis and Philadelphia*, xxii–xxiv, 254–257.

45. Donald F. Durnbaugh, "Work and Hope: The Spirituality of the Radical Pietist Communitarians," *Church History* 39 (1970): 72–90, esp. 85–90. Durnbaugh investigated a variety of groups, including "Woman in the Wilderness," "The Harmony Society," and "The Community of True Inspiration."

46. Wallmann, *Der Pietismus*, 144. Wallmann cites Emanuel Hirsch, *Geschichte der neuern Evangelischen Theologie im Zusammenhang mit den allgemeinen Bewegungen des europäischen Denkens* (Gütersloh: Gerd Mohn, 1975), 2:259.

47. Wallmann, *Der Pietismus*, 147–149.

48. Ibid., 148.

49. Hans Schneider, "Der radikale Pietismus im 18. Jahrhundert," in Martin Brecht, ed., *Der Pietismus im 18. Jahrhundert* (Göttingen: Vandenhoeck & Ruprecht, 1995), 115.

50. Johann Wilhelm Petersen, *Das Leben Jo. Wilhelmi Petersen, Der Heil. Schrifft Doctoris, Vormahls Professoris zu Rostock, nachgehends Predigers in Hannover an St. Egidii Kirche, darnach des Bischoffs in Lübeck, Superintendentis und Hof-Predigers, endlich Superintendentis in Lüneburg, Als Zeugens der Warheit Christi und seines Reiches, nach seiner grossen Oeconomie in der Wiederbringung aller Dinge* (1717), 345, 346, 347. Page numbers in the text refer to this source (*Das Leben*). Petersen wrote *Das Leben* in response to the many requests he received asking him to describe the course of his life and how he experienced the providence and leading of God (ibid., 1–2.). For Petersen's journeys to Altdorf, Nuremberg, Herolsberg and Württemberg, see ibid., 282–307; for his trip to Silesia, 308–322; and for his visits to Carlsbad, Zeitz, Halle, and Berlin, 324–333.

51. Herolsberg (Heroldsberg) is located in the Sebald Reichswald near Nuremberg. In 1806 it became part of Bayern. See Gerhard Köbler, *Historisches Lexikon der deutschen Länder*, 6th ed. (Munich: C. H. Beck, 1999), 250.

52. Petersen said his reason for moving from Nieder-Dodeleben to Thymer was that many of the people who came to visit him in the former residence came "in the name of Christ, yet did not have Christ in their heart." The move was also prompted by the restless farmhands on the estate at Nieder-Dodeleben. Petersen, *Das Leben*, 327.

53. Zeitz was at one time the seat of the Bishop of Naumberg. From 1653 to 1716, Zeitz was the seat of an alternate Saxon line, Sachsen-Zeitz. See Köbler, *Historisches Lexikon*, 745.

54. "God the Lord has wonderfully revealed to my wife and me this truth of the eternal Gospel . . . and has given us the joy of publicly confessing it. Therefore my wife first wrote about it, and had it published in octavo; then I wrote to defend

it in three volumes published in folio." Petersen, *Das Leben*, 297. Petersen's three volumes of *Wiederbringung aller Dinge* appeared between 1700 and 1710.

55. Ferdinand Helfreich Lichtscheid was the author of *Christliche Gedancken über das Büchlein vom ewigen Evangelio, der allgemeinen Wiederbringung aller Creaturen* (Zeitz: Melchior Hucho, 1700).

56. Eberhard Ludwig Gruber, *Nöthiges und nützliches Gespräch, von der wahren und falschen Inspiration* (1716). See Janet W. Zuber, ed. and trans., *Barbara Heinemann Landmann Biography: E. L. Gruber's Teachings on Divine Inspiration and Other Essays* (Amana, IA: Amana Church Society, 1981); Walter Grossmann, "Gruber on the Discernment of True and False Inspiration," *Harvard Theological Review* 81, no. 4 (1988): 363–387.

57. See references to letters of J. E. von Naumeister and of Carl Christian von Goldstein to August Hermann Francke in the manuscript databank of the Francke Foundations in Halle, http://192.124.243.55/cgi-bin/gkdb.pl.

58. Hans-Jürgen Schrader, "Traveling Prophets: Inspirationists Wandering through Europe and to the New World," in Jonathan Strom, Hartmut Lehmann, and James Van Horn Melton, eds., *Pietism in Germany and North America, 1680–1820* (Farnham, UK: Ashgate, 2009), 110–113, 121.

59. For studies of Rock and the True Inspiration, see Hans Schneider, "Inspirationsgemeinden," *Die Theologische Realenzyklopädie* 16 (1987): 203–206; Max Goebel and Theodor Link, *Geschichte des christlichen Lebens in der rheinisch-westfälischen evangelischen Kirche* (Koblenz: Karl Bädeker, 1860), 3:126–165; Noth, *Ekstatischer Pietismus*.

60. Paul Krauss, "Johann Friedrich Rock: Separatist und Inspirierter," in Max Miller, ed., *Lebensbilder aus Schwaben und Franken* (Stuttgart: W. Kohlhammer, 1983), 15:99. Wallmann cites Krauss's estimations of journeys made by Rock without acknowledgment. See Wallmann, *Der Pietismus*, 179.

61. Schneider, "Der radikale Pietismus im 18. Jahrhundert," 147. In the early years there may have been more than three hundred members. In the 1730s, Edelmann suggested the number was "scarcely fifty." Ibid., 151.

62. *Anfänge des Erniedrigungs-Lauffs Eines Sünders auf Erden in- und durch Gnade* (1707) and *Zweyter Aufsatz des Erniedrigungs-Lauffs Eines Sünders auf Erden* (1717). For an English translation, see Johann Friedrich Rock, *The Humble Way: An Autobiographical Account of God's Guidance*, trans. Janet W. Zuber (Amana, IA: Amana Church Society, 1999).

63. These autobiographical sources by Rock are available in a new critical edition. Ulf-Michael Schneider, ed., *Johann Friedrich Rock, Wie ihn Gott geführet und auf die Wege der Inspiration gebracht habe: Autobiographische Schriften* (Leipzig: Evangelische Verlagsanstalt, 1999).

64. See Hans-Jürgen Schrader, "Inspirierte Schweizerreisen," in Alfred Messerli and Roger Chartier, eds., *Lesen und Schreiben in Europa 1500–1900* (Basel: Schwabe Verlag, 2000), 351–382, esp. 363.

65. Johann Friedrich Rock, "Anfänge Des Erniedrigungs-Lauffs Eines Sünders auf Erden," in Schneider, *Johann Friedrich Rock,* 14–16.

66. Krauss, "Johann Friedrich Rock," 86.

67. Rock, "Anfänge Des Erniedrigungs-Lauffs," 14, 17.

68. Johann Friedrich Rock, "Zweyter Aufsatz Des Erniedrigungs-Lauffs Eines Sünders auf Erden," in Schneider, *Johann Friedrich Rock.* Page numbers in the text refer to this source ("Zweyter Aufsatz").

69. Krauss, "Johann Friedrich Rock," 90.

70. See ibid., 99, 101; Ulf Lückel, "Die Inspirierten in Wittgenstein und das prophetische Werkzeug Johann Friedrich Rock," *Wittgenstein: Blätter des Wittgensteiner Heimatvereins e.V.* 61, no. 4 (1997): 147–157, esp. 149–150.

71. Rock also traveled to Bayern—something Krauss did not mention.

72. Krauss, "Johann Friedrich Rock," 103, 112.

73. In Ysenburg in the early years, the Inspirationists came into conflict with the authorities. When some of the Inspirationists attacked the ruling elites, they were threatened with exile and, in some cases, this was carried out. Schneider, "Der radikale Pietismus im 18. Jahrhundert," 151.

74. Ibid., 115; Wallmann, *Der Pietismus,* 148.

75. Lehmann, "Die langfristigen Folgen der kirchlichen Ausgrenzung des radikalen Pietismus," 46–50.

76. Aaron Spencer Fogleman, *Hopeful Journeys: German Immigration, Settlement, and Political Culture in Colonial America, 1717–1775* (Philadelphia: University of Pennsylvania Press, 1996), 4–6, 101–107.

77. See J. Max Hark, ed., *Chronicon Ephratense: A History of the Community of Seventh-Day Baptists at Ephrata, Lancaster County, Pa. by Lamech and Agrippa* (Lancaster, PA: S. H. Zahm, 1889; reprint, New York: Burt Franklin, 1972).

78. Sangmeister's autobiography was first published in four parts between 1825 and 1827. For an English translation, see *Journal of the Historical Society of the Cocalico Valley* 4–10 (1979–1985).

79. Bach, *Voices of the Turtledoves,* 31–37, 43–44, 197–205. See Peter C. Erb, ed., *Johann Conrad Beissel and the Ephrata Community: Mystical and Historical Texts* (Lewiston, NY: Edwin Mellen Press, 1985).

80. Bach, *Voices of the Turtledoves,* 8–10.

81. Ibid., 10, 12–16.

82. Ibid., 16. Johannes Kelpius was a German Pietist, mystic, musician, and writer. In 1694, he and about forty followers created a settlement in Pennsylvania called the Society of the Woman in the Wilderness, based on Revelation 12:1–6: "The woman fled into the wilderness, where she has a place prepared by God." *The Holy Bible, New Revised Standard Version* (Oxford: Oxford University Press, 1989). They believed the end of the world would occur around 1700. See W. R. Ward, *The Protestant Evangelical Awakening* (Cambridge: Cambridge University Press, 1992), 44–45. Jonathan D. Scott has recently argued for a Kelpius birth date in 1667, www.middletonbooks.com/html/witw/witw_bio.html.

83. Schneider, *German Radical Pietism*, 112. In 1729, Alexander Mack migrated to Pennsylvania with a party of some two hundred New Baptists, setting out from Holland, where they had lived after fleeing Schwarzenau in 1720. The German "New Baptists" (*Neu-Täufer*) were so called because of their similarity to the sixteenth-century Anabaptists. They had no connection to early English Baptists.

84. Ibid., 17–19; Ward, *Protestant Evangelical Awakening*, 252–253.

85. Ephrath is identified as Bethlehem in Genesis 35:20. Jacob's wife, Rachel, died in childbirth and was buried on the road to Ephrath. For Beissel, the name *Ephrata* signified suffering, one of the marks of the true church. Bach, *Voices of the Turtledoves*, 42.

86. Ibid., 4, 19–23, 193–194.

87. Georg Conrad Beissel, "Collection of Maxims," in Erb, *Johann Conrad Beissel and the Ephrata Community*, 95, 102.

88. Conrad Beissel, *Some Theosophical Maxims, or, Rules of the Solitary Life* (1752), trans. Michelle S. Long (Ephrata, PA: Ephrata Cloister Associates, 1991).

89. Bach, *Voices of the Turtledoves*, 70, 85–90, 93–94. The last-named practices were common to both Ephrata and the Schwarzenau Brethren.

90. Ibid., 76–82.

91. Ibid., 97–114. In the *Dissertation on Man's Fall*, Beissel held Adam, not Eve, accountable for sin entering paradise.

92. Jeff Bach, "Maria Eicher of Ephrata: A Case Study of Religion and Gender in Radical Pietism," in David B. Eller, ed., *From Age to Age: Historians and the Modern Church*, special issue of *Brethren Life and Thought* 42, no. 3–4 (1997): 118–133. Maria Eicher and her older sister Anna were among Beissel's earliest followers. Beissel baptized them on Christmas Day, 1726.

93. Christian Neff, "Beisel, Johann Konrad," in *Mennonite Encyclopedia* (Scottdale, PA: Mennonite Publishing House, 1955), 1:267.

94. Ward, *Protestant Evangelical Awakening*, 253.

95. Bach, *Voices of the Turtledoves*, 18. Bach summarizes the key features of Beissel's thought as follows: "On a foundation of Boehmist thought transmitted through Gichtel and the Philadelphian Society, Conrad Beissel constructed his religious thought with Scripture read through the hermeneutics of Horch and direct religious experience . . . He created a unique synthesis of religious thought and practice from the Old World embodied in a singular religious community in the New World" (29).

96. Ibid., 177, 190–191; Neff, "Beisel, Johann Konrad," 267.

97. Bach, *Voices of the Turtledoves*, 36, 40–43.

98. Ibid., 16–17.

99. Schneider, *German Radical Pietism*, 95, 158.

100. Bach, *Voices of the Turtledoves*, 23.

101. Donald F. Durnbaugh, *The Believers' Church: The History and Character of Radical Protestantism* (New York: Macmillan, 1968).

102. Five distinct denominations have grown out of the Schwarzenau New

Baptists: Church of the Brethren (with 150,000 members, founded in 1708), the Fellowship of Grace Brethren Churches (41,000 members, founded in 1939), the Brethren Church (13,000 members, founded in 1882), the Old German Baptist Brethren (5,000 members, founded in 1881), and the Dunkard Brethren (about 1,000 members, founded in 1926). Together they comprise some 210,000 believers. These numbers are based on Hans Jörg Schmidt, Head of the City Archive in Schriesheim, "Religion made in Schriesheim: Der Kirchenbegründer Alexander Mack" (paper presented at the 300th Anniversary Celebration of the New Baptists in Schwarzenau, 2008), http://dpak.files.wordpress.com/2007/05/microsoft-word-religion-made-in-schriesheim.pdf.

103. Dale W. Brown, *Understanding Pietism*, rev. ed. (Nappanee, IN: Evangel Publishing House, 1996), 104–106.

Chapter 7. Pietism and Gender

1. Jeannine Kunert used these words in her review of Ulrike Gleixner and Erika Hebeisen, eds., *Gendering Tradition: Erinnerungskultur und Geschlecht im Pietismus* (Korb: Didymos-Verlag, 2007), H-Soz-u-Kult, Sept. 4, 2008, http://hsozkult.geschichte.hu-berlin.de/rezensionen/2008-3-134.

2. See Ulrike Gleixner and Marion W. Gray, *Gender in Transition: Discourse and Practice in German-Speaking Europe, 1750–1830* (Ann Arbor: University of Michigan Press, 2006); Gleixner and Hebeisen, *Gendering Tradition*.

3. Ulrike Gleixner, "How to Incorporate Gender in Lutheran Pietism Research: Narratives and Counternarratives," in Jonathan Strom, Hartmut Lehmann, and James Van Horn Melton, eds., *Pietism in Germany and North America 1680–1820* (Farnham, UK: Ashgate, 2009), 271–273.

4. Katherine M. Faull, "Temporal Men and the Eternal Bridegroom: Moravian Masculinity in the Eighteenth Century," in Katherine M. Faull, ed., *Masculinity, Senses, Spirit* (Lewisburg, PA: Bucknell University Press, 2011), 55–80. See the two recent articles by Paul Peucker: "Wives of the Lamb: Moravian Brothers and Gender around 1750," in Faull, *Masculinity, Senses, Spirit*, 39–54; and "Inspired by Flames of Love: Homosexuality, Mysticism, and Moravian Brothers around 1750," *Journal of the History of Sexuality* 15, no. 1 (2006), 30–64.

5. Peucker: "Inspired by Flames of Love," 34. "There were feelings of intense friendship between people of the same sex voiced in letters resembling love letters; there were men who longed for other men in a romantic way; there were cases of mutual masturbation among persons of the same sex and similar status; and there were cases where sexual contact took place between people of notably different status, in this case, between a teacher and a pupil" (33).

6. Ibid., 37–39.

7. Ibid., 64. For references to the poem for Christian Renatus and the Moravian hymnbook, see ibid., 51–52, 56, 57.

8. Hartmut Krüger, *Frauen im Pietismus* (Marburg: Francke, 2005), 73. Krüger

writes, "From the beginning, a distinguishing mark of Pietism was its character as a spiritual movement in large measure unleashed and borne along by women" (73).

9. Mirjam de Baar, "Internationale und interkonfessionelle Netzwerke: Zur frühen lutherisch pietistischen Rezeption von Anna Maria van Schurman und Antoinette Bourignon," in Gleixner and Hebeisen, *Gendering Tradition,* 100.

10. Gleixner, "How to Incorporate Gender in Lutheran Pietism Research," 271; Ruth Albrecht, "Frauen," in Hartmut Lehmann, ed., *Glaubenswelt und Lebenswelten des Pietismus* (Göttingen: Vandenhoeck & Ruprecht, 2004), 523–524.

11. Albrecht, "Frauen," 543. On marriage in Pietism, see Ulrike Gleixner, "Zwischen göttlicher und weltlicher Ordnung: Die Ehe im lutherischen Pietismus," *Pietismus und Neuzeit* 28 (2002): 147–184; Andreas Gestrich, "Ehe, Familie, Kinder im Pietismus. Der 'gezähmte Teufel,'" in Lehmann, *Glaubenswelt und Lebenswelten,* 498–521; Wolfgang Breul, "Marriage and Marriage-Criticism in Pietism: Philipp Jakob Spener, Gottfried Arnold, and Nikolaus Ludwig von Zinzendorf," in Strom, *Pietism and Community in Europe and North America,* 37–53.

12. Johannes Wallmann, *Der Pietismus* (Göttingen: Vandenhoeck & Ruprecht, 2005), 27. Wallmann observed that since Albrecht Ritschl, Pietist historiography has traditionally focused on three generations of male leaders, from Spener and Francke to Zinzendorf and Oetinger.

13. Ulrike Gleixner, "Erinnerungskultur, Traditionsbildung und Geschlecht im Pietismus," in Gleixner and Hebeisen, *Gendering Tradition,* 7–8. Gleixner writes, "The process of writing the lives of male authorities is assumed; women become the victims of a male writing of history" (7). See Kunert's review of *Gendering Tradition,* H-Soz-u-Kult, Sept. 4, 2008.

14. In traditional scholarship one finds no sense of women as prominent players in the movement. See Ulrike Witt, *Bekehrung, Bildung und Biographie: Frauen im Umkreis des Halleschen Pietismus* (Tübingen: Max Niemeyer Verlag, 1996), 4.

15. See de Baar, "Internationale und interkonfessionelle Netzwerke," 101n84. De Baar refers to Ruth Albrecht's chapter, "Frauen," in Lehmann, *Glaubenswelt und Lebenswelten,* 522–555.

16. Gleixner, "How to Incorporate Gender in Lutheran Pietism Research," 274.

17. Gleixner and Hebeisen, *Gendering Tradition,* 8–9.

18. Ulinka Rublack, "Introduction," in Ulinka Rublack, ed., *Gender in Early Modern German History* (Cambridge: Cambridge University Press, 2002), 14.

19. See the H-German Forum of Sept. 24, 2010, "New Perspectives on Religion in Eighteenth Century Germany," by Michael Printy of Wesleyan University, www.h-net.org/~german/discuss/early_modern/printy_em_forum. Gleixner shows how the household, the family, and community were central contexts for Pietism and for the formation of a new bourgeois culture.

20. Ulrike Gleixner, *Pietismus und Bürgertum: Eine historische Anthropologie der Frömmigkeit* (Göttingen: Vandenhoeck & Ruprecht, 2005), 393, 397.

21. Johanna Eleonora Petersen, née von Merlau, was discussed in chapter 3, so she is not included here.

22. Jutta Taege-Bizer, "Weibsbilder im Pietismus: Das Beispiel von Frankfurt am Main 1670–1700," in Leonore Siegele-Wenschkewitz, ed., *Frauen Gestalten Geschichte. Im Spannungsfeld von Religion und Geschlecht* (Hanover: Lutherisches Verlagshaus, 1998), 123. Taege-Bizer's study examines women's involvements in the Pietist network, their theological views, and how they negotiated these in terms of their social status in Frankfurt society.

23. Ibid., 125–126.

24. Ibid., 126–127. For more on Spener and Kißner, see Denise D. Kettering, "Pietism and Patriarchy: Spener and Women in Seventeenth-Century German Pietism" (PhD diss., University of Iowa, 2009).

25. Taege-Bizer, "Weibsbilder im Pietismus," 127.

26. Johann Jakob Schütz, *Lebens-Lauff und Abschieds-Reden einer recht Christlichen Witwe / Der Wohl-Edelgebohrnen / Viel Ehr- und Tugendreichen Fr. Mariae Julianae Baurin von Eyseneck / gebohrne von Hynßberg: Wie solches den 21. April. Anno 1684. bey dero ansehnlichem Leich-Begängnüß in Franckfurt am Mäyn abgelesen / und ferner nach der Wahrheit hierbey ergänzet worden; sampt Deroselben an ihre drey Kinder schrifftlich hinterlassenen Vermahn- und Erinnerungen; Wegen Rarität dergleichen lebenden Exempel / andern zu Trost und Erbauung / auf vieler Verlangen zum Druck befördert* (Hekel, 1691). The biography was reprinted by Johann Henrich Reitz in his collection *The History of the Reborn*. See Johann Henrich Reitz, "Historia von M. J. Bauerin von Eiseneck," *Historie der Wiedergebohrnen*, pt. 3 (Offenbach am Main: Bonaventura de Launoy, 1701; reprint, Tübingen: Max Niemeyer Verlag, 1982), 112–123.

27. Taege-Bizer, "Weibsbilder im Pietismus," 131.

28. Ibid., 129–130; Andreas Deppermann, *Johann Jakob Schütz und die Anfänge des Pietismus* (Tübingen: Mohr Siebeck, 2002), 103–104.

29. Taege-Bizer, "Weibsbilder im Pietismus," 132. ". . . Was ist euer Stand? Auß Dreck seid ihr (wie alle Menschen, Könige und Bettler) gebohren; Das ist euer Stand und kein anderer!"

30. Ibid., 133; Deppermann, *Johann Jakob Schütz*, 218. See also Hermann Dechent, "Johann Jakob Schütz, ein Frankfurter Liederdichter," in Hans-Jürgen Telschow, ed., *Ich sah sie noch die alte Zeit: Beiträge zur Frankfurter Kirchengeschichte* (Frankfurt: Evangelischer Regionalverband, 1985), 76–84.

31. Manfred Jakubowski-Tiessen, *Der Frühe Pietismus in Schleswig-Holstein* (Göttingen: Vandenhoeck & Ruprecht, 1983), 137. In 1700, Katharina Elisabeth Schütz granted four thousand acres of land in Pennsylvania to Georg Müller and Daniel Falckner. Müller was the leader of a separatist conventicle in Hamburg, Falckner a former student in Erfurt during Francke's time there. In 1700, Müller emigrated to Pennsylvania along with two hundred families from Friedrichstadt and Holstein. Falckner wrote *Curious News from Pennsylvania* (1702), encouraging more German friends to join them. See Johannes Wallmann, "Erfurt und der Pietismus im 17. Jahrhundert," in *Theologie und Frömmigkeit im Zeitalter des Barock: Gesammelte Aufsätze* (Tübingen: Mohr Siebeck, 1995), 348, 350.

32. Hans Schneider, "Der radikale Pietismus im 17. Jahrhundert," in Martin Brecht et al., eds., *Der Pietismus vom siebzehnten bis zum frühen achtzehnten Jahrhundert* (Göttingen: Vandenhoeck & Ruprecht, 1993), 112–113.

33. Deppermann, *Johann Jakob Schütz*, 218.

34. Taege-Bizer, "Weibsbilder im Pietismus," 133–134.

35. Deppermann, *Johann Jakob Schütz*, 220. Anna Elisabeth Kißner's letter to Countess Benigna von Solms-Laubach in 1690 contains a valuable account of Johann Jakob Schütz's last days.

36. Ibid., 219.

37. Claudia Wustmann, *Die "begeisterten Mägde": Mitteldeutsche Prophetinnen im Radikalpietismus am Ende des 17. Jahrhunderts* (Leipzig: Edition Kirchhof & Franke, 2008), 75.

38. de Baar, "Internationale und interkonfessionelle Netzwerke," 86.

39. Ibid., 100–101.

40. Mirjam de Baar, "Gender, genre and authority: Anna Maria van Schurman and Antoinette Bourignon," in Anne Bollmann, ed., *A Place of Their Own: Women Writers and Their Social Environments (1450–1700)* (Frankfurt am Main: Peter Lang, 2011), 138–139. Besides Latin, Greek, and Hebrew, van Schurman knew Syriac, Chaldean, Arabic, and Ethiopian and was fluent in Dutch, German, English, French, and Italian. See Pieta van Beek, *The First Female University Student: Anna Maria van Schurman (1636)* (Utrecht: Igitur, Utrecht Publishing & Archiving Services, 2010); Joyce Irwin, "Anna Maria Van Schurman: From Feminism to Pietism," *Church History* 46, no. 1 (1977): 50.

41. See Anna Maria van Schurman, *Whether a Christian Woman Should Be Educated and Other Writings from Her Intellectual Circle*, trans. Joyce L. Irwin (Chicago: University of Chicago Press, 1999). The book includes a translation of *Eukleria*.

42. de Baar, "Gender, Genre and Authority," 150, 155.

43. de Baar, "Internationale und interkonfessionelle Netzwerke," 89, 93.

44. Ibid., 93–94. Ten Latin letters from van Schurman to Schütz have survived, dated between July 1674 and February 1678, along with two letters from Schütz to van Schurman, dated in November 1676 and January 1677. Schütz also corresponded with Pierre Yvon, another Labadist member. Four of Schütz's letters to Yvon have survived in abstract form.

45. Both *L'Exercice prophetique* and *La Reformation de l'Eglise par le Pastorat* were sent to Schütz by the Labadists. See Wallmann, *Der Pietismus*, 141.

46. de Baar, "Internationale und interkonfessionelle Netzwerke," 94–95.

47. Klaus vom Orde, "Antoinette Bourignon in der Beurteilung Philipp Jakob Speners und ihre Rezeption in der pietistischen Tradition," *Pietismus und Neuzeit* 26 (2000): 59–60. For evidence of Jakob Böhme's influence on Bourignon, see Ernst Schering, "Adam und die Schlange: Androgyner Mythos und Moralismus bei Antoinette Bourignon. Ein Beitrag zum Einfluß Jakob Böhmes auf das französische Geistesleben," *Zeitschrift fuer Religions- und Geistesgeschichte* 10 (1958): 97–124.

48. de Baar, "Internationale und interkonfessionelle Netzwerke," 90–91. Bourignon continued to believe the Apostles' Creed, the Lord's Prayer, and the Ten Commandments.

49. de Baar, "Gender, genre and authority," 140–141. See also vom Orde, "Antoinette Bourignon in der Beurteilung Philipp Jakob Speners," 50–80; Phyllis Mack, "Die Prophetin als Mutter: Antoinette Bourignon," in Hartmut Lehmann and Anne-Charlott Trepp, eds., *Im Zeichen der Krise: Religiosität im Europa des 17. Jahrhunderts* (Göttingen: Vandenhoeck & Ruprecht, 1999), 79–100.

50. Mirjam de Baar, "Conflicting Discourses on Female Dissent in the Early Modern Period: The Case of Antoinette Bourignon (1616–1680)," *L'Atelier du Centre de recherches historiques*, Apr. 2009, published online Sept. 4, 2009, http://acrh.revues.org/index1399.html.

51. vom Orde, "Antoinette Bourignon in der Beurteilung Philipp Jakob Speners," 76–77. See Gottfried Arnold's *Unparteyische Kirchen- und Ketzerhistorie*, pt 4, chap. 3, art. 17.

52. vom Orde, "Antoinette Bourignon in der Beurteilung Philipp Jakob Speners," 50.

53. de Baar, "Internationale und interkonfessionelle Netzwerke," 95–97. Deppermann speaks only of contact between Bourignon and van de Walle. Deppermann, *Johann Jakob Schütz*, 152, 307.

54. Mirjam de Baar, *"I Must Speak": The Spiritual Leadership of Antoinette Bourignon (1616–1680)* (Zutphen, Netherlands: Walburg Pers, 2004), 812 and summary. De Baar writes, "Dutch, German, and Latin translations of her writings appeared, some during Bourignon's lifetime . . . There was even a series of English translations of her writings" (812).

55. de Baar, "Internationale und interkonfessionelle Netzwerke," 97, 98.

56. See Doris von der Brelie-Lewien, " 'Die Erlösung des Menschengeschlechts': Prophetinnen, Besessene, Hysterikerinnen (1690–1890)," in Karsten Rudolph and Christl Wickert, eds., *Geschichte als Möglichkeit: Festschrift für Helga Grebing* (Essen: Klartext, 1995), 394–421. A later instance of ecstatic prophecy is Ursula Meyer, from Bern, who first prophesied on March 16, 1715, and continued to prophesy for four years. Her prophecies took place mainly at the Ronneburg Castle in the Wetterau. The Inspirationists believed that the Spirit of God spoke to them in her prophecies. See Isabelle Noth, *Ekstatischer Pietismus: Die Inspirationsgemeinden und ihre Prophetin Ursula Meyer (1682–1743)* (Göttingen: Vandenhoeck & Ruprecht, 2005), 17–18, 266.

57. *Eigentliche Nachricht Von Dreyen Begeisterten Mägden, Der Halberstädtischen Catharinen, Quedlinburgischen Magdalenen, und Erffurtischen Liesen, Aus Zehen unterschiedenen eingelauffenen Schreiben zusammen getragen von M. August Herman Francken* (Leipzig, 1692). The book is a collection of ten letters on the subject of women prophets by Georg Heinrich Brückner, Andreas Achilles, and others. See Wustmann, *Die "begeisterten Mägde,"* 17–18, 22, 143, 156n226; Wallmann, "Erfurt und der Pietismus im 17. Jahrhundert," 346–347.

58. Crophius wrote an even-handed historical account of Pietism in 1700. Johann Baptist Crophius, *Wahrhafft- und Gründlicher Bericht Von der unter den Lutheranern neu-entstandenen Sect, Welche der Pietismus Oder die Pietisterey ins gemein genennt wird* (Vienna, 1700). See Wallmann, "Erfurt und der Pietismus im 17. Jahrhundert," 349; Friedrich de Boor, "Anna Maria Schuchart als Endzeit-Prophetin in Erfurt 1691/1692," *Pietismus und Neuzeit* 21 (1995): 148–149, 159.

59. Wustmann, *Die "begeisterten Mägde,"* 210–211.

60. Ibid., 88–89. Wustmann writes, "The born again Pietist saw herself as part of an elite community which assured her of a special status over against the rest of society" (23). When banished from one city, she would find fellowship and support in another and further affirmation.

61. de Boor, "Anna Maria Schuchart," 148–183. De Boor's article is based on Johann Baptist Crophius's *Bericht* (report) on Schuchart, dated November 24, 1692. As of 1995, this source had not yet been carefully examined. Ibid., 150, 160.

62. Wustmann, *Die "begeisterten Mägde,"* 131–134; de Boor, "Anna Maria Schuchart," 161–165.

63. Wustmann, *Die "begeisterten Mägde,"* 133, 134; de Boor, "Anna Maria Schuchart," 165–166.

64. Wustmann, *Die "begeisterten Mägde,"* 132.

65. de Boor, "Anna Maria Schuchart," 167, 173.

66. Wustmann, *Die "begeisterten Mägde,"* 137. Also see Wustmann 134–135; de Boor, "Anna Maria Schuchart," 168–169.

67. de Boor, "Anna Maria Schuchart," 169–170.

68. Crophius wrote, "I can testify that in various Christian conversations that I have had with her in the time she has been here, that she has uncovered for me the inmost ground of my heart and the state of my soul before God so accurately that I did not have to correct her in the least thing but found I had to accept it. But neither man, nor devil, nor angel can know the inmost state of the soul without the revelation of God." De Boor, "Anna Maria Schuchart," 182.

69. Wustmann, *Die "begeisterten Mägde,"* 137–138. For samples of Schuchart's verse, see ibid., 226–227.

70. Ibid., 139–140; Wallmann, "Erfurt und der Pietismus im 17. Jahrhundert," 347–348. These Pietists had been under the leadership of Johann Jakob Zimmermann of Württemberg; however, he died in Rotterdam just before the group's departure.

71. The best discussion of Elrichs is in the dissertation by Martin Schulz, "Johann Heinrich Sprögel und die pietistische Bewegung Quedlinburgs" (PhD diss., Halle, 1974), 59–60.

72. Wustmann, *Die "begeisterten Mägde,"* 143–144.

73. On Catharina Reinecke, see ibid., 145–158.

74. Ibid., 168–170.

75. Ibid., 171.

76. Cornelia Niekus Moore, "Die Darstellung der Frau im deutschen Pietis-

mus," in Udo Sträter, ed., *Interdisziplinäre Pietismusforschungen: Beiträge zum Ersten Internationalen Kongress für Pietismusforschung 2001* (Tübingen: Max Niemeyer Verlag, 2005), 38, 40.

77. Taege-Bizer, "Weibsbilder im Pietismus," 119–121.

78. Moore, "Die Darstellung der Frau im deutschen Pietismus," 41, 42. Moore refers to Paul Grünberg's biography of Spener.

79. Albrecht, "Frauen," 525–526.

80. Moore, "Die Darstellung der Frau im deutschen Pietismus," 42–43. Denise Kettering observes, "While his theological works espouse a position consistent with defined Lutheran categories for women's behavior, Spener's letters often encouraged Pietist women to become vigorous supporters of and participants in his reform movement." Kettering, "Pietism and Patriarchy," abstract.

81. Wustmann, *Die "begeisterten Mägde,"* 77–79, 113–114, 136, 166, 182–183, 196, 207, 209; Wallmann, "Erfurt und der Pietismus im 17. Jahrhundert," 347, 349.

82. Ulrike Gleixner, "Wie fromme Helden entstehen: Biographie, Traditionsbildung und Geschichts-schreibung," *Werkstatt Geschichte* 30 (2001): 38–39. Gleixner speaks of "eine biographische Kultur." See also Gleixner, *Pietismus und Bürgertum.*

83. Hans-Jürgen Schrader provides an overview of biographical literature within German Pietism in his "Die Literatur des Pietismus," in Lehmann, *Glaubenswelt und Lebenswelten,* 396.

84. Jeannine Blackwell, "Herzensgespräche mit Gott: Bekenntnisse deutscher Pietistinnen im 17. und 18. Jahrhundert," in Gisela Brinker-Gabler, ed., *Deutsche Literatur von Frauen, Erster Band, Vom Mittelalter bis zum Ende des 18. Jahrhunderts* (Munich: Verlag C. H. Beck, 1988), 265, 267.

85. Johann Henrich Reitz, "Vorrede an den Christlichen Leser," in *I. Theil der Historie Der Wiedergebohrnen* (Offenbach am Main: Bonaventura de Launoy, 1698).

86. Johann Henrich Reitz, "Zuschrifft," in *I. Theil der Historie Der Wiedergebohrnen.*

87. Of the thirty-five anonymous biographies in part 1, all but two were of women. In parts 2–5, twenty-one were of women, fifty-two of men.

88. Reitz, "Vorrede an den Christlichen Leser."

89. Douglas H. Shantz, "'Back to the Sources': Gottfried Arnold, Johann Henrich Reitz, and the Distinctive Program and Practice of Pietist Historical Writing," in Arnold Snyder, ed., *Commoners and Community* (Kitchener, ON: Pandora Press, 2002), 78, 83–85.

90. Gottfried Arnold, *Kirchen- und Ketzer-Historie Vierter Theil, Bestehend in allerhand nöthigen Documenten, Tractaten und Zeugnissen, Acten und Geschichten von vielen Religions-Streitigkeiten* (Frankfurt am Main: Thomas Fritschens sel. Erben, 1729), 1089–1090. Arnold cited Friedrich Breckling, *Catalogus testium veritatis post Lutherum* (1700).

91. Arnold, *Kirchen- und Ketzer-Historie Vierter Theil,* 1108.

92. Johann Heinrich Feustking, *Gynaeceum Haeretico Fanaticum*, ed. Elisabeth Gössmann (Munich: Iudicium Verlag, 1998), 57–61. All references to Feustking refer to this source.

93. Albrecht, "Frauen," 524; Blackwell, "Herzensgespräche mit Gott," 276–277.

94. Blackwell, "Herzensgespräche mit Gott," 278–279.

95. Ulrike Witt, "Eine pietistische Biographiensammlung: Erdmann Heinrich Graf Henckels 'Letzte Stunden' (1720–1733)," *Pietismus und Neuzeit* 21 (1995): 193. The full title of Henckel's work is *Die letzten Stunden einiger Der Evangelischen Lehre zugethanen und in diesem und nechste verflossenen Jahren selig in dem Herrn Verstorbenen Personen. Von unterschiedenem Stande, Geschlechte und Alter* (Halle, 1720–1733). The work is in four parts.

96. Witt, "Eine pietistische Biographiensammlung," 196, 197.

97. Ibid., 205, 208–209.

98. J. H. Feustking, *Gynaeceum haeretico fanaticum, Oder Historie und Beschreibung Der falschen Prophetinnen, Quäkerinnen, Schwärmerinnen, und anderen sectirischen und begeisterten Weibes-Personen, durch welche die Kirche Gottes verunruhiget worden; sambt einem Vorbericht und Anhang entgegen gesetzet denen Adeptis Godofredi Arnoldi* (Frankfurt: Gottfried Zimmermanns Buchladen, 1704); reprint of parts 1 and 2 edited by Elisabeth Gössmann are in her edited Feustking, *Gynaeceum Haeretico Fanaticum*.

99. Feustking was born on March 7, 1672, in the village of Stellau in Schleswig-Holstein, into a Lutheran pastor's family with a long tradition of Lutheran clergymen. In 1712, Duke Friedrich II of Saxon-Gotha called Feustking to be court preacher and confessor in the residence city of Gotha, "the most beautiful city in Thüringen." Feustking died in Gotha on March 23, 1713, at the age of forty-one. Ruth Albrecht, "Einleitung: Historisch-theologische Hinführung zu Person und Werk Feustkings," in Feustking, *Gynaeceum Haeretico Fanaticum*, xvii–xxii.

100. Ibid., xxv; Feustking, *Gynaeceum Haeretico Fanaticum*, 117.

101. Feustking devoted two entries to critiquing Johanna Eleonora Petersen. Feustking, *Gynaeceum Haeretico Fanaticum*, 458–482, 501–502.

102. Ibid., 359–360. Feustking writes, "According to Arnold and other fanatics . . . every Christian, including women, is free to preach and teach others so long as they are illumined within . . . One can see how everything in Arnold's damned *History of Heretics* is intended to bring suspicion upon the preaching office and make it hateful among the political leaders of our day" (359–360).

103. Albrecht, "Einleitung," xxxii.

104. Feustking, "Vorbericht," in *Gynaeceum Haeretico Fanaticum*, 50, 13–14.

105. Albrecht, "Einleitung," xxxiv.

106. Adelisa Malena, "Sectirische und begeisterte Weibes-Personen: On the *Gynaeceum Haeretico Fanaticum* by J. H. Feustking (1704)," *L'Atelier du Centre de recherches historiques*, Apr. 2009, 2, 4, published online Sept. 25, 2009, http://acrh.revues.org/index1402.html.

107. Orthodox Lutheran histories include August Pfeiffer's *Antienthusiasmus*

(1692), Ehregott Daniel Colberg's *Das Platonisch-Hermetische Christenthum* [The Platonic-Hermetic Christian world] (1690), Ernest Martin Plarrius's *Specimen Historiae Anabaptisticae* [Specimen of Anabaptist history] (1701), and Johannes Friedrich Corvinus's *Anabaptisticum et enthusiasticum Pantheon und geistliches Rüst-Hauss* [Pantheon and spiritual armory of Anabaptists and enthusiasts] (1702). See Albrecht, "Einleitung," xxxv–xxxvi.

108. Albrecht, "Frauen," 530–531.

109. See Wustmann, *Die "begeisterten Mägde,"* 142n136. Wustmann notes that in many records at the time, Magdalena Elrichs was identified by her mother's maiden name, as Magdalena Schultz.

110. Feustking, *Gynaeceum Haeretico Fanaticum,* 51–54.

111. Ibid., 57–61, 66.

112. Ibid., 413–416.

113. Wustmann, *Die "begeisterten Mägde,"* 48–50.

114. Elisabeth Gössmann, "Vorwort," in Feustking, *Gynaeceum Haeretico Fanaticum,* xv. Gössmann writes, "Of special value is Feustking's effort to provide the most complete listing possible of writings that originate from women in his day and from women at the time of the Reformation, whether Protestant or Catholic. This is what makes his writing so indispensable for feminist research. We learn much concerning old editions of works by these women, including accounts of their visions composed by male authors, the influence of women's writings and how they were received by men at the time" (xv).

115. Taege-Bizer, "Weibsbilder im Pietismus," 110, 134–135.

116. Whereas nineteenth-century scholars used the prominent role of women in Pietism to discredit it, twentieth-century historians, in an effort to rehabilitate Pietism, systematically eliminated women from their accounts. Max Weber and Carl Hinrichs portrayed an ascetic Pietism that had an economic and political impact. Mystical Pietism and women did not fit into their accounts. Witt, *Bekehrung, Bildung und Biographie,* 4–11.

Chapter 8. Pietism and the Bible

1. Johannes Wallmann, "Vom Katechismuschristentum zum Bibelchristentum: Zu Bibelverständnis im Pietismus," in Richard Ziegert, ed., *Die Zukunft des Schriftprinzips* (Stuttgart: Deutsche Bibelgesellschaft, 1994), 30–56; Richard Gawthrop and Gerald Strauss, "Protestantism and Literacy in Early Modern Germany," *Past and Present* 104 (Aug. 1984): 31–55.

2. Beate Köster, "'Mit tiefem Respekt, mit Furcht und Zittern': Bibelübersetzungen im Pietismus," *Pietismus und Neuzeit* 24 (1998): 115.

3. Ibid., 95–115. Aland identified "10 new translations in less than 50 years." Kurt Aland, "Bibel und Bibeltext bei August Hermann Francke und Johann Albrecht Bengel," in Kurt Aland, ed., *Pietismus und Bibel* (Witten: Luther-Verlag, 1970), 141.

4. Jonathan Sheehan, *The Enlightenment Bible: Translation, Scholarship, Culture* (Princeton: Princeton University Press, 2005), 62.

5. Hans-Jürgen Schrader, "Lesarten der Schrift: Die *Biblia Pentapla* und ihr Programm einer 'herrlichen Harmonie Göttlichen Wortes' in 'Fünf-facher Deutscher Verdolmetschung,'" in Ulrich Stadler, ed., *Zwiesprache: Beiträge zur Theorie und Geschichte des Übersetzens* (Stuttgart: Verlag J. B. Metzler, 1996), 201–202.

6. Martin Brecht, "Die Bedeutung der Bibel im deutschen Pietismus," in Hartmut Lehmann, ed., *Glaubenswelt und Lebenswelten* (Göttingen: Vandenhoeck & Ruprecht, 2004), 102.

7. See Heimo Reinitzer, *Biblia deutsch: Luthers Bibelübersetzung und ihre Tradition* (Wolfenbüttel: Herzog August Bibliothek, 1983), 305–306. On eighteenth-century discussions of the Bible, see Hans-Jürgen Schrader, *Literaturproduktion und Büchermarkt des radikalen Pietismus* (Göttingen: Vandenhoeck & Ruprecht, 1989), 523–526, 570–578.

8. Philipp Jakob Spener, *Pia Desideria: Deutsch-Lateinische Studienausgabe*, ed. Beate Köster (Giessen: Brunnen Verlag, 2005), 108, 110, 116.

9. Brecht, "Die Bedeutung der Bibel im deutschen Pietismus," 105.

10. A. H. Francke, "Vorrede," in Beate Köster, "Die erste Bibelausgabe des Halleschen Pietismus," *Pietismus und Neuzeit* 5 (1979): 155, 163.

11. Otto Podczeck, ed., *August Hermann Franckes Schrift über eine Reform des Erziehungs- und Bildungswesens als Ausgangspunkt einer geistlichen und sozialen Neuordnung der Evangelischen Kirche des 18. Jahrhunderts: Der Grosse Aufsatz* (Berlin: Akademie-Verlag, 1962), 151. See also Sheehan, *Enlightenment Bible*, 62.

12. Sheehan, *Enlightenment Bible*, 61.

13. Brecht, "Die Bedeutung der Bibel im deutschen Pietismus," 106; Martin Brecht, "August Hermann Francke und der Hallische Pietismus," in Martin Brecht et al., eds., *Der Pietismus vom siebzehnten bis zum frühen achtzehnten Jahrhundert* (Göttingen: Vandenhoeck & Ruprecht, 1993), 519–520; Sheehan, *Enlightenment Bible*, 62.

14. The full title of Horch's Bible (in English translation) is "Mystical and prophetical Bible, that is, the entire Holy Scripture of the Old and New Testament, newly and thoroughly improved, including an explanation of the most important Symbols and Prophecies, especially in the *Song of Solomon* and the *Book of Revelation*." For Horch, the *Song of Solomon* and the *Book of Revelation* provided the interpretive key to scripture and taught the stages leading up to Christ's millennial reign on earth.

15. See Douglas H. Shantz, "The Millennial Study Bible of Heinrich Horch: A Case Study in Early Modern Reformed Hermeneutics," in Peter A. Lillback, ed., *The Practical Calvinist: An Introduction to the Presbyterian and Reformed Heritage. In Honor of Dr. D. Clair Davis* (Fearn, Ross-shire, UK: Christian Focus, 2002), 391–414.

16. Brecht, "Die Bedeutung der Bibel im deutschen Pietismus," 106–107.

17. Hans-Christoph Hahn and Hellmut Reichel, *Zinzendorf und die Herrnhuter*

Brüder: Quellen zur Geschichte der Brüder-Unität von 1722 bis 1760 (Hamburg: Friedrich Wittig Verlag, 1977), 240; Brecht, "Die Bedeutung der Bibel im deutschen Pietismus," 107–108.

18. Hermann Ehmer, "Johann Albrecht Bengel," in Carter Lindberg, ed., *The Pietist Theologians* (Oxford: Blackwell, 2005), 233. Bengel said that the Moravians valued Zinzendorf's hymns more than the Bible.

19. Brecht, "Die Bedeutung der Bibel im deutschen Pietismus," 108–109.

20. Sheehan, *Enlightenment Bible*, 220. The Bible was liberated from theology and became "an instrument of culture in a post-theological age." "Sheehan focuses on one medium, translations of the Bible, and the associated scholarly developments, in England and Germany." Ritchie Robertson, "Religion and the Enlightenment: A Review Essay," *German History* 25, no. 3 (2007): 423.

21. Sheehan, *Enlightenment Bible*, 217.

22. Ibid., xiii.

23. Ibid., 29.

24. See Robertson, "Religion and the Enlightenment," 425; Roy Porter, *Enlightenment: Britain and the Creation of the Modern World* (London: Penguin Books, 2001), 99.

25. This view challenges Peter Gay, for whom the Enlightenment was marked by its "essential hostility" to religion. Gay's analysis focused mainly on France and the Philosophes. Peter Gay, *The Enlightenment: An Interpretation*, vol. 1, *The Rise of Modern Paganism* (New York: W. W. Norton, 1966).

26. Sheehan argues that we should understand the Enlightenment, not as "a set of doctrinal or philosophical precepts," but rather as "a new constellation of formal and technical practices and institutions." Jonathan Sheehan, "Enlightenment, Religion, and the Enigma of Secularization: A Review Essay," *American Historical Review* 108, no. 4 (2003): 1075.

27. In 1713, during the Great Northern War with Sweden (1700–1721), King Friedrich IV of Denmark renewed the special law of toleration for Altona, first decreed in 1664 by Friedrich III. Catholics, Reformed, Mennonites, and Jews, "of whatever faith they might be, [could live] in complete freedom of conscience, and in the free practice of their religions." Hermann Patsch, "Arnoldiana in der Biblia Pentapla: Ein Beitrag zur Rezeption von Gottfried Arnolds Weisheits- und Väter-Übersetzung im radikalen Pietismus," *Pietismus und Neuzeit* 26 (2000): 94. See also Michael Driedger, *Obedient Heretics: Mennonite Identities in Lutheran Hamburg and Altona during the Confessional Age* (Aldershot, UK: Ashgate, 2002); Franklin Kopitzsch, "Altona—ein Zentrum der Aufklärung am Rande des dänischen Gesamtstaats," in Klaus Bohnen and Sven-Aage Jørgensen, eds., *Der dänische Gesamtstaat. Kopenhagen-Kiel-Altona* (Tübingen: De Gruyter, 1992), 91–118.

28. Ingun Montgomery, "Der Pietismus in Norwegen im 18. Jahrhundert," in Martin Brecht and Klaus Deppermann, eds., *Der Pietismus im achtzehnten Jahrhundert* (Göttingen: Vandenhoeck & Ruprecht, 1995), 475.

29. The satire was entitled "Description of the Life of the False Apostle, Homiletic" (1706).

30. Christiania was originally called Oslo. It was renamed in honor of King Christian IV of Denmark and Norway, who rebuilt the city after a fire in 1624; the city retained the name *Christiania* until 1876. In 1877, the spelling was changed to *Kristiania*. In 1925, the name was changed back to *Oslo*. See www.visitoslo.com/en/history.52075.en.html.

31. Montgomery, "Der Pietismus in Norwegen im 18. Jahrhundert," 485. Lodberg was a reform-minded Lutheran who had supported the Halle mission to Tranquebar.

32. Carl Bertheau, "Glüsing, Johann Otto G.," *Allgemeine Deutsche Biographie* (Leipzig: Duncker & Humblot, 1879), 9:258ff.

33. The book is entitled *The Unstained Righteousness of the Followers of the Lamb, Set in Opposition to the Tainted Pharisaical Righteousness of This World* (1707). Patsch, "Arnoldiana in der Biblia Pentapla," 96.

34. *Monumenta Apostolica: Der Apostolischen Männer S. Barnabae, Hermae, Clementis, Ignatii, Polycarpi, Justini, Carpi, und anderer H. Zeugen der Ersten Kirchen, Briefe und Schriften. Zur Beförderung der Gottseligkeit, Verdeutschet, vermehret, und mit Registern versehen von Johann Otto Glüsing* (Hamburg, 1723). See Hans Haupt, "Glüsing, Johann Otto," *Neue Deutsche Biographie* 6 (1964): 472–473; Bertheau, "Glüsing, Johann Otto G.," 258ff.

35. Patsch, "Arnoldiana in der Biblia Pentapla," 96. See also Johann Adrian Bolten, *Historische Kirchen-Nachrichten von der Stadt Altona und deren verschiedenen Religions-Partheyen* (1791), 2:102–112; Haupt, "Glüsing, Johann Otto," 472–473; Hans Haupt, "Der Altonaer Sektierer Johann Otto Glüsing und sein Prozeß von 1725/26," *Schriften des Vereins für Schleswig-Holsteinische Kirchengeschichte*, 2nd ser., 11 (1952): 136–163; Manfred Jakubowski-Tiessen, *Der frühe Pietismus in Schleswig-Holstein* (Göttingen: Vandenhoeck & Ruprecht, 1983), 148–152, 155–156.

36. The map and index were prepared by Matthew Hiller (1646–1725), professor of oriental languages at Tübingen University and author of *Dissertatio De Antiquissima Gigantum Gente Eorumque Sedibus* (Tübingen: Johann-Conradi Reisii, 1701). See Hermann Patsch, "Verstehen durch Vergleichen: Die Biblia Pentapla von 1710–1712," in Manfred Beetz and Giuseppe Cacciatore, eds., *Die Hermeneutik im Zeitalter der Aufklärung* (Cologne: Böhlau Verlag, 2000), 11–12.

37. Patsch, "Arnoldiana in der Biblia Pentapla," 98. See also Schrader, "Lesarten der Schrift," 205.

38. Translation into Yiddish means translation into a form of German that uses Hebrew letters.

39. Sheehan, *Enlightenment Bible*, 73.

40. Patsch, "Arnoldiana in der Biblia Pentapla," 95, 97, 99–100, 102, 107–108, 115.

41. Johann Otto Glüsing, "Allgemeiner Vorbericht," in *Das Alte Testament, Der I. Theil* (Schiffbeck: Hermann Heinrich Holle, 1711).

42. Ibid. The Radical Pietist printer and publisher Johann Christoph Sauer (1693–1758), who in 1743 produced the first German Bible in America, greatly admired the *Biblia Pentapla*. See Schrader, "Lesarten der Schrift," 210n32.

43. Glüsing's dates are incorrect; the first edition was in 1679 and the second in 1687. Also, though Witzenhausen was well-educated, he was not a rabbi, as Glüsing suggested.

44. Glüsing, "Allgemeiner Vorbericht."

45. "Athias," in Isaac Landman, ed., *The Universal Jewish Encyclopedia* (New York: Varda Books, 2009), 1:580.

46. This edition is sometimes identified as the Leusden Hebrew Bible, since Leusden's name is prominent on the title page. Johannes Leusden (1624–1699) was professor of Hebrew at the University of Utrecht from 1650 to 1699. He studied with learned rabbis in the Amsterdam Jewish community and encouraged Christian scholars to consult rabbinic texts to better understand the Old Testament. His many writings included linguistic work (grammars and dictionaries), works on the Dutch Jews of his day, and editions of the Hebrew Bible. See L. Hirschel and A. K. Offenberg, "Johannes Leusden als Hebraist," *Studia Rosenthaliana* 1, no. 1 (1967): 23–50. Rabbis in the Amsterdam synagogue considered Leusden "a most expert professor of the Hebrew language." See William W. Brickman, "The Socio-cultural Context of Education in the Seventeenth-Century Netherlands," *Paedagogica Historica* 24:2 (1984): 393–394, 408n56.

47. L. Fuks and R. G. Fuks-Mansfeld, eds., *Hebrew Typography in the Northern Netherlands, 1585–1815* (Leiden: Brill, 1987), 2:290.

48. Maranos were crypto-Jews in Spain and Portugal. Catholic authorities suspected that Christianized Jews were still practicing their Jewish faith. "The name was applied to the Spanish Jews who, through compulsion . . . converted to Christianity in consequence of the cruel persecutions of 1391 and of Vicente Ferrer's missionary sermons. These 'conversos' (converts), as they were called in Spain, or 'Christãos Novos' (Neo-Christians) in Portugal, . . . or 'Anusim' (constrained) in Hebrew, numbered more than 100,000." www.jewishencyclopedia.com. *Auto de fé* (in Spanish) and *auto da fé* (in Portuguese) mean "act of faith." This refers to the ritual of public penance of condemned heretics during the Spanish and Portuguese inquisitions. See Henry Kamen, *The Spanish Inquisition: A Historical Revision* (New Haven: Yale University Press, 1999).

49. The 1667 edition of Athia's Hebrew Bible contains a Latin preface and apparatus directed to Christian scholars, written by Everardo van der Hooght (d. 1716).

50. Joseph Athia, "Eine Vorrede des Jüdischen Druckers," in *Das Alte Testament, Der I. Theil* (Schiffbeck: Hermann Heinrich Holle, 1711). See also Fuks and Fuks-Mansfeld, *Hebrew Typography in the Northern Netherlands*, 291–292, 296–298; Schrader, "Lesarten der Schrift," 212–213.

51. Athia, "Eine Vorrede des Jüdischen Druckers."

52. Schrader, "Lesarten der Schrift," 213–215.

53. Athia, "Eine Vorrede des Jüdischen Druckers."

54. Schrader, "Lesarten der Schrift," 215–216. Words added for the sake of German style, that were not in the original Hebrew, Witzenhausen placed in brackets.

55. Köster, "'Mit tiefem Respekt, mit Furcht und Zittern,'" 100.

56. Sheehan, *Enlightenment Bible*, 67; see also 68, 69. As contrasting examples, Sheehan cites the Lord's Prayer as rendered by Luther and Reitz. Ibid., 65n52, 66n54.

57. Köster, "'Mit tiefem Respekt, mit Furcht und Zittern,'" 113. This is taken from Luther's 1530 "Letter on Interpretation," *D. Martin Luthers Werke*, Weimar Ausgabe, 1883–1929, 30, 2.

58. Sheehan, *Enlightenment Bible*, 68.

59. Ibid., 69–70.

60. Ibid., 58.

61. Michael Berns, *Entdeckung Des Greuel Wesens, Welches Die so genandte Neue Christen Mit der biß dathin In Wandesbeck gedruckten Biblia Pentapla vorhaben, Allen rechtschaffenen Christen und geheiligten Seelen Zur Warnung und Verhütung auffgesetzet, Von Michael Berns, Past. zu Wandesbeck* (Hamburg, 1710). Berns published nine books between 1692 and 1724, all polemical works on atheism, heathenism, and Pietism. His last work was *Cabinet der Pietisten* (1724).

62. Berns, "Vorrede," in *Entdeckung Des Greuel Wesens*. "This work [the *Biblia Pentapla*] was undertaken completely without my knowledge and will and when I saw it in the early stages, I made clear my opposition to it, but with no effect . . . As soon as it appeared in print, I immediately came out against its abominations, warned my congregation about it, and . . . in a sermon undertook a public examination of it in church and demonstrated its ugly features and intentions and warned against its hellish poison."

63. Patsch, "Arnoldiana in der Biblia Pentapla," 104.

64. Berns, "Vorrede," *Entdeckung Des Greuel Wesens*.

65. Berns's concerns are evident from the headings of the first four chapters of the *Entdeckung*: Chap. I. "What is their view of God's Word and the original text [*Grund-Text*]?," Chap. II. "What is their view of the various versions [of the Bible]?," Chap. III. "The Gospel of Christ in Scripture is of Antichrist and from the Devil according to these new Christians." Chap. IV. "The Gospel according to the New Christians." For Berns, the Pietist *Biblia Pentapla* perpetuated a wrong understanding on each of these points.

66. Berns, *Entdeckung Des Greuel Wesens*, 3, 5, 6.

67. Ibid., 8–10.

68. ". . . denn wozu soll die *Biblia Pentapla*; sie wird keinem redlichen Menschen nütz / die Holländische lasse ich in ihren Würden / die Jüdische und Quäcker-Version ist vom Teufel / die Catholische und reformirte / was die Gutes haben / ist aus Lutheri Version entlehnet / und das übrige ist keines Hellers werth; so werden auch selbst die neue Christen wenig um dieselbe geben / als die sich nun vergnügen mit ihrem Babelischen N. Testament." Michael Berns, *Das natürliche Licht des Verstandes* (Hamburg, 1711), 22, HTM-Text 27.9.1997, ed. Hanns-Johann Ehlen, www.stjuergen-kiel.de/BernsLichtVT.htm.

69. Berns, *Entdeckung Des Greuel Wesens*, 12, 15, 16.

70. Ibid., 13, 15.

71. Schrader, "Lesarten der Schrift," 205.

72. This German polyglot Bible and its editor, Glüsing, are finally receiving the recognition they deserve as a unique and early example of Pietist engagement with the Bible, alongside the *Berleburg Bible* and the work of Bengel.

73. Patsch, "Verstehen durch Vergleichen," 129–130.

74. Patsch, "Arnoldiana in der Biblia Pentapla," 95.

75. Johannes Wallmann, *Der Pietismus* (Göttingen: Vandenhoeck & Ruprecht, 2005), 173.

76. Martin Hofmann, *Theologie und Exegese der Berleburger Bibel (1726–1742)* (Gütersloh: Verlag C. Bertelsmann, 1937), 200; Sheehan, *Enlightenment Bible*, 80. See also Sheehan, 73–74.

77. Sheehan writes, "In place of English tolerance, the Germans had geographical boundaries, inside of which religions flourished and perished through the exigencies of the princes who exercised sovereignty over the religious preferences of their subjects." Sheehan, *Enlightenment Bible*, 29. On English toleration, see John Coffey, *Persecution and Toleration in Protestant England, 1558–1689* (London: Longman, 2000).

78. Two early studies of eighteenth-century Berleburg's history are still valuable: Friedrich Wilhelm Winckel, *Aus dem Leben Casimirs, weiland regierenden Grafen zu Sayn-Wittgenstein-Berleburg* (Frankfurt am Main, 1842); Max Goebel, *Geschichte des christlichen Lebens in der rheinisch-westphälischen evangelischen Kirche*, vol. 2 (Koblenz: Karl Bädeker, 1852) and vol. 3 (Koblenz: Karl Bädeker, 1860). Goebel observed, "Only recently have Pastor Winkel and I together undertaken to research and portray the main features of this earlier time, which now appears attractive rather than terrible, and thereby to achieve for Berleburg its rightful place in the history of the Christian life in Germany." Goebel, *Geschichte des christlichen Lebens*, 3:125.

79. The northern county was Sayn-Wittgenstein-Berleburg and the southern county was Sayn-Wittgenstein-Hohenstein. Countess Hedwig exercised rule in the north after the death of her husband, Count Ludwig Franz, in 1694, until her son Casimir was ready to take over in 1712. See Hans Schneider, "Der radikale Pietismus im 18. Jahrhundert," in Brecht and Deppermann, *Der Pietismus im achtzehnten Jahrhundert*, 123–124.

80. Goebel, *Geschichte des christlichen Lebens*, 2:760.

81. Marcus Meier, *Die Schwarzenauer Neutäufer: Genese einer Gemeindebildung zwischen Pietismus und Täufertum* (Göttingen: Vandenhoeck & Ruprecht, 2008), 152–154; Ulf Lückel, "Berleburg as a Refuge for Religious Tolerance in the Eighteenth Century," in Otto Marburger, ed., *Schwarzenau 1708–2008* (Bad Berleburg: Druckerei Benner, 2008), 145, 147.

82. Goebel, *Geschichte des christlichen Lebens*, 2:762–763.

83. Ibid., 818. In *Theobald oder die Schwärmer* (1785), Heinrich Jung-Stilling portrayed Hochmnann von Hochenau as an impressive man. See Goebel, *Geschichte des christlichen Lebens*, 2:854–855. See also Schrader, *Literaturproduktion und Büchermarkt des radikalen Pietismus*, 179–182.

84. Goebel, *Geschichte des christlichen Lebens,* 2:761.

85. Hans Schneider, "Ein zeitgenössischer Bericht über den Wittgensteiner Pietismus zu Beginn des 18. Jhs," in Johannes Burkardt, ed., *Von Wittgenstein in die Welt* (Bielefeld: Luther-Verlag, 2009), 182.

86. Goebel, *Geschichte des christlichen Lebens,* 2:842. Hochmann von Hochenau built the small cabin in 1709. In 1849, Goebel visited the place where Hochmann's hut was located and was deeply moved. See Friedrich Wilhelm Bautz, "Hochmann von Hochenau," *Biographisch-Bibliographisches Kirchenlexikon* 2 (1990): 914–915. In 2009, a stone marker was set in Hüttenthal to honor the memory of Hochmann.

87. Meier, *Die Schwarzenauer Neutäufer,* 155.

88. The simple life of the countesses in Schwarzenau is offered in an anonymous report, dated in 1704. It is included in Goebel, *Geschichte des christlichen Lebens,* 2:764–771. See Ulf Lückel, "Sayn-Wittgenstein-Hohenstein, Henrich Albrecht Graf zu," in *Biographisch-Bibliographisches Kirchenlexikon* 19 (2001), 1213–1219.

89. Donald Durnbaugh, *Church of the Brethren: Yesterday and Today* (Elgin, IL: Brethren Press, 1986), 6–8. See the celebratory volume edited by Otto Marburger: *Schwarzenau 1708–2008.* See also Donald F. Durnbaugh, *European Origins of the Brethren* (Elgin, IL: Brethren Press, 1958).

90. Count Henrich Albrecht wrote these words in 1711. Goebel, *Geschichte des christlichen Lebens,* 2:736.

91. Ibid., 759–160.

92. Winckel, *Aus dem Leben Casimirs,* 58. Chapter 6 of Winckel's biography of Casimir deals with "those who were banished . . . from other countries whom the Count took in" (110–143).

93. Goebel, *Geschichte des christlichen Lebens,* 3:90–92; Winckel, *Aus dem Leben Casimirs,* 80, 86.

94. Winckel, *Aus dem Leben Casimirs,* 112–113.

95. Casimir himself played the flute. Goebel, *Geschichte des christlichen Lebens,* 3:92; Winckel, *Aus dem Leben Casimirs,* 80, 86–87.

96. Goebel, *Geschichte des christlichen Lebens,* 3:102. Jung-Stilling noted, "In the 1720s and 1730s, the expectation of the kingdom of Christ on earth was strong and widespread . . . Johann Christian Seitz was so bold as to maintain that the Lord would come in the year 1736. Any who would not believe him he rebuked as unbelievers." See Goebel, *Geschichte des christlichen Lebens,* 3:94–96, 101–102. On Seitz, see *Geistliche Fama* 17 (1735): 21–26, 72–74; 19 (1736): 111–115. Bengel came out against Seitz's calculations.

97. Schneider, "Der radikale Pietismus im 18. Jahrhundert," 161, 193n399; Lückel, "Berleburg as a Refuge for Religious Tolerance in the Eighteenth Century," 145–155.

98. Winckel, *Aus dem Leben Casimirs,* 115–143; Ulf Lückel, "Sayn-Wittgenstein-Berleburg, Casimir Graf zu," *Biographisch-Bibliographisches Kirchenlexikon* 19 (2001): 1196–1202. See also Martin Brecht, "Die Berleburger Bibel: Hinweise zu ihrem Verständnis," *Pietismus und Neuzeit* 8 (1982): 179.

99. A useful source for Schefer's career is Wilhelm Hartnack, ed., *Die Berleburger*

Chroniken des Georg Cornelius, Antonius Crawelius und Johann Daniel Scheffer, assisted by Eberhard Bauer and Werner Wied (Laasphe: Komm.-Verlag Buchhandlung Adalbert Carl, 1964), 133–142. The book offers a concise record of events relating to the local, cultural, and family history of Berleburg between 1488 and 1800.

100. Lückel writes, "The Count remained closely tied to his inspector, from whom he learned the faith, through whom he entered the Christian Church, and whom he loved as a father right to the end." Ulf Lückel, "Ein fast vergessener großer Berleburger: Inspektor und Pfarrer Ludwig Christof Schefer (1669–1731): Eine erste Spurensuche," *Wittgenstein: Blätter des Wittgensteiner Heimatvereins* 64, no. 4 (2000): 158.

101. Ulf Lückel, "Schefer, Ludwig Christof, ref. Pfr. und Inspektor in Berleburg, Hauptmitarbeiter an der Berleburger Bibel," *Biographisch-Bibliographisches Kirchenlexikon* 19 (2001): 1226–1230.

102. Johann Georg Hinsberg, *Geschichte der Kirchengemeinde Berleburg bis zur Regierungszeit des Grafen Casimir (18. Jh.)*, introduced, edited, and with commentary by Johannes Burkardt and Ulf Lückel (Bad Berleburg, 1999), 85–86; Hartnack, *Die Berleburger Chroniken*, 162n75.

103. Schrader, *Literaturproduktion und Büchermarkt*, 164, 188.

104. Brecht, "Die Berleburger Bibel: Hinweise zu ihrem Verständnis," 165–168; Schrader, *Literaturproduktion und Büchermarkt*, 163–164.

105. Haug published a book in Idstein in 1710, so may have been residing in Idstein by this time. Johann Friedrich Haug, *Theosophia Pneumatica, oder, Geheime Gottes-Lehre, Die Dinge Gottes vortragend im neuen Wesen des Geistes, abthuende Das alte Wesen des Buchstabens* (Idstein: Erdmann Andreas Lyce, 1710).

106. Schrader, *Literaturproduktion und Büchermarkt*, 164–176. Lyce founded the Idstein press in 1704 and served as court printer, but he was scarcely able to make a living from the small number of productions coming from the press.

107. Brecht, "Die Berleburger Bibel: Hinweise zu ihrem Verständnis," 170–174; Schrader, *Literaturproduktion und Büchermarkt*, 177, 187–198, 207. On the role of the Berleburg press in promoting Pietist and Philadelphian literature, see Schrader, *Literaturproduktion und Büchermarkt*, 183, 227–238.

108. Schrader, *Literaturproduktion und Büchermarkt*, 198.

109. Goebel, *Geschichte des christlichen Lebens*, 3:105.

110. Brecht, "Die Berleburger Bibel: Hinweise zu ihrem Verständnis," 181–182.

111. Ibid., 198–199.

112. Wallmann, *Der Pietismus*, 173–174.

113. Hofmann, *Theologie und Exegese der Berleburger Bibel*, 171–176.

114. Wallmann, *Der Pietismus*, 173–174.

115. Sheehan, *Enlightenment Bible*, 77–79.

116. Ibid., 79, 80. Both books embark on "a skeptical journey" on which "one never arrives."

117. Schneider, "Der radikale Pietismus im 18. Jahrhundert," 161, 193n399.

118. Sheehan, *Enlightenment Bible*, 82–84.

119. Brecht, "Johann Albrecht Bengel," 324. See J. A. Bengel, "The Author's Preface," in *Gnomon of the New Testament*, vol. 1, trans. Charlton T. Lewis and Marvin R. Vincent (Philadelphia: Perkinpine & Higgins 1862), xiii.

120. Martin Brecht, "Johann Albrecht Bengel," in Martin Greschat, ed., *Orthodoxie und Pietismus* (Stuttgart: Verlag W. Kohlhammer, 1982), 327; Brecht, "Die Berleburger Bibel: Hinweise zu ihrem Verständnis," 200; Brecht, "Die Bedeutung der Bibel im deutschen Pietismus," 108–109.

121. Aland, "Bibel und Bibeltext," 128–129.

122. Ehmer, "Johann Albrecht Bengel," 225; Johann Christian Friedrich Burk, *Dr. Johann Albrecht Bengel's Leben und Wirken meißt nach handscriftlichen Materialien* (Stuttgart: Johann Friedrich Steinkopf, 1831), 3. Burk was a great-grandson of Bengel. See Burk, "Vorrede," in *Dr. Johann Albrecht Bengel's Leben und Wirken*, iii. There is an English translation: J. C. F. Burk, *A Memoir of the Life and Writings of John Albert Bengel, Compiled Principally from Original Manuscripts Never before Published*, trans. Robert Francis Walker (London: William Ball, 1837).

123. Brecht, "Johann Albrecht Bengel," 317; Wallmann, *Der Pietismus*, 215.

124. Aland, "Bibel und Bibeltext," 130. These reflections are found in Bengel's letter to a student, dated February 24, 1721.

125. Burk, *Dr. Johann Albrecht Bengel's Leben und Wirken*, 4–7; Wallmann, *Der Pietismus*, 216.

126. Burk, *Dr. Johann Albrecht Bengel's Leben und Wirken*, 9–10, 32.

127. Martin Jung, "Johann Albrecht Bengel als Theologe des Pietismus: Textkritik und Biblizismus," in *Nachfolger, Visionärinnen, Kirchenkritiker* (Leipzig: Evangelische Verlagsanstalt, 2003), 76.

128. Burk, *Dr. Johann Albrecht Bengel's Leben und Wirken*, 14–15. Bengel resembles Arndt and Spener in his lack of a conversion experience.

129. Brecht, "Johann Albrecht Bengel," 318–319; Wallmann, *Der Pietismus*, 217.

130. Johann Christian Friedrich Burk, *Evangelische Pastoral-Theologie in Beispielen. Aus den Erfahurungen treuer Diener Gottes* (Stuttgart: Joh. Friedrich Steinkopf, 1838), 1:111.

131. Jung, "Johann Albrecht Bengel als Theologe des Pietismus," 77.

132. Burk, *Dr. Johann Albrecht Bengel's Leben und Wirken*, 39–43; Brecht, "Johann Albrecht Bengel," 320–322.

133. "Bengels Lebensbeschreibung," in Gerhard Schäfer, ed., *Gott hat mein Herz Angerührt: Ein Bengel-Brevier* (Metzingen: Ernst Franz Verlag, 1987), 169.

134. "He believed that by this delay he would find God's will with more certainty than by hasty acceptance or rejection." Burk, *Dr. Johann Albrecht Bengel's Leben und Wirken*, 145–146. See also Martin Brecht, "Der württembergische Pietismus," in Brecht and Deppermann, *Der Pietismus im achtzehnten Jahrhundert*, 252.

135. Doris Metzger, "Die Geschichte des Klosters Denkendorf, Bewohner und Gäste des Klosters," www.pastoralkolleg-wuerttemberg.de/geschichte.htm. Hart-

mut Lehmann observed, "Bengel encouraged his followers to take a leading part in society and to fulfill their roles to the best of their ability, until Christ returned. Bengel soon earned recognition as the prophet and patriarch of Württemberg Pietism. The 1743 *Reskript* established Pietism as a respectable player in state and society. It institutionalized conventicles under the oversight of the clergy." Hartmut Lehmann, *Pietismus und weltliche Ordnung in Württemberg vom 17. bis 20. Jahrhundert* (Stuttgart: Kohlhammer, 1969, 2001), 93–94.

136. Wallmann, *Der Pietismus*, 219.

137. John Weborg, "Bengel, Johann Albrecht (1687–1752)," in Donald K. McKim, ed., *Dictionary of Major Biblical Interpreters* (Downers Grove, IL: InterVarsity Press, 2007), 186–187.

138. Köster, "'Mit tiefem Respekt, mit Furcht und Zittern,'' 111; Wallmann, *Der Pietismus*, 221.

139. Sheehan, *Enlightenment Bible*, 111–112.

140. *Joannis Bengelii Gnomon Novi Testamenti, in quo, ex nativa Verborum Vi, Simplicitas, Profunditas, Concinnitas, et Salubritas sensuum coelestium, indicatur* (Tübingen 1742). The title translates as "Johann Albrecht Bengel's *Gnomon of the New Testament*, in which, from the natural force of the words, the simplicity, depth, harmony, and saving power of the heavenly meanings is indicated."

141. Bengel, "Author's Preface," xiv. "I have given the name *Gnomon* . . . to these explanatory notes, in the sense of a pointer or indicator, as of a sun-dial. The intention is briefly to point out the full force of words and sentences in the New Testament . . . The *Gnomon* points the way well enough."

142. Dennis Wayne Chadwick, "John Albert Bengel's *Gnomon* and 'Chiasmus,' " 16, www.mccks.edu/academics/wfps/review.html. Bengel wrote, "The entire perpetual spirit of the language of the New Testament is distinctly *Hebraizing*, and differs in this respect from the style of other Greek authors." Bengel, "Author's Preface," xxv.

143. Bengel, "Author's Preface," xxvii.

144. Ibid., xvi–xx. See appendix A for a list of Bengel's twenty-seven admonitions.

145. Johann Albrecht Bengel, *Gnomon: Auslegung des Neuen Testamentes in fortlaufenden Anmerkungen*, translated into German by C. F. Werner, 7th ed. (Berlin: Evangelische Verlangsanstalt, 1960), vol. 2, pt. 2, 591.

146. Weborg, "Bengel, Johann Albrecht (1687–1752)," 186.

147. Jung, "Johann Albrecht Bengel als Theologe des Pietismus," 80–81.

148. "Die Bibel ist ein Brief, den mein Gott mir hat schreiben lassen, wonach ich mich ausrichten soll und wonach mein Gott mich richten wird." See "Zitate von Johann Albrecht Bengel," www.bk-luebeck.eu/zitate-bengel.html.

149. "Nowhere [else] in Europe was so much scholarly energy, so much cultural capital, so many university positions, and so many publishing dollars devoted to the biblical text as in Germany." Sheehan, *Enlightenment Bible*, 116; see also 29–30.

Chapter 9. Pietism, World Christianity, and Missions to South India and Labrador

1. Peter Beyerhaus, *Er sandte sein Wort: Theologie der christlichen Mission*, vol. 1, *Die Bibel in der Mission* (Wuppertal: R. Brockhaus; Bad Liebenzell: Verl. der Liebenzeller Mission, 1996), 48–49. See also David Bosch, *Transforming Mission: Paradigm Shifts in Theology of Mission* (Maryknoll, NY: Orbis Books, 1991), 250–251. Examples of Orthodox Lutheran thinking on the great commission can be found in the *Wittenberger Gutachten* (1692) and in Johann Gerhard, *Loci Theologici* (1610–1622), arts. 23, 24.

2. Hermann Wellenreuther, "Pietismus und Mission: Vom 17. bis zum Beginn des 20. Jahrhunderts," in Hartmut Lehmann, ed., *Glaubenswelt und Lebenswelten des Pietismus* (Göttingen: Vandenhoeck & Ruprecht, 2004), 166–167.

3. Daniel Jeyaraj, "The Trailblazer," *Christian History and Biography*, July 1, 2005. For a comparison of the missionary methods of Ziegenbalg and Carey, see Daniel Jeyaraj, *Bartholomäus Ziegenbalg: The Father of Modern Protestant Mission—an Indian Assessment* (New Delhi: Indian Society for Promoting Christian Knowledge, 2006), 290–293.

4. Wellenreuther, "Pietismus und Mission," 168, 170.

5. Ibid., 176.

6. H. Gundert, *Die Evangelische Mission, ihre Länder, Völker und Arbeiten* (Stuttgart: Verlag der Vereinsbuchhandlung, 1886), 20–22. The journal *Pietismus und Neuzeit* devoted volume 7 (1981) to the Basler Christentumsgesellschaft; the articles were based on papers from a 1980 conference in Basel celebrating its two-hundredth anniversary.

7. Gundert, *Die Evangelische Mission*, 25–27. See also Julius Richter, *Geschichte der Berliner Missionsgesellschaft, 1824–1924* (Berlin: Verlag der Buchhandlung der Berliner ev. Missionsgesellschaft, 1924).

8. Wellenreuther, "Pietismus und Mission," 173.

9. Ibid., 173–174; Gundert, *Die Evangelische Mission*, 20–21.

10. Wellenreuther, "Pietismus und Mission," 174. On Spangenberg's "Instruction for Brothers and Sisters Who Serve the Gospel among the Heathen" (1784), see Theodor Bechler, *August Gottlieb Spangenberg und die Mission* (Herrnhut: Verl. Der Missionsbuchhandlung, 1933), 114–128.

11. One effort to address this neglect of German missions is the research group at the Institute for European History in Mainz, under Dr. Judith Becker: "Transfer und Transformation der Europabilder evangelischer Missionare im Kontakt mit dem Anderen, 1700–1970. Geisteswissenschaftliche Nachwuchsgruppe: Europa von außen gesehen." See also Judith Becker and Bettina Braun, eds., *Die Begegnung mit Fremden und das Geschichtsbewusstsein* (Göttingen: Vandenhoeck & Ruprecht, 2012).

12. For German sources on the Danish-Halle mission to India, see Heike Liebau, ed., *Die Quellen der Dänisch-Halleschen Mission in Tranquebar in deutschen Archiven:*

Ihre Bedeutung für die Indienforschung (Berlin: Verl. Das Arabische Buch, 1993); Erika Pabst and Thomas Müller-Bahlke, eds., *Quellenbestände der Indienmission 1700–1918 in Archiven des deutschsprachigen Raums* (Tübingen: Verlag der Franckeschen Stiftungen zu Halle [Saale], 2005). See also Heike Liebau, ed., *Geliebtes Europa // Ostindische Welt: 300 Jahre Interkultureller Dialog im Spiegel der Dänisch-Halleschen Mission* (Halle: Verlag der Franckeschen Stiftungen zu Halle, 2006).

13. Ziegenbalg wrote *A Detailed Report of a Royal Danish Missionary in Tranquebar on the Coromandel Coast, How He and His Colleague Heinrich Plütscho Are Carrying Out Their Ministry of the Gospel among the Heathen and Christians* (1710) and *Propagation of the Gospel in the East: Being a Further Account of the Success of the Danish-Missionaries* (London, 1710). Susannah Wesley read Ziegenbalg's accounts to her children to instill missionary-mindedness. See Jeyaraj, *Bartholomäus Ziegenbalg*, 260–261.

14. *Geneology of the Malabar (South-Indian) Deities from Their Own Writings, Including a Description of Popular Hinduism* (1713) and *Malabar Heathenism* (1713).

15. See Arno Lehmann, ed., *Alte Briefe aus Indien: Unveröffentlichte Briefe von Batholomäus Zigenbalg 1706–1719* (Berlin: Evangelische Verlagsanstalt, 1957).

16. "Der Königl. Dänischen Missionarien aus Ost-Indien eingesandter Ausführlichen Berichten, Von dem Werck ihres Amts unter den Heyden," pts. 1–9 (continuation 1–108) (Halle: Waisenhaus, 1710–1772). These are located in the Archive of the Francke Foundations, Halle, MISS:A 1; 121 K 1–9. All these reports have been digitalized and are available at http://192.124.243.55/digbib/hb.htm.

17. See Kurt Liebau, ed., *Die Malabarische Korrespondenz: Tamilische Briefe an Deutsche Missionare, Eine Auswahl* (Sigmaringen: Jan Thorbecke, 1998); Heike Liebau, *Die indischen Mitarbeiter der Tranquebarmission (1706–1845): Katecheten, Schulmeister, Übersetzer* (Tübingen: Max Niemeyer Verlag, 2008), 212.

18. Heike Liebau, "Die Halleschen Berichte," in Liebau, *Geliebtes Europa // Ostindische Welt*, 97.

19. D. Jeyaraj observed that "Ziegenbalg's palm-leaf writings are languishing in many places, including Halle. They are waiting to be researched. The Mission archives of the Francke Foundations houses them as crown jewels. They are looking for Indians to decipher them. There is a collection of his ethical principles titled 'Darmavazhi', which is also a palm-leaf manuscript. I hope scholars will come forward to study that, too." S. Dorairaj, "Of the German Who Took Tamil to Europeans: Interview with Daniel Jeyaraj, Professor at Liverpool Hope University," *Frontline: India's National Magazine* 27, no. 15 (2010).

20. See Heike Liebau, "German Missionaries as Research Workers in India: Their Diaries as Historical Sources (Benjamin Schultze)," *Studies in History* 11, no. 1 (1995): 114, 117; Liebau, *Die indischen Mitarbeiter der Tranquebarmission*, 38.

21. Liebau, *Die indischen Mitarbeiter der Tranquebarmission*, 18–20.

22. Ibid., 23–26, 41. The life stories were typically composed on the occasion of an ordination or death.

23. Jeyaraj, *Bartholomäus Ziegenbalg*, 35–37.

24. Heike Liebau, "Tranquebar um 1700," in Liebau, *Geliebtes Europa // Os-*

tindische Welt, 73; Daniel Jeyaraj, "The History of the Danish-Halle Mission in India," in Erika Pabst and Thomas Müller-Bahlke, eds., *Quellenbestände der Indienmission 1700–1918 in Archiven des deutschsprachigen Raums,* www.francke-halle.de/francke.htm/forschung/indmis.pdf.

25. On Ziegenbalg, see Jeyaraj, *Bartholomäus Ziegenbalg;* Arno Lehmann, *It Began at Tranquebar: The Story of the Tranquebar Mission and the Beginnings of Protestant Christianity in India* (Madras: Christian Literature Society, 1956).

26. Marianne Yaldiz, "Kunst und Religion in Südostindien," in Liebau, *Geliebtes Europa // Ostindische Welt,* 54–65; Sabine Bregy, "Zum Beispiel: Bartholomäus Ziegenbalg—Quellenkunde zur indischen Geschichte bis 1858," www.payer.de/quellenkunde/quellen1517.htm.

27. Liebau, "Tranquebar um 1700," 73; Liebau, *Die indischen Mitarbeiter der Tranquebarmission (1706–1845),* 80. See also Jeyaraj, *Bartholomäus Ziegenbalg,* 26–27.

28. Eugene F. Irschick, "Conversations in Tarangambadi: Caring for the Self in Early Eighteenth Century South India," *Comparative Studies of South Asia, Africa, and the Middle East* 23, no. 1–2 (2003): 256.

29. Ziegenbalg called the Tamil schoolmaster "Kanabadi Wathiar." The word for schoolmaster in Tamil is *Watthiar* or *Wathiar.* Some western scholars mistake "Wathiar" for the schoolmaster's name. See Brijraj Singh, *The First Protestant Missionary to India: Bartholomaeus Ziegenbalg* (Oxford: Oxford University Press, 1999), 17–18, 68.

30. Liebau, *Die indischen Mitarbeiter der Tranquebarmission,* 116; Albertine Gaur, "A Catalogue of B. Ziegenbalg's Tamil Library," *British Museum Quarterly* 30, no. 3–4 (1966): 100.

31. Erich Beyreuther, *Bartholomaeus Ziegenbalg—a Biography of the First Protestant Missionary in India,* trans. S. G. Lang and H. W. Gensichen (Chennai, India: Christian Literature Society, 1955, 1998), 30.

32. Jeyaraj, *Bartholomäus Ziegenbalg,* 68–70; Singh, *First Protestant Missionary to India,* 18. As of September 27, 1708, the church had 101 members; by 1712, it had 200. See Jeyaraj, *Bartholomäus Ziegenbalg,* 278–282.

33. Liebau, "Tranquebar um 1700," 73. The seventeenth-century Danish commander permitted the Portuguese to build a Catholic church in Tranquebar.

34. Werner Raupp, "PLÜTSCHAU, Heinrich, luth. Missionar," *Biographisch Bibliographisches Kirchenlexikon* 7 (1994), 757–758.

35. Kurt Liebau, "Einleitung," in Liebau, *Die Malabarische Korrespondenz,* 14–16.

36. Jeyaraj, *Bartholomäus Ziegenbalg,* 74.

37. Anders Norgaard, "Die Anfänge der Mission," in Liebau, *Geliebtes Europa // Ostindische Welt,* 20–21.

38. Jeyaraj, *Bartholomäus Ziegenbalg,* 235–237.

39. Ulrich Gäbler, "Die Anfänge der Mission in Tranquebar. Eine Skizze," http://gaebler.info/oekumene/mission.htm.

40. Jeyaraj, *Bartholomäus Ziegenbalg*, 186. In 1712, A. H. Francke and Heinrich Julius Elers in Halle sent fonts in Portuguese, Tamil, German, and English. The Tamil Old Testament was completed in 1726, after Ziegenbalg died.

41. Daniel Jeyaraj recently produced the first English translation of Ziegenbalg's Latin-Tamil Grammar, *Grammatica Damulica: Tamil Language for Europeans: Ziegenbalg's Grammatica Damulica (1716)*, trans. from Latin and Tamil, annotations and commentary by Daniel Jeyaraj, with the assistance of Sister Dr. Rachel Harrington, SND (Wiesbaden: Harrassowitz Verlag, 2010). On the earlier model for Ziegenbalg's grammar, see Daniel Jeyaraj, *Inkulturation in Tranquebar: Der Beitrag der frühen dänisch-halleschen Mission zum Werden einer indisch-einheimischen Kirche* (Erlangen: Verlag der Ev.-Luth. Mission, 1996), 84–91.

42. Dorairaj, "Of the German Who Took Tamil to Europeans."

43. Gaur, "Catalogue of B. Ziegenbalg's Tamil Library," 105n6.

44. Ibid., 99; Daniel Jeyaraj, ed., *Genealogy of the South Indian Deities* (New York: RoutledgeCurzon, 2005), 17.

45. Gaur, "Catalogue of B. Ziegenbalg's Tamil Library," 104. See also Will Sweetman, "The Prehistory of Orientalism: Colonialism and the Textual Basis for Bartholomäus Ziegenbalg's Account of Hinduism," *New Zealand Journal of Asian Studies* 6, no. 2 (2004): 21–23. Sweetman notes that in December 1715, Francke expressed a more positive view of Ziegenbalg's study of Hinduism. "If I did not consider it necessary to publish this book . . . nevertheless I could not by any means find fault with the great efforts which you for your part have expended on the accurate study of the heathen theology" (22).

46. Page numbers in the text refer to Irschick, "Conversations in Tarangambadi." The "siddhar" was a Hindu saint who taught a religious practice that undermined traditional temple rituals and the brahmanic religion of the Puranas. The teaching of the siddhars sought to overcome the sins of anger, lust, and egoism by moral behavior and care of the self and the body. They taught a yoga of silence and inner stillness through breath control; they emphasized holiness, vigilance, and knowledge of the self. While Hindu priests purchased the palm-leaf manuscripts of Civavaakiyar's writings in order to destroy them, because Civavaakiyar denounced traditional temple religion, Christians such as Ziegenbalg sought to preserve them. Ibid., 259, 263–264.

47. In reply, Ziegenbalg promised not to get angry. "I see myself bound to listen patiently to your objections to my teachings."

48. Liebau, *Die indischen Mitarbeiter der Tranquebarmission*, 89, 133; Jeyaraj, *Bartholomäus Ziegenbalg*, 67.

49. Liebau, *Die indischen Mitarbeiter der Tranquebarmission*, 114–116.

50. Ibid., 89–90; Singh, *First Protestant Missionary to India*, 36.

51. While back home, Ziegenbalg renewed acquaintance with Maria Dorothea Salzmann, the daughter of a teacher living in Halle and sister of Zinzendorf's friend Carl August Salzmann. Ziegenbalg and Maria Dorothea Salzmann were married in Halle on June 4, 1715, and she accompanied him on his return to India a year later.

They had three children, two of whom died in infancy. The widowed Maria would later marry the deputy governor of Tranquebar; they returned to Europe in 1720. See Singh, *First Protestant Missionary to India*, 36–39. On Maria Dorothea's letter writing, see Gita Rajan, "Labyrinths of the Colonial Archive: Unpacking German Missionary Narratives from Tranquebar, Southeast India (1706–1720)" (PhD diss., University of Michigan, 2001); Andreas Gross, "Maria Dorothea Ziegenbalg and Utila Elisabeth Gründler: The First Two Wives of Missionaries in Tranquebar," in Andreas Gross, Y. Vincent Kumaradoss, and Heike Liebau, eds., *Halle and the Beginnings of Protestant Christianity in India* (Halle: Franckesche Stiftungen, Aug. 2006), 2:705–718.

52. Liebau, *Die indischen Mitarbeiter der Tranquebarmission*, 83, 90–91, 143–144; Jeyaraj, *Bartholomäus Ziegenbalg*, 181–182.

53. Liebau, *Die indischen Mitarbeiter der Tranquebarmission*, 2–3, 128–129.

54. Daniel Jeyaraj, "Indian Participation in Enabling, Sustaining, and Promoting Christian Mission in India," in Richard Fox Young, ed., *India and the Indianness of Christianity: Essays on Understanding—Historical, Theological, and Bibliographical—in Honor of Robert Eric Frykenberg* (Grand Rapids, MI: Wm. B. Eerdmans, 2009), 30–38.

55. Liebau, *Die indischen Mitarbeiter der Tranquebarmission*, 119–120, 132–137.

56. Ibid., 94–95, 99.

57. Ibid., 2. Wallmann states that by the end of the eighteenth century, "80 missionaries from Halle were sent out to India." Johannes Wallmann, *Der Pietismus* (Göttingen: Vandenhoeck & Ruprecht, 2005), 132.

58. Liebau, *Die indischen Mitarbeiter der Tranquebarmission*, 2, 386–388.

59. Stephen Neill, *A History of Christian Missions* (Harmondsworth, UK: Penguin Books, 1964), 231.

60. Johann Lucas Niekamp's 1740 account of the Danish-Halle Mission to Tranquebar divided the first thirty years of the mission into three stages: the beginning phase of orientation under Ziegenbalg, 1706–1720; the work of Benjamin Schultz and completion of the Tamil Bible, 1720–1727; and the work of the Tamil catechist Rajanayakkan, 1727 onward. Anders Norgaard divided the entire history of the Pietist mission to India into three periods: the foundational period, 1706–1729; the established mission, 1730–1780; and the period of decline, 1780–1845. See Johann Lucas Niekamp, *Kurtzgefaßte Mißions-Geschichte oder Historischer Auszug Der Evangelischen Mißions-Berichte aus Ostindien von dem Jahr 1705 bis zu Ende des Jahres 1736* [A concise mission history or historical summary of the evangelical mission reports from East India from 1705 to the end of 1736] (Halle, 1740); Anders Norgaard, *Mission und Obrigkeit—Die Dänisch-hallische Mission in Tranquebar 1706–1845* (Gütersloh: Gütersloher Verlags-Haus Gerd Mohn, 1988); Liebau, *Die indischen Mitarbeiter der Tranquebarmission*, 81–82, 419.

61. On Schultze, see Heike Liebau, "Deutsche Missionare als Indienforscher. Benjamin Schultze (1689–1760)—Ausnahme oder Regel?," *Archiv für Kulturgeschichte* 76 (1994): 111–134; Heike Liebau, "Die Sprachforschungen des Mis-

sionars Benjamin Schultze unter besonderer Berücksichtigung der 'Grammatica Hindostanica'" (PhD diss., Martin Luther University, Halle-Wittenberg, 1988); Anders Norgaard, "Missionar Benjamin Schultze als Leiter der Tranquebarmission (1720–1726)," *Neue Zeitschrift für Missionswissenschaft* 33 (1977): 181–201.

62. Liebau, "German Missionaries as Research Workers in India," 113.

63. Ibid., 112. Schultze's grammars were more attentive to the spoken language, while Ziegenbalg was more attentive to the written language.

64. Hanco Jürgens, "Forschungen zu Sprachen und Religion," in Liebau, *Geliebtes Europa//Ostindische Welt*, 133; see also 126–128.

65. For the anniversary meeting, see "300-Jahr-Feier in Tranquebar: Lob für Wirken des ersten lutherischen Missionars," on the website of the Evangelisch-Lutherische Landeskirche Sachsens, www.evlks.de/aktuelles/spektrum/5951.html. Daniel Jeyaraj is professor of World Christianity at Liverpool Hope University.

66. Stephen Neill, *A History of Christianity in India, 1707–1858* (Cambridge: Cambridge University Press, 1985), 28.

67. Hans Rollmann, *Labrador through Moravian Eyes: 250 Years of Art, Photographs, and Records* (St. John's, NL: Special Celebrations Corporation of Newfoundland and Labrador, 2002), 10. Rollmann estimates that the Unity Archive in Herrnhut holds 250,000 pages of manuscript materials on Labrador alone. See also William H. Whiteley, "The Records of the Moravian Mission in Labrador," *American Archivist* 24 (1961): 425–430; William H. Whiteley, "Inventory of Moravian Mission Records from Labrador," 1960, Moravian Archives, Bethlehem, PA, www.moravianchurcharchives.org/labrador.pdf.

68. Thea Olsthoorn, *Die Erkundungsreisen der Herrnhuter Missionare nach Labrador (1752–1770)* (Hildesheim: Georg Olms Verlag, 2010), 13–16, 340–341. A comprehensive history of the Moravian mission to Labrador has yet to be written.

69. See *Graf Ohne Grenzen: Leben und Werk von Nikolaus ludwig Graf von Zinzendorf* [Count without borders: The life and work of Nikolaus Ludwig Count von Zinzendorf] (Unitätszarchiv in Herrnhut: Verlag der Comeniusbuchhandlung Herrnhut, 2000).

70. Jeyaraj, *Bartholomäus Ziegenbalg*, 260.

71. Rollmann, *Labrador through Moravian Eyes*, 52.

72. Peter Vogt, "Nicholas Ludwig von Zinzendorf (1700–1760)," in Carter Lindberg, ed. *The Pietist Theologians* (Oxford: Blackwell, 2005), 207.

73. Hans Schneider, "Nikolaus Ludwig von Zinzendorf als Gestalt der Kirchengeschichte," in Dietrich Meyer and Paul Peucker, eds., *Graf Ohne Grenzen: Leben und Werk von Nikolaus Ludwig Graf von Zinzendorf* (Herrnhut: Unitätsarchiv in Herrnhut, 2000), 10. See also Wallmann, *Der Pietismus*, 183.

74. Dietrich Meyer, "Zinzendorf und Herrnhut," in Martin Brecht and Klaus Deppermann, eds., *Der Pietismus im achtzehnten Jahrhundert* (Göttingen: Vandenhoeck & Ruprecht, 1995), 8. "His background in the upper nobility on the one hand and his complete identification with the artisan/craftsman class and uneducated on the other, in a way that superseded all social boundaries, was unusual for

his day . . . The extent of his writings [more than 67 volumes] points to his unusual energy" (8).

75. W. R. Ward, *The Protestant Evangelical Awakening* (Cambridge: Cambridge University Press, 1992), 141–142.

76. Vogt, "Nikolaus Ludwig von Zinzendorf," 210. Vogt writes, "Zinzendorf was not a trained theologian and never wrote a systematic exposition of his ideas. Instead, he expressed his views in hymns, sermons, letters, occasional pamphlets, and administrative instructions" (210).

77. Craig D. Atwood, "Introduction," in *Community of the Cross: Moravian Piety in Colonial Bethlehem* (University Park: Penn State Press, 2004), 6. Atwood notes, "The literature on Zinzendorf is enormous because his activities touched so many aspects of early modern German culture . . . His work influenced such luminaries as Goethe, Schleiermacher, Herder and Novalis" (6).

78. Wallmann, *Der Pietismus*, 183.

79. Ibid., 184.

80. Schneider, "Nikolaus Ludwig von Zinzendorf als Gestalt der Kirchengeschichte," 13.

81. Zinzendorf, "Kurze Generalidee meiner Absichten und Handlungen," in D. Meyer, ed., *Nikolaus Ludwig Graf von Zinzendorf: Er der Meister, Wir die Brüder* (Giessen: Brunnen Verlag, 2000), 17.

82. Wallmann, *Der Pietismus*, 185–187.

83. Craig D. Atwood, *Always Reforming: A History of Christianity since 1300* (Macon, GA: Mercer University Press, 2001), 213.

84. "In 1273 the Habsburg family became rulers of Austria, Styria and Carniola, a position they remarkably retained until 1918. From 1438 there was an almost continuous succession of Habsburg Emperors until the end of the Holy Roman Empire [under Napoleonic rule] in 1806." Mary Fulbrook, *A Concise History of Germany* (Cambridge: Cambridge University Press, 1994), 27.

85. "The religious boundaries created by the Peace of Westphalia lasted essentially until the population upheavals unleashed by the Second World War." Fulbrook, *Concise History of Germany*, 61.

86. Zinzendorf described a visit to his estates in 1722: "I found three kinds of subjects on my estates: the Lutherans, the Schwenkfelders, and the Moravian Brethren . . . The Moravian Brethren, founded some sixty years before the Protestant Reformation and accustomed to certain Church regulations, impressed three things upon my mind: their doctrine, the condition of their souls, and their regulations. In doctrine they were Reformed. But in 1725 after heartfelt discussion, they welcomed all the Evangelical Lutheran teaching that I presented to them." Zinzendorf, "Kurze Generalidee meiner Absichten und Handlungen," 22ff.

87. Dietrich Meyer, "Zinzendorf und Herrnhut," in Brecht and Deppermann, *Der Pietismus im achtzehnten Jahrhundert*, 21, 22. The "Moravian Church" took its beginnings as a pre-Reformation movement for reform under Jan Huss (1373–1415) in Bohemia and Moravia in the early fifteenth century. Hus followed John Wyclif

in criticizing the Roman Catholic doctrine of the seven sacraments. Scattered Moravians survived and joined religious refugees of other sorts in seeking refuge on the lands of the Berthelsdorf estate of Count Zinzendorf.

88. Ward, *Protestant Evangelical Awakening,* 124. Thanks to the preaching of Zinzendorf's Pietist friend in nearby Berthelsdorf, the Lutheran preacher Johann Andreas Rothe (1688–1758), Zinzendorf's estate became a gathering place for Pietist preachers.

89. Meyer, "Zinzendorf und Herrnhut," 21; Ward, *Protestant Evangelical Awakening,* 124; Wallmann, *Der Pietismus,* 188, 191.

90. Wallmann, *Der Pietismus,* 188.

91. Ibid., 188, 189; Meyer, "Zinzendorf und Herrnhut," 25–28.

92. "His wife's grandmother had been a highly prized friend of Spener, and the Ebersdorf court was in the inner circle of the policy-makers to the institutions at Halle, maintaining connexions across the Empire from the Wetterau to Silesia." Ward, *Protestant Evangelical Awakening,* 122.

93. J. G. G. Norman, "Moravians," in J. D. Douglas, ed., *The New International Dictionary of the Christian Church* (Grand Rapids, MI: Zondervan, 1974), 676. "As early as 1732 two members went to St. Thomas on the Virgin Islands; missions were also established in Greenland, North America (1734), South America (1735), South Africa (1736), Labrador (1752), Australia (1850), and Tibet (1856) . . . The proportion of missionaries to home communicants has been estimated as 1:60 compared with 1:5000 in the rest of Protestantism" (676).

94. Schneider, "Nikolaus Ludwig von Zinzendorf als Gestalt der Kirchengeschichte," 13.

95. Henry Ellis, *A Voyage to Hudson's Bay by the Dobbs Galley and California, in the Years 1746 and 1747, for Discovering a North West Passage* (London: H. Whitridge, 1748), 139, 232.

96. Rollmann, *Labrador through Moravian Eyes,* 5–6; Olsthoorn, *Die Erkundungsreisen der Herrnhuter Missionare,* 18–19.

97. Olsthoorn, *Die Erkundungsreisen der Herrnhuter Missionare,* 19–23; Rollmann, *Labrador through Moravian Eyes,* 6–7.

98. Rollmann, *Labrador through Moravian Eyes,* 6–7. Rollmann notes that the ruins of the 1752 house were discovered again in 2000 and excavated in 2001. See also David A. Schattschneider, "A 250-Year-Old Mystery: The Disappearance of J. C. Erhardt in Labrador," *Journal of Moravian History* 2 (spring 2007): 76–89.

99. Marianne P. Stopp, "Eighteenth Century Labrador Inuit in England," *Arctic* 62, no. 1 (2009): 47.

100. Olsthoorn, *Die Erkundungsreisen der Herrnhuter Missionare,* 107, 108. The mission journal included a conversation with the Inuit at the time: " 'We see now that you are not Europeans but rather are Inuit,' they said, and then asked us several times if we were afraid . . . Brother Jens Haven said, 'I am not afraid, for you are my friends and friends are not afraid of each other.' Then the Inuit said, 'Now we see

that you are our friends and are good people, for you come and sleep among us without weapons'" (107, 108).

101. J. C. S. Mason, *The Moravian Church and the Missionary Awakening in England, 1760–1800* (Woodbridge, UK: Boydell & Brewer, 2001), 47–48. A contemporary account describes how the ship was obtained: "A visit of a preliminary and exploratory character having been determined on in the early part of the year 1770, it became, therefore, one of the first objects of the Society [the Brethren's Society for the Furtherance of the Gospel among the Heathen], to procure such a vessel, and to engage the services of a trustworthy and experienced captain for the conduct of the expedition. After a good deal of inquiry in London and in other ports, a small sloop of eighty tons burden, called the *JERSEY PACKET*, was purchased and fitted out by the Society, or rather, by 'the ship's company,' and the command of her given to Captain Francis Mugford. She is described, in a MS. letter of Br. Benj. La Trobe to the Directing Board of the Unity, as not only 'a tight and sound ship, but also a prime sailer, readily obedient to the helm, and out-sailing all the vessels in the river on the passage down to Gravesend.'" *Brief Account of the Missionary Ships Employed in the Service of the Mission on the Coast of Labrador from the Year 1770 to 1877* (London, 1877), based on *Periodical Accounts* 21 (n.d.): 75–83, 120–133.

102. Olsthoorn, *Die Erkundungsreisen der Herrnhuter Missionare*, 30–31, 101–102; Rollmann, *Labrador through Moravian Eyes*, 8.

103. Rollmann, *Labrador through Moravian Eyes*, 8–9, 16–27. In 1970, the mission settlement in Hopedale was made a National Historic Site in Canada.

104. Olsthoorn, *Die Erkundungsreisen der Herrnhuter Missionare*, 105, 107.

105. Ibid., 176. Rollmann notes that only Haven and Drachardt have remained in collective memory. Christoph Brasen did not receive an entry in the *Dictionary of Canadian Biography* or in Joey Smallwood's *Encyclopedia of Newfoundland and Labrador*. See Hans Rollmann, "The Moravians in Labrador (I): Christoph Brasen (1738–1774)," www.mun.ca/rels/morav/texts/brasen.html.

106. Olsthoorn, *Die Erkundungsreisen der Herrnhuter Missionare*, 171–172.

107. Ibid., 172–173, 175.

108. "Retrospect of the History of the Mission of the Brethren's Church in Labrador for the Past Hundred Years (1771–1871)," *Periodical Accounts* 28 (1871): 1–19, 53–72, www.mun.ca/rels/morav/texts/brethren.html. The records of conversions and baptisms in Nain, Okak, and Hopedale are available in the Moravian Archive in Bethlehem, PA. Whiteley, "Inventory of Moravian Mission Records from Labrador," 9, 16, 28.

109. "Account of the Life of Brother Jens Haven," *Periodical Accounts Relating to the Missions of the Church of the United Brethren* 2 (1797): 111, www.mun.ca/rels/morav/texts/jhaven.html.

110. Mason, *Moravian Church and the Missionary Awakening*, 51.

111. According to "Account of the Life of Brother Jens Haven," "The American War raged at that time and the seas swarmed with privateers; but we ventured

upon God's help and sailed without convoy. We saw no enemy and met with no kind of disaster; but, when we came near the coast of Labrador, we discovered an ice-mountain of prodigious extent and height before us, and had scarce passed it in safety, before it fell to pieces with a tremendous crash, putting the surrounding sea into the most dreadful agitation and foam. Had this happened but a few minutes before, we must have perished in the immense ruin" (112).

112. Olsthoorn, *Die Erkundungsreisen der Herrnhuter Missionare,* 175–177.

113. Ibid., 177–178.

114. "Retrospect of the History of the Mission of the Brethren's Church in Labrador for the Past Hundred Years (1771–1871)," *Periodical Accounts* 28 (1871): 1–19, 53–72, www.mun.ca/rels/morav/texts/brethren.html.

115. Gundert, *Die Evangelische Mission, ihre Länder, Völker und Arbeiten,* 377.

116. Olsthoorn, *Die Erkundungsreisen der Herrnhuter Missionare,* 259.

117. Ibid., 262. Mikak is the subject of PhD research by Amelia Fay in the Department of Archaeology at Memorial University, Newfoundland. Fay's research project is entitled "An Extraordinary Woman, An Extraordinary Life: Excavating Mikak's House to Explore the Status of Women and the Effects of Colonialism in 18th Century Labrador." The focus of Fay's excavation is a dwelling on Black Island where Mikak lived, according to a 1776 census. The project was chosen in collaboration with the Inuit of Nunatsiavut. See Amelia Fay, "Searching for Mikak: Archaeologist Uncovering Story of First Labrador Inuit Woman to Earn a Place in Recorded History," *Labrador Life* 5, no. 4 (2011): 22–25.

118. Olaf Uwe Janzen, "Newfoundland and the International Fishery," in M. Brook Taylor, ed., *Canadian History: A Reader's Guide,* vol. 1, *Beginnings to Confederation* (Toronto: University of Toronto Press, 1994), 322. See also J. G. Taylor's "The Two Worlds of Mikak, Part I," *Beaver* 314, no. 3 (1983): 4–13; and "The Two Worlds of Mikak, Part II," *Beaver* 314, no. 4 (1984): 18–25.

119. Stopp, "Eighteenth Century Labrador Inuit in England," 47.

120. Olsthoorn, *Die Erkundungsreisen der Herrnhuter Missionare,* 259.

121. Stopp, "Eighteenth Century Labrador Inuit in England," 48.

122. "Account of the Life of Brother Jens Haven," 107.

123. Stopp, "Eighteenth Century Labrador Inuit in England," 49.

124. Olsthoorn, *Die Erkundungsreisen der Herrnhuter Missionare,* 260.

125. Ibid., 179, 261–266.

126. Stopp, "Eighteenth Century Labrador Inuit in England," 51.

127. Ibid., 52.

128. Taylor, "Two Worlds of Mikak, Part II," 22.

129. Stopp, "Eighteenth Century Labrador Inuit in England," 52–53.

130. Ibid., 54; Taylor, "Two Worlds of Mikak, Part II," 25.

131. Rollmann, *Labrador through Moravian Eyes.*

132. Hans Rollmann, ed., *Moravian Beginnings in Labrador: Papers from a Symposium Held in Makkovik and Hopedale,* Occasional Publication of Newfoundland and Labrador Studies, No. 2 (St. John's, NL: Faculty of Arts Publications, 2009).

133. Neill, *History of Christianity in India*, 28.

134. Mason, *Moravian Church and the Missionary Awakening*, 194, 196–197.

Chapter 10. The Contribution of German Pietism to the Modern World

1. Peter C. Erb, for example, investigated Gottfried Arnold's debts to late Medieval mystics such as Nicholas of Cusa, Hugh of Balma, and Jean Ruysbroc. Erb asserted that of all the early Pietists, Arnold had the most wide-ranging knowledge and made the most extensive use of late Medieval mystics. See Peter C. Erb, *Pietists, Protestants, and Mysticism: The Use of Late Medieval Spiritual Texts in the Work of Gottfried Arnold (1666–1714)* (Metuchen, NJ: Scarecrow Press, 1989). More recently, Marcus Meier has argued for the importance of Anabaptists, Mennonites, and the Amish in shaping German Radical Pietists such as Alexander Mack and the New Baptists of Schwarzenau. See Marcus Meier, *The Origin of the Schwarzenau Brethren*, trans. Dennis Slabaugh (Ambler, PA: Brethren Encyclopedia, 2008).

2. Peter Berger, *The Homeless Mind: Modernization and Consciousness* (New York: Vintage Books, 1974), 76, 184. Berger writes, "The pluralistic structures of modern society have made the life of more and more individuals migratory, ever-changing, mobile" (184).

3. Hans-Jürgen Schrader, "Traveling Prophets: Inspirationists Wandering through Europe and to the New World," in Jonathan Strom, Hartmut Lehmann, and James Van Horn Melton, eds., *Pietism in Germany and North America, 1680–1820* (Farnham, UK: Ashgate, 2009), 110–113, 121.

4. "Sheehan focuses on one medium, translations of the Bible, and the associated scholarly developments, in England and Germany." Ritchie Robertson, "Religion and the Enlightenment: A Review Essay," *German History* 25, no. 3 (2007): 423.

5. Jonathan Sheehan, *The Enlightenment Bible: Translation, Scholarship, Culture* (Princeton: Princeton University Press, 2005), 29.

6. Ibid., xiii.

7. Charles Taylor, *A Secular Age* (Cambridge, MA: Harvard University Press, 2007).

8. Karl Barth, *Die Protestantische Theologie im 19. Jahrhundert: Ihre Vorgeschichte und ihre Geschichte* (Zurich: Theologischer Verlag Zürich, 1947), 77–78. "In both the Pietist and the Rationalist we are dealing with the modern man and the modern citizen with the same perspective: that in every situation Christianity must serve the improvement of life" (77–78).

9. Thomas K. Kuhn, *Religion und neuzeitliche Gesellschaft: Studien zum sozialen und diakonischen Handeln in Pietismus, Aufklärung und Erweckungsbewegung* (Tübingen: Mohr Siebeck, 2003), 342.

10. See W. R. Ward, *Early Evangelicalism: A Global Intellectual History, 1670–1789* (Cambridge: Cambridge University Press, 2006); Mark A. Noll, *The Rise of Evangelicalism: The Age of Edwards, Whitefield, and the Wesleys* (Downers Grove, IL: InterVarsity Press, 2003); Donald F. Durnbaugh, *The Believers' Church: The History and Character of Radical Protestantism* (New York: Macmillan, 1968).

11. Martin Schmidt, "Der Pietismus als theologische Erscheinung," in *Der Pietismus als theologische Erscheinung* (Göttingen: Vandenhoeck & Ruprecht, 1984), 32.

12. Taylor, *Secular Age*, 18, 25–26.

13. Ibid., 77, 82–86. See Peter Burke, *Popular Culture in Early Modern Europe*, 3rd ed. (Farnham, UK: Ashgate, 2009).

14. Taylor, *Secular Age*, 143; see also 77, 300–303. The emphasis shifted from the object of faith to the genuineness of the feelings.

15. Douglas H. Shantz, "Pietist Autobiography and the Rise of Secular Individualism" (unpublished paper presented at the Annual Meeting of the Canadian Society of Church History, Congress of Humanities and Social Sciences, University of British Columbia, Vancouver, June 2, 2008).

16. Kuhn, *Religion und neuzeitliche Gesellschaft*, 342.

17. Albrecht Beutel, *Kirchengeschichte im Zeitalter der Aufklärung* (Göttingen: Vandenhoeck & Ruprecht, 2009), 93.

18. Martin Gierl, *Pietismus und Aufklärung: Theologische Polemik und die Kommunikationsreform der Wissenschaft am Ende des 17. Jahrhunderts* (Göttingen: Vandenhoeck & Ruprecht, 1997).

19. Ward, *Early Evangelicalism*, 21. Karl Gottfried Goebel describes Johann Christian Lange in Idstein as an eclectic thinker who developed a theology rooted in experiment and experience. Goebel presents Lange as a "trailblazer of the German Enlightenment." Karl Gottfried Goebel, *Johann Christian Lange (1669–1756): Seine Stellung zwischen Pietismus und Aufklärung* (Darmstadt: Verlag der Hessischen Kirchengeschichtlichen Vereinigung, 2004), 325, 331.

20. Beutel, *Kirchengeschichte im Zeitalter der Aufklärung*, 93–95.

21. Taylor, *Secular Age*; Kuhn, *Religion und neuzeitliche Gesellschaft*, 339, 342; Hartmut Lehmann, ed., *Glaubenswelt und Lebenswelten des Pietismus* (Göttingen: Vandenhoeck & Ruprecht, 2004), 15.

22. Kuhn, *Religion und neuzeitliche Gesellschaft*, 341.

23. Ibid., 10–11.

24. Martin Brecht, "Einleitung," in Martin Brecht et al., eds., *Der Pietismus vom siebzehnten bis zum frühen achtzehnten Jahrhundert* (Göttingen: Vandenhoeck & Ruprecht, 1993), 3. See Michel Godfroid, "Le Pietisme allemand a-t-il existe? Histoire d'un concept fait pour la polemique," *Etudes Germaniques* 101 (1971): 32–45.

25. W. R. Ward, *Early Evangelicalism: A Global Intellectual History, 1670–1789* (Cambridge: Cambridge University Press, 2006); W. R. Ward, *Christianity under the Ancien Regime, 1648–1789* (Cambridge: Cambridge University Press, 1999); W. R. Ward, *The Protestant Evangelical Awakening* (Cambridge: Cambridge University Press, 1992). Ward was coeditor of John Wesley's journals and diaries. W. Reginald Ward and Richard P. Heitzenrater, eds., *Journals and Diaries: The Works of John Wesley*, vols. 18–24 (Nashville, TN: Abingdon, 1988–2003).

26. Ward, *Early Evangelicalism*, 3–5, 24.

27. Mark Noll and Bruce Hindmarsh, "Rewriting the History of Evangelicalism: W. R. Ward, 1925–2010," *Books and Culture: Christian Review* 17, no. 2 (2011): 8.

28. Stephen J. Stein, "Some Thoughts on Pietism in American Religious History," in Strom, Lehmann, and Van Horn Melton, *Pietism in Germany and North America, 1680–1820*, 28–31.

29. J. Steven O'Malley, "Pietistic Influence on John Wesley: Wesley and Gerhard Tersteegen," *Wesleyan Theological Journal* 31, no. 2 (1996): 49–50, 63–64, 70.

30. See Frances Elizabeth Cox, *Hymns from the German* (London: Rivingtons, 1841, 1864); Catherine Winkworth, *Lyra Germanica: First and Second Series*, trans. from the German (London: Longman, Brown, Green and Longmans, 1855, 1858).

Conclusion. Reflecting on the Cultural and Religious Legacy of German Pietism

Epigraph. Michel de Certeau, *The Writing of History*, trans. Tom Conley (New York: Columbia University Press, 1988), 176.

1. Klaus Deppermann, "Pennsylvanien als Asyl des frühen deutschen Pietismus," *Pietismus und Neuzeit* 10 (1984): 192.

2. "As human products, religious beliefs, practices, and institutions are always in need of critical scrutiny. Their *effects*, not merely their intentions, must be acknowledged and examined." Margaret R. Miles, "Becoming Answerable for What We See: 1999 AAR Presidential Address," *Journal of the American Academy of Religion* 68, no. 3 (2000): 473.

3. Veronika Albrecht-Birkner, *Francke in Glaucha (1692–1704)* (Tübingen: Max Niemeyer Verlag, 2004), 19–28.

4. Veronika Albrecht-Birkner and Udo Sträter, "Die radikale Phase des frühen August Hermann Francke," in Wolfgang Breul, ed., *Der radikale Pietismus: Perspektiven der Forschung* (Göttingen: Vandenhoeck & Ruprecht, 2010), 61–63, 71, 80. Like the Labadists and Puritans, Francke sought to exclude those who did not give evidence of new birth and true Christianity.

5. W. R. Ward, *The Protestant Evangelical Awakening* (Cambridge: Cambridge University Press, 1992), 141–142.

6. A topic needing attention is Pietism and suicide. Numerous cases of suicide have been documented among the Pietists. The best known are Professor Joachim Feller of Leipzig University (d. 1691) and Georg Rudolf von Schweinitz of Magdeburg (d. 1707), a generous supporter of the Halle Foundations. See Tanya Kevorkian, *Baroque Piety: Religion, Society, and Music in Leipzig, 1650–1750* (Aldershot, UK: Ashgate, 2007), 153; Klaus Deppermann, *Der hallesche Pietismus und der preußische Staat unter Friedrich III. (I.)* (Göttingen: Vandenhoeck & Ruprecht, 1961), 29, 30.

7. Douglas H. Shantz, "Politics, Prophecy and Pietism in the Halberstadt Conventicle," in Fred van Lieburg, ed., *Confessionalism and Pietism* (Mainz: Philipp von Zabern, 2006), esp. 134–138.

8. Hartmut Lehmann, "Absonderung und neue Gemeinschaft," in Hartmut

Lehmann, ed., *Glaubenswelt und Lebenswelten* (Göttingen: Vandenhoeck & Ruprecht, 2004), 495. Lehmann describes Rock and other leaders of Radical Pietist groups as "Prophets." Pietists who offered spiritual direction (*führende Pietisten*), such as Spener, Francke, and Zinzendorf, he calls Pietist "Patriarchs."

9. The idea of the common priesthood of believers played "no significant role" in Radical Pietist circles. See Jonathan Strom, "The Common Priesthood and the Pietist Challenge for Ministry and Laity," in Christian T. Collins Winn, ed., *The Pietist Impulse in Christianity* (Eugene, OR: Pickwick, 2011), 54.

10. Johann Christian Edelmann, *Selbstbiographie*, new facsimile of C. R. W. Klose's 1849 Berlin edition (Stuttgart: Frommann-Holzboog Verlag, 1976), 249, 250.

11. See Douglas H. Shantz, "Conversion and Sarcasm in the Autobiography of Johann Christian Edelmann," in David M. Luebke, Jared Poley, and Dan Ryan, eds., *Conversion and the Politics of Religion in Early Modern Germany* (New York: Berghahn Books, 2011), 153–168.

12. Wolfgang Martens, "Nachwort," in Karl Philipp Moritz, *Anton Reiser: Ein psychologischer Roman* (Stuttgart: Philipp Reclam, 1972), 554–555, 558.

13. Dale W. Brown, *Understanding Pietism*, rev. ed. (Nappanee, IN: Evangel Publishing House, 1996), 25, 28, 56, 66. Brown's approach is evident in the following statement: "We conclude . . . with what may become a theme in reference to other issues: Spener and his followers opened the door for many manifestations of Protestant individualism; nevertheless, they did attempt to maintain a balance between their understanding of God's objective activity in Word and Sacrament and their stress on the individual" (30).

14. Roger E. Olson, "Pietism: Myths and Realities," in Winn, *Pietist Impulse in Christianity*, 3–16; Roger E. Olson, "Reclaiming Pietism," Mar. 16, 2011, www.patheos.com/community/rogereolson/2011/03/16/reclaiming-pietism.

15. Roger E. Olson, "Reclaiming Pietism Part 4," Nov. 19, 2010, www.patheos.com/community/rogereolson/2010/11/19/reclaiming-pietism-part–4.

16. Harold S. Bender presented "The Anabaptist Vision" as his presidential address to the American Society of Church History on December 28, 1943; it was published the following year. See Albert Keim, "History of the Anabaptist Vision," *Mennonite Historical Bulletin*, Oct. 1993, 1–7.

17. C. Arnold Snyder, *Anabaptist History and Theology: An Introduction* (Kitchener, ON: Pandora Press, 1995), 379.

Appendix A. Sources in Translation

1. Paracelsus, "Credo," in Jolande Jacobi, ed., *Paracelsus: Selected Writings*, 2nd ed., trans. Norbert Guterman (Princeton: Princeton University Press, 1957), 4–5.

2. Udo Benzenhöfer, *Paracelsus* (Hamburg: Rowohlt, 1997), 64–66; Charles D. Gunnoe, "Thomas Erastus and His Circle of Anti-Paracelsians: Appendix, The Letter from Johannes Oporinus," in Joachim Telle, ed., *Analecta Paracelsica: Sudien zum Nachleben Theophrast von Hohenheim im deutschen Kulturgebiet der frühen Neuzeit* (Stuttgart: Franz Steiner Verlag, 1994), 146–148.

3. Walter Pagel, *Paracelsus: An Introduction to Philosophical Medicine in the Era of the Renaissance*, 2nd rev. ed. (Basel: S. Karger, 1982), 31, 353.

4. Ms. in the Wolfenbüttel Archive, HAB Cod. Guelf. 13.7 Aug quarto, 231r–232v. See Carlos Gilly, " 'Theophrastia Sancta': Paracelsianism as a Religion in Conflict with the Established Churches," July 31, 2003, 13n18, available at the J. R. Ritman Library website, www.ritmanlibrary.nl/c/p/res/art/art_01.html.

5. Benzenhöfer, *Paracelsus*, 64–66; Gunnoe, "Thomas Erastus and His Circle: Letter from Johannes Oporinus."

6. Jakob Böhme, *Aurora, oder Morgenröte im Aufgang*, ed. Gerhard Wehr (Frankfurt: Insel Verlag, 1992). Page numbers in the text refer to this source (*Aurora*).

7. G. Wehr, *Jakob Böhme mit Selbstzeugnissen u. Bilddokumenten* (Hamburg: Rowohlt, 1971), 123, 118.

8. Zacharias Theobald, *Der alten und neuen Schwärmer, Widertäufferischer Geist, Das ist Glaubwürdiger und Historischer Bericht . . . Daraus zu schliessen Was man von denen jetziger Zeit aufs neue einschleichenden Schwärmern als David Joristen, Weigelianern, Rosencreutzern, Pansophisten, Böhmisten, Chiliasten, Enthusiasten, Quackern, Labadisten, Offenbahrungs-und Frey-Geistern, Quietisten, Träumern, Scheinheiligen neuen Falschen Propheten und Atheisten zugewarten habe weiln sie wie erwiesen einerley Lehre und Grund-Schätze führen . . . mit dazu dienlichen Kupfern vorgestellet* (1701).

9. www.passtheword.org/Jane-Lead/gospel.htm.

10. Lewis Bayly, *The Practice of Piety: Directing a Christian How to Walk, That He May Please God* (London: Hamilton, Adams, 1842), www.ccel.org/ccel/bayly/piety.html. Page numbers in the text refer to this source.

11. Gustav Adolf Benrath, "Der Mystiker Gerhard Tersteegen als Prediger und Seelsorger," *Monatshefte für Evangelische Kirchengeschichte des Rheinlandes* 58 (2009): 81–98, esp. 85.

12. Verses 1, 2, 4, and 8 were translated by Frederick W. Foster and John Miller (1789). I have made some changes to the wording in these verses and translated the remaining verses.

13. Max Goebel, *Geschichte des christlichen Lebens in der rheinisch-westphälischen evangelischen Kirche*, vol. 3, ed. Theodor Link (Koblenz: Karl Bädeker, 1860), 445–447.

14. Fende's letter can be found in Johannes Wallmann, ed., *Philipp Jakob Spener: Briefe aus der Frankfurter Zeit, 1666–1686*, vol. 4, *1679–1680* (Tübingen: Mohr Siebeck, 2005), 792–793. See also Andreas Deppermann, *Johann Jakob Schütz und die Anfänge des Pietismus* (Tübingen: Mohr Siebeck, 2002), 123–125, 187–189.

15. Jürgen Eichhoff, "The Three Hundredth Anniversary of the Germantown Protest against Slavery," *Monatshefte* 80, no. 3 (1988): 262.

16. Frances Elizabeth Cox, *Hymns from the German* (London: Rivingtons, 1864), 234–238.

17. Philipp Jakob Spener, *Pia Desideria: Deutsch-Lateinische Studienausgabe*, ed. Beate Köster (Giessen: Brunnen Verlag, 2005), 116, 118.

18. Ibid., 160, 162.

19. Johanna Eleonora Petersen, *Leben, von ihr selbst mit eigener Hand aufgesetzet Autobiographie* (1718), ed. Prisca Guglielmetti (Leipzig: Evangelische Verlagsanstalt, 2003).

20. Ibid., 29, 30.

21. Ibid., 39–41.

22. *Gerichtliches Leipziger Protocoll in Sachen die so genandten Pietisten betreffend; samt. Hn. Christian Thomasii berühmten J.C. Rechtlichem Bedencken darüber; und zu Ende beygefügter Apologi oder Defensions-Schrifft Hr. M. Augusti Hermanni Franckens an Ihro Chur-Fürstl. Durchl. zu Sachsen; . . . von einem vornehmen Freund communicirt und herauß gegebenen* (1692).

23. Miguel de Molinos (ca. 1628–1697) was a Spanish priest and mystical writer and the chief apostle of the religious revival known as Quietism. His best-known work, *Spiritual Guide,* appeared in 1675.

24. The report was first published in 1863. August Hermann Francke, Letter of April 27, 1700, in Gustav Kramer, ed., *Vier Briefe August Hermann Franckes: Zur zweiten Säcularfeier seines Geburtstags* (Halle: Verlag der Buchhandlung des Waisenhauses, 1863), 28–76. Page numbers in the text refer to this source.

25. In the forty-seven-page report, thirty-eight pages are devoted to the first two questions: how the Word of God is proclaimed and how the sacraments are being administered.

26. Francke runs through some forty-eight questions, of which a few are translated here.

27. Translation by Catherine Winkworth, in *Lyra Germanica,* 1st ser. (Longman, Brown, Green and Longmans, 1855), 236, www.hymnary.org/hymn/LG/95.

28. Ernst Bartz, *Die Wirtschaftsethik August Hermann Franckes* (Harburg-Wilhelmsburg: Wilhelm G. Frenk, 1934), 55–56.

29. Peter C. Erb, ed., *Pietists: Selected Writings* (New York: Paulist Press, 1983), 220, 226.

30. Barbara Hoffmann, *Radikalpietismus um 1700: Der Streit um das Recht auf eine neue Gesellschaft* (Frankfurt: Campus Verlag, 1996), 33. Some argue for 1702 as the year of founding.

31. Ibid., 34.

32. Ibid., 35.

33. Johannes Wallmann, *Der Pietismus* (Göttingen: Vandenhoeck & Ruprecht, 2005), 175.

34. Willi Temme, *Krise der Leiblichkeit* (Göttingen: Vandenhoeck & Ruprecht, 1998), 177, 209.

35. Klaus Breuer, "Buttlar, Eva Margaretha von," in Gerhard Krause and Gerhard Müller, eds., *Theologische Realenzyklopädie* (Berlin: Walter de Gruyter, 1981), 7:498.

36. Temme, *Krise der Leiblichkeit,* 185–186.

37. Wallmann, *Der Pietismus,* 175.

38. Temme, *Krise der Leiblichkeit,* 27–28.

39. Supplement no. 1, *Copia Eines Schreibens von Winter an die Jüngste Calebergerinnen in welchem dessen und der Hoffmeisterin Eva Theologische Meinung in etwas vorgelegt wird* (1703), in *Ausführliche Beschreibung des Neuen Unfugs* (1707), 19–27, Duke August Library Wolfenbüttel, HAB Ts 115 (11).

40. *Copia Schreibens eines guten Freundes vom 28ten Octobris Anno 1705. die in der Graffschaft . . . wohnende Pietisten betreffend*, in *Ausführliche Beschreibung des neuen Unfugs* (1707). Page numbers in the text refer to this source.

41. Ryoko Mori, *Begeisterung und Ernüchterung in christlicher Vollkommenheit* (Tübingen: Max Niemeyer Verlag, 2004), 225n992.

42. Max Goebel, "Der Separatismus in der Grafschaft Wittgenstein," book 9, in *Geschichte des christlichen Lebens in der rheinisch-westphälischen evangelischen Kirche* (Koblenz: Karl Bädeker, 1852), 2:820–824. See also Hans Schneider, "Der radikale Pietismus im 18. Jahrhundert," in Martin Brecht and Klaus Deppermann, eds., *Der Pietismus im achtzehnten Jahrhundert* (Göttingen: Vandenhoeck & Ruprecht, 1995), 124–125.

43. This background information is from William G. Willoughby, "Honors to Alexander Mack," www.cob-net.org/mack/honors.htm.

44. Alexander Mack, *The Complete Writings of Alexander Mack*, ed. William R. Eberly (Winona Lake, IN: BMH Books, 1991), 9–12. Eberly states that most of the translations in the book are by Donald Durnbaugh and appear in *European Origins of the Brethren* (1958) and *The Brethren in Colonial America* (1967).

45. R. W. Kelsey, "Letter of Christopher Sower, Written in 1724, Describing Conditions in Philadelphia and Vicinity, and the Sea Voyage from Europe," *Pennsylvania Magazine of History and Biography* 45, no. 3 (1921): 243–254.

46. The quotations in this background information are from ibid., 243, 244.

47. Anna Maria van Schurman, *Whether a Christian Woman Should Be Educated and Other Writings from Her Intellectual Circle*, trans. Joyce L. Irwin (Chicago: University of Chicago Press, 1999).

48. Ibid., 76, 79–80, 85, 92.

49. Johanna Eleonora Petersen, *Anleitung zu gründlicher Verständnis der Heiligen Offenbarung Jesu Christi . . . und in ihrer völligen Erfüllung in den allerletzten Zeiten denen wir nahekommen* (Frankfurt: Johann Daniel Müller, 1696), foreword and 294.

50. Ibid., foreword and 46, 294.

51. A. H. Francke, "Vorrede," in Beate Köster, "Die erste Bibelausgabe des Halleschen Pietismus," *Pietismus und Neuzeit* 5 (1979): 156–159, 162.

52. Martin Brecht, "Die Berleburger Bibel: Hinweise zu ihrem Verständnis," *Pietismus und Neuzeit* 8 (1982): 196–197.

53. J. A. Bengel, "The Author's Preface," in *Gnomon of the New Testament*, trans. Charlton T. Lewis and Marvin R. Vincent (Philadelphia: Perkinpine & Higgins, 1862), 1:xvi–xix.

54. Ibid.

55. Albertine Gaur, "A Catalogue of B. Ziegenbalg's Tamil Library," *British Museum Quarterly* 30, no. 3–4 (1966): 100.

56. Ibid., 103–104.

57. Arno Lehmann, ed., *Alte Briefe aus Indien: Unveröffentlichte Briefe von Bartholomäus Ziegenbalg 1706–1719* (Berlin: Evangelische Verlagsanstalt, 1957), 130–135.

58. Kurt Liebau, ed., *Die Malabarische Korrespondenz: Tamilische Briefe an Deutsche Missionare, Eine Auswahl* (Sigmaringen: Thorbecke, 1998). Page numbers in the text refer to this source

59. See also ibid., 270nn94, 95.

60. Marianne P. Stopp, "Eighteenth Century Labrador Inuit in England," *Arctic* 62, no. 1 (2009): 54. This passage is based on *Periodical Accounts* 2 (1790–96): 170–172.

61. Johann Christian Edelmann, *Selbstbiographie*, facsimile of C. R. W. Klose's 1849 Berlin edition (Stuttgart: Frommann-Holzboog Verlag, 1976).

62. Bernd Neumann, "Nachwort," in Edelmann, *Selbstbiographie*, 555.

63. Page numbers in the text refer to Edelmann, *Selbstbiographie*.

Appendix B. Translation of Georg Heinrich Neubauer's "183 Questions" (1697)

1. Ernst Bartz, *Die Wirtschaftsethik August Hermann Franckes* (Harburg-Wilhelmsburg: Wilhelm G. Frenk, 1934), 83–91.

2. Ibid., 83. The heading in German reads, "Der Zweck meiner Reyse soll seyn, zum Dienst und Besten des Waysen-Hauses, die Anstalten der Waysen und 'Armen' Häuser an unterschiedlichen Orten genau zu betrachten, und eine Steuer einzusamlen. Daneben die Zucht- Spinn- Krancken- Manufactur- und Doll-Häuser auch andere Anstalten zum Besten der Armen und menschlicher Gesellschaft insgemein, zu betrachten nicht weniger, was sonst obiter in jeder Stadt mit Nutzen wird können angemercket werden."

Appendix C. Discussion Questions

1. Michel Godfroid, "Le Pietisme allemand a-t-il existe? Histoire d'un concept fait pour la polemique," *Etudes Germaniques* 101 (1971): 32–45.

2. Udo Sträter, "Einführung in die Ausstellung," in Veronika Albrecht-Birkner and Bettina Citron, eds., *Hoffnung besserer Zeiten: Philipp Jakob Spener (1635–1705) und die Geschichte des Pietismus* (Halle: Verlag der Franckeschen Stiftungen, 2005), 14.

3. See Heinrich Bornkamm, *Mystik, Spiritualismus und die Anfänge des Pietismus im Luthertum* (Giessen: Alfred Töpelmann, 1926), 16, 18.

4. Ute Gause, *Paracelsus (1493–1541): Genese und Entfaltung seiner frühen Theologie* (Tübingen: Mohr Siebeck, 1993), 288.

5. Johannes Zachhuber's review of Hans Schneider, *Der Fremde Arndt*, is in *Sehepunkte* 7, no. 7–8 (2007), www.sehepunkte.de/2007/07/12608.html.

6. Jakob Böhme, *Aurora, oder Morgenröte im Aufgang*, ed. Gerhard Wehr (Frankfurt: Insel Verlag, 1992), 208–209.

7. Gerhard Wehr, "Einführung," in Böhme, *Aurora*, 11.

8. Johann Anselm Steiger, "Versuchung—orthodox und heterodox: *Tentatio* bei Luther und dem mystischen Spiritualisten Christian Hoburg," in Rainer Hering, ed., *Gottes Wort ins Leben werwandeln: Festschrift für Inge Mager zum 65. Geburtstag* (Hanover: Landeskirchliches Archiv Hannover, 2005), 224, 225.

9. Carl J. Schroeder, *In Quest of Pentecost: Jodocus van Lodenstein and the Dutch Second Reformation* (Lanham, MD: University Press of America, 2001), 44.

10. Hansgünter Ludewig, "Gerhard Tersteegen (1697–1769)," in Carter Lindberg, ed., *The Pietist Theologians* (Oxford: Blackwell, 2005), 203.

11. See Martin Brecht, "Philipp Jakob Spener, sein Programm und dessen Auswirkungen," in Martin Brecht et al., eds., *Der Pietismus vom siebzehnten bis zum frühen achtzehnten Jahrhundert* (Göttingen: Vandenhoeck & Ruprecht 1993), 371, 373; Erich Beyreuther, *Studien zur Theologie Zinzendorfs: Gesammelte Aufsätze* (Neukirchen-Vluyn: Neukirchener Verlag, 1962), 7.

12. Carter Lindberg, "Spener in English and Decadent Pietism," *Lutheran Quarterly* 22, no. 1 (2008): 76.

13. Carl Hinrichs, *Preußentum und Pietismus: Der Pietismus in Brandenburg-Preußen als religiös-soziale Reformbewegung* (Göttingen: Vandenhoeck & Ruprecht, 1971), 13.

14. Udo Sträter, "Soziales," in Hartmut Lehman, ed., *Glaubenswelt und Lebenswelten* (Göttingen: Vandenhoeck & Ruprecht, 2004), 619–620.

15. Juliane Dittrich-Jacobi, "Pietismus und Pädagogik im Konstitutionsprozeß der bürgerlichen Gesellschaft: Historisch-systematische Untersuchung der Pädagogik August Hermann Franckes (1663–1727)" (PhD diss., Faculty for Pedagogy, Philosophy, and Psychology, Bielefeld University, Apr. 1976), 129.

16. Frederick Herzog, ed., *European Pietism Reviewed* (San Jose: Pickwick, 2003), xv. Herzog observed that the Halle Pietists "lost their momentum by an uncritical alliance with the secular realm of government" (introduction).

17. Willi Temme, *Krise der Leiblichkeit* (Göttingen: Vandenhoeck & Ruprecht, 1998), 452.

18. Jeff Bach, *Voices of the Turtledoves: The Sacred World of Ephrata* (University Park: Penn State University Press, 2003), 29.

19. Ibid., 23.

20. Ibid., 197–198.

21. Claudia Wustmann, *Die "begeisterten Mägde": Mitteldeutsche Prophetinnen im Radikalpietismus am Ende des 17. Jahrhunderts* (Leipzig: Edition Kirchhof & Franke, 2008), 72.

22. Johann Heinrich Feustking, *Gynaeceum Haeretico Fanaticum*, ed. Elisabeth Gössmann (Munich: Iudicium Verlag, 1998), foreword and 50.

23. Jonathan Sheehan, *The Enlightenment Bible: Translation, Scholarship, Culture* (Princeton: Princeton University Press, 2005), 62.

24. Beate Köster, " 'Mit tiefem Respekt, mit Furcht und Zittern': Bibelübersetzungen im Pietismus," *Pietismus und Neuzeit* 24 (1998): 115.

25. Hans-Jürgen Schrader, *Literaturproduktion und Büchermarkt des radikalen Pietismus* (Göttingen: Vandenhoeck & Ruprecht, 1989), 189–190.

26. Martin Brecht, "Johann Albrecht Bengel," in Martin Greschat, ed., *Orthodoxie und Pietismus* (Stuttgart: Verlag W. Kohlhammer, 1982), 324. See "The Author's Preface," *Gnomon of the New Testament*, vol. 1, trans. Charlton T. Lewis and Marvin R. Vincent (Philadelphia: Perkinpine & Higgins 1862), xiii.

27. Kurt Aland, "Bibel und Bibeltext bei August Hermann Francke und Johann Albrecht Bengel," in Kurt Aland, ed., *Pietismus und Bibel* (Witten: Luther-Verlag, 1970), 130.

28. Herzog, *European Pietism Reviewed*, 106.

29. Hanco Jürgens, "Forschungen zu Sprachen und Religion," in Heike Liebau, ed., *Geliebtes Europa//Ostindische Welt: 300 Jahre Interkultureller Dialog im Spiegel der Dänisch-Halleschen Mission* (Halle: Verlag der Franckeschen Stiftungen zu Halle, 2006), 133.

30. Will Sweetman, "The Prehistory of Orientalism: Colonialism and the Textual Basis for Bartholomäus Ziegenbalg's Account of Hinduism," *New Zealand Journal of Asian Studies* 6, no. 2 (2004): 22.

31. Thea Olsthoorn, *Die Erkundungsreisen der Herrnhuter Missionare nach Labrador (1752–1770)* (Hildesheim: Georg Olms Verlag, 2010), 172–173.

32. Marianne P. Stopp, "Eighteenth Century Labrador Inuit in England," *Arctic* 62, no. 1 (2009): 51.

33. Karl Barth, *Die Protestantische Theologie im 19. Jahrhundert: Ihre Vorgeschichte und ihre Geschichte* (Zürich: Theologischer Verlag Zürich, 1947), 77–78.

Bibliographies and Further Reading

Bibliographies of Pietism Research

"Annotated Bibliography of Selected Sources for the Study of American Communal History." Spring 2004. Donald F. Durnbaugh, "Colonial Communal Settlements"; Peter Hoehnle, "The Amana Society"; Rod Janzen, "Hutterites and the Bruderhof"; Marlyn McGary Klee, "The Oneida Community (1848–1881)"; Elizabeth De Wolfe and Scott De Wolfe, "Shaker Historiography"; Kathleen Fernandez, "Zoar"; Rod Janzen, "Synanon Select Bibliography." www.communalstudies.org/resources.

Bach, Jeff. "Bibliographical Essay." In *Voices of the Turtledoves: The Sacred World of Ephrata*, 197–217. University Park, PA: Penn State University Press, 2003.

Burkart, Rainer W., Dennis L. Slabaugh, and Donald F. Durnbaugh. "History of Research on the Church of the Brethren from the Eighteenth Century to the Present." *Brethren Life and Thought* 45, nos. 1–2 (2000): 1–88.

Dreydoppel, Otto. "A Basic Bibliography of Moravian Studies." Moravian Theological Seminary, 2009. www.moravianseminary.edu/center/bibliography.html.

Durnbaugh, Donald F. "Bibliography of the Brethren." In Donald F. Durnbaugh and Dennis Martin, eds. *The Brethren Encyclopedia*. Vol. 3, 1857–2111. Ambler, PA: Brethren Encyclopedia, 1984.

Durnbaugh, Donald F. "Guide to Research in Brethren History." Revised by Jeffrey A. Bach, Donald F. Durnbaugh, Elaine L. Gibbel, William C. Kostlevy, and Kenneth M. Shaffer, Jr. Elgin, IL: Church of the Brethren, 2000. www.brethren.org/bhla/.

Heil, Andrew, Paul Peucker, and Lanie Graf. "Overview of Publications on the Moravian Church in English 2000–2010." *Journal of Moravian History*, no. 9 (2010): 89–121.

Janz, Bruce B. "Jacob Boehme Bibliography." 2009. http://pegasus.cc.ucf.edu/~janzb/boehme/boehmebib.htm and http://pegasus.cc.ucf.edu/~janzb/boehme/.

Strom, Jonathan. "Problems and Promises of Pietism Research." *Church History* 71, no. 3 (2002): 536–554.

Ward, W. R. "German Pietism, 1670–1750." *Journal of Ecclesiastical History* 44 (1993): 476–505.

Ward, W. R. "Select and User-Friendly Bibliography." In *Early Evangelicalism: A Global Intellectual History, 1670–1789*, 194–213. Cambridge: Cambridge University Press, 2006.

Collections of Primary Sources in English

Cox, Frances Elizabeth. *Hymns from the German.* London: Rivingtons, 1841, 1864. http://books.google.com/books/about/Hymns_from_the_German.html?id=lw4DAAAAQAAJ.

Durnbaugh, Donald F., ed. *European Origins of the Brethren: A Source Book on the Beginnings of the Church of the Brethren in the Early Eighteenth-Century.* Elgin, IL: Brethren Press, 1958.

Erb, Peter C., ed. *Pietists: Selected Writings.* New York: Paulist Press, 1983.

Faull, Katherine, ed. *Moravian Women's Memoirs: Their Related Lives, 1750–1820.* Syracuse, NY: Syracuse University Press, 1997.

Griffin, Emilie, ed. *The Pietists: Selected Writings.* Translated by Peter C. Erb. San Francisco: Harper Collins, 2006.

Herzog, Frederick, ed. *European Pietism Reviewed.* San Jose: Pickwick, 2003.

Lund, Eric, ed. *Documents from the History of Lutheranism, 1517–1750*, 216–310. Minneapolis: Augsburg Fortress, 2002.

Winkworth, Catherine. *Lyra Germanica: Hymns for the Sundays and Chief-Festivals of the Christian Year, First Series.* Translated from the German. London: Longman, Brown, Green and Longmans, 1855. www.ccel.org/ccel/winkworth/lyra.html.

Winkworth, Catherine. *Lyra Germanica, Second Series: The Christian Life.* Translated from the German. London: Longman, Green, Longman, and Roberts, 1858. www.ccel.org/ccel/winkworth/life.html.

Further Reading

The following publications are arranged by chapter, with primary and secondary sources listed separately.

Introduction. Issues in Defining and Describing the Pietist Movement

Secondary Sources

Brown, Dale W. *Understanding Pietism.* Rev. ed. Nappanee, IN: Evangel Pub., 1996. First published 1978.

Eshleman, H. Frank. *Historic Background and Annals of the Swiss and German Pioneer Settlers of Southeastern Pennsylvania, and of Their Remote Ancestors, from the Middle of*

the Dark Ages, down to the Time of the Revolutionary War 1600–1775; an Authentic History . . . by H. Frank Eshleman. Baltimore: Genealogical Pub. Co., 2000.
Fertig, Georg. "Migrations from the German-Speaking Parts of Central Europe, 1600–1800: Estimates and Explanations." Working Paper No. 38. Berlin: John F. Kennedy Institut für Nordamerikastudien, 1991.
Fogleman, Aaron Spencer. *Hopeful Journeys: German Immigration, Settlement, and Political Culture in Colonial America, 1717–1775.* Philadelphia: University of Pennsylvania Press, 1996.
Gerdes, Egon W. "Pietism: Classical and Modern: A Comparison of Two Representative Descriptions." *Concordia Theological Monthly* 39 (Apr. 1968): 257–268.
Gerdes, Egon W. "Theological Tenets of Pietism." *Covenant Quarterly* 34 (Feb./May 1976): 25–60.
Gillespie, Michele, and Robert Beachy, eds. *Pious Pursuits: German Moravians in the Atlantic World.* New York: Berghahn Books, 2007.
Lehmann, Hartmut, Hermann Wellenreuther, and Renate Wilson, eds. *In Search of Peace and Prosperity: New German Settlements in Eighteenth-Century Europe and America.* University Park: Penn State University Press, 2000.
Lindberg, Carter, ed. *The Pietist Theologians.* Oxford: Blackwell, 2005.
Lund, Eric. "Protestant Spirituality. I. Second Age of the Reformation: Lutheran and Reformed Spirituality, 1550–1700." In Louis Dupre, ed. *Christian Spirituality: Post-reformation and Modern,* 213–239. New York: Crossroad, 1989.
Miles, Margaret R. "Becoming Answerable for What We See: 1999 AAR Presidential Address." *Journal of the American Academy of Religion* 68, no. 3 (2000): 471–485.
Nolt, Steven M. *Foreigners in Their Own Land: Pennsylvania Germans in the Early Republic.* University Park: Penn State University Press, 2002.
Roeber, A. Gregg. *Palatines, Liberty, and Property: German Lutherans in Colonial British America.* Baltimore: Johns Hopkins University Press, 1993.
Sachse, Julius Friedrich. *The German Pietists of Provincial Pennsylvania.* Philadelphia: Julius F. Sachse, 1895. Reprint, New York: AMS Press, 1970.
Shantz, Douglas H. *Between Sardis and Philadelphia: The Life and World of Pietist Court Preacher Conrad Bröske.* Leiden: Brill, 2008.
Shantz, Douglas H., ed. *Brill Companion to German Pietism.* Leiden: Brill, forthcoming.
Stoeffler, F. Ernest. *The Rise of Evangelical Pietism.* Leiden: E. J. Brill, 1965, 1971.
Stoeffler, F. Ernest. *German Pietism during the Eighteenth Century.* Leiden: E. J. Brill, 1973.
Strom, Jonathan. "Problems and Promises of Pietism Research." *Church History* 71, no. 3 (2002): 536–554.
Strom, Jonathan, Hartmut Lehmann, and James Van Horn Melton, eds. *Pietism in Germany and North America 1680–1820.* Farnham, UK: Ashgate, 2009.
van Lieburg, Fred. "Bible Reading and Pietism in the Dutch Reformed Tradition."

In M. Lamberigts and A. A. den Hollander, eds. *Lay Bibles in Europe, 1450–1800*, 223–244. Louvain, Belgium: Peeters, 2006.

van Lieburg, Fred, ed. *Confessionalism and Pietism: Religious Reform in Early Modern Europe*. Mainz: Verlag Philipp von Zabern, 2006.

Wokeck, Marianne S. "The Flow and the Composition of German Immigration to Philadelphia, 1683–1776." *Pennsylvania Magazine of History and Biography* 105 (1981): 249–278.

Wokeck, Marianne S. "German Settlements in the British North American Colonies: A Patchwork of Cultural Assimilation and Persistence." In Hartmut Lehmann, Hermann Wellenreuther, and Renate Wilson, eds. *In Search of Peace and Prosperity: New German Settlements in Eighteenth-Century Europe and America*, 191–216. University Park: Penn State University Press, 2000.

Wokeck, Marianne S. *Trade in Strangers: The Beginnings of Mass Migration to North America*. University Park: Penn State University Press, 1999.

Yoder, Don, ed. *Pennsylvania German Immigrants, 1709–1786: Lists Consolidated from Yearbooks of the Pennsylvania German Folklore Society*. Baltimore: Genealogical Pub. Co., 1980.

Chapter 1. German Radicalism and Orthodox Lutheran Reform

Primary Sources

Arndt, Johann. *True Christianity*. Translated by Peter Erb. New York: Paulist Press, 1979.

Arndt, Johann. *True Christianity*. Edited by John Wesley. Introduction by Bruce Hindmarsh. Vancouver: Regent College Pub., 2012.

Boehme, Jacob. *The Way to Christ*. Translated by Peter Erb. New York: Paulist Press, 1978.

Gerhard, Johann. *Sacred Meditations*. Translated by C. W. Heisler. Philadelphia: Lutheran Publication Society, 1896. Reprint, Malone, TX: Repristination Press, 1998.

Gerhard, Johann. *Sacred Meditations*. Translated by Wade R. Johnston. Saginaw, MI: Magdeburg Press, 2008.

Gerhard, Johann. *Theological Commonplaces: On the Nature of Theology and Holy Scripture*. Translated from the original Latin by Richard J. Dinda. St. Louis, MO: Concordia Pub. House, 2006.

Jacobi, Jolande, ed. *Paracelsus: Selected Writings*. 2nd ed. Translated by Norbert Guterman. Princeton: Princeton University Press, 1957.

Oetinger, Friedrich Christoph. "Genealogy of the Well-Grounded Thoughts of a Theologian." In Frederick Herzog, ed. *European Pietism Reviewed*, 105–164. San Jose: Pickwick, 2003.

Taylor, Edward. *Jacob Behmen's Theosophic Philosophy Unfolded: In Divers Considerations and Demonstrations, Shewing the Verity and Utility of the Several Doctrines or Propositions Contained in the Writings of That Divinely Instructed Author. Also, the*

Principal Treatises of the Said Author Abridged; with a Short Account of the Life of Jacob Behmen. London: Printed for Thomas Salusbury, 1691.

Secondary Sources

Dixon, C. Scott. "Faith and History on the Eve of Enlightenment: Ernst Salomon Cyprian, Gottfried Arnold, and the *History of Heretics*." *Journal of Ecclesiastical History* 57, no. 1 (2006): 47–51.

Doan, Michael D. "Paracelsus on *Erfahrung* and the Wisdom of Praxis." *Analecta Hermeneutica* 1 (2009): 176.

Erb, Peter C. "Gottfried Arnold (1666–1714)." In Carter Lindberg, ed. *The Pietist Theologians*, 175–189. Oxford: Blackwell, 2005.

Erb, Peter C. "Introduction." In Johann Arndt. *True Christianity*. Edited by Peter C. Erb. New York: Paulist Press, 1979.

Erb, Peter C. *Pietists, Protestants, and Mysticism: The Use of Late Medieval Spiritual Texts in the Work of Gottfried Arnold (1666–1714)*. Metuchen, NJ: Scarecrow Press, 1989.

Fischer, Erdmann. *The Life of John Gerhard by Erdmann Fischer*. Translated by Richard Dinda and Elmer Hohle. Malone, TX: Repristination Press, 1999.

Gibbons, B. J. *Gender in Mystical and Occult Thought: Behmenism and Its Development in England*. Cambridge: Cambridge University Press, 1996.

Grell, Ole Peter, ed. *Paracelsus: The Man and His Reputation, His Ideas, and Their Transformation*. Leiden: Brill, 1998.

Hessayon, Ariel. "'The Teutonicks Writings': Translating Jacob Boehme into English and Welsh." *Esoterica* 9 (2007): 129–165. www.esoteric.msu.edu/Contents.html#VolumeIX.

Hirst, Julie. "The Divine Ark: Jane Lead's Vision of the Second Noah's Ark." *Esoterica* 6 (2004): 16–25.

Hirst, Julie. *Jane Leade: Biography of a Seventeenth-Century Mystic*. Aldershot, UK: Ashgate, 2005.

Hirst, Julie. "'Mother of Love': Spiritual Maternity in the Works of Jane Lead (1624–1704)." In Sylvia Brown, ed. *Women, Gender, and Radical Religion in Early Modern Europe*. Leiden: Brill, 2007.

Jacobi, Jolande. "Paracelsus: His Life and Work." In Jolande Jacobi, ed. *Paracelsus: Selected Writings*. 2nd ed. Translated by Norbert Guterman. Princeton: Princeton University Press, 1957.

Lund, Eric. *Johann Arndt and the Development of a Lutheran Spiritual Tradition*. Unpublished PhD diss., Yale University, 1979.

McDowell, Paula. "Enlightenment Enthusiasms and the Spectacular Failure of the Philadelphian Society." *Eighteenth-Century Studies* 35, no. 4 (2002): 515–533.

McIntosh, Christopher. *The Rose Cross and the Age of Reason: Eighteenth-Century Rosicrucianism in Central Europe and Its Relationship to the Enlightenment*. Leiden: Brill, 1997.

Nuttall, Geoffrey G. "Continental Pietism and the Evangelical Movement in Britain." In J. Van den Berg and J. P. Van Dooren, eds. *Pietismus und Reveil*. Leiden: Brill, 1978.

Osler, Margaret J. *Reconfiguring the World: Nature, God, and Human Understanding from the Middle Ages to Early Modern Europe*. Baltimore: Johns Hopkins University Press, 2010.

Penman, Leigh T. I. "The Unanticipated Millennium: Orthodoxy, Heterodoxy and Chiliastic Error in Paul Egard's *Posaune der göttlichen Gnade und Liechtes* (1623)." *Pietismus und Neuzeit* 35 (2009): 11–45.

Shantz, Douglas H. " 'Back to the Sources': Gottfried Arnold, Johann Henrich Reitz, and the Distinctive Program and Practice of Pietist Historical Writing." In C. Arnold Snyder, ed. *Commoners and Community*, 75–99. Kitchener, ON: Pandora Press, 2002.

Shantz, Douglas H. *Crautwald and Erasmus: A Study in Humanism and Radical Reform in Sixteenth Century Silesia*. Baden-Baden: Valentin Koerner, 1992.

Shantz, Douglas H. "David Joris, Pietist Saint: The Appeal to Joris in the Writings of Christian Hoburg, Gottfried Arnold and Johann Wilhelm Petersen." *Mennonite Quarterly Review* 78 (July 2004): 415–432.

Shantz, Douglas H. "The Origin of Pietist Notions of New Birth and the New Man: Alchemy and Alchemists in Gottfried Arnold and Johann Henrich Reitz." In Christian T. Collins Winn, ed. *The Pietist Impulse in Christianity*, 29–41. Eugene, OR: Pickwick, 2011.

Strom, Jonathan. *Orthodoxy and Reform: The Clergy in Seventeenth Century Rostock*. Tübingen: Mohr Siebeck, 1999.

Trueman, Carl. "Lewis Bayly (d. 1631) and Richard Baxter (1615–1691)." In Carter Lindberg, ed. *The Pietist Theologians*, 52–67. Oxford: Blackwell, 2005.

von Schlachta, Astrid. "Anabaptism, Pietism and Modernity: Relationships, Changes, Paths." In Fred van Lieburg and Daniel Lindmark, eds. *Pietism, Revivalism, and Modernity, 1650–1850*, 1–22. Newcastle upon Tyne, UK: Cambridge Scholars, 2008.

von Schlachta, Astrid. *From the Tyrol to North America: The Hutterite Story through the Centuries*. Translated by Werner and Karin Packull. Kitchener, ON: Pandora Press, 2008.

Voss, Karen-Claire. "Spiritual Alchemy: Interpreting Representative Texts and Images." In R. van den Broek and W. J. Hanegraaff, eds. *Gnosis and Hermeticism from Antiquity to Modern Times*. New York: State University of New York Press, 1998.

Wallmann, Johannes. "Johann Arndt (1555–1621)." In Carter Lindberg, ed. *The Pietist Theologians*, 21–37. Oxford: Blackwell, 2005.

Ward, W. R. *Christianity under the Ancien Regime, 1648–1789*. Cambridge: Cambridge University Press, 1999.

Ward, W. R. *Early Evangelicalism: A Global Intellectual History, 1670–1789*. Cambridge: Cambridge University Press, 2006.

Webster, Charles. *Paracelsus: Medicine, Magic, and Mission at the End of Time*. New Haven: Yale University Press, 2008.

Weeks, Andrew. *Boehme: An Intellectual Biography of the Seventeenth Century Philosopher and Mystic.* Albany: State University of New York Press, 1991.

Chapter 2. The Thirty Years War, Seventeenth-Century Calvinism, and Reformed Pietism

Primary Sources

de Labadie, Jean. "The Reformation of the Church by the Pastorate, 1667." In Frederick Herzog, ed. *European Pietism Reviewed.* San Jose: Pickwick, 2003.
Mortimer, Geoff, ed. *Eyewitness Accounts of the Thirty Years War, 1618–1648.* New York: Palgrave, 2002.
Teellinck, Willem. *North Star.* Translated by Annemie Godbehere. Edited by Joel R. Beeke. Grand Rapids, MI: Baker Book House, 2002.
Teellinck, Willem. *The Path of True Godliness.* Translated by Annemie Godbehere. Edited by Joel R. Beeke. Grand Rapids, MI: Reformation Heritage Books, 2006.
Tersteegen, Gerhard. "Important Rules of Conduct for a Community of Brothers Living Together" (1732). Reprinted in Winfried Zeller. "The Protestant Attitude to Monasticism, with Special Reference to Gerhard Tersteegen." *Downside Review* 93, no. 312 (1975): 188–192.
Tersteegen, Gerhard. *The Quiet Way: A Christian Path to Inner Peace—Selections from the Letters and Hymns.* Translated by Emily Chisholm. Bloomington, IN: World Wisdom, 2008.
Tersteegen, Gerhard. "Spiritual Letters" and "Spiritual Flower Garden." In Peter C. Erb, ed. *Pietists: Selected Writings,* 241–252. New York: Paulist Press, 1983.
van Lodenstein, Jodocus. *Tien Predicatie.* Translated by Iain Maclean. In William Stacy Johnson and John H. Leith, eds. *Reformed Reader: A Sourcebook in Christian Theology.* Vol. 1, 296–297, 322–324. Louisville, KY: Westminster, 1993.
Voetius, Gisbertus, and Johannes Hoornbeeck. *Spiritual Desertion.* Translated by John Vriend and Harry Boonstra. Grand Rapids, MI: Baker Books, 2003.
von Grimmelshausen, Johann Jakob Christoffel. *Simplicissimus.* Translated by Mike Mitchell. Sawtry, UK: Dedalus, 1999.

Secondary Sources

John Boldt. "Review of Carl J. Schroeder, *In Quest of Pentecost: Jodocus van Lodenstein and the Dutch Second Reformation* (Lanham, MD: University Press of America, 2001)." *Bulletin of the Institute for Reformed Theology* 4, no. 2 (2004): 8.
Collins, Kenneth J. "John Wesley's Critical Appropriation of Early German Pietism." *Wesleyan Theological Journal* 27 (1992): 57–92.
Damrau, Peter. *The Reception of English Puritan Literature in Germany.* Leeds: Maney, 2006.
de Baar, Mirjam, and Machteld Löwensteyn, eds. *Choosing the Better Part: Anna Maria van Schurman (1607–1678).* Dordrecht: Kluwer Academic, 1996.
de Certeau, Michel. "Labadie the Nomad." In *The Mystic Fable: The Sixteenth and*

Seventeenth Centuries, 271–294. Translated by Michael B. Smith. Chicago: University of Chicago Press, 1992.

Ella, George M. "Gerhard Tersteegen." *Leben, Journal of Reformation Life* 3, no. 4 (2007): 15–16.

Erb, Peter C. "Gerhard Tersteegen, Christopher Sauer and Pennsylvania Sectarians." *Brethren Life and Thought* 20 (1975): 153–157.

Govan, H. E. *The Life of Gerhard Tersteegen: With Selections from His Writings*. London: James Nisbet, 1898.

Jackson, Samuel, trans. *Life and Character of Gerhard Tersteegen, with Extracts from His Letters and Writings*. London: Black, Young, and Young, 1832.

Lehmann, Hartmut. "Lutheranism in the Seventeenth Century." In Ronnie Po-Chia Hsia, ed. *The Cambridge History of Christianity*. Vol. 6, *Reform and Expansion 1500–1660*. Cambridge: Cambridge University Press, 2007.

Ludewig, Hansgünter. "Gerhard Tersteegen (1697–1769)." In Carter Lindberg, ed. *The Pietist Theologians*, 190–206. Oxford: Blackwell, 2005.

Mackenzie, Edgar C. "British Devotional Literature and the Rise of German Pietism." Unpublished PhD diss., St. Andrews University, 1984.

Maclean, Iain. "The First Pietist: Jodocus van Lodenstein." In John Leith, ed. *Calvin Studies VI*, 15–34. Davidson, NC: Calvin Colloquium, 1993.

Medick, Hans. "The Thirty Years' War as Experience and Memory: Contemporary Perceptions of a Macro-Historical Event." In Lynne Tatlock, ed. *Enduring Loss in Early Modern Germany: Cross Disciplinary Perspectives*, 25–49. Leiden: Brill, 2010.

Niekus Moore, Cornelia. "Anna Hoyers' Posaunenschall: Hymns of an Empire at War and a Kingdom Come." *Daphnis* 13 (1984): 343–362.

Niekus Moore, Cornelia. "Anna Ovena Hoyers (1584–1655)." In Kerstin Merkel and Heide Wunder, eds. *Deutsche Frauen der Frühen Neuzeit: Dichterinnen, Malerinnen, Mäzeninnen*, 65–76. Darmstadt: Primus Verlag, 2000.

Noll Venables, Mary. "Pietist Fruits from Orthodox Seeds: The Case of Ernst the Pious." In Fred van Lieburg, ed. *Confessionalism and Pietism: Religious Reform in Early Modern Europe*, 95–104. Mainz: Philipp von Zabern, 2006.

O'Malley, J. Steven. "Pietistic Influence on John Wesley: Wesley and Gerhard Tersteegen." *Wesleyan Theological Journal* 31, no. 2 (1996): 48–70.

Saxby, Trevor J. *The Quest for the New Jerusalem, Jean de Labadie, and the Labadists, 1610–1744*. Dordrecht: Martinus Nijhoff, 1987.

Schroeder, Carl J. *In Quest of Pentecost: Jodocus van Lodenstein and the Dutch Second Reformation*. Lanham, MD: University Press of America, 2001.

Tanis, James. "The Heidelberg Catechism in the Hands of the Calvinistic Pietists." *Reformed Review* 24 (1971): 154–161.

van Asselt, Willem J. *The Federal Theology of Johannes Coccejus (1603–1669)*. Leiden: Brill, 2001.

van Beek, Pieta. *The First Female University Student: Anna Maria van Schurman (1636)*. Utrecht: Igitur, Utrecht Publishing and Archiving Services, 2010.

van Lieburg, Fred. "From Pure Church to Pious Culture: The Further Reformation in the Seventeenth-Century Dutch Republic." In Fred Graham, ed. *Later Calvinism: International Perspectives*. Kirksville, MO: Sixteenth Century Journal Pub., 1994.

Ward, W. Reginald. *The Protestant Evangelical Awakening*. Cambridge: Cambridge University Press, 1992.

Wilson, Peter H. *Europe's Tragedy: A History of the Thirty Years War*. London: Allen Lane, 2008.

Zeller, Winfried. "The Protestant Attitude to Monasticism, with Special Reference to Gerhard Tersteegen." *Downside Review* 93, no. 312 (1975): 178–192.

Chapter 3. Beginnings of Lutheran Pietism in Frankfurt, 1670–1684

Primary Sources

Merian, Maria Sibylla. *Flowers, Butterflies, and Insects: All 154 Engravings from "Erucarum artus."* New York: Dover, 1991.

Petersen, Johanna Eleonora. *The Life of Lady Johanna Eleonora Petersen, Written by Herself: Pietism and Women's Autobiography in Seventeenth-Century Germany*. Edited and translated by Barbara Becker-Cantarino. Chicago: University of Chicago Press, 2005.

Spener, Philipp Jakob. "On Hindrances to Theological Studies," "The Necessary and Useful Reading of the Holy Scriptures," "Meditations on the Suffering of Christ," "Resignation," "God-Pleasing Prayer," and "Christian Joy." In Peter C. Erb, ed. *Pietists: Selected Writings*, 65–96. Translated by Peter C. Erb. New York: Paulist Press, 1983.

Spener, Philipp Jakob. *Pia Desideria*. Translated by Theodore G. Tappert. Philadelphia: Fortress Press, 1964.

Secondary Sources

Albrecht, Ruth. "Johanna Eleonora Petersen in the Context of Women's and Gender Studies." In Jonathan Strom, Hartmut Lehmann, and James Van Horn Melton, eds. *Pietism in Germany and North America, 1680–1820*, 71–84. Farnham, UK: Ashgate, 2009.

Davis, Natalie Zemon. "Metamorphoses: Marie Sibylla Merian." In *Women on the Margins: Three Seventeenth-Century Lives*, 140–202. Cambridge, MA: Harvard University Press, 1995.

Eichhoff, Jürgen. "The Three Hundredth Anniversary of the Germantown Protest against Slavery." *Monatshefte* 80, no. 3 (1988): 262–267.

Erben, Patrick M. " 'Honey-Combs' and 'Paper-Hives': Positioning Francis Daniel Pastorius's Manuscript Writings in Early Pennsylvania." *Early American Literature* 37, no. 2 (2002): 157–194.

Heijting, Willem. "Hendrick Beets (1625?–1708), Publisher to the German Adherents of Jacob Böhme in Amsterdam." *Quaerendo* 3 (1973): 250–280.

Jung, Martin H. "Johanna Eleonora Petersen (1644–1724)." In Carter Lindberg, ed. *The Pietist Theologians*, 47–160. Oxford: Blackwell, 2005.
Learned, Marion Dexter. *The Life of Francis Daniel Pastorius, the Founder of Germantown*. Philadelphia: William J. Campbell, 1908. http://myweb.wvnet.edu/~jelkins/lp–2001/pastorius.html.
Reitsma, Ella. *Maria Sibylla Merian and Daughters: Women of Art and Science, June 10–August 31, 2008*. Los Angeles: Getty Publications, 2008.
Rowland, Ingrid D. "The Flowering Genius of Maria Sibylla Merian." *New York Review of Books* 56, no. 6 (2009).
Rücker, Elizabeth, and William T. Stearn. *Maria Sibylla Merian in Surinam*. London: Pion, 1982.
Schmidt-Loske, Katharina. *Maria Sibylla Merian, Insects of Surinam*. Los Angeles: Taschen Books America, 2009.
Shantz, Douglas H. "The Life and Thought of Johanna Eleonora Petersen in Recent Scholarship." *Perichoresis* 5, no. 1 (2007): 73–95. www.emanuel.ro/en.research.perichoresis.contents.
Stein, K. James. *Philipp Jakob Spener: Pietist Patriarch*. Chicago: Covenant Press, 1986.
Strom, Jonathan. "The Common Priesthood and the Pietist Challenge for Ministry and Laity." In Christian T. Collins Winn, ed. *The Pietist Impulse in Christianity*, 42–58. Eugene, OR: Pickwick, 2011.
Valiant, Sharon. "Maria Sibylla Merian: Recovering an Eighteenth-Century Legend." *Eighteenth-Century Studies* 3 (spring 1993): 467–479.

Chapter 4. Conventicles and Conflicts in Leipzig and the Second Wave, 1684 to 1694

Primary Sources

Francke, August Hermann. "From the Autobiography 1692." In Peter C. Erb, ed. *Pietists: Selected Writings*, 99–107. New York: Paulist Press, 1983.

Secondary Sources

Hindmarsh, D. Bruce. *The Evangelical Conversion Narrative: Spiritual Autobiography in Early Modern England*. Oxford: Oxford University Press, 2005.
Kevorkian, Tanya. *Baroque Piety: Religion, Society, and Music in Leipzig, 1650–1750*. Aldershot, UK: Ashgate, 2007.
Shantz, Douglas H. "Politics, Prophecy and Pietism in the Halberstadt Conventicle, 1691–1694." In Fred van Lieburg, ed. *Confessionalism and Pietism: Religious Reform in Early Modern Europe*, 129–147. Mainz: Verlag Philipp von Zabern, 2006.
Shantz, Douglas H. "Women, Men and Their Experience of God: Comparing Spiritual Autobiographies." *Canadian Evangelical Review*, no. 22 (autumn 2001): 2–18.
Stauffer, George. "Leipzig: A Cosmopolitan Trade Centre." In George Buelow, ed.

The Late Baroque Era: From the 1680s to 1740, 254–295. Englewood Cliffs, NJ: Prentice Hall, 1993.
Ward, W. R. *The Protestant Evangelical Awakening*. Cambridge: Cambridge University Press, 1992.

Chapter 5. Halle Pietism and Universal Social Reform, 1695 to 1727

Primary Sources

Francke, A. H. "Pietas Hallensis, or an Abstract of the Marvellous Footsteps of Divine Providence in the Building of a Very Large Orphanage or Spacious School for Charitable and Excellent Uses and in the Maintaining of Many Orphans and Other Poor People at Glaucha near Halle in the Dominions of the Kingdom of Prussia (1707)." In Frederick Herzog, ed. *European Pietism Reviewed*, 82–102. San Jose: Pickwick, 2003.
Francke, A. H. "Scriptural Rules of Life." Reprinted in Gary R. Sattler. *God's Glory, Neighbor's Good: A Brief Introduction to the Life and Writings of August Hermann Francke*, 199–237. Chicago: Covenant Press, 1982.

Secondary Sources

Cashin, Edward J. *Beloved Bethesda: A History of George Whitefield's Home for Boys, 1740–2000*. Macon, GA: Mercer University Press, 2001.
Fulbrook, Mary. *Piety and Politics: Religion and the Rise of Absolutism in England, Wurttemberg, and Prussia*. Cambridge: Cambridge University Press, 1983.
Gawthrop, Richard. "Lutheran Pietism and the Weber Thesis." *German Studies Review* 12, no. 2 (1989): 237–247.
Gawthrop, Richard. *Pietism and the Making of Eighteenth Century Prussia*. Cambridge: Cambridge University Press, 1993.
Grabbe, Hans-Jürgen, ed. *Halle Pietism, Colonial North America, and the Young United States*. Stuttgart: Franz Steiner Verlag, 2008.
Lindberg, Carter. "The Lutheran Tradition." In Ronald L. Numbers and Darrel W. Amundsen, eds. *Caring and Curing: Health and Medicine in the Western Religious Traditions*. 2nd ed., 185–188. Baltimore: Johns Hopkins University Press, 1998.
Marschke, Benjamin. *Absolutely Pietist: Patronage, Factionalism, and State-Building in the Early Eighteenth-Century Prussian Army Chaplaincy*. Tübingen: Niemeyer, 2005.
Marschke, Benjamin. "Halle Pietism and the Prussian State: Infiltration, Dissent, and Subversion." In Jonathan Strom, Hartmut Lehmann, and James Van Horn Melton, eds. *Pietism in Germany and North America, 1680–1820*, 217–228. Farnham, UK: Ashgate, 2009.
Matthias, Markus. "August Hermann Francke (1663–1727)." In Carter Lindberg, ed. *The Pietist Theologians*, 100–114. Oxford: Blackwell, 2005.
McCants, Anne E. C. *Civic Charity in a Golden Age: Orphan Care in Early Modern Amsterdam*. Urbana: University of Illinois Press, 1997.

McMullen, Dianne Marie. "The Geistreiches Gesangbuch of Johann Anastasius Freylinghausen (1670–1739): A German Pietist Hymnal." PhD diss., University of Michigan, 1987. Includes a critical edition of Freylinghausen's *Geistreiches Gesangbuch*, 2nd ed. (1705), and a transcription of the Wittenberg *Bedencken* (1716) with an annotated English translation.

Salo, Timothy. "Joachim Lange: Lutheran Pietist Theologian and Halle Apologist." In Christian T. Collins Winn, ed. *The Pietist Impulse in Christianity*, 82–93. Eugene, OR: Pickwick, 2011.

Smith, Samuel Clayton. "'Through the Eye of a Needle': The Role of Pietistic and Mystical Thought among the Anglican Elite in the Eighteenth Century Lowcountry South." PhD diss., Department of History, University of South Carolina, 1999.

Spaans, Joke. "Dutch Orphanages in the Golden Age." In Claus Veltmann and Jochen Birkenmeier, eds. *Kinder, Krätze, Karitas: Waisenhäuser in der Frühen Neuzeit*, 67–70. Halle: Verlag der Franckeschen Stiftungen, 2009.

Spaans, Joke. "Early Modern Orphanages between Civic Pride and Social Discipline: Francke's Use of Dutch Models." In Udo Sträter and Josef N. Neumann, eds. *Waisenhäuser in der Frühen Neuzeit*. Tübingen: Max Niemeyer, 2003.

van Eijnatten, Joris. *Liberty and Concord in the United Provinces: Religious Toleration and the Public in the Eighteenth-Century Netherlands*. Leiden: Brill, 2003.

Wilson, Renate. "Replication Reconsidered: Imitations, Models, and the Seeds of Modern Philanthropy." In Udo Sträter and Josef N. Neumann, eds. *Waisenhäuser in der Frühen Neuzeit*, 203–210. Tübingen: Max Niemeyer, 2003.

Chapter 6. Radical German Pietism in Europe and North America

EUROPE

Primary Sources

Durnbaugh, Donald F., ed. *European Origins of the Brethren: A Source Book on the Beginnings of the Church of the Brethren in Early Eighteenth-Century Europe*. Elgin, IL: Brethren Press, 1958.

Rock, Johann Friedrich. *The Humble Way: An Autobiographical Account of God's Guidance*. Translated by Janet W. Zuber. Amana, IA: Amana Church Society, 1999.

von Hochenau, Ernst Christoph Hochmann. "Letter to the Professors of Theology, Kirchmeier and Hottinger, at Marburg, dated December 12, 1716 in Schwarzenau." Reprinted in Hans Schneider. "Hochmann von Hochenau and Inspirationism: A Newly Discovered Letter." *Brethren Life and Thought* 25 (autumn 1980): 212–221.

Secondary Sources

Grossmann, Walter. "Gruber on the Discernment of True and False Inspiration." *Harvard Theological Review* 81, no. 4 (1988): 363–387.

Lehmann, Hartmut. "Continental Protestant Europe." In Stewart J. Brown and Timothy Tackett, eds. *The Cambridge History of Christianity.* Vol. 7, *Enlightenment, Reawakening, and Revolution, 1660–1815.* Cambridge: Cambridge University Press, 2006.

Meier, Marcus. *The Origin of the Schwarzenau Brethren.* Translated by Dennis Slabaugh. Ambler, PA: Brethren Encyclopedia, 2008.

Schneider, Hans. *German Radical Pietism.* Translated by Gerald T. MacDonald. Lanham, MD: Scarecrow Press, 2007.

Schrader, Hans-Jürgen. "Traveling Prophets: Inspirationists Wandering through Europe and to the New World—Mission, Transmission of Divine Word, Poetry." In Jonathan Strom, Hartmut Lehmann, and James Van Horn Melton, eds. *Pietism in Germany and North America, 1680–1820,* 107–123. Farnham, UK: Ashgate, 2009.

Shantz, Douglas H. *Between Sardis and Philadelphia: The Life and World of Pietist Court Preacher Conrad Bröske.* Leiden: Brill, 2008.

Shantz, Douglas H. "Communal Diversity in Radical German Pietism: Contrasting Notions of Community in Conrad Bröske and Johann Henrich Reitz." In Jonathan Strom, ed. *Pietism and Community in Europe and North America, 1650–1850,* 65–79. Leiden: Brill, 2010.

Shantz, Douglas H. "Homeless Minds: The Migration of Radical Pietists, Their Writings and Ideas in Early Modern Europe." In Jonathan Strom, Hartmut Lehmann, and James Van Horn Melton, eds. *Pietism in Germany and North America, 1680–1820,* 85–99. Farnham, UK: Ashgate, 2009.

Strom, Jonathan. "The Problem of Conventicles in Early German Pietism." *Covenant Quarterly,* 2004.

Zuber, Janet W., ed. and trans. *Barbara Heinemann Landmann Biography: E. L. Gruber's Teachings on Divine Inspiration and Other Essays.* Amana, IA: Amana Church Society, 1981.

NORTH AMERICA

Primary Sources

Beissel, Georg Conrad. *Some Theosophical Maxims, or, Rules of the Solitary Life (1752).* Translated by Michele Long. Ephrata, PA: Ephrata Cloister Associates, 1991.

Bornemann, Robert, ed. *Five Hymns from the Hymnbook of Magister Johannes Kelpius.* Philadelphia, PA: Fortress Press, 1976.

Doll, Eugene E., ed. *Ephrata as Seen by Contemporaries.* Allentown, PA: Schlechter's, 1953.

Durnbaugh, Donald F., ed. *Brethren in Colonial America: A Source Book on the Transplantation and Development of the Church of the Brethren in the Eighteenth Century.* Elgin, IL: Brethren Press, 1967.

Eberly, William R., ed. *The Complete Writings of Alexander Mack.* Winona Lake, IN: BMH Books, 1991.

Erb, Peter C., ed. *Johann Conrad Beissel and the Ephrata Community: Mystical and Historical Texts*. Lewiston, ID: Edwin Mellen Press, 1985.

Faull, Katherine, ed. *Moravian Women's Memoirs: Their Related Lives, 1750–1820*. Syracuse, NY: Syracuse University Press, 1997.

Hark, J. Max, ed. *Chronicon Ephratense: A History of the Community of Seventh-Day Baptists at Ephrata, Lancaster County, Pa. by Lamech and Agrippa*. Lancaster, PA: S. H. Zahm, 1889. Reprinted, New York: Burt Franklin, 1972.

Kelsey, R. W. "Letter of Christopher Sower, Written in 1724, Describing Conditions in Philadelphia and Vicinity, and the Sea Voyage from Europe." *Pennsylvania Magazine of History and Biography* 45, no. 3 (1921): 243–254.

Wellenreuther, Hermann, and Carola Wessel, eds. *Moravian Mission Diaries of David Zeisberger*. Translated by Julie T. Weber. University Park: Penn State University Press, 2005.

Secondary Sources

Bach, Jeff. "Maria Eicher of Ephrata: A Case Study of Religion and Gender in Radical Pietism." In David B. Eller, ed. *From Age to Age: Historians and the Modern Church*. Special issue of *Brethren Life and Thought* 42, nos. 3–4 (1997): 117–126.

Bach, Jeff. *Voices of the Turtledoves: The Sacred World of Ephrata*. University Park: University of Pennsylvania Press, 2003.

Curry, Thomas J. *The First Freedoms: Church and State in America to the Passage of the First Amendment*. New York: Oxford University Press, 1986.

Durnbaugh, Donald F. *Fruit of the Vine: A History of the Brethren, 1708–1995*. Elgin, IL: Brethren Press, 1997.

Durnbaugh, Donald F. "Work and Hope: The Spirituality of the Radical Pietist Communitarians." *Church History* 39 (1970): 72–90.

Landes, Wallace B., Jr., ed. *Radical Pietism in Contemporary Perspective*. Special issue of *Brethren Life and Thought* 43, nos. 3–4 (1998).

Levy, Leonard W. *The Establishment Clause: Religion and the First Amendment*. 2nd rev. ed. Chapel Hill: University of North Carolina Press, 1994.

Malbin, Michael J. *Religion and Politics: The Intentions of the Authors of the First Amendment*. Washington, DC: American Enterprise Institute, 1978.

McLoughlin, William G. *New England Dissent, 1630–1833: The Baptists and the Separation of Church and State*. Cambridge, MA: Harvard University Press, 1971.

Mead, Sidney E. *The Lively Experiment: The Shaping of Christianity in America*. New York: Harper and Row, 1963.

Rohrer, S. Scott. *Wandering Souls: Protestant Migrations in America, 1630–1865*. Chapel Hill: University of North Carolina, 2010.

Willoughby, William. *Counting the Cost: The Life of Alexander Mack*. Elgin, IL: Brethren Press, 1979.

Chapter 7. Pietism and Gender

Primary Sources

Petersen, Johanna Eleonora. *The Life of Lady Johanna Eleonora Petersen, Written by Herself: Pietism and Women's Autobiography in Seventeenth-Century Germany*. Edited and translated by Barbara Becker-Cantarino. Chicago: University of Chicago Press, 2005.

Peucker, Paul. "Inventory of the Records of the Choir of the Single Brothers in Bethlehem (1742–1844)." 2005. www.moravianchurcharchives.org/inventories.php.

Peucker, Paul. "Inventory of the Records of the Single Sisters' Choir in Bethlehem (1748–1844)." 2005. www.moravianchurcharchives.org/inventories.php.

van Schurman, Anna Maria. *Whether a Christian Woman Should Be Educated and Other Writings from Her Intellectual Circle*. Translated by Joyce L. Irwin. Chicago: University of Chicago Press, 1999.

Secondary Sources

Bollmann, Anne, ed. *A Place of Their Own: Women Writers and Their Social Environments (1450–1700)*. Frankfurt am Main: Peter Lang, 2011.

Breul, Wolfgang. "Marriage and Marriage-Criticism in Pietism: Philipp Jakob Spener, Gottfried Arnold, and Nikolaus Ludwig von Zinzendorf." In Jonathan Strom, ed. *Pietism and Community in Europe and North America, 1650–1850*, 37–53. Leiden: Brill, 2010.

Brown, Sylvia, ed. *Women, Gender, and Radical Religion in Early Modern Europe*. Leiden: Brill, 2007.

de Baar, Mirjam. "Conflicting Discourses on Female Dissent in the Early Modern Period: The Case of Antoinette Bourignon (1616–1680)." *L'Atelier du Centre de recherches historiques*, Apr. 2009. Online 4 Sept. 2009. http://acrh.revues.org/index1399.html.

de Baar, Mirjam. "Gender, Genre and Authority: Anna Maria van Schurman and Antoinette Bourignon." In Anne Bollmann, ed. *A Place of Their Own: Women Writers and Their Social Environments (1450–1700)*. Frankfurt am Main: Peter Lang, 2011.

Faull, Katherine M., ed. *Masculinity, Senses, Spirit*. Lewisburg, PA: Bucknell University Press, 2011.

Faull, Katherine M. "Relating Sisters' Lives: Moravian Women's Writing from Eighteenth Century America." *Transactions of the Moravian Historical Society* 31 (2000): 11–27.

Faull, Katherine M. "Temporal Men and the Eternal Bridegroom: Moravian Masculinity in the Eighteenth Century." In Katherine M. Faull, ed. *Masculinity, Senses, Spirit*, 55–80. Lewisburg, PA: Bucknell University Press, 2011.

Gleixner, Ulrike. "How to Incorporate Gender in Lutheran Pietism Research: Narratives and Counter-narratives." In Jonathan Strom, Hartmut Lehmann, and

James Van Horn Melton, eds. *Pietism in Germany and North America, 1680–1820*, 271–278. Farnham: Ashgate, 2009.
Gleixner, Ulrike, and Marion W. Gray, eds. *Gender in Transition: Discourse and Practice in German-Speaking Europe, 1750–1830*. Ann Arbor: University of Michigan Press, 2006.
Kettering, Denise D. "Pietism and Patriarchy: Spener and Women in Seventeenth-Century German Pietism." PhD diss., University of Iowa, 2009.
Lee, Bo Karen. "'I Wish to Be Nothing': The Role of Self-Denial in the Mystical Theology of Anna Maria van Schurman." In Sylvia Brown, ed. *Women, Gender, and Radical Religion in Early Modern Europe*. Leiden: Brill, 2007.
Peucker, Paul. "Inspired by Flames of Love: Homosexuality, Mysticism, and Moravian Brothers around 1750." *Journal of the History of Sexuality* 15, no. 1 (2006): 30–64.
Peucker, Paul. "The Songs of the Sifting: Understanding the Role of Bridal Mysticism in Moravian Piety during the Late 1740s." *Journal of Moravian History* 3 (2007): 51–87.
Peucker, Paul. "Wives of the Lamb: Moravian Brothers and Gender around 1750." In Katherine Faull, ed. *Masculinity, Senses, Spirit*, 39–54. Lewisburg, PA: Bucknell University Press, 2011.
Sensbach, Jon F. *Rebecca's Revival: Creating Black Christianity in the Atlantic World*. Cambridge, MA: Harvard University Press, 2005.
Shantz, Douglas H. "Anabaptist Women as Martyrs, Models of Courage, and Tools of the Devil." *Canadian Society of Church History: Historical Papers*, 2009, 21–34.
Shantz, Douglas H. "Women, Men and Their Experience of God: Comparing Spiritual Autobiographies." *Canadian Evangelical Review*, no. 22 (autumn 2001): 2–18.
Smaby, Beverly Prior. "Female Piety among Eighteenth Century Moravians." *Pennsylvania History* 64 (1997): 149–167.
Stitziel, Judd. "God, the Devil, Medicine and the Word: A Controversy over Ecstatic Women in Protestant Middle Germany 1691–1693." *Central European History* 29 (Sept. 1996): 309–338.
van Beek, Pieta. *The First Female University Student: Anna Maria van Schurman (1636)*. Utrecht: Igitur, Utrecht Publishing and Archiving Services, 2010.

Chapter 8. Pietism and the Bible

Primary Sources

Bengel, J. A. "The Author's Preface." In *Gnomon of the New Testament*. Vol. 1. Translated by Charlton T. Lewis and Marvin R. Vincent. Philadelphia: Perkinpine & Higgins, 1862.
Bengel, J. A. "Toward an Apocalyptic Chronology" (1740). In Peter C. Erb, ed. *Pietists: Selected Writings*, 272–74. New York: Paulist Press, 1983. Also in Eric

Lund, ed. *Documents from the History of Lutheranism, 1517–1750*, 301–304. Minneapolis: Augsburg Fortress, 2002.
Burk, J. C. F. *A Memoir of the Life and Writings of John Albert Bengel, Compiled Principally from Original Manuscripts Never before Published*. Translated by Robert Francis Walker. London: William Ball, 1837.

Secondary Sources

Brickman, William W. "The Socio-cultural Context of Education in the Seventeenth-Century Netherlands." *Paedagogica Historica*, 1984, 393–408.
Driedger, Michael. *Obedient Heretics: Mennonite Identities in Lutheran Hamburg and Altona during the Confessional Age*. Aldershot, UK: Ashgate, 2002.
Durnbaugh, Donald. *Church of the Brethren: Yesterday and Today*. Elgin, IL: Brethren Press, 1986.
Ehmer, Hermann. "Johann Albrecht Bengel." In Carter Lindberg, ed. *The Pietist Theologians*. Oxford: Blackwell, 2005.
Fuks, L., and R. G. Fuks-Mansfeld, eds. *Hebrew Typography in the Northern Netherlands, 1585–1815*. Vol. 2. Leiden: Brill, 1987.
Gawthrop, Richard, and Gerald Strauss. "Protestantism and Literacy in Early Modern Germany." *Past and Present* 104 (Aug. 1984): 31–55.
Porter, Roy. *Enlightenment: Britain and the Creation of the Modern World*. London: Penguin Books, 2001.
Robertson, Ritchie. "Religion and the Enlightenment: A Review Essay." *German History* 25, no. 3 (2007): 422–431.
Schneider, Hans. *German Radical Pietism*. Translated by Gerald T. MacDonald. Lanham, MD: Scarecrow Press, 2007.
Shantz, Douglas H. "The Millennial Study Bible of Heinrich Horch: A Case Study in Early Modern Reformed Hermeneutics." In Peter A. Lillback, ed. *The Practical Calvinist: An Introduction to the Presbyterian and Reformed Heritage. In Honor of Dr. D. Clair Davis*, 391–414. Fearn, Ross-shire, UK: Christian Focus, 2002.
Sheehan, Jonathan. *The Enlightenment Bible: Translation, Scholarship, Culture*. Princeton: Princeton University Press, 2005.
Sheehan, Jonathan. "Enlightenment, Religion, and the Enigma of Secularization: A Review Essay." *American Historical Review* 108, no. 4 (2003): 1061–1080. www.historycooperative.org/journals/ahr/108.4/sheehan.html.
Weborg, John. "Bengel, Johann Albrecht (1687–1752)." In Donald K. McKim, ed. *Dictionary of Major Biblical Interpreters*, 186–187. Downers Grove, IL: InterVarsity, 2007.

Chapter 9. Pietism, World Christianity, and Missions to South India and Labrador

SOUTH INDIA AND THE HALLE-DANISH MISSION

Primary Sources

Schwartz, C. F. *Remains of the Rev. C. F. Schwartz, Missionary in India; Consisting of His Letters and Journals; with a Sketch of His Life.* 2nd ed. Translated by Hugh Pearson. London: Jaques and Wright, 1826.

Ziegenbalg, Bartholomäus. *Geneaology of the South Indian Deities.* Edited by Daniel Jeyaraj. New York: Routledge Curzon, 2005.

Ziegenbalg, Bartholomäus. *Tamil Language for Europeans: Ziegenbalg's Grammatica Damulica (1716).* Edited by Daniel Jeyaraj. Translated from Latin and Tamil by Daniel Jeyaraj and Sister Dr. Rachel Harrington SND. Wiesbaden: Harrassowitz Verlag, 2010.

Secondary Sources

Benz, Ernst. "Pietist and Puritan Sources of Early Protestant World Missions (Cotton Mather and A. H. Francke)." *Church History* 20, no. 2 (1951): 28–55.

Beyreuther, Erich. *Bartholomaeus Ziegenbalg—a Biography of the First Protestant Missionary in India.* Translated by S. G. Lang and H. W. Gensichen. Chennai, India: Christian Literature Society, 1955, 1998.

DeJong, James A. *As the Waters Cover the Sea: Millennial Expectations in the Rise of Anglo-American Missions, 1640–1810.* Kampen, Netherlands: J. H. Kok, 1970. Reprinted, Laurel, MS: Audubon Press, 2006.

Dorairaj, S. "Of the German Who Took Tamil to Europeans: Interview with Daniel Jeyaraj, Professor at Liverpool Hope University." *Frontline: India's National Magazine* 27, no. 15 (2010).

Frykenberg, Robert Eric. *Christianity in India: From Beginnings to the Present.* Oxford: Oxford University Press, 2008.

Gaur, Albertine. "A Catalogue of B. Ziegenbalg's Tamil Library." *British Museum Quarterly* 30, nos. 3–4 (1966): 100.

Gertz, Steven, Robert Eric Frykenberg, Susan Billington Harper, and Keith J. White. "Christianity in India: A Faith of Many Colors." *Christian History,* no. 87 (2005).

Gross, Andreas. "Maria Dorothea Ziegenbalg and Utila Elisabeth Gründler: The First Two Wives of Missionaries in Tranquebar." In Andreas Gross, Y. Vincent Kumaradoss, and Heike Liebau, eds. *Halle and the Beginnings of Protestant Christianity in India.* Vol. 2, *Halle and the Beginning of Protestant Christianity in India,* 705–718. Halle: Francke Foundations, 2006.

Gross, Andreas, Y. Vincent Kumaradoss, and Heike Liebau, eds. *Halle and the Beginning of Protestant Christianity in India.* Vol. 1, *The Danish-Halle and the English-Halle Mission.* Vol. 2, *Halle and the Beginning of Protestant Christianity in India.* Vol. 3, *Communication between India and Europe.* Halle: Francke Foundations, 2006.

Hudson, D. Dennis. *Protestant Origins in India: Tamil Evangelical Christians, 1706–1835*. Grand Rapids, MI: Eerdmans, 2000.
Irschick, Eugene F. "Conversations in Tarangambadi: Caring for the Self in Early Eighteenth Century South India." *Comparative Studies of South Asia, Africa, and the Middle East* 23, nos. 1–2 (2003): 254–270.
Jeyaraj, Daniel. *Bartholomäus Ziegenbalg: The Father of Modern Protestant Mission—an Indian Assessment*. New Delhi: Indian Society for Promoting Christian Knowledge, 2006.
Jeyaraj, Daniel. "Indian Participation in Enabling, Sustaining, and Promoting Christian Mission in India." In Richard Fox Young, ed. *India and the Indianness of Christianity: Essays on Understanding—Historical, Theological, and Bibliographical—in Honor of Robert Eric Frykenberg*, 30–38. Grand Rapids, MI: Wm. B. Eerdmans, 2009.
Jeyaraj, Daniel. "The Trailblazer." *Christian History and Biography*, July 1, 2005.
Lehmann, Arno. *It Began at Tranquebar: The Story of the Tranquebar Mission and the Beginnings of Protestant Christianity in India*. Madras: Christian Literature Society, 1956.
Liebau, Heike. "Country Priests, Catechists, and Schoolmasters as Cultural, Religious, and Social Middlemen in the Context of the Tranquebar Mission." In Robert K. Frykenberg and Alaine Low, eds. *Christians and Missionaries in India: Cross-Cultural Communication Since 1500*, 70–92. Grand Rapids, MI: Eerdmans, 2003.
Liebau, Heike. "German Missionaries as Research Workers in India: Their Diaries as Historical Sources (Benjamin Schultze)." *Studies in History* 11, no. 1 (1995): 117.
Liebau, Heike. "Indian Pastors: 14 Short Biographies." In Andreas Gross, Heike Liebau, and Vincent Kumaradoss, eds. *Halle and the Beginning of Protestant Christianity in India (1706–1845)*. Vol. 3, *Communication between India and Europe*, 1543–1549. Halle: Francke Foundations, 2006.
Neill, Stephen. *A History of Christianity in India, 1707–1858*. Cambridge: Cambridge University Press, 1985.
Neill, Stephen. *A History of Christian Missions*. Harmondsworth, UK: Penguin Books, 1964.
Pierard, Richard V. "German Pietism as a Major Factor in the Beginnings of Modern Protestant Missions." In Christian T. Collins Winn, ed. *The Pietist Impulse in Christianity*, 285–295. Eugene, OR: Pickwick, 2011.
Rajan, Gita. "Labyrinths of the Colonial Archive: Unpacking German Missionary Narratives from Tranquebar, Southeast India (1706–1720)." PhD diss., University of Michigan, 2001.
Singh, Brijraj. *The First Protestant Missionary to India: Bartholomaeus Ziegenbalg*. Oxford: Oxford University Press, 1999.
Sweetman, Will. "The Prehistory of Orientalism: Colonialism and the Textual Basis for Bartholomäus Ziegenbalg's Account of Hinduism." *New Zealand Journal of Asian Studies* 6, no. 2 (2004): 12–38.

Young, Richard Fox, ed. *India and the Indianness of Christianity: Essays on Understanding—Historical, Theological, and Bibliographical—in Honor of Robert Eric Frykenberg.* Grand Rapids, MI: Wm. B. Eerdmans, 2009.

LABRADOR AND THE MORAVIAN MISSION

Primary Sources

"Account of the Life of Brother Jens Haven." *Periodical Accounts Relating to the Missions of the Church of the United Brethren* 2 (1797): 99–115. www.mun.ca/rels/morav/texts/jhaven.html.

Faull, Katherine, ed. *Moravian Women's Memoirs: Their Related Lives, 1750–1820.* Syracuse, NY: Syracuse University Press, 1997.

Peucker, Paul. "Labrador Records at the Unity Archives in Herrnhut, Germany." In Hans Rollmann, ed. *Moravian Beginnings in Labrador,* 152–161. St. John's, NL: Memorial University Faculty of Arts Pub., 2009.

"Retrospect of the History of the Mission of the Brethren's Church in Labrador for the Past Hundred Years (1771–1871)." *Periodical Accounts* 28 (1871): 1–19, 53–72. www.mun.ca/rels/morav/texts/brethren.html

von Zinzendorf, Ludwig Count. "Brotherly Union and Agreement at Herrnhut" (1727). In Peter C. Erb, ed. *Pietists: Selected Writings,* 325–330. New York: Paulist Press, 1983.

Secondary Sources

Atwood, Craig D. *Community of the Cross: Moravian Piety in Colonial Bethlehem.* University Park: Penn State University Press, 2004.

Demarée, Gaston R., and Astrid E. J. Ogilvie. "The Moravian Missionaries at the Labrador Coast and Their Centuries-Long Contribution to Instrumental Meteorological Observations." *Climatic Change* 91, nos. 3–4 (2008): 423–450.

Fay, Amelia. "Searching for Mikak: Archaeologist Uncovering Story of First Labrador Inuit Woman to Earn a Place in Recorded History." *Labrador Life* 5, no. 4 (2011): 22–25. www.mun.ca/labmetis/articles.html

Freeman, Arthur J. *An Ecumenical Theology of the Heart: The Theology of Count Nicholas Ludwig von Zinzendorf.* Bethlehem, PA: Moravian Church in America, 1998.

Hindmarsh, D. Bruce. "Moravian Narrative Culture." In *The Evangelical Conversion Narrative. Spiritual Autobiography in Early Modern England,* 162–192. Oxford: Oxford University Press, 2005.

Janzen, Olaf Uwe. "Newfoundland and the International Fishery." In M. Brook Taylor, ed. *Canadian History: A Reader's Guide.* Vol. 1, *Beginnings to Confederation.* Toronto: University of Toronto Press, 1994.

Mason, J. C. S. *The Moravian Church and the Missionary Awakening in England, 1760–1800.* Woodbridge, Suffolk, UK: Boydell & Brewer, 2001.

Rollmann, Hans. "Johann Christian Erhardt and the First Moravian Exploration of Labrador in 1752." In Hans Rollmann, ed. *Moravian Beginnings in Labrador: Papers from a Symposium Held in Makkovik and Hopedale*, 53–68. Occasional Publication of Newfoundland and Labrador Studies, No. 2. St. John's, NL: Memorial University Faculty of Arts Pub. 2009.

Rollmann, Hans, ed. *Labrador through Moravian Eyes: 250 Years of Art, Photographs, and Records*. St. John's, NL: Special Celebrations Corporation of Newfoundland and Labrador, 2002.

Rollmann, Hans, ed. *Moravian Beginnings in Labrador: Papers from a Symposium Held in Makkovik and Hopedale*. Occasional Publication of Newfoundland and Labrador Studies, No. 2. St. John's, NL: Memorial University Faculty of Arts Pub., 2009.

Schattschneider, David A. "A 250-Year-Old Mystery: The Disappearance of J. C. Erhardt in Labrador." *Journal of Moravian History* 2 (spring 2007): 76–89.

Sensbach, Jon. " 'Don't Teach My Negroes to be Pietists': Pietism and the Roots of the Black Protestant Church." In Jonathan Strom, Hartmut Lehmann, and James Van Horn Melton, eds. *Pietism in Germany and North America, 1680–1820*, 83–198. Farnham, UK: Ashgate, 2009.

Shantz, Douglas H. "A Church Ahead of Its Time: The 18th century Moravian Community on Gender, Worship and Ecumenism." *Hinge: Journal of Christian Thought for the Moravian Church* 12, no. 1 (2005): 2–18, 32. www.moravianseminary.edu/center/hinge12.1.htm

Stopp, Marianne P. "Eighteenth Century Labrador Inuit in England." *Arctic* 62, no. 1 (2009): 45–64. www.mun.ca/labmetis/articles.html.

Taylor, J. Garth. "In the Wake of the *Hope*: Jens Haven's 1764 Reconnaissance Journey in Northern Newfoundland and Southern Labrador." In Hans Rollmann, ed. *Moravian Beginnings in Labrador: Papers from a Symposium Held in Makkovik and Hopedale*, 87–103. Occasional Publication of Newfoundland and Labrador Studies, No. 2. St. John's, NL: Memorial University Faculty of Arts Pub., 2009.

Taylor, J. Garth. "The Two Worlds of Mikak," Parts I and II. *Beaver* 314, no. 3 (1983): 4–13; 314, no. 4 (1984): 18–25.

Vogt, Peter. "Nicholas Ludwig von Zinzendorf (1700–1760)." In Carter Lindberg, ed. *The Pietist Theologians*, 207–223. Oxford: Blackwell, 2005.

Ward, W. R. *The Protestant Evangelical Awakening*. Cambridge: Cambridge University Press, 1992.

Whiteley, William H. "The Establishment of the Moravian Mission in Labrador and British Policy, 1763–1783." *Canadian Historical Review* 45, no. 1 (1964): 29–50.

Whiteley, William H. "Inventory of Moravian Mission Records from Labrador." Moravian Archives, Bethlehem, June 1960. www.moravianchurcharchives.org/inventories.php and www.moravianchurcharchives.org/labrador.pdf.

Whiteley, William H. "The Moravian Missionaries and the Labrador Eskimos in the Eighteenth Century." *Church History* 35, no. 1 (1966): 76–92.

Whiteley, William H. "The Records of the Moravian Mission in Labrador." *American Archivist* 24 (1961): 425–430.

Chapter 10. The Contribution of German Pietism to the Modern World

Secondary Sources

Bradley, James E., and Dale K. Van Kley. *Religion and Politics in Enlightenment Europe.* Notre Dame, IN: Notre Dame University Press, 2001.

Carlsson, Eric. "Pietism and Enlightenment Theology's Historical Turn: The Case of Johann Salomo Semler." In Christian T. Collins Winn, ed. *The Pietist Impulse in Christianity,* 97–106. Eugene, OR: Pickwick, 2011.

de Certeau, Michel. *The Writing of History.* Translated by Tom Conley. New York: Columbia University Press, 1988.

Gregory, Jeremy. "Introduction: Transforming 'the Age of Reason' into 'an Age of Faiths': Or, Putting Religions and Beliefs (Back) into the Eighteenth Century." *Journal for Eighteenth-Century Studies* 32, no. 3 (2009): 287–305.

Hunter, Ian, Frank Grunert, and Thomas Ahnert, eds. *Christian Thomasius, Essays on Church, State, and Politics.* Translated by Ian Hunter. Indianapolis: Liberty Fund, 2007.

Noll, Mark, and Bruce Hindmarsh. "Rewriting the History of Evangelicalism: W. R. Ward, 1925–2010." *Books and Culture: Christian Review* 17, no. 2 (2011): 8.

O'Malley, J. Steven. "Pietistic Influence on John Wesley: Wesley and Gerhard Tersteegen." *Wesleyan Theological Journal* 31, no. 2 (1996): 48–70.

Printy, Michael. "New Perspectives on Religion in Eighteenth-Century Germany." H-German Forum: New Perspectives on Eighteenth-Century History. Published by H-German, 24 Sept. 2010. www.h-net.org/~german/discuss/early_modern/printy_em_forum.

Shantz, Douglas H. "Conversion and Revival in the Last Days: Hopes for Progress and Renewal in Radical Pietism and Gottfried Wilhelm Leibniz." In Fred van Lieburg and Daniel Lindmark, eds. *Pietism, Revivalism, and Modernity, 1650–1850,* 42–62. Newcastle upon Tyne, UK: Cambridge Scholars, 2008.

Shantz, Douglas H. "The Place of Religion in a Secular Age: Charles Taylor's Explanation of the Rise and Significance of Secularism in the West." Christian Thought Lecture, University of Calgary, 16 Mar. 2009. www.ucalgary.ca/christchair/2009_events.

Sorkin, David. *The Religious Enlightenment: Protestants, Jews, and Catholics from London to Vienna.* Princeton: Princeton University Press, 2008.

Stein, Stephen J. "Some Thoughts on Pietism in American Religious History." In Jonathan Strom, Hartmut Lehmann, and James Van Horn Melton, eds. *Pietism in Germany and North America, 1680–1820,* 28–31. Farnham, UK: Ashgate, 2009.

Taylor, Charles. *A Secular Age.* Cambridge, MA: Harvard University Press, 2007.

Wagner, Paul S. "John Wesley and the German Pietist Heritage: The Development of Hymnody." ThD diss., Toronto School of Theology, University of Toronto, 2004.

Ward, W. R. *Early Evangelicalism: A Global Intellectual History, 1670–1789.* Cambridge: Cambridge University Press, 2006.

Winn, Christian T. Collins, ed. *The Pietist Impulse in Christianity*. Eugene, OR: Pickwick, 2011.

Conclusion. Reflecting on the Cultural and Religious Legacy of German Pietism

Secondary Sources

Goa, David J., ed. *Pietism and the Challenges of Modernity: Lectures by David J. Goa, Cam Harder, and Eugene L. Boe*. Camrose, AB: Ronning Centre for the Study of Religion and Public Life, 2011.
Keim, Albert N. "History of the Anabaptist Vision." *Mennonite Historical Bulletin*, Oct. 1993, 1–7. www.mcusa-archives.org/library/anabaptistvision/keim-historyofvision.html.
Olson, Roger E. "Pietism: Myths and Realities." In Christian T. Collins Winn, ed. *The Pietist Impulse in Christianity*, 3–16. Eugene, OR: Pickwick, 2011.
Olson, Roger E. "Pietism and Postmodernism: Points of Congeniality." *Christian Scholar's Review* 41, no. 4 (2012): 367–380.
Shantz, Douglas H. "Conversion and Sarcasm in the Autobiography of Johann Christian Edelmann." In David M. Luebke, Jared Poley, and Dan Ryan, eds. *Conversion and the Politics of Religion in Early Modern Germany*, 153–168. New York: Berghahn Books, 2012.
Shantz, Douglas H. "Politics, Prophecy and Pietism in the Halberstadt Conventicle." In Fred van Lieburg, ed. *Confessionalism and Pietism*, 129–147. Mainz: Philipp von Zabern, 2006.
Snyder, C. Arnold. *Anabaptist History and Theology: An Introduction*. Kitchener, ON: Pandora Press, 1995.
Strom, Jonathan. "The Common Priesthood and the Pietist Challenge for Ministry and Laity." In Christian T. Collins Winn, ed. *The Pietist Impulse in Christianity*, 42–58. Eugene, OR: Pickwick, 2011.

Index of Persons and Places

Young Center Books in Anabaptist & Pietist Studies

Charles E. Hurst and David L. McConnell, *An Amish Paradox: Diversity and Change in the World's Largest Amish Community*

Rod Janzen and Max Stanton, *The Hutterites in North America*

Karen M. Johnson-Weiner, *Train Up a Child: Old Order Amish and Mennonite Schools*

Peter J. Klassen, *Mennonites in Early Modern Poland and Prussia*

James O. Lehman and Steven M. Nolt, *Mennonites, Amish, and the American Civil War*

Steven M. Nolt and Thomas J. Meyers, *Plain Diversity: Amish Cultures and Identities*

Douglas H. Shantz, *An Introduction to German Pietism: Protestant Renewal at the Dawn of Modern Europe*

Tobin Miller Shearer, *Daily Demonstrators: The Civil Rights Movement in Mennonite Homes and Sanctuaries*

Richard A. Stevick, *Growing Up Amish: The Teenage Years*

Susan L. Trollinger, *Selling the Amish: The Tourism of Nostalgia*

Diane Zimmerman Umble and David L. Weaver-Zercher, eds., *The Amish and the Media*

Center Books in Anabaptist Studies

Carl F. Bowman, *Brethren Society: The Cultural Transformation of a "Peculiar People"*

Perry Bush, *Two Kingdoms, Two Loyalties: Mennonite Pacifism in Modern America*

John A. Hostetler, ed., *Amish Roots: A Treasury of History, Wisdom, and Lore*

Julia Kasdorf, *The Body and the Book: Writing from a Mennonite Life*

Donald B. Kraybill, ed., *The Amish and the State*, 2nd edition

Donald B. Kraybill, *The Riddle of Amish Culture*, revised edition

Donald B. Kraybill and Carl Desportes Bowman, *On the Backroad to Heaven: Old Order Hutterites, Mennonites, Amish, and Brethren*

Donald B. Kraybill and Steven M. Nolt, *Amish Enterprise: From Plows to Profits*, 2nd edition

Werner O. Packull, *Hutterites Beginnings: Communitarian Experiments during the Reformation*

Benjamin W. Redekop and Calvin W. Redekop, eds., *Power, Authority, and the Anabaptist Tradition*

Calvin Redekop, ed., *Creation and the Environment: An Anabaptist Perspective on a Sustainable World*

Calvin Redekop, Stephen C. Ainlay, and Robert Siemens, *Mennonite Entrepreneurs*

Steven D. Reschly, *The Amish on the Iowa Prairie, 1840 to 1910*

Kimberly D. Schmidt, Diane Zimmerman Umble, and Steven D. Reschly, *Strangers at Home: Amish and Mennonite Women in History*

David Weaver-Zercher, *The Amish in the American Imagination*

Diane Zimmerman Umble, *Holding the Line: The Telephone in Old Order Mennonite and Amish Life*